D0363564

Area Redevelopment Policies in Britain & the Countries of the Common Market

A seven part essay prepared under contract to the Area Redevelopment Administration by the Institute of Industrial Relations, University of California at Los Angeles.

U.S. DEPARTMENT OF COMMERCE
John T. Connor, *Secretary*

AREA REDEVELOPMENT ADMINISTRATION
William L. Batt, Jr., *Administrator*

January / 1965

Library of Congress Catalog Card Number 65-60021

For sale by the Superintendent of Documents, U.S. Government Printing Office
Washington, D.C., 20402 - Price $1.25

Foreword

Modern technology is a paradox that brings general material affluence and yet leaves pockets of economic disadvantage. To solve the problems of some of these pockets we can sometimes rely on past experience. But as technology advances the accompanying distress presents many new problems which are beyond the current frame of social and economic experience.

The Area Redevelopment Act of 1961 anticipated this need with the inclusion of section 27 which provides for research into the "hows," "whys," and "wheres" of these new perplexities.

In seeking answers is it necessary for us to delve into movements of people from one place to another? How they move? Why they move? Is it necessary for us to inquire into the population, labor force, and unemployment in chronically depressed areas? Should we look to our neighbors across the seas as well as to our people at home?

Exploration into seemingly divergent areas of social and economic activity is uncovering valuable information to form the equations which will lead to the solutions we seek. One thing is certain: we are irretrievably involved with each other. If we are to understand and influence the smallest part, we are obliged to understand the whole.

A part of that whole is "Area Redevelopment Policies in Britain and the Countries of the Common Market."

William L. Batt, Jr., *Administrator,*
Area Redevelopment Administration.

Contents

Part 1

Preface & Introduction

Frederic Meyers

Preface

This series of studies was done under a contract between the U.S. Area Redevelopment Administration and the University of California, Los Angeles. The Institute of Industrial Relations at UCLA was the agency through which the University acted in directing the study.

The Institute of Industrial Relations was fortunate in that it had previously established a continuing association with the Centre de Recherches of the Institut des Sciences Sociales du Travail at the Université de Paris. When the contract proposal was submitted, it was proposed that the research should be organized through this association between the two institutes. Accordingly, I was designated project director, and M. Yves Delamotte, directeur adjoint in charge of the Centre de Recherches of the Paris Institut, was designated European project director.

M. Delamotte was largely responsible for recruitment of the national experts on the Continent, and the Institut served as European headquarters for the project. As we had expected, this arrangement contributed greatly to the efficiency with which the studies were made, and we are most grateful to the staff of the Institut for its assistance in the completion of the work.

The studies of the distinguished team of experts who reported on their countries speak for themselves. But the authors should be identified by their positions. M. Pierre Bauchet, who wrote the French report, is Directeur des Etudes at the Ecole National d'Administration. Mrs. Erika Georges, who collaborated with M. Delamotte on the section on the role of the European Coal and Steel Community and the European Economic Community, is assistant professor of economics at San Fernando Valley State College. Dr. L. H. Klaassen, who wrote the reports on the Benelux countries, is a member of the staff of the Netherlands Economic Institute. Dr. Ettore Massacesi was formerly manager of the Labor Affairs Division of the Coal and Steel Community High Authority, Chief of the Office of Labor Affairs for an important holding company of state participation, and now directs his own research organization. Mr. A. J. Odber, who did the study of Britain, is director of the business research unit at the University of Durham. Dr. Dietrich Storbeck, who wrote the study of West Germany, is a member of the staff of the Dortmund Sozialforschungstelle associated with the University of Münster. We are, of course, grateful for their contributions.

Mrs. Georges translated the German and Italian studies, and I did a first editing of these translations. I translated M. Bauchet's study. Dr. Klaassen wrote in English, and I partially edited his work. Cartography was done by Mr. Terence Thomas and Mr. J. Blok of the UCLA Geography Department. The staff of the Institute of Industrial Relations did yeoman work in typing and reproducing the studies under most difficult circumstances. Mrs. Anne Cook of the institute did the demanding job of final editing.

For all these contributions we are most grateful. All of us associated with the project hope that it will be helpful in the formulation of effective redevelopment policies in the United States. The ARA's decision to finance this research was, of course, based on the hope that European experience might contribute something to American policy. It is my belief that it can, and in the introduction I have given my personal views on the kinds of lessons to be learned. It is, however, a necessary by-product that the relevant lessons be learned by any interested national administration.

At our initial planning meeting held in Paris in November 1962, a fairly lengthy discussion was held on the kind of report each expert was to prepare. It was obvious that a great deal of descriptive material on techniques should be included. But it was agreed also that each report should include some historical discussion of the development of policy and the reasons for changes in direction, since it seemed that here was where experience expressed itself. Further, it was agreed that substantial space should be devoted to critical evaluation, as description unrelated to results would be of relatively little use. But, while there was a briefing on U.S. problems and policies, it was not expected that the national experts would attempt to assess the relevance of their experience for the United States; this must be the task of those who formulate or assist in the formulation of American policy. Thus direction of the studies toward critical evaluation of national policies in national terms was deliberate. It was thought then, and I believe the results demonstrate the wisdom of the choice, that this would be the most effective use of the distinguished group of scholars who had agreed to collaborate.

Most of the authors prepared extensive bibliographies of the relevant literature. Copies of these bibliographies may be obtained from the UCLA Institute of Industrial Relations.

Finally, I wish to express my personal satisfaction in the opportunity to participate in this collaborative international research effort. It was a most pleasant and, I believe, productive experience, and I am thankful to all who contributed to it.

FREDERIC MEYERS.

PARIS, *September 1963.*

Introduction

This brief introduction is followed by six essays on redevelopment policies in each of the Common Market countries and in the United Kingdom, and on the role of the European Economic Community and the Coal and Steel Community. These were commissioned by the Institute of Industrial Relations of the University of California, Los Angeles, under a contract with the U.S. Area Redevelopment Administration. The object was to explore the lessons to be learned from experience in these countries in their attempts to deal with problems analogous to those to which the U.S. redevelopment legislation is directed.

Each of the countries studied has incorporated regional development programs in its kit of economic policies. To describe their magnitude with any precision is extremely difficult. Policies that have a redevelopment orientation are not always categorized in national budgets as such; for example, budgets for infrastructures may be administered in part by ordinary departments of government, and though they may emphasize development in less well-endowed regions, accounting may not identify the effort as a redevelopment one. Various aids to mobility of labor or capital may not be entirely accountable in money terms. Likewise, policies such as those in France and Britain which restrict building in congested areas may have a substantial redevelopment effect without any possible measure of cost. The impact of the Italian requirement that the mixed and public holding companies make specified proportions of their investments in the South is not measurable.

It will be apparent that the massive Italian effort to solve the problems of unemployment, underemployment, and low incomes in the Italian South is, at least relatively, much the largest and most comprehensive program described. Appropriations as of June 12, 1961, for the Cassa per il Mezzogiorno for the 15-year period 1950–65 totaled nearly \$3½ billion. That is, the Cassa has spent or will spend, on the average each year, a sum equal to about 3 percent of 1961 total gross capital formation in the economy. And this does not measure the whole of the Italian redevelopment effort. Furthermore, the Cassa's program is the only one which from its beginning has been oriented toward a regional approach, treating the problems of the South, at least in concept, as an integrated whole. To be sure, implementation has not always been consistent with the concept. But this is the direction toward which the other Italian programs, conceived as more or less ad hoc measures to deal with problems in particular areas, are tending.

The French program has also been of major proportions. Again, it cannot be measured as a whole, but some indication of its size may be indicated by the fact that redevelopment loans by two central Government agencies, plus those of local communities, from 1955–61 averaged annually about 0.2 percent of gross domestic capital formation, and loan guarantees by regional development corporations also averaged annually about 0.2 percent of gross domestic capital formation. State investment subsidies for redevelopment purposes averaged annually about 0.1 percent of gross domestic capital formation. Financing from these three sources, then, came to the substantial sum of 0.5 percent of gross domestic capital formation. These programs, of course, do not describe the totality of the French effort, which has gradually and imperfectly been integrated into the total planning program.

The British programs have been of somewhat lesser magnitude. Britain has been engaged in redevelopment activities perhaps longer than any of the other countries, but there was a considerable deemphasis in the years 1949–59. However, by 1961–62, official Treasury and Board of Trade expenditures on factory buildings, grants, and loans had risen sharply to about three-fourths of 1 percent of gross domestic capital formation. Since Mr. Odber's study was completed, a new program for the northeast of England has been projected which will expand activity and meet many of the conceptual objections to past programs.

Programs in Germany and in the Benelux countries are smaller, at least in financial magnitudes. The German problems have been of a different sort, often of political origin. Inherently, there are differences in the meaning of cost and expenditure measures for small countries such as Belgium, Holland, and Luxemburg, than for large. In some ways, perhaps, they are more comparable to a region within one of the larger countries in which there is a large city.

But from an American point of view, one of the most interesting aspects of the European programs is the fact that such extensive and determined efforts have been made in economic environments of relatively sustained high levels of employment. In all of the countries studied, unemployment rates are well below those of the United States.[1] In all but Italy, full employment has prevailed for all or most of the postwar period. Yet, in each of the countries, attention to the kinds of problems with which we are concerned in the United States, and to the solution of which the Area Redevelopment Act is directed, is also expressed in extensive measures of public policy.

Professor L. H. Klaassen, in his essay on the Benelux countries, proposes a theoretical model which makes measures to develop disadvantaged areas consistent with the purely economic criterion of maximizing national product in an environment of generally full employment. The model seems to be realistic and useful; indeed, others of the authors might well have had a similar model in mind in organizing their reports. Mr. Odber did in fact have this specific model at hand.

While full employment does not, apparently, eliminate the problems to which these studies are directed, it does make them more easily susceptible to solution, and makes available, both economically and politically, certain tools more difficult to use in an environment of general underemployment.

So far as the specific instruments for creating new employment and more adequate incomes in the problem areas are concerned, those that appear in the British and European arsenals but not in the American are available only in an environment of full employment. The American policymaker will find little new, otherwise. He is, of course, familiar with the necessity of an adequate infrastructure. The particular measures for developing or redeveloping this kind of social capital are so intimately tied to the particular needs and possibilities of a region that little can be learned from the detailed programs for its provision. The devices for making investment in a problem region attractive are also well known. Making credit available

---

[1] See Robert J. Myers and John H. Chandler, "Explaining International Unemployment Rates," *Monthly Labor Review,* September 1962.

at low-interest rates, the development of industrial sites, outright subsidies for the initial costs of investment, tax exemptions—all these are obvious and universal.[2] The differences from country to country are differences of detail and depend upon the political, economic, and financial structure of each country. The final effect of these measures, whatever their particulars may be, is to give some kind of subsidy to attract industrial location to the desired area by making it relatively profitable.

The general principle enunciated in all the studies that such subsidies should be "once-and-for-all" needs reiteration. If the criteria upon which redevelopment policy is based are to be fundamentally economic, that is, to assure long-run increases in net national product, only that industry or employment should be created which can survive once the initial investment disadvantages, real or merely apparent, are overcome. If this is the criterion there is no point in commitment to continuing subsidies for operating costs.

In most of the countries, and under certain rules of the Coal and Steel Community and of the Common Market, relocation allowances may be given to workers moving out of areas of relatively high unemployment or low incomes. These are, in principle, familiar to policymakers in this field. But full employment permits more discrimination in the use of relocation allowances. When the whole emphasis is on insufficient employment, and when general unemployment prevails, relocation is difficult to use in any event, and tends to become largely a device for evening out rates of unemployment by moving unemployed out of redevelopment areas to areas with lower rates of unemployment just as retraining, as some of the evidence cited by Mr. Odber indicates, tends to become the employment of unemployed skilled workers to teach other unemployed skilled workers their unneeded skills.

Moreover, as virtually all the studies show, voluntary migration is selective and greatly reduces the quality of the labor force remaining in redevelopment areas. With its age distribution becoming progressively poorer, the labor force deteriorates into a pool of obsolete skills. Mobility is so low that relocation allowances may well be ineffective, and even if people are induced to leave, their chances of employment remain doubtful. However, in a situation of full employment, when net new investment is high, the existence of a labor pool, even of poor quality, would serve as an important locational inducement. The attraction would become even stronger if relocation allowances were available to move *into* the redevelopment area the labor force ingredients, in terms of skill and age, necessary to maximize its usefulness. This is made an explicit part of Dr. Klaassen's model.

It seems apparent from the experience of the several countries studied, then, that long periods of full employment do not result in the disappearance of problems of depressed areas. Indeed, unless one assumes a much higher degree of mobility of labor and of capital than can realistically be anticipated, there is no reason to expect such a result in a dynamic economy. Declines of employment, under technological or market pressures, or both,

[2] The impact of pricing policies for such services as rail transportation and energy is discussed in several of the studies, and there are examples of deliberate subsidies given through these means—sometimes, as in Germany, for reasons of political causation of local economic problems. But given the criterion of "once-and-for-all" aid, as Professor Bauchet points out, the problem is to assure that inadvertent subsidies are not given by economically irrational rate structures. Short-term aid can be defended, as Dr. Storbeck says, on the analogy of the "infant industries" argument. As all American readers will know, the impact of the freight rate structure on regional development has been productive of long controversy, of which the Georgia freight rate case is only one of the striking evidences.

in coal mines, textiles, agriculture, and shipyards, reinforced by the extraordinary locational pressures on market-oriented industries created by the progressive reduction of tariff barriers under the terms of the Treaty of Rome, and further augmented in the Federal Republic of Germany by the creation of a new frontier, have left pools of hardship and poverty behind them. They have added to differences in well-being such as those between the South and the rest of Italy, and between the poorer agricultural areas of France and the wealthier industrial sections, especially Paris. There are analogues not only in the other countries studied but also in the United States, which have persisted over very long historic periods. Full employment by itself cannot solve these problems; indeed, it may well aggravate them by the progressive deterioration resulting from selective mobility. It does, however, permit a refocusing of redevelopment policy.

Rather than specific instruments, what may be of significance to the American reader are the major directions and problems of European policies. These may be categorized as (1) concern with the criteria for identification of redevelopment areas; (2) the continuing tendency toward regionalization of policy; (3) as a corollary of regionalization, increasing concentration of assistance in development nuclei; (4) the relating of redevelopment policy to programs to deal with urban congestion; and (5) the problem of maintaining the differentiating character of development aids and of preventing their dilution by the application of local and general economic policies.

Each of the countries studied has wrestled with the problem of the criteria by which redevelopment areas are to be identified. In these economies of full employment, unemployment rates, even in those areas with greatest unemployment, with rare exceptions are equal to or below those which would be regarded as acceptable in the United States. This happens because sufficient mobility exists to maintain low unemployment rates, or because the rate of natural population growth is low or negative, or both. It is true both of areas in which the slow and long-term release of labor from agricultural employment is the source of the problems, and of areas where the more dramatic decline of particular industries, for example coal and textiles, has created regional crises.

Thus the focus of attention tends to be on islands of low incomes and low standards of living in generally prosperous economies, on their depopulation, and on the concomitant of increasing congestion in great urban agglomerations. It was a revelation, at least to this writer, to see how closely the problems of congested and depressed areas are related in British and continental thought.

Problem areas, then, are identified by the twin criteria of relatively high rates of unemployment and relatively low incomes. In some instances there is associated the criterion of excessive emigration. But, as Professor Bauchet has pointed out, mere differences in income are insufficient as a criterion for the application of special treatment. Since there are bound to be structural differences among areas, there are necessarily differences in average incomes. Consequently, increasing attention is paid in European thought, and also in policy, to the criterion of "development-worthiness." In terms of Dr. Klaassen's model, this means an attempt to compare the marginal changes in net national product, taking into account not only the private but also the social costs of an additional unit of investment in developed as against underdeveloped or depressed areas.

It is apparent that none of the national experts believes that even in economies of full employment is complete governmental nonintervention in the domain of regional policy the way to achieve maximization of national income and rates of growth. A most persuasive case is made that once-and-for-all assistance to rationally selected private investment, accompanied by the development of the necessary infrastructure, in development-worthy areas contributes more to the long-term growth of national income than to do nothing. This extends even to the encouragement of decentralization, that is, the movement of some industry out of congested areas. The latter contrasts with the American legal prohibition of assistance to industry moving to redevelopment areas, originating no doubt in the problem of general unemployment and in the often well-founded suspicion that such movements are motivated principally by a desire to escape union organization.

But the external economies of location in industrially developed areas, the often large hidden subsidies to industry resulting from social investment in infrastructure, subsidies which may become cumulatively large as the community can increasingly afford them,[3] and the indications that many locational decisions are not based solely on economic considerations, all lead to the conclusion that governmental measures to offset the initial disadvantages of development-worthy areas are consistent with the purely ecomonic criterion of maximization of national income.

This has led the governments of most of the countries studied to move away from the identification of small zones with critical problems, to which redevelopment assistance is made available on an equal basis, toward the examination of the potentials of whole regions. Indeed, the first planning conference on this project identified the subject of investigation as the policies directed at the redevelopment of areas of high unemployment and/or low incomes. But the finished essays came in as studies of *regional* policies.

This tendency is, at least on the policy level, still far from fully developed in any of the countries. In each, public policy is a melange of special policies to deal with critical problems in small local areas and of beginning efforts to define more or less homogeneous regions in terms of their economies, problems, and potentials and to deal with them as a whole. The outstanding case is the Italian Mezzogiorno, but French policy also seems far advanced, at least to American if not to critical French eyes.

The identification of regions and the examination of problems on a regional scale seem the first, necessary steps toward manageable solutions, and away from futile arguments in principle about whether a job should be brought to each worker, or whether the worker should be moved to a job consistent with prevailing patterns of, and incentives to, industrial location. This procedure permits an integrated evaluation of the economic potential of a region and of its infrastructure. It leads almost necessarily to the identification of the most promising and probably most efficient centers around which the economy of the region may be developed. It permits the concentration of development assistance in these centers, or nuclei, or growth points, or poles, as they may variously be called. Again, Professor Klaassen's model shows the circumstances in which development policy oriented in this fashion may be economically efficient. And this approach to regional development seems more likely to succeed than a laissez-faire dependence

[3] It is recognized that whether this occurs depends in considerable measure on the tax and political structure of the community and the state. It is apparent that many urban communities in the United States are starved for the support necessary to maintain municipal services as they grow.

upon mobility of labor toward existing jobs, since intraregional movement is certainly easier to stimulate than interregional. And however more mobile capital may be, its movement can apparently be better organized by regional policy than by competitive efforts to attract new industry to a multiplicity of small and inefficient development areas.

There is another possible consequence of a regional approach to development problems. An examination of regional economies, particularly in a context of full employment, permits a focus not only on presently critical problems, but also on the future. That is, preventive as well as remedial policies can be more easily pursued. This is so because the nature of a regional aproach is such that the entire economies of the several regions should be under continuous examination. Of the several countries studied, only in France is there explicit recognition of this possibility—a recognition to which not only the regional approach but the planning approach no doubt contributes.

The change in approach is undoubtedly the outstanding fundamental and common characteristic of development policy in the several countries. In general, they began with an effort to identify and treat problems of relatively high unemployment or low incomes in each small locality in which they appeared—to bring industrial jobs to each group of workers jobless either because they had been released from agriculture or because the industry in which they worked was in decline. In general this appeared to be as inefficient and ineffective as complete reliance on the market. The direction of development policy in every case has been toward regional development around regional development centers—a direction pursued farthest, perhaps, in Italy, Holland, and France, and least far in Belgium, Britain, and Germany. A major point of criticism by each of the national experts is the failure each observes in the policies of his own country to go more rapidly toward this approach.

The most difficult obstacle to the attainment of a regional approach to development policy is the fact that in no country do political and administrative boundaries correspond with the economic. The difficulties thus presented are perhaps more easily overcome in politically centralized countries like France and Italy than in federal Germany or in Britain with its strong traditions of local government. Certainly in the United States this problem is of crucial importance. Nevertheless, the major lesson to be learned from experience in the countries studied is that unrelated efforts to develop every problem community are, at best, a dissipation of resources and at worst, virtually doomed to failure.

The regionalization of development policies and their integration into an overall consideration of the economy lead naturally to a relating of development problems to those of congestion in urban agglomerations. Professor Klaassen's model shows the circumstances under which—again from the point of view of the purely economic criterion of cost of investment, including social as well as private cost—new investment, which on the basis of private cost alone might locate in an agglomeration, ought better to be directed elsewhere. There are circumstances under which a dollar of social expenditure on subsidy to entrepreneurs to locate outside an agglomeration might save more than a dollar in social cost in a congested urban agglomeration.

The positive expressions of this kind of policy appear in the control of new locations in Paris and in London. Though Mr. Odber is critical of the unwillingness to control new office building in the London area, at least there are the requirements for Industrial Development Certificates for new industry. New industrial locations outside the development areas, and particularly in London, are closely limited. As for Paris, not only is new commercial and industrial construction closely controlled, but a premium is granted for the destruction of existing buildings (though, as M. Bauchet remarks, the latter has been of little effect). In Holland there is explicit recognition of this problem, although outright restrictions such as those in France and Britain are not applied.

Such policies are conceivable only in an environment of full employment; even then, it would clearly be difficult to gain political acceptance for them in the United States. But full employment reduces, if it does not eliminate, competitiveness among local communities for new industry. Thus it provides an environment in which area redevelopment policies are more likely to be effective.

As most of the national studies indicate, even under full employment it is difficult to maintain the differentiating character of redevelopment policies; that is, to prevent their being offset either by policies of subordinate units of government intended to further their own development or by general economic policies of the central government.

As Dr. Storbeck's analysis makes clear, it is often the communities least needful of development which can best afford it, and their individual efforts may well counteract national assistance to the areas chosen for redevelopment. Dr. Storbeck's comments have particular point for the United States which, like west Germany, has a federal system.

In the other countries of the Common Market, centralization of authority permits greater control. To be sure, the situation in France, where some local policies escape the control of its highly centralized government to the detriment of consistent redevelopment measures, indicates that centralization is not sufficient answer. Indeed, as Professor Bauchet points out, it brings its own problems with it. But France's experience also shows the strength of local drives for economic aggrandizement.

In addition to the diluting effects of actions taken by local units of government, a universal problem seems to exist in the failure to coordinate such policies of central government as public works, housing, education, monetary and fiscal measures, procurement, etc., with development policy. The consequence often is that the differentiation in locational advantages intended to be created is neutralized. Apparently it is one of the most difficult political problems in any country to get coordination of policy between special development agencies and the permanent departments of the central government, and to get the latter to incorporate development criteria into their decisions. But failure to do so obviously weakens the development effort and results in unnecesary dissipation of resources.

Not one of the national experts evaluates highly the success of the policies pursued in his country. With respect to evaluation it should first be noted that it proved impossible to assess the usefulness of any particular instrument by itself. That is, it cannot be said that tax exemption is more successful than low-interest-rate loans, or that either is more useful than the development of industrial sites to be sold or rented at low cost. Area development policy is, or should be, an integrated whole. Policies are applied in conjunction with each other. When they take hold in a community or region, they become cumulative, and no single policy can be given major credit. For this reason, uniform measures to compare the effectiveness of particular policies in isolation proved infeasible.

Mr. Odber was able to single out one important deterrent to successful application of development policy in Britain, that is, the tendency to decertify a small area once it achieved an unemployment rate less than the critical figure. He makes a strong case that long-term assurance of availability of development measures, until the area has clearly become self-sustaining, is essential to the success of a policy. Again, all the authors attribute some degree of failure to the fact that growth-point policies were pursued with insufficient vigor, and development policies were dissipated in attempting to meet the problems in all the specific localities in which they arose. In general, also, there was a failure to coordinate general economic policies with development policies, so that the differentiating effect of development measures was often diluted. As noted above, this problem arose not only out of the independent policies of local communities or areas, but also out of conflicts between various policies of the central government.

Techniques of evaluation of the success of development policies are difficult to find. In general, the authors used measures of relative change in well-being in the development areas, as compared with the rest of the country. The question asked was simply whether the disparities in well-being were reduced or increased over the time period considered. Such measurements often were difficult because of the state of economic statistics by regions. As Professor Klaassen points out, it seem a little absurd that much information is available about the Grand Duchy of Luxemburg because it happens to be a sovereign nation, but little is available about much larger and more important regions within other countries. This is noted, not because it is of particular concern to the United States, but because it explains the relatively unsophisticated measures of the impact of development policies.

European economies have been under great strains in the postwar period. Among the factors producing these strains have been the reconstruction of war damages, the disruption of accustomed trade relations caused by political circumstances, the locational impacts of the organization of the Coal and Steel Community, the Common Market, and the European Free Trade Association, the generally high rates of change in productivity and growth, compared, for example, to the United States (though there are substantial differences among the countries studied in this respect), and the relatively rapid rate of increase in prices, again compared to the United States. Most of these, save the price increases, are deliberate and desirable. But they often accentuate local and regional problems; for example, the high rates of increase in productivity produce the same problems of manpower displacement in Europe as they do in the United States.

Considering these circumstances, the external observer would probably evaluate the impact of development policies more positively than do the experts themselves. To bring to a halt the increase in discrepancies between the advantaged and the disadvantaged segments of the economy, as seems to be the general conclusion from the crude measures of evaluation available, was no mean achievement. Indeed, unemployment rates in the equivalents to "section 5a" areas under the U.S. Area Redevelopment Act are, in Europe, often far lower than the U.S. national average rate.

But, as we have said, general full employment, though it may reduce the meaningfulness of the employment criterion, does not eliminate the necessity for area or regional development policies. It does, however, require a refocusing on different criteria and more fundamental objectives. In terms of philosophy, our authors regard the policies of their countries as partial failures because they have not progressed far or fast enough toward this refocus. In terms of achievement, fundamentally they seem to believe that because of this failure to focus clearly, the contributions which depressed regions could make to national welfare and income have been less than they should have been. The theme runs through all the studies that concentration on the purely economic objective yields, as a byproduct, better "social" results than if a direct attack is made on the problems of social welfare. But it should be underlined that this does not mean sole reliance on the market, laissez faire, and worker and entrepreneurial response to economic motivations in accordance with existing locational inducements. It does mean changing locational inducements by governmental action so as to maximize national income. In the views of the authors, generally speaking, such failures as they see flow from internal inconsistencies of policies judged by these standards.

These studies may be commended to students and policymakers in the field of development of disadvantaged areas within advanced industrial societies. Done by outstanding scholars of Europe and Britain, most of whom have had direct experience in formulating policy and who are deeply interested in the problem principally from the point of view of policy, they should be most provocative of ideas for the improvement of policy outside their own countries, as they have been within them. They are worthy of careful attention.

For reference purposes, the appendix to this introduction provides certain national income data for each of the seven countries, from 1955 to 1960 or 1961. These are shown in the national currency, and translated into dollar equivalents by means of the average exchange rate prevailing during the year.

SELECTED NATIONAL INCOME STATISTICS FOR THE STUDY COUNTRIES

	1955	1956	1957	1958	1959	1960	1961
FRANCE							
In billions of new francs:							
Gross national product	170.5	188.3	210.6	239.6	260.0	286.0	309.1
Gross domestic fixed capital formation	29.9	33.8	39.8	44.1	46.2	49.9	55.1
General government consumption expenditure	22.2	27.4	31.1	34.2	38.9	40.9	45.0
Fixed capital formation—							
By general government only	3.8	4.4	4.8	5.3	5.8	6.1	7.0
By general government, public corporations and government enterprises	n.a.	n.a.	n.a.	n.a.	19.1	19.7	21.2
Exchange rate, new franc in U.S. dollars	.286	.286	.238	.237	.204	.204	.204
In billions of U.S. dollars at current exchange rate:							
Gross national product	48.7	53.8	50.0	56.9	53.0	58.3	63.0
Gross domestic fixed capital formation	8.6	9.7	9.5	10.5	9.4	10.2	11.2
General government consumption expenditure	6.3	7.9	7.4	8.1	7.9	8.3	9.2
Fixed capital formation—							
By general government only	1.1	1.3	1.1	1.3	1.1	1.2	1.4
By general government, public corporations and government enterprises	n.a.	n.a.	n.a.	n.a.	3.9	4.0	4.3

761-932 O—65——2

SELECTED NATIONAL INCOME STATISTICS FOR THE STUDY COUNTRIES—Continued

	1955	1956	1957	1958	1959	1960	1961
GERMANY							
In billions of marks:							
Gross national product	178.3	196.4	213.6	228.5	247.9	282.4	310.4
Gross domestic fixed capital formation	41.0	45.0	46.7	50.3	57.1	67.7	77.9
General government consumption expenditure	23.8	25.3	27.3	30.6	33.6	38.4	43.7
Fixed capital formation, general government only	4.8	5.5	5.7	6.3	7.9	9.4	10.3
Exchange rate, mark in U.S. dollars	.238	.238	.238	.238	.239	.240	.249
In billions of U.S. dollars at current exchange rate:							
Gross national product	42.4	46.7	50.8	54.5	59.3	67.7	77.3
Gross domestic fixed capital formation	9.7	10.7	11.1	12.0	13.6	16.2	19.4
General government consumption expenditure	5.6	6.0	6.5	7.3	8.1	9.2	10.9
Fixed capital formation, general government only	1.1	1.3	1.4	1.5	1.9	2.3	2.6

BELGIUM							
In billions of Belgian francs:							
Gross national product	482.4	520.4	554.2	551.0	572.4	608.0	....
Gross domestic fixed capital formation	74.7	86.4	95.2	89.6	98.5	106.5	....
General government consumption expenditure	53.2	55.6	58.2	62.8	67.0	72.3	....
Fixed capital formation—							
By general government only	8.2	9.7	10.0	9.0	10.4	10.7	....
By general government, public corporations and government enterprises	17.3	19.2	19.2	19.5	21.4	20.7	....
Exchange rate, franc in U.S. dollars	.020	.020	.020	.020	.020	.020	....
In billions of U.S. dollars at current exchange rate:							
Gross national product	9.6	10.4	11.0	11.0	11.5	12.2	....
Gross domestic fixed capital formation	1.5	1.7	1.9	1.8	2.0	2.1	....
General government consumption expenditure	1.1	1.1	1.2	1.3	1.3	1.4	....
Fixed capital formation—							
By General Government only	.2	.2	.2	.2	.2	.2	....
By General Government, public corporations and government enterprises	.3	.4	.4	.4	.4	.4	....

SELECTED NATIONAL INCOME STATISTICS FOR THE STUDY COUNTRIES—Continued

	1955	1956	1957	1958	1959	1960	1961
ITALY							
In billions of lire:							
Gross national product	13, 807	14, 885	15, 992	17, 114	18, 290	19, 937	21, 912
Gross domestic fixed capital formation	2, 750	3, 046	3, 434	3, 481	3, 786	4, 441	5, 058
General government consumption expenditure	1, 887	2, 099	2, 233	2, 501	2, 695	2, 950	3, 225
Fixed capital formation, general government only	361	333	372	455	514	577	636
Exchange rate, lira in U.S. dollars	.0016	.0016	.0016	.0016	.0016	.0016	.0016
In billions of U.S. dollars at current exchange rate:							
Gross national product	22. 1	23. 8	25. 6	27. 3	29. 5	32. 1	35. 3
Gross domestic fixed capital formation	4. 4	4. 9	5. 5	5. 6	6. 1	7. 1	8. 1
General government consumption expenditure	3. 0	3. 4	3. 6	4. 0	4. 3	4. 8	5. 2
Fixed capital formation, general government only	.6	.5	.6	.7	.8	.9	1. 0

NETHERLANDS							
In millions of guilders:							
Gross national product	30, 273	32, 542	35, 283	35, 911	38, 385	42, 470	44, 380
Gross domestic fixed capital formation	6, 798	8, 119	9, 044	8, 060	8, 913	9, 970	10, 800
General government consumption expenditure	4, 337	4, 913	5, 282	5, 197	5, 184	5, 750	6, 160
Fixed capital formation—							
By general government only	1, 084	1, 245	1, 496	1, 395	1, 587	1, 730	1, 970
By general government, public corporations and government enterprises	2, 235	2, 476	3, 131	2, 779	2, 975	3, 230	3, 430
Exchange rate, guilder in U.S. dollars	. 262	. 261	. 262	. 264	. 265	. 265	. 276
In billions of U.S. dollars at current exchange rate:							
Gross national product	7. 94	8. 50	9. 24	9. 48	10. 17	11. 25	12. 25
Gross domestic fixed capital formation	1. 78	2. 12	2. 37	2. 13	2. 36	2. 64	2. 98
General government consumption expenditure	1. 14	1. 28	1. 38	1. 37	1. 37	1. 52	1. 70
Fixed capital formation—							
By general government only	. 28	. 32	. 39	. 37	. 42	. 46	. 54
By general government, public corporations, and government enterprises	. 59	. 65	. 82	. 73	. 79	. 86	. 95

SELECTED NATIONAL INCOME STATISTICS FOR THE STUDY COUNTRIES—Continued

	1955	1956	1957	1958	1959	1960	1961
LUXEMBURG							
In millions of francs:							
Gross national product	18, 448	20, 296	21, 935	21, 810	22, 482	24, 413	....
Gross domestic fixed capital formation	4, 124	4, 030	5, 230	5, 227	5, 247	5, 125	....
General government consumption expenditure	2, 423	2, 297	2, 477	2, 797	2, 608	2, 534	....
Fixed capital formation—							
By general government and government enterprises	1, 232	965	1, 175	1, 517	1, 693	1, 267	....
By general government, public corporations and government enterprises	1, 467	1, 231	1, 525	1, 915	1, 957	1, 567	....
Exchange rate, franc in U.S. dollars	. 020	. 020	. 020	. 020	. 020	. 020	....
In millions of U.S. dollars at current exchange rate:							
Gross national product	367	407	437	437	450	490	....
Gross domestic fixed capital formation	82	81	105	105	105	103	....
General government consumption expenditure	46	46	49	56	52	51	....
Fixed capital formation—							
By general government and government enterprises	25	19	24	30	34	25	....
By general government, public corporations and government enterprises	29	25	30	38	39	31	....

UNITED KINGDOM							
In millions of pounds:							
Gross national product	19, 163	20, 836	21, 944	22, 927	23, 957	25, 313	26, 738
Gross domestic fixed capital formation	2, 751	3, 045	3, 307	3, 436	3, 673	4, 083	4, 499
General government consumption expenditure	3, 278	3, 569	3, 692	3, 797	4, 014	4, 251	4, 630
Fixed capital formation—							
By general government only	249	295	321	337	374	412	492
By general government, public corporations and government enterprises	1, 300	1, 379	1, 474	1, 474	1, 577	1, 660	1, 793
Exchange rate, pound in U.S. dollars	279. 13	279. 57	279. 32	280. 98	280. 88	280. 76	280. 22
In billions of U.S. dollars at current exchange rate:							
Gross national product	53. 5	58. 2	61. 3	64. 4	67. 3	71. 1	75
Gross domestic fixed capital formation	7. 7	8. 5	9. 2	9. 7	10. 3	11. 5	12. 6
General government consumption expenditure	9. 2	10. 0	10. 3	10. 7	11. 3	11. 9	13. 0
Fixed capital formation—							
By general government only	. 7	. 8	. 9	. 9	1. 1	1. 2	1. 4
By general government, public corporations and government enterprises	3. 6	3. 9	4. 1	4. 1	4. 4	4. 7	5. 0

Sources: United Nations Statistical Yearbook. For exchange rates, Federal Reserve Bulletin.

Part 2

Regional Policy in the Benelux Countries

L. H. Klaassen*

*The author wishes to express his deep gratitude to all those who contributed in one way or another to this study. He is much indebted to Mr. E. F. Mendoza Berrueto of Mexico City, Mexico, and Professor A. J. Odber of the University of Durham, England, who gave valuable criticisms on ch. 1. The description of Dutch regional economic policy was very much improved by incorporating the remarks of Mr. F. J. J. H. M. van Os of the Ministry of Economic Affairs, The Hague, Holland, and Mr. H. Kuipers of the Netherlands School of Economics, while the Belgian part profited by the comments of Dr. N. Vanhove of the West Flemish Economic Research Bureau at Bruges, Belgium.

Mrs. S. van Willigenburg, secretary at the Netherlands Economic Institute in Rotterdam, took care of the administrative part of the work and the typing of the manuscript. I am grateful to her for the patience with which she responded to my many requests.

Contents

Introduction

In order to make the objectives of regional economic policy in the Low Countries understandable and also to make clear why the instruments used in this policy deviate in some respects from those used elsewhere, it seems useful to start this report with a short theoretical argument on regional differences in income and employment in general and then, more specifically, to discuss the application of this argument to the actual situation in the Benelux countries. It will become apparent then that there are no *basic* differences in the objectives and tools of regional economic policy in the Benelux countries as compared with other European countries, but that fundamental differences in fact exist only (to confine ourselves to the Western World) between Europe and the United States. This holds particularly for the policy with regard to large urban agglomerations in many countries in Europe, which constitute a basic factor in many decisions taken in the field of regional economic policy in both Western and Eastern Europe.

We will concentrate first on the theory of regional differences in income and employment that underlies the policies actually followed. This theory was not formulated explicitly either in Belgium or in Holland. Its main ideas, however, can be found in official papers, though sometimes not very clearly stated and often vaguely formulated.

This theoretical treatment of the problem will be followed by a description of the regional policies adopted in Holland and the changes and adjustments in these policies during the postwar years. Some indication will be given of their effectiveness and of the magnitude of the changes in regional distribution of employment and income that have taken place as a result.

Since Belgian regional policy is a very recent development, it will be difficult to follow exactly the same line in the chapter on Belgium. Nevertheless, an attempt will be made to give some idea of the effectiveness of that country's regional policy.

After a short chapter on Luxemburg some general conclusions will be drawn.

A Theory of Regional Distribution of Income and Employment

General

The aim of this theoretical model is certainly not to explain all the extremely complicated developments that actually take place, but only to show the context in which the basic ideas on regional planning in the low countries should be placed.

Let us start with an economy where three kinds of individuals exist: workers, suppliers of capital, and entrepreneurs. The objective of each entrepreneur is to combine labor and capital in such a way that his total profits are maximized. This implicitly means that his demand for labor and capital has to be defined not only in terms of total quantities required but also on a *regional* basis.

In general he will be inclined to shift to regions where his chances of getting the maximum profit will be highest. These, of course, are not necessarily the regions where *production* costs are lowest, because transportation and marketing costs, especially in regions far from the larger markets, might considerably exceed those elsewhere. This would mean that his profits in those regions would be lower in spite of the fact that production costs are lower.

Assuming for the moment that the differences in production costs are decisive for the differences in profits, we may start from the simplified supposition that the location of demand for labor and capital, which means the location of industries, is regulated by the level of total costs, i.e., wage costs, the remuneration of capital, and the prices of raw materials and semifinished products. We may start then from an equilibrium situation in which all regional incomes are equal and there is no unemployment in any region. Now suppose that some exogenous factor changes; for instance, assume an increase in foreign demand for products produced in region I. As a result of this, the demand for labor and capital as well as the remuneration of both factors of production increases. Labor and capital flow from all other regions to region I. This flow will continue until a new equilibrium is reached (on a higher level) in which again there is no reason for anybody, worker or supplier of capital, to shift his actual supply from one region to another. Nor is there any incentive for the entrepreneur to change the regional distribution of his demand for the factors of production.

If this mechanism worked, there would be no reason to worry about regional problems. Equilibrium would be restored automatically.

Rigidities

However, in this unrealistic classical theory a very important rigidity was neglected. Workers do not react immediately to differences in wages. Their reaction is slow and lags behind actual demand. This means that the demand for labor as a result of the foreign demand for products produced in region I will probably increase more rapidly than the working population in region I, including migration to that region. The reaction is too slow to supply the necessary additional labor. Wages will then rise more in region I than in other regions, and regional differences in income appear. This situation is often found in industrial versus agricultural regions. The much higher income elasticity for industrial products than for agricultural products causes a premanently higher demand for workers in industry than in agriculture. In combination with the relative immobility of labor this may cause substantial and permanent differences in regional incomes and wages.

The question immediately arises, however, whether the mobility of capital is so high that, as soon as the wage difference between region I and other regions is such that production outside region I can take place at lower costs than inside region I, enterpreneurs would immediately shift their demand for labor and capital to other regions where production costs are lower. Here, too, there is considerable rigidity in the reaction of capital to differences in production costs. However, one should distinguish between the mobility of capital already invested, which because of extremely high costs of relocation is almost zero, and the mobility of new capital, of current investments. It may be safely assumed that the mobility of investments is relatively high compared with that of the existing capital stock.

One example will make this point clear. Gross investment equals savings plus the funds resulting from depreciation of the existing capital stock. Since the second source of capital to be reinvested is given, the total amount depends on changes in the rate of net investments. If the reinvestments amount to, say, 5 percent of the total capital stock annually, this means, with a gross capital coefficient of 3.0, that about 15 percent of total gross production is needed for replacement. If net investments amount to, say, 10 percent of gross production, this category covers about 40 percent of the total gross investments. The higher the net investment rate, the larger the amount of capital that may be reinvested elsewhere. The mobility of capital, therefore, is itself a function of the rate of expansion of the economy. The lower the rate of expansion, the lower the capital mobility; the higher this rate, the higher also the mobility of capital.

These two rigidities, then—the relatively low mobility of labor (i.e., the very slow reaction of workers to changes in the regional distribution of demand for labor) and the low mobility of capital—are the most important factors causing regional differences in income and employment. The demand for labor exceeds supply in the expanding area, causing inflationary pressures there, and the supply of labor exceeds demand in the less expanding area, causing unemployment in that region. Both evils, inflation and unemployment, go hand in hand as a result of insufficient mobility of labor and capital.

It should be remarked here that the higher the average rate of expansion of the whole economy, the lower is the average rate of unemployment. At or near full employment, profit expectations in the different regions are determined not only by the level of costs, wages, and prices per region but also by the *availability of labor as such.* The mobility of capital in this situation is thus influenced by whether workers in a given region are available or not. We will see later that this point plays an important role in the decentralization of industry in the Netherlands.

For theoretical reasons we assumed that maximum profits do not, geographically speaking, coincide with minimum costs of production and marketing. However, in very small countries like the Benelux countries price differences from region to region are very slight, and therefore in these countries the two policies, maximization of profits and minimization of production and marketing costs, for all practical purposes may be considered identical.

Regional Policy

It follows from the foregoing that a government policy designed to decrease regional differences in income and employment should aim at—

- Furthering the mobility of labor, for instance, by subsidizing the costs of moving and by supplying good housing facilities and other amenities in the expanding area.
- Furthering the mobility of capital (and keyworkers connected with it) toward lower cost regions by increasing cost differences between regions. This can be done by subsidizing directly or indirectly the industries locating or expanding in the areas to be developed.

The effectiveness of such a regional economic policy is measured by the total difference in national income with and without the policy. Since this procedure is a very complicated one and, moreover, no quantitative measurements of the reaction coefficients of workers and entrepreneurs are available, a number of measures are usually taken simultaneously and their effectiveness later assessed. Eventually, some changes in policy may be made on the basis of this new knowledge.

Geographical Differentiation of Regional Policy

The question to be solved immediately, of course, is which workers should receive financial support, and which entrepreneurs in what region. Not all less developed areas have the same possibilities for future economic growth. Such factors as geographical position or defectiveness of infrastructure may play an important role in the the failure of some areas to develop. Since the costs of development of the regions are very different, as are their development possibilities, a choice should be made on the basis of general economic and social research as to which areas are to receive help in the form of labor subsidies and which in the form of capital subsidies. This decision implies a determination of those regions from which workers should be encouraged to migrate to jobs elsewhere and those to which jobs should be brought. That is, research is needed to find out which regions can be developed by investing capital in them and which regions cannot. An efficient policy presupposes that a choice is made, the "best" regions are selected, and the movement of labor and capital to these regions is furthered.

It must be stressed that the regions selected are not necessarily either the developed or the less developed regions. Development is a dynamic process and not always one of regular long-run expansion; a developed region of today may be an underdeveloped region of tomorrow. Activities therefore should be directed toward *future* possibilities and not be undertaken solely because a particular region is or is not developed at the moment.

The policy described above is illustrated by graph I.

Area A is the developed area; B and C together are the underdeveloped area. Since development possibilities in area C are greater than in area B, this area is chosen for development. The movement of capital from A to C is subsidized, but not from A to B.

Labor movement from B to A is subsidized, but not from C to A. In the

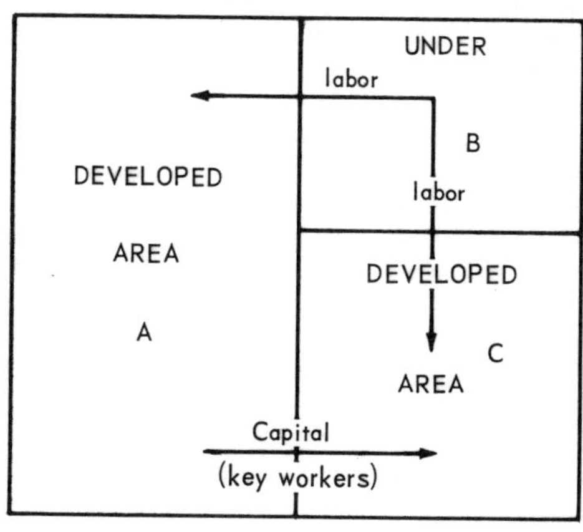

longer run, labor movement from B to C might also be subsidized. Moreover, since keyworkers are always needed to accompany capital movements, subsidies for movement of specialized labor from A to C might be given.

Social Elements in Regional Policy

Very often in practice a different procedure is followed, and areas are selected simply because they are less developed. Holland's social policy, for instance, sought a redistribution of income in favor of the areas with the highest unemployment and consequently, very often, the lowest income. The choice was not made on the basis of development possibilties. That a number of the areas chosen coincide with areas that might have been chosen if the policy were strictly economic does not mean that its basic principles are economic.

In this case, clearly, a price is paid for the more equal regional income distribution in the form of a lower total national product than might have been attained if the policy were more economically oriented. Justification for this policy is partly found in the fact that population in the areas with "heavy and persistent" unemployment is often immobile, so that the subsidies necessary to move this population to other areas would be relatively large. Expenses might actually be so high that it is cheaper to move capital to the area. Frequently sociological factors are also brought into the picture, often of a doubtful nature, such as the affection of the people for the region where they were born. Arguments like this are important perhaps in the short run but definitely not in the long run. They might hold for the parents but not for the children.

The Larger Agglomerations

In the Netherlands and many other European countries there is another factor which plays an important role in the choice of areas to be developed. The argument runs as follows: Areas that are already developed normally show very high population densities. Larger cities (agglomerations) lie in these areas, and the population increases of these large agglomerations exceed those of the smaller nuclei. They tend to get bigger and bigger, with all the disadvantages of such growth and in fact very few advantages. Hence we must stop or at least slow down the growth of these large agglomerations in favor of the smaller ones, which usually lie in the less developed areas.

The argument on this point could be treated in a somewhat different way, and might run as follows:

The growth of a large city brings about many economies of large-scale production which are nonexistent in the smaller cities and towns. This holds not only in the economic field but also in the cultural and the educational fields. Moreover, in a large city, the expansion of public services is possible because of the large demand.

This large-scale expansion of public services and production generally will lead to a higher nominal gross urban income per capita the larger the city is. However, the increments in income are likely to decrease as the growth proceeds; that is, the additional advantages become relatively smaller. Nevertheless, as far as nominal income per capita is concerned, the increase continues, even if the agglomeration becomes very large.

On the other hand, operating costs of the community increase too, particularly the costs of transportation for the manufacturer as well as for the worker, whose journey to work increases not only in distance but even more in time. Congestion in the downtown area brings the need for costly freeways, while at the same time there will be a trend toward decentralization with consequent capital losses in the downtown area.

The Optimum Size of a City

If we call these costs the operating costs of a city, there must clearly be a point where the difference between gross income per capita and operating costs (this difference to be called disposable income) is at a maximum. This is the point where the city reaches its optimum size. This point is shown in graph II.

From this point onward disposable income per head will decrease although the nominal gross income is still increasing, because operating costs are increasing even more.

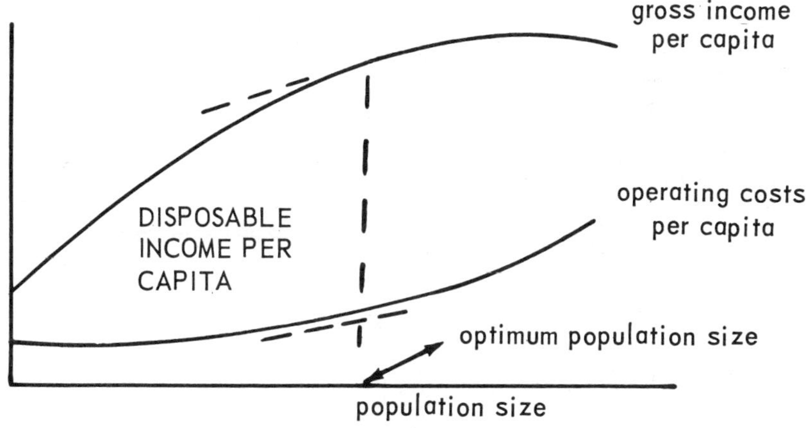

In building cities one should aim at maximizing the contribution of all cities together to the total national income. The distribution of population over the existing nuclei, therefore, should be such that marginal disposable income in all of them is equal.

As a matter of fact, each individual nucleus has its own geographical and economic characteristics leading to different total income and operating cost functions. The criteria stated above mean, therefore, that cities in which operating costs are low and income created is high, grow to a much higher level than cities where the reverse is the case (agricultural nuclei).

This analysis leads to the conclusion that the central government should not indiscriminately support migration from less developed to developed areas. In Holland the overcrowding of large agglomerations is considered so disastrous for the efficient functioning of the whole economy that not only are no measures taken to promote migration to these agglomerations but some are taken to prevent a further influx of workers. This is not the

761-932 O—65——3

case in Belgium; however, at least no explicit statements can be found in Belgian regional policy.

Degree of Centralization of the Tax System

The problem is aggravated when, as in the Netherlands, the tax system of the country is centralized. The main taxes—income and property—are paid to the central government and then redistributed to the local governments. Since the formulas on which this redistribution is based imply that larger agglomerations receive considerably more per capita than smaller ones, the fact that they may be much more costly to operate and that their contribution to disposable income per head in the country may be lower than that of the smaller cities is hidden by the tax system. In actual fact everybody earning income in the country is paying for the high cost of the larger agglomerations.

Normal economic laws of equilibrium would work, of course, if each agglomeration had to pay its own operating costs and if everybody behaved in accordance with purely economic rationality. Then the relatively expensive large agglomerations would have very high tax rates. This would immediately influence the decision to live in that city and its growth would be slowed down. Since in no country is the tax system completely decentralized, however, almost everywhere the whole country contributes to the operating costs of the large agglomerations. The more centralized the tax system is, the more this holds true.

Our first graph changes as a result of these considerations. Because of the need to avoid further overcrowding of the larger agglomerations, no arrow will be shown pointing from area B to area A for labor. In graph III capital flows from area A to area C and labor from area B to area C.

"Nuclei" Policy

Graph III, however, does not take into account that an effort should be made to distribute the total population of the country as efficiently as

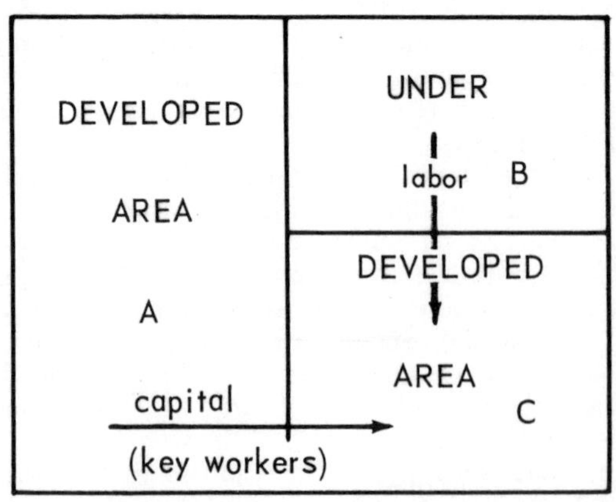

possible over the existing or even new nuclei. Graph II suggests that disposable income created by additional population increases as the nucleus grows (up to the optimum-size point). This means that a higher contribution to total income is obtained by developing the nuclei in which marginal disposable income is highest than by developing the whole area or, even worse, the smaller, economically inefficient nuclei. For this reason activities and subsidies should be confined to the larger and more efficient nuclei in the development area. This again changes our graphical representation of regional policy into the final graph IV.

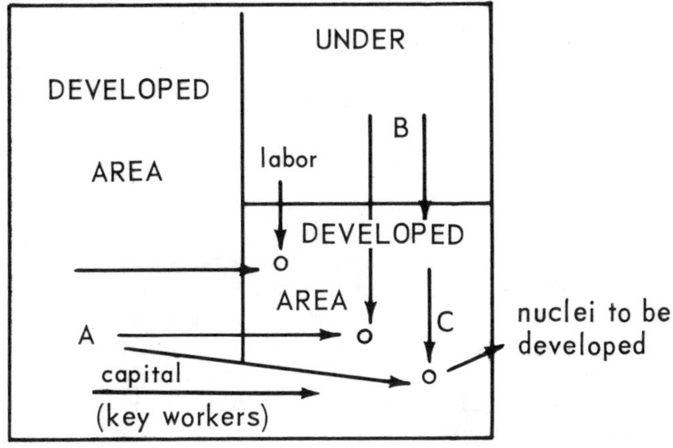

Conclusion

The foregoing sections give the basic theoretical background of regional policy in the low countries, as well as some insight into the problems existing in these areas. In actual practice many additional factors and considerations come into play. These will be discussed in the following sections on individual countries.

One further point, however, should be made here: very often it is not sufficient to subsidize workers moving from one area to another; it may also be necessary to train them for new jobs created in the developing area. This training is clearly needed insofar as moving from one region to another implies moving from one sector of the economy to another, which, of course, is not always the case. Training of workers is a fundamental problem in sectorial analysis and a secondary, but in some cases still very important, problem in regional analysis. As such it will be treated in the following sections.

Some Income Data About Benelux

The three Benelux countries cover an area of 25,400 square miles, of which 50 percent lies in the Netherlands, 46.5 percent in Belgium, and 3.5

percent in Luxemburg. The total population of the three countries is 21 million (Belgium 9.2 million, Holland 11.5 million, and Luxemburg 0.3 million). In Holland the working population amounts to 36 percent of total population, in Belgium 40 percent, and in Luxemburg 45 percent.

In 1960 the gross national product of the three countries together equaled $23.8 billion. As per capita of the working population, this amounts to $3,010 for Benelux, $2,689 for Holland, $3,380 for Belgium, and $2,990 for Luxemburg.

Map I shows the income differences within the Benelux countries. The highest income per capital of the working population is found in the Belgian provinces of Brabant and Liège. This average is heavily influenced by the presence there of the agglomerations of Brussels and Liège. Generally speaking the Belgian level is somewhat higher than that of the Netherlands. On the other hand, the Dutch province with the highest per capita income is about 48 percent above the lowest, while in Belgium this percentage is 78. The distribution in Belgium, therefore, is more unequal than in Holland.

Although much more relevant data, such as exports, imports, consumption, investment, etc., are available, for the three countries as a whole, none of these macroeconomic data exist for regions. Statistical data of a macroeconomic character are always collected on a national basis and seldom on a regional basis. This leads to the somewhat ridiculous situation that everything is known about very small countries like Luxemburg but almost nothing about the Ruhr, Southern California, or London areas, for example. Beginnings have been made in the collection of better regional data for Holland and Belgium.

Regional Policy in the Netherlands

Some General Information; Regional Income Differences

The Netherlands, with a population of 11.5 million and a gross national product of $11.2 billion in 1960, is situated in northwestern Europe. It has a relatively long coastline along the North Sea and occupies, broadly speaking, the delta of the Rhine, the Meuse, and the Schelde rivers. The main part of this delta proper lies below sea level and is protected against the sea by dunes and dykes. Because of the country's geographical position and lack of raw materials, the Dutch concentrated from the 16th century on shipping and trade. Imported raw materials were partly used in local industry. Shipbuilding and repair were concentrated in and around the larger ports, with financial institutions and insurance activities flourishing in the main centers of economic activity.

The industrial revolution gave rise to rapid industrial development in Holland's hinterland, West Germany. The Ruhr area became a large importer of all kinds of raw materials, and as the Rhine was the natural connection between the Ruhr and the sea, a new impulse was given to the development of Dutch ports, especially Rotterdam.

The central government is located in The Hague at a distance of about

Benelux Regional Income Distribution

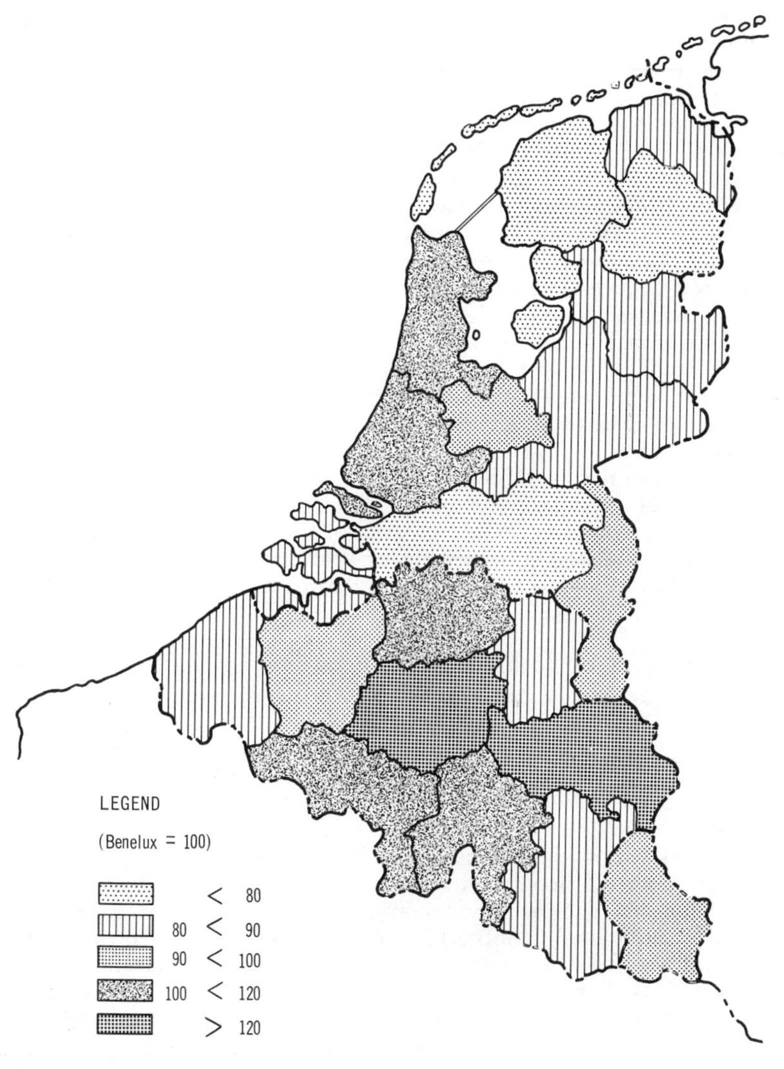

15 miles from the center of Rotterdam and some 35 miles from the center of Amsterdam.

Roughly speaking, therefore, the three largest cities in Holland each concentrated on specific activities: Amsterdam on trade and finance, but also on shipping (general cargo); Rotterdam on shipping (bulk products) and industry based on deep navigable water; and The Hague on the affairs of the central government and of many head offices of national and international enterprises. Although some industrial nuclei existed in other parts of the country (Amersfoort, Tilburg, Enschede, South Limburg), the main activities in the northern, eastern, and southern parts of the country were in agriculture.

Recent developments have stimulated the further growth of the western part of the country. During the postwar years Europe rapidly shifted from European to non-European raw materials (oil, iron ore), and the larger ports in Holland, especially Rotterdam, tended to become the European ports of entry for these raw materials. The creation of a harbor west of Rotterdam (Europort), whose construction is now well under way and which will enable very large ships (up to 120,000 tons) to enter the harbor, will be another stimulus. Further rapid industrial development is likely.

The consequence of historical developments has been a heavy concentration of population in West Holland. A ring of cities including the three already mentioned and also Leiden, Haarlem, Hilversum, Utrecht, Gouda, and Dordrecht, with a total population of about 4 million, is concentrated in a relatively small area in the west of the country. It is called the conurbation Holland or, better, the Rimcity. Its population density is about 8,000 to the square mile.

In contrast to this well-developed area, several regions, especially in the north and east, have shown a relatively small population increase and a lagging average income, mainly because of the lack of development possibilities in agricultural activities. This problem was fully recognized immediately after World War II and was the reason for the introduction of regional policy in the Netherlands.

Basic Elements of Industrialization Policy in the Netherlands [1]

INTRODUCTION

It seems useful before entering into the details of Dutch regional policy to treat first some basic elements of the measures taken in Holland to promote industrialization in general. Unlike Belgium the industrialization policy in Holland does not provide the basis on which regional policy has been built. In Belgium, as will become clear later, a so-called general act provides the basis for the general industrialization policy while the regional act provides for additional facilities for certain areas within the framework of the general act and of the same character as the facilities given under the general act. In Holland, however, the regional act is of a more specific character. Nevertheless, it is desirable to treat Dutch general legislation first as background for a better understanding of the specifically regional

[1] Coal and Steel Community, *Massnahmen zur erleichterten Schaffung neuer Betaetigungsmoeglichkeiten* (also in English, Italian, Dutch, and French), 1962. This recent publication gives a systematic review of all measures in the field of industrialization in the EEC countries and the United Kingdom. Dutch expert F. J. J. H. M. van Os, Belgian expert A. Detroz, Luxemburg expert P. Camy.

legislation, and then to outline some of the major incentives to regional development before discussing them in more detail.

FACILITIES FOR INDUSTRIES

Facilities for industries in the Netherlands are given in five forms: (*a*) Loans to industries, (*b*) guarantees, (*c*) general tax facilities, (*d*) accelerated depreciation, and (*e*) facilities to promote development of new products.

Loans to industries

The Dutch Government may support industries developing new machinery or new production processes which are not able to bear the full risk of the undertaking themselves. Requirements for a loan are that the undertaking be of general interest and that the industry itself make a satisfactory contribution to it.

The maximum to be given per applicant is $140,000 and is granted on the basis of real cost invested by the industry in the project. Whether repayment will be demanded or not depends on the outcome of the investment.

The "development loans" are given by the Ministry of Economic Affairs.

Guarantees

There are three groups of guarantees that may be given:

(1) Guarantees given by the Ministry of Economic Affairs on loans of the *Nederlandse Middenstandsbank N.V.* (Dutch Bank for smaller industries). These guarantees are intended especially for the financing of the purchase, renewal, or improvement of equipment as well as for the related renewal of buildings. The guarantees are given on loans between $11,000 and $27,000. Hardly any use of these facilities has been made.

(2) Guarantees given by the Ministry of Finance on loans of the *Maatschappij tot Financiering van het Nationaal Herstel N.V.* (Herstelbank—Reconstruction Bank). Originally this institution was meant mainly for financing special postwar industrial reconstruction projects, but now general projects are financed with guarantees by the Ministry of Finance. The importance of these guarantees is small.

(3) Guarantees given by the *Stichting Industrieel Garantiefonds* (Industrial Guarantee Fund). These guarantees are given through two financing corporations, especially to small and medium-sized industries and new industries unable to obtain the funds needed for expansion on the regular capital market. The capital of the fund has been made available by the central government. To corporations other than the two financing corporations, dividend guarantees may be given to a maximum of 5 percent annually to a maximum period of 10 consecutive years.

Finally, mention should be made of special guarantees given by the government on specific projects of generally recognized importance as basic industries. Two examples are the guarantee for a $7 million loan for an extension of the steel plant in Ijmuiden and a guarantee for a $6 million loan for the soda industry in Delfzijl (special laws).

General tax facilities

General tax facilities to all sorts of enterprises in the Netherlands are given in two ways:

(1) Before profit taxes are paid, remaining losses of the preceding 6 years may be deducted. Also it is possible to deduct losses expected for

the coming year. For new enterprises all losses incurred during the first 6 years of the existence of the industry may be deducted in any of the following years.

(2) New investments or costs of improvements of equipment may be partially deducted from profits in the year of investment and the following year (each year 5 percent).

Accelerated depreciation

The general rule is that one-third of the total costs of investments in manufacturing as well as other industries may be depreciated at a maximum rate of 8⅓ percent annually for equipment and 6 percent for buildings. This facility is, of course, low-cost financing just in the first period of investments because lower depreciation later will lead to higher profits and thus higher taxes then.

Facilities to promote development of new products

Important financial support is given by the government to TNO (Central Organization for Applied Physical Research), a large organization of which the industrial research department alone includes 27 research institutions.

FACILITIES FOR WORKERS

Training

In the Netherlands there are 25 regional training schools for adults, each covering a certain geographical area. They are open to workers between 18 and 50 years of age and have a threefold purpose:

(1) To *train* persons in a trade for the first time.
(2) To *retrain* persons with a skill for which there is no more demand.
(3) To *train* persons who have left their trade for several years and want a "refresher course."

Training is given in those trades which attract an insufficient number of young people and in which in-plant training possibilities are inadequate. Participants are first given medical and psycho-technical tests. They receive compensation for wage loss, for travel expenses, and for costs of board and lodging.

In addition to these facilities, indirect support to workers is given by subsidizing industries that hire and train unemployed workers. These subsidies equal 50 percent of the product of the number of training weeks and the weekly wage rate (after deduction of the estimated value produced by the worker at the beginning of the period) to a maximum of $250 per worker.

Compensation for cost of moving

Workers moving from one locality to another may get governmental support if there is a lack of employment where they were living and a demand for workers in the new locality. They fall into two main categories:

(1) Married workers migrating to a place not designated as a "development nucleus." These workers may get (if not migrating to the Rimcity) full compensation for travel costs for themselves and their family and for costs of moving, as well as $67 plus $11 per child for resettlement expenses.

(2) Married workers migrating to a "development nucleus." These workers may get the same facilities as those in group 1 and in addition, for a maximum of 1 year, 50 percent of the costs of board and lodging or 50 percent of the costs of their daily traveling.

Although regional policy will be examined in detail in the following sections, the main facilities provided to industries in the so-called development areas may be listed here:

(1) *A system of premiums and price reductions* for existing and new industries in development nuclei.

(2) *Provision of industrial land and industrial sites.* By the Act of 1952 about $1.5 million was provided for the opening up of industrial sites in the development nuclei. Out of this amount subsidies were given to local governments of 50 percent of the investments made to a maximum price of $0.07 per square foot and a maximum area of 25 acres. Recently the facilities were substantially widened by dropping the maximum per square foot and fixing the subsidy at 25 percent of total investments to a maximum of $55,000 per applicant (municipality). Annually $550,000 is made available for this purpose.

(3) *Construction of houses.* Since the construction of housing in the Netherlands is rationed per province by the Central Government and per municipality by the Provincial Government, the concentration of residential construction in development nuclei forms an effective instrument for regional policy. Nevertheless, only a modest use of this instrument is made (2,000 houses annually).

In addition to these elements of regional policy, measures of a more general nature are taken to improve the relative position of the "development areas." The most important is probably the improvement of road connections within the development areas and between them and the developed areas. For this program some $52.5 million is available for a 4-year period (from 1960), with $17 million of this earmarked for the accelerated construction of state highways to the development areas.

In the social and cultural field also, important stimuli are given. From 1960 to 1963 about $7 million was made available. A priority scheme for educational institutions stimulated the improvement of education in the problem areas.

Finally, an extensive program for land reform in the agricultural sector should be mentioned.

The First Stage of Regional Policy in the Netherlands [2]

During the years immediately after World War II, average unemployment in the Netherlands amounted to about 2.5 percent of the total active population. Actually, there were large variances from this overall average, especially in five regions in the north and the south. These regions were, in the north, southeast Drenthe (15.5 percent unemployment in 1950), east Groningen (6.6 percent), and east Friesland (3.9 percent), and, in the south, southwest North-Brabant (8.3 percent) and northeast North-Brabant (4.5 percent). Southeast Drenthe particularly showed a very high unemployment rate, and it was considered necessary to investigate in detail the

[2] In 1962 Dr. N. Vanhove published his study on the efficiency of the regional economic policy in the Netherlands: *De doelmatigheid van het regionaal-economisch beleid in Nederland,* Gent-Hilversum. His description of the principles of this policy are so clear and to the point that large parts of it are used in this and the following section. Use is also made of the seventh Memoranda on Industrialization of the Ministry of Economic Affairs and Mr. van Os' contribution to the "Seminar on Urban Development Policy and Planning": F. J. J. H. M. van Os, M.A., "Economic Basis of Urban Development," Seminar Warsaw, September 19–29, 1962.

economic problems of this area. The study was done by the Ministry of Economic Affairs in collaboration with the local government of the town of Emmen. It was concluded that the basic problems of the area were of a structural character, resulting from stagnation in the demand for peat (on which employment in the area was largely based) and from a very rapid natural increase of population.

The first regional development plan resulted from this study. It was aimed partly at improving the production and marketing of peat, and partly at preparing measures to stimulate the industrial development of the area. By the Act of 13 July 1951 a sum of roughly $1.5 million was voted for development of the area. As a reference, it might be noted that average annual government expenditures during the decade of the fifties was slightly under $2 billion, translated at prevailing rates of exchange.

This marked the beginning of further research on underdeveloped areas, and the following criteria were formulated for designating a "development area":

(1) The problem of structural unemployment must be acute.
(2) A solution by means of migration seemed impractical.
(3) A solution by means of industrialization of the area seemed possible.
(4) The total costs of the development plan could be kept within reasonable limits.[3]

On the basis of these criteria, nine development areas were designated:

In the northeast

(1) Southwest Groningen
(2) East Groningen
(3) East Friesland
(4) Southwest Drenthe

In the east

(5) Northeast Overijssel

In the southeast

(6) Northeast North-Brabant
(7) North Limburg

In the southwest

(8) Southwest North-Brabant

In the northwest

(9) East West-Friesland in North Holland

The Act on Development Plans of 23 June 1952 voted about $2.5 million for regional investments. Dutch policy at this stage was clearly directed toward improvement of the employment situation in the development areas. Although it was hoped that decentralization of industry might result as well, this was not stated explicitly. Financial support was given to move unemployed workers from the development areas to other areas of the country, and the mobility of capital was stimulated by a number of measures:

(1) creation of industrial sites
(2) improvement of infrastructure
(3) improvement of public utilities
(4) construction of industrial buildings
(5) training and retraining of workers
(6) construction of houses for workers in new industries in the development areas

[3] Tweede Kamer, Zitting 1951–52. Bijlage 2322–1.

An essential feature of the first-stage policy was some concentration of the development in a limited number of "nuclei" in order to obtain the economies of large-scale production. A special premium was paid to industries newly locating or expanding in the designated nuclei. This consisted of 25 percent of the building costs to a maximum of $0.70 per square foot of effective floor space. Payment of the premium was subject to the condition that at least one unemployed person in the area must be hired for every 500 square feet of new floor space. The total number of workers employed had to be not less than 10.

Some General Conclusions

It is evident that during the first stage the Government based its regional policy on the following principles:

(1) The main criterion for designation of a development area was the structural character and extent of unemployment. This unemployment might be caused by a rapid population growth that exceeded a normal rate of increase in jobs or by a low increase in employment and a more or less normal increase in population. In general, the areas in the northern part of the country fell in the second category, and the areas in the south in the first.

(2) Improvement of the situation was sought in two ways: (*a*) by furthering migration of workers to the more developed areas by subsidizing their costs; and (*b*) by furthering industrial development in the development areas by subsidizing industry newly locating or expanding there.

(3) Since economies of scale were considered to be of importance, concentration was stimulated by the payment of special subsidies to industries in a limited number of nuclei in the development areas.

It appears that during the first stage of regional policy, which lasted from 1951 to 1958, little or no attention was paid to the "agglomeration" aspect of the problem, since workers moving to the large agglomerations could also apply for a subsidy in their costs of moving. The stimulation of labor mobility was an essential feature of the first stage, and the stimulation of the mobility of capital formed a natural and necessary complement.

Another essential feature was that the choice of the development areas was based upon *negative* criteria. The more unemployment, which very often means the less development possibilities, the greater the probability that an area was chosen as a development area. The policy, therefore, did not start from the principle of distinguishing the less developed areas that could be stimulated most efficiently from the purely economic point of view, but only from the principle that assistance should be specially devised for those areas where the unemployment level was highest and of a structural character.

The only indication of even shortrun economic criteria can be found in the formulation of the second and fourth criteria on page 38: a solution by means of migration did not seem possible, and the total costs of the development plan could be kept within reasonable limits. Even taking these into account, the general conclusion remains that the Dutch regional policy from 1951 to 1958 was directed toward developing areas where conditions were worst, and completely neglected the question whether these particular regions were the most suitable for development. *It was a shortrun social policy without a longrun economic view and in which economic considerations played only a partial role.*

During the period 1951–58, migration from the development areas to the developed parts of the country contributed substantially to the solution of the problem of excess labor supply in the development areas. About 70,000 people migrated from the three northern provinces of Groningen, Friesland, and Drenthe to other parts of the country. Of these, about 47,000, or roughly 68 percent, settled in the most developed part of the Netherlands, the western Provinces. About 9,000 people from the east and 7,000 people from Zeeland also came to the west. About 3,800 people went from the west to the south and southeast.

During discussions of regional policy in the years 1956–59, more and more attention was paid to this increasing concentration in the west and especially in the Rimcity. It was argued that in the long run it would lead to intolerable economic and social consequences, and various specific objections were advanced.

The objections of an *economic* character were as follows:

(1) From a certain point on, large agglomerations are relatively very expensive. Decentralization would help avoid the extra costs involved. An indication of the differences in social costs is given by a study made by Dr. C. van den Berg [4] in 1956 on the structure of municipal expenditures. He calculated that the average difference in expenditures of a town with 20,000 compared with a town of 250,000 inhabitants might be estimated at about $10 per capita per year. Indications are that this ratio holds good also for the largest cities in Holland: Amsterdam, Rotterdam, and The Hague.

(2) Valuable agricultural and horticultural land in the west with very high net returns (bulb fields, Westland—very capital-intensive vegetable production) has to be sacrificed with increasing population growth.

(3) Building costs in the west are very high compared with those elsewhere as a result of bad soil conditions making foundations extremely expensive.[5]

(4) Rapid development of *all* industries in the west will, because of the resulting lack of industrial sites, prevent the future growth of industries that can develop *only* in the west.

The objections of a *noneconomic* character were:

(1) Concentration of population in large cities is undesirable from a sociological, public health, and recreational point of view.

(2) Further concentration of population in an area below sea level under constant threat of floods is ill advised.

(3) Concentration of population and industry is undesirable from the defense point of view.

All these arguments, many of which can be found in a Central Planning Office and Government Physical Planning Service publication, "The Development of the Western Part of the Country," [6] contributed to a change in the regional economic policy of the Netherlands. It was considered essential to prevent further unnecessary growth of the Rimcity, although the

---

[4] Dr. C. van den Berg, *De structuur van de gemeentelijke uitgaven,* Leiden, 1956.

[5] Rijksdienst voor het Nationale Plan en Centraal Planbureau, *Het Westen en overig Nederland,* The Hague, 1956.

[6] *De ontwikkeling van het Westen des lands,* The Hague, 1956.

objections were not scientifically balanced against the advantages that, up to a certain point, characterize large agglomerations in the economic, social, and cultural fields.

Also, no precise research was done with regard to the exact level of the total private and social costs of locating industries in different areas. It was taken for granted that the incomplete data available were proof enough of the enormous differences in social costs, and these differences evidently were much larger than those in private costs could possibly be.

Some research on the differences in private costs has been done by the Netherlands Economic Institute in Rotterdam.[7] In this study total costs were divided into (*a*) wages and salaries, (*b*) transportation costs of raw materials and finished products, (*c*) land and building costs, and (*d*) costs of energy. Generally speaking, the costs under categories (*a*) and (*c*) decline with increasing distance from the Rimcity, while those under category (*b*) increase, and under (*d*) remain constant. In order to estimate the quantitative importance of these factors a study was made for an enterprise more or less typical of manufacturing industry. A factory with 100 workers producing steel doors and windows was given 7 alternative locations in different parts of the country. The differences in costs expressed as a percentage of total value produced by such an enterprise were, for different cities: Rotterdam, +1.7 percent (west of the country); Eindhoven, +0.6 percent (south); Amersfoort, +0.3 percent (center); Leeuwarden, −0.1 percent (north); Meppel, −0.6 percent (north); Purmerend, −0.7 percent (northwest); and Steenderen, −1.0 percent (southwest).

Although the differences are small, in general the level of cost decreases with the size of the city and the distance from the west. In fact, however, this industry is very much concentrated in the western part of the country so that evidently a high preference for the larger agglomerations (secondary factors of location) exists.

An additional question arises here with regard to regional policy in general. If it is in fact true that underdeveloped areas make production of certain products possible at lower cost but entrepreneurs will locate their industries in those areas only if they are subsidized, then the actual difference in costs is made larger. This conflicts with the general opinion that the subsidy to the entrepreneur is given in order to compensate him for the economic *disadvantages* of locating in an underdeveloped area because of defectiveness of the infrastructure, low productivity of labor, etc. Further research on this point would be extremely useful in order to prevent competition between firms in developed and underdeveloped areas from being complicated by a system of subsidies from the Central Government in favor of firms that already have lower costs.

Returning to our main discussion, we find that the two problems—the underdeveloped nature of certain areas and the need to prevent, within the limits of normal freedom for worker and entrepreneur, the further unnecessary growth of the larger agglomerations—were combined in one policy that was expected to bring an overall solution for both problems. It was to do so by stimulating growth in the heavily underdeveloped areas and by simultaneously preventing unnecessary growth of the Rimcity. One might ask why the solution was sought in the extremes rather than in the medium-developed areas most promising from the point of view of economic de-

[7] *Onderzoek naar enige vestigingsfactoren van de bedrijven welke stalen ramen en deuren vervaardigen,* Netherlands Economic Institute, Rotterdam, 1959.

Development Regions in Benelux

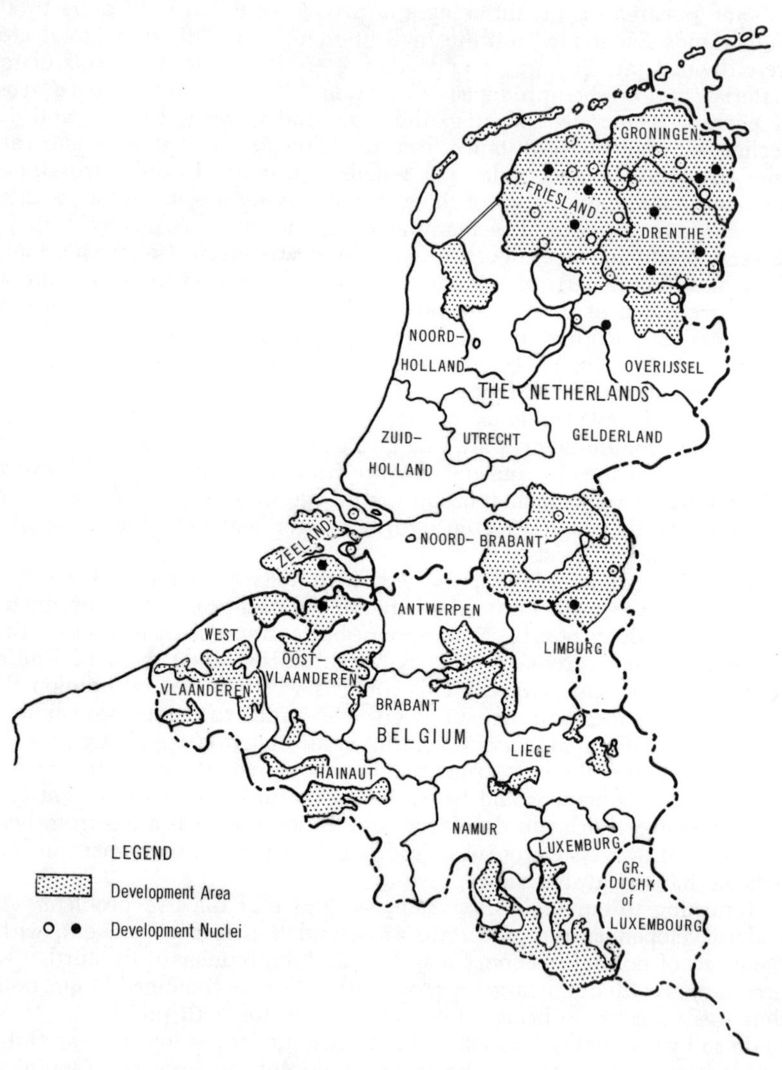

velopment. We will consider this matter later after a look at the actual regional policy.

The new policy was directed to areas larger than those of the first stage. At the presentation of the 1959 budget for the Ministry of Economic Affairs, development areas and nuclei were designated as shown in map II. Instead of "development areas" the regions were called "problem areas."

It would have been possible to pursue the policy objectives by a system of permits for new industries locating in the Rimcity. The Dutch Government, however, preferred to allow industry complete freedom of location, arguing that industry itself was best able to judge the advantages and disadvantages of being located in a given place. Policy therefore concentrated on positive measures in the problem areas more than on negative measures in the Rimcity.

The measures taken to promote the development of the problem areas were:

(1) Improvement of the infrastructure (*a*) by creating efficient, fast connections between the problem areas and the developed parts of the country, and (*b*) by accelerating the construction of industrial sites.

(2) Improvement of the "housing climate" in the problem areas by building modern houses for employees.

(3) Improvement of the social, cultural, and medical "climate" of the problem areas.

(4) A subsidy for the costs of migration of workers living outside the nuclei in a problem area to the nuclei in any one of the problem areas, or more generally to places where there is a net demand for workers. *Migration to the Rimcity was excluded from this subsidy.*

(5) For the period April 1959 on, a new subsidy system for the nuclei in the problem areas. This subsidy system consists of two parts: A premium and a price reduction.

Under the new system, the premium is a subsidy on the costs of new buildings and expansion of old buildings on condition that the industry will employ at least one man per 1,000 square feet if the industry is newly located and one man per 500 square feet if it is an expanding, already existing industry. The amount of the premium for new industries in 1959 was:

$1 per square foot effective floor space for the first 10,000 square feet newly built.

$1.25 per square foot for an additional 10,000 square feet.

$1.50 per square foot for each additional 10,000 square feet up to 40,000 square feet. For the floor space exceeding 40,000 square feet the additional premium is about $2 per square foot.

In the expansion of old industries the premium was first set at $1 per square foot, regardless of the size of the floor space. It is apparent that the premium is a progressive one, making it much more important for larger factories than the old system was.

The question arises whether it is wise to restrict the subsidy to industries where a given minimum of workers will be employed. It might be argued that in any case demand for capital goods and raw materials in the industry would indirectly stimulate demand for labor in other industries. It is not just direct employment but rather the total—or direct plus indirect—employment[8] that is important. The validity of this argument depends on the regional distribution of the indirect demand for labor. If this were exerted in the Rimcity, it would not contribute very much to the solution of the regional differences in employment. If, however, indirect demand were to be exerted locally, that is, in the underdeveloped area itself, the argument would be of some importance. A closer study of the input-output relations of industry in the underdeveloped areas seems necessary in order to draw a definite conclusion.

In 1962 the minister of economic affairs officially reduced the amount of the premium.[9] Since September 1, 1962, it has been as follows for new industries:

$1 per square foot for the first 20,000 square feet newly built.
$1.10 per square foot for the second 20,000 square feet.
$1.20 per square foot for the third 10,000 square feet.
For additional space the premium increases correspondingly to a maximum of $2 per square foot. The maximum subsidy to be given is $350,000.

In the case of expansion the premium amounts to $0.70 per square foot to a maximum of $70,000.

The premium evidently was made less discriminatory by size of industry. The basic reason for the reduction was the unexpectedly large sums needed for subsidies to industries in problem areas.

The regulation on *price reduction* made it possible to reduce the price of municipal land by 50 percent. In the case of industrial land, the entrepreneur would receive 50 percent of the total price from the central government on condition that at least one-fifth of the total land bought would immediately be used for industrial buildings.

This regulation was also changed in 1962 in such a way that, for areas larger than 25 acres, the reduction to be applied will be multiplied by $\frac{25}{x}$ in which x is the total acreage bought by the entrepreneur. Here, too, the subsidy is somewhat restricted. Contrary to the change in the premium, however in this case the larger the industry or, more precisely, the larger the area it needs, the larger the restriction is, i.e., the smaller the price reduction.

Up to January 1, 1963, the premium and price reduction facilities had been used to employ 19,825 workers in new industries and 13,651 in expanded industries. At that date negotiations were going on concerning some 7,750 additional workers.

Some General Conclusions

Summarizing our description of the second stage, we find that the "agglomeration argument" played an important role in the consideration surrounding the "new look" in regional policy. However, as we have said, too much stress was laid on the higher operating costs of agglomerations and hardly any attention was paid to the higher income created by them, although this factor was recognized, as far as the smaller ones were concerned, and in fact led to the principle of concentration. The concept of

---

[8] Credit Professor A. J. Odber, Durham University, Durham, England.
[9] Nederlandse Staatscourant, Aug. 1, 1962, No. 147.

the optimum size of a city, therefore, did not enter the discussions. Nor did other economic arguments as, for instance, the contribution of industries in different areas to the balance of payments. Since Holland's international trade accounts for roughly 50 percent of its total national product, even slight percentage deviations from the normal relationship of exports and imports create serious balance-of-payments problems. Because of the lack of statistical data, no precise estimate of the contribution of the Rimcity to total exports and imports is available, but this contribution is probably very high. Slowing down the development of this area indirectly by stimulating development elsewhere in the country could have an unfavorable influence on the balance-of-payments position. It must be admitted however, that natural tendencies toward decentralization already exist.

Apart from this aspect, the major change in policy was the abolition of subsidies to workers moving to the Rimcity. Instead, a subsidy was paid to workers moving from the problem areas outside the nuclei to the nuclei in order to promote concentration.

The main features of the second stage, therefore, can be summarized by stating that the *policy pursued decentralization of industrial activities by furthering mobility of capital to the problem areas without furthering migration of labor to the developed areas.*

Again, it should be stressed that in this second stage, too, not enough attention was paid to the question *where* industrial development could be stimulated most efficiently. It was considered self-evident that this stimulation should take place in the least developed areas. In this regard the Dutch regional policy lost none of its social character, though it pretended to be an economic policy.

Neither in the first nor in the second stage of regional policy were measures recommended with regard to the commuting of workers. In general, this is regarded as a normal economic phenomenon. As we will see later, in Belgium one of the criteria for selecting development areas is "seasonal, weekly, or daily commuting of an important part of the active population under unfavorable conditions."

Although commuting is not mentioned anywhere in official Dutch papers, questions were raised in Parliament in 1961 especially with regard to the heavy daily commuting from the northern part of North Holland to Amsterdam and the iron and steel factories in Velsen, and from west North Brabant to the Rotterdam area. Those questions, together with the urging of the provincial governments of North Brabant and North Holland, resulted in a study by the Netherlands Economic Institute [10] and the Institute of Labor Problems at the request of the Ministry of Economic Affairs and the Ministry of Social Affairs.

This report found that, of itself, commuting by large numbers of workers was an insufficient motive for the creation of new employment in the area where they lived. Only if (a) commuting time was exceptionally long, and (b) employment of commuters fluctuated heavily, did there seem to be reason to interfere. The report concluded that in general these criteria did not apply to commuting in the two areas studied, and therefore no special measures were recommended.

[10] Drs. J. A. Bourdrez en Professor Dr. J. Godefroy, *Het pendelverschijnsel in Noord-Noordholland en West-Noordbrabant,* Rotterdam/Tilburg, December 1962.

The Effectiveness of Dutch Regional Policy

In this section we will consider whether it is possible to measure the effects of Dutch regional policy. This test implies answers to three basic questions:

(1) Does industry tend to decentralize and can the extent to which decentralization takes place be measured?

(2) To which areas is this decentralization directed and is there a significant difference between the development of industry in the problem areas and development in other areas, taking into account locational factors characteristic of each area?

(3) If there is greater development in the problem areas, is this an additional growth, or is it merely the result of the concentration of industry in those areas at the expense of the developed areas?

The answers to these questions are examined in detail by Dr. N. Vanhove in his recent book on the effectiveness of Dutch regional economic policy.[11]

THE DECENTRALIZATION OF MANUFACTURING INDUSTRIES

Dr. Vanhove first created a decentralization index (D), defined as the relative difference in employment of the western part of Holland between 1953 and 1960 per branch of industry. Suppose that the employment in a given branch in the western part of the country in 1953 is 25 percent of the total employment in Holland, and in 1960 is 20 percent; then his decentralization index is

$$D = \frac{25-20}{25}\, 0.100 = 20$$

He further assumed that the tendency to decentralize was different for different branches, but this could be explained by a number of measurable variables, as components of total production costs of the particular branch. These variables were—

(1) The fraction of wages in total value added (X_1);

(2) The raw material weight per worker employed (X_2);

(3) The fraction of skilled workers in the total number of workers (X_3);

(4) The rate of growth of the industry considered (X_4).

He confined himself to manufacturing industries.

The assumption about the variables requires some further explanation. As already stated, Holland's international trade accounts for about 50 percent of its total national product. This means that the role the large ports of Rotterdam and Amsterdam play in those imports and exports is considerable. Hence it may be safely assumed that industries located further away from the west generally have higher transportation costs than those located in the west. The more transport-intensive, therefore, the less the particular industry will be inclined to locate far from the west. This is the background of variable X_2.

Further, since the west is the most developed part of Holland, wages are considerably higher there than in other areas. The average skill of the

[11] N. Vanhove, *De doelmatigheid van het regionaal-economisch beleid in Nederland*, Gent-Hilversum, 1962, pp. 59 ff.

workers is also higher. A labor-intensive industry, therefore, will tend to decentralize more than a capital-intensive industry unless a very highly skilled worker is required (variables X_1 and X_3).

Finally, if an industry is inclined to decentralize, this tendency can be effectuated much more easily if its rate of growth is high rather than low, since with more new plants more locational decisions are to be made (variable X_4).

It follows from the foregoing that the influence of variable X_1 should be positive (the more labor, the more decentralization), that of variables X_2 and X_3 negative, and that of variable X_4 again positive.

A statistical test by means of regression analysis for 20 branches leads to the following result:

$$D^{x}=\underset{(0.248)}{0.556X_1}-\underset{(0.149)}{0.327X_2}-\underset{(0.105)}{0.211X_3}+\underset{(0.062)}{0.118X_4}-20.63 \qquad R=0.782$$

The influence of each of the variables can be compared by the product of the regression coefficients and their standard deviation. If the influence of the fraction of skilled workers is put equal to 100, the result is:

Fraction of wages	141
Raw material weight	119
Fraction of skilled workers	100
Rate of growth	100

It appears that the largest influence is exerted by the fraction of wages in total value added and by raw material weight per worker.

The constant in the equation equals 20.63 which means that, *ceteris paribus*, there is a tendency for industry to be located in the west of the country. Decentralization results from the fact that this negative constant is overcompensated by other factors working in favor of decentralization.

The tendency toward decentralization is greatest for the following industries:

Industry	*Index (D)*
Leather	32. 5
Shoe	29. 1
Electrotechnical	23. 9
Clothing	21. 2
Wooden wares	20. 2

and smallest for:

Chemical	0. 8
Cocoa and chocolate	2. 3
Wool	2. 5
Carpentry	5. 2
Paperware	5. 6

Summarizing Dr. Vanhove's answer to the first question, we find that there is a measurable tendency toward decentralization from the western part of the country to other areas (problem areas and others). The variables explaining the degree of decentralization per branch are found in the major cost components of the manufacturing industries and in the rate of growth of the particular industry.

The second question is concerned with the choice the entrepreneur will make among the different regions. This choice, of course, is influenced by the characteristics of the areas with regard to the regional wage level, the availability of labor, and the structure of industry in the region.

The factor of availability of labor plays a very important role in Holland because unemployment during the last 10 years has been well under 1 percent of the working population, and the shortage of workers, particularly in the west, is one of the main bottlenecks in the expansion of production.

Dr. Vanhove incorporated in his analysis the following variables:

Y=the relative growth of employment in manufacturing in 42 regions during the period 1950–1960.

Z_1=the average unemployment per region during this period.

Z_2=the proportion of the chemical and metal industries in total industry in the region as an average from 1950 to 1960.

Z_3=the degree of industrialization in 1950.

Z_4=the average wage level (=income level) in 1955.

The choice of the variables requires some explanation. First, the variable Y was chosen as representing the industrial growth of the region. Since all regions in principle have their own growth potential, which is greater if more growth industries (of which chemical works and metal works are the most important) are represented, this factor should be taken into account (variable Z_2). The entrepreneur will be attracted more easily to an area that already has at least some industrial experience; hence he will prefer, *ceteris paribus*, a region with a higher degree of industrialization to one with a lower degree of industrialization (variable Z_3). Finally, he will be interested in the availability of labor (variable Z_1) and the wage level (Z_4).

The *a priori* expectations about the variables are that Z_1, Z_2, and Z_3 exert a positive influence and Z_4 a negative influence on the relative increase in industrial employment in a given region.

In testing the influence of these variables, Dr. Vanhove found that the proportion of chemical industry and metal industry (Z_2) and the degree of industrialization (Z_3) played only an insignificant role. His final result, therefore, explains the differences in Y by the differences in Z_1 and Z_4 only. His result is

$$Y^{x}=\underset{(1.30)}{7.61}\,Z_1-\underset{(3.86)}{10.18}\,Z_4+43.80 \qquad R=0.815$$

Putting the influence of Z_4 (wage level) equal to 100, Dr. Vanhove finds the influence of Z_1 (availability of labor) to be 209. This factor is therefore twice as important as the wage level in explaining the regional growth of employment in manufacturing.

Thus we have the basic answer to the second question. The next step taken by Dr. Vanhove was to compare the actual increase in employment in manufacturing industries in the problem areas with the theoretical increase indicated by this formula. If the actual increase is larger than the theoretical expectation, it seems likely that this should be attributed to the regional policy directed toward stimulating the growth of these regions.

Since the second stage of regional policy was introduced only in 1959, the comparison was made for the "development areas" of the 1951–58 policy. Dr. Vanhove set forth the differences he found in a table which we reproduce here in full, as table 1.

TABLE 1.—*The actual and theoretical rate of growth of employment in manufacturing industries in the development areas, 1950–60, in percent*

Development area	Actual growth	Theoretical growth	Difference
1. Southwest Groningen	11. 2	17. 0	−5. 8
2. East Groningen	20. 5	36. 0	−15. 5
3. East Friesland	63. 1	42. 6	+20. 5
4. Southeast Drenthe	64. 8	64. 0	+. 8
5. Northeast Overijssel	51. 2	37. 1	+14. 1
6. East West-Friesland	7. 9	13. 2	−5. 3
7. Southwest North-Brabant	28. 8	20. 0	+8. 8
8. Northeast North-Brabant	86. 4	23. 5	+62. 9
9. North Limburg	77. 8	20. 3	+57. 5

Source: N. Vanhove, *De doelmatigheid van het regionaal-economisch beleid in Nederland*, Gent-Hilversum, 1962, p. 103.

The unweighted average of the actual growth is 45.7 percent and the theoretical average expectation is 30.4 percent. The actual growth, therefore, exceeds the theoretical growth by 15.3 percent; that is, on the average the growth was 50 percent larger than was to be expected on theoretical grounds. However, in three of the nine areas actual growth was smaller than the theoretical expectation.

From these results, Dr. Vanhove draws the "careful conclusion" that in east Friesland, northeast Overijssel, northeast North-Brabant and northern Limburg the regional policy resulted in increases in total employment in manufacturing that would not have been obtained without it.[12] Thus, the regional policy during 1951–59 may be called an effective one.

THE INFLUENCE OF REGIONAL POLICY ON THE CONCENTRATION OF INDUSTRY IN THE DEVELOPMENT AREAS

The final question is whether the regional policy created additional employment or merely caused a concentration of employment in development areas which otherwise would have shown a more dispersed regional distribution. It is very difficult to answer this question and Dr. Vanhove devoted only a few lines to it. Statistical research in this field is very difficult. By definition the sum of the differences between actual growth and theoretical growth for all regions equals zero. No definite conclusion, therefore, can be drawn from this. The only way to get to the bottom of the problem is to investigate directly whether or not the development of the problem areas takes place at the expense of the neighboring areas. Dr. Vanhove comes to the conclusion that, generally speaking, statistics do not support the assumption that such development takes place at the expense of surrounding areas.

Conclusion

Our conclusion must be that the regional policy of the Dutch Government so far has resulted in a marked increase in employment in manufacturing in

[12] *Ibid.*, p. 103.

five of the original nine development areas. It may be hoped that the Minister of Economic Affairs will find this a good reason to restrict the regional policy to those areas where it seems effective. In doing so, he will be able to turn his policy more from a social to an economic direction. In addition, further research is needed to designate new development areas with a more favorable outlook than the regions that are lagging behind, in order to increase the effectiveness of the regional policy that has already proved so beneficial for five less-developed areas.

Regional Policy in Belgium

Some General Information

Belgium has a total population of about 9.2 million and a gross national product of $12.2 billion (in 1960). It has a short coastline on the North Sea with Antwerp as the major port. About 16 percent of its total population resides in the arrondissement of its capital, Brussels. Belgium has a language problem, and difficulties arise from the political contrasts between its Flemish and Walloon inhabitants. Roughly speaking, the Flemish part of the country is the northwest (including Antwerp and the agglomeration of Gent) and the Walloon part is the southeastern and central area. Brussels is half Walloon, half Flemish; its employment is mainly administrative, financial, and industrial.

The population of the Flemish-speaking part has expanded considerably more than that of the Walloon part. "From the eighties of the last century until 1955, Brussels grew by 150 percent, the Flemish-speaking country by 80 percent and Wallonia by 30 percent. Great changes also took place in the ratios between the shares which those parts held in total population. Brussels grew from 11 to 16 percent, Flanders from 46 to 50 percent, whereas Wallonia fell from 42 to 35 percent. A closer study of data shows that the growth of Brussels is mainly due to an immigration surplus (the natural increment being very small) and that the growth of the Flemish parts is accounted for by the high birth rate and the comparatively low death rate, whereas Wallonia is beginning to evince distinct signs of aging as a consequence of the steadily falling birth rate and the migration to other parts." [13]

Unlike Holland, Belgium started its industrial production early on the basis of coal. The raw materials were found at the French border (Charleroi) and the region of Liège near the German border, giving rise not only to coal mining on a large scale but also to the growth of heavy industry in both areas. Nevertheless, the structure of the Belgian economy has remained a relatively unfavorable one. In section 4.3 we will consider this point more in detail.

Postwar Economic Developments in Belgium

The gross national product in Belgium during the postwar years was maintained at a high level, relative to the other countries in the Common Market.

[13] Van Os, "Economic Basis of Urban Redevelopment," Seminar Warsaw, Sept. 19–29, 1962.

In 1960 it amounted to $1,331 per capita for the total population. In the same year, the level of GNP per capita in West Germany was $1,268, in France $1,276, in Italy $650, and in the Netherlands $975. The per capita figures for the working population in 1960 were: Belgium, $3,380; West Germany, $2,673; France, $3,065; Italy, $1,618; and the Netherlands, $2,689.[14]

Though gross national product per capita is higher in Belgium than in other Common Market countries, the relatively slow rate of growth in recent years has been of great concern to the Belgian Government.

Figures taken from the EEC document cited in note 14 illustrate this point. The growth of GNP per capita of the working population in the EEC countries, 1955–60, was as follows: Belgium, 11.6 percent; West Germany, 24.8 percent; France, 21.8 percent; Italy, 20.8 percent; the Netherlands, 15.6 percent; and the EEC, 20.7 percent. The same document expresses the opinion that for the period 1960–70 the Belgian growth rate will continue to be well under the average of the EEC countries.

The main reason for this unfavorable development is no doubt the relatively low level of investment in Belgium (11.1 percent of GNP). This is well under that of West Germany (15.3 percent), Italy (14.0 percent), and the Netherlands (15.4 percent), and under the EEC average (13.5 percent). Although the investment ratio in France is about the same as that of Belgium (11.0 percent), the capital coefficient in this country is also low (2.5), so that the low level of investment is more than offset by the high productivity of the investments.

A second problem in Belgium, clearly related to the relatively low level of investment, is the high level of unemployment. In 1960 unemployment amounted to 4.3 percent of the working population as against 0.9 percent in West Germany, 1.2 percent in France, and 1.2 percent in the Netherlands. Because of the very unfavorable circumstances in southern Italy, the percentage for that country was 4.8.[15]

There can be little doubt that this relatively high unemployment level in Belgium is due to the unfavorable structure of the Belgian economy. "Regionally * * * structural unemployment is clearly a problem caused by a lack of employment in the insufficiently expansive, traditional sources of subsistence." [16]

Trends in Employment

The most recent data about the Belgian labor force and its distribution by industrial sectors are to be found in the official postcensal estimates for 1956. The total labor force at that date amounted to well over 3.5 million workers, of whom roughly 50 percent were employed in the industrial sector. This percentage is relatively high compared with France (1957, 37 percent), the Netherlands (1958, 41 percent), Italy (1958, 36 percent), and Luxemburg (1947, 40 percent), and even higher than the figure for West Germany (1957, 48 percent). Although few recent statistical data are available, it is possible to give some idea of the labor force in the manufacturing industries. In 1956 this percentage for Belgium was

---

[14] *Bericht over de vooruitzichten voor de economische ontwikkeling in de EEG van 1960 tot 1970,* EEC document II (4344) 1/62–N Rev. 1.

[15] OECD working papers; monthly Bulletin of Statistics UNO.

[16] Van Os, *op. cit.*

37 percent, for France in 1954, 26 percent; the Netherlands in 1947, 28 percent; and Italy in 1951, 23 percent. The figure for West Germany in 1950 was 32 percent and for Luxemburg in 1947, 29 percent; both well under the Belgian figure.

The labor force in mining and quarrying in Belgium amounted to 4.7 percent in 1956. The corresponding figures for the other EEC countries are: France, 1954, 2.2 percent; West Germany, 1950, 3.2 percent; Italy, 1951, 0.9 percent; the Netherlands, 1947, 1.4 percent; Luxemburg, 1947, 2.8 percent. Although the Belgian figure is again well over those for the other EEC countries, the percentage of the labor force working in mining, as well as the number of workers, is declining. In 1930 the percentage was 6.0 percent, in 1950, 5.3 percent. Between 1950 and 1956 the total number of people employed in this industry declined from 186,000 to 167,000. In 1961 the number employed was 111,000. This number decreased further in recent years and the decline is expected to continue.

Regional Income Differences in Belgium

Regional income differences in Belgium are considerable. The data in table 2 give a clear picture of the present situation. By far the highest income is earned in the Brussels arrondissement in the province of Brabant where the income per capita is 45 percent higher than the average for Belgium as a whole. This means that the Brussels average income is almost 60 percent higher than that of the rest of Belgium.

The two other provinces with large agglomerations, Liège in Wallonia

TABLE 2.—*Product by province in Belgium*

Province	Gross product 1959		
	Total (billion francs)	Per inhabitant (1,000 francs)	Index (Belgium=100)
Antwerp	82.58	58.3	104
Brabant	139.62	71.6	128
Arrondissements of:			
Brussels	113.55	80.7	145
Louvain	15.99	46.1	83
Nivelles	10.10	51.4	92
East Flanders	58.87	46.4	83
West Flanders	46.58	44.0	79
Hainaut	68.12	53.6	96
Liège	63.59	62.9	113
Limburg	22.94	40.7	73
Luxemburg	8.74	40.1	72
Namur	18.39	49.6	89
Belgium	509.50	55.8	100

Source: G. Chaput, *Les produits intérieurs provinciaux, 1948, 1953, 1959*, Cahiers Economiques de Bruxelles, January 1962.

and Antwerp in Flanders, are the only others that lie above the national average: Liège 13 percent and Antwerp 4 percent. The remaining six provinces lie below the national average, though income in Hainaut, with the industrial towns of Mons and Charleroi, is only 4 percent below. The per capita income in the Brussels arrondissement is twice that of Limburg and of Luxemburg.

Defining the underdeveloped areas as areas where the per capita income lies 15 percent or more below the national average, we find three main zones:

(1) East and West Flanders.
(2) Luxemburg.
(3) Limburg.

In the northern area a large part of the province of Antwerp, excluding the agglomeration of Antwerp, might also be considered. It would then be more appropriate to distinguish two main zones of low incomes:

(1) The northern area of the country (excluding Antwerp) roughly coinciding with the Flemish-speaking part of the country.
(2) The southeastern part of the country.

The more developed part of Belgium, apart from Brussels as the capital, is a long axis stretched along the rivers Meuse and Sambre running from Liège in the east to the Borinage in the west. The extreme ends of this axis are the most developed; the center in the province of Namur is relatively less developed.

This axis is continued in a western direction on French territory with considerable economic activity in Artois (cities of Lille, Roubaix, and Tourcoing) immediately over the Belgian border. A large number of Belgian commuters (25,000) in this area daily cross the French frontier to work, mainly in the textile industries.

Roughly speaking, therefore, the distribution of income coincides with the distribution of employment in manufacturing.

It is possible to give a somewhat more sophisticated explanation of regional income differences in Belgium by comparing the character of industry in different provinces.

We will do it in the following way:

(1) From the National Bureau of Statistics we use the indices of production for different branches in mining and manufacturing to define an industry in this group as a declining industry (absolute decrease in production), a stagnating industry (growth less than the average growth), or a growth industry (growth more than the average). The results are set forth in table 3, which gives the level of production for 1961 and the weight of the particular branch in the index of industrial production; for manufacturing industries these weights are a fraction of the total weight for manufacturing.

(2) On the basis of these figures and using statistical data from a publication by G. Chaput,[17] we are able to derive the percentage of total value-added produced in each province, divided among declining, stagnating, and growing industries. The results are shown in table 4 (after agriculture has been added to declining industries).

[17] Les produits intérieurs provinciaux, 1948, 1953, 1959, Cahiers Economiques de Bruxelles, January 1962.

It appears that the concentration of declining industries is low in the provinces of Brabant and Antwerp (particularly low in Brussels) and extremely high in Limburg and Luxemburg. The concentration of growing industries is high in Antwerp, Hainaut, and Liège and very low in Flanders, Limburg, and Luxemburg. The situation in Flanders improved somewhat as a result of the location of several growth industries since 1959.

(3) Assuming that services do not belong among declining or stagnating industries, we are now able to compare the percentage of total value-added per province in declining and stagnating industries with the average gross income per province (see table 5). It is clear that in general a low percentage in declining and stagnating industries gives rise to a high income level, while a low income level results from a high percentage in declining and stagnating industries.

TABLE 3.—*Production level, 1961, and weights of industries*

Industries	Production index 1961 (1953=100)	Weight
Declining industries:		
Mining	77.6	23.3
Stagnating industries:		
Food	114.0	1.4
Spinning	125.6	8.8
Clothing	105.9	6.6
Leather	115.5	.7
Coke	121.6	1.0
Earthenware	117.6	1.8
Cement	102.8	.8
Growing industries:		
Hosiery	163.9	2.8
Weaving	130.9	8.1
Shoe industry	151.3	2.2
House shoes	140.0	.3
Paper	184.7	3.5
Chemical	190.1	4.2
Oil refineries	249.9	.3
Electricity	165.6	2.4
Glass	186.7	2.8
Iron and steel	148.8	9.0
Nonferrous metals	150.8	3.0
Metalworking	156.5	33.0
Declining industries	77.6	23.3
Stagnating industries	116.6	21.8
Growing industries	157.7	54.9
Total industry (mining + manufacturing)	130.2	100.0

TABLE 4.—*Percentage of total value-added produced in industry by region*

Province or arrondissement	Declining industries	Stagnating industries	Growing industries	Subtotal	Services and small industries	Total
Antwerp	4.3	12.4	23.9	40.6	59.4	100.0
Brabant	4.2	11.5	17.0	32.7	67.3	100.0
Arrondissement Brussels	1.8	10.2	17.2	29.2	70.8	100.0
Arrondissement Louvain	13.1	21.1	9.9	44.1	55.9	100.0
Arrondissement Nivelles	17.1	11.5	28.1	56.7	43.3	100.0
West Flanders	12.0	21.6	9.0	42.6	57.4	100.0
East Flanders	12.2	25.2	14.1	51.5	48.5	100.0
Hainaut	17.1	11.0	28.8	56.9	43.1	100.0
Liège	12.4	10.3	31.1	53.8	46.2	100.0
Limburg	38.7	8.4	8.1	55.2	44.8	100.0
Luxemburg	20.7	7.8	11.8	36.4	63.6	100.0
Namur	13.4	9.1	19.0	41.5	58.5	100.0
Belgium	12.3	12.7	18.5	42.0	58.0	100.0

Regional Distribution of Unemployment

Since unemployment results from a difference between the demand for labor and the supply of labor, it is necessary to look at the natural rate of growth of the population per province and to compare this figure with the rate of growth of total production per province. The data for 1961, which was a normal year as regards population growth, are given in table 6.

We find that the natural as well as the total net increase is highest in the Flemish regions of Antwerp, Louvain, West Flanders, East Flanders, and Limburg, while the Walloon provinces stay far below the Flemish percentages. Only the total increases in Brussels and Nivelles are relatively high, although their natural increase in population is extremely low.

Actually, a high population growth exerts pressure on the whole economic development as long as the number of jobs does not increase correspondingly. Largely for this reason, a number of Flemish provinces show an income that lags far behind the Belgian average.

In table 7 the provinces and the arrondissements of Brussels, Louvain, and Nivelles are classified according to two characteristics: High or low natural increase of population (compared to 5.6 percent, the Belgian average) and high or low percentage of declining and stagnating industries (compared to 25 percent, the Belgian average). The indices of unemployment for the year 1957 and of income for 1959 (Belgium=100) are also given for these regions, the income figures being in parentheses.

TABLE 5.—*Economic structure and gross income by region*

Province or arrondissement	Production of declining and stagnating industries (percent of total value-added), 1959	Gross income per capita, 1959 (Belgium=100)
Arrondissement Brussels	12.0	145
Brabant	15.7	128
Antwerp	16.7	104
Namur	22.5	89
Liège	22.7	113
Hainaut	28.1	96
Luxemburg	28.5	72
Arrondissement Nivelles	28.6	92
West Flanders	33.6	79
Arrondissement Louvain	34.2	83
East Flanders	37.4	83
Limburg	47.1	73

As expected, in the case of income the provinces with high percentages in both categories take a relatively unfavorable position, while those with low percentages have the most favorable (with the exception of Namur). The other two groups take an intermediary position. More or less the same picture results if the unemployment figures are used instead of income. The relatively favorable position of areas with low natural population growth is perhaps even more striking here than for income.

Summarizing, we find that the considerable income differences in Belgium are due to a lack of growth industries in some areas combined with significant differences in population growth among regions. Very heavy long-distance commuting is another consequence of this unequal distribution of growth industries and population growth.

Commuting in Belgium

It has been pointed out already that about 25,000 Flemings commute daily between Belgium and the French industrial agglomeration of Lille-Roubaix-Tourcoing. Commuting over long distances is common in Belgium. "Of the total number of socially insured workers (about 1,300,000 in 1947), about 320,000 or 25 percent commute between their homes in one district and their jobs in another. One-third of them found employment in Brussels; 25,000 Flemings worked in Wallonia. Of the 175,000 workers in the Liège industry, 30,000 came from outside this area, four-fifths of them being natives of the Dutch-speaking territories lying to the west and north. According to the returns of the Belgian railways (which give an incomplete picture) an average distance of over 20 miles is traveled to and from work. These shuttle movements are encouraged by the exceptionally low rates charged for workers' season tickets by the public transport companies. One might speculate how far this transport system has contributed to the uneven distribution of employment and whether it may not still tend to enhance it.

"The number of 'frontier workers' is also considerable. It is estimated that 50,000 people shuttle to northern France, some 60 percent of whom are Flemish, and 10,000 to the Netherlands from the provinces of Antwerp and Limburg. This employment, especially in northern France, is highly susceptible to cyclical fluctuation." [18]

Like all commuting, that in Belgium may be judged from two viewpoints. On the one hand, commuting may be considered an evil, lengthening working hours with travel hours and keeping workers from their families much longer than would be the case if industry were spread more evenly over the country. On the other hand, commuting to the larger agglomerations prevents them from becoming too large and enables the worker to live in familiar surroundings which he may enjoy at least on weekends.

It is difficult to pass judgment on this development. It is certain, however, that mobility of labor on such a scale contributes considerably to the solution of employment problems in the less developed areas as well as to the solution of the problem of labor shortages in the industrial areas of Belgium, in French Artois, and in the southern Netherlands.

Regional Policy in Belgium

INTRODUCTION [19]

As we have said, industrial activity in Belgium is heavily concentrated in Wallonia. This concentration has been made possible partly by the employment of non-Walloon labor. And since large amounts of capital already have been invested in these regions, there is an unmistakable tendency to further concentration, which is intensified by the typical structure of Belgian industry, controlled as it is by a number of powerful holding companies, such as the "Société Général." The Flemings object that many opportunities for industrial development are thus lost to them and Flemish workers are doomed to accept jobs far from home. It must be added that this complaint is also heard in Walloon circles, notably in agricultural areas and in regions where employment is declining as a result of structural changes.

It is understandable, then, that interest in regional problems should have appeared first in labor circles, leading to requests for intervention by the Government. As scientific circles and the inhabitants of the regions gradually became aware of the problems, regional economic councils were formed. Sometimes they comprise a whole province, sometimes smaller areas. Among their membership are to be found not only government authorities, but also industrialists, agrarians, and representatives of trade unions and of tradesmen's organizations. These bodies first applied themselves to regional investigation, and as a result Belgium now possesses a growing number of regional monographs. Armed with this knowledge, the councils try to draw the attention of industrialists to the opportunities for industrial development in their regions. Their most important function is to promote regional development.

Opposing them are the managements of several industrial agglomera-

[18] Van Os, *op. cit.*
[19] This section is taken from van Os, *op. cit.*, pp. 16–17.

TABLE 6.—*Population increase by region*

Province or arrondissement	Natural increase in percent	Migration in percent	Net increase in percent	Total population in 1,000 Dec. 31, 1961
Antwerp	8. 41	+1. 54	9. 95	1, 444
Arrondissement Brussels	2. 32	+6. 96	9. 28	1, 438
Arrondissement Louvain	7. 47	+1. 98	9. 45	353
Arrondissement Nivelles	1. 29	+10. 21	11. 50	202
West Flanders	8. 48	−1. 95	6. 53	1, 073
East Flanders	5. 80	−1. 90	3. 90	1, 277
Hainaut	2. 13	−5. 44	−3. 31	1, 260
Liège	1. 74	−. 81	. 93	1, 011
Limburg	16. 85	−4. 06	12. 79	579
Luxemburg	6. 06	−4. 65	1. 41	219
Namur	4. 21	−. 68	3. 53	373
Belgium	5. 63	−. 12	5. 51	9, 229

tions, captains of industry, financiers, and even some economists who hold that Belgian industrialization is best served by as great a concentration as possible. There are a few areas which, they claim, offer far and away the best chance of an economically favorable development. The factories established there would be in the strongest competitive position vis à vis foreign manufacturers. The State, it is argued, should promote concentration there and waste no money on areas where industry is artificial and therefore unsound.

Under such circumstances it is hardly surprising that a bill introduced in 1952, which aimed to provide facilities for the establishment of new industrial enterprises and the extension and modernization of existing ones in areas where economic growth had come to a standstill or extensive structural unemployment existed, was never passed. Successive Belgian governments, however, have not allowed themselves to become discouraged. Between 1952 and 1959 a number of statutory acts and royal decrees of a general tenor were enacted to promote economic expansion, providing for financial grants to aid in the establishment, extension, or rationalization and renovation of factories. Although these acts were of a general nature, in their application regard was paid to the varying regional situations.

In the same period the government financed a number of regional studies, entrusted to several universities and other institutes or private groups. Moreover, an American institute made a study on the subject, bearing the title of "Current Belgian Economic Development Efforts."

In 1959 the old acts were superseded by a general act to promote economic expansion and the establishment of new industries. It applies to the whole Belgian territory and its objectives are to stimulate industry and combat structural unemployment over the long term, to promote the rationalization and expansion of production, to adapt production to the perspectives opened up by the Common Market, and to encourage local action for the replacement of dying enterprises or industries.

TABLE 7.—*Economic structure and population growth by region*

Percentage of declining and stagnating industries	Natural population growth					
	High			Low		
High	Luxemburg	(72)	97	Hainaut	(96)	48
	Limburg	(73)	86	Nivelles	(92)	48
	West Flanders	(79)	157			
	East Flanders	(83)	158			
	Louvain	(83)	124			
Low	Antwerp	(104)	137	Brussels	(145)	73
				Liège	(113)	58
				Namur	(89)	64

Figures in parentheses: income (Belgium=100). Source: Table 2, above.

Other figures: unemployment (Belgium=100). Source: *Bijdragen tot de studie* van de ruimtelijke welvaartsverschillen in Belgie, Leuven 1961, p. 172.

THE GENERAL ACT ON ECONOMIC EXPANSION

This important act, dated July 17, 1959, is called the "act to introduce and regulate measures taken to promote economic expansion and erection of new industries."[20] The next day, July 18, the regional act came into force; it is officially called the "act to introduce specific measures to combat economic and social difficulties in certain areas." Both 3-year acts have been prolonged for an additional 3 years since 1962.

The general act and the regional act have several regulations in common. In both cases help is given to industries in four different forms: (*a*) Low interest rates (*b*) government guarantees on loans, (*c*) direct financing by the government, and (*d*) tax exemption. This help, which is not restricted to Belgian nationals or Belgian companies, is given to six categories of enterprises, persons, and/or institutions:

(1) Manufacturing industries or handicrafts.
(2) Persons or institutions carrying out activities in the general interest (specified below).
(3) Trading companies contributing directly to the economic expansion of manufacturing industries.
(4) Provinces.
(5) Municipalities.
(6) Regional economic institutions providing facilities for industries.

The facilities are given if the person, enterprise, or institution is carrying out activities with regard to (*a*) the creation, (*b*) the extension, (*c*) the reorientation, or (*d*) the modernization of enterprises in manufacturing or handicraft. Thus, help is given to new industries as well as existing ones. The criteria for granting facilities may be summarized under the heading "the general interest," which includes specifically—

[20] Former acts to promote investments are the Act Duvieusart (Aug. 7, 1953) and the Act Rey (July 10, 1959). For a detailed description of the general and regional acts see *Belgisch Staatsblad,* Aug. 29, 1959. See also *Uw belangen bij economische expansie,* edited by N. V. Ebes, Gent.

(1) Creation of new employment in accordance with the employment policy;
(2) Creation of new industries or production of new products;
(3) Development of existing industries that adjust themselves to new market conditions;
(4) Improvement of stagnating sectors in the economy;
(5) More rational use of the country's economic resources;
(6) Improvement of labor conditions and of production conditions of enterprises by increasing productivity or profitability as well as improvement of the quality of the products;
(7) Extension of research departments of enterprises.

The conditions on which facilities are given are as follows:

(1) The future profitability of investments within a reasonable time must be assured. This means that the entrepreneur is expected to prove (within reasonable limits) the profitability of the planned investments.
(2) The project should be satisfactory from both an economic and a social point of view.
(3) The applicant is expected to contribute satisfactorily to the financing of the project.

Within the framework of the regional act an additional criterion for financial aid is that the firm is handicapped as a result of undertaking a project in a development area. Clearly this criterion is analogous to the "infant industry tariff" enabling a new industry to develop in a country by protecting it in its early stages against foreign competition. In this case the government is giving financial help for extra costs resulting from location in the development area, as, for instance, higher prices for certain services or higher salaries paid to specialists to compensate them for working in a development area.

Low interest rates

The aid given in the form of low interest rates depends on certain conditions. It consists of the following:

(1) *General aid.* This consists of a government contribution in the rate of interest of 2 percent.

(2) *Specific aid.* This may be given in the form of an additional contribution of 2 percent if by doing so the net rate of interest to be paid by the enterprise, after deduction of the general 2 percent plus the specific 2 percent, would not fall below 1 percent. This specific aid is given *only to existing industries* in order to enable them to face new market conditions in the international market (Common Market). Investments in this field may not be less than $20,000. This minimum is not applicable to the development areas, as we will see later.

(3) *Additional aid.* This is to aid investments during a period of recession. The year 1959 was considered to be a year of recession; the years 1960 and 1961 were not. If the entrepreneur is eligible for general aid, with this additional aid the interest rate could reach a minimum of 3 percent, and if he is eligible for the general and the specific aid, then this minimum may reach 1 percent.

Low interest rates hold for 3 years; in certain cases the period may be prolonged for an additional 2 years.

Government guarantees

The government guarantee is given for loans and interest payments, and may be given separately or combined with low interest rates. If the loan is given by a public institution (mentioned by name), the guarantee covers 100 percent, and if by a private institution, 50 percent, of the part of the loan not covered by the guarantees the industry itself is able to give.

Direct financing by the government

This form of aid (which covers the construction or purchase of industrial buildings and leasing or selling them to industrial enterprises) is given only in "exceptional and urgent cases" if required in the general interest. In that event, the municipalities have authority to buy land and build industrial buildings on it in order to put them at the disposal of industrial firms. The local governments are entitled to the same support (low interest rates and government guarantees) that private industries may obtain. Here, also, the general interest is the main criterion.

The same rules hold for local or regional public corporations working in the general interest. They too are entitled to buy land, build industrial buildings, and rent or sell them to industries, using the same facilities as local governments.

Tax exemption

Regardless of whether or not an industry has received any government support in the form of low interest rates or State guarantee, a firm is exempt from real estate tax on investments completed after January 1, 1959, and made in order to meet international competition or in a recession period. These tax exemptions may be given for a period of 5 years reckoned from January 1 after completion of the investments.

Under certain conditions, provincial and local governments may grant exemptions from taxes on personnel employed and on horsepower, for new as well as expanding industries.

An additional facility may be given in the form of advances without interest on investments in research departments up to a maximum of 50 percent of the capital invested.

THE REGIONAL ACT ON THE DEVELOPMENT OF CERTAIN AREAS

The main function of the regional act is to give industries *additional* support if located in certain areas, additional in the sense of on top of the support already provided by the general act.

The criteria for an area to be considered a development area are one or more of the following conditions:

(*a*) Considerable, persistent unemployment or permanent lack of employment;

(*b*) Heavy migration causing underpopulation, defined as a population too small for the normal functioning of existing public and social services;

(*c*) Seasonal, weekly, or daily commuting by an important part of the active population under unfavorable conditions;

(*d*) Existing or expected stagnation of important economic activities implying unfavorable consequences.

A secondary condition is that a development area should have a satis-

761-932 O—65——5

factory infrastructure or that improvement of the existing infrastructure is possible at reasonable cost.

The application of these rules resulted in the designation of a large number of usually small [21] areas in Flanders, the Borinage, eastern Liège, the Ardennes, and the southern part of Namur. The act explicitly states that the Government support given to these areas is not limited to industries within their boundaries but also may be given to industries in the neighborhood insofar as they contribute substantially to the solution of the problem of the development area. The areas chosen are given in table 8. See also map II.

It may be concluded that the unemployment criterion was especially applicable to the Flemish part of the country. The migration criterion held good for several Flemish as well as Walloon areas. The commuting criterion applied more particularly to Flemish areas (commuting to Antwerp and Brussels). The stagnation criterion, finally, was of most importance to the Walloon areas.

TABLE 8.—*Development areas in Belgium*

No.	Development area	Population in 1,000	Criterion on the basis of which the area was chosen
1	Borinage	221	d
2	Hogeland-Zuiderkempen	242	a-c
3	Center	99	d
4	Eeklo	67	a-c
5	Luxemburg and southern part of province of Namur	91	b-c-d
6	Lokeren-Dendermonde	118	a-c
7	Veurne-Tielt	211	b-c
8	Verviers	54	a-b
9	Aalst	82	a-c-d
10	Ieper	37	c
11	Doornik-Aat	38	c-d
12	Hoei	39	c
13	Oudenaarde	44	a
14	Geraardsbergen	15	b
15	Neder Maas	....	d

The facilities of the regional act are not granted automatically. The central government decides whether a given industry or project is of general interest and will promote the economic expansion of the development area.

The development areas were selected for a period of 3 years from December 16, 1959, to December 16, 1962. The facilities might be granted to investments from January 1, 1959, on and to applications before Decem-

[21] According to the act the population of a development area should not exceed 15 percent of the country's population.

ber 16, 1962. Both periods have recently been prolonged by an additional 3 years.

The facilities offered correspond closely to those given by the general act, with the exception of (*c*). They are: (*a*) Low interest rates, (*b*) Government guarantee, (*c*) provision of capital, (*d*) industrial buildings, and (*e*) tax exemptions. These facilities may be given in any combination.

Low interest rates

A support may be given of a maximum of 4 percent in the interest rate. This 4 percent may be given to new as well as existing industries (in the general act, for new industries the general aid maximum is 2 percent). There is no requirement with respect to international competition or to size of investment. The period of support varies from 5 to 8 years (general act 3 to 5 years). Additional help is given in periods of recession, when the minimum interest rate may be fixed at 1 percent. Recession is defined as a recession for the whole of Belgium, not for the specific area.

Government guarantee

The only difference between the general act and the regional act is that in the regional act no restrictions are to be found with regard to the percentage of the loan the government may guarantee (the general act sets a maximum of 50 percent of private loans). The guarantee, of course, is for the period of the loan, which may be longer under the regional act than under the general act.

Provision of capital

This facility is mentioned only in the regional act. Its main aim is a grant to cover part of the investments in buildings and equipment. The provision will not exceed 20 percent of the investment costs in buildings and 7.5 percent of those in equipment (in a recession period 30 percent and 10 percent respectively) and has a maximum of $20,000. The capital is provided immediately after completion of the investments, though an advance may be secured for buildings. The capital provided is exempt from tax.

Industrial buildings (direct financing by the government)

The difference between the general act and regional act is that the latter does not state that support in the form of provision for industrial buildings is given only in exceptional and urgent cases.

Tax exemption

The regulations with regard to tax exemptions are the same for both acts, except that in the development areas no requirements are made as to international competition or recession. The exemption from the real estate tax is given for a 5-year period and is automatic if the industry is supported in one way or another by the government.

A comparison between the two acts seems useful, particularly to show that the regional act merely gives *additional* support to industries located in the development areas. Restrictions are fewer and the periods for which support is given are longer. Table 9 gives the comparison.

Apart from the facilities for industries, Belgian regional policy offers support to workers in regard to training and migration.

Training

In 1961 it was decided that the National Office of Employment might provide the following facilities for new, expanding, or converting industries:

(1) Assistance in the selection of workers;
(2) A short retraining program for new workers;
(3) A subsidy if retraining takes place in the industry itself;
(4) A subsidy of 50 percent for training of Belgian workers in foreign countries.

Moreover, the office is empowered to:

(1) Create retraining centers;
(2) Subsidize existing retraining centers;
(3) Provide workers during retraining with financial means up to 90 percent of their gross wage rate.

These facilities are granted (under certain conditions regarding former employment) to workers over 18 years of age.

Migration

The migration of unemployed workers to more favorable areas is subsidized. The National Office of Employment pays the travel and moving costs of the unemployed and his family and provides a fixed sum for all other costs. This support is given on condition that the new residence is 20 miles or more from the original one, that dailv commuting would keep the worker from home more than 12 hours daily, and that the costs of commuting would exceed 40 cents daily.

The Effectiveness of Belgian Regional Policy

One could say that the emphasis in Belgium even more than in Holland lies on the *social* aspects of the problem of regional distribution of employment. Belgian policy is in addition a *short-run* policy. Improvement of the general investment climate of the development areas does not receive any attention. Furthermore, the policy in itself does not seem completely consistent from an economic point of view.

It is rather difficult to assess the economic effect of Belgian regional policy to date, for two reasons. First, the additional advantages given by the regional act are relatively small compared to those already given by the general act, and second, the acts are of very recent date so that no major structural changes as a consequence of them can be expected. However, there are some data available on the regional distribution of employment in industries that have made use of the facilities of either the general or the regional act, and also on the kinds of facilities granted to industries in different regions of Belgium.

First, we will look at the regional distribution of additional employment in industries receiving financial support from the Government under either of the acts. The data on actual and expected employment by these firms

TABLE 9.—*Comparison between facilities given by the regional and general acts*

Facilities	General act, July 17, 1959	Regional act, July 18, 1959
1. *Low interest rates*	1.1. 3–5 year period.	5–8 year period.
	1.2. General aid 2 percent, specific aid 2 percent additional.	4 percent aid.
	1.3. Existing industries.	Existing and new industries.
	1.4. To meet international competition.	No specific purpose.
	1.5. Investment minimum $20,000.	No minimum.
	1.6. Application before Dec. 31, 1961 (prolonged).	Application before Dec. 16, 1962 (prolonged).
	1.7. Additional aid (recession period); in case of general aid to a minimum of 3 percent,	Additional aid (recession period) to a minimum of 1 percent.
	in case of specific aid to a minimum of 1 percent.	To a minimum of 1 percent.
2. *Government guarantee*	2.1. 3–5 year period.	5–8 year period.
	2.2. Restriction (50 percent) in case loan is given by a private bank.	No restriction.
3. *Provision of capital*	3.1.	$20,000. 20–30 percent for buildings. 7.5–10.0 percent for equipment.
4. *Industrial buildings*	4.1. Exceptional and urgent cases.	No restrictions.
5. *Free loans*	5.1. For industrial research.	Same.
6. *Tax exemption*	6.1. Real estate tax— a. To meet international competition. b. In recession periods.	Real estate tax—No restrictions.
	6.2.	Capital provided under (3) tax exempt.

Source: N. V. Ebes, ed., *Uw belangen bij economische expansie*, Gent.

as of October 1, 1962, were supplied by the Ministry of Economic Affairs and Energy in Brussels and are presented in table 10. We have added the distribution of the population to the employment data and have constructed an employment ratio showing whether the additional employment in the area exceeds, relatively speaking, the proportion of population in that area (index>100) or not (index<100).

It appears that in relation to the population, Flanders is receiving considerably more additional employment than Wallonia and Brussels. Of the total additional employment, it has received 64.5 percent. Its population represents 51.2 percent of the total population. In Flanders additional employment is concentrated in West Flanders, East Flanders, and Antwerp. Limburg and Louvain lag behind.

TABLE 10.—*Actual and expected additional employment as of Oct. 1, 1962*

Province (1)	Population in 1,000 (2)	Population in percent (3)	Additional employment (4)	Additional employment in percent (5)	Employment ratio (5):(3)
Antwerp	1, 444	15. 6	14, 062	17. 5	112
West Flanders	1, 073	11. 6	19, 244	23. 9	206
East Flanders	1, 277	13. 8	12, 832	16. 0	116
Limburg	579	6. 3	4, 228	5. 2	83
Arrondissement Louvain	353	3. 8	1, 521	1. 9	50
Flanders	4, 726	51. 2	51, 887	64. 5	126
Arrondissement Brussels	1, 438	15. 6	6, 407	8. 0	51
Hainaut	1, 260	13. 7	9, 528	11. 8	86
Liège	1, 011	11. 0	8, 266	10. 3	94
Luxemburg	219	2. 4	1, 137	1. 4	58
Namur	373	4. 0	1, 028	1. 3	33
Arrondissement Nivelles	202	2. 2	2, 154	2. 7	123
Wallonia	3, 065	33. 2	22, 113	27. 5	83
Belgium	9, 229	100. 0	80, 407	100. 0	100

In Wallonia only the arrondissement of Nivelles has an employment ratio of more than 100. All other areas fall behind, particularly the provinces of Namur and Luxemburg.

In table 11 these data are compared with the unemployment ratios of the different provinces and arrondissements. Horizontally the unemployment data are given for each area (Belgium=100) divided into low unemployment (less than 100 percent of the Belgian average) and high unemployment (≧100 percent). Vertically the employment ratios are given, also divided into low and high ratios with the division at 100 percent of the average.

In the table the double line separates Wallonia and Brussels from Flanders.

The provinces of Wallonia and Brussels (except Nivelles), covering 96 percent of the total population of Wallonia and Brussels, lie in the upper left corner of the table (low unemployment—low employment ratio). The major part of Flanders (93 percent of its population) is in the lower right corner (high unemployment—high employment ratio). The conclusion from this table is that the additional employment created by industries making use of the facilities of the general and regional acts, taken together, tends to concentrate in areas with higher unemployment. The question whether this will actually decrease unemployment in these areas can be answered only if natural population growth in these areas is also taken into account. A study of the development of each area separately will therefore be necessary.

Further information on the effects of the general act and the regional act separately is available from the Ministry of Economic Affairs and Energy. These data concern the sort of facilities used and the amounts of capital involved.

TABLE 11.—*Unemployment and employment ratios in provinces and arrondissements*

Employment ratio	Unemployment: Low <100		Unemployment: High ≥100	
Low <100	Namur	33–64	Louvain	50–124
	Brussels	51–73		
	Luxemburg	58–97		
	Limburg	83–86		
	Hainaut	86–48		
	Liège	94–58		
High ≥100	Nivelles	123–48	Antwerp	112–137
			East Flanders	116–158
			West Flanders	206–157

To begin with the general act, it appears that, in total, *low interest* facilities were given on capital amounting to about $268 million for 667 applicants. This is roughly $400,000 per applicant. Of this total of $268 million, about 41 percent was granted to Flanders, 9 percent to Brussels, and 50 percent to Wallonia. The capital on which low interest rates were given amounts to $314,000 per applicant in Flanders, $214,000 in Brussels, and $670,000 in Wallonia. Thus, by this measure the projects in Wallonia were more than twice as large as those in Flanders and more than three times as large as those in Brussels.

The figures concerning cases in which *low interest rates and government guarantees* or only a *government guarantee* were given show a total of about $94 million (Flanders 43.5 percent, Brussels 44.5 percent, and Wallonia 12 percent). Of the capital involving *only* a government guarantee ($47 million), 86 percent went to Brussels.

These figures show that Wallonia profited most from the low interest facilities and Flanders most from the government guarantees combined with low interest rates. The government guarantees proper mainly benefited Brussels.

The data about the regional act should be judged in the light of the fact that of the total population of the development areas, about 60 percent is Flemish and 40 percent Walloon. Here, too, only low interest rates and government guarantees are important. The grants of capital took place on such a small scale ($250,000, half Flemish, half Walloon) that they may be disregarded here.

The total number of applicants for *low interest rates* was 507, of which 382 were located in Flemish provinces and 125 in Walloon provinces. Of the total capital involved ($128 million), 63 percent was invested in Flemish and 37 percent in Walloon provinces. This corresponds roughly with the distribution of population in these areas. The amount of capital per applicant was again much larger in Wallonia than in Flanders ($380,000 against $210,000).

Of the facilities consisting of *low interest rate combined with government guarantee* or *government guarantee alone,* use was made in Flanders of a capital amounting to $25 million (99 applicants) and in Wallonia of $58 million (150 applicants). The amount per applicant in Flanders was $250,000 and in Wallonia $385,000. Again, the amount approved per applicant is much higher in Wallonia than in Flanders.

To sum up, we can say that:

(1) In proportion to its population, Wallonia profited most from the general facilities for low interest rates (50 percent), and Brussels profited most from the government guarantees alone (86 percent) and in combination with low interest rates (44.5 percent).

(2) Flanders' benefits from the regional facilities for low interest rates corresponded to the Flemish population in development areas (63 percent). Wallonia profited most from the regional facilities for government guarantees alone or combined with low interest rates (70 percent). Here Flanders received only 30 percent.

(3) The amount per applicant in Flanders is on the average much lower than in Wallonia.

In order to compare these results with those concerning additional employment, table 12 was constructed. From it we may draw the following final conclusions:

(1) From the application of the general act and the regional act, Flanders profited by 45 percent as far as capital is concerned and 64.5 percent as far as labor is concerned (population 51.2 percent of the total).

(2) For Brussels these figures are 11.5 percent of capital and 8 percent of additional employment (population 15.6 percent of the total).

(3) For Wallonia the figures are 43.5 percent of capital and 27.5 percent of employment (population 33.2 percent of the total).

(4) Capital per applicant approved in Brussels and Wallonia amounted to more than double that in Flanders.

The percentage share of additional employment in Wallonia is smaller than its percentage of the population, while its share in facilities is much larger. For Flanders the proportion of additional employment is larger than its population share, but its share in facilities considerably smaller. For Brussels the shares in facilities and additional employment are both much lower than its population share.

TABLE 12.—*Investments and newly created employment in Belgium facilitated by the general and regional acts*

Region	Capital						Additional employment		Capital per worker
	General act		Regional act		Total				
	Millions	*Percent*	*Millions*	*Percent*	*Millions*	*Percent*	*Number*	*Percent*	
Flanders	$152	42. 0	$105	50. 0	$257	45. 0	51, 887	64. 5	$4, 950
Brussels	67	18. 5	....	....	67	11. 5	6, 407	8. 0	10, 400
Wallonia	143	39. 5	106	50. 0	249	43. 5	22, 113	27. 5	11, 300
Belgium	362	100. 0	211	100. 0	573	100. 0	80, 407	100. 0	7, 150

These figures are understandable in the light of the relative capital richness of Wallonia and its industrial tradition. Generally, larger and more capital-intensive projects [22] will be undertaken there, while smaller projects are more likely in Flanders because of its relatively abundant labor and its agricultural tradition. It remains to be seen, however, whether in the long run regional policy in Belgium, with its relatively favorable conditions for capital-intensive projects and no restrictions as to labor per unit of capital, will sufficiently decrease the regional income differences in the country.

Provincial and Local Action [23]

During the fifties regional action was initiated in those areas where high unemployment and excessive commuting exist. This resulted in the establishment of a number of boards, especially in Flanders. The most important of these are:

Limburg Economic Board (1951);
West Flemish Economic Board (1954);
Economic Board for East Flanders (1956);
Economic Board for Antwerp (1957).

Meanwhile (in 1952) the Economic Board for Flanders grew out of cooperation between provincial governments and social organizations.

In Wallonia the *Conseil Economique Wallon* had already been in existence for some time; the *Institut de Recherches Economiques du Hainaut* had been established as early as 1936. Gradually this *Conseil Economique* organized provincial sections.

The Economic Board for Brabant was started in 1959. Thus the whole territory of Belgium has become covered with provincial organizations designed to stimulate the economic growth of their regions. They consist of representatives of the provincial government and private persons from all sectors of the economy, with the governor of the province as chairman.

Recently, on the basis of the regional act, intermunicipal organizations have been created with the aim of promoting economic expansion and investment in their areas. Both general and regional acts gave rise to the establishment of many intermunicipal organizations on a smaller scale, such as Veneco (Gent—45 municipalities), Leiedal (Courtrai—21 municipalities), S. V. Land van Aalst (Alost—2 municipalities), and Zuiderkempen (13 municipalities). They usually concentrate on specific objects (larger agglomerations, ports) or restricted objectives.

One may argue about the question whether provincial boundaries are appropriate for delimiting efficient areas for regional economic policy. Since in Belgium provincial economic policy is of a supplementary character, this argument is actually not very important.

Although their policy aims are limited, provincial organizations have contributed substantially to the growth and quality of investment in some areas by giving information and service to foreign firms willing to locate there and by promoting the expansion of existing industries. An important function of these organizations is the promotion of economic re-

[22] Especially noteworthy are the $30 million investments in heavy industry in the Liège region.
[23] See O. Vanneste, *Onderneming en regionaal overheidsbeleid,* Brugge, April 1963.

search in the area as proposals for improvement of the infrastructure of the region are based on this research. This task is especially important since the central government pays only limited attention to infrastructural problems.

Recent Developments in Belgian Regional Policy [24]

In 1962 certain changes were introduced in regional policy in Belgium. The two main purposes of these changes were:

(1) to keep more strictly to the fundamental intent of the act than has been done so far

(2) to give a higher priority to certain nuclei in development areas than to other places

The first point implies still further promotion of those industries that show a rapid expansion, that offer promising possibilities for specialization within the Common Market or in world trade, or that are expected to have a favorable influence on other industries. On the basis of these criteria a list was made of industries to be promoted. This list will be adjusted to actual economic development.

Insofar as this was possible, nuclei were indicated in the development areas to which special facilities should be given. Thus the Dutch principle of "decentralization by means of regional concentration" was adopted.

With these two changes Belgian policy turns more in an economic direction. However, no policy has yet been formulated with respect to the larger agglomerations or a better selection of areas to be developed. The basis of regional policy in Belgium, therefore, remains primarily social and secondarily economic.

Regional Policy in Luxemburg

Some General Information [25]

The area covered by Luxemburg corresponds roughly to that of a small Dutch or Belgian province (1,000 square miles). The population is about 325,000, and the working population 147,000, or 45 percent of the total. Estimates for 1958 indicate that the agricultural population represents about 22 percent of the working population. Total national product amounts to about $500 million, or $1,350 per capita and $2,990 per capita of the working population.

The largest town in the country is Luxemburg City with 70,349 inhabitants as of January 1, 1958. The five towns next in size are Esch sur Alzette, 29,818; Differdange, 18,063; Dudelange, 14,728; Pétange, 11,485; and Kayl, 6,192. It is evident that there is only one major town in Luxemburg.

---

[24] See Professor Dr. P. Frantzen, *De expansie-wetten als instrument van de economische politiek der Belgische regering,* "E.–S.B.," Dec. 12, 1962.

[25] *Essai de délimitation régionale de la communauté économique européenne,* Brussels, Jan. 30, 1961.

The country may be divided into two main regions. The northern region, called Oesling, covers one-third of the total area. This region is primarily agricultural, with a population of 45,000. Roughly speaking, this area belongs to the geographical region of Eifel-Ardennes. The southern region, called Gutland, occupies two-thirds of the country. A continuation of the Lorraine basin, it includes the capital and the most important activities of the country, particularly mining and the connected iron and steel production. The relative importance of this production is indicated in the EEC document cited in note 14 by comparing the production of steel per capita in Luxemburg (about 10,000 kg) with that of the United States of America (638 kg) and France (291 kg). Other economic activities are of relatively minor importance.

Thus, although the country is a very small one, the economic structures of the two main regions are very different. This is accentuated by the fact that a number of stagnating smaller industries are located in Oesling (textile, leather, shoes, timber, and furniture). The contrast between Oesling and Gutland is, indeed, the principal regional problem in Luxemburg. An additional problem is the imminent exhaustion of iron ore deposits, which, it is estimated, will peter out before the end of the century. This is a second reason for the Luxemburg Government to stimulate industries other than iron and steel. Even more than in the other two Benelux countries, Luxemburg's regional problems are sectoral ones, for the solution of which retraining of workers is a necessary condition.

With regard to the concentration of population in the capital, which compared to that in other countries is very modest, further density in the capital is considered undesirable.[26]

Regional Policy in Luxemburg [27]

Recently the Luxemburg Parliament approved a master act on development and expansion of industry in the country. This act provides facilities for the creation of new industries and for the enlargement, reorientation, and rationalization of existing industries. The act also facilitates measures for improvement of the general structure of the economy and its regional equilibrium.

The following facilities are provided: (*a*) subsidies and premiums, (*b*) loans, (*c*) low interest rates, (*d*) guarantees, and (*e*) tax exemptions.

Subsidies

These are as follows:

(1) Partial subsidies for investment costs in buildings, equipment, and materials.

(2) Partial or full subsidies for the cost of retraining workers.

(3) Partial or full subsidies for the cost of training workers in the case of new industries. If an existing industry starts production of new products, this is considered the creation of a new industry.

The amount of the subsidies for investments in buildings, eqiupment,

---

[26] Pierre Camy, *Possibilités de développement régional au Grand-Duché de Luxembourg,* Bulletin Benelux, 1961–62.

[27] Coal and Steel Community, *Massnahmen zur erleichterten Schaffung neuer Betaetigungsmoeglichkeiten,* Luxemburg, 1962.

and materials will not exceed 15 percent for buildings and 7.5 percent for equipment and materials. The subsidies are paid immediately after completion of the investments, though an advance of 50 percent in building investments is possible. Facilities will be given to industries in temporary difficulties and to those with structural problems that want to convert, rationalize, or expand. The funds available for these subsidies for 1962 amounted to $200,000.

Additional subsidies are provided for research, $24,000 in 1961; promotion of tourism, $100,000; and export promotion, $26,000.

Loans

Loans are not given to heavy industry or trade. They are given by banking institutions to industries whose own means do not exceed $1,000,000. The interest rate may not exceed 4 percent.

To get a loan, the industry must (1) be located in Luxemburg and (2) employ mainly Luxemburg workers. The equipment so financed may not be exported. The minimum loan is fixed at $5,000. Loans may also be given to handicraft and tourist industries.

It should be noted that these facilities have been available for more than 10 years and do not actually form part of the new act.

Low Interest Rates

The Minister is authorized by the act to subsidize banking institutions in order to enable them to give loans at lower interest rates. These loans may be used for investments in land, buildings, equipment, and materials or for the financing of intangible investments (organization studies, research, or promotion of new products or production processes). The interest may be lowered by 4 percent to a minimum of 1 percent.

The expenses for 1961 were $40,000 and estimated at $70,000 for 1962.

Guarantees

The central government is authorized to guarantee loans to a maximum of 50 percent of the total amount left after deduction of the value of the securities given to the banking institutions. The maximum to be guaranteed is fixed at $4 million. If economic conditions make it necessary, this amount may be increased to $8 million.

Tax Exemptions

A part of the cost of new investments in equipment and materials may be deducted from profits if these investments are made within a period of 5 years from the effective date of the act. The plant and equipment must remain in the country and the value per plant may not be smaller than $200,000. For the first part of the investments (to $40,000), the reduction is 30 percent, for the second part (from $40,000 to $5 million) 20 percent, and for the third part (more than $5 million) 10 percent.

Additional facilities may be given to:

(1) *New enterprises* if their capital comes from abroad and they do not compete with Luxemburg industries. The facilities given apply for a 10-year period and consist of reduced tax rates for direct taxes or accelerated depreciation.

(2) *Existing enterprises* if they have already invested in productive equipment and materials in 1959, 1960, or 1961. The reduction

is 30 percent for the first investment part (to $40,000), 20 percent for the second part (from $40,000 to $1.2 million), and 10 percent for the third part (over $1.2 million), to be spread over a 4-year period.

Facilities are not provided for plant and equipment with a lifetime of less than 1 year.

The new act also enables the minister of economic affairs (with the cooperation of local government) to purchase land and buildings for industrial enterprises. The land and/or buildings may be leased or sold to industries. The funds provided for these activities for 1961 and 1962 were $240,000.

Finally, the new act provides for the retraining of workers by means of subsidies given to industries and/or workers. In 1961, $40,000 was available for this purpose; in 1962, $80,000.

Conclusion

The Luxemburg regional legislation is largely a copy of Belgian legislation. Here, too, capital-intensive industries are promoted relative to labor-intensive industries. This might be desirable from the macro economic point of view but it very probaby stimulates further growth of industry in the traditional industrial areas and not specifically in the less developed areas. Within the framework of the small Luxemburg economy, however, the problem does not seem to be of major importance.

A Comparison of Belgian and Dutch Regional Policy

A general comparison of two regional policies is a complicated task since these policies are usually so complex that the comparison is between two n-dimensional quantities. The outcome, therefore, cannot be a conclusion that one policy is better or more effective than another but only an indication of what the main differences are and what effect they will have on actual development. Our simple theory of regional distribution of income and employment will help us in finding some systematic differences.

General Objectives

The basic objectives of regional policy in Belgium and in Holland are really the same, namely, to obtain a more equal distribution of employment over the country by stimulating the demand for labor (industrialization) in the most underdeveloped parts.

This is not as logical as it might seem at first sight. It seems much more effective to stimulate development where development possibilities are most favorable, in order to attract labor and capital to those places where the contribution of additional activities to total income will be at a maximum. This does not mean that development should always be stimulated in the most developed parts of the country since, even if private cost considerations would lead to such a policy, the social costs involved in a further growth of these often densely populated and urbanized areas may be so high that private cost advantages are largely offset. We do not find this argument anywhere in Belgian regional policy. On the contrary, the system of cheap rail transport to the larger agglomerations for workers points in the opposite direction, although it is well known that these same agglomerations always show a deficit budget as a result of the very high social costs.

In Holland, in the second phase of regional policy, it was recognized that it might be unjustified from a national economic point of view to stimulate further *unnecessary* growth of the Rimcity, since this would not lead to a maximum contribution to national income. Thus an economic element was introduced into the discussions and into the regional policy.

Although in Holland the Rimcity was explicitly excluded from any special stimuli, this does not alter the fact that basically the development was stimulated in the most underdeveloped areas. Neither in Holland nor in Belgium was any systematic research done on the question of which areas could be developed best from the national economic or, even better, the Benelux point of view.

One of the arguments for the policy adopted has always been that the mobility of workers in the underdeveloped areas is so low that only a limited effect could be expected from an increased demand outside those regions. Although this might be true in the short run, it hardly holds for the long run. Moreover, it does not justify the principle of developing *only* underdeveloped regions. A middle way could be found by determining which economic and social criteria or, better, which positive as well as negative economic together with social criteria should play a part in the choice of the areas.

Specific Objectives

Before discussing the instruments used in regional policy in Belgium and Holland, it seems useful to classify them, in accordance with our theory, as measures that increase the mobility of capital and those that increase the mobility of labor. With regard to labor mobility a subdivision into three categories seems useful:

(1) Long-distance regional mobility (migration).
(2) Short-distance regional mobility (commuting).
(3) Social and sectoral mobility.

With regard to capital two categories may be mentioned:

(1) Regional mobility.
(2) Sectoral mobility.

In practice, long-distance commuting as well as short-distance migration takes place. In Belgium especially the former is a normal occurence. Still, the average distance over which people migrate is larger than that over which they commute. For this reason migration is indicated as long-distance regional mobility and commuting as short-distance regional mobility.

Social mobility indicates the willingness of the worker to accept a different occupation, in the same industry or elsewhere, while sectoral mobility indicates the tendency to shift from one sector or branch of the economy to another. Since the two mobilities often coincide in practice, they are taken as one group.

With regard to capital, regional mobility indicates the tendency of an industry to invest in another region (migration of capital), and sectoral mobility indicates the propensity to invest in another branch or sector of the economy.

Instruments

A broad classification of instruments is given in a recent publication of the Coal and Steel Community.[28] It is as follows:

GENERAL MEASURES

Direct measures in favor of industries

11. Financial support
    111. subsidies and premiums
    112. loans
    113. low interest rates
    114. guarantees
    115. financing
    116. advances
    117. professional associations
12. Tax reductions
    121. tax exemptions and reductions
    122. accelerated depreciation
    123. lower import duties
13. Tariff reductions
14. Support for the production of new products

Indirect measures in favor of industries

21. Infrastructure, industrial sites, industrial land
22. Prefabricated factories
23. Decentralization of scientific and research institutes
24. Construction of houses for workers

Measures in favor of workers

31. Training
32. Retraining
33. Subsidy for migration

Other measures

41. Restrictions on locating of new or expansion industries in certain areas
42. Facilities for foreign investment

Not all these measures form part of regional policy proper; many relate much more to general industrialization policy. However, in Belgium especially, general and regional legislation are so closely connected and interwoven that it is very hard to separate the two. For this reason we will consider both together. Tables 13 and 14 show the relevant measures taken in Belgium and in Holland, classified by type and by objective.

Conclusion

Our comparison may be summarized as follows:

(1) In Belgium the accent is on direct measures in favor of industries. In Holland more attention is paid to coordinated infrastructural improve-

[28] *Massnahmen zur erleichterten Schaffung neuer Betaetigungsmoeglichkeiten*, Luxemburg, 1962.

ment, in the widest sense of the word, together with financial facilities for industries.

(2) In both countries attention is given to the training and retraining of workers, industrial research, and improvement of the infrastructure, though the last seems to be of higher quality in Holland.

(3) In Belgium the larger agglomerations do not get special treatment. In Holland no subsidy is given for migration to the Rimcity, and financial support is limited more to development nuclei than is the case in Belgium.

(4) In Belgium low railway rates are arranged for commuters; at the same time, "heavy commuting" is a criterion for an area to be designated as a development area. This seems to be an inconsistency in Belgian policy.

(5) In Holland subsidies to industries are given on a larger scale in development areas only on condition that a certain number of new workers are employed. No such restriction exists in Belgium, with the result that capital-intensive industries are more heavily subsidized than labor-intensive industries. Hence the subsidized capital invested per worker in Wallonia is much higher than in Flanders.

(6) No physical restrictions exist in Belgium with regard to location of industry. In Holland entrepreneurs may build only on special industrial sites, though exceptions are sometimes made.

(7) In Belgium regional policy recently shifted in the direction of "regional concentration" in development nuclei. In Holland the principle of mainly stimulating certain nuclei within the development areas was adopted in 1952.

International Influences on Future Regional Development in Benelux

Future regional development in the Benelux countries is difficult to predict. It seems likely that, on the one hand, regional policy in the three countries will have some success, but, on the other hand, this success will be needed just to offset the unfavorable developments taking place in stagnating or declining industries, especially in Wallonia but also in certain parts of Holland.

Two factors will probably have considerable influence in the future: the Benelux Treaty and the Common Market.[29] It seems worthwhile to consider the impact of these two customs unions on regional developments.

The intensity of the relations between two regions generally depends on two factors:

(1) *The distance* between the regions. With increasing distance the intensity of contacts decreases considerably—a phenomenon well known from international trade studies.

(2) *The import duties* on the products sold from one area to the other. These duties are analogous to transportation costs. They increase the "distance" between two regions in the economic sense of the word.

---

[29] See L. H. Klaassen, *De economische structuren en de interregionale ontwikkeling in Noord-West Europa*, Liège, 1958.

761-932 O—65——6

TABLE 13.—*Important measures taken in Belgium according to type and objectives*

Measures	Mobility of labor			Mobility of capital	
	Migration	Commuting	Social mobility	Regional	Sectoral
1. Direct measures in favor of industries.	....	....	....	Regional act—low interest rates + state guarantees $210 million (July 1959–October 1962).	General act—low interest rates + state guarantees $360 million (July 1959–October 1962).
				80,407 workers	
2. Indirect measures in favor of industries.	....	Infrastructural improvements development areas.	....	Infrastructural improvements development areas.	Development fund $2 million (3 years).
3. Measures in favor of workers.	Subsidies for training and retraining. Subsidies for migration.	Low railway rates for commuters to larger agglomerations.	Subsidies for training and retraining.	Subsidies for training and retraining.	Subsidies for training and retraining.
4. Other measures....	....	....	....	....	

TABLE 14.—*Important measures taken in Holland according to type of measures and objectives*

Measures	Mobility of labor			Mobility of capital	
	Migration	Commuting	Social mobility	Regional	Sectoral
1. Direct measures in favor of industries.	....	....	....	Premium and price reduction in development nuclei. $58 million (July 1959–August 1960) 10,403 workers $184 million 33,476 workers (July 1959–December 1962). Minimum 1 worker per 1,000 sq. ft. new industries; 1 worker per 500 sq. ft. experimental industries.	State guarantees. Tax reductions. Accelerated depreciation. Research institutes.
2. Indirect measures in favor of industries.	2,000 houses annually built in development nuclei.	Infrastructural improvements development areas ($53 million for 3 years).	....	Infrastructural improvements ($53 million for 3 years).	Research institutes.

TABLE 14.—*Important measures taken in Holland according to type of measures and objectives*—Continued

Measures	Mobility of labor			Mobility of capital	
	Migration	Commuting	Social mobility	Regional	Sectoral
3. Measures in favor of workers.	Subsidy for migration cost.	....	Subsidy for training and retraining.	Subsidies for training and retraining.	Subsidies for training and retraining.
	2,000 houses annually built in development nuclei. No subsidy for migration to Rimcity.	....	Regional training centers.	Regional training centers.	Regional training centers.
4. Other measures	....	....	....	Restrictions on location in areas not designated for industrial location.	

Since import duties are the same for a given product regardless of origin or destination as long as the countries of origin and destination are the same, they are relatively of less importance for areas far apart than for areas very close to each other. For this reason their influence on international trade between areas in different nations but close to the common border will be considerably larger than on trade between regions much farther apart. Thus the abolition of import duties within the framework of Benelux or EEC will exert a relatively large influence on common frontier areas in all member countries.

The lowering of tariff walls will also favorably influence the tendency of industries to locate in frontier areas. So far, location close to a border has meant a disadvantage for the industry since the area covered by the industry, given a certain price for its product, was limited to a semicircle if import duties were high, or to a semicircle in one country and a much smaller semicircle in the second country whose radius was dependent upon the level of import duties to be paid at the border. Only when no import duties exist is the area covered a complete circle.

In general, on the basis of this argument, one would expect frontier areas to be less developed than areas farther from the border. This hypothesis was tested by the author in 1955 for the border areas of Holland in the study cited in note 29. Table 15 relates the income of border provinces to the average income of Holland.

With the exception of the municipalities in Zeeland (actually economically related to Belgium more than to Holland) all border places lie considerably, according to Dutch standards, below the Dutch average. Moreover, the difference for the municipalities at the German border is larger than for those at the Belgian border. This conforms to expectations. Benelux has already made considerably more progress than the EEC, so that im-

TABLE 15.—*Income of border municipalities as a percentage of average Dutch income*

Province in which border municipalities are located	Income as a percent of Dutch income	
	1955	1958[1]
A. *German border:*		
Groningen	94.0	93.4
Drenthe	83.5	87.8
Overijssel	96.5	92.2
Gelderland	82.0	92.6
Limburg	86.0	}
B. *Belgian border:*		} 93.4
Limburg	95.0	}
Noord-Brabant	90.0	91.8
Zeeland	110.0	95.3

[1] Calculations of Dr. M. van Overeem, "The Impact of the Common Market on Dutch Regional Policy," presented at the 1963 meeting of OECD, Paris, N.E.I., 1963.

port duties at the Dutch-Belgian border are correspondingly lower than at the Dutch-German border.

Finally, table 16 gives data concerning the income of border municipalities as a percentage of the average income of the province in which the municipality is located.

TABLE 16.—*Income of border municipalities as a percentage of average income in the corresponding province*

Province in which border municipalities are located	Income as a percent of the corresponding province	
	1955	1958[1]
A. *German border:*		
Groningen	96.0	90.0
Drenthe	91.0	92.0
Overijssel	102.0	97.5
Gelderland	90.0	93.9
Limburg	91.0	100.0
B. *Belgian border:*		
Limburg	100.0	97.8
Noord-Brabant	92.5	97.1
Zeeland	105.0	99.8

[1] Dr. M. van Overeem, *op. cit.*

These figures also indicate that the original hypothesis is correct. This means that the impact of the Common Market in regions close to a *common* border probably will be greater than in other areas of the member countries (including areas bordering nonmember countries).

A second future development may be expected from the fact that western European industry is gradually substituting raw materials from abroad for domestic raw materials. This particularly holds for coal (replaced by oil) and iron ore. As a result the large ports are becoming depositories of cheap raw materials and therefore also favorable locations for basic industries. Recent developments on the Dutch and Belgian coasts indicate that the actual situation is adjusting rapidly to this new trend.

Needless to say, this stimulus for the coastal areas will increase economic development in the Rimcity. This means that an efficient regional policy will be needed more than ever to prevent unbalanced growth in the country.

In Belgium, on the contrary, the new trend will stimulate parts of Flanders that so far have been relatively less developed. This is especially true of the area around the Terneuzen-Gent canal which will be accessible to very large ships, up to 50,000 tons. Large basic industries have already shown interest in this area.

The same development, therefore, may show completely different regional influences in Belgium than in Holland.

Basic economic research is needed to ascertain where new developments will exert their influence and what are the possibilities of finding an optimal combination of regional requirements and actual developments. If theory is perfected and more statistical regional data become available, it will be possible to refine regional policy so as to maintain the delicate equilibrium between optimum growth of the whole economy and regionally balanced distribution of employment and income.

Appendix

Theoretical model of the regional income differences in the Netherlands

(1) $$P_t = P_{t-1} + {}^{\Delta}_{n}P_{t-1} + M_t$$ (definition)

in which P_t is working population at point of time t for a given region, ${}^{\Delta}_{n}P_{t-1}$ is the natural increase of the population during the period t and M_t is the net migration during the same period. If $M_t > 0$ there is net inmigration, if $M_t < 0$ there is net emigration.

(2) $$M_t = \alpha(Y_t - \overline{Y}_t)$$ (migration)

in which Y_t stands for the per capita income of the region under consideration and $\overline{Y}_t$ for the average income of the country. Y_t is considered to be identical with the wage rate.

(3) $$L_t^D = \beta_1 Y_t + \beta_2 Z_t + \beta_3 A_t$$ (labor-demand)

L_t^D stands for the demand for labor in the region, Y_t for the wage level. Z is a structural variable determining the demand for labor in the region. It represents in fact the structure of the region. A is an agglomeration factor introduced on the assumption that demand for labor, given the structure of the economy and the wage level is a positive function of the degree of urbanization.

(4) $$L_t^S = P_t$$ (labor-supply)

L_t^S is the supply of labor which is supposed to be equal to working population.

(5) $$L_t^S = L_t^D$$ (equilibrium equation)

It is assumed in this long-run model that there is full employment.

The solution for Y_t from this model is

(6) $$Y_t = -\frac{1}{\alpha+\beta_1}(P_{t-1} + {}^{\Delta}_{n}P_{t-1}) + \frac{\beta_2}{\alpha+\beta_1}Z_t + \frac{\beta_3}{\alpha+\beta_1}A_t + \frac{\alpha}{\alpha+\beta_1}\overline{Y}_t$$

This formula implies:

(*a*) Population growth has a negative influence on per capita income.

(*b*) A better structure of the economy and a higher degree of urbanization lead to a higher per capita income.

Attention may be drawn to the fact that α and β_1 play a very important role in the model.

As may be seen easily α is a measure for the propensity to migrate. A large α means a strong reaction to even small income-differences and a small α that even large income-differences do not lead to migration of some importance. β_1 gives the reaction on demand for labor of differences in wage rates between the area and the average of the country.

If α approaches zero the influence of population growth is a maximum. At the same time the influences of Z_t and A_t become large.

If α approaches infinity Y_t becomes equal to $\overline{Y}_t$. In that case the (infinite) mobility of labor (propensity to migrate) is so high that regional income differences disappear.

Before statistical testing two corrections on (6) have to be made. First the variable Y_t in (6) is the average income of persons actually employed. Data, however, include unemployed persons as well. This unemployment may be considered exogenous. Since this influence in fact should be represented by a multiplicative factor an approximation is used by linearization.

The second correction is a very simple one and in fact implies that sizes of regions are eliminated by using relative data instead of absolute figures.

Part 3

Regional Development Policies in France

Pierre Bauchet

Contents

Introduction

Zones which are the object of special measures are of various dimensions, from the urban agglomeration to the economic region defined by decree.[1] But they have in common such characteristics as inadequate incomes or levels of living, excessive emigration or too great population concentration, and disequilibria between the supply of and demand for labor.

The history of regional development policies is a long one. Before the second world war the idea of attempting to revive the depressed regions, then those of the south of France, was advanced. The growth of armament industries, particularly aviation, provided the opportunity to apply these notions.

In the immediate postwar period, the urgency of reconstruction and the scarcity of manpower disguised the inequalities in regional rates of growth. But they reappeared in the early years of the decade of the fifties, particularly with the slowing down in 1952 and 1953, so that greater attention was paid to regional problems, and the legislative arsenal began to develop. However, contemporary policies and institutions really began with the decrees of June 30, 1955, and this analysis begins with that date.

To permit a better understanding of French regional policies, it is necessary to make a quick examination of the problems giving rise to those policies, and then to evaluate the results.

Regional Problems

The years beginning in 1954 were marked by inequalities in regional development, notably between Paris and the rest of France. Regional policies tended to remedy the most striking inequalities by attacking the effects, though not the causes, of distortion. After a brief description of the relative situation of the regions in 1954, certain aspects of regional problems will be considered.

The Relative Situation of the Several Regions in 1954

It would not be possible to make an exact map of underdeveloped regions in France. Their definition is too imprecise to permit such a classification.

---

[1]Arrêté, Nov. 28, 1956 (Journal Officiel, Dec. 6, 1956, p. 11649); Décret No. 60–516, June 2, 1960 (Journal Officiel, June 3, 1960, p. 5007). We will speak of several kinds of regions, of which the principal are:

(1) The departments, administrative jurisdictions originating with Napoleonic legislation of the beginning of the 19th century. They are 90 in number. In each are the principal local authorities representing the central government, especially the prefect.
(2) The program regions, 21 in number, which are economic areas serving as the framework for the application of regional programs. Each includes several departments.
(3) The so-called socioeconomic regions defined by the European Economic Community. Nine in number, each includes several program regions.

For the boundaries of these several kinds of regions, see map 1.

Map I

France: Large Socio-Economic Regions and Program Regions

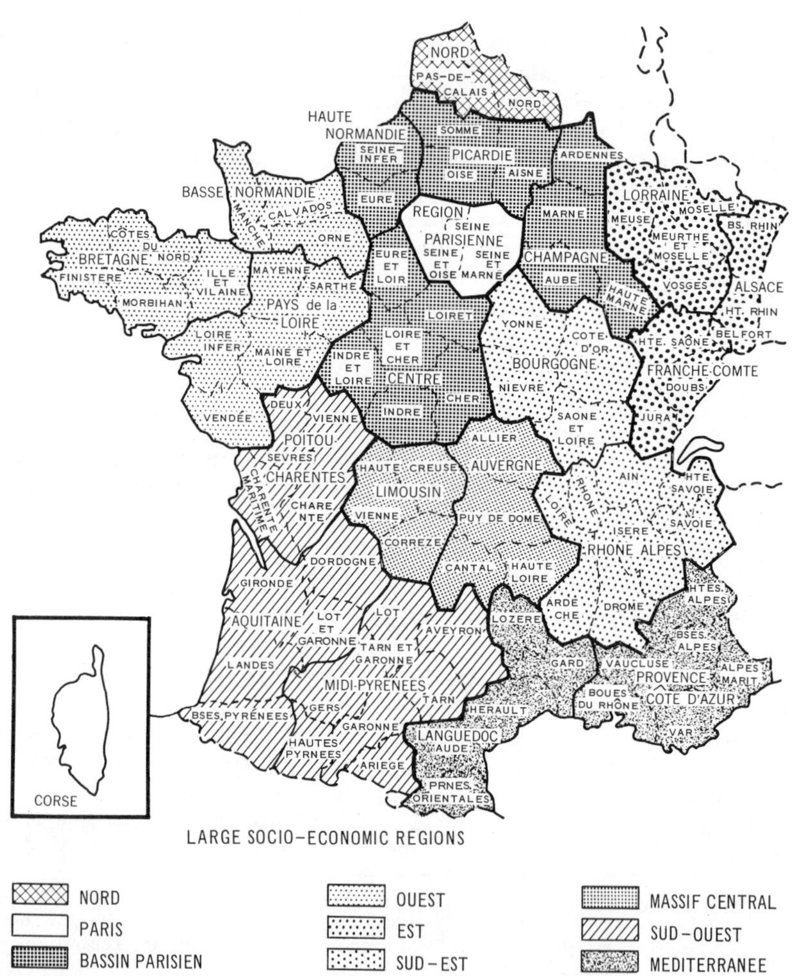

Departments and Program Regions appear by name on the map

The relative situation of the several departments and regions in France in 1954, that is, before the adoption of regional development measures, can, however, be roughly portrayed by means of three criteria. The disparities existing at that date can be measured in order to see if they were moderated later. The disparities to be considered concern:

(1) The active industrial population (map II—index of the relative growth of the active industrial population between 1946 and 1954).[2] It may be said, in gross terms, that growth of industrial production is a sign of progress.

(2) The average level of wages (map III). Lacking a measure of all incomes, a knowledge of wages and salaries permits a determination of an important part of income in each department.

(3) The number of job seekers, that is, persons registered as wishing employment, without jobs in each department (map IV). This is one factor in an estimate of unemployment, although not a completely satisfactory measure.

MAP II.—*Index of the Relative Change in Active Industrial Population, 1946–54*

[All of France=100]

Category 1—Index 113.8 and Above

Department	Index	Department	Index
Moselle	144. 3	Seine et Oise	114. 3
Haute Savoie	130. 8	Savoie	113. 8
Ardennes	116. 3		

Category 2—Index 107.0 Through 113.7

Seine, Seine et Marne, Haute Marne, Meurthe et Moselle, Meuse, Vosges, Bas Rhin, Haut Rhin, Doubs, Belfort, Drôme, Isère, Charente Maritime, Hautes Alpes.

Category 3—Index 100.2 Through 106.9

Aisne, Marne, Eure et Loir, Loir et Cher, Loiret, Loire Atlantique, Sarthe, Vendée, Haute Saône, Ain, Ardèche, Puy de Dôme, Basses Pyrénées, Lozère, Alpes Maritimes.

Category 4—Index 93.4 Through 100.1

Nord, Pas de Calais, Oise, Aube, Cher, Indre, Indre et Loire, Eure, Maine et Loire, Morbihan, Jura, Côte d'Or, Rhône, Haute Vienne, Deux Sèvres, Dordogne, Lot et Garonne, Aveyron, Tarn, Vaucluse.

Category 5—Index 86.6 Through 93.3

Somme, Mayenne, Côtes du Nord, Finistère, Ille et Vilaine, Saône et Loire, Yonne, Loire, Allier, Cantal, Haute Loire, Corrèze, Charente, Vienne, Gironde, Landes, Haute Garonne, Lot, Hautes Pyrénées, Tarn et Garonne, Gard, Basses Alpes.

Category 6—Index 79.8 Through 86.5

Calvados, Orne, Nièvre, Ariège, Hérault, Bouches du Rhône, Var.

---

[2] See appendix I, a note explaining the maps, and appendix II, the data used for construction of the maps.

Map II

Change in the Active Industrial Population by Departments, 1946 to 1954

Actual Compared to Hypothetical Projections Based on National Average Growth by Industries, 1946 to 1954

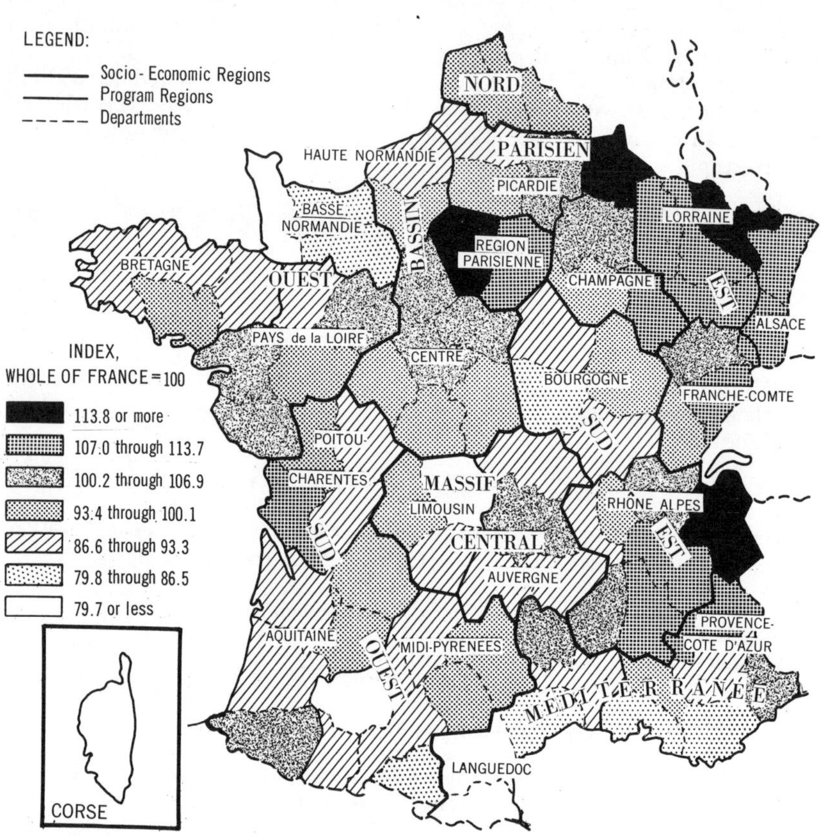

Departments Showing Least Growth In Active Industrial Population:	
Creuse	75.2
Manche	79.0
Pyrénées Orientales	79.3
Aude	79.6
Gers	79.7

Departments Showing Greatest Growth In Active Industrial Population:	
Moselle	144.3
Haute Savoie	130.8
Ardennes	116.3
Seine et Oise	114.3
Savoie	113.8

Category 7—Index less than 79.8

Gers	79.7	Manche	79.0
Aude	79.6	Creuse	75.2
Pyrénées Orientales	79.3		

Map III.—*Relative Wage Levels, 1954*

[All of France=100]

Category 1—Index 102 and Above

Seine	130	Bouches du Rhône	104
Seine et Oise	122	Meurthe et Moselle	102
Rhône	104		

Category 2—Index 96 Through 101

Seine et Marne, Seine Maritime, Moselle, Doubs, Belfort, Savoie.

Category 3—Index 89 Through 95

Nord, Pas de Calais, Oise, Loire Atlantique, Ardennes, Sarthe, Haut Rhin, Isère, Haute Savoie, Allier, Puy de Dôme, Gironde, Haute Garonne, Basses Alpes, Alpes Maritimes.

Category 4—Index 82 Through 88

Aisne, Marne, Cher, Eure et Loir, Indre et Loire, Loiret, Eure, Calvados, Meuse, Bas Rhin, Côte d'Or, Nièvre, Saône et Loire, Ain, Drôme, Loire, Hautes Pyrénées, Gard, Hérault, Pyrénées Orientales, Var, Tarn.

Category 5—Index 75 Through 81

Somme, Aube, Haute Marne, Indre, Maine et Loire, Côtes du Nord, Finistère, Ille et Vilaine, Morbihan, Vosges, Jura, Haute Saône, Yonne, Ardèche, Corrèze, Haute Vienne, Charente, Charente Maritime, Vienne, Dordogne, Landes, Lot et Garonne, Basses Pyrénées,, Ariège, Aveyron, Lot, Aude, Vaucluse, Corse, Hautes Alpes.

Category 6—Index 68 Through 74

Loir et Cher, Manche, Orne, Mayenne, Cantal, Haute Loire, Deux Sèvres, Tarn et Garonne.

Category 7—Index Less Than 68

Lozère	67	Vendée	64
Creuse	67	Gers	61

Map IV—*Average Number of Jobseekers, 1954*

(Number per 10,000 active industrial population)

[All of France=242]

Category 1—50 or Fewer

Deux Sèvres	23	Haute Marne	42
Meuse	29	Hte Saône+Belf	50
Vosges	33		

Map III

Relative Wage Levels by Departments, 1954

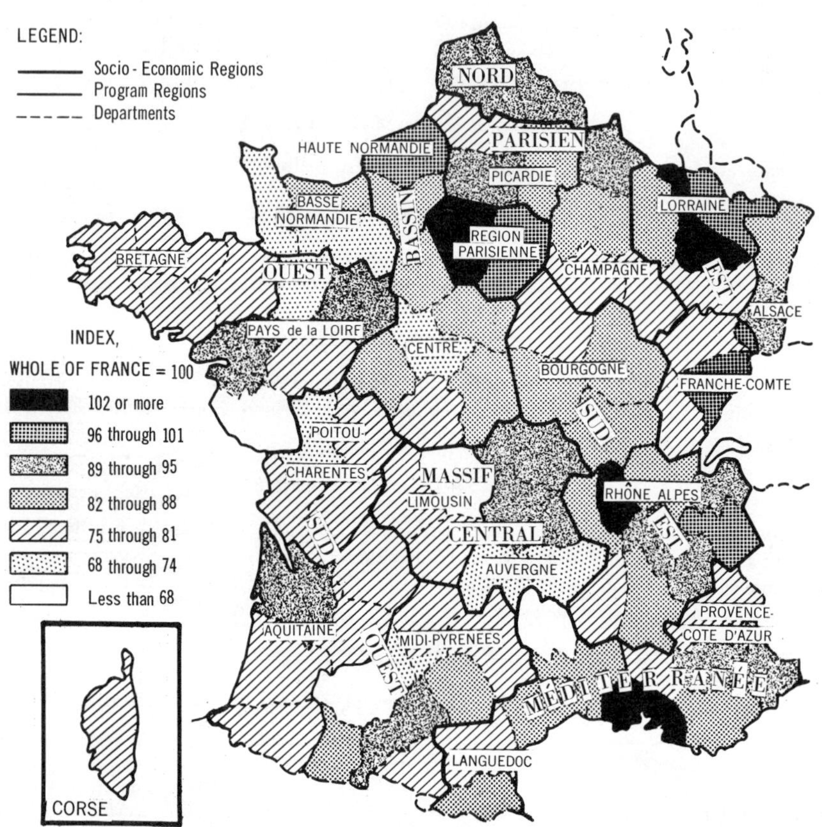

Departments With Highest Wages:

Seine	130
Seine et Oise	122
Rhône	104
Bouches du Rhône	104
Meurthe et Moselle	102

Departments With Lowest Wages:

Gers	61
Vendée	64
Creuse	67
Lozère	67

Category 2—51 Through 165

Nord, Seine et Marne, Aisne, Oise, Ardennes, Aube, Indre, Loir et Cher, Loiret, Eure, Orne, Maine et Loire, Vendée, Meurthe et Moselle, Moselle, Haut Rhin, Doubs, Jura, Nièvre, Saône et Loire, Yonne, Ain, Isère, Haute Savoie, Charente, Landes, Aveyron, Gers, Lot, Lozère, Basses Alpes, Hautes Alpes, Var.

Category 3—166 Through 281

Pas de Calais, Seine et Oise, Somme, Marne, Cher, Eure et Loir, Indre et Loire, Calvados, Manche, Mayenne, Finistère, Bas Rhin, Côte d'Or, Drôme, Loire, Rhône, Savoie, Allier, Haute Loire, Puy de Dôme, Corrèze, Creuse, Haute Vienne, Charente Maritime, Dordogne, Hautes Pyrénées, Tarn.

Category 4—282 Through 397

Seine, Seine Maritime, Loire Atlantique, Côtes du Nord, Ille et Vilaine, Morbihan, Ardèche, Cantal, Vienne, Lot et Garonne, Basses Pyrénées, Haute Garonne.

Category 5—398 Through 513

Tarn et Garonne, Sarthe.

Category 6—514 Through 628

Gironde, Artiège, Gard, Pyrénées Orientales, Vaucluse.

Category 7—More Than 628

Bouches du Rhône	628	Aude	1148
Alpes Maritimes	643	Hérault	1597
Corse	670		

Such as they are, these criteria bear largely on the industrial activity of the departments. It is not possible to measure precisely the other sectors.

Though the classification of the departments in accordance with these criteria does not give an exact idea of their relative situation in 1954, it presents at least an approximation, a picture which a knowledge of the economic facts shows to be valid. The salient features of this picture will be summarized by the large social and economic regions, beginning with the north and the west.

The north

This region was homogeneous, since the situation of the two departments composing it was comparable in 1954. It was below the national average in wages and in the growth of active industrial population. Unemployment was relatively low because of continuous emigration. Its then stagnant situation is to be explained by the importance of the declining textile and coal mining industries and by the small number of modern industries.

The west

In 1954 this region appeared to be one of the most underdeveloped, principally at the extreme of Bretagne and in the departments of Basse Normandie. Though certain parts of the Pays de la Loire, particularly Loire-Atlantique and Sarthe, had a less unsatisfactory level of employment and wages, throughout the region the level of wages and salaries and the

Map IV

Number of Jobseekers Per 10,000 Active Industrial Population, by Departments, 1954

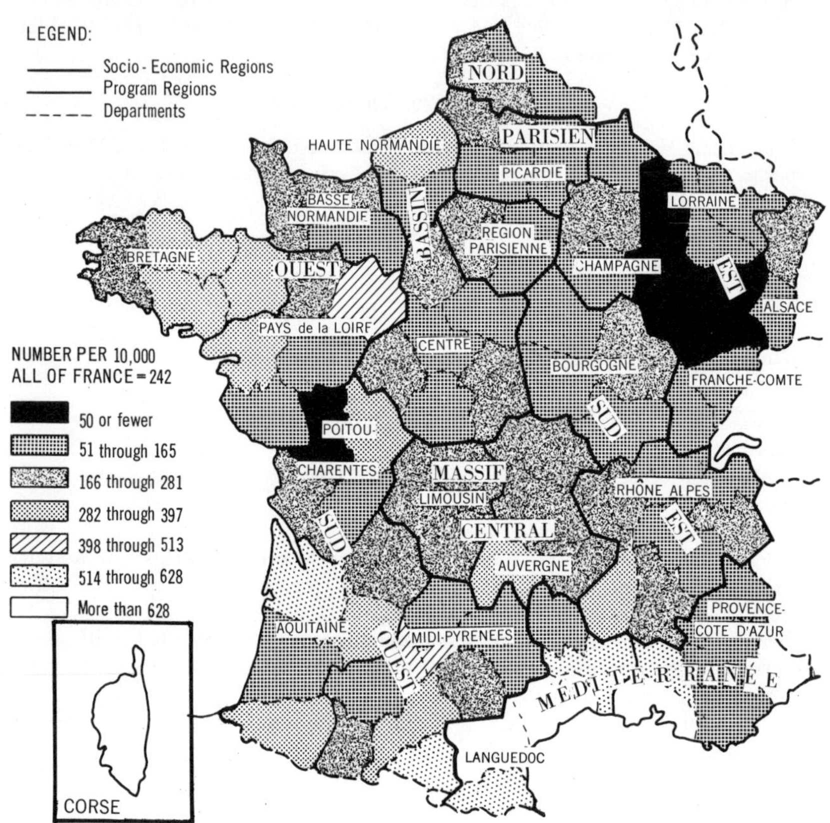

Departments With Highest Rates:	
Hérault	1597
Aude	1148
Corse	670
Alpes Maritimes	643
Bouches du Rhône	629

Departments With Lowest Rates:	
Deux Sèvres	23
Meuse	29
Vosges	33
Haute Marne	42
Haute Saône	50
Belfort	50

growth of the active industrial population put it in the lowest group. A low level of industrial activity, except for the shipyards which by 1954 were not yet in serious difficulty (which explains the less unfavorable situation of Loire-Atlantique), agricultural poverty, and a decline of the artisan trades accounted for the problems of the west.

The southwest

The situation of the southwest was, in some ways, like that of the west: Low wages and slow growth of industry. Basses Pyrénées was an exception, accounted for by the opportunity to exploit natural gas at Lacq. The relatively low number of job seekers in certain departments resulted largely from a low birth rate and rapid emigration.

The massif central

This was another of the same type of region. Limousin had very low wages, a very large number of job seekers, and one of the slowest rates of industrial growth. Only the department of Puy-de-Dôme in Auvergne showed a certain vitality, due to tourism.

The Mediterranean

Though Languedoc was among the most backward regions, Provence-Côte d'Azur showed a somewhat better picture, particularly in the department of Hautes-Alpes. But despite the rather high level of wages in Bouches du Rhône and the small number of job seekers, again due to demographic factors, no significant industrial development had appeared. Tourism alone produced the relatively higher wage level.

The southeast

Though Bourgogne seemed to be stagnating, the Rhône-Alpes region, with the exception of Loire, showed signs of vitality: Growth of active industrial population, relatively high wages, particularly in Rhône, and few job seekers despite a high birth rate.

The east

Since 1954 the east has been in a privileged situation: High wages particularly in Meurthe et Moselle, increase in the active industrial population, and very few job seekers. The development of the steel industry, and of heavy metallurgical and metal processing industries, tended to compensate for the decline in textiles and the traditional artisan trades. However, the situation of Vosges, Meuse, a part of Franche-Comté, and Bas Rhin did not seem particularly good so far as wage levels were concerned.

The Parisian basin and the region of Paris

The ring which surrounds Paris from Champagne to the Centre did not benefit greatly from its closeness to Paris because, apart from Haute Normandie, wages there were quite low. Growth of the active industrial population had not been rapid. The number of job seekers was not significant by reason of any attraction exercised by Paris. The Parisian region, on the other hand, had exceptionally high wages and a very rapid rate of growth of industrial population. All the signs of rapid growth were combined.

This contrast between a center of development and its surroundings illustrates one of the propositions of classical location theory; in the first phase the development of the center feeds on its surroundings.

This rapid tour shows that since 1954 a contrast has existed between the east of France, which encompasses a number of developing zones, and the west which, from Basse Normandie to Languedoc, is in a particularly unfavorable situation. This rudimentary division of France into two contrasting parts is doubtless too simple, but it reflects quite well the realities which seem to have been maintained over the years. Of course, the particularly dynamic Parisian region must be set apart, and it must be remembered that some departments are exceptions to this division of France into two parts.

Some Aspects of Regional Problems

One source of problems is to be found in industries whose markets are declining, or simply growing less rapidly than overall output. Problems of this kind arise from the textile industries, the coal mines, and the shipyards. To these must be added the particular problems of agriculture. Entire regions live on these activities and suffer from their relative decline.

Second, problems peculiar to certain regions, such as distance from the great centers of development and lack of resources, have produced a relatively low rate of growth in certain parts of France.

Finally, population movements have accentuated the disparities. Population is concentrated around Paris and the overpopulated Parisian region. In contrast, entire regions, notably in the center of France, are suffering a real depopulation, both rural and urban.

Other explanations might be added to these three most important causes. Deserving of special mention are certain policies relating to the pricing of public services and of transportation or energy, tax policies, and public investment which, without deliberately discriminating against certain zones, have had the effect of penalizing them. But for the purpose of describing the general context in which regional policy in France is placed, this introductory discussion will be limited to the three important causes.

THE SECTORS THAT GENERATE REGIONAL DISEQUILIBRIA

As noted above, the regons in difficult situations are often those that are predominantly agricultural, or those whose industrial activity is dominated by the textile industries, by shipyards and military arsenals, or by coal mining.

Agricultural production is certainly not declining: It increased more than 30 percent between 1949 and 1959 at a fairly regular rate. But accompanying this progress there has been a massive migration of workers out of agricultural employments, averaging about 2 percent a year.[3] The fourth plan for the French economy, covering the years 1961–65, projects a further decrease of 440,000 persons employed in agriculture for those 4 years. Most of the emigrants from agriculture seek jobs which are not available in the region in which they have lived.

It is well known that mechanization of agriculture, while increasing productivity and production, brings pressure on prices and reduces the number of workers. Some regions, such as Alsace, Rhône-Alpes, and Haute Normandie, can place these workers in other employments in their home regions.

---

[3] Rapport Général de la Commission de la Main-d'Oeuvre du IVe Plan, Imprimerie Nationale, Paris, 1961, pp. 18 and 44.

However, others such as Bretagne, Pays de la Loire, Basse Normandie, the Nord, and Bourgogne have, for decades, sent former agricultural workers in search of employment to the great cities, particularly Paris. Some farmers continue to live on very poor and very small plots of land. Thus the agricultural population made excess by improved productivity brings in its train an accumulated emigration of former farm workers and persons formerly providing services to agriculture, or unemployment camoufiaged by the continuance on the farm of a population which cannot be employed elsewhere.

The textile industry is also responsible for the difficulties encountered in certain regions. Although textile production increased by 35 percent between 1949 and 1959, this rate of increase is less rapid than that of the other great industrial sectors. But more important, it has been accompanied by a qualitative change in the structure of jobs and by a significant reduction in the number of unskilled workers.

Furthermore, textile activity is subject to fluctuations in demand which were accentuated by the past wars. Before 1940, orders of an army largely composed of infantrymen brought about an increase in production. Losses from wartime destruction and the need to rebuild family stocks permitted the textile industry to maintain its expansion during the immediate postwar period. But from 1950 onward problems began to appear, accentuated by the shutting off of colonial markets in Indo-China and north Africa. Furthermore, the increase in production expected in the fourth plan for the period 1959–65 will be accompanied by a further reduction in employment, estimated at 19,000 employees, particularly in jute, cotton, and wool. These branches of the textile industry which anticipate further reductions in employment are concentrated particularly in the Nord and in Lorraine.

So far as coal mining is concerned, the exhaustion of certain mines and the competition of liquid hydrocarbons and gas have brought about a reduction in the use of solid fuels. Reduction in coal mining activity has begun to be felt in the decade of the 1960's. However, even before this date certain pits, especially those in the Centre and in the Nord, closed down, bringing about a sharp decrease in employment. Furthermore, mechanization of mining has reduced employment.

This reduction continues. The number of workers employed in the coal mining industry diminished from 358,240 in 1947 to 232,000 in 1959. It is anticipated that total employment will not exceed 175,000 in 1965. This massive reduction in employment has brought about serious consequences for the regions of the Centre and the Nord.

Shipyards and military arsenals have been another source of employment problems. The former experienced a considerable prosperity in the immediate postwar period resulting from the need to replace marine transport destroyed in the war. This expansion was prolonged by the Suez crisis because of the need to build tankers.

However, since 1955 orders have stabilized or even been reduced. Reconstruction has been completed. Shipyards in the new countries are increasingly competitive. A policy of reconversion and concentration of ship construction, scarcely begun but to be continued in the coming years, has already had the effect of reducing the number of employees from 52,800 in 1955 to 48,000 in 1961, a reduction of 6 percent. Moreover, shipyards are concentrated particularly in the coastal regions of Provence, Aquitaine, Bretagne, Haute Normandie, and the Nord. Their problems will accentuate the difficulties of these regions. Similarly, changes in armaments have brought about the closure of military arsenals often situated close to naval shipyards, particularly in Bretagne.

More generally, industrial activities which, though not undergoing true crises, are growing at a very modest rate and do not substantially increase employment, have multiple effects in moderating the expansion of the regions in which they are located. W. W. Rostow correctly emphasized that such industries as coal mines, iron, steel, and heavy machinery which formerly played a preponderant role in western industry, have, as the economies become mature, lost ground relative to chemistry, electronic industries, and heavy consumer goods industries such as automobiles.[4] Although regions like the Nord and the high valley of the Loire, in which the older industries are located, are not really experiencing a depression, they suffer from a lack of dynamism which may be the prelude to more serious crises.

UNFAVORABLE REGIONAL STRUCTURES

Regional difficulties are not always related to the presence of industries which are either mature or in decline. Some regions with declining industries have not suffered particularly. The Rhône-Alpes region is well known for its silk industry, now in decline, watchmaking, and agriculture which has left its high valleys. Nevertheless, it has had a remarkable expansion as a result of other activities such as electrical and chemical industries and tourism.

In such regions declining industries represent a relatively small part of total employment. Moreover, the other industries located there do not rely mainly on local markets. It may thus be concluded that declining industries provoke a regional crisis only when two conditions exist:

(1) A large proportion of the employed population of the region is employed in the declining industries.

(2) The other industries depend on them, either as suppliers to them or as producers of consumer goods for the workers employed.

But there are also regions whose decline cannot be explained solely by the presence of industries in difficulties. Such is the case for Languedoc, the Centre, and Champagne. Their problems are more related to the fact that they have not been able to attract expanding modern industries, and to the factors that are responsible for this state of affairs.

Such natural factors as climate, the lack of subsoil resources, the poor quality of the soil, and the broken character of their geography, which makes communication difficult, have played a role, particularly in Bretagne and in Auvergne. The lack of a dynamic local elite which might have taken the initiative to attract industry and, more broadly, the lack of general characteristics in the population favorable to industrialization have slowed down development in some regions. The absence of factors that might attract the necessary skilled managerial and technical personnel as well as younger workers, housing problems, and the lack of appropriate urban organization, all have contributed to the reluctance of new industry to locate in certain regions.

Distance from the large centers of decision and development also handi-

[4] W. W. Rostow, *Les Etapes de la Croissance Economique,* Editions du Seuil, Paris, 1962, p. 24.

caps numerous regions in which industries hesitate to locate because of high transportation costs for the supply of materials and for delivery to market of the goods which they produce. All the western parts of France, from Basse Normandie to Aquitaine, have been hurt by their distance from the centers of the Common Market and from the Parisian region. It is striking how the eastern regions have, on the average, suffered less from lack of development.

POPULATION MIGRATION

Much of the population of whole zones has been emigrating. By reason of a high birth rate (the Nord) or lack of sufficient regional employment (Bretagne) much of the active population is moving, particularly toward the Paris region. Except in the Centre, the rate of migration is not sufficiently high to offset the birth rate and to make these regions completely depopulated areas or "deserts," but it deprives them of their most dynamic elements, bringing in its train a mass movement from the west to the east and from the north to the south of France.

Such regions as Paris with a 9 percent immigration from 1954 to 1962, Rhônes-Alpes with 5 percent, and Provence with 11 percent, have been the recipients of this mass migration. The absolute numbers of persons involved have not been so large as to create serious difficulties except in the Paris region, to which more than a million persons have come in 7 years.

Even greater problems may arise in a particular locality. The closing of a single enterprise can bring about unemployment which is relatively very important to a particular town. But it is quite evident that the Government need not intervene in each such case, since in a developing region the dismissed workers can often find jobs by moving to neighboring localities. However, the Government has considered it necessary to intervene on occasion in particular localities or somewhat larger zones when important enterprises have threatened to close their doors and the general employment situation has already been unfavorable.

These aspects of regional problems in France explain some of the characteristics of the policies adopted:

Policies are not concerned only with particular industrial sectors. Assistance given to particular industries, shipyards, and arsenals does not suffice to revive the region. Broader measures, especially the development of the infrastructures, are also necessary, partly to overcome those obstacles not wholly related to the existence of declining industries.

The object of regional policy has been less to solve a current unemployment problem which up to the present has been quite marginal, and more to offset the threat of future unemployment. It thus tends to direct and control future migrations between regions or even to suppress them.

An analysis of all the French regions disclosed that virtually all have problems, though they are particularly difficult in the west. Even the Parisian region is not without its problems, which arise from its overpopulation. It is impossible to find zones without difficulties; all have greater or lesser ones. For this reason regional policy is beginning to be considered in France as an aspect of general policy. All the regions must be considered and treated simultaneously. Further, it is not possible to resolve the difficulties of some regions without affecting others: To slow down migration to Paris presupposes development in such regions of emigration as Bretagne.

Regional policies in France cannot be understood except in the particular framework of the French administrative structure, the heritage of Napoleonic centralization. The development of policy has given rise to a search for a rational choice of the regions to be developed, that is, for criteria of underdevelopment. Further, the means that may be applied in the framework of a generally liberal economic policy are both diverse and not greatly restrictive.

Local administrative structure in France is composed of two superimposed jurisdictions: the commune and the department. At the head of the department are the prefect, named by the Central Government, and the elected general council. In the commune are the mayor and the municipal council, both elected.

There are two reasons for this administrative structure: On the one hand it is necessary that representatives of the central authority supervise the management of the large national services throughout the country. On the other hand there are local services. National and local services are often brought together in the department. Furthermore, the prefect and the mayor are not solely representatives of either the central administration or of the department or the commune. They act as representatives both of the French state and of the department or commune.

At present the territorial administrative framework is the department, a creation of the French Revolution. Many consider it obsolete in an epoch when most economic problems are posed on a larger scale. But in 1955 there existed no other regional administrative framework bringing together within it the several administrative services. Where there were larger administrative jurisdictions going beyond the bounds of the department, they were overlapping and so checked and bridled as to render regional policy impossible of administration.

It was necessary, then, to consider a regrouping if regional institutions were to be efficient. To this end there were created, in 1956, 24 program regions (*régions de programmes*), of which 2 were in overseas departments and Algeria.[5] But the confusion remained because these program regions were only for purposes of application of a single decree, that of June 30, 1955, on regional action. The next step was taken in 1959 when a new law set forth the principle of harmonization of administrative jurisdictions in metropolitan France with a view to setting in motion programs of regional action.[6] But it was not until 1960 that the number of program regions was set at 21 and the overlapping of jurisdictions in program regions for the approximately 30 administrative agencies concerned was set straight.[7] Finally, the decree of December 12, 1961, fixed the boundaries of 19 educational jurisdictions, most of which coincide with the program regions.

These tasks accomplished, a twofold evolution has characterized the regionalization of economic action of the Government: First, regional institutions have been either established or improved in order that those who best know the needs of each region can make those needs known and even

---

[5] Arrêté, Nov. 28, 1956 (Journal Officiel, Dec. 6, 1956, p. 11649).
[6] Décret No. 59–171, Jan. 7, 1959 (Journal Officiel, Jan. 11, 1959, p. 761).
[7] Décret No. 60–516, June 2, 1960 (Journal Officiel, June 3, 1960, p. 5007).

make decisions; and second, a more precise analysis of the regional economies has been developed.

The Institutions

The administrative structure of France has guided the development of regional economic institutions into two parallel paths: Decentralization of administration and deconcentration of authority. But the level of centralization remains quite high in that numbers of institutions and authorities concerning regional development are concentrated, at the governmental level, in Paris.

INSTITUTIONS AT THE LEVEL OF THE REGION

The decentralization movement

When the legislature by Law No. 54–809 of August 14, 1954, [8] authorized the Government to initiate a program directed toward financial equilibrium, economic expansion, and social progress and to take all measures relative to "the pursuit of economic expansion and increase of national income by means of a regional, departmental or local organization charged with effectuating the economic development of the regions within the framework of the plan in cooperation with qualified representatives of banks, of agriculture, of commerce, of industry, of fishing, of transport, of the artisan trades, of local groups and of the most representative unions of workers," certain organizations already existed at the local level. These included, for example, the *Comités d'Etudes Economiques* spontaneously created since 1950 on the initiative of the general councils and the chambers of commerce. The decree of December 11, 1954,[9] provided for *Comités d'Expansion Economique,* departmental or interdepartmental, which were to be consulted in order to effectuate economic and social development within the framework of national economic policy. Further, these committees were to be grouped into regional coordinating commissions when the problems raised went beyond the jurisdiction of one or several committees. The committees are composed of interested and competent persons from the sectors enumerated in the law.

Decree No. 55–873, of June 30, 1955,[10] concerning the establishment of programs of regional action was silent as to the institutions which were to prepare these programs. It merely emphasized the necessity of coordinating the work of the administrations and of public and private establishments benefiting from the assistance of a public agency. It seems that the Government still hesitated to associate the interested groups in the conception of the regional plan. As far as the means of execution are concerned, it was content with facilitating the creation of *Sociétés de Développement Régional,* charged with stimulating private saving and its investment in underdeveloped regions, and *Groupements Professionels,* or regional trade associations having as goals rationalization and conversion with approval of the state.

Up to this time, the decentralization movement was quite limited. Not until the 1959 measure [11] concerning harmonization of administrative jurisdictions in metropolitan France, enacted with a view to activating the pro-

---

[8] Journal Officiel, Aug. 15, 1954, p. 7858.

[9] Décret No. 54–1231, Dec. 11, 1954 (Journal Officiel, Dec. 12, 1954, p. 11645).

[10] Journal Officiel, July 2, 1955. See also Décrets Nos. 55–876 and 55–877 of the same date.

[11] Décret No. 59–171, Jan. 7, 1959 (Journal Officiel, Jan. 11, 1959, p. 761).

grams of regional action, did a new period begin, however timid it may have been, oriented toward a more precise definition of the role and powers of existing institutions.

The *Comités d'Expansion Economiques* seeking to organize themselves at a departmental or interdepartmental level could obtain the approval of the ministry on condition that they adhere to certain patterns of occupational and geographical composition. Their principal reason for being was to obtain the greatest possible participation of economic and social groups in the region concerned. The functions of these committees were expanded in 1961 [12] to include a consultative role on the development of the regional plans and of the *tranches opératoires* [13] and on the modifications that might be made in the projections of regional plans. Further, they were to give advice to the interdepartmental conference on the execution of regional plans, described below. Their mission, then, was one of consultation and stimulation, the role which the leadership of the region was to play.

Commissions Départementales de l'Equipement were created in 1961 [14] and were charged with coordinating public works and with establishing an order of priority among investment projects. They also had a consultative role, that of transmitting information to interdepartmental conferences and giving them advice on the development or revision of regional development plans. They were also to be kept advised on the realization of these plans.

This decentralization movement, which tends to associate local interests with the regional development planning, is accompanied by a deconcentration movement, which tends to associate with the same planning certain local public authorities.

The deconcentration movement

In the French province, the prefect is the only agent of the national state with general authority. It was his functions and his role which it was desirable to reinforce. But the prefect is at the head of a single department. Since regional action concerns several departments, it was clearly necessary to institute some kind of organ of coordination and of supervision or decision bringing together the authority of several prefects. Recourse was had at first to the *Inspecteur Général de l'Administration en Mission Extraordinaire* (IGAME).

The prefects can exercise little initiative in economic matters. Each is responsible in his own department for the carrying out of the measures provided for in the regional plans.

The two institutions created at the regional level are the interdepartmental conference, created in 1959, and the coordinating prefect. The circular of December 18, 1961, assigned three tasks to the interdepartmental conference:

(1) To participate in the establishment of development plans for the regions which heretofore had had none.

(2) To complete the programs of regional action established under the regime of the decree of June 30, 1955, which dealt with economic development only by giving directives concerning regional economic balance.

---

[12] Décret No. 61–72, Jan. 20, 1961, modifying Décret No. 54–1231 (Journal Officiel, Jan. 21, 1961, p. 867).

[13] See below, p. 36.

[14] Circulaire du Premier Ministre, Dec. 18, 1961 (Journal Officiel, Dec. 19, 1961, p. 11619).

(3) To bring up to date the first programs undertaken.

The conference is composed of the prefects of the interested departments and of local civil servants and is presided over by the coordinating prefect. Its role is precise in the division of investment credits: Upon the preparation of the budget of each ministry, the conference transmits to the ministries specific propositions on the most urgent operations, with reasons therefor, after having taken great care to select and to coordinate proposed investments. The conference is concerned with proposed departmental projects when they present a regional interest, and such programs, once developed, are submitted to it. Finally, it is up to the interdepartmental conference, after consultation with the committee on expansion, to present annual reports on the execution of the regional plan, which formerly were prepared by the *Commissariat Général du Plan.*

At first it was the duty of the IGAME to stimulate action by those regional services that were obligated, under the decree of July 14, 1956, to coordinate the measures providing programs in their jurisdiction. The 1959 measure establishing the interdepartmental conference provided that a later special decree would designate which of the prefects should preside over it. This coordinating prefect was designated for each of the 21 program regions by the special decree of January 20, 1961. He was to be the prefect of the most important of the several departments. His powers are identical with those that the IGAME previously had.

It is apparent from the description of his functions that the coordinating prefect is not a "regional authority," but that he remains the equal of the other prefects. He does not possess any superior power over any of them. It is necessary, however, to qualify this general statement somewhat. In five departments (Corrèze, Eure, Seine-Maritime, Vienne, and Isère) there has been in progress for a year an experiment whose general goal is, under the authority of the prefects, to seek a greater unification of action of regional services, notably by regrouping, reassignment of function, and reinforcement of the means of coordination. In this experiment the prefects concentrate in their hands the entire powers exercised by the State within the department. More recently, a decentralized procedure has been established for the administration of investment grants and exemption from local taxes, discussed later, in the Pays de la Loire, Bretagne, Basse Normandie, Aquitaine, Limousin, and Languedoc.

Taken literally, the decentralization and deconcentration measures as a whole seem weak and inefficient. This weakness certainly hinders the development and success of regional plans. But close attention must be paid to the experiments in progress. They are true tests of possible administrative reconstruction and clearly are of significant value. They have aroused among the interested groups and persons a feeling for the region and a concern for all that affects it. These groups are likely to bring pressure on the Government someday to give to the regional bodies the powers which they now lack.

NATIONAL INSTITUTIONS

National institutions play an essential role in regional development because the power to make decisions remains in fact in the hands of the central authority.

The administrative organs

Certain ministerial departments traditionally exercise great influence on regional policy because of the very nature of their activities. In the sectors which they control they make decisions which have geographic repercussions. These decisions are independent, though there are several consultative organs, such as the *Comité National d'Orientation Economique,* the *Haut Conseil de l'Aménagement du Territoire,* and the *Comité de Décentralisation des Etablissements Publics.* In order to remedy in part this strict vertical structure of French administration and the anarchy which might well result from it, and to promote the necessary unity of point of view and conception, special agencies were created charged particularly with consideration of regional policy as a whole.

It was the *Commissariat Général du Plan* which first had the idea of coordinating the several decisions taken by the ministries, and it was hoped to accomplish this coordination within the *Commissariat.* Charged with administration of the plan, it is a small agency divided into sections corresponding to the several economic sectors. In the drafting of each successive plan it is assisted by tripartite *Commissions de Modernisation* (including representatives of the Government, of management, and of workers). These *Commissions de Modernisation* have the duty of developing for the plan proposals concerning particular sectors.

The decree of December 31, 1958 (modified on February 14, 1963) [15] created within the *Commissariat Général du Plan* a committee called the *Comités des Plans Regionaux.* It is composed of the *Commissaire Général du Plan* as chairman, the *Directeur de 'lAménagement du Territoire,* and representatives of the several interested ministries, of the Executive Council of the *Fonds de Developement Economique et Social,* of the *Comité National d'Action Economique,* of the *Haut Conseil de l'Aménagement du Territoire,* and of the *Comité de Décentralisation.* It is charged with the establishment and coordination of regional economic development plans and the plans for land use, and with the duty to maintain liaison between the several institutions concerned with regional economic action.

As a parallel at the ministerial level there was created, in November 1960,[16] an Interministerial Committee for problems of regional action and land use planning (*aménagement du territoire*). Its structure and function, as modified in 1961 and 1963, for the first time permitted overall consideration of such diverse questions as soil legislation, the construction of markets and national slaughterhouses, and the system of public aid for industrialization. It is charged with preparing governmental decisions on regional matters and is composed of certain ministers, with the participation of the *Commissaire Général du Plan* and of the *Délégué à l'Aménagement du Territoire.*

But the need for an overall view of regional problems quickly made it apparent that a dual structure, including the plan for economic development established under the authority of the *Commissaire Général du Plan,* on the one hand, and the plan for land use conceived by the *Conseil Supérieur de la Construction,* on the other, did not suffice. Hence there was

---

[15] Journal Officiel, Jan. 4, 1963, p. 263, modified by Décret No. 63–116, Feb. 14, 1963.

[16] Décret No. 60–1219, Nov. 19, 1960 (Journal Officiel, Nov. 20, 1960, p. 10363); Décret No. 61–728, July 16, 1961; Décret No. 63–112, Feb. 14, 1963 (Journal Officiel, Feb. 15, 1963).

created in February 1963 [17] a *Délégation à l'Aménagement du Territoire et à l'Action Régionale,* an agency for coordination and stimulation whose function, apart from the general objectives defined by the plan, is to prepare and coordinate the elements necessary for governmental decisions in matters of land use planning and regional action, and to see to it that the interested ministries act accordingly. This implies the possibility of recourse to the final decision of the Prime Minister and explains why the *Délégué is* directly attached to him. The *Délégué* has access to the interministerial committee, of which he is in a way the executive. He follows the progress of the plan in the region. He is, in a word, the authority responsible for regional action and it is to him that the coordinating prefects and the interdepartmental conferences turn. He has at his disposition a special fund to finance supplemental operations which might be judged necessary for the achievement of the investment policy. It should also be noted that other agencies have been created and attached to the *Délégation.* An example is the *Mission Interministériella pour l'Aménagement Touristique* for the Languedoc-Roussillon coastal area.

The financial organs

In 1955 [18] there was established the *Fonds de Développement Economique et Social,* better known as the FDES. This fund replaced a number of funds established earlier for construction, for the retraining of workers, and for industrial decentralization. The FDES has a double function. It is, on the one hand, a special account of the treasury and, as such, serves as a lender. A special account, "Loans of the FDES," was organized in 1960.[19] The fund has handled the granting of loans to various specialized establishments. On the other hand, FDES is an agency directed by an executive council which does many things other than lending. It is presided over by the director general of the *Caisse des Dépôts et Consignations.* The council is divided into special committees, of which the principal one, so far as our study is concerned, is Committee No. 1. This Committee, created on June 30, 1960, coordinates the financial aids granted in regional matters. It is a sort of financial executive for regional policy, or at least for an important part thereof: Regional development, community tourist facilities, and productivity. However, about 50 percent of the total granted for regional policy does not come under its jurisdiction. A subcommittee gives tax and license fee exemptions in accordance with certain national fiscal policies.

Alongside the FDES, the *Fonds National d'Aménagement du Territorie,* which became the *Fonds National d'Aménagement Foncier et d'Urbanisme,* facilitates the land management necessary to urban and industrial operations. The *Fonds de l'Intervention pour l'Aménagement du Territoire,* created in February 1963,[20] has as its function the financing of complementary investment operations considered necessary for the functioning of the land use planning policy in accordance with a decision taken by the interministerial committee on November 19, 1960.

Finally, it should not be forgotten that each ministry has its own budget which, by reason of decisions taken by the ministry, has an influence on

[17] Décret No. 63–112, Feb. 14, 1963 (Journal Officiel, Feb. 15, 1963).

[18] Décret No. 55–875, June 30, 1955; Décret No. 55–1367, Oct. 18, 1955 (Journal Officiel, Oct. 19, 1955, p. 10351).

[19] Décret No. 60–703, July 15, 1960.

[20] Décret No. 63–112, Feb. 14, 1963.

regional policy: The creation of a hospital, for example, has a substantial effect on the region in which it is placed. Moreover, the execution of measures included in regional plans which fall normally within the functions of the several administrations is financed, according to the normal procedure, by credits against the respective budgets of the interested services.

The Development of the Analysis of Regional Economies

Alongside the construction of regional institutions, and in order to reinforce their powers and their means of action, the analysis of regional economies has been continuously refined. These two movements are inseparable, because the very participation of interested persons and groups leads to an improvement in the analysis of problems, while this greater understanding of the problems itself leads the regional interests to be more demanding so far as their participation is concerned.

Three stages may be distinguished: The programs of regional action, regional development plans and land use planning, and the *tranches opératoires.*

THE PROGRAMS OF REGIONAL ACTION

Growing regional disequilibria, the uncontained growth of Paris, and the slow death of certain regions have led the public authorities to interest themselves in regional problems. But the dispersion of efforts, the wish to stimulate local initiative, and the desire to control the funds distributed have centered increasing attention on the coordination of measures to be taken and their inclusion in a plan.

Past evolution

Geographic considerations were gradually introduced into the national plan. The first plan only suggested in passing certain problems of regional equilibrium. The second provided for three specific actions. There was created in Moselle a *Comité Départmental du Plan,* transformed in November 1951 to a *Comité d'Aménagement du Plan d'Equipement de la Moselle.* The planning for the Bas Rhône-Languedoc region gave rise to a special commission. Finally, in January 1955 there was created a commission for the use of gas resources and industrial development of the southwest.

In order to integrate these actions into a national framework, the decree of June 30, 1955, provided for the elaboration of regional programs. The "exposition of reasons" for this decree indicates that besides a coordination of public and private resources within the regional framework, these programs had as their object the completion of the *Plan de Modernisation et d'Equipement,* within whose framework they were to be developed. As is characteristic of French planning, the text insists, moreover, that it is important that representatives of private institutions existing in each region should participate in the development, and become interested in its activation and the exploitation of its possibilities.

The method of effectuation

The method of effectuation of these programs is not without weakness and scarcely bears out its promises of decentralization. Very generally, the preparation of the reports for each of the 19 regions was first done by Parisian civil servants who, in order to avoid collusion, were required not to visit the regions. But without real power and without sufficient means of information in Paris, they gradually abandoned their task. Under the new arrangements, those who develop the reports for the *Commissariat Général du Plan* maintain contacts with local authorities, who furnish a part of the basic information. In certain cases, particularly in the case of the Bretagne plan, the essential information is provided by local committees and study groups. Then a "synthesis group," including, besides the *Commissaire Général Adjoint du Plan,* representatives of the ministries, prefects, and local civil servants, brings together all the studies and proposals coming not only from central and local administrations but also from committees for expansion and for land-use planning. This synthesis is the object of local consultation which has grown over the years. In the course of this consultation the original document, a simple sketch, is filled in and sometimes doubled in size. Finally, the national committee and the interministerial committee for economic orientation look it over before its approval by ministerial decree.

Although this procedure marked considerable progress over the earlier situation, the regional programs developed in this fashion did not fully meet expectations. Analysis of the regions was often carried out too quickly, and was insufficiently coordinated with the objectives of the national plan. The decree of January 5, 1955, set out specific governmental decisions to accelerate regional development. These did not define new objectives and means, but were limited in general to partial measures rather than setting forth the lines of a true regional policy.[21]

REGIONAL DEVELOPMENT PLANS AND LAND-USE PLANNING

The decree of December 31, 1958, fused into a single document—*Le Plan Régional de Développement Economique et Social et d'Aménagement du Territoire*—the programs of regional action under the decree of June 30, 1955, and the regional plans under the Loi-Cadre of August 7, 1957, on construction. This was done so that all regional problems might be considered together as fully as possible and so that the policies of land-use planning would be incorporated. The procedure was not significantly altered. The preparatory work and the documentation developed by the study centers and the local administrative authorities were brought together by the secretariat of the committee on regional plans in the *Commissariat Général du Plan*. This committee on regional plans replaced the "synthesis" committee. Where local initiative was important, a preliminary plan was developed locally and then submitted to the committee. The growing importance of local initiative, manifested in the committees on expansion or the study groups, should be noted. These programs were all to be set in motion by the end of the year 1962. In addition to the nine previous programs of regional action, only four new plans were developed.[22] Nothing more was done, as the organization of the *tranches opératoires* came along to modify the line traced up to this point.

THE TRANCHES OPÉRATOIRES

The fourth plan for modernization and equipment emphasized the requirements of regional policy and set forth new procedures for their develop-

[21] Several programs were initiated in 1956 and 1957. They concerned Bretagne, Alsace, Aquitaine, Corsica, Languedoc, Lorraine, and the regions of the south, the north, and Poitou-Charentes.

[22] Nord, Rhône-Alpes, Provence-Côte d'Azur, Champagne.

ment. An interministerial circular of December 18, 1961,[23] gives the general directives on the preparation and content of the *tranches opératoires.*

The *tranches opératoires* fill in the national plans at the regional level and make specific the content of the regional plans. The latter only set out long-term objectives, without setting a timetable for the operations and the means of financing. The *tranches opératoires* are valid for the duration of the Fourth Plan.[24] Thus they have the same executory character as the national plan,[25] neither more nor less. Their preparation is entrusted to the Interdepartmental Conference, "whose mission is to evaluate, taking account of the over-all provisions of the national plan and of the orientation of the regional plan, the order of priorities and the location of investments within the totality of the recommendations of the latter."

a. *Purposes*

The *tranches opératoires,* then, have two objects:

1) *To sketch out the objectives of the development of the region in the four-year period of the Plan.* Lacking a general knowledge of actual regional economic circumstances, the accent is placed particularly on problems of employment (a study of probable surpluses and scarcities of manpower and the fixing of employment objectives to be attained) in the whole region or at certain specified points,[26] and on the outlook for development (production, investment, and so forth) in the basic economic sectors. The statistics and regional income accounting are still too imperfect to permit the fixing of objectives of industrial production or income by regions.

2) *To determine public investments during the same period (1962–1965).* On the basis of proposals made within the framework of the Plan by the several ministries, consultation, however limited, goes on locally in order to assure coherence in the work to be done and to avoid either too sketchy or too detailed examination of the problems. The information contained in the *tranches opératoires* concerns only the large operations and not the detail fixed in annual budgets.

Three categories of investments may be distinguished:

(*a*) Investments specified in the national plan to be made over a period of years by sectors, such as large-scale energy investments, hydroelectric and thermal stations, the aerial, port, and navigable river infrastructure, highways, railroads, large telecommunication investments, university building, the principal sanitary facilities installations, and certain agricultural investments. So far as these matters are concerned, the interdepartmental conference can only point out the existence of certain local conditions affecting their accomplishment and propose priorities among the several operations of this type.

(*b*) Investments specified at the regional level for the period of the fourth plan.[27] Even for these, local authorities are free only within certain financial

---

[23] Journal Officiel, Dec. 19, 1961, p. 11620.

[24] However, certain analyses were requested for a period extending to 1970.

[25] See interministerial circular, Dec. 18, 1962.

[26] The studies made by the *Commissariat Général du Plan* are supplied to the regions. The regional study groups and particularly the committees on expansion fill in or, as the need may be, correct the data which are communicated to them.

[27] For example, urban facilities in the important urban agglomerations, large housing developments, equipment of primary industrial zones, secondary industrial establishments, cultural equipment, tourist facilities, sanitary investment, social investment, and secondary telecommunication matters.

limitations. Most frequently the central services allocate the expenditures provided for in the plan among the regions. Sometimes they even send lists of operations to the regional authorities. The interdepartmental conferences propose to the central authority modifications which seem desirable to them, so as to substitute some operations for others within the limits of the sums allocated. They may also propose an order of priority of operations, taking into account the characteristics of the regions, or indicate priorities in favor of certain portions of the region under consideration, or examine complementary local investments in the planned operations and the possibilities of local financing. Conferences can also increase or diminish the total of the expenditures provided for by as much as 20 percent.

(*c*) Investments to be included in total sums in the *tranches opératoires*. These are investments which it is neither desirable nor possible to specify at the regional level, but rather by department.[28] The role of the interdepartmental conference is to synthesize the proposals of the departmental commissions and to suggest priorities within the financial limits suggested by the national authority.

Procedures

Interdepartmental conferences charged with developing the *tranches opératoires* receive not only the information contained in the plan but also the dossiers established by each ministry on its projects, or circulars developed jointly by the *Commissariat Général du Plan* (General Planning Commission) and the several ministries.[29] The conferences study this information and initiate complementary studies by regional authorities of the several administrations, by the designated committees on expansion, and, more generally, by the several agencies with jurisdiction in economic matters. The specific role played by the *Trésoriers Payeurs Généraux* should be noted. They indicate to the conferences the basic numerical data relative to the level and rate of operations in progress and their opinion on the future financing of these operations.

The conference provides a provisional draft of the *tranches opératoires* to the planning commission and to each interested ministry. The total volume of public investment by region and by sector is then specifically decided on and communicated to regional authorities, who are then called upon to make certain modifications in their original proposals. These modifications may bear particularly on complementary financing to be asked of local communities for certain works. The specific drafts are approved by the *Comité Interministériel pour l'Action Régionale et l'Aménagement du Territoire*.

In sum, the *tranches opératoires* set out, by region, the schedule of operations and the financial prospectus within the period of the plan (in contrast

---

[28] For example, housing, basic urban equipment, elementary and kindergarten classes, recreation facilities, investments of a rural character, departmental, and community roads.

[29] In particular, conferences are given information on the criteria for the distribution of public investments established by the several ministries. For example, for the distribution of secondary schools, the Ministry of National Education takes account principally of the number of the population falling within the age group 11–17 years, in 1958–59 and in 1970.

to the programs of regional action which give only long-term objectives). The financial prospectus includes not only the state-provided funds but also local financing and funds contributed by the offices and companies for low-cost housing, by the chambers of commerce and of agriculture, and by the companies of mixed private and government ownership. It is, therefore, a quadrennial program of investment and not annual detailed budgetary proposals.

It is necessary to underline the nature of these proposals. Even when they are approved by national authorities such as the planning commission and the ministries, their executory character is no greater than that of the plan. They do not constitute a budgetary commitment, at least until the proposals are included in a subsequent legislative program.

Finally, it should be noted that the *tranches opératoires* will be developed for the fifth plan (1965–69) in a different manner than that employed initially. They will be integrated within this plan. In effect, the plan will be developed simultaneously by sector and by region. The regional authorities will be consulted at the same time as the national *Commissions de Modernisation,* and these two groups together will develop the regionalized plan.

Thus, France is arriving at the end of an evolution which, from an analysis of regional economic data made in cooperation with the planning commission but quite independent of the plan, has led to the development of a regionalized plan, that is, a plan in which development and investment are located geographically.

But a number of problems remain to be solved. The French administrative structure continues to obstruct the development of regional policy. Although the planning commission has an incontestable role today, thanks to the committee on regional plans and the very active presence of the assistant commissioner general, the harmonization of measures of local interest, though progressing, is still partial. The absence of a true coordinating agency and the vertical structure of French administration obstruct the development of regional programs rather more than that of national plans.

Within the regions similar problems exist. At the level of research, the competent people do not always have the power to effectuate and to coordinate the research or inquiries made by public or private bodies whose dispersion reduces the usefulness of their work. At the level of execution, the functions of the coordinating prefect who presides over the interdepartmental conference do not give him the necessary authority over his colleagues from the other departments, nor indeed over the directors of departmental services other than those of the Ministry of the Interior. Important decisions are taken in Paris by each ministry and executed within the departmental hierarchy despite the sometimes vigorous resistance of the prefects. The regional program is thus divided up among several regional and national authorities.

Moreover, the absence of a truly regional administrative structure having at its head some authority unifying the departmental administrations compromises the development of the *tranches opératoires* and, for the future, that of a decentralized plan. The interdepartmental conference would have greater influence if it were a true regional conference supported by an appropriate apparatus. Otherwise, with respect to public and private interests at the regional level, no one has the same means of action as the general planning commission has at the national level, that is, the opportunity to conciliate and to direct them within the commissions.

It should not be deduced from this first stage of evolution that the development of the plan is likely to be largely decentralized. Though the local authorities are consulted and though this consultation constitutes considerable progress compared to the past and has stimulated a renewed sense of regional obligation, local power is exercised only within the quite strict financial limits set by national authorities. The relatively small scale of local budgets implies almost necessarily a substantial centralization of decision. Only financial decentralization could give greater latitude to regional authorities. Deconcentration remains limited.

Finally, the question arises whether the boundaries of regions have not been set too narrowly to permit a true decentralization. Numbers of large-scale projects such as regional land-use planning programs, roads and means of communication, go beyond present administrative boundaries and can be examined only at the national level. If the regions were larger, it would be possible to leave more to the competence of local authorities. Moreover, such cities as Paris, Lyon, and Marseilles have zones of influence which extend beyond the framework of the program regions and are cut up by them. For these reasons, it might be well to consider giving more importance to the 9 socioeconomic regions sketched out by the European Economic Community, corresponding to the 11 *Laender* of Federal Germany and to the 11 regions of the English board of trade.

The Criteria

The criteria for regional policy were developed very slowly. In a first phase, designation of problem regions was quite casual and rested primarily on difficulties peculiar to each other rather than on an overall evaluation: the needs of agriculture in Bas Rhône-Languedoc, and the textile crisis in Lorraine. It was not until 1955 that general criteria began to be developed for the identification of problem regions. But 6 years of application of these criteria show that, within the French context, they do not suffice to set off sharply the regions to be assisted. Now, however, the responsible authorities seek less to identify such regions and more to specify the objectives of regional development and appropriate location policies.

THE GENERAL CRITERIA FIXED BY THE LAW

Three periods may be distinguished: In 1955–59 legislation referred to general criteria based on the current situation of the region. Beginning in 1960, it referred more specifically to relative employment data, though these were provisional. Finally, after 1961 an effort was made to add a second criterion, the standard of living.

(1) Decree No. 873 of June 30, 1955, designates as regions to be developed those that "suffer from underemployment or insufficient economic development." It will be noted how vague this definition is. However, it was repeated in almost identical form in Decree No. 878 of the same date concerning localities or zones more restricted than the regions of the preceding decree and in which the situation called for urgent measures. These "critical zones," 26 in number, were those that "were suffering from serious and permanent underemployment or from insufficient economic develop-

ment." Later in the same year [30] another measure made these criteria more specific and fixed them at three:

(*a*) The existence of an excess of manpower relative to existing industrial installations, resulting in partial or complete unemployment of a permanent character, or in a high and permanent number of workers seeking jobs and not finding them.
(*b*) The likelihood of the appearance in the near future of an excess of manpower by reason of actual or expected decisions to shut down particular businesses or of a reduction in the level of their activity.
(*c*) The existence of a large excess of rural manpower.

It will be seen that these criteria served rather as a pretext for aid to be given to certain zones rather than as the basis for a systematic and fundamental analysis of those regions that disclosed these characteristics. Moreover, in 1959 [31] a system of fixed investment grants was instituted in eight new zones called "special conversion zones" in which economic difficulties had become apparent. Further, in the same year [32] another measure used practically the same language to define the conditions under which investment grants would be given to enterprises that created new employment in localities other than the "critical zones" and the "special conversion zones." Such localities were defined as those "in which there existed exceptionally large, partial, or total unemployment or a particularly large number of job seekers, or when such a situation may arise in the near future because of the likely or actual closure of factories or of a significant reduction in the level of their activity." In sum, rather than the vague notion of insufficient economic development, it was the criterion of current or likely future insufficient employment which prevailed.

(2) In 1960,[33] in an effort to obtain greater coherence and flexibility, the criteria for the making of investment grants were enlarged. So that the Government might not be taken unawares by unforeseen local difficulties, it was decided that in the future the premium would be granted outside the special reconversion zones, in accordance with economic and demographic criteria. The localities or regions to be concerned were those that displayed the following characteristics: Exceptionally high total or partial unemployment, or a very large number of job seekers; the likelihood that such a situation might arise because of the closure of businesses or the expected reduction in their activities, or by reason of the existence of a particularly high number of young people finishing their school careers in relation to the number of job opportunities in existing enterprises or in new enterprises whose establishment was decided upon or expected; and a continuing excess of rural manpower, taking into account the foreseeable development of production and improvement in agricultural methods.

This measure emphasized current and, particularly, expected manpower problems. Future disequilibria between the number of job offers and the number of job seekers by region are the subject of special studies by the planning commission. These studies take into consideration the natural increases in population, expected occupational distribution by sex and age group, the development of industry, and agricultural migration. The ab-

---

[30] Arrêté, Aug. 28, 1955 (Journal Officiel, Oct. 8, 1955).
[31] Arrêté of Mar. 27, 1959. See below, p. 64.
[32] Décret No. 59–483, Apr. 2, 1959. (Journal Officiel, Apr. 3, 1959).
[33] Décret No. 60–370, Apr. 15, 1960.

sence of significant unemployment by reason of the overemployment which still prevails in France, and the fear of sharp changes in this situation in certain regions because of the increase in the number of young people, account for the importance attached to forecasting. The law relied on the work undertaken by the general planning commission beginning in 1959 in order to specify systematically which regions merited particular attention.

Since there is no real present unemployment, the research of the planning commission must relate to basic disequilibria which may threaten to show up in employment problems in the near or distant future. Such studies explore possible imbalance between job offers and the number of job seekers in nonagricultural employment by regions as far ahead as 1965 or even 1975.

The starting point is the determination of the growth of the active population between 1960 and 1965, by region, taking account of changes forecast in labor force participation by age and by sex; school attendance and the length of military service are factors that are considered with particular attention. Consideration is also given to the number of economically active people who are likely to leave agriculture, given the migration trends which seem to be fairly constant. This manpower, of course, will have the effect of increasing the number of people seeking work in nonagricultural sectors.

On the other side, the industrial development foreseen by the commissions of the general planning commission permits the determination of employment in the several activities which are likely to be offered in each region.

A comparison of this supply of and demand for jobs gives an approximate idea of the problems that are likely to appear and especially those that may create unemployment in certain regions. In this way it is hoped to specify those regions to which the attention of public authority should be turned.

(3) The law of August 4, 1962,[34] supplemented the employment criterion with that of the standard of living. This measure, which approved the fourth plan of modernization and equipment, established a distinction between two types of regions: Those "whose economic development in relation to national growth is proceeding with sufficient vigor" that they require only a "policy of accompaniment"; and those which, "on the other hand, cannot develop their resources and increase their standard of living sufficiently unless the state acts more boldly and undertakes in them very great assistance and projects of the broadest scope." For these the governmental policy is to be "a policy of bringing along." The fourth plan does not give a list of the regions included in these two categories. It merely cites the west of France as being in the second category.

During the parliamentary debates on the fourth plan a revision was adopted providing that general criteria be established to separate the two large categories of French regions. The work group charged with developing these criteria finally arrived at two very general ones:

(1) The criterion of current or future employment disequilibrium, as defined by the decree of April 15, 1960.

(2) The standard of living criterion. The regions to be considered as subject to the "policy of bringing along" were those whose income and expenditures per capita were less than the national average. Incomes to be taken into consideration were those in the agricultural sector, incomes of

[34] Journal Officiel, Aug. 7, 1962.

industrial and commercial professions, of noncommercial professions, and wages and salaries. The last category, of course, is the most precise and by far the most significant. Measures of expenditures are various: Energy consumption, number of automobiles of less than 5 years of age, telephone traffic, the number of general medical practitioners per capita, the quality of housing, and so forth.

Before evaluating the validity of these criteria, we shall examine how they have been applied, that is, the designation of the regions.

APPLICATION OF THE CRITERIA—THE REGIONS CONSIDERED AS UNDERDEVELOPED

It will be remembered that until the 1960's the designation of criteria served to legitimize the choice of regions assisted rather than to determine in a rigorous way those that should have been. Regional policy suffered from an orientation toward critical individual situations rather than being guided by considerations of general equilibrium and welfare.

Mention should first be made of certain large-scale regional renewal programs, some of which were begun in the 1950's and have not yet been finished: The restoration of Bas Rhône-Languedoc, the hills of Gascogne, the wastelands and marshes of the west. These large projects involve the preservation and enrichment of soil, particularly by irrigation. With the development of French agriculture and the resulting overproduction, these programs have lost much of the importance originally attributed to them.

It should further be noted that the decree of January 5, 1955,[35] provided that in certain zones construction of enterprises occupying more than 500 square meters of floor space, or additions to existing enterprises of more than 10 percent of their floor space, required prior approval of the Minister of Construction on advice of a competent commission. These measures particularly concerned the Parisian region.

The decree of June 30, 1955, provided for special assistance to 26 critical zones. Certain of these were seriously affected by the decline of traditional industries, particularly textiles and shoes (Aubusson, Castres, Fourmies, Fougères, Ganges, Lodève, Romorantin, Vallée des Vosges, Vienne). In others the problems arose because of the exhaustion of mineral resources, either oil or coal (Autun, Béthune, Commentry, Decazeville, Saint-Etienne, Péchelbronn). In some, the completion of reconstruction activities and the slowing down of various industries were a source of difficulty (Alès, Amiens, Béziers, Brest, Châtellerault, Lorient, Saint-Malo, Tarbes). Finally, in others the problems arose from exceptionally high rural overpopulation (the zones of Rennes, of the Rance River, and of Saint-Brieux-Guingamp).

The program regions in which these critical zones lay are the following: Nord (Fourmies, Béthune), Lorraine (especially the Vosges region), Bretagne (Fougères, Brest, Lorient, Saint-Malo), Auvergne (Saint-Etienne, Decazeville, Commentry), Languedoc (Béziers, Alès, Norbonne) and, to a lesser degree, the regions of the center and of the southwest. Furthermore, beginning in 1959 the declining rate of growth in particular industries disclosed the vulnerability of certain regions in which those industries were concentrated, for example, in the north, Béthune with its coal basin, Calais with lace, and Fourmies with wool. In the west the decline in naval construction at Nantes and Saint-Nazaire created difficulties. In the Vosges

[35] Journal Officiel, Jan. 8, 1955.

valley of Lorraine it was cotton; in Poitou-Charentes the problems arose out of the shoe and porcelain industries at Limoges; and in Languedoc wine culture created difficulties. For these reasons, an Arrêté of March 27, 1959, designated these regions as "special conversion zones" and provided a decentralized and rapid procedure for the making of investment grants. Moreover, a decree of April 2 of the same year permitted the extension of the benefits of this premium to all localities outside the critical zones in which serious unemployment either existed or was foreseeable.

The urgency of certain situations, the necessity of continuous revision in the successive measures, and, finally, the generalization of regional analyses led to a more systematic designation of the problem regions. Studies carried on by the planning commission on the disequilibria which might be forecast between the supply and demand for manpower led to an extension and a changed definition of the regions to receive special assistance. Disequilibria appeared dangerous in the whole of the west, particularly in Bretagne, and, to a lesser degree, in the north, the southwest, and the center. For these reasons the decree of April 15, 1960, provided:

(*a*) Four special conversion zones centered on Nantes-St.-Nazaire, Limoges, Montpellier, and Bordeaux.

(*b*) Special measures of assistance for localities threatened with unemployment by reason of an excess of manpower, particularly in the departments of Bretagne.

The critical zones in the north and the east were established only on a provisional basis until October 30, 1960. An Arrêté of June 15, 1961, extended the special measures provided by the decree of April 15, 1960, for the Breton departments to the departments of Manche, Mayenne, Loire-Atlantique, and Vendée, as well as for two arrondissements of Maine-et-Loire. Thus the west (Bretagne, a part of Basse Normandie, and the Pays de la Loire) was given special attention. This was supplemented by the creation of special zones of rural action [36] situated almost without exception in the same regions, and by the creation of two new special reconversion zones at Brest and Lorient.[37]

It should be added that at the time of writing the attention of the public authorities is being directed to the whole western part of France, that is, those regions situated to the west of a line from Caen to Montpellier. This is being done for two reasons. Immigration of numerous refugees from north Africa has substantially modified the situation. Until this migration these regions, though not particularly dynamic, were not seriously threatened with large-scale unemployment because of their poor demographic situation. But now it seems more urgent to create employment and to stimulate industrial development, particularly in Aquitaine and Midi-Pyrénées.

Of more importance, however, is the fact that henceforth France will be greatly affected by the influence of the Common Market. The eastern part of the country will undoubtedly benefit greatly as a result of the lowering of tariff walls. By contrast, the west will be handicapped by its distance from the central industrial regions of the Common Market.

In sum, the attention of governmental authority, which at first was diffused among several zones including some in the eastern part of the country, has slowly become concentrated on Bretagne and the regions of the west and the southwest.

---

[36] Décrets of May 15, June 13, and Sept. 14, 1961.

[37] Décrets of June 16, 1961, and Jan. 17, 1962.

Current criteria are not satisfactory. The first criticism is their inability to lead to exact conclusions. In the present situation of full employment in the French economy, forecasts of future employment disequilibria cannot always be very precise. Certainly the regions of the west will have a surplus of manpower which will call for urgent measures. But elsewhere the figures do not show this clearly. In the center of France, in the north, and in the regions of the southwest the probable surpluses are not so different from those in other regions that the former areas clearly require greater assistance. Doubtless the immigration of north African refugees to Aquitaine and Midi-Pyrénées will also necessitate state intervention. But unless full employment is followed by future underemployment, the criterion of population excess will not suffice except in occasional cases for the designation of those regions in which intervention is necessary.

The standard of living criterion seems no more adequate. The measure of income, except for wages and salaries, are unreliable, and those of expenditures include too small a portion of the total. Though in some regions such as Bretagne there is both a considerable threat of underemployment and a low standard of living, inequalities in the standard of living showing up among other regions are too small to permit distinction with any degree of confidence between those regions that should receive substantial aid and those that should not.

A second criticism may be levied against the criteria. They imply objection of regional policy whose values may be questioned.

To assist those regions in which excesses of manpower are likely to show up is to restrict interregional migration or even to maintain the present geographical population distribution. Such a policy might be warranted if the migration were so great as to risk the depopulation of entire regions. In a Europe of limited space, it is difficult to be resigned to the death of certain regions. But often population movements do not have such serious consequences. Before 1955, when there was pressure to avoid local unemployment, the interventionist policy with its tendency to reduce migration could be explained. But now when there is no serious unemployment, the prevention of regional manpower disequilibria and the reduction or cessation of migration can bring about serious consequences. They tend to create artificial and sometimes irrational industrial location. They may even obstruct spontaneous population movements toward the regions in which people prefer to live, particularly those of especially good climate.

The criteria of inequalities in living standards and especially in incomes are also questionable. Certainly, exceptionally low incomes in a particular region call for some measures. But intervention where the differences are not great leads toward an equalization which is contrary to the nature of things. Interregional differences in income distribution result in part from differences in industrial structures.

But with what should the present criteria be replaced? Rather than to fix criteria, it would be better to set out the objectives of development. The first goal of regional policy is not to combat disequilibria, but rather to induce optimal location of enterprises, of urban networks, and of large public works.

The location of certain enterprises

The relative reduction in the cost of transportation makes the location of modern industries much less predictable than in the past. Today a market for the product and adequate manpower are sufficient conditions of location for a considerable number of industries. It is, therefore, not possible to forecast *a priori* all locations.

However, there are certain industries for which natural circumstances or tradition are the definitive factors. High transportation costs of either semifinished or finished products limit the possible location of steel plants or petroleum refineries. The location of such traditional industries as textiles, cutlery, and hats, whose rate of expansion is relatively low, is fixed in zones from which they are unlikely to move. Finally, extractive industries such as mining and activities related to them, particularly chemicals, are fixed in their location by their very nature.

Taking account of the rate of economic expansion forecast for the nation and of the special conditions of each region, it is possible to forecast the probable development of these several activities. This development would constitute given data for the regional model.

The definition of regional metropolises and of urban networks

A certain number of sanitary, administrative, educational, and social functions provided by Government should be placed at a distance not greater than 300 kilometers from the consumers. For the maximum convenience of those who use them, specialized hospitals, universities, centers of administration, and head offices of business should not be too far away. Experience shows that these functions attract and reinforce one another in the same center and that they do not develop adequately in isolation. The lack of regional metropolises with this kind of complex leads to the demand that they all be in the national capital. There then develops in the capital a multitude of tertiary activities which depend on the others. Great consumers of manpower, these activities, such as headquarters offices, laboratories, insurance companies, and publishing houses, empty the provinces of their skilled management and supervision and overpopulate the capital.

The necessity of grouping such functions together in a single zone seriously limits the number of regional metropolises which could be developed. The Government must choose centers in which it will establish its own functions, so as to encourage tertiary activity to remain in the regions. In France five or six such centers ought to be designated. These choices, which will require considerable expense for the development of infrastructures, can only be made by the state, in consideration of such factors as population, the comparative development of towns, and administrative requirements.

Large public works

The designation of regional metropolises will require certain public works, such as roads radiating from the center and various kinds of building construction. Other large public works such as dams and irrigation depend on soil and subsoil conditions. When several sites are competitive, their location and execution will depend on calculations of relative profitability. Expected productivity should be compared, that is, the expected rate of growth of the several sectors of the economy, direct and indirect costs of investments, manpower movements required, and supply of raw materials.

Conclusion

In the France of 1963 in which regional disequilibria are difficult to define with precision, it would be better to define the objectives to be obtained through planned land management broadly conceived, than to attempt to direct policy toward righting these regional disequilibria.

The Means of Execution

Policies for regional development are often confused with those required for national economic development. Though theoretically the distinction seems simple—regional policies having as their object the stimulation of growth in specific regions or the treatment of a crisis in these regions—numerous well-conceived national policies have considerable regional impact. The distribution of hospitals, for example, is not used for the purpose of solving such problems as appear in Bretagne or in Languedoc. Nevertheless, the existence of hospitals in these regions has an influence on their position. It may be said that the concern for regional development in France during the past 10 years is such as to have greatly influenced national policy and that the latter can no longer be understood without considering its regional consequences and repercussions. At the extreme, a rational national policy would in fact be the ideal regional policy.

This stage has not yet been reached in France. There will always remain some regions whose problems are sufficiently critical to demand specific policies. The policies which will be examined here, then, are principally those directed at remedying particular difficult regional situations. However, certain of them already involve a general regional policy.

These policies are not all the full responsibility of the Central Government. Though the Central Government as such originated many of them, it may either undertake, directly or indirectly, the responsibility for their operation or it may only participate in operations conducted by others, such as public businesses, local communities, and enterprises of part Government ownership. It may also set certain requirements of a prohibitory character, such as construction permits. On the other hand, it may stimulate by means of tax or other benefits the accomplishment of the desired policies. Thus, its intervention is varied, both on the legal and on the psychological level.

Regional policies have a double aspect: They may attempt to change the character of a region so that enterprises will be interested in locating there; these are policies affecting the environment. They may also stimulate or restrict enterprises in their location within a particular region. These are the policies that directly and specifically affect the enterprises.

POLICIES HAVING TO DO WITH THE ENVIRONMENT

It is clear that those measures which tend to give to a region either a satisfactory infrastructure or adequate collective regional facilities contribute to regional development. Four groups of such policies may be distinguished: (1) Those concerning development of the infrastructure, (2) those having to do with the creation of industrial zones, (3) pricing policies, and (4) construction permits and the problem of the Parisian region. Except for the last, whose effect, as we shall see, has been limited, these policies are restricted to assistance in the expense of first establishing an enterprise, and not in the cost of continuing production. French policies thus seek to prepare the way for businesses and not to replace them in the management of their own affairs.

Development of the Infrastructure

It is perhaps unnecessary to underline the attraction to industry which is exercised by good road, rail, and aerial communications, the presence and rational exploitation of energy sources such as coal, gas, and oil, and the existence of comfortable housing, educational institutions at all levels, and centers of culture such as theaters and concert halls.

The development of certain infrastructures must be the task of national authority. The great highway networks, the universities, and the hospitals are the responsibility of the central government. On the other hand, some are left to local authority. Decisions concerning the former have an incontestable effect on the development of regions even when the central authorities are not primarily concerned with regional growth and when they act without regard for it. Until recent years, the several ministries have acted largely without regard for the regional consequences of their decisions. This explains in part certain of the disequilibria existing today.

So far as educational facilities are concerned, the southern half of France has been greatly favored over the northern part, except for the Parisian region and the east, both of which are well equipped. Since modern industries require more and more skilled manpower, the recent development of the southeast and the Mediterranean regions has been greatly encouraged by the existence of good educational facilities, particularly in Alpes Maritimes, one of the departments with the highest educational achievement. In contrast, the difficulties of the northern regions are in large part related to undereducation.

The efforts toward centralization of the July Monarchy and the Second Empire produced a star-shaped pattern of rail transportation, with its center at Paris. This pattern has markedly favored the development of Paris to the disadvantage of the peripheral regions, which cannot connect with each other except through Paris. Many enterprises, as would be expected, establish themselves in or move toward the center of the star in order to avoid transportation costs. The modernization of the railroads and their recent electrification, moreover, have, reinforced the effect of this star, at least insofar as large-scale traffic moves by rail. The character of the railroad network, then, constitutes an important fundamental factor, though presently unintended, in the rapid development of the Parisian basin.

Since the 18th century the highway structure also has had the same pattern of a star around Paris. The new program of fast highways duplicates in large measure the same structure. This only reinforces those advantages of the Parisian region which result from the railway pattern. However, for several years now particular attention has been given to the development of transverse means of communication. Despite this, 80 percent of the airport development has been in the Parisian region.

Only recently have the ministries begun to realize the importance of infrastructure development on regional growth. New norms for road construction and for sanitary, social, and urban facilities are under study. But it will take a long time before administrative ways of thinking adapt themselves to the new view that the planning of large public works programs must be done with regard for the harmonious development of the regions systematically, and not merely exceptionally.

Alongside these works of the Central Government, there are others originating in the local communities or the agencies developed by them to achieve their aims. Among these are the six large regional development organizations: the Compagnie Nationale du Bas-Rhône-Languedoc, the Société pour la Mise en Valeur Agricole de la Corse (SOMIVAC), the Compagnie d'Aménagement des Landes de Gascogne, the Société des Friches et Taillis de l'Est, and the Société Centrale d'Aménagement Foncier Rural, the last created in 1960 in order to provide for the reception of immigrants from agriculture.

So far as the economics of their projects are concerned, the communities usually do not have the facilities to make the necessary studies on profitability and investment costs to accomplish the operations for which they are responsible. This problem is further complicated, at the administrative level, by the necessity for several communities to cooperate to carry on those projects whose scale exceeds the jurisdiction and the resources of any one of them.

Mixed companies, called *Sociétés d'Equipement,* have been created. For the most part they are federated in the *Société Centrale de l'Equipement du Territoire* (SCET),[38] a subsidiary of the *Caisse des Dépôts et Consignations.* The SCET has the responsibility for large-scale regional development projects, for housing developments, for tourist facilities, for highways, for markets having national interest, as well as for industrial zones, as we shall see below. Some of these companies construct and manage toll roads, of which the first goes from Fréjus (Var) to Nice (Alpes Maritimes), and the second, which is under construction, from Vienne (Isère) to Valence (Drôme). At the end of the year 1961, there were 72 companies in the 21 program regions. Two examples will show the diversity of their activities. The *Société d'Equipement* for the department of Vaucluse is concerned with urban renewal at Avignon, Carpentras, and Cavaillon. The *Société du Marché d'Intérêt National* of Nord-Finistère is concerned with the construction of a market in the Morlaix region, at Saint Pol de Léon.

The creation of industrial zones

It was indicated that the *Sociétés d'Equipement* and the SCET have as one of their purposes the creation of industrial zones. Actually, the urban plans which, in principle, all communities of more than 10,000 inhabitants should have, include zoning for one or more industrial zones depending on the expected development of the community.

Besides the SCET, the *Fonds Nationale d'Aménagement Foncier et Urbain* (FNAF), which is simply a special treasury account, has as its sole object "the location of industrial enterprises and the planning of housing zones." Under the responsibility of the Minister of Construction, it has sometimes intervened directly to develop industrial zones such as those of Chalon-s-Saône, Chalon-s-Marne, and Rennes. But its major role is that of a financial organization which gives short-term loans at an interest rate of 2½ percent to local communities, to *Sociétés d'Equipement,* and to public establishments, and gives them assistance in the form of interest premiums. This permits these bodies to acquire and develop lands for industrial zones by the installation of roads, water, gas, and electricity lines, drainage systems, and other such requirements. The FNAF has assisted in the creation of industrial zones of more than 4,000 hectares (about 10,000 acres) in area by the granting of 2-year loans, twice renewable, at the 2½ percent rate, and by the resale of 500 hectares of developed lands. There are currently about 100 industrial zones that have been developed with the assistance of FNAF.

---

[38] The SCET was created under the sponsorship of the *Caisse des Dépôts,* a semi-public financial organization, for the purpose of assisting local communities to solve problems of housing and management of water, gas, and electricity distribution. For the most part it acts through mixed investment companies whose creation it encourages. SCET is also responsible for the construction of toll roads and of facilities for mountain sports.

The FNAF is not the only financial organization contributing to these purposes. The *Caisse des Dépôts et Consignations* also grants loans to local communities for the development of industrial zones. And local communities finance a substantial portion of them themselves.

This policy, in which local communities are deeply interested, is not without its risks. It is never certain that the lands, whose development may be onerous for the community, will find buyers. Nevertheless, the debt must be borne for long years by the taxpayers of the community. The problem is aggravated when the lands are sold below cost or when factories are constructed or acquired by a system of rent with an option to buy. The risks undertaken may exceed those which the community involved ought normally to support. This explains why the lending organizations, such as SCET, counsel caution to communities desirous of undertaking such operations. A 1962 circular of the Minister of the Interior [39] limits the participation of the communes to 50 percent of the total cost of the land and of the building shell, a limit which may be exceeded in the regions requiring a special development effort. It conditions construction on the assurance that the plants will be occupied by industry. It requires a standard building which may be used by different kinds of firms. Finally, it requires that the employment created by the new factories will not exceed the available manpower.

Pricing policies

The pricing policies of the large public services have profound effects on regional development, even when they do not have this as one of their objectives. Energy and transportation are examples.

The case of electricity is particularly interesting. Until the application of a new rate schedule called "the green rate," France lived under a system of rates whose principles were developed between the wars. There were very few variations in rates, and the rates were not especially low except near the sources of hydroelectric power, particularly in the Alps, and near the coal mines, particularly in the north. This explains the concentration of electrochemical industries in Savoie. The application of a new rating system, based on the production costs of the marginal unit, has somewhat modified the relative prices and thus has stimulated development in the several regions. Similarly, coal and fuel prices were set in accordance with the usual rules of pricing, particularly including transportation costs. This had the effect of benefiting the regions near the mines such as the Nord and Lorraine, and those with petroleum refineries, such as Provence, Basse Bretagne, and Aquitaine.

Transportation pricing policies have also had a great influence on regional development. Several examples will suffice to show this. Before 1930, the rail transportation rates were fixed "ad valorem": For the same transportation service and for equal weights, more valuable merchandise was carried at higher rates. Thus, heavy goods such as raw materials benefited from a rate lower than the real cost of its transportation. This gave a relative advantage to industries situated far from the sources of raw materials, particularly Parisian industry. Similarly, low passenger rates on the suburban lines of Paris constituted an advantage for the industries of this region, which did not need to pay as high wages as they would have if their employees had had to pay the usual transportation rates.

---

[39] Cited by M. Bloch-Lainé, Directeur General de la Caisse des Dépôts et Consignations in his article "Sept années d'initiation à l'expansion régionale: Bilan et Lecons, "*Revue de Développement du S.O.*, 1962.

In 1946, a new system of freight rates tended to equalize the charges. The basic principle was that the kilogram/kilometer should have the same price on all lines, whatever might be the real cost of transportation. This system gave an advantage to the less developed regions in which the traffic volume was low and whose costs were therefore relatively high.

In order to further harmonious regional development, pricing systems now try to reflect everywhere the marginal production cost of the services sold. Without discussing the merits, such prices have the advantage of reflecting the true relative situation of the regions with respect to each other and of avoiding all camouflaged subsidy.

Even though the Electricité de France and, in large measure, the railroads are willing to apply this basic principle, it remains to be determined whether it would not be better to give preferential rates to certain zones or industries. Parts of France such as Bretagne, with quite special problems, urge the central authority to grant them preferential energy and transportation prices in order to stimulate their development.

In the energy field, examples of special consideration given to the regions for development purposes are rare and unimportant. Those concessions in the matter of electrical energy granted especially in the southwest are actually an anticipation of expected development which will reduce the real costs to the level of the prices given. However, in the matter of transportation, especially by rail, material reductions have been granted, particularly to Bretagne and the regions of the center.

These reductions are exceptions to the general principles of pricing, and the Government is properly reluctant to grant them. They present a double problem. The first is that they establish an undesirable precedent: What is granted to one cannot be refused to another and slowly the rate schedules lose all rationality. The second is that they induce development on the basis of artificial costs: If and when the special benefit is withdrawn, the firms benefiting from it may be in difficulty and the region may experience a new recession.

Construction permits and the problem of the Parisian region

For management of the total environment as well as industrial zones, the Ministry of Construction has a specific instrument available, the construction permit. The ordinance of October 27, 1945, makes it a prerequisite for all construction. Thus, in a negative way, it permits control of the distribution of enterprises throughout the country.

This device has not yielded the results expected of it. From 1949 to 1953, two-thirds of the industrial permits were given in the Parisian region and nine great industrial agglomerations. Furthermore, the number of new buildings constructed was least in those areas in which the ratio of vacant factories to the number of active factories was highest, and the resulting unemployment was the greater the more the declining industry had dominated the region. It was thus necessary to control further the construction or the extension of industrial establishments. A 1955 measure which sought to encourage a better distribution of industry throughout the country[40] required ministerial approval, given on the advice of an *ad hoc* commission, for the construction or extension of industrial buildings employing more than 50 persons or occupying a surface area greater than 500 square meters or exceeding 10 percent of existing surface area.

---

[40] Décret No. 55–36, Jan. 5, 1955 (Journal Officiel, Jan. 8, 1955, p. 385).

The problem was particularly great for the congested Parisian region. For this reason a series of measures in 1955, 1958, 1959, and 1960 dealt specially with the Parisian problem.[41] These extended the requirement of ministerial approval to all installations or extensions in the Parisian region of services depending on the Government, including scientific and technical establishments. Similarly, approval was required for all construction or extension in the Parisian region of industrial establishments of a scientific and technical nature but under private control. Finally, a special levy was placed on the construction of office or industrial buildings in the Parisian region and a premium was given for their abolition.

POLICIES DIRECTLY AFFECTING THE ENTERPRISES

These policies all have in common the fact that they are subsidiary with respect to the effort which must be made by the enterprises themselves which either convert or decentralize. Indeed, the Government never had the intention to support regional development by itself. Among these measures, however, it is useful to distinguish between those which are specific and those which are general.

Specific policies

These policies are essentially financial and fiscal, and include six different types of benefits: The special investment grant, Government loans, interest rate premiums, guarantees of the state and of the regional development companies, tax exemptions, and measures concerning manpower.

(1) The special investment grant

As we have seen, a 1955 measure instituted a special investment grant for enterprises locating or existing in "localities or zones which are suffering serious and permanent underemployment or insufficient economic development." These were designated as critical zones in another measure of the same year. A 1959 measure extended the benefits of the grant to the "special conversion zones." In the former case the rate of the grant was negotiable and varied between 8 and 12 percent for each operation. For the special conversion zones the grant was at a fixed rate: 15 percent of investments for the extension or partial conversion of industrial installations existing in the zone; 20 percent of investment for the creation of a new installation or the complete conversion of the type of manufacturing. A 1959 decree extended the grant case by case to zones other than the critical and special conversion zones.[42] The new zones to which the benefits of the grant were extended had to have less special conditions. In 1960 [43] the system of grants was substantially modified. The critical zones were abolished and the special conversion zones were limited to four: Nantes-St.-Nazaire, Bordeaux, Limoges, and Montpellier. In these four specially designated areas the rate of the grant continued to be at a fixed level. At the same time the benefit was extended to all activity creating new employment, not only manufacturing but also service industries, in any locality or zone in which there was an immediate threat of total or partial unemployment or exceptionally great rural

[41] Décret No. 55–883, June 30, 1955; Décret No. 58–1461, Dec. 31, 1958 (Journal Officiel, Jan. 4, 1959, p. 264); Décret No. 58–1460, Dec. 31, 1958 (Journal Officiel, Jan. 4, 1959, p. 264); Law No. 60–790, Aug. 2, 1960 (Journal Officiel, Aug. 4, 1960, p.7215).

[42] Décret No. 59–483, Apr. 2, 1959 (Journal Officiel, Apr. 3, 1959, p. 3861).

[43] Décret No. 60–370, Apr. 15, 1960 (Journal Officiel, Apr. 16, 1960, p. 3545).

overpopulation. The four departments of Bretagne were presumed to have satisfied these conditions and there the grant was set at a minimum of 10 percent of the amounts of investment. Furthermore, the new measure provided that investment programs eligible for assistance had to anticipate the creation of not less than 20 new jobs, and that the amount of the grant could not exceed NF 5,000 ($1,000) for each job created in the case of a partial conversion or extension, or NF 7,500 ($1,500) in the case of a new industry or complete reconversion. These latter conditions were imposed to avoid the risk of the establishment in these zones of enterprises which, in order to benefit as much as possible from the grant, overinvested and thus employed few workers. Henceforth, the assistance was related to the number of jobs created.

(2) Government loans

The Government grants loans to enterprises which, when they are undertaking operations of conversion, concentration, specialization, or deconcentration, do not wish to assume such exceptionally high risks as may be presented, or cannot obtain the necessary financing by recourse to the usual procedures, either because they do not offer sufficient security or because the risks are considered too high. In these cases the State grants, through the FDES, loans for a period varying, in general, between 7 and 15 years according to the normal amortization rate of the investments, at an interest rate of 6 percent. The specific terms are established in a contract with the beneficiaries.

Though these FDES loans were very successful during the period when the financial market was too restricted for the demand for such funds, now the FDES prefers to refer those seeking long-term credit to the *Crédit Nationale* or the *Crédit Hotelier* or other specialized agencies which act as intermediaries of the Treasury. The *Crédit Hotelier* particularly is granting more and more loans, and three-fourths of them are for operations in the Provinces. Nevertheless, production loans granted by the FDES have been used to serve the ends of regional expansion, though originally they did not have this purpose.

(3) Interest rate premiums

These are granted to enterprises undertaking the operations described above with respect to Government loans. They serve to reduce the rate of interest on loans secured in the financial market or at the banks to a real rate as near as possible to 6 percent, but never below that on loans granted by the State. This procedure was practically abandoned after 1960.

(4) Guarantees by the state and by the societies for regional development

The exposition of reasons for the 1955 Décret establishing these guarantees [44] said that the object of the guarantees was "to permit enterprises whose creation, extension or transformation appeared justified from the economic point of view, to have recourse to credit from financial establishments managing public funds whose charters did not provide for the direct financing of private investment." The guarantees are granted for long- and medium-term loans for the purpose of reducing the interest rate. The guarantees apply either to the capital sum borrowed as well as the interest or to the interest alone.

Actually, the guarantees have been granted only to the regional development societies (SDR) which now number 15 in France, distributed through-

[44] Décret No. 55–874, June 30, 1955.

out the country except in the Parisian region. These societies were the result of one of the decrees of June 30, 1955. They had as their purpose the encouragement of private savings and investment in the less developed regions, particularly investment operations within the framework of programs of regional action. For this reason, certain advantages were granted to them: exemption from the tax on corporations and from the proportional tax on distributed profits, and a guarantee by the state to their shareholders of minimum annual dividends of 5 percent for 12 years. They may participate temporarily in the capital of businesses on condition that they never provide more than 35 percent of the capital and do not obligate in this way more than 25 percent of their own capital. They may also grant long-term loans financed by bonds sold to the public. These bonds are guaranteed by the state and their proceeds are divided among businesses whose programs of investment are subject to a required prior study.

(5) Tax exemptions

The tax exemption policy involves both national and local levies.

(*a*) *National taxes.* Decree No. 55–879 of June 30, 1955, provides for an exemption from the tax on the transfer of buildings for building acquisitions approved in advance and made with a view to decentralization or the creation of a new industry. Decree No. 55–877 of the same date provides for exemption from the income tax on individuals or from the tax on corporations for contributions made to approved *Groupements Professionels,* groups of enterprises "established without a profit purpose with a view to undertaking rationalization or conversion." The decree of August 29, 1957, reduced the tax on corporations when they increased their capital. Finally, the ordinance of February 4,1959, gives to enterprises belonging to *sociétés conventionnées,* that is, mutual small-business agencies to improve methods, the right to a special amortization equal to the ratio of their subscription to the capital of the society. Since the law of January 31, 1962, this right has been extended to companies making fixed investments in certain areas, particularly mining.

(*b*) *Local taxes.* The decree of June 30, 1955, permitted local communities to grant partial or total exemption from license fees, generally for a period of 5 years, to enterprises which were undertaking transfers or creation of new establishments. This exemption is automatic because it is tied to the granting of reduction in the building transfer tax. In addition, there may be exemptions granted as a result of special agreement.

(6) Measures concerning manpower

The decree of September 14, 1954, assists in the retraining and placement of manpower affected by decentralization or conversion operations. So far as the employer is concerned, the Government grants a subsidy which covers the wages of the workers affected and of the trainers, as well as the necessary material for a maximum period of 6 months. So far as the worker is concerned, the Government reimburses him for his transportation costs and those of his family necessary for the change in residence to a different locality in order to find employment, following one of these operations. He is also granted a relocation allowance.

Technical colleges and centers of vocational training have been established in the provinces. These are essential both to motivate the industries which might be willing to move and to insure the success of decentralizaiton operations. Often the manpower in the region does not have the necessary skills. This is especially true in the zones in which industrial traditions do

761–932 O—65——9

not exist and in which skilled manpower is an essential factor of success.

Mention should also be made of the indemnities for transfer of residence furnished by the European Coal and Steel Community to aid miners and steelworkers who have had to change their place of residence. These have so far benefited but a few hundred workers, however.

The general term "vocational training" (*formation professionelle*) includes the technical training given under the direction of the Ministry of Education to adolescents from 14 to 17 years of age, as well as the adult vocational training (*Formation Professionelle des Adultes*—FPA) provided under the direction of the Ministry of Labor to workers at least 17 years of age. FPA originally represented an attempt by the Government during prewar economic difficulties to give adults a trade quickly. It was continued for the same purpose during the period of international tension and the war, and then to meet the needs of the reconstruction. The relating of these programs to regional policies, themselves of recent origin, has not been considered until very recently. Neither the manpower nor the general planning commission was concerned with adult vocational training during the preparation of the basic documents of the fourth plan.

It was not until 1962 that an *ad hoc* working commission met in the planning commission and decided that adult vocational training should be doubled during the period of the fourth plan. The building construction commission had furnished a report on the subject for its sector. It seems that the Ministry of Labor itself did not, until 1962, have any liaison with the planning commission, perhaps in part because it was nót particularly desired by the Ministry.

Although until now there has been little connection between the regional and sectoral objectives of the plan and the FPA, this gap will be filled in the fifth plan. The manpower commission has undertaken studies to estimate, by region and sector, the needs for skilled personnel and for the extension or creation of FPA centers.

Though it has been decided to orient the programs of the adult vocational training services more toward the needs of regional expansion, the accomplishment of this objective will not be easy. Currently, the FPA centers do not respond to the needs of regional policy except at a time of crisis in a particular locality or sector, as was the case in the iron mines of Lorraine.

Of course, the forecasts of the plan by sectors serve to give some employment information for vocational training purposes, if only in general outline. But despite the flexibility of its organization, a center for adult vocational training begins to operate as late as 2 years after the request for it is first made. Furthermore, in France as in other countries, statistics of the responsible agency—in France the *Commission de la Main d'Oeuvre* for the plan and its subcommission on "Qualifications"—give only the numbers of skilled and highly skilled workers and engineers required for the growth envisaged, and do not break the data down by occupations. But the adult training centers train for specific occupations. There is scarcely any of the necessary information in the programs of regional action. This work remains to be done.

Nevertheless, though the instrument does not yet serve the ends of regional policy, it exists and appears to be doing its general job well. There are three types of centers for adult vocational training: Approximately 100 managed by the *Association Nationale Interprofessionelle pour la Formation Rationelle de la Main d'Oeuvre* (ANIFRMO); approximately 30 directly subsidized; and 30 under technical supervision of the Ministry of Labor.

(*a*) The centers managed by the ANIFRMO are old, having been created before the Second World War by associations of employers and workers, particularly in the metal and building trades. They grew very rapidly and began to receive financial support from the Government. At the time of the Liberation, the Ministry of Labor, in an effort to rationalize their efforts, provided that most of them should be managed by the ANIFRMO. Though this is legally a nonprofit association organized under the law of 1901, it resembles in general a public administrative establishment. It is directed by a tripartite council, composed of representatives of the Ministry of Labor, of employers' associations, and of workers' organizations. It is placed under the general supervision of the Ministry of Labor from which it receives subsidies. It is accountable financially to both the Ministry of Labor and the Ministry of Finance. The tie with specific occupations is maintained through the *Commissions Nationales Paritaires Professionelles* which advise the Minister on the study programs and the accomplishments of the FPA centers.

ANIFRMO cooperates both financially (part payment of trainers, pay to students) and technically (development of programs and of teaching techniques, training of future instructors). But it is not merely a management association. The unique aspect of the French system concerns the two organisms attached to it.

First is the *Institut National de Formation Professionelle,* sometimes called the *Centre de Formation des Moniteurs,* which serves to train trainers. These people become most effective parts of the FPA after an 8-week course of instruction, which was preceded by intensive trade examinations corrected by bipartite boards. The *Institut* also improves training methods, establishes the progressions and programs, and develops the types of examinations taken in the centers.

Second is the *Centre d'Etudes et de Recherches Psychotechniques,* which systematically examines for research purposes about 50,000 psychotechnical tests taken each year by the candidates for places at the FPA centers, as well as the approximately 30,000 tests taken on completion of the training program. It studies occupations and jobs.

(*b*) The centers directly subsidized by the Ministry of Labor receive their support under various legislation, such as *Promotion Sociale* [45] and *Sécurité Sociale*—assistance to the handicapped, for example. The Government provides for payment to students and for the compensation of trainers as well as for the technical cooperation of the ANIFRMO.

(*c*) Finally, because they give a diploma, the other centers are under the technical control of the Ministry of Labor. They are generally concerned with training for such special cases as juvenile delinquents, institutionalized persons, or the physically abnormal.

Vocational training, retraining, and placement of adults take place under various other schemes than the FPA, including that done with the aid of the FDES mentioned above, the Coal and Steel Community program discussed elsewhere in this volume, and activities under the legislation providing for *Promotion Sociale.*

In 1959, legislation [46] concerning *Promotion Sociale* established means to

---

[45] See below.

[46] Law No. 59–960, July 31, 1959 (Journal Officiel. Aug. 6, 1959); also Décret No. 59–1424, Dec. 18, 1959 (Journal Officiel, Dec. 19, 1959).

facilitate the promotion of workers to higher jobs or their change to new industries. The law provides for occupational training "of the first degree" designed to train semiskilled and skilled workers. But it also provides for the enrichment of the FPA with a "second degree" intended for the training of higher level technicians, research workers, and economic and administrative staff. For this purpose, financial support was substantially increased. With this aid, the second-degree centers in FPA provide support while training for persons without employment, or supplement the incomes of employed persons undergoing training whose employers do not pay them full wages during the training period. In this way, the FPA trains technicians in nuclear physical chemistry, topographers, beginning electronic technicians, executive secretaries, works supervisors, etc.

Thus adult vocational training is, in France, an integral part of the world of work. It is carried on in close relation with the interested organizations of employers and workers, who together solicit financial support, who make known their needs and advice through the several national and regional commissions with which consultation is required by the regulations, and who participate in the management of the ANIFRMO.

The fact that vocational training is given in a true work environment as close as possible to the factory or workshop, so that the students will not be separated from their usual environment, integrates it into industrial life. The philosophy of training is that it should be adapted to the personality of workers and devoted to concrete techniques directly related to industrial work. However, it should not have as its goal narrow specialization but rather a kind of polyvalence designed to facilitate later reorientation and readaptation. Because the greater part of the trainers themselves come from industry, they know industrial conditions.

General policies

Public funds, not including the operation of public and semipublic credit institutions, provide more than a fifth of the investments made in France each year, either in the form of public investments or as aid to productive activity. It has been seen in the discussion of the infrastructure how this investment policy has influenced regional development and how other types of aid such as tax exemption, loans, and subsidies, also have an effect on regional development.

The Government, when it encourages certain activities, favors the regions in which they are established. Conversely, it may hesitate to discontinue assistance to activities whose disappearance would compromise regional equilibrium. Doubtless it is difficult to separate out the influence of this assistance, since it concerns sectors of industrial activity whose location is diverse.

Probably all the subsidies and loans granted to the energy sector have had little regional influence. This is so although the Electricité de France has taken great care to locate its enterprises in an optimal way and particularly to develop new sources of energy (nuclear) in the least developed regions (Bretagne and those in the center).

But steel, shipyards, aircraft, and tourism have more specific locational characteristics. The second of these particularly, which benefits from substantial assistance under the law of May 24, 1951, includes four yards in the west, which account for 40 percent of the employment of industry, and two in the southwest. To reduce the assistance granted to these would work greatly to the disadvantage of these already disadvantaged regions.

Considering the effect which these subsidies have, it might be hoped to direct the investment of all the assisted enterprises toward locations favorable to regional development. But this objective has not generally been adopted.

The Effectiveness of the Policies

The effectiveness of the policies may be evaluated in two different ways. The first, the extent to which the interested groups make use of the means placed at their disposal by the Government, such as loans, subsidies, and facilities, represents some measure of their appropriateness, or rather their usefulness. But more fundamentally, an analysis of the development of the less developed regions provides a measure of the effectiveness of the policies undertaken. Therefore, these two aspects will be discussed in turn.

Utilization of the Means Offered by the Government

The first difficulty arises from the difference between specific regional policies and those that do not have as their prime objective correction of an abnormal situation in some region or another. In the latter group fall such policies as the more rational distribution of social investments in the country, or logical price policy for transportation or energy. It is much more difficult to evaluate the utilization of these than to measure the extent to which the first type are employed. We will limit ourselves to an examination of the utilization of the specific means, although the general policies are not without effect.

Good information is not available on the operations supervised by Specialized Committee No. 1 of the FDES. Data are particularly poor on the importance of measures undertaken by local communities. Insofar as possible, we will examine successively the amounts involved and then their location, dealing with the amount of loans, of subsidies, and of tax advantages.

THE AMOUNT OF ASSISTANCE

Loans and guarantees

(1) Information is based on the direct loans of the FDES. The growth of these loans since 1955, in thousands of dollars at 5 NF=$1, is as follows:[47]

1955	1956	1957	1958	1959	1960	1961	1962	Total
$3, 200	$6, 800	$9, 200	$7, 500	$4, 100	$9, 800	$4, 200	$11, 700	$56, 500

The rate of growth of loans has exceeded considerably the 10 percent rate of growth in investment. The decline in 1961 was due to the fact that committee No. 1 was required to limit loans of public funds to those operations which could not be financed by other means and to direct requests toward specialized institutions and the regional development companies.

[47] Most of the information given here comes from the annual report of the Conseil de Direction of the Fonds de Développement Economique et Social, which publishes in an appendix a report of the activity of committee No. 1 (see the seventh report for 1961–62).

Up to 1961 the apparent rate of growth permits the first conclusion that the rate of reconversion and decentralization was proceeding more rapidly than the rate of total investment. Next it is necessary to discuss the growth of other sources of specific financing.

(2) The advances made by the *Fonds Nationale d'Aménagement du Foncier et Urbain* (FNAF) and credits granted by local communities for factory building are less well known. The first, granted exclusively to local communities for the development of industrial zones, reached a total amount of about 150 million N.F. ($30 million) by 1961, that is, an amount slightly less than the loans made by FDES to enterprises. Similarly, some estimates put the credits granted by local communities for the construction of industrial structures for businesses at about 40 million N.F. ($8 million) annually, that is, approximately equal to the rate of credits given by FDES.

(3) Guarantees and various loans. The state has intervened in regional development by encouraging the growth of regional development companies which, as we have seen, assist local enterprises in obtaining credit, either by direct participation or by loans. The government both guarantees bonds issued by the regional development companies to give them means of financing, and makes advances which assure the payment of dividends.

Though it is not now possible to obtain details on the operatons of the regional development companies, two facts permit some measure of their importance. At the end of 1961 [48] 15 regional development companies covered the total territory of France. Moreover, from 1957 to 1962, the total of guaranteed bonds issued by the regional development companies amounted to 488 million NF ($100 million). As table 1 shows, the regional development companies in the less developed regions have been very active, particularly the Société de Développement Régional de l'Ouest and the Société Toulousaine Financière et Industrielle du Sud-Ouest.

It is a question whether mention should be made here of FDES loans whose primary object is not regional development. The treasury makes certain loans to enterprises whose object is not in the first instance the development of less developed regions, but rather merely assistance to one or another sector or simply the effort to find profitable investment. Such are the loans granted through specialized intermediary institutions (semipublic institutions such as the *Caisse des Dépôts,* the *Crédit National,* the *Crédit Foncier,* the *Crédit Agricole,* the *Crédit Hôtelier*). The total of such loans amounted to about $350 million in 1963. Similarly, loans made to increase productivity amounted to about $20 million.

Currently, the treasury, through these institutions, assumes responsibility for operations which were formerly the function of Specialized Committee No. 1. Furthermore, the high volume of these loans compared to those made through Committee No. 1 ($350 million against $44 million), the fact that a substantial part of them are made in the regions and not in Paris, and the fact that considerations of regional development may play a role in the decisions of the specialized institutions and in the granting of productivity loans, all lead to the conclusion that these loans should be considered as part of the policies of combating regional underdevelopment. But this objective may be ignored in loans made by these institutions. Though they are semipublic, they do not always act in accordance with governmental objectives.

In sum, the volume of loans granted for regional development by 1961

[48] See Rapport Annuel sur l'Execution du Plan de Modernisation et d'Equipement (1961 T II), pp. 16 ff.

amounted to $44 million by the FDES (Committee No. 1), $30 million by the FNAF, and an annual rate of $8 million by local communities. Guarantees of loans made by the regional development companies amounted to $100 million for the 1957–61 period.

As a final note on the subject of loans, it should be observed that they do not equal in amount those granted by the special credit institutions of a

TABLE 1.—*Summary of bonds issued by the SDR*

[In thousands of dollars at 5 NF=$1]

	1957	1958	1959	1960	1961	Total
Société Alsacienne de Dévelopement et d'Expansion (SADE)	$1, 800	....	$3, 000	....	$4, 500	$9, 300
Société Lorraine de Développement et d'Expansion (LORDEX)	....	....	3, 200	....	4, 000	7, 200
Société de Développement Régional du Nord et du Pas-de-Calais	....	....	3, 400	$3, 600	4, 500	11, 500
Société de Développement de la Région Méditerranéenne	2, 400	....	....	4, 000	....	6, 400
Société Toulousaine Financière et Industrielle du Sud-Ouest (TOFINSO)	....	$3, 000	....	3, 400	5, 800	12, 200
Société pour l'Expansion Economique du Sud-Ouest (EXPANSO)	....	....	2, 000	....	2, 500	4, 500
Société de Développement Régional du Sud-Est	....	3, 600	....	3, 500	....	7, 100
Société de Développement Régional de la Bretagne	....	....	....	1, 200	1, 500	2, 700
Société de Développement Régional de l'Ouest (SODERO)	....	....	4, 100	4, 300	6, 400	14, 900
Société de Développement Régional de Normandie	....	....	....	3, 000	1, 400	4, 400
Société de Développement Régional du Centre-Est (CENTREST)	....	....	3, 200	3, 000	....	6, 200
Société pour le Développement Economique du Centre et du Centre-Ouest (SODECCO)	....	....	....	2, 200	4, 200	6, 400
Société Champenoise d'Expansion (CHAMPEX)	....	....	....	....	2, 900	2, 900
Société de Développement du Languedoc-Roussillon (SODLER)	....	....	....	....	2, 100	2, 100
Société de Développement Régional de la Picardie	....	....	....	....	....	....
Total	4, 200	6, 600	19, 000	28, 200	39, 800	97, 700

semipublic character. These make their loans with at best an imperfect consideration of regional development policy.

Subsidies

(1) State subsidies

The state subsidies include in the first place special investment grants whose amounts, in thousands of dollars at 5 NF=$1, have grown as follows:

1956	1957	1958	1959	1960	1961	Total
$1, 600	$1, 100	$1, 100	$9, 200	$17, 700	$10, 600	$41, 300

It will be noted that the amount of grants increased very sharply in 1960, by reason of the size of the decentralization operations of Citroën at Rennes. When these are deducted, a continuous growth in grants made appears, resulting from a growing number of operations and a broadening of the conditions under which the grant is made and its rate fixed under the 1959 measures discussed above.

Assistance to workers (granted by the FDES) is the second type of state subsidy. There has been a tendency for this kind of assistance to increase, particularly in 1961. The amount of assistance for occupational retraining as well as the indemnities for change of residence have doubled in the period 1960–61. Furthermore, the number of workers retrained rose from 3,918 in 1959 to 9,861 in 1961.[49]

	1955–57	1958	1959	1960	1961	Total
Assistance for occupational retraining (thousands of dollars at 5 NF =$1)	$700	$400	$500	$500	$1, 300	$3, 400
Changes of residence (thousands of dollars at 5 NF=$1)	90	90	120	90	240	630

Thus the necessary training of manpower in the regions in which industries are locating or developing seems to be progressing. In order to have a better measure it would be necessary to know the number of FPA centers, on which unfortunately we do not have precise information.

Mention should be made of the assistance given by the general planning commission under the heading of productivity, which has amounted to some $6 million since 1954, and of the interest premiums granted to enterprises undertaking a program of regional development, which now have fallen into disuse.

(2) Local subsidies

In this area as in that of loans and tax exemptions it is extremely difficult to

[49] See Rapport du Conseil de Direction du Fonds de Développement Economique et Social pour 1961–62, p. 187.

estimate the amount of aid actually granted. In their anxiety to attract industry, the departments and the communes undertake direct and indirect sacrifices. Aside from sums of money, they give to businesses on very advantageous conditions either land or factory buildings constructed by them, sometimes, though not necessarily, through the Sociétés d'Equipement. This assistance, which does not necessarily involve particularly critical zones, has been granted without significant control despite the efforts of the supervisory authorities. It probably has exceeded by large amounts the subsidies granted under the direction of Committee No. 1 of the FDES. But the desire of the communities to act without control has often led them to conceal the total amount of this assistance.[50]

C. Tax exemptions

(1) National taxes

Contributions made to *Groupements Professionels* approved by Committee No. 1 of the FDES whose function is to encourage regional development are deductible from the tax on income. Since only about a dozen groups have benefited from this privilege, it does not seem to have had great importance for regional development.

Exemptions from the tax on building transfers given to enterprises which regroup, reconvert, or decentralize have had greater importance. For the 4 years 1958–61, more than 1,039 exemptions were granted, with the total amount of exemptions being about $8 million.

Other tax exemptions exist, but since they are not primarily intended to assist in the problem of development of less developed regions, it is not worthwhile to attempt to draw any conclusions from their application.

(2) Local taxes

These are the exemptions from license fees granted for a period of 5 years. Since the rate and the basis of the tax vary from commune to commune, it is not possible to evaluate the effect of this privilege. It is automatically granted to enterprises which enjoy the exemption from the building transfer tax, as well as to a number of others. Nevertheless, it appears that the amount of exemptions granted has been considerably larger than the total of national tax exemptions.

THE LOCATION OF CERTAIN ASSISTANCE

Because of the imprecision of the data, it is possible to generalize only on the location of assistance granted through Committee No. 1 of the FDES. Although that assistance constitutes only a part of the measures designed to stimulate regional development, it is a useful index. It will be noted that it appears to be diffused more and more generally throughout the country and particularly that it is less concentrated than it was in the special reconversion zones.

(1) The following figures show the relative decline in the amount of assistance granted to the special reconversion zones.

One reason for this relative reduction in assistance granted to the special zones is the progressive abolition of some of them, particularly in the Nord.

---

[50] Before leaving this subject, mention should be made of the premiums given for the abandonment of industrial locations in the Parisian region under the law of Aug. 2, 1960. Since the total premiums granted have amounted to only about 4 million NF, they probably have had relatively little importance.

		Special zones	Rest of France
Number of aids granted	1959	83	65
	1961	57	202
Loans granted in thousands of dollars at 5 NF=$1	1959	1, 000	3, 100
	1961	1, 200	3, 000
Investment grants in thousands of dollars at 5 NF=$1	1959	4, 800	9, 200
	1961	2, 600	10, 600

(2) As one measure of the effect of assistance granted up to October 31, 1961, a very rough classification of program regions into three groups has been made: (*a*) Those in which the amount of assistance was probably least, (*b*) a middle category, and (*c*) those in which the amount of assistance granted was greatest. The following regions fall into the first group: Auvergne, Bourgogne, the Centre, Franche-Comté, Languedoc, Limousin, Basse Normandie, Haute Normandie, Picardie, Poitou-Charentes, and Provence-Côte d'Azur. Into the second group fall the following: Alsace, Aquitaine, Bretagne, Champagne, Lorraine, Midi-Pyrénées, and Rhône-Alpes. The third group consists of the Pays de la Loire and the Nord.

To these approximations there may be added the list of departments benefiting from the investment grants shown in table 2.

From these two sets of data the following conclusions may be drawn:

The most critical regions such as those of the center (Auvergne and Limousin) or Bretagne have not made maximum use of the assistance available. Nevertheless, the classification of departments benefiting from the investment grants shows more satisfactory results. Though the departments of the center of France have scarcely used this aid, those of the west and of the north have profited greatly from it. It should further be noted that the measures recently taken to assist the west seem to be bearing fruit, since in the single year 1961 the four Breton departments have benefited as greatly from grants as in the whole period 1955–60.

On the other hand, the dynamic regions of the southeast (particularly Rhône-Alpes) and the east have received a substantial portion of the assistance, particularly in the form of loans. More generally, most of the French regions, even those in good economic condition, have benefited from the aid of the Government. This shows, on the one hand, that the Government and particularly the members of Committee No. 1 have not hesitated to grant benefits even to operations to be undertaken in regions which really have no need of simulation.[51] On the other hand, it shows that assistance, particularly in the form of investment grants, has not sufficed to stimulate greatly the number of installations in the special reconversion zones. Limousin and Auvergne in particular have benefited from only a few operations despite the relatively high rate of grants in these areas.

These conclusions are limited. It is known that probably half the assistance does not come under the jurisdiction of Committee No. 1 of the FDES and thus is not included in this study of regional distribution. The

[51] It is in the spirit of the several legal texts that assistance may be granted outside of special reconversions zones wherever difficult local and temporary situations may appear by reason of the closure of factories or of rural migration.

TABLE 2.—*Principal departments receiving investment grants up to Dec. 31, 1961*

	Jobs created
Ille-et-Vilaine	6, 926
Nord	6, 066
Loire-Atlantique	5, 668
Vosges	5, 617
Pas-de-Calais	5, 108
Somme	3, 452
Hérault	3, 000
Saône-et-Loire	2, 691
Gironde	2, 676
Vienne	2, 482
Bas-Rhin	2, 464
Loire	2, 332
Haute-Vienne	1, 778
Finistère	1, 242
Seine-Maritime	690

Source: Rapport sur l'Exécution de Plan en 1961 et 1962, p. 249.

same is true for loans granted through the semipublic financial institutions of a specialized nature, whose importance is growing and which have not necessarily granted credits according to criteria of regional development. Moreover, local authorities, anxious to attract industry at any price, have acted in a quite unorganized way, without a general plan and without regard for their own financial means. That is, the assistance whose distribution we do not know has probably been given with little regard for the objective of revival of the less developed regions, of the critical zones, or of the special reconversion zones.

A general conclusion could not be drawn from statistics of the use of governmental assistance at various levels even if they were available. The attraction of industries seeking credit and the utilization of industrial lands do not necessarily imply a lasting revival of an entire region. It would be necessary to know if the new industrial installations had multiplying effects and if they stimulated the development of other activities and a demand for credit not specifically granted for regional development.

It is desirable, therefore, to attempt to discover if the regional development resulting from French regional policy has or has not reduced the disparity existing in 1954.

Development of the Regions from 1954 to 1962

We shall attempt to measure whether the two principal objectives of regional policy—to reduce the disparities between Paris and the provinces and to develop the regions that have problems—are being achieved.

THE RELATIVE GROWTH OF PARIS AND OF THE REST OF FRANCE

A fairly exact sketch of the development may be traced with the assistance of the documents contained in the annual reports of the modernizaion and equipment plans concerning decentralization operations and construction permits.

Decentralization operations

Transfers or extensions outside of Paris of enterprises formerly situated in the Paris region have increased perceptibly during the past several years, as a result not only of the assistance granted but also of the prohibitions,[52] and perhaps simply because of the various difficulties and the high prices required to purchase land in the Parisian region. Whatever the reasons may be, several conclusions are evident:

(1) The number of decentralization operations is growing rapidly.

(2) The geographic distribution of decentralization operations shows that the regions which have benefited most from this movement are the Centre (particularly Eure-et-Loir, Loiret, Loir-et-Cher), Picardie (particularly Somme and Oise), Bourgogne, and Haute Normandie (Eure and Seine-Maritime). (See table 3.)

	Number of decentralizations	Jobs created
1950–1954	49	25, 500
1954–1958	375	80, 480
1959	140	31, 000
1960	184	30, 000
1961	289	39, 000
Total	1, 037	205, 980

Construction permits

As confirmation of the tendency toward industry decentralization it suffices to compare the number of permits issued in the Parisian region with those in the provinces in percentages, taken from the reports of the plan.

	Number of permits, percent		New employment, percent		Cumulative surface area, percent	
	Province	Parisian region	Province	Parisian region	Province	Parisian region
1956	80	20	84	16	73	27
1957	85	15	84	16	80	20
1958	80	20	83	17	79	21
1959	83	17	88	12	82	18
1960	83	17	90	10	81	17
1961	85	15	94	6	87	13

[52] Décrets of Dec. 31, 1958, requiring prior approval for the creation and extension of offices in the Parisian region, and the law of Aug. 2, 1960, on premiums and levies.

A clear tendency will be noted toward the reduction of development in the Parisian region, particularly of industries that employ large numbers of workers, in favor of industries located in the provinces.

It appears that the decentralization movements were directed primarily to an area within 200 kilometers of Paris. However, it can be seen from a more extended study of the issuance of construction permits that the movement of industry now extends beyond this range. Significant decentralizations are currently taking place in the west (departments of Calvados, Mayenne, Loire-Atlantique, Côtes du Nord, and Morbihan) and in Bourgogne.

It remains to be seen whether the assistance for decentralization has played a large role in the movement from Paris toward increasingly distant regions. It seems that outside frequent requests for a reduction in registration fees, the operations giving rise to direct state aid are in the minority. It may be concluded that this aid has not played as fundamental a role as one might have thought in inducing entrepreneurs to locate their enterprises at greater distances from Paris. It seems indeed that other factors have been more important.

First, the expansion of businesses leads them to develop new installations. Because of the difficulty of obtaining construction permits in Paris and the high price of land there, the industrialist prefers to extend elsewhere and can often find available industrial buildings. Second, removal to the provinces often permits significant economies in manpower and general costs.

The reasons for the decentralization of industry to areas farther and

TABLE 3.—*Geographic Distribution of Decentralizations to Dec. 13, 1961*

Region	Number of operations	Number of jobs created
Nord	46	8, 540
Picardie	134	24, 500
Champagne	64	12, 360
Lorraine	20	3, 600
Alsace	23	6, 720
Franche-Comté	13	5, 970
Bourgogne	94	16, 010
Auvergne	21	3, 450
Rhône-Alpes	75	13, 420
Provence-Côte d'Azur-Corse	19	3, 150
Languedoc	11	1, 380
Midi-Pyrénées	9	2, 070
Aquitaine	21	2, 380
Limousin	15	1, 140
Poitou-Charentes	21	4, 360
Pays de la Loire	57	15, 430
Bretagne	28	11, 220
Basse Normandie	62	12, 700
Haute Normandie	88	23, 800
Centre	210	28, 220
Total	1, 031	200, 420

farther from Paris are in part the exhaustion of Parisian building capacity and the lack of manpower within a reasonable distance from the capital, in addition to the legislative provisions reducing the number of special conversion zones too close to the capital. Thus, though the industrial decentralization movement is pronounced, legislative measures are not the only causes.

THE RELATIVE DEVELOPMENT OF THE SEVERAL REGIONS

To evaluate the relative development of the several regions the disparities between them will be compared for the years 1962 and 1954. For these purposes [53] the following factors are considered:

(1) The average level of wages (maps V and IX), which constitutes a partial index of changes in incomes between 1954 and 1962.

(2) Changes in the total population between 1954 and 1962. Doubtless, changes in the active population would be more informative, but the present state of census data does not permit this analysis (map VII).

(3) The changes in the surface area represented by construction permits issued, which show the places in which development, principally industrial, has occurred (map VIII).

(4) Changes that have occurred in the number of jobseekers. The significance of this factor is, of course, not great because of the very low levels of unemployment in France, much below 3 percent and showing relatively little regional variation (maps VI and X).

In maps XI and XII these four indices have been recapitulated.[54]

By means of these factors the relative situation of the regions will be examined to see if it has changed since 1954, that is, if there appears to be any real effectiveness of regional measures. Beginning with the north, we shall examine the nine socioeconomic regions one by one.

The north

The north has shown scarcely any relative progress over the period under consideration. Wages in Pas de Calais do not seem to have followed the national increase. Construction permits have also increased less in the two departments than in the rest of France. Only the factor of the number of jobseekers seems to have substantially improved. Emigration has wiped out the manpower surplus. The northern region includes declining industries such as mines and textiles and mature industries such as steel and heavy metals. The assistance available has not permitted this area, industrialized since the 19th century, to attract new industries in sufficient number to change its character significantly.

MAP V.—*Relative Wage Levels, 1961*

[All of France=100]

Category 1—Index 104 or Greater

Seine	135	Bouches du Rhône	106
Seine et Oise	127	Seine et Marne	104
Rhône	108		

[53] App. I contains a note explaining how the maps were constructed, and app. II contains the figures on which they are based.

[54] See app. III.

Map V

Relative Wage Levels by Departments, 1961

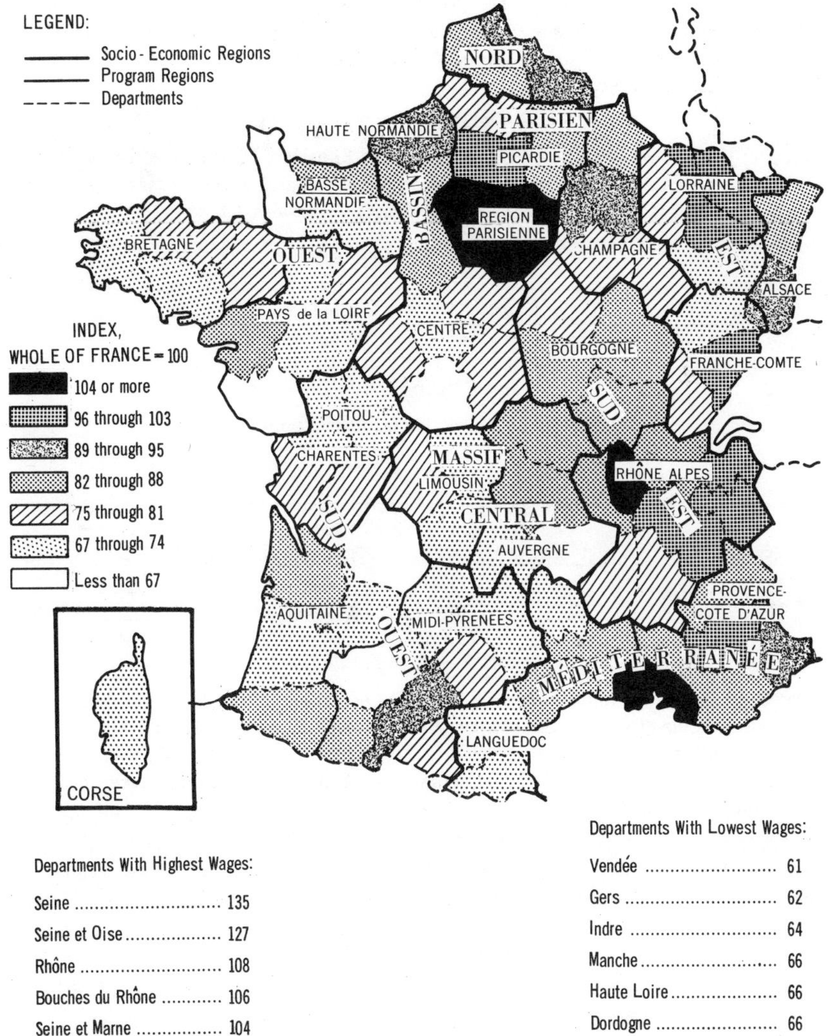

Departments With Highest Wages:

Seine	135
Seine et Oise	127
Rhône	108
Bouches du Rhône	106
Seine et Marne	104

Departments With Lowest Wages:

Vendée	61
Gers	62
Indre	64
Manche	66
Haute Loire	66
Dordogne	66

Category 2—Index 96 Through 103

Oise, Meurthe et Moselle, Doubs, Isère, Savoie, Haute Savoie, Basses Alpes, Moselle.

Category 3—Index 89 Through 95

Nord, Marne, Seine Maritime, Haut Rhin, Belfort, Haute Garonne, Alpes Maritimes.

Category 4—Index 82 Through 88

Pas de Calais, Aisne, Ardennes, Eure-et-Loir, Eure, Calvados, Loire Atlantique, Bas Rhin, Côte d'Or, Nièvre, Yonne, Ain, Loire, Allier, Puy de Dôme, Gironde, Basses Pyrénées, Hautes Pyrénées, Gard, Hérault, Hautes Alpes, Var, Vaucluse.

Category 5—Index 75 Through 81

Somme, Aube, Haute Marne, Cher, Indre et Loire, Loiret, Sarthe, Côtes du Nord, Ille et Vilaine, Meuse, Jura, Yonne, Ardèche, Drôme, Haute Vienne, Charente, Charente Maritime, Ariège, Tarn.

Category 6—Index 67 Through 74

Loir-et-Cher, Orne, Maine et Loire, Mayenne, Finistère, Morbihan, Vosges, Haute Saône, Cantal, Creuse, Corrèze, Deux Sèvres, Vienne, Landes, Lot et Garonne, Aveyron, Lot, Tarn et Garonne, Aude, Lozère, Pyrénées Orientales, Corse.

Category 7—Index Less Than 67

Dordogne	66	Indre	64
Haute Loire	66	Gers	62
Manche	66	Vendée	61

MAP VI.—*Average Number of Jobseekers, 1962*

(Number per 10,000 active industrial population)

[All of France=132]

Category 1—34 or fewer

Moselle	13	Hte Saône+Belf	31
Meuse	22	Ardennes	34
Nord	30	Meurthe et M	34

Category 2—35 Through 112

Pas de Calais, Seine, Seine et Marne, Seine et Oise, Aisne, Oise, Aube, Haute Marne, Eure-et-Loir, Loir-et-Cher, Loiret, Eure, Orne, Vosges, Bas Rhin, Haut Rhin, Doubs, Jura, Côte d'Or, Saône et Loire, Yonne, Ain, Drôme, Loire, Rhône, Isère Haute Savoie, Haute Loire, Puy de Dôme, Charente, Dordogne, Landes, Aveyron, Lot, Lozère, Basses Alpes.

Category 3—113 Through 189

Somme, Marne, Cher, Indre, Indre et Loire, Seine Maritime, Calvados, Maine et Loire, Nièvre, Ardèche, Savoie, Corrèze, Creuse, Haute Vienne, Gers, Tarn, Gard, Hautes Alpes.

Category 4—190 Through 266

Manche, Mayenne, Vendée, Ille et Vilaine, Allier, Cantal, Charente Maritime, Deux Sèvres, Lot et Garonne, Ariège, Hautes Pyrénées, Var, Vaucluse, Vienne.

Category 5—267 Through 343

Loire Atlantique, Sarthe, Côtes du Nord, Finistère, Basses Pyrénées, Haute Garonne, Corse.

Map VI

Number of Jobseekers Per 10,000 Active Industrial Population by Departments, 1962

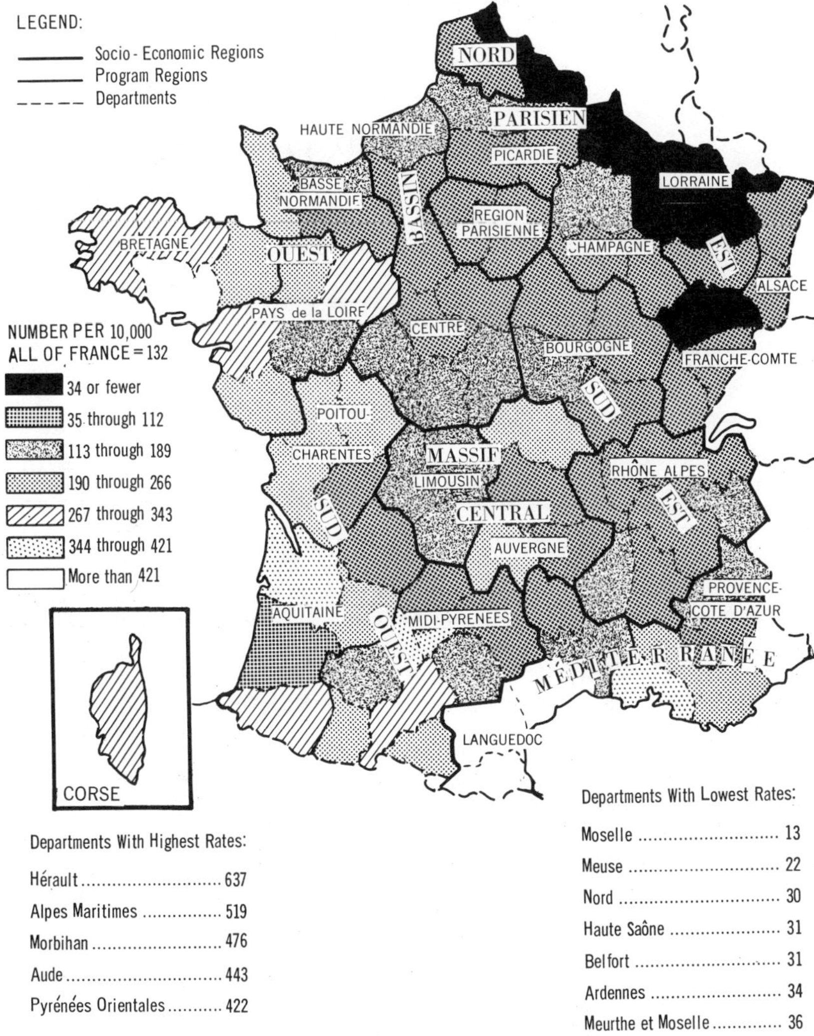

761–932 O—65——10

Category 6—344 Through 421

Gironde, Tarn et Garonne, Bouches du Rhône.

Category 7—421 or more

Pyrénées Orientales	422	Alpes Maritimes	519
Aude	443	Hérault	637
Morbihan	476		

Map VII.—*Change in Total Population, 1954 to 1962*

(Index, 1954=100)

[All of France=108]

Category 1—Index 117 or Greater

Seine et Oise	135	Bouches du Rhône	118
Moselle	120	Var	117
Alpes Maritimes	119	Doubs	117

Category 2—Index 113 Through 116

Seine et Marne, Rhône, Isère, Haute Savoie, Haute Garonne.

Category 3—Index 109 Through 112

Oise, Seine Maritime, Meurthe et Moselle, Belfort, Drôme, Basses Pyrénées, Gard, Hérault, Pyrénées Orientales, Basses Alpes, Vaucluse, Corse.

Category 4—Index 106 Through 108

Nord, Pas de Calais, Seine, Ardennes, Marne, Eure-et-Loir, Indre-et-Loire, Loiret, Eure, Calvados, Loire Atlantique, Maine et Loire, Bas Rhin, Haut Rhin, Côte d'Or, Puy de Dôme.

Category 5—Index 102 Through 105

Aisne, Somme, Aube, Haute Marne, Cher, Loir-et-Cher, Sarthe, Vendée, Finistère, Ille et Vilaine, Meuse, Vosges, Jura, Saône et Loire, Ain, Loire, Savoie, Allier, Haute Vienne, Charente, Charente Maritime, Vienne, Gironde, Landes, Lot et Garonne, Hautes Pyrénées, Tarn, Hautes Alpes.

Category 6—Index 98 Through 101

Indre, Manche, Orne, Mayenne, Côtes du Nord, Morbihan, Haute Saône, Nièvre, Yonne, Ardèche, Corrèze, Deux Sèvres, Dordogne, Aveyron, Lot, Tarn et Garonne, Aude, Lozère.

Category 7—Index, Less Than 98

Gers	97	Cantal	96
Ariège	97	Creuse	94
Haute Loire	97		

Map VII

Change in Total Population, by Departments, 1954 to 1962

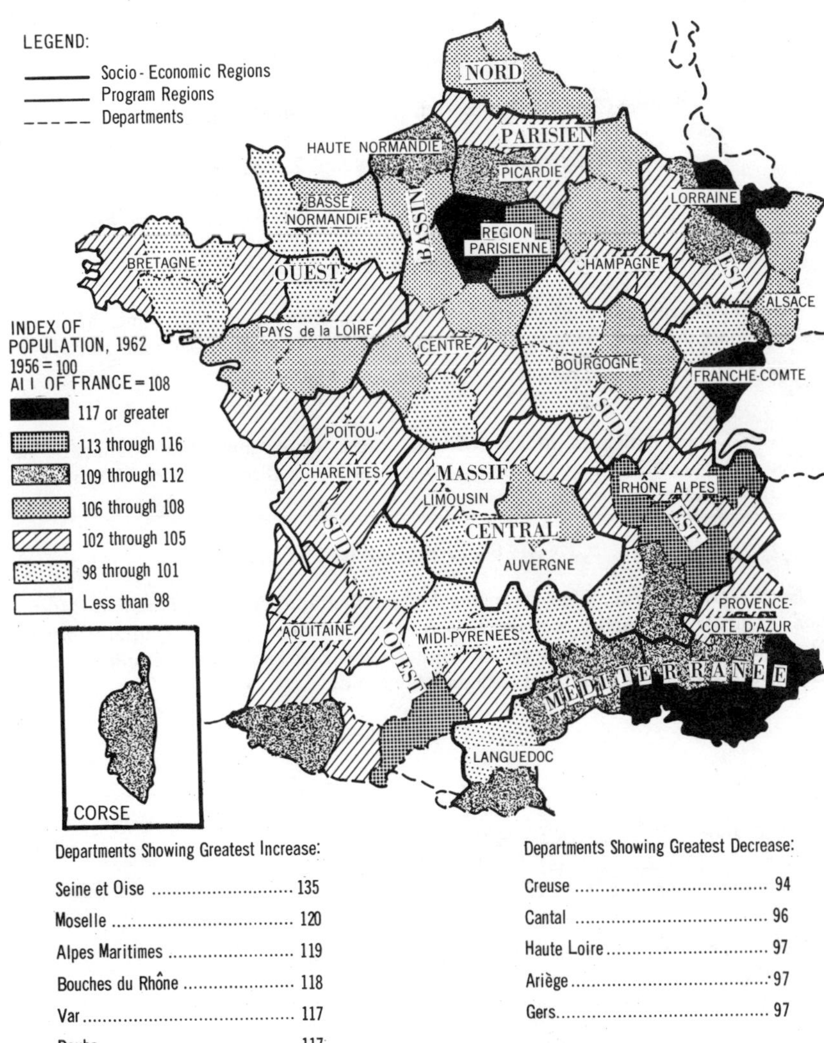

Departments Showing Greatest Increase:	
Seine et Oise	135
Moselle	120
Alpes Maritimes	119
Bouches du Rhône	118
Var	117
Doubs	117

Departments Showing Greatest Decrease:	
Creuse	94
Cantal	96
Haute Loire	97
Ariège	97
Gers	97

MAP VIII.—*Change in Area of Construction Permits Granted, 1953–55 to 1959–61*

(Difference in square meters per capita of 1954 active industrial population)

[All of France=+0.8 m2]

Category 1—2.8 m2 or more

Eure-et-Loir	+4.3	Haute Loire	+3.1
Ille et Vilaine	+3.9	Loiret	+2.8
Mayenne	+3.4	Charente	+2.8

Category 2—From +2.3 to +2.7 m2

Aisne, Oise, Loir et Cher, Bas Rhin, Yonne, Vienne, Lot et Gar.

Category 3—From +1.8 to +2.2 m2

Aube, Indre et Loire, Orne, Sarthe, Nièvre, Haute Savoie, Basses Pyrénées.

Category 4—From +1.2 to +1.7 m2

Seine et Marne, Somme, Haute Marne, Indre, Eure, Seine Maritime, Maine et Loire, Côtes du Nord, Doubs, Côte d'Or, Ain, Drôme, Isère, Deux Sèvres, Haute Garonne, Gers, Lot.

Category 5—From +0.7 to +1.1 m2

Pas de Calais, Ardennes, Marne, Meuse, Vosges, Haut Rhin, Haute Saône, Saône et Loire, Rhône, Allier, Puy de Dôme, Creuse, Dordogne, Gironde, Ariège, Tarn, Tarn et Garonne, Aude, Hautes Alpes, Vaucluse.

Category 6—From +0.2 to +0.6 m2

Nord, Seine et Oise, Cher, Manche, Loire Atlantique, Vendée, Finistère, Morbihan, Meurthe et Moselle, Moselle, Belfort, Ardèche, Loire, Savoie, Cantal, Corrèze, Haute Vienne, Charente Maritime, Aveyron, Hautes Pyrénées, Gard, Hérault, Pyrénées Orientales, Alpes Maritimes, Bouches du Rhône, Var.

Category 7—Less Than +0.2

Landes	+0.1	Basses Alpes	([1])
Jura	+0.1	Corse	−0.2
Calvados	+0.1	Lozère	−0.3
Seine	+0.05		

[1] No permits in either of the two periods.

MAP IX.—*Change in Relative Wage Levels, 1954 to 1961*

[All of France=100]

Category 1—Index 105 or Greater

Haute Savoie	110	Basses Alpes	106
Hautes Alpes	110	Seine et Marne	105
Basses Pyrénées	108		

Map VIII

Change in Total Area of Construction Permits Issued, 1953-55 to 1959-61

Square Meters of Difference Between Two Periods Per Capita of Active Industrial Population.

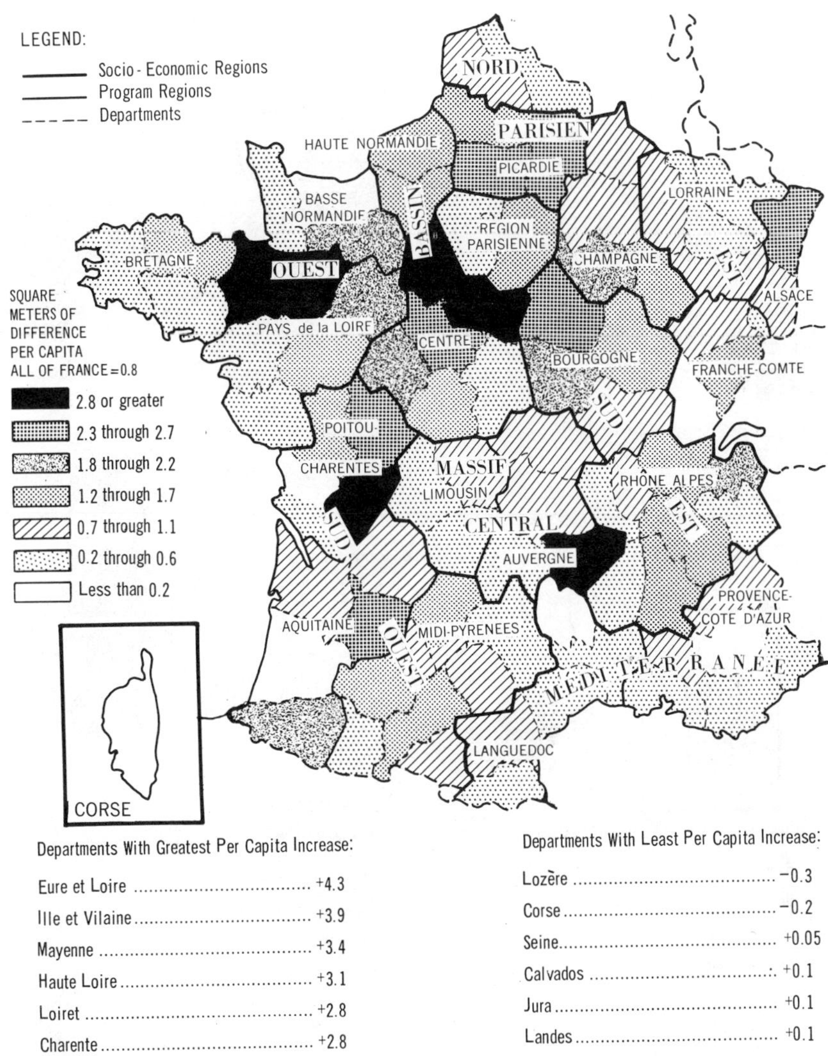

Departments With Greatest Per Capita Increase:	
Eure et Loire	+4.3
Ille et Vilaine	+3.9
Mayenne	+3.4
Haute Loire	+3.1
Loiret	+2.8
Charente	+2.8

Departments With Least Per Capita Increase:	
Lozère	−0.3
Corse	−0.2
Seine	+0.05
Calvados	+0.1
Jura	+0.1
Landes	+0.1

Map IX

Relative Change in Average Annual Wages by Departments, 1954 to 1961

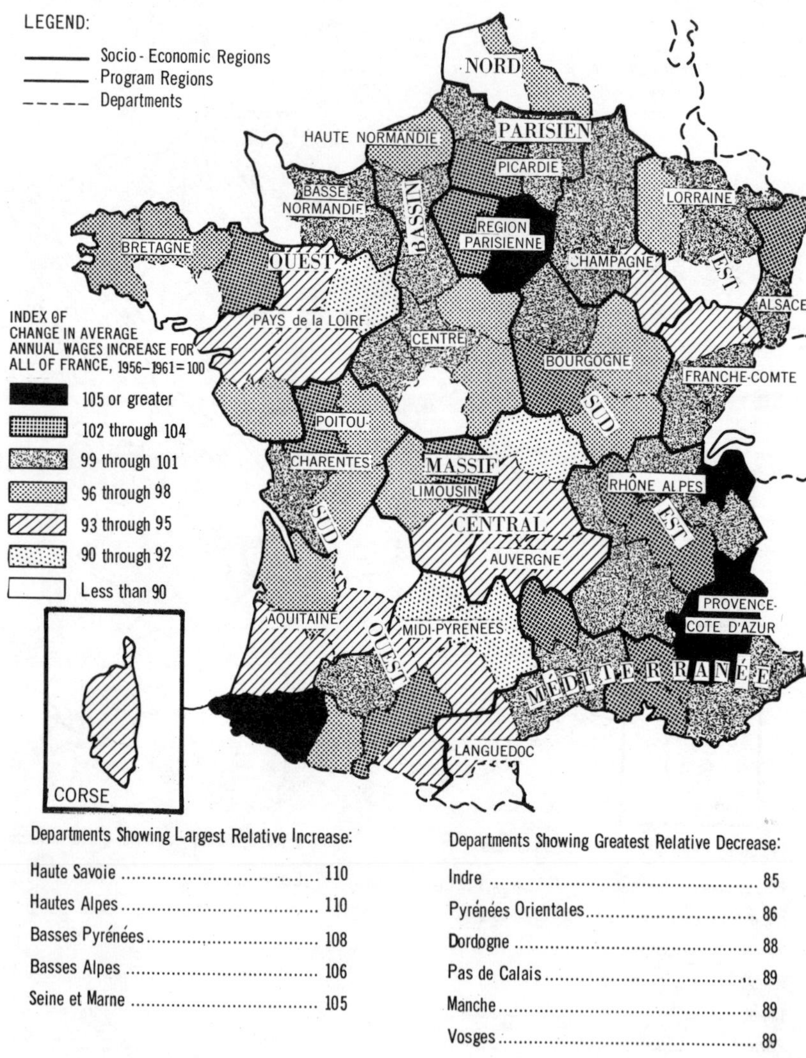

Departments Showing Largest Relative Increase:

Haute Savoie	110
Hautes Alpes	110
Basses Pyrénées	108
Basses Alpes	106
Seine et Marne	105

Departments Showing Greatest Relative Decrease:

Indre	85
Pyrénées Orientales	86
Dordogne	88
Pas de Calais	89
Manche	89
Vosges	89

Category 2—Index 102 Through 104

Seine, Seine et Oise, Oise, Ille et Vilaine, Bas Rhin, Nièvre, Rhône, Isère, Creuse, Deux Sèvres, Haute Garonne, Bouches du Rhône, Vaucluse, Lozère.

Category 3—Index 99 Through 101

Aisne, Somme, Aube, Ardennes, Marne, Eure et Loir, Indre et Loire, Loir et Cher, Eure, Calvados, Orne, Meurthe et Moselle, Moselle, Haut Rhin, Doubs, Jura, Yonne, Ain, Ardèche, Drôme, Loire, Savoie, Charente Maritime, Gers, Gard, Hérault, Alpes Maritimes, Var.

Category 4—Index 96 Through 98

Nord, Cher, Loiret, Seine Maritime, Vendée, Côtes du Nord, Finistère, Meuse, Côte d'Or, Saône et Loire, Haute Vienne, Charente, Vienne, Gironde, Hautes Pyrénées.

Category 5—Index 93 Through 95

Haute Marne, Loire Atlantique, Maine et Loire, Mayenne, Haute Saône, Belfort, Cantal, Haute Loire, Puy de Dôme, Corrèze, Landes, Lot et Garonne, Ariège, Tarn, Tarn et Garonne, Aude, Corse.

Category 6—Index 90 Through 92

Sarthe, Allier, Aveyron, Lot.

Category 7—Index, Less Than 90

Vosges	89	Dordogne	88
Manche	89	Pyrénées Oles	86
Pas de Calais	89	Indre	85

Map X.—*Change in Number of Jobseekers, 1954 to 1962*

(Index, 1954=100)

[All of France=55]

Category 1—Index, 29 or less

Moselle	20	Aube	25
Nord	23	Drôme	29
Bas Rhin	23		

Category 2—Index 30 Through 35

Pas de Calais, Seine, Seine et Marne, Seine et Oise, Aisne, Oise, Somme, Ardennes, Marne, Eure et Loir, Loiret, Seine Maritime, Orne, Meurthe et Moselle, Jura, Ardèche, Loire, Rhône, Haute Loire, Puy de Dôme, Creuse, Haute Vienne, Ariège, Aude, Gard, Hérault, Lozère, Bouches du Rhône, Vaucluse, Corse.

Category 3—Index 56 Through 80

Cher, Indre et Loire, Loir et Cher, Sarthe, Ille et Vilaine, Meuse, Haut Rhin, Doubs, Haute Saône et Belfort, Côte d'Or, Saône et Loire, Yonne, Isère, Savoie, Haute Savoie, Allier, Cantal, Corrèze, Vienne, Dordogne, Gironde, Landes, Lot et Garonne, Lot, Hautes Pyrénées, Tarn, Tarn et Garonne, Pyrénées Orientales, Basses Alpes.

Map X

Change in Number of Jobseekers by Departments, 1954 to 1962

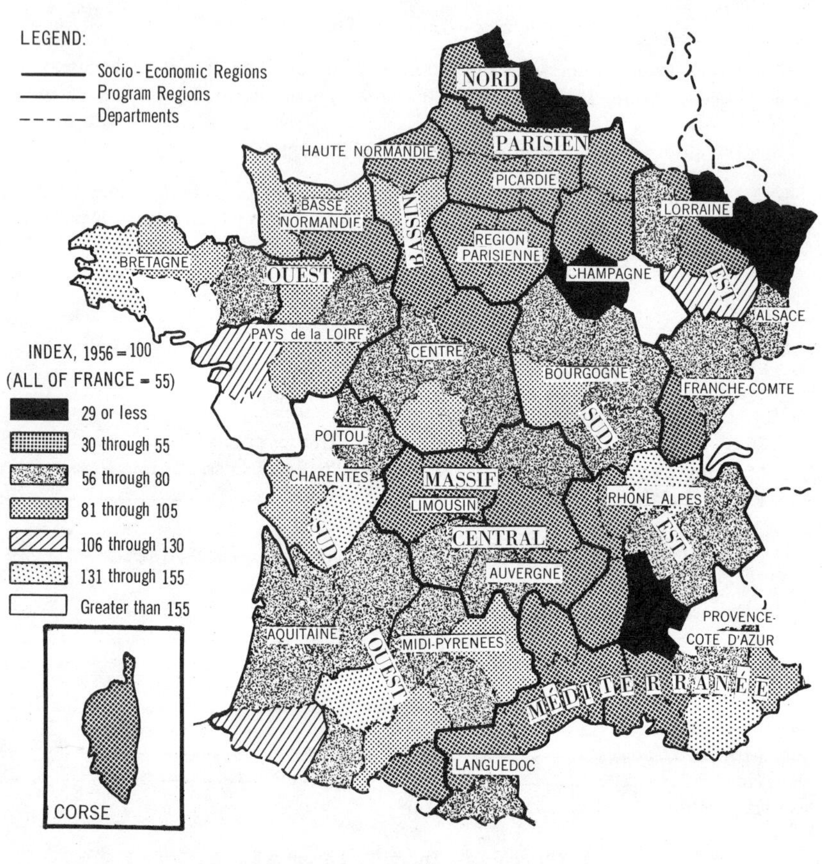

Departments With Greatest Decrease:

Moselle	20
Nord	23
Bas Rhin	23
Aube	25
Drôme	29

Departments With Greatest Increase:

Deux Sevres	1016
Vendée	371
Hautes Alpes	186
Haute Marne	158
Morbihan	156

Category 4—Index 81 Through 105

Indre, Eure, Calvados, Manche, Maine et Loire, Mayenne, Côtes du Nord, Nièvre, Charente Maritime, Aveyron, Haute Garonne, Alpes Maritimes.

Category 5—Index 106 Through 130

Loire Atlantique, Vosges, Basses Pyrénées.

Category 6—Index 131 Through 155

Finistère, Ain, Charente, Gers, Var.

Category 7—Index 155 or Greater

Morbihan	156	Vendée	371
Haute Marne	158	Deux Sèvres	1016
Hautes Alpes	186		

MAP XI.—*Recapitulation of the Indices of Change, 1954–62*

(Sum of the rank categories for the 4 indices studied)

Category 1—Total 10 or less

Seine et Marne	9	Haute Savoie	9
Oise	9	Eure et Loir	10
Bas Rhin	9		

Category 2—Total 11 Through 12

Seine et Oise, Aisne, Aube, Loiret, Ille et Vilaine, Moselle, Doubs, Drôme, Rhône, Isère, Basses Pyrénées, Haute Garonne, Bouches du Rhône, Vaucluse.

Category 3—Total 13 Through 14

Somme, Ardennes, Marne, Indre et Loire, Loir et Cher, Seine Maritime, Orne, Meurthe et Moselle, Yonne, Vienne, Gard, Hérault, Basses Alpes, Alpes Maritimes.

Category 4—Total 15 Through 17

Nord, Seine, Eure, Maine et Loire, Mayenne, Sarthe, Meuse, Haut Rhin, Jura, Belfort, Côte d'Or, Nièvre, Saône et Loire, Ardèche, Loire, Savoie, Haute Loire, Puy de Dôme, Creuse, Haute Vienne, Charente, Gironde, Lot et Garonne, Lozère, Var, Corse.

Category 5—Total 18 Through 19

Pas de Calais, Cher, Calvados, Côtes du Nord, Haute Saône, Ain, Allier, Corrèze, Charente Maritime, Deux Sèvres, Ariège, Lot, Hautes Pyrénées, Tarn, Tarn et Garonne, Aude, Pyrénées Orientales, Hautes Alpes.

Category 6—Total 20 Through 21

Haute Marne, Indre, Loire Atlantique, Finistère, Cantal, Dordogne, Landes, Gers.

Category 7—Total Greater Than 21

Aveyron	22	Manche	23
Vosges	22	Morbihan	26
Vendée	22		

Map XI

Recapitulation of the Indices of Change, by Departments, 1954 to 1962

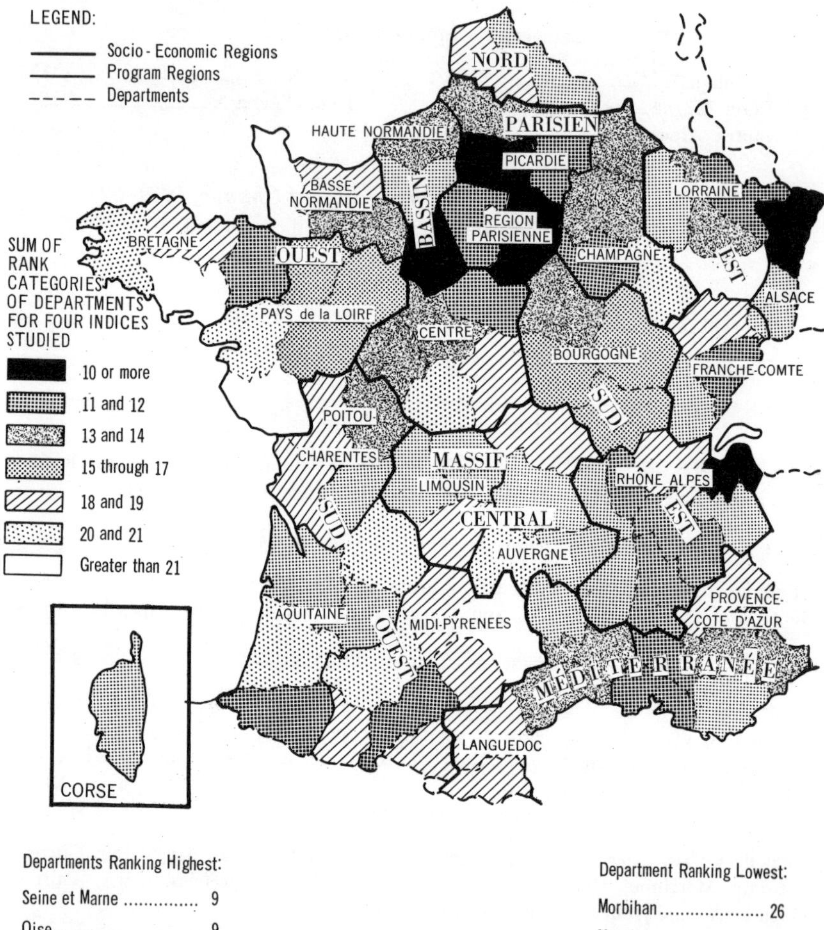

Departments Ranking Highest:	
Seine et Marne	9
Oise	9
Haute Savoie	9
Bas Rhin	9
Eure et Loire	10

Department Ranking Lowest:	
Morbihan	26
Manche	23
Vendee	22
Vosges	22
Aveyron	22

Map XII.—*Recapitulation of the Indices of Change, 1954–62*

(Number of indices above the national average)

Above the National Average for All Four Indexes

Seine et Marne, Oise, Rhône.

Above the National Average for Three of the Four Indexes

Seine et Oise, Eure et Loir, Seine Maritime, Bas Rhin, Drôme, Isère, Haute Savoie, Creuse, Basses Pyrénées, Haute Garonne, Gard, Vaucluse.

Above the National Average for Two of the Four Indexes

Seine, Aisne, Somme, Ardennes, Aube, Marne, Loiret, Orne, Ille et Vilaine, Meurthe et Moselle, Moselle, Doubs, Nièvre, Ardèche, Haute Loire, Puy de Dôme, Deux Sèvres, Ariège, Gers, Aude, Hérault, Lozère, Basses Alpes, Hautes Alpes, Bouches du Rhône, Corse.

Above the National Average for One of the Four Indexes

Nord, Haute Marne, Indre, Indre et Loire, Loir et Cher, Eure, Maine et Loire, Mayenne, Sarthe, Côtes du Nord, Meuse, Vosges, Haut Rhin, Jura, Belfort, Côte d'Or, Yonne, Ain, Loire, Haute Vienne, Charente, Vienne, Dordogne, Gironde, Lot et Garonne, Lot, Tarn, Tarn et Garonne, Pyrénées Orientales, Alpes Maritimes, Var.

Above the National Average for No Index

Pas de Calais, Cher, Calvados, Manche, Loire Atlantique, Vendée, Finistère, Morbihan, Haute Saône, Saône et Loire, Savoie, Allier, Cantal, Corrèze, Charente Maritime, Landes, Aveyron, Hautes Pyrénées.

The west

In none of the three program regions in the west (Basse Normandie, Pays dela Loire, Bretagne) did the situation seem to have improved markedly by 1961. Only three departments, Orne, Mayenne, and Ille et Vilaine, which are closest to the Parisian region and have benefited from its expansion, show a significant increase in wages and an increase above the average for all of France in the issurance of construction permits. But the number of persons seeking jobs remains high and emigration large.

The change in 1962 and the spring of 1963, not reflected in the maps, seems more favorable. But except in the parts near the Parisian region, the west remains substantially behind the growth of the rest of France.

The massif central (Limousin and Auvergne)

The situation of the massif central, another great region in serious difficulty in 1954, does not seem to have improved relatively. Aside from a considerable increase in the number of construction permits in Haute Loire and an increase in wages in Creuse, the stagnation of this region does not seem to have been overcome. The stationary total population, weaker wage movements than elsewhere, and construction permits at a low level are evidence of this stagnation. We have noted elsewhere that this region has made little use of the assistance made available to it.

Map XII

Recapitulation of the Indices Position of the Departments Compared to the National Average for the Four Indices of Change Studied, 1954 to 1962

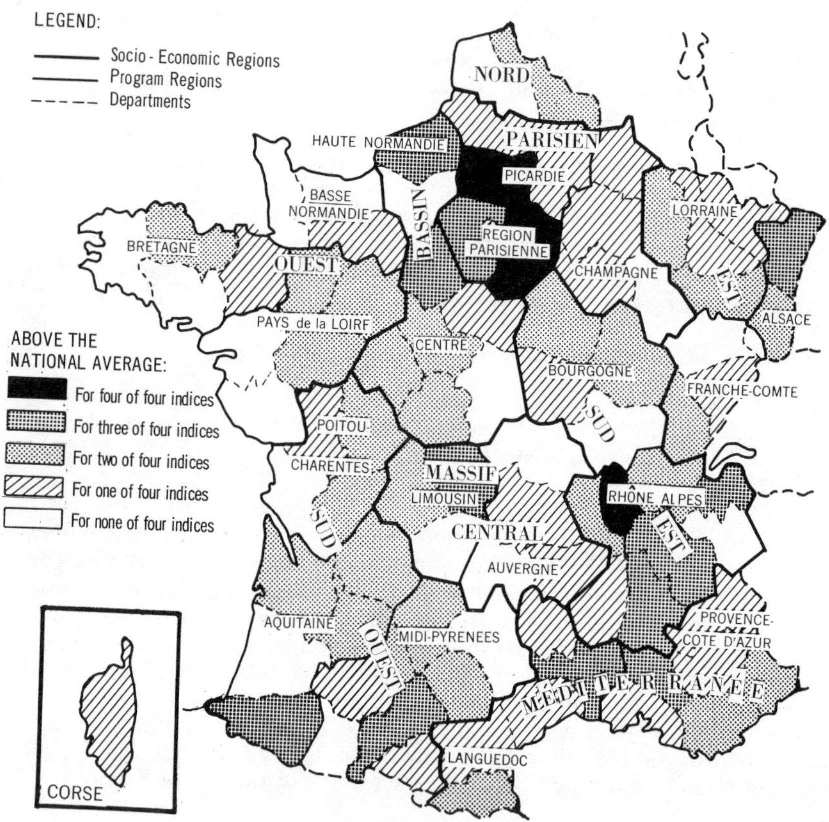

The southwest (Poitou-Charentes, Aquitaine, Midi-Pyrénées)

Certain zones in the southwest, particularly Basses Pyrénées, a part of the program region of Midi-Pyrénées, and Poitou-Charentes, seem to show relative progress. Total population has grown more rapidly than elsewhere, as have the levels of wages, and sometimes construction permits. But elsewhere in the region progress in these variables is below the French average.

The Mediterranean

Though the greater part of Languedoc, except for the department of Gard, has not shown any significant sign of recovery, Provence is progressing both in total population (augmented by large immigration) and in wage levels. The low surface area represented by construction permits is explained by the largely tertiary character of the development. Provence is the only French region whose relative rate of population growth is larger than that of Paris.

The southeast

Aside from the department of Saône-et-Loire, the program regions of the southeast, both Bourgogne and Rhône-Alpes, show wage increases and industrial locations in a number of departments. Since the new industries are modern and dynamic, it may be judged that this region is continuing the growth shown since 1954.

The east

Apart from the departments of Vosges and Haute Saône, which have been in difficulty since 1954, the east shows greater than average dynamism, particularly in Lorraine and Alsace.

The Parisian basin and the Parisian region

Though the Parisian region continues its expansion (despite a reduction in the number of construction permits issued, demonstrating the effectiveness of the legal prohibitions), the new fact is the involvement of the whole Parisian basin in this growth. The expansion extends further and further from Paris, from Champagne to the Centre, and sometimes even beyond the limits of the Parisian Basin, particularly in the west and in Bourgogne, industries increasingly go these distances in order to find industrial sites and manpower at reasonable prices. Wage levels and the surface area represented by construction permits are growing. It is true, however, that population is increasing in the basin less rapidly than the average because of the attraction which Paris and its high salaries exercise in the area.

Two concluding questions remain: Have the regions said to be underdeveloped surmounted their handicaps since 1954? And have the aids provided by law and public authority played a role?

A look at the maps suggests a pessimistic answer. The difference between the situation of eastern France,[55] to the right of a line Rouen-Marseille, and that of the west does not seem to have been eradicated or even much reduced since 1954. The former, better endowed with natural resources and close to the heart of the Common Market, has even increased its advantage over the other zones, particularly the southeast, which were already behind. Except for certain areas such as Basses Pyrénées and Gard,

[55] The north of France is not classified with the west.

the west does not seem to have improved its situation fundamentally, handicapped as it is by distance from the industrial centers of Europe. With respect to such factors as total population,[56] the rate of industrial location, and level of wages the divergencies between the developed regions of the east and the less developed regions of the west remain as great as they were.

Nevertheless, a significant change has occurred between 1954 and 1962. The Parisian basin has been brought along by the development of the Parisian region. Such critical zones as Picardie and the Centre have been gaining relatively.

The contagion has even extended to certain peripheral regions such as Bretagne, Basse Normandie, and Bourgogne. In this way parts of the country which were formerly in an unfavorable situation have entered the current of expansion.

But have the aids available played a role?

So far as the critical zones are concerned, one observation must be made. Their reconversion has not always gone well. Certainly, public assistance has permitted avoidance of the worst, that is, generalized unemployment. But the northern region, affected by the closing of coal mines and the textile crisis (critical zones of Fourmies and Béthune), has not been fundamentally changed. Though it does not now have unemployment, few new industries have located there to provide jobs for young people. In Lorraine, Vosges, as our maps show, is in a poorer situation than the rest of the region. The reconversion of the coal mines of the center is only half accomplished, and the critical zones of Auvergne show no more dynamism than those of the north. Similarly, the southwest and the west remain least developed. On the other hand, the situation in Alsace and in Picardie has changed profoundly since the critical zones were created in 1955.

Elsewhere we have noted that though certain kinds of assistance, particularly the investment grants, go as a matter of priority to zones with problems, others have worked to the greater benefit of spontaneously dynamic regions, particularly in the east and the southeast.

Thus, French regional policies have permitted a slowing down in the decline of the critical zones. The stabilization of differences between the most favored regions and the others is to the credit of specific policies and the public assistance which attracted new industries, coming particularly from the Parisian region, and prevented any increase in the threat of unemployment. But the policies have not led to any profound change in the less industrialized regions (the west and the southwest) or in those in which mature industries dominate (the north and a part of Auvergne).

The assistance granted, weak as it was (1 percent of the budget), was not without effectiveness. Is it sufficient? This question raises the whole problem of regional policy in general.

At a time when French planning is being regionalized and when, as a consequence, regional policies as distinguished from national policies lose their particular meaning, it may be asked what is the objective of regional policies: To maintain full employment? To give all citizens an equal income? To permit each region to develop best?

The first objective, invoked for a long time, is legitimate only when serious underemployment exists. This is no longer the case today in France.

[56] It will be noted that, instead of diminishing, migration to Paris doubled between 1954 and 1962 as compared with the period 1946–54.

Furthermore, it encourages immobility of labor, which is already too great, and a sort of regional Malthusianism. The second is utopian because it presupposes a uniform distribution of industries throughout the country. Only the third objective, to develop everywhere industries appropriate to the region, can serve both regional and national interests. But it raises theoretical difficulties which French planners will encounter on their way.

Appendix I

Explanation of the Maps

Maps 2 to 4 concern the relative situation of the departments in 1954 with respect to:

Map 2—active industrial population (index of change from 1946).

Map 3—average level of wages.

Map 4—the number of jobseekers.

Maps 5 and 6 concern the relative situation of the departments in 1961 or 1962 with respect to:

Map 5—average level of wages.

Map 6—the number of jobseekers.

Maps 7 through 12 concern the relative change of the departments from 1954 to 1961 or 1962 with respect to:

Map 7—total population.

Map 8—the surface area of construction permits granted.

Map 9—average level of wages.

Map 10—the number of jobseekers.

Maps 11 and 12—the recapitulations of the four indices.

Classification of the departments into seven categories is done in the same fashion for all the maps, whether they are derived from absolute numbers or index numbers. The five positions at the upper and at the lower extremes make up, respectively, the first and seventh categories. The interval between these extremes is divided into five categories spaced equally. Of course, for the maps portraying the number of jobseekers, the higher positions refer to the departments having the least number, and vice versa.

Maps 2 and 7—Population:

Census data for 1954 and 1961 were used as one measure of industrial development in each region.

It would have been interesting to see how the distribution of the active population between the primary, secondary, and tertiary sectors by departments had changed. Such a comparison, however, would be distorted by the historical circumstances surrounding the 1946 census. The numbers of the agricultural population were artificially inflated at the expense of the other sectors. The war had slowed down the movement out of agriculture, and workers from other sectors had taken up agriculture work by reason of such circumstances as the special food rations for heavy labor. Likewise, the tertiary sector was artificially inflated for reasons connected with the war. Such reasons included the relative increase in incomes in commerce because of inflation, the difficulty of finding stable employment elsewhere, and the possibilities of fraud which induced certain individuals to declare themselves as working in employments in the tertiary sector.

Thus, only the change in total active industrial population between the two censuses was examined. It appeared that the dynamism of each department could be shown quite well by the relation between the actual active industrial population reached in 1954 with that which it would have been if each kind of employment had increased at the national average rate. This was measured by multiplying for each department the number of persons employed in each industry in 1946 by the index of national average increase in that industry from 1946 to 1954. These were totaled for each department, and divided by the actual 1954 active industrial population. The resulting index is greater or less than 100 depending on whether industries in the department changed at a rate greater or lesser than the national average. If the index is greater than 100, it may be concluded that the department developed more rapidly than might have been expected, taking account of its 1946 industrial structure; i.e., its growth had accelerated, relatively. If the index is less than 100, the reverse is the case.

The results of these calculations appear in appendix II. After grouping these indexes into the seven categories, map 2 was constructed. It shows in the darker shades the regions more dynamic in this earlier period, and the lesser in the lighter.

Unfortunately it was not possible to study the change in active industrial population from 1954 to 1962 in a similar way. The breakdowns of the 1962 census data is still in progress and has been delayed. Consequently, data on active industrial population are still not available. For this reason, map 7 simply shows the growth in total population of the department from 1954 to 1962 (base of 100=total population of the department according to the 1954 census). Of course, this growth is not necessarily a sign of economic development; a more satisfactory index will be that of active population by industry when that is known.

The data for population by department have been published in various places. For these purposes they were taken from the review, *L'Usine Nouvelle,* supplement of January 1963, pp. 70 and 71.

Maps 3, 5, and 9—Wages:

Maps 3, 5, and 9 use statistics prepared by the Institut National des Statistiques et des Etudes Economiques (INSEE) and derived from the declarations of wages by employer for tax purposes. The 1954 data are published in the journal *Etudes Statistiques,* quarterly supplement to the monthly statistical bulletin of INSEE, No. 3, July–September 1956, p. 61. Those for 1961 were given by INSEE before publication. The data for 1962 are not yet ready at this writing.

These data give, for each department, the nominal net full-time annual wage for both sexes for industry and commerce. Excluded are the agricultural industries (farming, forestry, fishing), domestic service, and public employment. They do, however, include wages in the nationalized industries such as the railroads, electricity, gas, coal mines, etc.

Maps 3 and 5 show, for 1954 and 1961 respectively, the relative wage level in each department with respect to the national average. The index was computed by dividing the average wage in each department by that for France as a whole. The national average, then is the base (=100) of the index. Map 9 shows the relative change in average wages in each department from 1954 to 1961. The increase in wages in each department was related to that for all of France (or an increase of 201.36 percent in money wages). This national average increase represents the base of 100 for the index.

Maps, 4, 6 and 10—The number of jobseekers:

These maps are based on statistics of the Ministry of Labor showing the distribution by departments of the number of persons registered as wanting jobs with the employment offices. The data for 1954 are published in the *Revue Française du Travail,* published by the Ministry of Labor, No. 1, 1956, pp. 70 and 71. Those for 1962 were communicated directly by the statistical services of the Ministry of Labor.

The figures are the annual averages of unsatisfied job requests at the end of each month. For the year 1962 job requests of repatriates from North Africa were excluded.

To construct maps 4 and 6 there was taken, for 1954 and 1962 respectively, the annual average of the number of jobseekers by department. This was related to the active industrial population of the department according to the 1954 census. The data are in number of jobseekers per 10,000 active industrial population. It was not possible to relate the number of jobseekers in 1962 to the active population according to the 1962 census, since, as was indicated above, this latter is not yet available.

Map 10 shows the index of change in the number of jobseekers, by departments, from 1954 to 1962.

Map 8—Change in surface area of construction permits granted:

This map is based on statistics published by the Ministry of Construction giving, by department, the floor surface of industrial construction permits granted annually by the Ministry. The jurisdiction of the Ministry extends to requests for permits for establishments occupying more than 500 square meters or employing more than 50 wage earners. They are published in the statistical bulletin of the Ministry of Construction, the January and August number of 1960 for the year prior to 1960; June 1961 for the year 1960, and the July–August 1962 number for the year 1961. The data for 1962 are not yet available.

To show the relative change in the granting of permits for the period considered, there was calculated for each department the difference between the surface area of permits granted during the 3 years 1959 to 1961 and that for the 3 years 1953 to 1955. This difference was then divided by the active industrial population of the department according to the 1954 census, so as to obtain the change in square meters per capita. Three-year periods were chosen for comparative purposes in order to eliminate so far as possible random variations.

Maps 11 and 12—Recap of the four indexes of change, 1954 to 1962:

Finally, a crude recapitulation of the relative change in the departments from 1954 to 1962 (maps 7 through 10) was attempted. This recapitulation was done in two ways:

Map 11 was constructed by adding for each department the four figures representing the category (from 1 to 7) in which the department fell for each of the four indexes. Then the departments were again classified, according to the method used throughout, into seven categories. The better positions are those of the departments which total the least number of points (the extreme positions theoretically possible being 4—a department ranking in the first category for all indexes—and 28—a department ranking in the last category for all indexes).

Map 12 classifies the departments in five groups according to whether they lie above the national average for 0, 1, 2, 3, or all 4 of the indexes.

It should be emphasized that these recapitulations are necessarily arbitrary in that they are derived from indexes whose significance is quite unequal. Given this reservation, the results are nevertheless of interest.

Appendix II

STATISTICS BEHIND THE MAPS

	Total population			Average annual wages, wage earners in industry and commerce			Area of construction permits, 3 years 1959–61 less 3 years 1953–55 divided by active industrial population, 1954, square meters per capita	Number of jobseekers without jobs		
	1954 Census	1962 Census	Index 1954=100	Relative level, 1954, France =100	Relative level, 1961, France =100	Change, 1961 to 1964, (5)+(4)		Per 10,000 active industrial population 1954	Per 10,000 active industrial population 1962	Index, 1954=100
	(1)	(2)	(3)	(4)	(5)	(6)	(7)	(8)	(9)	(10)
Nord	2, 098. 6	2, 274. 2	108	95	92	97	+0. 5	131	30	23
Pas de Calais	1, 276. 8	1, 348. 2	106	93	83	89	+0. 7	175	96	55
Région Nord	(3, 375. 4)	(3, 622. 4)	(107)	(94)	(89)	(94)	(+0. 6)	....	....	....
Seine	5, 154. 8	5, 575. 3	108	130	135	104	+0. 05	307	108	35
Seine et Marne	453. 4	525. 8	116	99	104	105	+1. 5	153	79	52
Seine et Oise	1, 708. 8	2, 301. 7	135	122	127	104	+0. 4	210	97	46
Région parisienne	(7, 313. 0)	(8, 402. 8)	(115)	(127)	(132)	(104)	(+0. 2)	....	....	....
Aisne	487. 1	510. 4	105	84	84	100	+2. 3	128	70	54
Oise	435. 3	482. 1	111	95	96	102	+2. 3	107	51	48
Somme	464. 2	481. 9	104	80	80	101	+1. 4	254	140	55
Picardie	(1, 386. 6)	(1, 474. 4)	(106)	(86)	(87)	(101)	(+2. 0)	....	....	....

Ardennes	280. 5	297. 1	106	89	88	99	+0. 9	77	34	44
Aube	240. 8	252. 0	105	77	77	100	+1. 8	158	39	25
Marne	415. 1	443. 6	107	88	89	101	+0. 8	264	121	46
Haute Marne	197. 1	206. 6	105	80	75	94	+1. 7	42	66	158
Champagne	(1, 133. 5)	(1, 199. 3)	(106)	(85)	(84)	(99)	(+1. 2)	....	....	....
Cher	284. 4	291. 4	102	83	79	96	+0. 5	200	122	61
Eure et Loir	261. 0	276. 7	106	84	85	101	+4. 3	208	103	49
Indre	247. 4	248. 6	100	75	64	85	+1. 2	143	148	103
Indre et Loire	364. 7	392. 5	108	82	81	99	+2. 0	256	158	62
Loir et Cher	239. 8	248. 4	104	72	71	100	+2. 7	84	46	56
Loiret	360. 5	389. 8	108	84	81	96	+2. 8	130	66	51
Centre	(1, 757. 8)	(1, 847. 4)	(105)	(81)	(78)	(97)	(+2. 2)	....	....	....
Eure	332. 5	360. 5	108	84	83	99	+1. 2	82	84	102
Seine Maritime	941. 7	1, 024. 6	109	97	94	97	+1. 5	362	122	34
Haute Normandie	(1, 274. 2)	(1, 385. 1)	(109)	(95)	(92)	(97)	(+1. 4)	....	....	....
Calvados	443. 0	477. 2	108	86	85	99	+0. 1	166	162	97
Manche	446. 9	442. 8	99	74	66	89	+0. 4	277	223	81
Orne	274. 9	277. 6	101	73	73	100	+1. 9	159	67	42
Basse Normandie	(1, 164. 8)	(1, 197. 6)	(103)	(80)	(78)	(97)	+0. 6	....	....	....
Loire Atlantique	733. 6	794. 3	108	94	88	93	+0. 2	296	317	107
Maine et Loire	518. 2	554. 4	107	79	74	93	+1. 3	164	170	103
Mayenne	251. 5	247. 0	98	71	68	95	+3. 4	273	223	81
Sarthe	420. 4	441. 0	105	90	81	90	+2. 1	407	303	74
Vendée	395. 6	403. 1	102	64	61	97	+0. 3	62	229	371
Pays de la Loire	(2, 319. 3)	(2, 439. 8)	(105)	(86)	(79)	(92)	(+1. 1)	....	....	....

STATISTICS BEHIND THE MAPS—Continued

	Total population			Average annual wages, wage earners in industry and commerce			Area of construction permits, 3 years 1959–61 less 3 years 1953–55 divided by active industrial population, 1954, square meters per capita	Number of jobseekers without jobs		
	1954 Census	1962 Census	Index 1954=100	Relative level, 1954, France =100	Relative level, 1961, France =100	Change, 1961 to 1964, (5)+(4)		Per 10,000 active industrial population 1954	Per 10,000 active industrial population 1962	Index, 1954=100
	(1)	(2)	(3)	(4)	(5)	(6)	(7)	(8)	(9)	(10)
Côtes du Nord	503. 2	497. 9	99	80	76	96	+1. 6	298	271	91
Finistère	727. 9	739. 3	102	77	74	96	+0. 3	213	305	143
Ille et Vilaine	586. 8	609. 8	104	79	81	102	+3. 9	381	260	68
Morbihan	521. 0	527. 4	101	79	70	89	+0. 5	305	476	156
Bretagne	(2, 338. 9)	(2, 374. 4)	(102)	(78)	(76)	(97)	(+1. 4)	....	....	....
Meurthe et Moselle	607. 0	678. 1	112	102	101	99	+0. 4	77	34	44
Meuse	207. 1	217. 6	105	84	81	97	+1. 0	29	22	76
Moselle	769. 4	922. 5	120	98	99	100	+0. 5	64	13	20
Vosges	372. 5	380. 0	102	78	69	89	+1. 1	33	42	127
Lorraine	(1, 956. 0)	(2, 198. 2)	(112)	(95)	(93)	(98)	(+0. 6)	....	....	....
Bas Rhin	707. 9	764. 4	108	84	86	103	+2. 6	173	40	23
Haut Rhin	509. 7	534. 8	107	93	92	99	+1. 1	82	54	66
Alsace	(1, 217. 6)	(1, 308. 2)	(107)	(88)	(89)	(101)	(+1. 9)	....	....	....

Doubs	327. 2	383. 0	117	96	96	100	+1. 6	59	44	74
Jura	220. 2	224. 5	102	80	79	99	+0. 1	81	40	49
Haute Saône	209. 3	207. 5	99	78	73	93	+0. 8 }	50	31	62
Terr. de Belfort	99. 4	110. 3	111	101	94	93	+0. 4 }			
Franche-Comté	(856. 1)	(925. 3)	(108)	(91)	(88)	(97)	(+0. 9)	....	....	....
Côte d'Or	356. 8	386. 4	108	87	84	97	+1. 3	171	103	60
Nièvre	240. 1	242. 7	101	84	86	102	+1. 9	165	160	97
Saône et Loire	511. 2	530. 2	104	86	84	97	+0. 7	91	57	62
Yonne	266. 4	268. 9	101	79	79	100	+2. 6	138	78	56
Bourgogne	(1, 374. 5)	(1, 428. 2)	(104)	(85)	(84)	(98)	(+1. 4)	....	....	....
Ain	331. 9	328. 1	105	82	883	100	+1. 2	62	91	146
Ardèche	249. 1	245. 6	99	79	79	101	+0. 6	394	149	38
Drôme	275. 3	303. 5	110	82	81	99	+1. 2	257	74	29
Loire	654. 5	686. 6	105	87	86	99	+0. 2	204	89	44
Rhone	966. 8	1, 110. 2	115	104	108	103	+0. 9	209	84	40
Isère	626. 1	725. 7	116	94	98	104	+1. 6	99	73	74
Savoie	252. 2	265. 8	105	97	97	100	+0. 2	181	121	67
Haute Savoie	293. 9	332. 6	113	90	99	110	+1. 8	61	37	60
Rhône Alpes	(3, 629. 8)	(3, 998. 1)	(110)	(94)	(97)	(102)	(+0. 9)	....	....	....
Allier	327. 7	379. 0	102	89	82	92	+0. 7	258	192	75
Cantal	177. 1	170. 9	96	73	68	94	+0. 5	293	222	76
Haute Loire	215. 6	209. 6	97	71	66	94	+3. 1	210	93	44
Puy de Dome	481. 4	509. 2	106	93	88	95	+1. 0	181	90	50
Auvergne	(1, 246. 8)	(1, 268. 7)	(102)	(87)	(82)	(94)	(+1. 2)	....	....	....

STATISTICS BEHIND THE MAPS—Continued

	Total population			Average annual wages, wage earners in industry and commerce			Area of construction permits, 3 years 1959–61 less 3 years 1953–55 divided by active industrial population, 1954, square meters per capita	Number of jobseekers without jobs		
	1954 Census	1962 Census	Index 1954=100	Relative level, 1954, France =100	Relative level, 1961, France =100	Change, 1961 to 1964, (5)+(4)		Per 10,000 active industrial population		Index, 1954=100
								1954	1962	
	(1)	(2)	(3)	(4)	(5)	(6)	(7)	(8)	(9)	(10)
Corrèze	242. 8	238. 7	98	80	74	94	+0. 5	201	149	74
Creuse	172. 7	162. 5	94	67	68	102	+0. 9	270	136	50
Haute Vienne	324. 4	329. 4	102	78	85	96	+0. 2	256	136	53
Limousin	(739. 9)	(730. 6)	(99)	(78)	(74)	(96)	(+0. 4)	....	....	....
Charente	313. 6	324. 8	104	81	77	96	+2. 8	70	100	142
Charente Maritime	448. 0	471. 3	105	78	78	99	+0. 4	219	193	88
Deux Sèvres	312. 8	316. 9	101	71	84	104	+1. 2	23	235	1, 016
Vienne	319. 2	329. 2	103	75	72	96	+2. 3	347	217	62
Poitou-Charentes	(1, 393. 6)	(1, 442. 2)	(103)	(77)	(76)	(98)	(+1. 6)	....	....	....

Dordogne	337. 9	370. 4	98	75	66	83	+1. 1	175	109	62
Gironde	896. 5	936. 1	104	90	88	97	+0. 9	528	346	66
Landes	248. 9	260. 0	104	76	72	94	+0. 1	125	74	59
Lot et Garonne	265. 6	271. 5	102	76	71	93	+2. 3	308	246	80
Basses Pyrénées	420. 0	469. 5	112	78	84	108	+2. 0	302	330	109
Aquitaine	(2, 208. 9)	(2, 307. 5)	(104)	(84)	(82)	(98)	(+1. 2)	....	....	....
Ariège	104. 0	135. 1	97	80	75	94	+0. 9	522	206	39
Aveyron	292. 7	287. 1	98	80	73	92	+0. 6	107	89	83
Haute Garonne	525. 7	592. 1	113	90	94	104	+1. 2	349	314	90
Gers	185. 1	179. 5	97	61	62	101	+1. 5	84	126	151
Lot	147. 8	148. 6	101	77	71	92	+1. 5	139	99	71
Hautes Pyrénées	203. 5	212. 0	104	83	82	98	+0. 3	251	201	80
Tarn	308. 2	318. 4	103	82	77	93	+1. 1	218	163	75
Tarn et Garonne	172. 4	174. 6	101	73	69	94	+1. 0	487	384	79
Midi-Pyrénées	(1, 975. 4)	(2, 047. 4)	(104)	(84)	(82)	(98)	(+1. 0)	....	....	....
Aude	268. 3	267. 9	100	78	73	94	+1. 0	1, 448	1, 443	39
Gard	396. 7	433. 1	109	84	85	101	+0. 4	538	183	34
Hérault	471. 4	512. 5	109	86	85	99	+0. 5	1, 597	637	40
Lozère	82. 4	80. 9	98	67	69	103	−0. 3	136	69	51
Pyrénées Orientales	230. 3	252. 1	109	84	72	86	+0. 4	590	422	72
Languedoc	(1, 449. 1)	(1, 546. 5)	(107)	(84)	(81)	(97)	(+0. 5)	....	....	....
Basses Alpes	84. 3	92. 2	109	91	96	106	(1)	105	84	80
Hautes Alpes	85. 1	88. 6	104	80	88	110	+1. 0	95	176	186
Alpes Maritimes	515. 5	613. 7	119	90	90	100	+0. 5	643	519	81

STATISTICS BEHIND THE MAPS—Continued

	Total population			Average annual wages, wage earners in industry and commerce			Area of construction permits, 3 years 1959–61 less 3 years 1953–55 divided by active industrial population, 1954, square meters per capita	Number of jobseekers without jobs		
	1954 Census	1962 Census	Index 1954=100	Relative level, 1954, France =100	Relative level, 1961, France =100	Change, 1961 to 1964, (5)+(4)		Per 10,000 active industrial population 1954	Per 10,000 active industrial population 1962	Index, 1954=100
	(1)	(2)	(3)	(4)	(5)	(6)	(7)	(8)	(9)	(10)
Bouches du Rhône	1, 048. 8	1, 241. 4	118	104	106	102	+0. 4	629	347	55
Var	413. 0	485. 1	117	83	83	100	+0. 2	136	203	150
Vaucluse	268. 3	301. 8	112	79	82	103	+0. 7	528	207	39
Corse	247. 0	275. 6	112	77	72	93	−0. 2	670	267	40
Provence	(2, 662. 0)	(3, 098. 4)	(116)	(96)	(97)	(101)	(+0. 4)	....	....	....
All of France	42, 777. 2	46, 242. 5	108	100	100	100	+0. 8	242	132	55

Column 3: See map 7.
Column 4: See map 3.
Column 5: See map 5.
Column 6: See map 9.
Column 7: See map 8.
Column 8: See map 4.
Column 9: See map 6.
Column 10: See map 10.

[1] Basses Alpes: No construction permits issued in either of the 2 periods.

INDEX OF CHANGE IN THE ACTIVE INDUSTRIAL POPULATION 1946–54

[Excluding food and agricultural industries]

	Population 1946 (1)	Projected 1954 population based on national average growth by industry (2)	Actual 1954 population (3)	Index: (3)÷(2)
NORD				
Région du Nord:				
Nord	399, 496	485, 570	462, 657	95. 3
Pas-de-Calais	217, 209	235, 083	226, 017	96. 1
PARIS				
Région parisienne:				
Seine	846, 903	1, 018, 888	1, 095, 393	107. 5
Seine-et-Marne	47, 789	57, 710	63, 656	110. 3
Seine-et-Oise	225, 356	227, 861	317, 688	114. 3
BASSIN PARISIEN				
Picardie:				
Aisne	48, 223	58, 677	61, 319	104. 5
Oise	52, 502	64, 707	62, 601	96. 7
Somme	56, 505	68, 875	60, 889	88. 4
Champagne:				
Ardennes	33, 328	42, 412	49, 330	116. 3
Aube	37, 480	46, 560	44, 884	96. 4
Marne	36, 191	43, 150	43, 418	100. 6
Haute-Marne	20, 117	24, 288	26, 133	107. 6
Centre:				
Cher	32, 649	38, 875	38, 210	98. 3
Eure-et-Loir	21, 950	25, 652	26, 102	101. 8
Indre	24, 861	27, 187	27, 048	99. 5
Indre-et-Loire	35, 527	40, 127	37, 951	94. 6
Loir-et-Cher	21, 564	24, 048	24, 232	100. 8
Loiret	37, 246	43, 682	45, 233	103. 6
Haute Normandie:				
Eure	38, 275	46, 000	45, 254	98. 4
Seine-Maritime	127, 932	157, 852	142, 783	90. 5
OUEST				
Basse Normandie:				
Calvados	46, 468	57, 108	48, 216	84. 4
Manche	37, 324	43, 114	34, 061	79. 0
Orne	26, 181	30, 541	25, 493	83. 5
Pays de la Loire:				
Loire-Atlantique	81, 403	97, 330	100, 266	103. 0
Maine-et-Loire	55, 617	61, 596	61, 448	99. 8
Mayenne	20, 130	22, 721	20, 353	89. 6
Sarthe	34, 016	38, 962	41, 454	106. 4
Vendée	26, 649	28, 931	30, 316	104. 8

INDEX OF CHANGE IN THE ACTIVE INDUSTRIAL POPULATION 1946–54—Continued

	Population 1946 (1)	Projected 1954 population based on national average growth by industry (2)	Actual 1954 population (3)	Index: (3)÷(2)
OUEST—continued				
Bretagne:				
Côtes-du-Nord	30, 254	33, 345	30, 183	90. 5
Finistère	59, 384	68, 111	59, 336	87. 1
Ille-et-Vilaine	51, 959	56, 926	52, 741	92. 6
Morbihan	36, 136	41, 434	40, 866	98. 6
EST				
Lorraine:				
Meurthe-et-Moselle	84, 987	107, 249	121, 233	113. 0
Meuse	19, 419	23, 596	26, 693	113. 1
Moselle	96, 357	116, 167	167, 685	144. 3
Vosges	64, 221	77, 997	84, 918	108. 9
Alsace:				
Bas-Rhin	83, 569	101, 010	110, 781	109. 7
Haut-Rhin	83, 096	105, 165	115, 887	110. 2
Franche-Comté:				
Doubs	45, 557	57, 781	63, 265	109. 5
Jura	25, 092	31, 093	30, 478	98. 0
Haute-Saône	22, 866	27, 022	28, 698	106. 2
Territoire de Belfort	16, 933	21, 822	23, 810	109. 1
SUD-EST				
Bourgogne:				
Côte-d'or	31, 267	37, 245	25, 195	94. 4
Nièvre	24, 383	29, 166	25, 194	86. 3
Saône-et-Loire	64, 331	76, 117	70, 931	93. 1
Yonne	23, 692	27, 408	23, 847	87. 0
Rhône-Alpes:				
Ain	33, 319	40, 216	40, 789	101. 4
Ardèche	24, 027	29, 075	29, 630	101. 9
Drôme	29, 641	33, 639	36, 455	108. 3
Loire	142, 092	171, 335	157, 909	92. 2
Rhône	180, 230	216, 380	210, 965	97. 4
Isère	100, 309	122, 022	131, 063	107. 4
Savoie	25, 153	31, 270	35, 603	113. 8
Haute-Savoie	24, 756	30, 159	39, 451	130. 8
MASSIF CENTRAL				
Auvergne:				
Allier	39, 176	47, 227	42, 403	89. 7
Cantal	10, 306	11, 542	10, 493	90. 2
Haute-Loire	20, 966	24, 955	21, 928	87. 8
Puy-de-Dôme	57, 767	72, 124	73, 402	101. 7

INDEX OF CHANGE IN THE ACTIVE INDUSTRIAL POPULATION 1946–54—Continued

	Population 1946 (1)	Projected 1954 population based on national average growth by industry (2)	Actual 1954 population (3)	Index: (3)÷(2)
MASSIF CENTRAL—continued				
Limousin:				
Corrèze	20, 776	24, 183	22, 047	91. 1
Creuse	12, 624	14, 700	11, 067	75. 2
Haute-Vienne	40, 089	45, 450	44, 233	97. 3
SUD-OUEST				
Poitou-Charentes:				
Charente	30, 145	36, 308	32, 561	89. 6
Charente-Maritime	31, 940	37, 166	40, 285	108. 3
Deux-Sèvres	21, 947	24, 223	23, 981	99. 0
Vienne	25, 403	29, 145	25, 609	87. 8
Aquitaine:				
Dordogne	27, 482	31, 550	30, 971	95. 3
Gironde	91, 639	106, 518	95, 118	89. 2
Landes	21, 135	24, 057	22, 325	92. 8
Lot-et-Garonne	19, 607	22, 721	21, 231	93. 4
Basses Pyrénées	39, 574	43, 260	44, 070	101. 8
Midi-Pyrénées:				
Ariège	15, 653	19, 546	15, 689	80. 2
Aveyron	26, 339	28, 510	26, 706	93. 6
Haute-Garonne	59, 336	71, 699	62, 935	87. 7
Gers	8, 772	10, 076	8, 035	79. 7
Lot	8, 617	10, 018	9, 045	90. 2
Haute-Pyrénées	22, 838	29, 271	25, 830	91. 3
Tarn	40, 228	47, 110	44, 093	93. 5
Tarn-et-Garonne	11, 342	13, 038	11, 449	87. 8
MEDITERRANEE				
Languedoc:				
Aude	19, 214	21, 778	17, 354	79. 6
Gard	45, 651	50, 134	46, 159	92. 0
Hérault	35, 990	41, 679	33, 896	81. 3
Lozère	3, 324	3, 848	3, 901	101. 3
Pyrénées-Orientales	17, 759	20, 269	16, 093	79. 3
Provence-Côte D'Azur:				
Basses-Alpes	6, 556	7, 947	6, 993	87. 9
Hautes-Alpes	4, 950	5, 851	6, 589	112. 6
Alpes-Maritimes	48, 377	55, 291	57, 062	103. 2
Bouches-du-Rhône	120, 424	144, 030	122, 363	84. 9
Var	44, 200	54, 256	46, 003	84. 7
Vaucluse	21, 069	25, 183	24, 514	97. 3

Appendix III

RECAPITULATION OF THE POSITION OF THE DEPARTMENTS WITH RESPECT TO THE 4 INDEXES OF CHANGE, 1954–62

The figures give the classification of the department in the distribution into seven categories of rank used in construction of maps.

The sign shows the position of the department with respect to the national average:

= equal to the national average.

+ greater than the national average.

— less than the national average.

	Criteria				Sum of the 4 ranks, map XI
	Total popula-tion, map VII	Construc-tion permits, map VIII	Average wages, map IX	Number of job-seekers, map X	
NORD					
Région du Nord:					
Nord	4=	6—	4—	1+	15
Pas de Calais	4—	5—	7—	2=	18
PARIS					
Région parisienne:					
Seine	4=	7—	2+	2+	15
Seine et Marne	2+	4+	1+	2+	9
Seine et Oise	1+	6—	2+	2+	11
BASSIN PARISIEN					
Picardie:					
Aisne	5—	2+	3=	2+	12
Oise	3+	2+	2+	2+	9
Somme	5—	4+	3+	2=	14
Champagne:					
Ardennes	4—	5+	3—	2+	14
Aube	5—	3+	3=	1+	12
Marne	4—	5=	3+	2+	14
Haute Marne	5—	4+	5—	7—	21
Centre:					
Cher	5—	6—	4—	3—	18
Eure et Loir	4—	1+	3+	2+	10
Indre	6—	4+	7—	4—	21
Indre et Loir	4=	3+	3—	3—	13
Loir et Cher	5—	2+	3=	3—	13
Loiret	4=	1+	4—	2+	11
Haute Normandie:					
Eure	4=	4+	3—	4—	15
Seine Maritime	3+	4+	4—	2+	13
OUEST					
Basse Normandie:					
Calvados	4=	7—	3—	4—	18
Manche	6—	6—	7—	4—	23
Orne	6—	3+	3=	2+	14

RECAPITULATION OF THE POSITION OF THE DEPARTMENTS WITH RESPECT TO THE 4 INDEXES OF CHANGE, 1954–62—Con.

	Criteria				Sum of the 4 ranks, map XI
	Total population, map VII	Construction permits, map VIII	Average wages, map IX	Number of job-seekers, map X	
OUEST—continued					
Pays de la Loire:					
Loire Atlantique	4=	6−	5−	5−	20
Maine et Loire	4−	4+	5−	4−	17
Mayenne	6−	1+	5−	4−	16
Sarthe	5−	3+	6−	3−	17
Vendée	5−	6−	4−	7−	22
Bretagne:					
Côtes du Nord	6−	4+	4−	4−	18
Finistère	5−	6−	4−	6−	21
Ille et Vilaine	5−	1+	2+	3−	11
Morbihan	6−	6−	7−	7−	26
EST					
Lorraine:					
Meurthe et Moselle	3+	6−	3−	2+	14
Meuse	5−	5+	4−	3−	17
Moselle	1+	6−	3=	1+	11
Vosges	5−	5+	7−	5−	22
Alsace:					
Bas Rhin	4=	2+	2+	1+	9
Haut Rhin	4−	5+	3−	3−	15
Franche-Comté:					
Doubs	1+	4+	3=	3−	11
Jura	5−	7−	3−	2+	17
Haute Saône	6−	5=	5−	} 3−	19
Territoire de Belfort	3+	6−	5−		17
SUD-EST					
Bourgogne:					
Côte d'or	4=	4+	4−	3−	15
Nièvre	6−	3+	2+	4−	15
Saône et Loire	5−	5−	4−	3−	17
Yonne	6−	2+	3=	3−	14
Rhône-Alpes:					
Ain	5−	4+	3=	6−	18
Ardèche	6−	6−	3+	2+	17
Drôme	3+	4+	3−	1+	11
Loire	5−	6−	3−	2+	16
Rhône	2+	5+	2+	2+	11
Isère	2+	4+	2+	3−	11
Savoie	5−	6−	3=	3−	17
Haute Savoie	2+	3+	1+	3−	9
MASSIF CENTRAL					
Auvergne:					
Allier	5−	5−	6−	3−	19
Cantal	7−	6−	5−	3−	21

RECAPITULATION OF THE POSITION OF THE DEPARTMENTS WITH RESPECT TO THE 4 INDEXES OF CHANGE, 1954–62—Con.

	Criteria				Sum of the 4 ranks, map XI
	Total population, map VII	Construction permits, map VIII	Average wages, map IX	Number of job-seekers, map X	
MASSIF CENTRAL—con.					
Auvergne—Continued					
Haute Loire	7−	1+	5−	2+	15
Puy de Dôme	4−	5+	5−	2+	16
Limousin:					
Corrèze	6−	6−	5−	3−	18
Creuse	7−	5+	2+	2+	16
Haute Vienne	5−	6−	4−	2+	17
SUD-OUEST					
Poitou-Charentes:					
Charente	5−	1+	4−	6−	16
Charente Maritime	5−	6−	3−	4−	18
Deux Sèvres	6−	4+	2+	7−	19
Vienne	5−	2+	4−	3−	14
Aquitaine:					
Dordogne	6−	5+	7−	3−	21
Gironde	5−	5+	4−	3−	17
Landes	5−	7−	5−	3−	20
Lot et Garonne	5−	2+	5−	3−	15
Basses Pyrénées	3+	3+	1+	5−	12
Midi-Pyrénées:					
Ariège	7−	5+	5−	2+	19
Aveyron	6−	6−	6−	4−	22
Haute Garonne	2+	4+	2+	4−	12
Gers	7−	4+	3+	6−	20
Lot	6−	4+	6−	3−	19
Hautes Pyrénées	5−	6−	4−	3−	18
Tarn	5−	5+	5−	3−	18
Tarn et Garonne	6−	5+	5−	3−	19
MEDITERRANEE					
Languedoc:					
Aude	6−	5+	5−	2+	18
Gard	3+	6−	3+	2+	14
Hérault	3+	6−	3−	2+	14
Lozère	6−	7−	2+	2+	17
Pyrénées Orientales	3+	6−	7−	3−	19
Provence:					
Basses Alpes	3+	7−	1+	3−	14
Hautes Alpes	5−	5+	1+	7−	18
Alpes Maritimes	1+	6−	3=	4−	14
Bouches du Rhône	1+	6−	2+	2=	11
Var	1+	6−	3=	6−	16
Vaucluse	3+	5−	2+	2+	12
Corse	3+	7−	5−	2+	17

Part 4

Area Redevelopment in the Federal Republic of Germany

Dietrich Storbeck*

*This study does not concern itself with aid to the economy of West Berlin, inasmuch as such aid is extended exclusively for political reasons. This special situation demands and justifies extraordinary development measures (tax exemptions and subsidies) which are not part of the Federal area redevelopment policy. Their inclusion would lead beyond the scope of this study and create a wrong impression of the German area redevelopment policy.

Contents

Development Areas in Germany

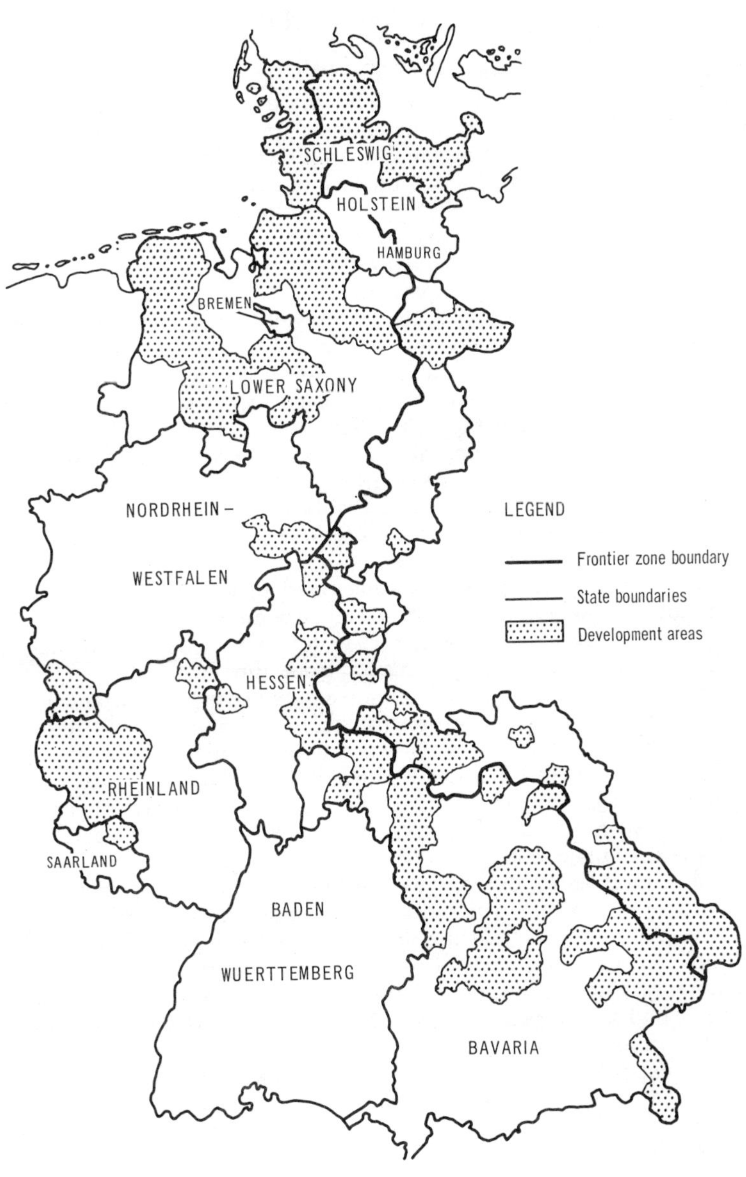

761-932 O—65——12

Regional Economic Development Since the War

General Development

The economic development of the Federal Republic of Germany has, to a large extent, been determined by population changes resulting from World War II and its aftermath. These changes have considerably altered the size, composition, and regional distribution of the population. During the war plants were closed down for lack of raw materials, loss of jobs as a result of war damage was heavy, and regional shifts of particular production processes led to a decrease in the number of jobs. However, because of the simultaneous fall in the labor supply, these developments had no disruptive effects on employment.

From 1939 to 1950, in spite of the losses suffered in the war, the population increased by 7.3 million to a total of 49.4 million, an increase of 17.3 percent. This increase was due mainly to an influx of expellees from the German areas in the east, and only slightly to the natural rate of increase, which had fallen during the war. The determining factor, therefore, in the change in the population structure was the immigration of expellees and their demographic composition and regional distribution. The ratio of females to males increased considerably (in 1939 it was 105 to 100; in 1950, 114 to 100), and though the labor force increased in size, it decreased as a percentage of total population.[1]

In subsequent years, population increased further through immigration and natural growth. Immigration still accounted for about 52 percent of the total increase in the period 1951–60 (5.5 million). In these years the immigrants were mainly refugees from the Soviet Zone (DDR) of Germany; the immigration of foreign workers became important only after 1959. As the younger generation predominated among these immigrants, the age structure of the West German population improved considerably (at the expense of the DDR). By the end of 1959 approximately 37.6 million inhabitants, or 68 percent of the total population, were of working age, that is, between 15 and 65 years. This constant inflow of labor and its more intensive use opened the way to economic expansion.

In the immediate postwar years, however, despite a pent-up demand for consumer goods, the demand for labor, which had fallen because of war damage, plant closures, and the dismantling of war production plants, was not sufficient to provide employment for the enlarged supply of labor. It was impossible to use the additional labor in agriculture, as the family farms generally had sufficient farm labor. Nor could the tertiary industries absorb the mass unemployment; commerce, transportation, and other services could be expanded only with the increase of purchasing power. In public employment there was, temporarily, overemployment, due to political changes. On the other hand, almost all handicrafts and the construction industry were expanding as a result of the war damage and the pent-up demand in general. Since these constituted a fairly small part of the West German economy, however, their expansion did not greatly affect other sectors.

[1] In 1939, there were 68.8 percent of the total population between 15 and 65 years of age; in 1950, only 67.2 percent.

By 1950 the labor force[2] exceeded its 1939 total by 12 percent. The census of September 1950 showed about 2 million more in the labor force than before the war, while there were 1.7 million unemployed (according to the statistics of the unemployment offices). At the same time, the agricultural labor force had decreased by 280,000.[3] The increase in the labor supply was in industry and the services, and the large number of unemployed came from these sectors.

As the labor force grew, it also changed in character. Before the war one-third of the nonagricultural labor force of 19.7 million had been self-employed.[4] After the war, despite the large proportion of formerly self-employed among the refugees, the percentage of wage and salaried employees increased steadily since the refugees had of necessity to join their ranks. By 1950 the proportion had risen to about 72 percent. From 1950 to 1960 the increase of wage and salaried employees (4.3 million) was greater than that of the total nonagricultural labor force (3.4 million). In September 1960 the Federal Republic had a labor force of 25,464,000, of which 20,665,700 (or 79 percent) were employed by others. Thus the susceptibility to crises and to the threat of unemployment has increased considerably in the German economy.

Between 1950 and 1960, however, unemployment was almost completely eliminated in the Federal Republic. In the fall of 1960 there were about 5.4 million more persons employed in industry than in 1939. The increase in total nonagricultural employment was even greater, since the decline in agriculture continued. As a result of the general mechanization of agriculture and policy measures to improve the agricultural structure, and especially because of low incomes in agriculture, the number of people employed on farms decreased by about 1.6 million from 1950 to 1960. This decline was completely absorbed by the expanding economic sectors.[5]

In this decade, manufacturing and mining showed the greatest increase in employment; they employed workers who could no longer find employment in the declining handicrafts. Between 1950 and 1960 total nonagricultural employment increased by 2.5 million to a total of 12.3 million. With the industrial expansion, employment in commerce and transportation also increased considerably—1.6 million in the last decade. Finally, employment in the service sectors rose substantially, particularly in the private services. The employment developments within the German economy, therefore, correspond to the general trend in developed countries. In contrast to a decline in the primary sectors (in this case, agriculture), there was an increase in the secondary industries and a great increase in the tertiary sector.

The immigration of expellees and refugees from the east played a decisive part in determining the nature of the reconstruction. Having lost all they possessed, these people worked particularly hard, in order to reestablish themselves as rapidly as possible. Their initiative, together with the mass-production processes of modern industrial society, impelled the economic expansion even more than the general drive for reconstruction. Apart from

---

[2] This includes the temporarily unemployed.

[3] This decline was mainly due to war losses among the agricultural population.

[4] Census of occupations of May 17, 1939.

[5] The agricultural policies hastened, to some extent, the elimination of older farmers, who made their estates available for new enterprises in exchange for an appropriate pension ("natural rent").

this, the loss of property suffered by many West Germans and the general shortage of commodities awakened economic ingenuity and industriousness in the local population. These factors, combined with the expansion of industry induced by sound economic policies and the impact of mass consumption of industrial goods, led to the rapid economic recovery which became known as the "German miracle."

Simultaneously with the reconstruction of the German economy, every effort was made to combat unemployment. Here the Marshall plan constituted a great help. By 1950 the number of unemployed had fallen to 1.69 million, though the unemployment rate [6] was still 10.2 percent in September 1950.[7] The rate fell below 10 percent for the first time in September 1952, to 6.4 percent (1,050,600). When in 1955 it fell below 3 percent, by general standards the Federal Republic had reached full employment (less than 3 percent). However, a further fall in unemployment brought the rate below 2 percent in September 1957, and below 1 percent in September 1959.[8] In September 1961 the rate was only 0.5 percent of all employees, while over half a million foreign workers were employed in the Federal Republic.

The amount of unemployment existing at the present time is therefore very small, and even in the underdeveloped areas it has fallen to levels that allow us to speak of full employment within the entire Federal Republic. The unemployment figures, of course, give only the number of statistically unemployed and not the total potential supply of labor.[9] Actually almost every labor market still contains silent reserves, i.e., a latent labor supply that becomes effective only with appropriate conditions (wage level, proximity to place of work, working hours, etc.). The growing proportion of women workers indicates the increasing importance of these silent reserves in a state of full employment. In general, however, employment has reached such a high level that endeavors to eliminate the remaining regional unemployment are of secondary importance compared with efforts to augment the labor supply by hiring foreign workers. Great unemployment 10 years ago has been followed by an acute shortage of labor, which was not apparent before 1961 because of the constant flow of refugees from the DDR, but which has definitely been felt since the complete separation of East Germany.[10]

---

[6] Unemployed as a percentage of the total labor force (employed and unemployed).

[7] The level of unemployment decreases seasonally in winter (e.g., in the construction industry) and is, therefore, lower in spring than in autumn (end of September).

[8] With the decrease of unemployment, the number of "homeworkers" has declined, too: in September 1959, there were about 177,000 "homeworkers" (mainly women). "Bericht ueber die Arbeitsmarktlage in der Bundesrepublik und in Berlin-West im Jahre 1959," *Bundesarbeitsblatt,* 11. Jg. (1960), No. 8, pp. 269 ff.

[9] Cf., "Die Struktur der restlichen Arbeitslosigkeit in der Bundesrepublik Deutschland (eine Untersuchung ueber Angebot und Nachfrage auf dem Arbeitsmarkt vom Herbst 1958)," *Amtliche Nachrichten der Bundesanstalt fuer Arbeitsvermittlung und Arbeitslosenversicherung,* 7. Jg. (1959), No. 3, Beilage, pp. 5 ff.

[10] Since 1959, problems connected with the hiring of foreign workers have been in the foreground in the *Amtliche Nachrichten der Bundesanstalt fuer Arbeitsvermittlung und Arbeitslosenversicherung* (subsequently cited as *Amtliche Nachrichten der Bundesanstalt*).

Regional Development

The war and its consequences also affected the regional distribution of the population. During the war some of the nonworking population was evacuated from the large cities. The destruction of residential areas in industrial centers further contributed to the depopulation of the cities. At the end of the war the expellees from the eastern territories [11] went at first to the rural areas, rather than to the bombed cities. Consequently, there was a large increase in the rural and a decrease in the urban populations. These changes in the regional distribution made the elimination of unemployment particularly difficult, as additional jobs could be found only in the course of reconstruction of the cities and their industries. With only a few exceptions, reconstruction was started at the old sites, as it was here that quick results might be expected.

The chance to change the regional structure of the population over the long term by establishing new residential and industrial centers was not seized upon. As reconstruction was left almost completely in the hands of the private economy, the old regional structure of industry soon predominated again. Extensive migrations brought the maldistributed population to the newly created industrial jobs, so that by 1950 many West German cities had already regained their prewar population. These migrations usually occurred in stages—from the country to the small towns, to the larger towns, and finally to the cities. Communities of all sizes increased in population in the period 1939–60, particularly the cities of 10,000 to 100,000 inhabitants. Often these cities lie close to the industrial centers, whose importance thus increased even more. From 1939 to 1960, the increase of the rural population was much less than that of the urban population.

The country-to-city movement was especially characteristic of the expellees. However, the immigrants from the DDR were often directed to those areas that had been left by expellees in the course of this migration.[12] At first the reason for such a distribution policy may have been the presumed temporary nature of the movement of refugees from the DDR; later, however, it could have been only the fact that housing facilities were available in these areas. At any rate, developments have shown that these areas could hold neither the expellees nor the refugees.

Between 1956 and 1961 there were population decreases especially in the east and the north of the Federal Republic, i.e., in the depressed areas of today. This means that the previous migrations had not sufficiently corrected the relationship between the existing labor supply in certain areas and their employment capacity and that it remains uncorrected. The greatest part of the population increase between 1956 and 1961 occurred in the urban industrial centers, while in the areas with a mixed economic structure population increased at the average rate. In the depressed areas along the border of the Eastern Zone, and in the agricultural depressed areas, population stagnated or decreased.[13]

---

[11] Areas beyond the Oder/Neisse line.

[12] W. Nellner, "Die Wanderungsbilanz der Vertriebenen und Zugewanderten in den Kreisen des Bundesgebietes," *Informationen des Instituts fuer Raumforschung,* 6. Jg. (1956), No. 16, pp. 407 ff., esp. p. 414.

[13] W. Sahner, "Aspekte der regionalen Differenzierung der Bevoelkerungsentwicklung in der Bundesrepublik Deutschland von 1956 bis 1961," *Informationen des Instituts fuer Raumforschung,* 12. Jg. (1962), No. 14, pp. 334 ff.

The original maldistribution of the expellees is evident not only in their subsequent migrations, but also in the obvious discrepancy between employment capacity and population of the areas affected, which showed high rates of unemployment. The most important regions for the settlement of expellees and refugees were the rural areas, with work opportunities determined by the extent of the cultivated areas, unless additional employment was made available through industrialization. Such jobs, however, were seldom created because reconstruction was left to private initiative. The refugee enterprises that were established in the agricultural areas soon ran into difficulties; many of these small businesses were given up because of the relative backwardness of the regions in which they were located. The correcting migration, or redistribution of the population, was, of course, retarded by such undertakings.

Statistics for 1950 and 1955 show the effect of the movement of expellees on the rate of unemployment in various *Laender*. In 1950 Schleswig-Holstein, Lower Saxony, and Bavaria, which had a large number of expellees, had the highest rates of unemployment.[14] In Schleswig-Holstein, for example, 57 percent of all unemployed and 68 percent of the long-term unemployed were expellees. In this *Land*, whose population had increased by two-thirds after the war through the admittance of expellees and refugees, 30 percent of all registered employees were still without work in the spring of 1950, and almost 22 percent in the autumn of 1950. Because of the extensive emigration of expellees from Schleswig-Holstein [15] to areas with better employment possibilities, the unemployment rate decreased to about 7 percent by the fall of 1955.[16] The general economic growth had led to expansion particularly in the industrial centers of the Federal Republic, which attracted the unemployed from areas with less employment. Aided by Federal resettlement funds (under the policy of "passive area redevelopment"), the emigration brought about a decrease of regional unemployment rates.

A serious consequence of these "correcting migrations" was the fact that the most unproductive and immobile immigrants stayed in the depressed areas. The employment opportunities in the industrial cities were seized mainly by the younger workers, while the older unemployed remained, their immobility being fortified by their increasing security through social policy measures.[17] Consequently, while the overall unemployment decreased, the proportion of the younger unemployed (those under 45 years of age) decreased even more. The possibilities of absorbing the older unemployed were rather restricted because of their limited occupational and regional mobility. A further difficulty arose from the often low occupational skills of the immigrants, who came predominantly from the agricultural areas of East Germany.[18] Their absorption in industry demanded a switch to industrial work, which was difficult for the older persons.

[14] "Die Struktur der Arbeitslosigkeit im Bundesgebiet," *Bundesarbeitsblatt*, 1. Jg. (1950), No. 12, pp. 440 ff.

[15] H. P. Kuehl, "Entwicklung und Struktur der Arbeitslosigkeit in Schleswig-Holstein," *Informationen des Instituts fuer Raumforschung*, 6. Jg. (1956), No. 9, pp. 232 ff.

[16] At this time, the average for the Federal Republic was 2.7 percent.

[17] Measures within the scope of the "Equalization of War Burdens" (compensation for war damages), recognition and gradual increase of the rights to rents, recognition of pension rights, and the revaluation of insurance claims and stocks.

[18] This holds for the immigrants to the north of the Federal Republic (Schleswig-Holstein), at least.

Consequently, the effects of immigration were particularly grave for the areas that were already depressed before the war. These are mainly the agricultural areas in the low mountains where gainful employment is limited by the unfavorable conditions of production.[19] Inadequate transport and public utility services have rendered industrial development in these areas more difficult, while agriculture already has a surplus of labor on the small family farms. These areas with relatively high unemployment rates stand out in the otherwise fully employed German economy. For instance, the average rate of unemployment in September 1959 was 0.9 percent,[20] while the unemployment rates of the Laender ranged from 0.2 percent (Baden-Wuerttemberg) to 2.2 percent (Schleswig-Holstein). The differences were even greater for smaller districts (districts served by one employment office), with a range of 0.1 percent to 5.7 percent.

The unemployment rate, of course, tells us little about the economic use of the regional labor potential, as the unemployment figure encompasses only the registered unemployed.[21] It does not include the latent labor reserves who, under favorable conditions, are ready to work. Area redevelopment policies, therefore, should not be based only on the unemployment rate, since then the areas with below average use of their potential labor supply might possibly be left out.[22] Apart from farm workers released by structural improvements in agriculture, additional workers who had not been offered employment before may be available in the course of industrialization. A small number of women workers is typical of areas with insufficient employment opportunity. The one-sided structure of the economy of these areas is not adequate to employ the resident population. Further, both the unemployed and the latent reserves are to a great extent immobile, because of family ties, part-time employment, and small farms, so that they are unaffected by "passive area redevelopment," that is, resettlement assistance.

Consequently, effective economic development and simultaneous elimination of the remaining unemployment can be achieved only through active area redevelopment policies, i.e., through assistance in the creation of new jobs adapted to the existing labor potential. The area redevelopment measures of the Federal Republic, therefore, are directed primarily to these areas, in an effort to reduce employment in agriculture through structural improvements, to raise nonagricultural employment through industrialization, and to further general economic development through improving transport systems and public utilities by means of public funds.

With the general fall in unemployment in the course of West Germany's industrial expansion, regional differences have diminished. They still exist,

---

[19] G. Mueller, "Ursachen geminderter Arbeitstaetigkeit und Moeglichkeiten zur Behebung geringerer Erwerbstaetigkeit," *Bundesarbeitsblatt,* 12. Jg. (1961), Heft 13, pp. 414 ff. Also cf., "Arbeitskraftreserven in schwach industrialisierten Gebieten der Bundesrepublik," *Informationen des Instituts fuer Raumforschung,* 11. Jg. (1961), No. 18, pp. 499 ff.

[20] "Bericht ueber die Arbeitsmarktlage in der Bundesrepublik und in Berlin-West im Jahre 1959," *op. cit.,* pp. 269 ff.

[21] T. Galland, *Statistik der Beschaeftigten und Arbeitslosen in der Bundesrepublik Deutschland.* Schriftenreihe des Bundesarbeitsministeriums, Heft 3. Stuttgart, 1956. pp. 56 ff.

[22] Cf., "Die Struktur der restlichen Arbeitslosigkeit in der Bundesrepublik Deutschland (eine Untersuchung ueber Angebot und Nachfrage auf dem Arbeitsmarkt vom Herbst 1958)," *op. cit.,* pp. 5 ff.

however, as the structural causes of regional unemployment have by no means been eliminated. Further redevelopment measures will be necessary to eliminate the depressed areas' susceptibility to adverse effects from even a small decrease in the rate of economic growth. The uneven regional economic structure of the Federal Republic and the regional distribution of particular jobs (e.g., for foreign workers) point to the necessity of such stabilization measures. Because of the high mobility of the refugees and the use of foreign workers, industry has not so far had to tap the labor reserves by means of new investments in the depressed areas. This explains, in part, the small success of area redevelopment policy to date.

The Present Regional Structure

As indicated above, the events of the war have not evened out the regional economic structure of the Federal Republic. Population concentrations in the industrial areas contrast with the lightly settled areas in the great agricultural regions. The greatest difference in population density in 1960 was between 42 inhabitants per square kilometer in the Land district [23] of Pruem/Eifel and 767 inhabitants per square kilometer in the Land district of Aachen. With a total area of 247,954 square kilometers and a population of 53,372,600, the average density of the Federal Republic was about 213 inhabitants per square kilometer. Even the average figures for the Laender differ greatly: For Bavaria the average is 129, and for Nordrhein-Westfalen it is 436 inhabitants per square kilometer. The differences are due mainly to the irregular distribution of the great cities and the agglomerations within the Federal Republic. There are nine major agglomerations,[24] which in 1960 had about 22.6 million inhabitants, or 43.5 percent of the population. These population centers are: Rhein-Ruhr (10.4 million inhabitants), Rhein-Main (2.5 million), Hamburg (2.3 million), Stuttgart (1.8 million), Rhein-Neckar (1.4 million), Muenchen (1.4 million), Hannover (1.0 million), Nuernberg (1.0 million), and Bremen (.8 million). Although the cities had regained their former peak populations by about 1950, these high-density centers still had a relatively greater population increase than the rest of the Federal Republic from 1956 to 1960; almost half the increase during this period occurred in the heavily populated centers.

The importance of the large cities in the regional population structure is also indicated by the distribution of the population according to size of community. The 52 cities with over 100,000 inhabitants had, by 1960, about 16.5 million inhabitants, or almost 31 percent of the total population of the Federal Republic; the communities with 10,000 to 100,000 inhabitants had about 12.7 million inhabitants or almost 24 percent of the total population; and the communities with less than 2,000 inhabitants also had about one-fourth.[25] During the war and postwar periods, it was the middle group which had gained relatively.

The uneven distribution of the population is due basically to the differences in regional economic structure, which are the result of the natural

---

[23] The Laender are divided into *Regierungs*—districts (33), and the latter again into county districts and urban districts (434,130).

[24] G. Isenberg, *Die Ballungsgebiete in der Bundesrepublik.* Vortraege des Instituts fuer Raumforschung, No. 6. Bad Godesberg, 1957.

[25] *Statistisches Jahrbuch fuer die Bundesrepublik Deutschland, 1961,* p. 45.

conditions of production and of historical events. The most important of these differences is the ratio of industrial employment;[26] only industry can expand basic production (primary and secondary sectors) in view of the fact that most agricultural lands have been developed. The tertiary sector can develop only on the basis of prior existence of employment in the primary and secondary sectors. Their increase depends on the increase in industrialization. The concentration of the population in a few high-density centers is, therefore, usually a consequence of the concentration of industrial jobs.

A recent analysis[27] has distinguished, apart from the urban agglomerations, agricultural zones (where agriculture is dominant), mixed zones (where agriculture is still dominant, but industry is represented to a greater degree), and industrial zones (where industry dominates). The agricultural zones occupy almost one-third of the total area of the Federal Republic with 13.7 percent (6.8 million) of the population, and an average population density of 90 inhabitants per square kilometer. A little more than one-third of the total area is occupied by the mixed zones, which have 10.9 million inhabitants, a population density of 120, 21.6 percent of the total population, and 14 percent of the total industrial employment. The number of inhabitants in the industrial zones is almost as large, but they have 28.3 percent of all industrial employees and a much greater population density (230). If one adds the industrial zones to the urban agglomerations, together they take up almost one-third of the total area of the Federal Republic, represent two-thirds of the total population, and contain over 80 percent of all industrial employees. Judging from the developments to date, there will be further migrations from the agricultural zones, whereas the mixed zones have a good chance of population increases, if industry expands further. Without significant agriculture or industry, some areas have tourism as a primary source of income.[28]

Within the particular economic zones, economic development has been by no means the same. The depressed areas of the Federal Republic include agricultural, mixed, and industrial zones. The concurrence of several unfavorable circumstances hindered the economic growth of these areas, so that structural weaknesses have become obvious. The regional differences in the unemployment rate still existing today are predominantly caused by such structural defects, and only in the frontier areas by special political circumstances. Though boom conditions have decreased them, there are still large differences in regional unemployment rates.

According to a report of October 1958,[29] the Rhein-Ruhr and Rhein-Main agglomerations, as well as the entire southwest of the Federal Republic, suffered from a serious labor shortage, as their unemployment rates of below 1 percent showed. On the other hand, there were higher unemployment rates in the north (Schleswig-Holstein and Lower Saxony), and in the southeast (Bavaria), which betrayed the economic underdevelop-

---

[26] Number of industrial employees per 1,000 inhabitants.

[27] *Die Raumordnung in der Bundesrepublik Deutschland.* Gutachten des Sachverstaendigenausschusses fuer Raumordnung. Stuttgart, 1961, pp. 35 ff.

[28] G. Isenberg, "Bemerkungen zu einer Karte der oekonomischen Strukturzonen in der Bundesrepublik Deutschland," *Informationen des Instituts fuer Raumforschung,* 7. Jg. (1957), No. 19, pp. 475 ff.

[29] At this time the average unemployment rate for the Federal Republic was 1.7 percent.

ment of these areas. At that time, the depressed area Bayrischer Wald had the highest unemployment rates with an average of 8 percent followed by East Friesland with 5.5 percent and the northern part of Schleswig-Holstein, the area around Kassel, and a few areas in the southeast of Bavaria with average unemployment rates of about 3.5 percent. Areas of high unemployment with about the same economic structure are often found right next to each other. This points to the structural cause and the long-term significance of this type of unemployment.

The large number of registered foreign workers, approximately 650,000 in 1962,[30] emphasizes the great labor shortage in the economy as a whole. The areas of heavy foreign employment are the agglomerations and industrial zones, except where special circumstances in the frontier areas increase the exchange of labor with neighboring countries (e.g., Switzerland).[31] The use of foreigners in the depressed areas is very limited. Only in the more industrialized central portion of the frontier with East Germany are they used to a somewhat larger extent. The distribution of foreign workers therefore corresponds to the tightness of the regional labor markets. There can be no doubt that the loosening of the labor market by the hiring of foreigners has diminished the tapping of both the open and the silent labor reserves in the depressed areas. The general economic development and the Federal economic policy supporting this development, therefore, have not made full use of the available possibilities to even out the regional structure, and may even have destroyed some of them.

Regional Economic Policy

Federal Economic Policy

At the end of the war and up to the currency reform (1948), the German economy was centrally administered. This state of affairs had its origin in the general price freeze of the planned economy before the war and in the rationing measures of the war economy. Distribution of raw materials and consumer goods in short supply was achieved by nationwide rationing, while black markets to a small extent evened out the deficiencies. Before the formation of the "united economic area," a uniform economic policy was impossible because of the separation into Laender and Allied occupation zones, though each had an administered economy. Thus, a postwar German economic policy came into being only after the currency reform had established a common basis and when simultaneously the price freeze was ended for most commodities.

The basic concept of the economic policy that followed was the idea of the "Social Market Economy." It lead to an economic program that was liberal, but also directed toward social justice, and which generally encouraged private enterprise to help reconstruct the economy. Anticipating high

[30] In addition, there are presumably numerous foreigners employed who are not registered.

[31] G. Isbary, "Auslaendische Arbeitnehmer und inlaendischer Arbeitsmarkt," *Informationen des Instituts fuer Raumforschung,* 12. Jg. (1962), No. 24, pp. 629 ff.

profits in view of the generally low levels of consumption, entrepreneurs, on the one hand, were very willing to invest. Employees, on the other hand, were stimulated to work by the expected increase in consumption due to the currency reform and the end of rationing. Both of these influences led to a quick stabilization of the new currency and of the general economic situation. Nevertheless, in the following years numerous policy measures were taken to increase the GNP, in order to direct the productive capacity of the destroyed economy as fast as possible toward the needs of the enlarged population. Extensive measures to create jobs [32] and to increase the volume of investment were consequently the most important aspects of economic policy in these years.

However various bottlenecks could not be eliminated immediately, so that key prices (rents, coal, power, etc.) were still frozen, and the respective industries had to be expanded with Federal aid. Some measures had already been taken to relieve economic distress in areas hard hit by the war. Special redevelopment programs to create more jobs were carried out in areas with unemployment rates far above the average, in order to prevent increasing differences in the standard of living within the Federal Republic.[33] The early successes in the general reawakening of the economy raised hopes that Federal aid could quickly eliminate unemployment in these areas, too. In view of the rapid economic expansion, structural weaknesses of particular industries were paid as little attention as the weaknesses of particular areas.

The goal of the social market economy was also realized to a large extent with respect to the role of the state in the economy. Together with the currency reform, an independent Federal bank was created, whose policies sometimes had a strong impact on the economic system and occasionally were even directed against the objectives of the Government. After the attainment of full employment (1955) [34] Federal intervention in the economy was decreased in connection with social welfare measures, so that the ability of the state to influence economic development was considerably lessened. On the other hand, the share of the Government in the GNP grew, because no noticeable tax cuts were made; the increases in revenue stimulated Parliament's willingness to spend. Tax cuts would have helped the consumer in particular (e.g., by reduction in the rate of the turnover tax), and would have weakened the trend toward industrial integration and concentration which later became evident.

The state was particularly cautious and generally refrained from direct investment in the course of reconstruction, which came about largely through private initiative once Federal assistance by way of credit extension and the job creation program had ended. On the one hand, tax exemption for new capital investments led to high rates of investment and so stimulated the economy; on the other hand, it made possible the rapid formation of large concentrations of property in the private economy, which caused an overvaluation of the achievements of the latter and, at times, vain expectations.

---

[32] E.g., the job creation program of 1950.

[33] Epping, "Wirtschaftsbelebung und Arbeitsbeschaffung," *Bundesarbeitsblatt,* 1950, No. 10, pp. 370 ff.

[34] In 1955, for the first time, an unemployment rate of less than 3 percent was attained (September 1955: 2.7 percent).

With the economic expansion, based on increasing mass consumption and increasing exports, the goal of economic security and therewith the policies of stabilization and structural improvement became more important. Among these policies were constant endeavors to stabilize the currency, which sometimes even pushed the policies directed toward economic growth into the background. In spite of this, the boom led to continuous price increases, which had already caused export difficulties in some sectors.[35] In connection with these stabilization policies structural improvements in the depressed areas, which up to then were subject to employment policies only, gained greater significance.

At the same time, programs aiming at improvement of the general economic structure were developed. The best known among them is the "Green Plan,"[36] designed to aid agriculture. Whereas earlier policies had sought only the elimination of bottlenecks (in housing, energy, etc.) through the improvement of public utilities, now specific policies were directed at the elimination of structural deficiencies. These policies, often rather costly, aim at establishing a structure of production that is stable even under competitive pressures. Of course, they are mixed with other policies resulting from the pressures of special interest groups, which are neither "free enterprise" nor "social" in the sense of the basic concept.

The liberal principles of Germany's economic policy after the war extend to its foreign economic policy. The Federal Republic quickly accepted the idea of the economic integration of Europe and showed its willingness to participate in a free world market. Though the international situation seemed to warrant this policy, it also had its disadvantages. An especially good example is the situation of German agriculture, i.e., the clumsy Federal policies regarding structural improvements.

It is more difficult to characterize the social policy of the Federal Republic in a short paper. Improving social justice has created many difficulties for the "social market economy." On the one hand, economic reconstruction was brought about by favoring private capital; on the other hand, because of the war there was need for much more state aid than in normal times. Simultaneously, in the endeavor to increase social security for the entire population, state aid was increased greatly (rent reform, expansion of the health insurance program, etc.). These moves toward the "welfare state" have created problems for a free enterprise economy. By decreasing individual initiative and limiting the competitive market, the state assumes increasing responsibility. Recent developments have clearly shown that the social policy is also falling more and more under the influence of special interest groups, so that its basic principle can scarcely be realized. Social and economic policy becomes limited to particular measures, according to the particular pressures of individual groups or to the assumed wants of special blocks of voters. The full extent and the effect of such a dissipated policy cannot always be clearly foreseen and analyzed. Such measures often work against each other. Among these, area redevelopment constitutes only a small part.

---

[35] To some extent, however, these are sectors having export difficulties because of changes in demand.

[36] "Landwirtschaftsgesetz vom 5. September 1955," *Bundesgesetzblatt*, 1955, Teil I, pp. 565 ff.

The term "regional economic policy" may denote the Federal area redevelopment policy or it may denote the economic policies of the Laender and the communities. In the German literature it has been used mostly in the former sense.[37] Because of the differences between the Federal Government, the Laender, and the communities, the objectives, means, and effects of their regional economic policies differ, too. There are also differences in their constitutional and legislative authority.

The Federal Republic of Germany is a Federal state in which the Laender and the communities have important rights of legislation regarding regional policy. According to the Constitution, the Laender may "exercise governmental authority and carry out governmental responsibilities" unless the Constitution provides otherwise by special regulations. As to regional policy, such special regulations give the Federal Government authority with respect to territorial changes of the Laender,[38] exclusive legislative power for the Federal railways, air traffic, and the postal and telecommunications systems, and concurrent power of legislation for all other communications systems, for land tenure rights, and for housing regulations. In addition, the Federal Government has concurrent power of legislation for the tax system.[39] Finally, the Constitution authorizes the Federal Government to pass broad legislation regarding problems of spatial planning (*Raumordnung*).[40]

Apart from the basic rights of the individual, the Constitution guarantees the power of the communities "to regulate and bear the responsibility for all local affairs, within the framework of the law."[41] Hence local economic development is left to the communities, as well as developmental planning, which is mostly done by groups of communities (land planning associations). The power of the Federal Government to pass broad legislation regarding spatial planning does not encompass concrete and detailed planning of individual spatial development projects, but may concern itself only with the institutions and the form of such planning and with the determination of major objectives, in view of the equality of rights within the Federal Republic. Consequently, the Central Government can directly influence regional economic policy beyond its own sphere of authority only through its investments. Within the scope of its policy, it must encourage uniformity of the regional economic policies of the Laender and the communities.

The consequence of this situation is the existence of redevelopment areas

---

[37] Cf., *Zur Frage regionaler Wirtschaftspolitik.* Denkschrift des Instituts fuer Raumforschung. Bad Godesberg, 1954; and "Moeglichkeiten und Grenzen regionaler Wirtschaftspolitik" (Gutachten des Wissenschaftlichen Beirats beim Bundeswirtschaftsministerium), *Bulletin des Presse und Informationsamtes der Bundesregierung,* Jg. 1955, No. 59, pp. 481 ff.

[38] Article 29 of the Constitution (Grundgesetz).

[39] With the exception of taxes with purely local basis and impact. Of course, the Federal Government cannot determine the rates of the "real taxes" (profit and property taxes); consequently, there are great differences in these rates among different communities within the Federal Republic (article 105 of the Constitution).

[40] Article 75 of the Constitution.

[41] Article 28 of the Constitution. The article continues: "Associations of communities, too, have the right of self-government within the scope of their legal obligations."

of the Laender apart from those of the Federal Government;[42] and various instances show that there is also competition among the Laender.[43] The lack of uniform Federal regulations leads to differing development policies for two reasons:

(1) There is no general measuring rod with which to determine when an area is to receive redevelopment assistance; this leads to discrimination in the selection of redevelopment areas in the different Laender.

(2) The varying financial positions of the Laender, determined mainly by their respective economic structures, lead to differences in the extent of redevelopment measures that are not coordinated with Federal policies.

In practice, the differences between the Federal redevelopment policies and those of the Laender become especially important if the Federal and the Laender governments are run by different political parties.

Since the financial strength and thereby the policy of the Laender as well as of the Federal Government depend mainly on their tax revenues, the development of their economy constitutes a significant factor in their economic policy. Inasmuch as numerous Federal economic policy measures are carried out by the administrations of the Laender (e.g., housing policies, the "Green Plan"), and inasmuch as the Laender make certain investments of their own, the influence of Laender governments on economic development is often great. And the individual Land's role in determining Federal economic policy [44] is proportionate to its financial ability.

In order to prevent overlapping and contradiction, coordination of the measures of the Federal Government and the Laender is essential, but this cannot always be achieved.[45] The Federal Government can enforce coordination only regarding policies that it initiates. Moreover, even in this case the manner of implementation is sometimes left to the Laender. For instance, early in 1950, the Federal Government proclaimed a job creation program, for which funds amounting to DM 3.4 billion (about $800 million at prevailing rates of exchange) were appropriated. Although the Laender received general directives on implementation of the program, in several instances these funds were used for overdue public investment or special support for particular branches of industry.[46] In other instances the Federal development policies have missed their objective. In the case of credit

---

[42] A rich Land, like Nordrhein-Westfalen, could therefore enact extensive development programs (East Westfalen plan, Frontier program, "Randgebiets-program"), which included almost all frontier areas of this Land, only some of which are identical with Federal frontier areas. In view of the above-average income of employees, employment rate, and tax revenues in Nordrhein-Westfalen, these programs included areas which would not have been counted among redevelopment areas according to the standards of other Laender. E. Dittrich, "Haben wir eine konkrete raumpolitische Leitlinie?" Informationen des Instituts fuer Raumforschung, 10. Jg. (1960, No. 17, pp. 403 ff.

[43] E.g., the different developments in neighboring parts of Bavaria (west Mittelfranken) and Baden-Wuerttemberg (Hohenloher Land). Cf., *Die Raumordnung in der Bundersrepublik Deutschland, op. cit.*, p. 71.

[44] Through the "Bundesrat" (Senate), which must vote on all legislation.

[45] Dittrich, "Haben wir eine konkrete raumpolitische Leitlinie?" *op. cit.*, pp. 403 ff.

[46] "Das Arbeitsbeschaffungsprogramm der Bundesregierung fuer die finanzschwachen Laender," *Bundesarbeitsblatt*, 1. Jg. (1950), No. 8, pp. 290 ff.

extension to refugee enterprises, for example, the Laender were asked to guarantee these funds, but they demanded the usual financial securities.

The communities exert a stronger influence than the Central Government on the realization of regional economic policies through their local activities, though these are oriented toward completely different objectives. This orientation derives not only from the constitutional autonomy of the communities, but also from their peculiar position within the German financial system. Business taxes, whose level depends on either capital or payroll, form the largest part of community revenues.[47] Consequently, local budgets are determined mainly by the extent of industrialization, and so the communities attempt, by the most varied methods, to attract new and to enlarge existing industries.[48] However, in general only the communities that are financially well situated, due to their already high degree of industrialization, can afford to carry out such a policy.[49] The advantages offered to the companies they want to attract often surpass the stimulus to investment provided by the Federal development policy. The financially weak communities, on the other hand, need their revenues in full for current expenditures. Finally, the communities can attract industry also by means of general economic and social policy (e.g., "aid to the middle class").

In general, the financially weak communities, which lack the opportunities for industrial development, are found in the redevelopment areas. Inasmuch as the financially strong communities (large cities) with their urban facilities are already attractive to industry, local economic policy undermines the development measures of the Federal Government and of the Laender [50] and increases the divergencies between the rural and the industrial communities.[51] Thus an active redevelopment policy for the depressed areas becomes even more urgent. This situation also explains the economic policies through which the Laender attempt to decrease their internal differences in development.

In its regional economic policy, the Federal Government has other problems as well. Its policies necessarily take effect within the Laender and alongside the development measures of the Laender, while at the same time it must apply general standards, i.e., standards valid for the entire Federal area.[52] It has to limit its redevelopment measures to areas whose distress is above average or which are in a special emergency situation. Under the constitution, the Federal Government does not have the power to coordinate the various redevelopment measures of the Laender; it can only compensate for differences in development arising from divergent Laender policies by large offsetting Federal expenditures.

---

[47] Isenberg, "Bemerkungen zu einer Karte der oekonomischen Strukturzonen in der Bundesrepublik," *op. cit.*

[48] Even illegal tax exemptions have been offered.

[49] The communities guarantee investments, provide inexpensive industrial sites, and often offer additional support (construction of houses and roads, etc.).

[50] From an economic point of view, such a policy would be correct if it were based on actual productive advantages. Since, however, there are great differences among the "social costs" (which are not borne by the entrepreneurs), fictitious cost advantages often induce long-term investments (though these cost advantages are real for the private entrepreneur).

[51] The worker communities in the neighborhood of large industrial cities, who do not receive direct revenues from the profit tax, constitute a special problem.

[52] Cf., Dittrich, "Haben wir eine konkrete raumpolitische Leitlinie?" *op. cit.*, pp. 403 ff.

A further difficulty is the fact that general economic measures (i.e., those not regionally directed) have different regional effects because of structural differences.[53] For instance, the Federal development policies for small business (credits) are of practically no importance in regions with a high percentage of large corporations, while they are very significant in areas where small business predominates. Regional coordination of the general Federal policies is particularly difficult because their objectives—at least in recent years—have been determined more by political than by economic considerations. The "Green Plan" is such a general policy measure, an amply financed Federal program for the long-term structural improvement of German agriculture. Aside from the funds for general use, the Laender receive funds for particular policy measures (farm reorganization, road construction, protection of soil and watersheds, etc.). Therefore, within the framework of general directives, the Laender decide on the regional distribution of these funds according to their own standards, once the "development-worthiness" has been determined under the plan. This results in differences among the Laender in the realization of the plan; perhaps even greater differences if in the distribution of the funds the Laender are aided by the communities, which from their limited horizon always strive to obtain the largest possible share.

This fact is of even graver significance because the Federal Government depends on the aid of the communities in the realization of practically all policy measures. Consequently, it depends on the communities' judgment regarding the merit of particular activities. This difficulty cannot be prevented by the use of a different type of development measure unless the Federal Government establishes regional and local development offices—an unlikely event. The inclusion of district administrative authorities which are not influenced by the financial interests of the local community does not look very promising either, in view of the political relations between neighbor communities. Nor will matters be improved by the use of administrations at a higher level.[54] A basic change in this difficulty, or its elimination, can be expected only when the financial interests of the communities become organically connected with the fiscal interests of the higher authorities (Laender and Federal Government) through participation in other than business taxes. The present distribution of the tax revenues forces the communities into their present regional economic activities, the faults of which become evident only when they are analyzed in a wider context.

Spatial Planning

The term "regional policy" is not common in the Federal Republic,[55] although it is better than the more recently proposed *Raumordnungspolitik,*

---

[53] D. Storbeck, *Die wirtschaftliche Problematik der Raumordnung—eine Untersuchung ueber Notwendigkeit, Ziele und Mittel der Raumordnung im System der Marktwirtschaft.* Berlin, 1959, pp. 72 ff.

[54] Cf., E. Dittrich, "Der Beitrag der Landkreise in der Raumordnung," *Informationen des Instituts fuer Raumforschung,* 12. Jg. (1962), pp. 1 ff.

[55] Storbeck, *Die wirtschaftliche Problematik der Raumordnung, op. cit.,* p. 22.

or "spatial planning policy." [56] Spatial planning is often misunderstood to mean total planning. However, according to all the literature,[57] neither total nor partial planning is meant thereby, but only the creation of order through the establishment of criteria for development policy, taking account of the total space of the nation. The use of such criteria, of course, implies certain restrictions on the freedom of individual choice, as, for example, restrictions on the use of land. "Order means in this connection the elimination of tensions due to present use of space, harmonization in light of the principles of general welfare, establishing priorities among the various liberties claimed, according to the merits of each individual case, changing the contest between individual interests into a system of coordinated rights, and thus realizing the principles." [58] Inasmuch as such limitations of individual freedom will occur mainly in the area of economic decisions, the question (which has not to date been answered by the advocates of spatial planning) arises whether all the means consistent with a liberal economic policy have already been employed for the spatial planning objective, and whether such a policy cannot achieve it.[59]

It must be understood that the principles of spatial planning are derived from ideas of democratic freedom, and that it attempts to realize the concepts of "social justice" and of "social security" in the spatial interrelations of society. Nevertheless, the German public—which is very sensitive to such comprehensive planning—has strongly opposed the concept of spatial planning.[60] Against this opposition, no analysis of the principles of spatial planning, i.e., of their translation into concrete measures, which would allow economic calculations, has been undertaken to date.

Apart from the much earlier "land planning," [61] which consists of individual planning on the technical level and so varies in the different Laender, spatial order has not, until now, been a factor in the political practice of the Federal Republic. Spatial planning is mentioned once in the Constitution (art. 74), but no legislation has been enacted.[62] A general regional policy has not been formed, although in the course of the regional distribution of materials for housing construction and the resettlement of expellees and refugees connected therewith, the Federal Republic actually did undertake spatial planning measures. In the summer of 1952, when a bill on land acquisition for defense objectives was under consideration, the necessity of coordination of the Federal regional policy was emphasized for the first time. One year later, legislation was demanded by the representatives

---

[56] *Die Raumordnung in der Bundesrepublik Deutschland, op. cit.*, p. 11.

[57] *Loc. cit.*

[58] Ibid., p. 53. Also cf., E. Dittrich, "Das Leitbild einer zielbewussten Raumordnungspolitik in Stadt und Land," *Informationen des Instituts fuer Raumforschung* 12. Jg. (1962), No. 12, p. 540.

[59] Storbeck, *Die wirtschaftliche Problematik der Raumordnung, op. cit.*, pp. 85 ff. and pp. 139 ff.

[60] This is expressed in a particularly impressive way in "Moeglichkeiten und Grenzen regionaler Wirtschaftspolitik," *op. cit.*, pp. 481 ff. Also cf., *Die Raumordnung in der Bundesrepublik Deutschland, op. cit.*, p. 66.

[61] H.-W Klamroth, *Organisation und rechtliche Grundlage der Landesplanung in der Bundesrepublik Deutschland und in Berlin.* Mitteilungen aus dem Institut fuer Raumforschung, No. 16. Bad Godesberg, 1952.

[62] At the present time, the Federal Government is preparing a "Federal Spatial Planning Law."

of the Federal ministry concerned with these questions. Subsequent competition among the different ministries involved nipped the Federal initiative in the bud.

Another move came in 1954 from the ranks of science in the form of a lengthy publication of the *Institut fuer Raumforschung,*[63] which, about a year later, was the subject of a detailed expert analysis by the scientific commitee of the Federal Ministry of Economic Affairs.[64] However, this analysis limited the possibilities of regional economic policy to a few cases and rejected the concept of spatial planning in view of its "autonomous regional objectives." Because of the principle of the uniformity of Federal economic policy, regional economic policy had to be an integral part of the general Federal economic policy. Federal measures were limited to those permissible in a free enterprise economy. Consequently, the committee especially emphasized means to develop the system, i.e., measures furthering the market mechanism, the mobility of economic factors, and marginal-cost pricing. Direct subsidies for particular areas were rejected in principle, while particular development measures through credit extension, etc., were favored only if the investments promised a higher than average productivity. The only exceptions should be the "political" depressed areas, including West Berlin as a special case. While tax exemptions for the areas along the border of the DDR should be only temporary and for the purpose of stimulating investment, the political situation of West Berlin necessitated continuous subsidies by means of a general tax exemption. Apart from these exceptions, the analysis of the scientific committee limited regional economic policy to means conforming to the market mechanism and to objectives determined by economic criteria. Thus noneconomic criteria (e.g., better population distribution, deglomeration, rural-urban balance) were rejected as standards for regional economic policy if economic reasons did not justify them.

While this analysis increased discussion about spatial planning, it decreased political activity regarding it. Thus, it was not until May 1956, that there was a report on the steps taken to activate spatial planning.[65] These were as follows:

(1) Formation of an Expert Committee for Spatial Planning (SARO) to establish criteria.

(2) Formation of an Interministerial Committee for Spatial Planning (IMARO) to coordinate the Federal measures affecting spatial problems.

(3) Conclusion of an administrative agreement with the Laender regarding spatial planning, as well as a preliminary administrative agreement regarding the regulation of supraregional land planning.

Since then, without much public discussion, work in this area has progressed further. In May 1961 the Expert Committee for Spatial Planning completed an extensive report, which contained basic criteria for Federal spatial planning.[66] Based on this report, *Principles for Spatial Policy Meas-*

---

[63] *Zur Frage regionaler Wirtschaftspolitik, op. cit.*

[64] "Moeglichkeiten und Grenzen regionaler Wirtschaftspolitik," *op. cit.* pp. 481 ff.

[65] "Aktivierung der Raumordnung," *Bulletin des Presse- und Informationsamtes der Bundesregierung,* Jg. 1956, No. 96, p. 926.

[66] *Die Raumordnung in der Bundesrepublik Deutschland, op. cit.*

ures of the Federal Government and Their Coordination[67] referring to Federal plans and investments was published in 1962. In view of the goal of uniform living conditions, the following criteria were set out:

(1) Avoidance of further geographical concentration both of population and of economic activity.
(2) Improvement of the agricultural structures.
(3) Raising of the productive power of badly structured regions.
(4) Stimulation of well-organized and decentralized population centers.
(5) Provision of sufficient areas of recreation.
(6) Prevention of water and air contamination.
(7) Preservation of soil and natural scenery.

In addition to these criteria, the committee emphasizes "intercommunity cooperation" and "broad water plans" as important means toward good use of space.

Encompassing so many areas, these criteria give an impressive picture of the variety of the problems and of the difficulty of spatial planning as a whole. It is clear that their application cannot be limited to public investments, but also involve sections of the private economy. Concrete measures and the harmonization of spatial planning with the general economic policy are not mentioned. Even if these criteria should be limited to public investments at first, difficulties in implementation will arise because of the constitutional autonomy of the communities, whose unequal financial strength is one of the main reasons for regional differences. In addition, the urgent investment needs of the heavily populated centers which are also the most active economic centers, cannot be neglected. The "raising of the productive power of badly structured regions" will necessarily be second in importance for a long time. Moreover, it should be pointed out that several concepts used in the statement of the criteria have not yet been defined in a generally accepted manner.[68] Therefore, the established criteria can be only a preliminary basis for discussion, though they show the intended direction of policy. At the present time there is a lack of basic knowledge about the interrelations of regional economic developments and about the impact of various regional policies, which must be carefully analyzed in the context of the economic system and the present tax structure.

The SARO report, in an effort to establish a scientific basis for the "Criteria for Spatial Planning Policy," stated the following postulates:[69]

(1) A region's use and structure (which is based on use) are determined by its comparative advantage.
(2) The size of a region's population and labor force must be in a healthy relation to its capacity for employment.

---

[67] "Grundsaetze fuer die raumbedeutsamen Massnahmen des Bundes und ihre Koordinierung" (Bundesministerium fuer Wohnungsbau, Staedtebau und Raumordnung), *Informationen des Instituts fuer Raumforschung,* 12. Jg. (1962), No. 17, pp. 413 ff.

[68] This holds; e.g., for concepts like "uniformity of living conditions," improvement of the agglomeration centers," "loosely organized structure of settlement," "healthy plant size," and also for the characteristics and the definitions of the agglomeration centers, redevelopment areas, etc.

[69] *Die Raumordnung in der Bundesrepublik Deutschland, op. cit.,* pp. 73 ff.

(3) The community conditions necessary for spatial planning include the following in particular:
   (*a*) Adequate transport for workers.
   (*b*) Appropriate income opportunities.
   (*c*) Sufficient provision of the private and public establishments necessary for the customary standard of living.
   (*d*) Location of secondary occupations so that communication problems are minimized.
   (*e*) An appropriate relationship between primary and secondary industries.

(4) The environment must meet basic needs; sufficient educational facilities are especially important.

(5) The employment capacity in the sense of the primary productive capacity of a region, should be based on a variety of industries.

(6) The eastern frontier areas of the Federal Republic need particular development aid, to prevent the desolation that might result from their politically unfavorable location.

It is proposed that these postulates, which are to be related to concrete cases, be included in the economic policy as a whole, and that their realization be adapted to the general development. They are intended as the basis of a definite concept of spatial planning for the whole Federal Republic, to be developed in cooperation with the Laender. The measures recommended have been classified into four groups: [70]

(1) Direct regional policy actions.
(2) Coordinated regional application of policies of the several ministries.
(3) Harmonization of differences in productive capacity.
(4) Spatial planning.

The first group includes "regional economic development," or the use of public funds to bring about a balance between the resident labor force and the number of jobs within a region. The second group concerns the use of public funds for structural improvements in various sectors of the economy (agriculture, housing, small business, etc.) while regional structures are being changed. The harmonization of differences in productive capacity aims at a regional leveling of public expenditures through improved financial cooperation at the Federal and Laender levels. The institutionalization of spatial planning is to make possible the preparation and coordination of Federal investments which have regional effects.

Viewed in this manner, these proposals do not contain any far-reaching changes, except that the regional economic effects of all public investments and of the Federal economic policy shall be taken into consideration and be given due weight. The situation will be different, of course, if this new aspect comes into conflict with the "general economic policy." It seems likely that these far-reaching proposals and comprehensive objectives will be considerably reduced once they are put into practice.

Spatial planning and land planning decisively affect labor markets. One must therefore consider the importance of particular regional measures [71] for labor markets, as follows:

(1) Measures that prevent a further increase of the agglomerations serve at the same time to decrease tensions in their labor markets,

---

[70] *Loc. cit.*

[71] Cf., H. Schnaas, "Raumordnung und Arbeitsmarkt," *Bundesarbeitsblatt,* 11. Jg. (1960), pp. 464 ff.

once the establishment of further industries is discouraged. As long as employment opportunities increase in the agglomeration centers, their population, too, will increase.

(2) Connected with halting concentration are measures for the underdeveloped, predominantly agricultural areas. These industrialization measures, along with improvement of the agricultural structure, can tap labor reserves which are set free from agriculture (if labor is optimally used). In order to prevent the emigration of these workers, the development of industrial jobs in these areas must be an integral part of the agricultural structural improvement policy. In addition, silent labor reserves will be tapped.

(3) Both policies are limited by the effects of the dissolution of industrial monostructures; i.e., agglomerations based on a single industry, which endangers the economic stability of several agglomerations unless new and diverse industries are located there. The location of industries in the single-industry agglomerations, which will employ those parts of the labor potential that had been little demanded before, is another possible means of harmonization.

Regional Policy and European Integration

One peculiarity of the regional economic policy of the Federal Republic within the European Community must be pointed out.[72] Among the present members of the Community, the Federal Republic of Germany is the only federal state. Therefore, the coordination of regional economic policy in Germany with the objectives and provisions of the EEC is rendered more difficult, because the Laender and the communities as well as the Federal Government can make regional and local economic policy. Federal authority may not always be sufficient to insure that Laender and local actions are completely integrated with EEC principles. Thus, the Federal Government is confronted with the problem of enforcing coordination on several levels, a problem that no other member country has to face.

Area Redevelopment Policy

Federal Area Redevelopment Policy

Area redevelopment policy is made within the framework of the general economic policy and according to the principles of the "social market economy." The general economic-political goal is to increase individual incomes of the population in the redevelopment areas. Reliance is placed on the market mechanism. While no restrictions are to be placed on locational decisions, investment in development areas is to be encouraged by active measures. Though direct subsidies are excluded, income opportunities are to be enlarged and stabilized through structural improvements, so that incomes can be increased by means of productivity increases. Behind this policy lies the belief that the more efficient use of productive resources in the redevelopment areas contributes also, in the long run, to the maximization of the social products, for in a free enterprise economy

[72] *Ibid.*, pp. 112 ff.

the location of production does not lead automatically to the "optimal use of space." [73]

The fact that redevelopment policy works within the framework of the free market economy by no means excludes regionally directed actions on the part of the Federal Government; for "development-worthiness" can be judged much better on the basis of an area's particular situation than on the basis of a global policy oriented to general characteristics of distressed areas.[74] The designation of redevelopment areas for extended periods creates, at the same time, the necessity for continuity of Federal measures. The rapid success of redevelopment measures should not lead to the termination of a program planned for a given period, because it is on the basis of that period that local and newly established businesses make their own calculations. On the other hand, there must be a guarantee that with the termination of the program the new industries can stand on their own feet. Therefore, the object of redevelopment measures is only the acceleration of structural adjustment processes and the attraction and support of new economic activities whose success cannot be doubted under normal conditions of production. Hence, direct assistance to firms is in general limited to credit extension and to temporary assistance. The criteria established by the Scientific Committee of the Federal Ministry of Economics, however, go even further: Private production should be aided by public funds only if thereby an above-average productivity increase can be achieved.[75] Thus the committee aims directly at maximization of the social product.

The first objective is to provide more of those public services that are lacking in the redevelopment areas because of their low tax revenues. Thus, redevelopment begins in the public sector and in those areas where the general conditions of production can be improved by such means as opening up roads, improving the water and energy systems, raising the natural productive conditions (soil rehabilitation, tapping of raw materials), and improving the local labor force. This is indirect development. It creates equality of economic opportunities and only on this basis can production be increased and permanent success assured. The lack of productive power in the redevelopment areas is a consequence of their lack of sufficient employment capacity,[76] evidenced by labor surplus in the primary production sectors. This capacity is insufficient to provide adequate (average) incomes for the population. Thus redevelopment policy is faced with the choice between active and passive policies. An active redevelopment policy

---

[73] Storbeck, *Die wirtschaftliche Problematik der Raumordnung, op. cit.*, pp. 85 ff. and 113 ff.

[74] The frequent alterations of the characteristics of redevelopment areas, and the discussion among experts started thereby, point up how questionable such global lists of characteristics are. With their generalizations regarding individual spatial structures, they paralyze redevelopment policy; and in a dynamic economy these characteristics must be continuously reexamined. Cf., G. Mueller, "Grundlagen fuer eine Neuabgrenzung der Foerdergebiete," *Raumforschung und Raumordnung,* 16 Jg. (1958), Heft 1, pp. 15 ff.

[75] "Moeglichkeiten und Grenzen regionaler Wirtschaftspolitik" (Gutachten des Wissenschaftlichen Beirats beim Bundeswirtschaftsministerium), *op. cit.* The same expert report recognizes, however, that the shifting of private costs to the public sector causes a general distortion of the social costs, which renders the productivity comparison rather questionable. According to the literature on this problem, the social costs are probably low in the redevelopment areas.

[76] G. Isenberg, *Tragfaehigkeit und Wirtschaftsstruktur.* Bremen-Horn, 1953.

is directed toward enlarging the productive capacity; i.e., toward creating additional jobs in the primary and secondary sectors, while the passive policy encourages a decrease of the population through emigration.

As the general population density in Germany is rather high, the capacity of agriculture has been exhausted, and so an active development policy must consist of industrialization. Enlargement of the existing industries and attraction of new ones are to be encouraged by Federal measures to increase public services, which in turn leads to a leveling of the local disadvantages resulting from the general backwardness of the areas. However, since entrepreneurial willingness to invest can be influenced only after complete equalization of these opportunities—which will require a considerable period—and even then probably slowly, the Federal redevelopment policy includes industrial development. Policies intended to encourage investment and adjustment can become effective only when the requisite basic conditions exist.

The Federal redevelopment policy has been limited mainly to credit policies, although the use of retained earnings normally represents a very high share of investments. However, the smaller the advantages for industrial establishments in a redevelopment area, the more likely that marginal firms will come into the area, because marginal firms have to calculate profitability closely whereas large ones do not and are attracted only by large differences. If the general state of business is good, the profit opportunities made possible through redevelopment measures (which always carry the risk, difficult to evaluate, that the whole program will not succeed) will influence investment decisions of entrepreneurs even less. On the other hand, boom conditions can increase the attractiveness of the redevelopment areas because of the availability of labor reserves and other advantages, while in the industrial centers labor shortages prevail.

Apart from the industrialization policy, structural improvements in agriculture are also a very important part of area redevelopment policy, in view of the predominantly agricultural character of the redevelopment areas. Agriculture in these areas usually faces unfavorable production conditions and many of the farms are traditionally too small to be economically profitable. Here, Federal measures are directed to improving the conditions of cultivation and to eliminating the fragmentation of farms. These structural adjustments include the merging of farms and the bringing together of scattered parcels of land (*Flurbereinigung*). They can create the necessary prerequisites for the mechanization and organization (through agricultural associations) of agriculture, but require governmental support by means of credit policies and technical assistance as well as by the improvement of marketing facilities.

Development measures affecting different economic spheres must be integrated to take account of the interdependencies within the economy. For instance, the agricultural policies release part of the agricultural labor force, which must be absorbed by the enlargement of existing industries and the establishment of new ones if unemployment and emigration are not to increase and the area is to remain stable. Retraining and rehabilitation within the framework of the Federal employment policy [77] should facilitate the transition.

The economic sectors of commerce and services expand with the general improvement of goods production in the redevelopment areas. Their de-

---

[77] Federal Office for Employment Exchange and Unemployment Insurance.

velopment needs assistance only where they constitute a primary industry within the regional economic structure, for example, tourism. Sometimes an increase in administrative offices, educational institutions, military establishments, and the like can help to raise the productive power of an area. Apart from these exceptions, the commerce and service sectors do not need particular development aid.

Each area redevelopment measure must be related to economic development as a whole and to general economic policies. The general economic situation determines to a large extent the amount of funds available for redevelopment; they are greatest under boom conditions unless an anticyclical financial policy reverses this relationship. Therefore, the business cycle especially influences public investments in the redevelopment areas. The danger of the establishment of marginal firms in redevelopment areas in the rising phase of the cycle has already been pointed out; on the other hand, in a depression the redevelopment areas should not become oases within the economy. Related to the state of business is the general level of employment, which determines the chances of emigration from the redevelopment areas. At the same time, most recent developments have shown that labor reserves in the redevelopment areas are an important investment incentive.

Coordination of redevelopment policies with the general economic policy is also very important. Long-run development programs may fail if the general economic policy provides competing incentives not limited to particular regions. This can happen very easily in the case of credit and financial measures, which are the most important means of redevelopment policy. For instance, credit measures favoring small business [78] constitute such incentives that they almost offset the incentives provided by the redevelopment measures. Similarly, general measures of fiscal policy (e.g., increased depreciation allowances) can spread the advantages which were earlier limited to particular regions and thereby undermine their effect in the redevelopment areas.[79]

Finally, redevelopment measures must be adjusted to the structure of the redevelopment areas. Only a knowledge of the causes of underdevelopment makes possible a rational decision between active and passive redevelopment policies.

The more redevelopment measures are concentrated in time and space, the greater is their success and their further stimulus to the economy. In addition, regional development objectives can be pursued by concentrating particular measures in selected localities and combining them according to individual requirements. Such a concentration makes it possible for municipal administrative agencies to establish longrun development plans, which constitute an important means of orientation for the industries to be attracted, without limiting their freedom of choice. The combination of settlement of new industries, opening up communication networks, improving public utilities and housing, and retraining the agricultural labor in one area can lead to rapid successes whose multiplier effects constitute further stimuli and bring about further expansion in the region. The

---

[78] Small business has a particular disadvantage in the credit market and should receive Federal assistance in this regard. P. Adenauer, *Mittelstaendische Investitionsnanzierung in der sozialen Marktwirtschaft*. Muenster, 1961, pp. 41 ff.

[79] Therefore, redevelopment policies should not concentrate on interest, tax, or amortization rates, but rather on relative rates; i.e., compared with the average rates.

"Central Points Program"[80] is a beginning of such concentration of redevelopment measures.

In this regard, the attraction of large firms and of branches of large companies is important, as they can be expected to stimulate the local economy to an especially large extent. The formation of branches has the additional advantage that the apparent companies themselves can extend assistance in the beginning. Hence the establishment of large firms which will have a concentrating effect is to be preferred to the dispersal of funds which, up till now, has predominated in the area redevelopment policy.

Redevelopment Areas

The criteria for the selection of redevelopment areas have changed over the years. This is indicated by the various designations, which refer to the economic situation rather than to the geographical region. At first, the term "distressed areas" (*Notstandsgebiete*), common before the war,[81] was used. *Notstand* designates an exceptional situation which urgently needs help. Although the general economic expansion eliminated most of the distress fairly early, there were still economic imbalances in some areas which caused personal incomes to be far below the average. In view of the need to correct the underlying structural imbalances, these areas were now called "rehabilitation areas" (*Sanierungsgebiete*). Yet, since development assistance was also provided in special cases to counteract disadvantages caused by the political situation, the term "redevelopment areas" (*Foerdergebiete*) was used concurrently. The latter term is used today to denote both rehabilitation areas and "zone frontier areas," i.e., areas along the border of the Soviet Zone. The zone frontier areas and other border regions constitute a special group. Inasmuch as all the areas obtain the same types of development assistance, the different designations have no practical significance.

Since distress and underdevelopment are measured by comparison with average values for the economy as a whole, the demarcation of redevelopment areas must always be related to a specific time and space. With the growth of the total economy, differences in regional structure increase, and standards and marginal values change with the general economic situation. However, an overall economic policy demands as much uniformity and continuity in the demarcations of the redevelopment areas as possible, and for the implementation of the policies a few practical patterns are preferred. In view of the differing causes of the imbalances, these requirements can be only partially fulfilled. Moreover, classification of the areas according to identical symptoms does not indicate their relative importance,[82] which may, for example, be determined by the location of the area (frontier area or proximity to an agglomeration).

In all areas appropriate for redevelopment there are economic emergencies or imbalances due to structural causes, which cumulate without

---

[80] Cf., "Foerderung wirtschaftlich schwacher Gebiete," *Bulletin des Presse und Informationsamtes der Bundesregierung,* 1961, No. 44, p. 399.

[81] E. Dittrich, "Die deutschen Notstandsgebiete," *Grundfragen deutscher Raumordnung* (Mitteilungen aus dem Institut fuer Raumforschung, Heft 21). Bad Godesberg, 1955, pp. 30 ff.

[82] E. Dittrich, "Notstandsgebiete in der Bundesrepublik," *Wirtschaftsdienst,* 42. Jg. (1962). Heft 10, p. 433.

outside assistance. The economic symptoms of these areas are: Well above average unemployment, low personal incomes, low purchasing power, and, due to the continuous emigration, decreasing demand, an aging population, decline or stagnation of industry, unprofitable agriculture with underemployment, insufficient tax revenues in the communities, and declining municipal expenditures. These symptoms appear together since they are causally related. Declining industry and unprofitable agriculture cause low incomes, purchasing power, and municipal tax revenues. Declining purchasing power and insufficient municipal services hinder industrial development.

Although the characteristic symptoms are the same for all redevelopment areas, regional economic imbalances have different causes:

(1) Noneconomic causes:
  (*a*) Danger of, or damage by, natural catastrophies.
  (*b*) Insufficient buildings, equipment, and public utilities due to extensive war damage.
  (*c*) Difficulties due to political causes.

(2) Economic causes:
  (*a*) Impact of business fluctuations.
  (*b*) Structural defects.

Areas with imbalances due to noneconomic causes can be demarcated relatively easily. In this group are the coast and flood areas, some border areas with heavy war damage, and the zone frontier areas. These are imbalances which can either be eliminated with a once-and-for-all intervention, or which cannot, because of their political origins, be eliminated, so that continuous assistance is necessary. The areas with imbalances falling in the second group, however, are much harder to demarcate. Though the symptoms can be measured by individual indexes, the causes are difficult to identify because of their interelationships. Declining industries, low personal incomes, and high unemployment are usually indications of structural imbalances. Therefore, this category includes in the main those areas with underemployment in agriculture (mostly small scale) and insufficient industry.

To date, there have been no redevelopment areas whose problems have been caused by imbalances in particular branches of industry or by the business cycle, although individual branches have temporarily been in great difficulties, in spite of the general economic expansion. Although the firms in these branches are concentrated in a few economic areas, Federal area redevelopment measures have not been designated even for problems related to the changes in the bituminous coal and the textile industries.[83] The textile regions affected had already been assisted by redevelopment measures of the Land (Muensterland) or by earlier Federal action (parts of Overfranken). The often very large decreases in employment in the bituminous coal industry [84] were counterbalanced through the expansion of other industries in the area affected (the Ruhr).[85]

As already noted, the demarcation of areas with structural imbalances presents difficulties. As early as 1951, the IMNOS established the following criteria for the demarcation of "rehabilitation areas":

---

[83] *Die Raumordnung in der Bundesrepublik Deutschland, op. cit.*, pp. 105 ff.

[84] In 13 selected cities of the Ruhr area, from 1956 to 1960, employment decreased by 63,000, or 19.3 percent.

[85] Cf., K. J. Meyer, "Soziale Probleme bei der Stillegung von Zechen," *Informationen des Instituts fuer Raumforschung*, 11. Jg. (1961), No. 3, pp. 37 ff.

(1) In an area with a population of at least 100,000, the average unemployment rate (of wage and salary earners) for five specified keydates must be 25 percent or more (according to the official unemployment statistics); or

(2) In an area at least as large as a Land district in 1950 or at the time of the last census, no less than 80 persons (including family members of farmers) per DM 100,000 (about $24,000) of agricultural assets must be employed in agriculture, with no opportunities for part-time work; or

(3) In an area at least as large as a Land district, the total war damage must amount to at least 30 percent of the total agricultural assets.[86]

In the following years, the marginal unemployment rate was lowered from 25 to 19 percent. In addition, areas that showed several of these characteristics only partially were included. Since then, various proposals have been advanced regarding the basis of selection,[87] but no new criteria have been issued, although the conditions in the redevelopment areas have changed considerably. Consequently, the selection of areas is a political decision of the IMNOS, and the inflexible statistical characteristics have been waived in favor of allowing the decision to be adjusted to the dynamic economic changes that may take place. Thus, the Expert Committee's *Report on Spatial Planning* states the following prerequisites for Federal redevelopment assistance:

"(1) Great damage due to political causes, especially at the frontier, to be expected particularly in the 40 k.m.-wide frontier area along the border to the Soviet Zone (zone frontier areas and other frontier areas).

"(2) Great distress due to a disproportion between population and productive capacity which has been caused by the longrun economic development or by the events after the war (rehabilitation areas).

"(3) The political necessity of total reconstruction in the case of Heligoland Island.

"(4) Large development projects which can be expected to be successful and which cannot be financed by the Land (Emsland, Coast Plan Area, Northern Program)." [88]

On the basis of these prerequisites, about one-third of the area of the Federal Republic is included within the designated redevelopment areas,[89] which have increased considerably in number since the start of redevelopment measures in 1951.[90] The zone frontier areas and other border areas, which include numerous rehabilitation areas, constitute the largest part.[91] The other redevelopment areas are mainly in the north of the Federal Re-

---

[86] Listed in Mueller, "Grundlagen fuer eine Neuabgrenzung der Foerdergebiete," *op. cit.*, pp. 15 ff.

[87] Th. Dams, "Agraroekonomische Aspekte zur Methode der Abgrenzung von wirtschaftlichen Notstands- und Foerderungsgebieten," *Berichte zur Landwirtschaft*, 34. Jg. (1956), Bd. 3, pp. 437 ff. Mueller, "Grundlagen fuer eine Neuabgrenzung der Foerdergebiete," *op. cit.*, pp. 15 ff.

[88] *Die Raumordnung in der Bundesrepublik Deutschland*, *op. cit.*, p. 99.

[89] W. Sahner, "Ein Drittel der Bundesrepublik Foerderungsgebiete," *Informationen des Instituts fuer Raumforschung*, 12. Jg. (1962), No. 1, pp. 167 ff.

[90] *Die deutschen Notstandsgebiete 1951*. Sammelband der Informationen des Instituts fuer Raumforschung. Bad Godesberg, 1952.

[91] Cf., Map of the Redevelopment Areas assisted by the Federal Government in 1960. Dittrich, "Haben wir eine konkrete raumpolitische Leitlinie?" *op. cit.*, pp. 403 ff.

public—all of Schleswig-Holstein and large parts of Lower Saxony, which received a large number of immigrants after the war and which, in addition, are burdened with comprehensive development projects. There are some in the western frontier area (Eifel, Saar frontier area, and Pfalz); these include war damage and agricultural problem areas. The rest of the rehabilitation areas are agricultural regions in the low mountains adjacent to the zone frontier or other border areas (Bavaria and North Hessen). The more industrialized regions included among the redevelopment areas are to be found only in the zone frontier area. Their often one-sided structure of production and their agricultural problems have complicated the imbalances created by the zone frontier.

Area Redevelopment Measures and Means

Since 1951 the Federal Government has taken measures for the development of the rehabilitation areas.[92] In addition to the creation of new industrial jobs, improvement of the structure of agriculture has been an important part of the program. Since 1956 the "Green Plan" of the Law for Agriculture has extended rehabilitation policies to agriculture as a whole.

The measures of the Federal Office for Labor Exchange and Unemployment Insurance also began very early; they were directed mainly toward rapid elimination of unemployment. The means used were "value-creating unemployment assistance" (work relief) and the resettlement of unemployed persons through the interregional employment offices. Later, the Federal Government and the Laender instituted policies attempting to eliminate the backwardness of the redevelopment areas.

The long list of redevelopment measures can be divided into two categories: Passive and active rehabilitation policies. The passive development policy subsidizing the emigration of surplus labor by various measures[93] was carried out mainly by the Federal Office for Labor Exchange and Unemployment Insurance. These measures included reimbursement for travel and moving expenses and (in case of need) "separation assistance"; grants and loans to employers for the purchase of work clothing and equipment; "transition funds" to replace temporary losses of earnings; and economic assistance to agricultural workers for the purchase of equipment necessary for a part-time job.[94]

These measures of the Federal office were supplemented by development aid to housing and by construction of hostels for young and old workers at the site of employment.[95] This increased the mobility of labor in general and encouraged emigration from the backward areas. The expellees and refugees, as well as younger persons who were not tied to one place by property and family, were particularly willing to emigrate. The consequence of this policy was an increasing aging of the labor supply remaining

---

[92] K. Schneider, "Agrarreform durch regionale Wirtschaftspolitik," *Informationen des Instituts fuer Raumforschung,* 9. Jg. (1959), No. 5, pp. 99 ff.

[93] L. Pompernelle, "Methoden zur Ueberwindung der Immobilitaet von Arbeitskraeften in Gebieten mit struktureller Arbeitslosigkeit," *Informationen des Instituts fuer Raumforschung,* 7. Jg. (1957), No. 14, pp. 359 ff., esp. pp. 367 ff.

[94] "Richtlinien des Verwaltungsrates der Bundesanstalt fuer Arbeitsvermittlung und Arbeitslosenversicherung zur Foerderung der Arbeitsaufnahme vom 17. Dezember 1953," *Amtliche Nachrichten der Bundesanstalt,* 2. Jg. (1954), No. 9, p. 571.

[95] "Vorschriften ueber Arbeitsvermittlung und Lehrstellenvermittlung im Auftrage der Bundesanstalt fuer Arbeitsvermittlung und Arbeitslosenversicherung," *Amtliche Nachrichten der Bundesanstalt,* 8. Jg. (1960), No. 3, p. 109.

in the rehabilitation areas. In the early years the less productive workers, who because of deficient occupational training had no great employment opportunities in other localities, also tended to remain. Viewed only from the point of view of the unemployment rate, however, this policy was a definite success. Unemployment in the redevelopment areas rapidly decreased to the level of the average for the entire Federal Republic a few years earlier.[96]

In contrast, the active rehabilitation policy attempts to improve the regional economic structure by means of increasing employment in the areas with high unemployment or declining industries. It alone, therefore, deserves to be called "redevelopment policy." Corresponding to the various objectives and to the differing authorities (Federal Government and Laender), different development measures have been employed, whose impact has depended on the general state of business, the economic structure of the affected areas, and the assistance extended concurrently to other sectors of the economy. The general state of business, in particular, is of great importance for the means and the extent of area redevelopment policies, because the creation of new jobs in the redevelopment areas presupposes a general increase in employment. In all their variations and their differing impacts, all redevelopment measures aim at the same goal: To increase personal incomes and to raise productive capacity through more efficient use of the regional labor potential. This requires a twofold approach:

(1) *Structural improvement.* This means greater security or higher wages and salaries in existing jobs, or higher profits in the firms providing these jobs. The majority of industrial enterprises in the redevelopment areas are marginal firms which, because of structural weaknesses or deficient adjustments, lag behind general economic development. Up to now, the general economic expansion and the personal efforts of entrepreneurs (in family businesses) have been able to cover up these weaknesses.

(2) *Creation of new jobs.* Through the expansion of existing enterprises and the attraction of new ones, the employment capacity of the redevelopment areas can be increased and their economy revitalized. Such an increase in employment is an essential supplement to the structural improvement measures in agriculture which release numerous agricultural employees for other work. In addition, the settlement of new enterprises may improve the economic structure through the use of parts of the labor potential that had not been employed before (e.g., female labor).

In the pursuit of this goal, advantages are created in the redevelopment areas relative to the rest of the economy. The measures taken correspond in each case to the specific policy objectives.

Very important, but barely visible in the official programs, are the subsidies which the communities in the redevelopment areas obtain to improve their productive power, i.e., the *indirect assistance.* This is to counterbalance the financial weakness of these communities and to strengthen their infrastructure. The Federal Government and the Laender participate in "development-worthy" projects in the areas of roadbuilding, water systems, education, health services, etc., in short, in investments that constitute

[96] In this connection, one should note that the tasks of the Federal Office for Labor Exchange and Unemployment Insurance do not include area redevelopment policies. Cf., 'Gesetz ueber Arbeitsvermittlung und Arbeitslosenversicherung in der Fassung vom 3. April 1957," *Bundesgesetzblatt,* 1957, Teil I, pp. 322 ff.

important prerequisites for industrialization. This group of measures also includes loans and grants for public utilities and other public services that are basic to the development of the local economy.

Direct assistance, as in the credit policies, provides incentives to private enterprise in the redevelopment areas. A crucial point is assistance to agriculture (which is given also in the rest of the Federal Republic) for improvement of the structure of production (creation of farms of adequate size, mechanization, and rationalization, increase of productivity and quality). Since the employment capacity of agriculture has been exhausted and there is underemployment, the incentives to industry are of special importance. This type of assistance is given to modernize, rationalize, and enlarge existing enterprises as well as start new enterprises in the redevelopment areas.

Finally, special assistance is given to individuals in order to facilitate adjustments to structural change. These measures include retraining, training of the local labor, and aid for the settlement of skilled labor through provision of housing, reimbursement for moving expenses, etc. Preferences regarding personal taxes are limited to the special case of West Berlin.

The different policies involve various economic means, which are only rarely coordinated within an organic program. The basic principle in the choice of means is to avoid dictation. Thus, a typical redevelopment policy is technical assistance, providing information and advice. The measures facilitating the establishment of new industries, investment aids, and the like are offered by the Federal Government to private entrepreneurs who are completely free to accept or reject these offers. This is of significance, because area redevelopment overlaps with measures of general economic assistance. A good example is the large number of credit policy measures in the Federal Republic.[97] In 1963 there were 17 credit measures based on ERP funds, 22 based on Federal funds, and 82 measures of the Laender; only about one-fifth of these measures relate to the Federal and Laender redevelopment areas. Redevelopment measures compete particularly strongly with the general assistance to expellees and refugees from the Soviet Zone, with compensation for war damages, and with small business measures not related to particular regions. These groups obtain the same type of credit assistance as firms in the redevelopment areas, while they are not limited in their choice of location—not even by the bureaucratic means of credit refusal. It is, therefore, up to private enterprises whether they will participate in redevelopment in view of the fact that they can obtain assistance from other sources.

The following Federal economic redevelopment measures have been used:

(1) Improvement of the infrastructure

As previously noted, the communities in the redevelopment areas have fallen behind in their municipal services because of the lack of sufficient funds. Since many redevelopment areas are old "rehabilitation areas," this situation often has existed for decades, so that there is great deficiency in public investments.[98] The increase of municipal services in the industrial areas has widened the differences between them and the communities in the redevelopment areas. The development measures, which are shared by the Federal and the Laender governments, subsidize municipal investments

[97] H. Dittes, "Die Kredithilfen des Bundes und der Laender an die gewerbliche Wirtschaft," *Zeitschrift fuer das gesamte Kreditwesen.* Sonderausgabe, 1963.

[98] Storbeck, *Die wirtschaftliche Problematik der Raumordnung, op. cit.,* pp. 172 ff.

through grants and long-term loans, which are sometimes extended without interest.[99] Aid is also provided by the acceleration and concentration of Federal and Laender investments in these areas, particularly investments in communications (which, however, are carried out mostly in the agglomerations because of their higher demand). Since this type of aid is limited, the backwardness of the redevelopment areas compared to the average for the Federal Republic can be corrected only gradually. Hence measures to improve the infrastructures hardly constitute an increased stimulus to private enterprise. In some cases, however, they have had a temporary employment effect by providing work for the unemployed on public projects.

(2) Credit policies for private enterprises

The credit policies of the Federal Government and the Laender regarding private business are of much greater significance. They include loans for investments and short-term loans for working capital and are in the form of low-interest-rate loans, interest subsidies (in the case of bank loans), and Federal guarantees for loans.[1] The low-interest loans of the state are to make possible long-term financing of new industries and expansions of existing firms, the economic success of which seems guaranteed in general, but not in the short run. These are loans for up to 15 years (with no repayment for 2–3 years) at an interest rate of 5 percent. They are intended particularly for firms who do not have enough capital to meet the amount of self-financing generally demanded by the banks, and therefore cannot obtain any credit otherwise. The terms of the loans are especially long and enable the firms to synchronize repayments of the loan and amortization of the investment. Furthermore, credits are extended for the settlement of industrial and handicraft enterprises in the redevelopment areas, which may cover up to 50 percent of the costs of the investment and which may run for 15 years at an interest rate of 3½ percent. In general, these credits are extended to new enterprises which are branches of firms outside the redevelopment areas, which can support the new branches by means of their own capital or by securing credits for them in the free market.

In addition, interest subsidies are extended for loans for rationalization purposes in industrial sectors that are important for the economic structure; they amount to 3 percent per year toward the normal amount of interest to be paid to the banks, and are extended for 3 years. This short-run Federal assistance is intended for investments that promise profitable returns within a short period.

Finally, the Federal and the Laender governments guarantee loans for investments in the redevelopment areas, in order to strengthen the weak competitive position in the credit market of small- and middle-sized enterprises. This indicates the willingness of the state to share the risks of new enterprises and expansions of existing enterprises in the redevelopment areas. In most Laender the conditions and the amount of the guarantee are not specified in detail.

(3) Government orders

Another measure assisting the economy of the redevelopment areas is the preferential allocation of Government orders to enterprises in those areas. Administrative agencies of the Federal and the Laender Govern-

[99] Of course, similar types of aid are extended to financially strong large cities, so that the particular advantage to the redevelopment areas is relatively small.

[1] Dittes, "Die Kredithilfen des Bundes und der Laender an die gewerbliche Wirtschaft," *op. cit.*

ments, as well as public-service enterprises, are directed to give preference to bids from the redevelopment areas. Of course, this policy can be applied only to a limited extent, inasmuch as orders can be given only to those enterprises that produce the required products. Apart from the fact that administrative agencies usually make their small purchases from local firms, the extent of specialization in modern industry considerably narrows the applicability of this policy.[2] Only in exceptional cases will it be possible to extend long-run and adequate assistance to an enterprise by such means. Thus, this measure alone cannot constitute a stimulus; it is only a supplementary aid.

(4) Freight allowances

The Federal and the Laender governments share (at 80 percent and 20 percent respectively) the financing of freight allowances for enterprises in the zone frontier and other frontier areas, in which the demarcation of the frontier after the war has increased freight costs. These are direct subsidies with the intention of counterbalancing unfavorable vocational conditions which might cause emigration of local industrial enterprises and thereby increase the relative backwardness of these areas. Their effect, however, is difficult to assess since railroad tariffs are often not related to costs.[3] This policy helps to keep in the redevelopment areas enterprises that on the basis of a long tradition and experience produce products of high quality, as well as enterprises that are an essential part of the economic strength of the areas.

(5) Structural improvement of agriculture

The means provided within the "Green Plan" are of great significance for the redevelopment areas in general, because of their small farms and unfavorable conditions of cultivation—the criteria for application of the "Green Plan." Thus they must be included in the special redevelopment measures, though they are also available for agriculture outside the redevelopment areas. These measures are long-term credit aids for rationalization investments as well as Federal grants to improve the general agricultural conditions of production, for example, for building roads, improving soil and water systems, and applying measures against erosion. At the same time, individual agricultural enterprises receive credits for structural adjustments and for the mechanization of production.[4] For the redevelopment areas, the measures improving farm size are of special significance, because they are directly connected with other redevelopment measures, such as the setting free of agricultural labor through mergers of farms or through reorganization of the structure of land holdings and uses.

(6) Organization of redevelopment

The help of governmental administrative agencies in the implementation of particular redevelopment measures is essential for their success. For instance, structural improvements of agriculture cannot very well be carried

[2] A special example of this type of assistance is West Berlin with its highly developed electrical industry, which has obtained a large part of the orders of the Federal post office (telephone and telegraphic service), and probably would have without special policy measures. Sometimes defense orders (uniforms and equipment) have been of special interest to specific locations.

[3] Cf. P. Schulz-Kiesow, *Eisenbahngueterpolitik in ihrer Wirkung auf den industriellen Standort und die Raumordnung.* Heidelberg, 1940.

[4] Other agricultural subsidies for special production costs and special productive successes within the scope of the "Green Plan" are of a general nature, and therefore not of special significance for the redevelopment areas (e.g., subsidies for fertilizers, for diesel-power fuel, and premiums for special-quality products).

out without the cooperation of public surveyors and their advice and arbitration in property disputes. The cooperation of the officials responsible for land planning and of the ministries for economic affairs of the Laender is particularly important. In view of the varied economic development measures, advice on available assistance by the respective administrative experts has a significant impact on the location of new enterprises. Of course, to date, the "policy of technical assistance in matters of location" has barely been developed within the Federal Republic.[5] Thus, it is often left to the ingenuity of the entrepreneur to discover the possibilities of development assistance and to make his choice accordingly.

(7) Tax exemptions

Other means of Federal redevelopment policy are tax exemptions for economic processes that are especially desirable.[6] Tax exemptions amount to direct subsidies and must therefore be critically analyzed. The Federal Government can allow them only for taxes falling within its jurisdiction (turnover tax, income, and corporation taxes). Direct tax exemptions have been applied only for the economy of West Berlin. Here the rebate of the turnover tax on purchases from West Berlin is of particular importance. This measure is to stimulate purchases from West Berlin in order to counterbalance its marketing problems.

A policy measure that has been rather effective in stimulating total investment is tax exemption or accelerated depreciation allowances for certain investments. Such tax exemptions have had a greater impact on the volume of investment than have special redevelopment policies. To apply them *only* to redevelopment areas would promise great success, but this has not been done, to date.

Tax exemptions on personal incomes of the residents of an area can also be given, in order to prevent emigration or encourage immigration. This measure has been used only in the special case of West Berlin, in order to counterbalance, at least partly, the many disadvantages and political risks for residents of West Berlin. It has not been applied in the redevelopment areas of the Federal Government and of the Laender.

(8) Training and retraining of labor

An important measure is retraining as well as training of the young workers, which is usually necessary because of the structural changes in the redevelopment areas and their industrialization. The Federal Government provides funds for construction and organization of the necessary training facilities to administrative agencies and associations on the basis of a program of the Federal Office for Labor Exchange and Unemployment Insurance. Therewith the labor potential of the redevelopment areas is generally improved in relation to the particular demands of industry. Funds are available also to subsidize traveling connected with training and the construction of boarding houses for apprentices. In view of the predominantly agricultural structure of the redevelopment areas of the Federal Republic, this measure is of great significance as a preparation for industrialization; of course, it misses its purpose if the trained workers cannot get jobs in new industries in these areas.

[5] There is no real advertising, informing entrepreneurs about the possibilities for investments and developments in redevelopment areas.

[6] This policy has been rejected by the Scientific Committee at the Federal Ministry of Economic Affairs, except for special political cases (West Berlin). Cf., "Moeglichkeiten und Grenzen regionaler Wirtschaftspolitik," *op cit.*

761-932 O—65——14

(9) Increasing labor mobility

Increasing the mobility of labor is only partly a measure of active redevelopment policy. If the mobility of the resident labor force is encouraged through measures facilitating the finding of new homes, this policy becomes passive policy, inasmuch as it encourages the emigration of labor from the redevelopment areas. Only if this policy helps to settle highly qualified workers (foremen, master craftsmen, etc.) is it active restoration policy. Such aids constitute an important prerequisite for the establishment of new industries, since highly qualified labor can rarely be found among the labor reserves of the redevelopment areas. In addition, this type of assistance decreases the competition for highly qualified labor among enterprises already in the area, and thus prevents possible difficulties with its supply.

This list demonstrates that redevelopment policy has a large number of measures at hand to improve the economic structure and expand the economies of the redevelopment areas. Their effects are clear in each individual case, and they are obviously selected according to the relative needs of these areas. Each special policy measure serves to improve particular processes, and cannot alone achieve basic structural improvement; this results only from coordinated application of all policies. And whether structural improvement is actually achieved depends on whether these measures are applied exclusively for redevelopment and not also for other economic or social policy objectives.

Some measures can even have a double effect, i.e., they can support both active and passive restoration policy.[7] However, because of the interrelationships of the important means of redevelopment policy, their coordinated application is an essential prerequisite for success. This holds especially for measures improving the agricultural structure, which make sense only if they are accompanied by the establishment of new industries to absorb the labor set free. However, coordination of measures is not a task of the Federal redevelopment policy, which is limited to the provision of general means.

Coordination is primarily the duty of the Laender in establishing the redevelopment programs for the several redevelopment areas. These programs are usually set up by the governments of the Laender (land planning agencies), which possess the necessary knowledge of the preconditions and possibilities of an effective redevelopment policy on the basis of their collection of local data. Though the land-planning agencies sometimes show dirigistic tendencies in the implementation of their plans, they are at this time the only possible coordinating bodies.

The Federal Government itself has not instituted any coordination of the redevelopment measures it supports, even though its actions have been called "programs" from time to time.[8] Actually these programs contained only the public announcement of the above-described measures. They did not even contain recommendations to the Laender for effective action to coordinate the Federal funds in special redevelopment programs. Gradually, of course, the Laender followed with their own redevelopment activities and included, apart from the redevelopment areas as demarcated by the Federal Government, additional areas which were backward relative

[7] E.g., the measures to increase mobility and those subsidizing training.

[8] Such a program is the assistance to the zone frontier area, which is suffering from special difficulties the Federal Government considers "temporary."

to the average for the respective Land. They used the same measures as the Federal Government. Thus, these programs usually specified only the sequence in time and the regional distribution of public investments, but not the priorities of particular economic areas within the redevelopment policy of the Federal Government and of the Laender.

Such a program is the "Coast Program," which was established as a 10-year program in 1954 by the Land Lower Saxony. Apart from improvements of coastal protection measures, it provides for investments for water supplies and soil improvements, on the basis of which the structural improvement of agriculture is to be carried out.[9] In this way, the preconditions for the establishment of new industries within the scope of the redevelopment policy are to be created simultaneously.

Similarly the "Programm Nord" was established in 1953 for the northern parts of the Land Schleswig-Holstein for a period of 25 years and with funds in the amount of DM 1.167 billion (about $280 million).[10] Because of the agricultural structure of these areas, improvement of agriculture is most important.[11] Simultaneously efforts are made to create agricultural "central towns," which can be developed as the sites for service industries. The general goal of these programs is the elimination of the backwardness of these areas relative to the rest of the Federal Republic. By June 1960, almost DM 480 million ($115 million) from Federal and Land funds had been invested in measures to improve the agricultural structure. The amount spent for municipal measures following these primary investments was estimated at DM 75 million ($18 million).[12] By June 1960, however, hardly any new industrial jobs had been created.

The "Emslandplan" is also due to the initiative of the Land government (Lower Saxony). This plan is based on the particular development possibilities of the Emsland. Extensive oil discoveries in these areas are the bases for industrialization. They are to be supplemented by measures encouraging industrialization, in particular the opening up of roads, improvement of the water supplies, and investments to increase public services. In addition, agricultural structural improvements and cultivation measures are to raise the general productive power of this region.

The Federal Government initiated a new method of area redevelopment with the "Central Points Program," which started in 1959 in 16 selected small cities in small-farm areas with underemployment. Acting upon a proposal of the Laender, the Inter-Ministerial Committee for Problems of Distressed Areas selected these cities to exercise the functions of "central towns" so that their development can stimulate the economy of the surrounding areas. Two of these central points are in the zone frontier area, six in other Federal redevelopment areas, and eight in redevelopment areas of the Laender. In 1961, 15 more small towns were added, 3 of which were in the zone frontier area, 5 in the Federal redevelopment areas, and 7 in the redevelopment areas of the Laender. Of this total of 31 towns, 10 are in Bavaria, 7 in Lower Saxony, 5 in Rheinland-Pfalz, 4 in Hessen, 3 in

---

[9] G. Mueller and H. Goeben, "Kuestenprogramm und Landesplanung," *Raumforschung und Raumordnung,* 15. Jg. (1957), Heft 1, pp. 1 ff.

[10] C. Bielfeldt, "Programm Nord. Stand, Erfahrungen und Lehren," *Informationen des Instituts fuer Raumforschung,* 8. Jg. (1958), No. 8, pp. 191 ff.

[11] G. Keil, "Programm 'Nord'—Aus der Arbeit der Landasplanung Schleswig-Holstein," *Raumforschung und Raumordnung,* 11. Jg. (1953), Heft 1, pp. 37 ff.

[12] "Kommunal-wirtschaftliche Folgemassnahmen im Programm Nord-Gebiet," *Informationen des Instituts fuer Raumforschung,* 12. Jr. (1962), No. 17, p. 428.

Schleswig-Holstein, and 2 in Baden-Wuerttemberg.[13] The program provides for low-interest loans to private enterprises and to municipal governments. Loans to private enterprises are for a period up to 15 years at 3.5 percent, and are used for investments which are to provide at least one permanent job for each DM 10,000 ($2,400) of Federal funds. The communities obtain loans for up to 20 years at 2 percent per annum for the development of industrial sites, etc.[14] In addition, the Laender may provide further assistance, e.g., in the distribution of public aid for the construction of housing or by grants for municipal investments (water, roads, etc.).

Since 1961, no new towns have been added to the Central Points Program, whose success is shown by the fact that assistance will be terminated for nine of the previously selected small towns in 1963. Evidently the large amount of public investment and of industrial development in a period of general economic development has achieved such good results after only 2 to 3 years that further redevelopment measures do not seem necessary. In view of this, it is surprising that no new small towns have been selected, although the other redevelopment measures of the Federal Govrnment and of the Laender have not been reduced.

One often gets the impression that development programs have been set up predominantly for budgetary reasons, in order to secure their long-term financing. In addition, land-planning activities have led to the initiation of redevelopment programs where it was possible to coordinate economic problem areas into one planning area by means of development programs.

Results and Critical Analysis

Since 1951 there have been Federal redevelopment measures for redevelopment areas, the number and financing of which have increased over the years.[15] If the special programs (Emsland and Nord programs) are included, by 1960 about DM 2 billion (nearly $500 million) have been spent on Federal development measures. As a reference, total Government expenditures in 1960 were $18.7 billion, rising steadily from $3.7 billion in 1951. However, these expenditures have had limited success, despite the contribution of general economic expansion to the area redevelopment policy. The Federal Government itself [16] calls the results achieved over all these years rather unsatisfactory. The lack of success is demonstrated in part by the fact that no redevelopment area could be excluded from the redevelopment policy; compared to the areas selected in 1951, their number has actually been increased.[17] While Government revenues have risen, redevelopment expenditures have not increased correspondingly, though since 1956, on the average, DM 233 million ($55 million) have been spent annually on a larger number of redevelopment areas, compared to an annual average of DM 165 million ($40 million) from 1951 to 1955. The increase in total expenditure thus amounts to about 40 percent. In spite of the unsatisfactory results, no new redevelopment measures have been applied to accelerate the adjustment processes.

---

[13] In the Saar and in Nordrhein-Westfalen no "central points" were selected.

[14] "Foerderung wirtschaftlich schwacher Gebiete," *op cit.*, p. 399.

[15] Cf., *Die Raumordnung in der Bundesrepublik Deutschland, op. cit.*, pp. 100 ff.

[16] E.g., "Bundeshilfe fuer die Bauern in den Notstandsgebieten," *Bulletin des Presse- und Informationsamtes der Bundesregierung,* 1956, No. 11, pp. 97 ff.

[17] Only redevelopment measures for some of the selected small towns within the central points program will be terminated in 1963.

Of course, the results of redevelopment policy can be measured only partially for various reasons. This is so particularly with respect to improvements of the infrastructure of the redevelopment areas, inasmuch as the extent of the investments cannot be established statistically because of differing methods of financing these improvements. Nor are the results measurable. There can be no doubt that the great underdevelopment of public services in the redevelopment areas, compared to the average for the Federal Republic, has only been reduced, and not eliminated, as the large cities and industrial centers have been able to increase their public services in the meantime.

Sufficient data do not exist to judge the results in agriculture. The annual Report on Agriculture and further policy measures within the "Green Plan" show that the structural improvements have not had sufficient impact to date. Since the redevelopment areas are usually small-farm agricultural areas with an imbalanced economic structure, they are still rather underdeveloped. Not until the regional data of the census of 1961 are available can the success of the agricultural structural improvement policies be properly evaluated.

The results of industrialization, the most important objective of area redevelopment, can be estimated fairly precisely; indirectly, these results also indicate the expansionary impact of the improved facilities and the increased productivity of the communities in the redevelopment areas. Since the period of reconstruction of old industrial sites overlapped the first years of redevelopment policy, the industrialization successes since 1955–56 are particularly important for a critique of the redevelopment policy. From 1956 to 1960, the number of industrial employees in the Federal Republic [18] increased by 713,000 or 10.3 percent. Simultaneously, the Land districts [19] of the zone frontier area had an increase of approximately 47,250 industrial employees, or 13 percent. Their proportion of the increase in total employment was somewhat over 6 percent, or a little higher than their share in total industrial employment in 1956 (5.3 percent). Most of the increase over the Federal average came after 1958, due particularly to the increasing labor shortage in the industrial centers and the consequent efforts to tap the reserves in the redevelopment areas by establishing industries in these areas.

The situation in the other redevelopment areas of the Federal Republic was similar.[20] Between 1956 and 1960 there was a 19 percent increase in employment; i.e., almost twice the average increase. In total, this increase amounted to about 50,000 industrial employees, so that the increase in the redevelopment areas constituted 7 percent of the total increase in the Federal Republic; their percentage of total industrial employees in the Federal Republic thereby increased from 3.8 percent (1956) to approximately 4 percent in 1960.

Thus, in both groups of redevelopment areas, there were small increases in industrial employment compared to the increase in industry outside those areas. The relative backwardness of the redevelopment areas therefore was only slightly reduced. The percentage of industrial employees in the

---

[18] Excluding the Saar and West Berlin.

[19] The city districts have been omitted in this calculation because of their more advanced industrialization.

[20] This calculation, too, is only for Land districts. Parts of the zone frontier areas are included among the restoration areas.

zone frontier areas (5.3 percent) still remained below their percentage of the total population, which amounted to 8.7 percent in 1960. This relationship was even more unfavorable in the reconstruction areas, which with 4 percent of total industrial employment had 9.2 percent of the total population in 1960.

The small impact of the redevelopment policy is shown especially well in an analysis of the choice of sites for new or migrating industries for the periods 1955–57 and 1958–60.[21] In total, 1,724 enterprises with 247,565 employees were studied.[22] In the first period, 1955–57, the average size of enterprise was 174 employees, much higher than in the second period, when it was 117 employees per enterprise. In addition, the total number of employees in the first period (138,000) was higher than in the second (109,000). These differences show a gradual decline in the establishment of large enterprises and in the size of employment increases. Apart from adjustments of capacities, a labor shortage was the most important factor in this development. In both periods employment increases were greatest in the metal, the electrical, and the clothing industries. With approximately 174,000 employees, their employment amounted to 70 percent of the total number of employees in the new industries. The majority of the new enterprises located in Bavaria, Nordrhein-Westfalen, Baden-Wuerttemberg, and Niedersachsen; employment in the new industries in these Laender was 80 percent of the total of new employment. Among them, Bavaria led in both periods, with a total of 66,000 new employees.

In both periods, new industries in the redevelopment areas constituted a larger proportion of all new industries than their share in the general increase in industrial employment, but the increase in industrial employment in the rest of the Federal Republic was to a larger extent due to expansions of existing enterprises, not considered in this study. The choice of redevelopment areas as sites for new business was not—as might be supposed—due to the redevelopment policy, but rather was due to the increased labor shortage. Two hundred and forty-three, or 74 percent, of the 330 new enterprises in the redevelopment areas indicated that the labor supply was the determining factor in their choice of location.[23] One hundred and twenty-seven enterprises (38 percent) stated that future possibilities of expansion was a major reason, while about 10 percent indicated transportation or market factors. Only 16 enterprises (or 8 percent) chose their new location because of the redevelopment measures offered.

The importance of the labor supply in the choice of location increased in the second period. While 60 percent of the firms had made their choice on account of the labor supply in the 1955–57 period, 80 percent did so in 1958–60. Simultaneously, the proportion of firms with predominantly female labor increased considerably. In the first period, 52 out of 98 new enterprises had predominantly female employment (in 30 enterprises more than 75 percent); in the second, 166 out of 232 new firms employed women predominantly and in 128 of these firms women constituted over 75 percent of the total number of employees. Thus, on the whole, in the years 1958–60 the labor market became much more important as a locational factor than

[21] *Die Standortwahl der Industriebetriebe in der Bundesrepublik Deutschland im Zeitraum von 1955 bis 1960*, published by the Federal Ministry for Labor and Social Order, Bonn, 1961.

[22] Excluding the Saar and West Berlin. Only establishments with over 50 employees are included.

[23] In some cases more than one reason was given, so that, in total, there are 454 reasons from 330 enterprises.

before.[24] Expansion in the redevelopment areas also occurred in this period.

To date, the measures of the Federal Government directed toward the industrialization of the redevelopment areas have evidently had only a small impact, since their degree of industrialization has not increased much more than the average for the Federal Republic. And in those areas in which the degree of backwardness has been reduced, the tight labor market in the industrial areas has contributed much more than the area redevelopment policy.[25] In view of the long-term efforts and considerable funds expended on regional economic development, one must ask the reason for the small success. The reason may be found, not in a lack of funds, but rather in their poor use.

The greatest defect is probably the lack of exclusiveness of the policies for area redevelopment. The preferential treatment given to private industry as a stimulus to investment in the redevelopment areas is also provided for such other purposes as assistance to small business and assistance to expellees and refugees, purposes unconnected with redevelopment. In addition, the Federal financial policy has created such favorable conditions for investment financing (tax exemption for retained earnings) that the preferential treatment of the redevelopment areas becomes almost insignificant. The small number of large enterprises that were established in the redevelopment areas indicates this clearly. As long as similar or greater advantages can be had outside the redevelopment areas, it is not the redevelopment measures, but the advantages of location in relation to the general economic situation, which determine the choice of site for an industry.

The exclusiveness of area redevelopment policies is reduced even further by the special redevelopment measures of the Laender, since their redevelopment areas are regarded as additional redevelopment areas. They receive in general the same type of preferential treatment as the Federal redevelopment areas. Since the Laender have closer contact with their industries, they can direct entrepreneurs willing to invest to their own redevelopment areas first, and only after this to the Federal redevelopment areas. The greater the choice between redevelopment areas, the greater the regional distribution of private investments.

Finally, the Federal area redevelopment policy competes with the economic policy of the communities in the rest of the Federal Republic. As the communities can directly influence the establishment of industries, this competition is of special significance. Apart from the effect of small changes in the regional financial structure, the communities of the redevelopment areas have usually not been capable of effective competition because of their weak financial structures. Federal financial assistance to the communities in the redevelopment areas is limited to special municipal investments. These communities are, consequently, more limited and controlled in their expenditure policy than their financially stronger competitors outside the redevelopment areas.

A further weakness of the area redevelopment policy is the isolation of individual policies. The need for coordination of policies has already been pointed out with the example of the workers released through structural improvements in agriculture. The retraining and training measures

[24] The great increase in the number of foreign workers did not come until 1960.

[25] Cf., Die Industrialisierung passiver Raeume," *Informationen des Instituts fuer Raumforschung,* 6. Jg. (1956), No. 1, pp. 23 ff.

in the redevelopment areas make sense only if accompanied by the establishment of appropriate industries. The extent of the redevelopment areas, however, permits a vast regional distribution of industrial settlements and of other redevelopment measures. Consequently, the coordination of policies must be accomplished mainly in the local or regional unit. However, this does not happen, even for public investments, because responsibility rests in various administrative levels.

The lack of coordination of the individual redevelopment measures leads to their regional dissipation. Thus a large number of areas receiving redevelopment aid cannot be helped very much by these measures alone. Industrial undertakings stimulated by the redevelopment measures are scattered over the many redevelopment areas and, therefore, do not provide mutual interaction and support. To limit the redevelopment policies to smaller and fewer areas would promise much more success. The apparently rapid and satisfactory results of the central points program clearly argue against the present dispersion of area redevelopment measures.

A more concentrated redevelopment policy could be fruitfully supplemented by activating a policy of technical assistance for the location of industry,[26] especially if this policy is directed toward the establishment of large enterprises in central locations in the redevelopment areas. In general, large enterprises bring about rapid industrialization, and their development attracts additional firms and thus causes cumulative local growth. It is true that the choice of these large firms is related to their general economic policy problems; however, increased advertising of the redevelopment measures may assist in directing such firms to central locations in redevelopment areas.

The obscurity of redevelopment policy to date has constituted a great hindrance to area redevelopment. A lack of clarity in the policy results mainly from the involvement of innumerable authorities of the Federal and the Laender governments.[27] It is typical of economic policy since the war that the individual measures are not easily accessible even to the interested person, because they are announced by different ministries and institutions. German administrators do not publicize their policies sufficiently. There are, for instance, no official publications either on the preferential treatment of investments in area redevelopment policy or about the areas affected by this treatment. The administrative agencies have limited themselves in general to giving information only in response to inquiries.

In enumerating these deficiencies, this assessment of the German area redevelopment policy is directed not against its objectives or policies, but rather against the method of application. This method results from preoccupation with a generally successful economic policy, whose measures are directed mainly toward the large economic sectors that determine general economic growth. To publicize such policy measures is often neither desirable nor necessary. In addition, the backwardness of the redevelopment areas is no longer considered an emergency within the full employment economy, so that special policy measures do not seem to be necessary.

These weaknesses of the Federal Republic's area redevelopment policy have apparently been covered up by events. On the one hand, the great

---

[26] E. Ebner, *Wirtschaftliche Raumordnung in der industriellen Welt.* Veroeffentlichung der Akademie fuer Raumforschung und Landesplanung, Bd. XVI. Bremen, 1950, p. 32.

[27] Cf., *Die Raumordnung in der Bundesrepublik Deutschland, op. cit.*, p. 97.

labor shortage in the industrial centers pushes new enterprises into the redevelopment areas; on the other hand, the passive redevelopment policy noticeably decreased unemployment in the redevelopment areas—especially in the early 1950's. As a result of this policy, the population of the redevelopment areas has declined. Emigration, however, began to decrease after 1956; after 1958 the population even increased somewhat. The population index for the zone frontier areas and for the rehabilitation areas stood at 89.6 in 1960 (1950=100).

The great impact of the general labor shortage on the establishment of new industries in the redevelopment areas can be seen also in the changing choices of location of new enterprises resulting from the increased use of foreign workers in the industrial centers.[28] A comparison of the 650,000 (registered) foreign workers with the 44,500 employees in new enterprises in the redevelopment areas, or with the increase of 377,000 industrial employees in the Federal Republic from 1958 to 1960, shows the magnitude of this development. The foreign workers were hired predominantly in the industrial centers and thus reduced the tightness of these labor markets. This lessened the pressure on industries employing a relatively large amount of labor to invest in the redevelopment areas. This situation seems to continue.

The further success of the area redevelopment policy in the near future has become questionable, if new methods are not employed. One of these is the central points program, which does not have some of the defects mentioned above; an increase in this program could assure greater success. Evidently, however, for 1963 no increases and no changes in the other redevelopment policies are planned so that continued expansion in the redevelopment areas (as from 1958 to 1960) is not now assured. In the present phase of general economic development, dominated by investments for rationalizations because of the increase in competition, measures to encourage new enterprises or enlargement of existing enterprises in the redevelopment areas will be even less successful without new stimuli.

The above exposition should indicate that even a continuation of the successes of the redevelopment measures up to date will not be sufficient to eliminate underdevelopment in these areas. The relatively high seasonal unemployment in these areas points to the still persisting instability of their economic structure. It is surprising that the Federal Government does not take more advantage of the present boom situation to eliminate the structural imbalances in these areas and to stabilize their economies permanently. In the application of the concept of the "social market economy," area redevelopment policy in the Federal Republic of Germany is certainly deficient.

---

[28] Dittrich, "Notstandsgebiete in der Bundesrepublik," *op. cit.*, pp. 431 ff.

Part 5

Regional Economic Development Policies in Italy

Ettore Massacesi

Contents

Italy

VALLE
D'AOSTA
PIEMONTE
TORINO
MILANO
LOMBARDIA
Bergamo
Brescia
TRENTINO-
ALTO
ADIGE
Verona
VENETO
Padova
Venezia
FRIULI-
VENEZIA
GIULIA
Trieste
LEGEND
(Population of Cities)
• 100,000 to 500,000
★ 500,000 and over
Parma
Reggio
Modena
Ferrara
EMILIA - ROMAGNA
Bologna
LIGURIA
GENOVA
La Spezia
Firenze
Livorno
TOSCANA
MARCHE
Perugia
UMBRIA
ABRUZZI
E
MOLISE
LAZIO
ROMA
Bari
PUGLIA
CAMPANIA
NAPOLI
BASILICATA
Taranto
SARDEGNA
Cagliari
CALABRIA
Messina
Reggio Calabria
PALERMO
SICILIA
Catania
SCALE
1:4,500,000
0
100
200 KM.

The Italian South

Socio-Economic Background

Regional Policies in Italy: Definition

Italy's problem of economic development is often conceived of essentially as the problem of the dualism of the poor agricultural south and the richer industrial north. Such a statement, leading simply to a policy of industrialization of the south conceals important factors of sectoral disequilibria within each region. As Professor Marrama indicates, merely to concentrate on industrialization of the south may aggravate misery rather than alleviate it.[1]

Historically, differences in the well-being of the people were largely, though of course not solely, related to geophysical differences in the areas in which they lived. And such differences exist within as well as between large regions. In general, the wealth of an area has been related to the predominance of the plains over the hill zone, and of the latter over the mountain zone, and to the relative fertility of each.

Obviously, one cannot present an adequate picture of the entire economic situation of Italy by correlating the predominance of the plains or the fertile hills with the relative wealth of a region. But it is a fact that the standard of living of the population residing in the plain areas is much higher than that of the population of the mountains. And it is true that the economic development of the regions in which the plains or fertile hills predominate began much earlier and has become much more firmly established. Thus, all the major economically developed areas are situated in the Plain of the Po between the Alps and the Apennines. This part of Italy—due to its climate and its vegetation—does not differ very much from the central European countries with their relatively high rainfall and dependable rivers. These areas, consequently, have a rich agriculture and adequate pastures for the raising of livestock. But within this area in Italy, there are also noticeable regional differences: for instance, until about a decade ago, the region of Veneto was relatively much poorer than Lombardia and Piemonte. And in the interior of Veneto—a region from which important migrations, a sign of a low standard of living, flow toward foreign countries and toward other parts of Italy—there are areas like the Po Delta and Basso Polesine which have all the conditions that, even today, make for a kind of poverty comparable to that of the south.

Liguria is a rather uneven area from the geographic point of view, but it has been favored by natural ports such as Genova and Savona which offer promise for industrial development, as well as by natural beauty which has led to the rise of tourism of remarkable economic importance.

In the south of the Plain of the Po, between two eastern and western extensions of the Apennines, the countryside changes and the climate becomes Mediterranean. The weather cycle is completely different from that of northern Italy. There is not much rain and the rivers are dry during large parts of the year. However, three hill regions of cental Italy; i.e., Toscana, Umbria, and the Marche, and among these Toscana in particular—according to Luzzato—"represent, in general, greatest economic balance: of course, they are not wealthy areas, but they are reasonably well off; however, vast areas of desolate poverty can also be found in these

[1] Vittorio Marrama, *La Riduzione Degli Squilibri fra Regioni e Settori.* Relazione al: V Convegno Di Studi Di Economia e Politica Del Lavoro.

regions, such as the highest part of the Umbro-Marchigiano Apennines; there is also the Maremma Toscana, which has been one of the most desolate regions of Italy for about 2,000 years, and which today owes its fast, though not yet quite completed, development to the successful struggle against malaria." [2]

Since the war, the relative equilibrium of these three regions has been altered to the disadvantage of Umbria. This region does not possess any outlet to the sea and it is far from the most heavily used lines of communication. Furthermore, it is situated beyond the limits of the area assisted by the *Cassa per il Mezzogiorno* (the institution set up to develop the south). As Umbria has no particular natural advantages, and as it cannot take advantage of the economic development aid of the Cassa, this region has shown clear signs of economic stagnation.

Lazio lies next to Umbria. It is a classical example of a region with the most marked economic and social imbalance. Actually, the area is divided into three parts, one of which is the urban area of the city of Rome.

The city of Rome has a very high per capita income, but its economy is predominantly one of tertiary industries, because of its administrative activities as the capital and its attraction for tourists. The Latian area north of Rome shows clearly the symptoms of a depressed economy, with a poor agriculture and a lack of industrial activities; while to the south of Rome the agriculture of the Pontine Plain and the assistance to industrialization extended by the Cassa per il Mezzogiorno have created the preconditions for a relatively balanced economic and social development, already underway. Further south begins that part of Italy which has the most serious problems of economic and social underdevelopment. This is the Mezzogiorno of Italy.

In the publication cited above, Luzzato states:

> To the south of Lazio, the most striking contrast offers itself to the eyes of the less prepared visitor when he goes from the coast to the interior areas. Not only along the shores of the Gulf of Gaeta, Naples, and Salerno, but also further to the south along the coast of the Tyrrhenian Calabrium which is much less known, one finds a varied and rich vegetation, extreme density of population, especially around Naples, and ideal climatic conditions, which, since ancient times, have made it the preferred residence of the wealthy Romans. We find an analogous situation—although in less accentuated form and with some exceptions—along the Adriatic Sea, from the river Tronto down to the south, while, on the other hand, the Ionian coast, west of Taranto, which was once rich due to the numerous and flourishing cities of Magna Grecia, has been depopulated by malaria and left desolately abandoned. However, even the person from the less fortunate areas who turns toward the interior finds himself confronted with a completely different picture: these areas are only sparsely populated, with bare or burned mountains, with scarcely any trees, predominantly extensive grain farming with low returns, and little and extremely inconvenient ways of communication. Consequently, markets for the agricultural products are either completely lacking or exist only to a very limited extent.
>
> The same contrast exists in Sicily, perhaps to an even greater degree, particularly between the eastern and the northern coast and the entire interior of the island. On the coast, there are small landed properties, possibilities of irrigation—even if only through strenuous labor—extremely intensive citrus fruit cultures, wine, and almond trees, a rather high population density, and numerous cities, which are the seat of at least modest commercial and handicraft activities. In the interior, on the other hand, it is completely dry for many months; there is extensive wheat farming on large estates, little pasture and livestock, and agglomerations of the rural population in large and miserable centers which have nothing in common with cities but the name.

[2] Gino Luzzato, "Gli squilibri economici fra regione e regione e l'Unità nazionale," in *Gli Squilibri Regionali e l'Articolazione dell'Intervento Pubblico*. Reports of the National Center for the Social Protection of Milan, Italy, Lerici, ed., 1962.

Similar remarks can be made about Sardinia. All this confirms the general impression that in Italy there are marked differences within regions as well as between north and south.

It is necessary to take account of these facts in the following analysis of Italian regional policies since the war. Thus, in addition to the vast ecnomic depression of the south of Italy, there are certain areas in central and northern Italy with local problems of underdevelopment similar to those of the Mezzogiorno. This holds in particular for the mountain areas.[3]

In the following analysis, particular attention will be paid to the regional development policies of the south for the reason that these policies have an organic character and are based on regional rather than on sectoral considerations. On the other hand, the assistance extended to depressed local economies in the central and northern regions has predominantly sectoral characteristics. It consists of intervention in favor of agriculture in these areas, or of subsidization of particular industrial activities, but never treats the region as a whole. Italian economic policy has traditionally been oriented toward sectoral intervention in accordance with the division of authority between the various ministries (Agriculture, Industry, Public Services, Transport, etc.). There is, however, a tendency in more recent concepts of Italian regional policy toward policies framed more from a regional point of view than from considerations of particular sectoral disequilibria.

The most important, indeed until now unique, attempt to institute policy measures based on a predominantly regional perspective, is that of the Cassa per il Mezzogiorno. At the time of its creation, it represented a new institutional solution; as we shall see, this new entity—to whose conception the scheme of the Tennessee Valley Authority contributed to a considerable extent—serves also to overcome the sectoral specialization of authority of the various ministries, developing an organic and homogeneous approach to regional problems.

In the countries with developed, if not yet completely mature, economies, regional policies are usually directed toward the problems of relatively declining areas; i.e., those areas which, having an economic structure based predominantly on a single industry, suffer directly and immediately from the contraction of its major industry. This is true of some coal basins and of some areas with heavy concentration in the textile industry. It should be emphasized at the outset that this phenomenon is not a major source of problems in Italy.

Particular problems do exist for individual industries, difficulties which transcend narrow geographic limits. But the troubles of an industrial sector rarely assume such importance as to constitute regional difficulties in the usual broad meaning of the term "regional." Excepting agriculture, whose problems have caused the decline of entire regions, extensive migration of labor, and great social problems, in Italy there is no industry which so dominates the economy of a region that a crisis in it would cause pronounced depression in the whole region.

Although the Italian industrial system appears to be concentrated geographically, in reality the regions with the greatest industrial concentration—and not only the industrial triangle of Milano-Torino-Genova—are characterized by a marked industrial diversity. Historically, this is due to

[3] See, in particular, the reports of the International Study Congress on the Problems of Backward Areas. Giuffre, ed., Rapporto della Commissione Italiana, 1954, pp. 49–59.

761-932 O—65——15

the fact that the Italian economy not possessing natural resources of any importance, has never developed an entrepreneurial class psychologically conditioned to the predominance of one industry. It is true that there are zones in Lombardia, for instance, where the textile industry, wool, cotton, or silk, has been dominant. But when there was a crisis in this sector which eliminated antiquated enterprises, reconversion was almost automatic because of the ability of the local entrepreneurs to turn to new productive sectors.

In a few cases an industry is of such importance that a crisis could cause difficulties in the regional economic system in spite of its diversity. This is the case in Torino, where the automobile industry is concentrated and where great problems could arise if production should be sharply reduced. Fortunately, however, this industry is presently expanding greatly.

It must be said that crises of particular industries have had local effects of some importance, though the impact is not truly regional. The most important of these industries are:

(1) The sulfur industry, which is undergoing a process of modernization and of reconversion causing employment difficulties in the provinces of Enna Agrigento and of Caltanisetta in Sicily.

(2) The coal, lead, and zinc mining industries, which are concentrated in the area of Sulcis Iglesiente in Sardinia and which are undergoing reconversion as a consequence of the treaty provisions that respectively instituted the European Coal and Steel Community—regarding coal production—and the European Economic Community—regarding the production of lead and zinc.

(3) The iron mining industry in the area of the Monte Amiata and on the Island of Elba.

(4) The shipbuilding industry, which suffers from the diffculties common to this industry all over the world and which in some areas, as for instances the provinces of Trieste and Gorizia, also has a dockyards crisis brought about by the political and geographic consequences of the Peace Treaty of 1947.[4]

Thus, in Italy the problem of declining industrial areas is not as important as in many other western countries. But there are areas, apart from the Mezzogiorno, in which problems of underdevelopment do exist and they may assume regional importance.

In recent years, regional, provincial, and local administrations have increased their efforts to analyze the socioeconomic regional structure, and today there is no region in Italy which does not have voluminous data on local economic and social conditions. However, these studies rarely result in action because the local entities do not normally possess sufficient administrative authority or the financial capability necessary to effective support of local economic activities.[5]

---

[4] The Italian shipbuilding industry is located in 11 different centers in which industrial employment is greatly concentrated in shipbuilding. According to the data of the census of 1951, the industry represented the following percentages of total manufacturing industries: Gorizia 59 percent, Trieste 25 percent, La Spezia 22 percent, Genoa 13 percent, Venice 6 percent, Savona 5 percent, Ancona 14 percent, Livorno 13 percent, Taranto 65 percent, Palermo 27 percent, Naples 8 percent; since that date the percentages have greatly decreased.

[5] See Giacomo Corna-Pellegrini, "Esperienze di studi e pianificazione regionale in Italia," in *Gli Squilibri Regionali e l'Articolazione dell'Intervento Pubblico.* Reports of the National Center for the Social Protection of Milan, Lerici, ed., 1962, pp. 381–415. This report constitutes a systematic and well-documented study of the most significant experiences in Italy in the past 15 years. It contains an extensive bibliography.

Italy consists of 19 regions only 4 of which are constitutionally recognized as such (namely, the regions of "Special Status": Valle d'Aosta, Trentino-Alto Adige, Sicily, and Sardinia), while the others are, at present, only geographical designations and await legislative action. One of the most controversial subjects during the recent electoral campaign, and an issue likely to be of importance in Italian politics in the future, is that of regional constitutions within the national constitutional framework.

In concluding these preliminary remarks, the following characteristics of Italian regional economic policies should be emphasized:

(1) They are to develop the economically and socially backward areas, rather than to assist reconversions in declining industrial areas.

(2) With the single important exception of the development policy of the Mezzogiorno, based on a regional conception concerning the entire area, they are implemented predominantly by measures of a sectoral character.

(3) There are some pressures for greater differentiation of economic policy and for its conception and implementation on a regional basis, but these tendencies have not yet been sufficiently crystallized on the operational level.[6]

Historical Premises of Italian Regional Policies

HISTORICO-INSTITUTIONAL ASPECTS OF REGIONAL PROBLEMS

A consideration of utmost importance to an understanding of regional economic differences in Italy is the fact that national unity was achieved only a century ago, and that before unification Italy was divided into seven national states of extremely diverse size and political and economic institutions. The fusion of these systems into a unified economy took long to achieve and has had continuing effects on relative regional development. Each national state was a more or less closed economic system. For example, the railroad network, then a most important determinant of economic development, was extremely unequal in density from state to state, and communications between states were not continuous.

A controversy has existed as to whether economic differences between the north and the south grew largely after unification, or whether they preceded it, and were perhaps aggravated in subsequent years. In one of the more careful examinations of the problem, Eckaus comes to the second conclusion, estimating that at the time of unification per capita income in agriculture was higher in the north than in the south by about 20 percent, and for all activities the differences was between 12 percent and 25 percent. He further concludes:

> As to the relative capacity for further development of the two regions, looked at either *a priori* or *a posteriori,* I believe that one has to arrive at the conclusion, that it was greater in the North. The data on its social capital and the types—apart from the quantity—of its agricultural and industrial production lead us to think that, in the North, the change from the ancient to the modern form of life had been well completed at a time when it was still in its most primitive beginnings in the South.

---

[6] Of special interest is the speech by the Minister of Finance, Ugo La Malfa, in Parliament on May 22, 1962, entitled "Problemi e Prospettive dello Sviluppo Economico Italiano," which is the basic document of the program developed for the realization of a policy of economic planning in Italy.

In addition, the North had the advantage of its silk production, a product that was exported in large quantities and therefore furnished foreign exchange. Finally, although this is a less concrete element and even more subject to individual judgment, it seems that the North was also, at that time, superior from the point of view of intelligence, enthusiasm, and expectations. With few exceptions, the major part of the South seems to have been stagnant. In the North, on the other hand, it appears that in 1860 economic changes were spreading slowly but surely from the ctities to the provinces.[7]

Since unification, the political and economic history shows an accentuation of the initial divergencies. These were intensified by various political conflicts between the north and the south.[8]

The economic history of Italy, of interest as background for our analysis, may be summarized as follows: By the time of unification and for a rather long time before, the agriculture of the Po Plain had reached a state of development which could compare with the most developed in central Europe. This was true of Piemonte, due largely to the foresight of Cavour—the man of Piemonte who "made the Italian Risorgimento and led the country to unity"; and it was also true of Lombardia and Veneto, in part because the Austrian monarchy saw clearly in the historical setting of the time the political profitability of extending special favors to the agricultural propertied class. In addition, agriculture flourished in Toscana as a result of the far-reaching application of the *mezzadrile* (sharecropping) system in that region, and it was rich in the area of Naples because of the natural fertility of the soil and its climate.

These same economic areas contained the relatively more advanced industrial systems. In Piemonte, Lombardia, and Liguria—the areas now called the industrial triangle—were found the most important industrial activities: textiles, mechanical industries, steel, and the extractive industries based on the small existing deposits, which were then of sufficient importance to constitute an effective stimulus to industry, though subsequently they became practically insignificant. This industrial progress was reinforced by the development of improved transportation facilities, including transalpine lines through the St. Gotthard Pass (1884) and the Simplon Tunnel (1906) as well as a dense internal railway network.[9]

In Toscana, the textile industry predominated—in Prato it was wool, in Pontedera and Pisa, cotton. In the south, however, there were only a few mechanical and textile activities in the area of Naples. Apart from this, mainly handicraft industry was to be found.

The protective tariff concessions made in 1887 to industry, on the one hand, and to grain producers, on the other, had a very damaging impact on the Mezzogiorno. According to Luzzatto, "it was in the period of the full application of the tariff of 1887, and of the more apparent manifestations of its effects on the national economy, that the Mezzogiorno made a great sacrifice in favor of the industrial interests of some regions of the north, which has been considered an immediate consequence of national unity and the elimination of internal customs."[10] While the most typical and most abundant products of the diversified agriculture of the south encountered major export difficulties, the manufactures of the northern industries have

[7] L. S. Eckaus, "L'esistenza di differenze economiche tra Nord e Sud d'Italia al tempo dell'unificazione," *Moneta e Credito*, 1960, pp. 347 ff.

[8] See Umberto Zanotti-Bianco, "Introduzione alla questione meridionale," *Nord e Sud*, 1960.

[9] Luzzato, *op. cit.*, pp. 77–80.

[10] *Ibid.*

had a secure, though small, market in the Mezzogiorno in which they did not have foreign competition.

Finally, the problems created by customs policy were aggravated by the demographic situation. Population pressure increased, partly because of the increase in the birth rate, partly because of the decrease in mortality. But these tendencies appeared in different degrees in the north and in the south. In the south, the situation tended to worsen and finally brought about that phenomenon of migration which was to be another cause of the widening of the economic differences between north and south. Luzzato says:

> The movement of emigrants from the entire kingdom to the transoceanic countries, which after having reached a maximum of 200,000 in 1888 and in 1892 * * * decreased in the following 8 years to a much lower figure, only to increase again much more rapidly in the first 13 years of the new century, reached a maximum of over 800,000 emigrants in 1907 and in 1913, 650,000 of whom came from the continental Mezzogiorno and from Sicily.
>
> This enormous exodus, which in some regions, like Basilicata, led to a noticeable diminution of the already-scarce population, was, first of all, a symptom of the tragic situation of the great masses of fieldworkers, who had never before left their country and who, having learned that some groups of farmers had found in America, and particularly in the United States, more tolerable living conditions, faced the risks and troubles of a long sea voyage, not to secure a fortune, but to escape misery and hunger * * *. In sum, while recognizing that emigration represented a temporary alleviation of a situation that had become intolerable, one cannot hold with certainty that it has led to an effective solution of the problem of the South.[11]

Actually, the alleviation of immediate economic and social tensions made less urgent and less evident the need for an economic policy directed toward harmonization of the economic conditions of the Italian regions. Furthermore, the emigrants were usually the more enterprising men, so that the south of Italy was deprived of its more important, even if only potential, human capabilities. An analogous phenomenon can be found in other regions in central and northern Italy, for example, in the Marche and in Veneto. Thus the differences between regions were accentuated, at least from a longrun point of view.

The aspect of entrepreneurial capacity cannot be overstressed. As has been seen, in recent years the reconstruction of the Italian economy took place in the northern region where there is an environment conducive to the development of intellectuals and entrepreneurs capable of initiating new industrial enterprises; in contrast, the process of industrialization of the Mezzogiorno has been and will be retarded because of a deficiency of the human factor, that is, of men able to assume the risks of industrial enterprise and to organize the instruments of production.

In conclusion, the retarding effect of the autarkic Fascist policy on the entire Italian economy in the period between the two world wars must not be neglected. In a country with an economic structure like Italy's, which necessarily implies trade with other countries if only because of its insufficiency of natural resources, the attempt to establish a self-sufficient economy could not have failed to retard progress and so was bound to lead to crystallization, if not actual accentuation, of the imbalances between regions. Furthermore, Fascist policies prohibiting emigration, seriously impeding internal migration, and suppressing trade-union activity in defense of workers aggravated the problems.

This is, in substance the historical background of an economic policy which seeks to attain equilibrium on the regional economic level—a policy

[11] *Ibid.*, p. 80.

applied at first hesitantly and then with greater determination in the new Italian democracy. It is an economic policy that will assume greater dimensions in the future.

NATURAL RESOURCES AND OTHER FACTORS DETERMINING THE LOCATION OF ECONOMIC ACTIVITIES

Aside from geographical and historico-institutional factors, the distribution of natural resources, as already noted, is one of the basic reasons for the disparities between regions. It is, of course, true that natural resources have always been scarce in Italy, and that this deficiency was one of the causes for the slow development of the Italian economy in the 19th century. Nevertheless, the few available natural resources gave rise to some industrial activity in the processing of these resources, which in turn encouraged the growth of new industries based on them as raw materials. This was the origin of entrepreneurial and industrial traditions on which subsequent and more far-reaching economic development could be founded.

For instance, the few small iron-mining establishments in the valleys of the Prealpi in Lecco and Bergamo gave rise to the Falck iron firm which represented, until 1946–48, the major basis of Italian steel production. Since then, with the adoption of the large northern development programs of the steel companies with Government participation—known now as "Italsider"—and with the establishment of the steelworks on the coast, the center of the industry has been pushed more toward the south. And under the development policy of the Mezzogiorno a great steel center is rising at Taranto, which already constitutes a pole of industrial development.

Hydroelectric energy is another locational factor that has augmented the regional disequilibria. It has influenced the development of the steel industry described above, as well as that of smaller centers based on the iron mines of the Island of Elba, of Piombino, and of Livorno. Indeed, once again the availability of water, which caused the development of the two different types of agriculture in the north and in the south, is a determinant for the concentration in the north—with some exceptions, of course—of important hydroelectric establishments using the huge quantities of glacial water of the Alps. In the period between the two world wars, the exceptional stimulus given to the production of hydroelectric energy had great impact on the different developments of the regional economies. And when technological progress and the reopening of international trade stimulated thermoelectric energy, the discovery of natural gas in the Po Plain gave further impetus to the northern region. Only later—as we shall see, it is always much later in the Mezzogiorno—did the discovery of natural gas in the south create new hopes for economic development there.

Finally, while the availability of water in the northern and central regions has made possible the development and use of all the economically profitable resources, in the south the problems of the water supply for cities and provinces remain largely unsolved, notwithstanding the great efforts of the Cassa per il Mezzogiorno to construct an organic and rational water system. For some industrial establishments which have been able to maintain themselves in the south, the provision of water for industrial uses still constitutes a difficulty. It can, of course, be surmounted, but only at high costs, through the establishment of the necessary infrastructure.

Another locational factor that is important for industry, as well as for the development of agriculture, is the condition of roads. The geographic, geological, and orographical structures have been serious obstacles to the construction of an organic net of railroads and roads in the south. It is significant that the secondary railroads, according to the classification of the Italian Railway Administration, are concentrated in the Mezzogiorno.

The system of roads in the south, too, has such quantitative and qualitative inadequacies as to be a positive determinant of the attraction of economic activities to the north rather than to the south. Many of the southern roads are old and bad, leading to great communication difficulties and increasing maintenance costs. The first step to solve this problem has been taken by the Cassa per il Mezzogiorno, which has concentrated on improvement of road surfaces by increasing the proportion of asphalt roads. On the national level, the *autostrade* to be built in the south should constitute a most important element in the process of industrialization. Those along the Adriatic Sea, which will link Milan and Bologna with Pescara and Bari, will have particular importance, as will the *autostrada* from Milan to Rome and Naples, with an extension into Calabria and with one branch going from Naples to Bari so as to lessen the isolation of the Basilicata region.

To these causes of natural origin, or involving natural factors, and to the economic policy measures which have consciously or unconsciously favored the already-developed regions, there must be added the consequences of the war. The destruction of productive capacity during the Second World War was much greater in the South than in the Centro-Nord, for Sicily and the continental Mezzogiorno first became battlefields and then territories of occupation. Voechting estimates, for example, that while 35 percent of the economic assets of Abruzzi and Campania was destroyed, the proportion was only 12 percent in the valley of the Po and that the capacity for electric power output was reduced by 55 percent and 50 percent in southern Italy and Sicily, respectively, compared to only 10 percent in the north. In the south, the lack of electrical energy alone caused losses of income over four times as great as those in the north.[12]

Another locational factor of importance is the availability of skilled labor. The high degree of illiteracy in the Mezzogiorno until a few years ago certainly constituted a deterrent to new industrial activity in the south. Special efforts have been made, within the scope of the regional development policy, to provide the regions that are at a disadvantage from this point of view with sufficiently qualified manpower. This is true both for the south and for other regions in which work traditions are less developed.

THE HUMAN ASPECTS OF REGIONAL DIVERSITY

Demographic evolution and economic development are interacting phenomena, though it is difficult to establish to what exent they affect each other. It is certain that the interaction of these two phenomena in Italy has led to important consequences from the point of view of regional disequilibria. The natural demographic increase, which varies from region to region, has always been high in the Mezzogiorno and in some regions of central Italy.

In the 3 years from 1861 to 1863, the average national birth rate was 37.8 per thousand inhabitants and the death rate was 30.3 per thousand. In both births and deaths the entire south was much above the national

[12] Friedrich Voechting, *La Questione Meridionale,* Istituto Editoriale del Mezzogiorno, 1955, p. 593.

average during that period, while the north was below the national average. The central regions, on the other hand, had about average birth and death rates.

In the 3 years from 1959 to 1961—one century later—both the birth and the death rates had decreased to 18.2 per thousand and 9.7 per thousand, respectively; but there are again significant differences between regions. The birth rate is very low—10 to 12 per thousand inhabitants—in the central and northern regions, with the exception of Veneto and Trentino-Alto Adige, while it is still very high—22 to 24 per thousand inhabitants—in the southern regions, with the exception of Abruzzi e Molise. At the same time, the death rate is slightly higher in the Centro-Nord—10 to 13 per thousand inhabitants—while it is lower than the national average in the south—about 8 per thousand. Obviously, this is due to the diverse age structure of the population, which is, on the average, older in the north than in the south. Consequently, the actual rate of increase is lowest in the north—it is even negative in Piemonte and Liguria—while, relative to the national average of 8.5 per thousand, it is very high in the south, about 15 per thousand.

Following are the regional rates of natural population increase, per thousand, for 1959–61:

Calabria	16.5	Marche	6.0
Campania	15.9	Umbria	5.9
Basilicata	15.8	Lombardia	5.1
Sardinia	15.5	Emilia-Romagna	3.9
Puglia	15.3	Toscana	3.6
Sicily	13.9	Valle d'Aosta	2.1
Lazio	11.1	Friuli-Venezia Giulia	.8
Trentino-Alto Adige	8.3	Liguria	−0
Veneto	8.2	Piemonte	−0.5
Abruzzi e Molise	8.1		

The effects of the natural population increase, however, are greatly modified by the phenomenon of migration. It has been calculated that in the period between the unification of Italy and the Second World War about 6 million citizens emigrated to America or to other parts of Europe.[13] In the the period since 1945 the streams of emigrants, which had practically stopped during the Fascist period, have again begun to flow. The following groups of migrants can be distinguished:

(1) A persistent stream of transoceanic emigration.
(2) Another large stream into the European countries; this stream increased during 1950–60 and assumed much greater significance than before.
(3) A stream, which will become of greater and greater importance, from the poorest to the more wealthy regions of Italy.
(4) A series of intertwining streams within particular regions, especially in the south, and within particular provinces and communities.

The following figures will give some idea of the diverse role which these migratory streams have played in the last decade. From 1951 to 1961 the natural increase of the Italian population was 4,142 million, while the

[13] *Introduzione ai Problemi del Lavoro,* Istituto Sociale Ambrosiano, 1952, vol. I, p. 58.

effective increase for the same period was 2,948 million. Therefore, always assuming that one can derive a useful estimate of the extent of emigration from a comparison of the natural with the effective population increase, there has been a net migratory movement of 1,194 million, or about 120,000 persons per year.

Considering the differences between natural and effective increases by groups of regions, the northwest has had an estimated positive immigration of about 1,029 million. On the other hand, central Italy and Veneto have had an estimated positive emigration of about 457,000. The Mezzogiorno, finally, has had a natural increase of 2,650,000 but an effective increase of 884,000; that is, almost 190,000 persons move every year from the south to other regions of Italy and abroad.

TABLE I.—*Natural and Effective Population Increase, by Regions, 1861 to 1936*

Region [1]	Natural increase	Effective increase	Difference	Percent effective increase of natural
Piemonte	1, 363, 179	741, 871	−621, 308	55. 35
Liguria	469, 415	695, 442	+226, 027	148. 28
Lombardia	2, 279, 101	2, 575, 342	−153, 759	94. 37
Venezia Euganea	3, 132, 591	1, 947, 526	−1, 185, 065	62. 18
Emilia	1, 702, 978	1, 333, 224	−369, 754	78. 33
Toscana	1, 477, 240	1, 007, 372	−469, 868	68. 20
Marche	755, 712	394, 998	−360, 714	52. 22
Umbria	446, 349	212, 899	−233, 495	47. 73
Lazio	847, 909	1, 904, 063	+1, 056, 154	224. 54
Meridione [2]	6, 131, 603	3, 463, 972	−2, 667, 631	56. 50
Sicilia	2, 503, 968	1, 607, 664	−896, 304	64. 30
Sardegna	524, 612	446, 142	−78, 470	85. 14
Total	22, 084, 702	16, 330, 515	−5, 754, 187	73. 84

1 Excluding Venezia Tridentina and Giulia, for which data are lacking.

2 Abruzzi, Molise, Campania, Puglia, Lucania and Calabria have been consolidated. Separate data begin only on June 1, 1882.

Source: Coppola d'Anna F., *Popolazione, Reddito e Finanze Pubbliche d'Italia dal 1860 ad oggi*, p. 26.

The census also shows that while the Italian population increased by about 6 percent, on the average, that of the major cities increased by 20.1 percent. This vast expansion of the cities appears to be higher than average in the north (with the exception of Liguria) and in Lazio, and below average in the other regions (with the exception of Basilicata and Sardinia). In certain industrial zones, immigration has caused problems of congestion.

If one considers zones of attraction to be those which, over a relatively long period, for instance a decade, have a strong positive balance of immigrants over emigrants, the following conclusions may be drawn:

Among the Italian regions, the only ones for which this condition holds are Piemonte, Lombardia, Liguria, and Lazio. Other regions, such as Emilia-Romagna and Toscana, have a very high number of immigrants, but also an almost equal number of emigrants. * * * If we except Lazio (or Rome), which should be analyzed by itself, we have left only the three regions of the Northwest of Italy. And even in these three regions there are provinces which, for years, have had a negative migratory balance: these are the provinces of Cuneo in Piemonte, of La Spezia in Liguria, of Sondrio Brescia, Cremona, and Mantova in Lombardia. A look at the map confirms that all these areas are provinces at the periphery of the area of maximum industrial concentration within the three regions—an area which is no more a triangle as it used to be, but a kind of rough quadrangle * * *. Finally, it must not be forgotten that in the interior of the provinces with a large positive migratory balance, such as the provinces of Milano and Torino, there is a marked transfer of people from the zones on the periphery, mostly the hills and mountain areas, to the industrial zones. * * * To establish precisely the region of origin of the immigrants in the industrial quadrangle is just as difficult as to determine their exact number. Here, too, however, if we refer again to some estimates * * * it seems possible to state * * * that perhaps 35% of the immigrants come from the South and the islands, 20% from Veneto, 20–25% from the mountain and hill zones adjacent to the industrial quadrangle, 10–15% from Central Italy, and the last 5–10% from the other "flight-areas" of the North, like the Delta Ferrarese or from areas of rapid demographic exchange, like the Appennino Tosco-Emiliano.[14]

The phenomenon of zones of rapid demographic exchange is a significant indication of the events that have occurred in Italy in recent years. They exist not only in some areas of the Appennino Emiliano and Toscano, but also in the "Riviera dei Fiori" in Liguria. These are zones to which the southern farmers migrate in order to take up the jobs left vacant by the indigenous people, who have emigrated to the city with the intention of changing both their residence and their occupation.

A careful student of the economic problems of the Mezzogiorno, Francesco Compagna,[15] has stated that the problem of agriculture, the problem of the south, and the demographic problem are one and the same, and should be attacked as such. This opinion could be extended to all regional disequilibria. In effect, the widespread opinion that internal migration constitutes a natural adjustment to regional disequilibria must be corrected in view of the dimension of the phenomenon and some of its qualitative aspects. In other words, a fundamental cause of the emigration from the underdeveloped to the more advanced areas may be found in the regional disequilibria, but it would be a gross oversimplification to conclude that the emigration itself constitutes the solution for the disequilibria.

Actually, in Italy, there is an ever clearer superposition of an industrial society upon a rural society. While the population actively engaged in agriculture decreases, that engaged in industry and the services increases. This is a phenomenon of industrializing society but one that sometimes occurs together with others of a more pathological character. And it is for this reason that the corrective measures of economic policy must continuously be applied, regionally or by sectors.

In 1936 the population working in agriculture in Italy constituted almost 50 percent of the total labor force. In 1951 there were still 6,800,000 persons working in agriculture, or about 40 percent of total employment; in 1961 the agricultural labor force had diminished to about 5.8 million, which was a little less than 30 percent of total employment. But this phenomenon has, obviously, different dimensions in the north and in the south. Those employed in agriculture in the north and in central Italy

---

[14] Luciano Gallino, "Problemi inerenti alle zone di attrazione," in *Gli Squilibri Regionali e l'Articolazione dell'Intervento Pubblico, op. cit.*, pp. 279 ff.

[15] See, particularly, Francesco Compagna, *I Terroni in Città,* Editori La Terza, 1959.

constituted 34 percent of total employment in 1951, and have decreased to 23 percent in 1961, while in the south total agricultural employment in 1951 was 52 percent of total employment, and still about 45 percent in 1961. During the same period, industrial employment in the Centro-Nord increased from 4.2 to 5.7 million, while the increase in the south was from 1.3 to 1.6 million. We can conclude from this, again, that the divergencies between Centro-Nord and south have not diminished, but rather increased.

During the same period and in subsequent years unemployment has decreased, a phenomenon which is not easy to measure because Italian unemployment was the result of two components: Unemployment in the usual sense of the term, and underemployment, which was particularly high in agriculture and in the services, especially the commercial services. Progressively, this underemployment became complete employment. Subsequently, the members of wholly unemployed decreased, and have now reached a level which, though still substantial, is nevertheless tolerable. Today there exist, in addition, some scarcities of skilled manpower, which at certain times and places become real bottlenecks.

As a result of those changes, regional disequilibria have been accentuated, at least in the short run, and, lacking the necessary economic countermeasures, also in the long run. Although some "flight zones," because of their natural characteristics, are destined to be unpopulated or thinly populated, or—under a more favorable hypothesis—to be useful only after reforestation or as pasture, in others it is necessary that a labor force remain available. In these, continuing emigration of the labor force in the age groups of highest productivity has damaging effects which may prejudice the tentative beginnings of solutions of the regional problems.

This is the reason why demographic problems and the social movement of the population, on the one hand, and regional economic development, and particularly the economic development of the south, on the other hand, are the subject of great debate.[16] Migration will certainly be one of the fundamental considerations in the possible reform of the operations of the Cassa per il Mezzogiorno and in the application of the policy of economic planning on the regional level.[17]

General Outline of Economic Development Policy

All the preceding historical and institutional factors, all the technical, economic, and social circumstances briefly mentioned, together with the effect of war destruction on productive capacity and the structure of production, combine to emphasize the immediate need for the best possible economic policy measures to solve the regional problems of underdevelopment, depression, and economic stagnation.

---

[16] See G. Ackley and L. Spaventa, "Emigrazione e Industrializzazione nel Mezzogiorno: un commento allo studio di Vera Lutz," *Moneta e Credito,* June 1962, p. 135; Vera C. Lutz, "Il processo di sviluppo in un sistema economico 'dualistico,' " *Moneta e Credito,* December 1958, p. 459; Vera C. Lutz, "Alcuni aspetti strutturali del problema del Mezzogiorno: La complementarità dell'emigrazione e dell'industrializzazione," *Moneta e Credito,* December 1961, p. 407; "Una polemica di fondo sulla politica meridionalista," *Bancaria,* November 1960; Vera C. Lutz, "Reply," *Moneta e Credito,* June 1962, p. 144.

[17] See "Emigrazione e sviluppo economico," *Sintesi Economica,* October 1962, an article by Pasquale Saraceno, an economist with direct responsibilities in the formation of the policy of planning in Italy. See also *L'Italia verso la Piena Occupazione,* Feltrinelli, 1963.

The starting point of the new economic policy with regional "overtones" coincides with the end of the period of postwar reconstruction—at least in its major aspects. La Malfa writes:

The operations of reconstruction, which, among other types of assistance, profited from support by UNRRA, as well as from other United States aid in the amount of 1200 billion lire, can be said to have been completed around 1950, the year in which the per capita income once more regained the highest prewar level. But once the prewar productive capacity was regained, this made more obvious the elements of weakness in our economic system: the modest per capita income, about 160,000 lire, did not leave a margin large enough for adequate formation of new capital. The productive structure, particularly that of the manufacturing industries, was underdeveloped.

And it is at this starting point that the policy of development began which gave rise to what has been called "the Italian economic miracle." [18]

Though beginnings have been made in the solutions of certain problems, those that have not been solved are posed again in new terms. La Malfa continues:

After a period of intensive development which, in its essential aspects, has come without directives of total planning, it has become necessary again to consider the problem of the kind of policy most suitable for our present requirements for economic development. And this has become necessary for two reasons: First, although many situations of underdevelopment have been alleviated to some extent in absolute terms, they have nevertheless become less tolerable for our society because of the contrast * * * with situations which have not only improved much faster, but which continue to have the most favorable prospects for further development. Second, the level of income achieved in the country allows us today to face the old problems with much less pressure on the national resources than would have been necessary ten years ago.[19]

The object of this investigation, then, is to examine the direction of the regional economic development policy applied in Italy between 1950 and 1962, and, at least briefly in the conclusions, to indicate the prospects for the future of this policy. The progress already achieved in dealing with regional and sectoral imbalances has accentuated rather than decreased the necessity to set out, once more, the objectives of regional economic policy and the techniques of intervention to be applied in the future, in order to complete the solution of the problem.

The outstanding manifestation of the policy of economic development on the regional level is certainly the creation of the Cassa per il Mezzogiorno. And this is so for conceptual reasons, because creation of the Cassa involved the achievement of a completely new economic policy, as well as for material reasons, given the magnitude of intervention and of the financial means committed. In the following investigation we shall give special attention to the Cassa per il Mezzogiorno, in view of its central position in the regional development program and the special characteristics of its policies. But the Cassa does not represent the entire development policy of the south during the 12-year period to be examined. Certain other measures of territorial and of sectoral character, which have been stressed particularly in the southern regions, are part of development policy.

The first or territorial category includes the provisions and funds for the Sicilian region under the law instituting the *regione autonoma.* It also includes the provisions for Calabria, made after a tragic flood, which are to alleviate the grave geological difficulties of this area. These provisions have assumed such great importance from the techno-economic point of

[18] Ugo La Malfa, "Problemi e Prospettive dello Sviluppo Economico Italiano," presented to Parliament on May 22, 1962, on behalf of the Ministry of Finance.

[19] *Ibid.*

view that they have been transformed, beyond what was originally intended, into a program for regional development.

In this category also is the plan for the "rebirth of Sardinia," which, because it was more recently adopted and implemented, is more elaborate and complete in its techniques and has greater political and institutional significance. The special law for Naples also falls in this category of territorial intervention. It provides the *Comune* of Naples with large financial means, though with few institutional and administrative directions regarding the expenditures of the funds, in order to rehabilitate a city of such importance for the cultural and economic life of the continental Mezzogiorno.

In the second group of sectoral policy measures, which are of special significance for the south, fall certain laws concerning agriculture, particularly the law for the mountain zones and the 5-year "Green Plan" for the development of agriculture (*piano verde*), as well as certain provisions requiring that industrial enterprises with Government participation reserve some part of their new investments for the southern region.

Thus, since 1950, the problem of the south has entered a new phase based on the acceptance of principles which can be summarized as follows:

(1) Economic policy for the Mezzogiorno is designed to counteract those natural tendencies and forces which, if left to themselves, would aggravate the dualism, the asymmetry, and the differences which have worked to the disadvantage of the Mezzogiorno.

(2) The economic development of the south must be promoted and sustained not only in the interest of the south alone, but also in the interest of further development of the north, and consequently, by definition, in the interest of harmonization, constantly pushing the entire Italian economy toward higher levels of income, employment, and welfare.

(3) An adequate policy of development for the southern regions must not only work within the framework of, and in coordination with, a wider and organic development policy for the entire Italian economy, but must also, above all, be sustained with resources received from a common national fund, to which the whole country, including particularly the more advanced regions, should contribute in their own interest.

(4) The policy measures and the aid to the development of the south constitute a real and proper productive investment which the Italian economy makes for its own advantage, and are not mere grants made only for charitable or "social" reasons.

(5) The ultimate goal of the development policy is not to take away something from the north in order to give it to the south, but to add to the economic capacity of both. With the start in the south of a process of economic growth which can feed on itself and proceed under its own power, this region should lose its traditional character as the "second-rank" Italy (*Italia minore* in contrast to *Italia maggiore*), which only served to slow down the general development. The south must become an integral, essential, and equally dynamic part of one single economic system, which can grow at a faster rate and with much greater stability than in the past.

To complete the general picture of economic policy adopted on the regional level, it is necessary to emphasize that it is not limited to the Mezzogiorno. Certain territorial policies have also been applied in the Centro-

Nord, but with less conviction and firmness. This group of territorial measures includes, particularly, the law for the development of the depressed areas of the Centro-Nord, though it has been of only limited importance. In addition, there are some specific measures in the special legislation establishing the autonomous regions of Trentino-Alto Adige and Valle d'Aosta. As to the sectoral measures, the law for the mountain zones and the "Green Plan" for agriculture apply to the Centro-Nord as well as to the south.

Development Policy in the Mezzogiorno

Nature and Extent of Government Policy and the Executive Organs

Though a development policy for the Mezzogiorno had been attempted earlier, it was less a policy than a series of measures, sometimes rather confused and often uncoordinated. Real development began in 1950, that is, when the reconstruction of the country, though not yet completed, was well underway.

Rossi Doria summarized the situation in the Mezzogiorno at that time as follows: Of its 18 million inhabitants, over 50 percent were still working in agriculture, while the remainder were engaged in activities which, for the most part, were rather different from those common in a modern industrialized civilization. The average per capita income was 110,000 lire, or about $176, which was 50 percent or less of that of the northern Italian regions. The number of permanently unemployed amounted to 15 percent of the labor force, and underemployment in agriculture to 30 percent or more of total agricultural labor.[20]

The outstanding manifestations of misery and unemployment were in the agricultural regions which—apart from the imbalance between population and resources—suffered from the maldistribution of landed property and the resulting pattern of social relations. Barely one-third of the cultivated land was in the hands of the farmers, and the remaining agricultural workers were kept in the insecure situation of day laborers, *compartecipanti,* a form of sharecroppers, and small tenant farmers.

Therefore, when in 1950—after the liberation, the restoration of democracy, and the beginning of reconstruction—an attack was begun on the problems of the depressed south, the prospects for rapid economic development were not very promising. Mass emigration to foreign countries seemed improbable; successful industrialization was hindered by the general backwardness of the country and by the low purchasing power of the internal markets. Consequently, a policy directed toward the improvement of agriculture seemed to be the only means which could both meet the needs of the most backward sector and start the process called "preindustrialization."

Thus the policy of 1950 was above all agricultural. On the one hand, it sought through the creation of the Cassa per il Mezzogiorno to increase the productive capacity of the natural agricultural resources (by means of land rehabilitation, irrigation, afforestation, and the construction of roads, aqueducts, and electricity networks), while at the same time increasing employ-

[20] "Il Mezzogiorno agricolo negli anni 60," *Nord e Sud,* June 1962, pp. 62 ff.

ment; and, on the other hand, with the land reform legislation, to correct the social injustices in the country, to increase and consolidate agricultural properties, and thus to accelerate the transformation of the organizational structure of agriculture into more intensive and more profitable enterprises. As time passed, greater effort was made in nonagricultural sectors.

Vera Lutz, a non-Italian observer who had given great attention to the problems of the Italian Mezzogiorno and who had contributed considerably to the discussion on the conceptual improvement of southern development policy, described the evolution of this policy as follows:

> The effort made after the Second World War to promote industrialization in the South of Italy, and to raise living standards there closer to parity with those in the North, has exceeded, in respect both of the financial resources devoted to it, and the variety of the methods used, all previous attempts in this direction. The period witnessed intense legislative activity in favour of the Mezzogiorno, the foundation of a number of new institutions, and the allocation of a very substantial amounts of government funds. The whole body of law relating to the subject is by now very complex. A volume compiled by SVIMEZ contains some 340 laws, passed by the national or regional Parliaments during the period 1947 to 1957; since then the number has grown. Here we can only give a brief sketch of the main lines of the policy.
>
> It is customary to speak of the measures as forming two "cycles." The first cycle, spanning roughly ten years from the end of 1947, comprised fiscal relief, special credit facilities, and other incentives to private enterprise; the setting up (in 1950) of the Cassa per il Mezzogiorno; and the first big operations of the latter in the field of public investment. The second cycle was initiated by the new Law on Provisions for the Mezzogiorno of July 1957. This, besides extending the period of validity of the earlier concessions, broadened their scope. It also provided for new forms of government aid (including grants towards the capital costs of private industrial enterprise) and for new types of public investment. A supplementary law of July 1959 and a law of the same month providing "new incentives in favour of medium and small industries" added further force to the continuous crescendo of Southern development aids. Under the later series of laws the Cassa per il Mezzogiorno—supervised by a Committee of Ministers for the Mezzogiorno—continues to be one of the chief instruments of the policy.[21]

Thus the vital centers of the new development policy for the Mezzogiorno were the Cassa per il Mezzogiorno, the new executive institution, and the Ministerial Committee for the Mezzogiorno, the new political institution. The reasons for the creation of these two institutional instruments clearly show the novelty of the measures taken, the kinds of obstacles that had to be surmounted, and the nature of the difficulties which, earlier, had impaired the effectiveness of the legislative measures encouraging the development of the Mezzogiorno. It was said that these measures were uncoordinated, piecemeal and sometimes contradictory; in fact, they could not become operative because, lacking a specific and organic program for the south, the more industrialized regions of the north dictated, and to some extent still dictate, the rhythm and tone of economic policy for the entire country. In sum, the north had enough bargaining power to channel economic policies in the directions more conducive to the development of the established economy in the north.

Thus it was necessary to formulate a specific policy for the Mezzogiorno alone, stated in such a way as to guarantee that the "normal" economic policy measures would be maintained, that is, a policy which could not be distorted in favor of the more developed areas. The plan was conceived with these objectives, and it included the law that established the Cassa per il Mezzogiorno. It has an "adjunctive" character in the sense that the

[21] *Italy: A Study in Economic Development,* London, Oxford University Press, 1962, p. 101.

ministries had to continue to do for the Mezzogiorno what they did for the other Italian regions.

The principle was established, subsequently extended to much other legislation, that 40 percent of the "normal" economic activity of the Government had to be devoted to the Mezzogiorno; the activity of the Cassa per il Mezzogiorno and its planned expenditures are additional measures (thus the criterion "di aggiuntiva") over and above the basic 40 percent. This percentage arises from the fact that the population of southern Italy constitutes a little less than 40 percent of the total population of the country.

The *specific* measures for the south were to be administered outside the procedures normally employed by the Government through the various ministries. The administrative activity of the Italian State is usually carried on through the ministries within the limits of their respective institutional spheres of authority. The rhythm of bureaucratic activities is slow and cumbersome, due to the rigid financial laws and the extreme pressure of formal controls. Since the end of the war, the need for thoroughgoing administrative reform has become apparent. The reasons for the failure to accomplish it are not relevant to this study. However, since it has not been achieved, economic actions by the state are almost always implemented by means of new *ad hoc* executive organs, outside the old administrative apparatus though linked to it by extremely fine threads.

The so-called normal policies of the Government extend over the entire national territory. Each ministry intervenes in the sectors that lie within its own sphere of authority, very often without taking prior coordinating action with other ministries dealing with interrelated sectors. Because the policies are not coordinated, their potential economic effects become dispersed; consequently, under the "normal" procedures, the Mezzogiorno cannot get the massive, detailed application required by the nature of the problem.

The Cassa per il Mezzogiorno was created because of two considerations: The idea that the south required a specific policy, distinct in form and substance from the normal economic policy measures; and the recognition that this specific policy had to progress with a new rhythm, within new dimensions, and by means of new forms in order really to change the basic conditions of the economic and social life of the Mezzogiorno; in other words, in order to create that self-propelling economic mechanism which is the final objective of the policy for the south.

The law which constitutes the starting point of the new development policy for the Mezzogiorno was approved and went into effect on August 10, 1950. This law created the two new institutions: the political institution, the ministerial committee for the Mezzogiorno, and the executive institution, the Cassa per il Mezzogiorno. The ministerial committee was composed of the Ministers of Agriculture and Forestry, the Treasury, Industry and Commerce, Public Works, Labor and Social Welfare, and Transport. It was subsequently enlarged to include also the Minister of State Holdings, the Minister of Tourism, and the Minister of Public Education. The last was put on the committee in 1957 on a limited basis, with respect to policies concerning vocational education. As an indication of the importance of cultural and vocational education for the population of the south and for the efficacy of the development policy of the Mezzogiorno, he was made a coequal member in 1962.

Under the original law of 1950, the ministerial committee, which is presided over by the president of the council of ministers or, more often, by a minister designated by the council of ministers, had the task of formulating a general plan for the decade 1950–60, later to become the 15-year plan 1950–65, for the execution of special works encouraging economic and social progress in southern Italy, in coordination with the already planned public works program of the relevant ministries. Thus, the special policies had to be coordinated with the so-called ordinary measures of the Government in such a manner as to constitute one single program. The plan was to be entirely organic, that is, it was not to consist of individual actions, but of actions that were technologically and economically coordinated, including those related to:

(1) The water system in the mountains and the respective rivers.
(2) Land improvement.
(3) Irrigation.
(4) The transformation of agriculture, including land reform.
(5) The road systems of the provinces and communes.
(6) Aqueducts and sewage systems.
(7) Establishments to improve the marketing of agricultural products.
(8) Facilities for tourists.
(9) Special measures for the improvement of the southern long-distance railroad system (this became an objective of the Cassa with Law No. 949 of July 25, 1952).
(10) The raising and utilization of foreign loans (which became a goal of the Cassa with Law No. 166 of March 22, 1952).
(11) Credit facilities for industry developed by special medium-term institutions [22] (established by Law No. 298 of April 11, 1953).
(12) The extraordinary provision for the construction of schools [23] (made an objective of the Cassa by Law No. 654 of August 9, 1954).
(13) The facilities for industrial development and for vocational education (established by Law No. 634 of July 29, 1957).

On September 20, 1962, Law No. 1462, in addition to certain substantive changes, established the following new objectives for the Cassa per il Mezzogiorno:

(1) The construction of housing for workers employed in industries in the area and in the nuclei of industrialization.
(2) The financing of the construction, completion, and improvement of certain harbors and airports.
(3) The implementation of certain policies regarding hospitals and nursery schools and kindergartens.

However, these new policies have been established without a corresponding increase in funds for the Cassa per il Mezzogiorno; rather, the general plan as revised, was further changed so as to permit these new investments. This will obviously affect other investments which had been planned earlier. The most recent law implies an extension of the activity of the Cassa till 1965, an extension which cannot, of course, be implemented without further increases in the funds at the disposition of the Cassa.

The creation of the Cassa has thus led to an attack, with aggressive new methods and techniques, on the problem of the underdeveloped area of the

---

[22] These are the Institute for the Economic Development of Southern Italy (ISVEIMER) for the continental south of Italy, the Regional Credit Institute for Medium and Small Enterprises in Sicily (IRFIS), and the Industrial Credit Institute for Sardinia (CIS).

[23] See Gabriele Pescatore, *L'Intervento Straordinario nel Mezzogiorno d'Italia,* A. Giuffre, 1962, p. 4.

south, in such a way as not to affect unfavorably the general development of the Italian economy, but rather to accelerate it to the greatest possible extent as a consequence of the interdependence between the development policy for the southern regions and the general economic policy. Pescatore states:

> In providing this institution with these extraordinary functions, the legislators intended to create not only a unitary direction of ends and means, but also a technical and administrative organization which could not have been realized within the channels of the public administration. The program of special policies which was thus created is characterized by the institutional dialectic between the Ministerial Committee, which formulates the plan, and the Cassa per il Mezzogiorno which implements it. But if one considers its relations with other institutions, i.e., its relation with the ordinary administration of the State, another task which the South poses for the Ministerial Committee becomes apparent. This is the so-called goal of coordination: that is, the legislators took care to assure the necessary harmonious cooperation between the ordinary administrative institutions and the Cassa per il Mezzogiorno, by means of the activities of the group of ministers united in the Ministerial Committee for the Mezzogiorno. This Committee, which is politically responsible to Parliament for the activities of the Cassa, also has—aside from the planning of the measures to be taken—the task of coordinating the special policies within the sphere of authority of the Cassa with the ordinary policies of the public administration which are financed through the ordinary administrative budgets.[24]

As we shall see, this essential objective of coordination has largely failed of achievement.

Another important aspect of the program of special policies is the unification of action. The region of the south is considered as a single area, in which the economic development problems must be attacked as a unit, avoiding the fragmentation of policies which characterized the programs undertaken before the establishment of the Cassa.

The areas of activity of the Cassa include Abruzzi, Molise, Campania, Puglia, Basilicata, Calabria, Sicily, Sardinia, the Provinces of Latina and Frosinone, some zones of the Province of Rome, and some communes of the Province of Rieti in Lazio. Also included are some communes of the land reclamation zone of the River Tronto in the Province of Ascoli Piceno and the islands of Elba, Giglio, and Capraia.

In order to implement the plan, the Cassa has been provided with funds in the amount of 2,107.5 billion lire, or about $3.4 billion. These come from a first appropriation of 1,000 billion lire in the original legislation, a subsequent appropriation of 280 billion lire, and, by Law No. 634 in 1957, a third appropriation of 760 billion lire. Other funds have been provided for the Cassa by Laws No. 1349 of 1957 in the amount of 8.5 billion, No. 622 of 1959 in the amount of 99 billion, and No. 454 of 1961 (the law which established the 5-year plan for the development of agriculture) in the amount of 30 billion lire. The annual expenditures, which in 1950 were limited to 100 billion lire, or about $160 million, have been increased to 190 billion lire, because of the extension of the period of activity of the Cassa and the above-mentioned increases in financial appropriations. The total expenditures have been distributed among the various measures as shown in table II.

In later sections we will examine the type and the extent of the policies of the Cassa in each sector. Here we will indicate only the general organization of the plan and the general distribution of the funds. Pescatore writes:

> The fundamental outline of the plan can be summarized as follows: In the agricultural sector, land reclamation and agricultural reorganization constitute the most important task of the Cassa, inasmuch as agriculture is still the principal economic activity in the South. The major policies are based on the irrigation of

[24] *Ibid.*

550,000 hectares of land, partly to be realized through public reclamation of 350,000 hectares, and partly through private agricultural improvements of another 200,000. The agricultural reorganization encompasses investments in land of approximately 2 million hectares, in particular, investments for the cultivation of more profitable products (olives and fruits) and for livestock specialization and the raising of specialized breeds. These policy measures are expected to bring about an annual increase in agricultural production giving rise to total sales of 250 billion lire, and to create annual employment of 60 million workdays.

With respect to the water supply, it is planned to "normalize" the drinking water situation in all the Southern communities. This plan requires a huge and unified water system, a task which requires an accurate hydrological analysis of all the existing sources of water, in order to be able to see the possibilities of their integrated utilization. And as the normalization is planned for the needs in the year 2000, the conditions for an adequate time sequence of the individual projects, whether technical or economic, had to be established, while at the same time attempting to equalize the costs of the water supplies for the large and the small centers.

In the communication sector, the program envisages the improvement of the provincial and communal systems of roads, through improvement and paving of 15,000 kilometers and new construction of 3,500 kilometers, apart from 500 kilometers of interregional roads which lead to the autostrade and 7,000 kilometers of small roads connecting farms with communal and provincial roads (*strade di bonifica*). In addition, the plan further envisages augmentation and modernization of the most important Southern railroads, the development of tourism by measures improving the natural beauty of certain areas, subsidizing artistic and archeological endeavors, and adding to and renewing hotels and mineral springs. * * *

Particular attention must be paid to the so-called second period of the Southern policy which began with Law No. 634 of July 1957, which established new incentive measures for the industrialization of the Mezzogiorno. Regarding this objective, of the total funds of 139 billion lire appropriated, 59 billion were destined for medium and small enterprises as grants, 55 billion for reductions in interest rates on loans, and 25 billion as incentive measures for the creation of areas and nuclei of industrial development. * * *

Regarding the investment in human capital, the funds appropriated amounted to 37 billion lire and were to be used for all levels of education: From primary education to the preparation for professional careers, from technical, agricultural, and industrial training to the preparation of the appropriate University degrees in engineering, in agronomy and forestry, in economics and business administration, etc.[25]

The industrial and some of the agricultural activities financed by the Cassa have profited indirectly from the funds the Cassa has obtained through foreign loans, which amounted to a total of 250.3 billion lire ($400 million). The Cassa has received such loans from the International Bank of Reconstruction and Development, from the European Investment Bank, and from Morgan Stanley and Co. The president of the Cassa per il Mezzogiorno stated in the publication cited above that these loans are a "sign of the confidence placed in the institution (i.e., the Cassa) by the financial, international, public, and private organizations, confirmed by the favorable judgment of the technicians and economists of the World Bank who had to analyze the structure and efficiency of the development programs of the Cassa. The President of the World Bank, in his examination of the various requests for financial support, has always expressed his preference for those presented by the Cassa, as they were based on criteria of productivity and chosen only after serious economic analyses.[26]

The program, which we have considered in its essential outline, has had to be modified to a certain degree, primarily because of the changes made by Law No. 1462 of 1962, and also because of the long-term increase in the

[25] *Ibid.*, pp. 7–8.
[26] *Ibid.*, p. 9.

TABLE II.—*Progressive Increases in Financing of the Cassa per il Mezzogiorno*

(Billions of lire)

Sector	10-year plan 1950–60: initial appropriation, Aug. 10, 1950	12-year plan 1950–62: appropriation, July 25, 1952	15-year plan, 1950–65		
			Appropriations, July 29, 1957	Appropriations, July 24, 1959	Appropriations June 12, 1961
Infrastructure:					
Roads	90.0	115.0	166.5	166.5	225.8
Railways and ferries	...	75.0	93.0	93.0	105.4
Aqueducts and drains	115.0	117.5	312.0	312.0	324.5
Land improvement and mountain stabilization	380.0	478.0	650.0	662.0	662.2
Land reform	280.0	280.0	280.0	280.0	280.0
Tourism	25.0	25.0	40.0	51.0	64.0
Incentives to private initiative:					
Subsidies for land improvement	110.0	129.5	188.0	188.0	188.0
Credit for agrarian improvement	...	...	20.0	20.0	29.0
Industry	...	...	244.5	244.5	139.0
Fishing	...	...	5.0	5.0	...
Artisan trades	...	...	5.0	5.0	15.0
Hotel and tourist credit	...	...	4.5	5.5	18.0
Improvement of the human factor:					
Contributions for the construction of nursery and elementary schools, vocational training, etc	...	...	31.5	36.5	56.6
Total	1,000.0	1,280.0	2,040.0	2,069.0	2,107.5
Total in billions of dollars	1.6	2.1	3.3	3.3	3.4

Source: Cassa per il Mezzogiorno.

costs of the public works the Cassa is to carry out, which obviously will decrease, in real terms, the actual content of the program.

There are Italian observers who think that the Government should intervene in the depressed areas not only by undertaking public works important for private enterprise, but also as an entrepreneur itself. This is also the view of many Italian politicians, particularly those who favor a policy of economic planning. And their hopes have been realized to a certain extent. The Italian Government, through its special agencies called *Enti di Gestione*—in particular the *Istituto per la Ricostruzione Industriale* (IRI) and the *Ente Nazionale Idrocarburi* (ENI)—is a large stockholder in industrial enterprises which were established with governmental participation, but which nevertheless are organized as private industrial corporations and may also have private shareholders. These enterprises with governmental participation operate in the market using the criterion of economic profits. But in their investment policies they are directed by the *Enti di Gestione,* which are institutions pursuing public ends. Law No. 634 of 1957, which increased the authority of the Cassa and initiated the second phase, the so-called industrialization phase, of the development policy of the Mezzogiorno, provides for direct intervention by the Government in support of industrialization through these enterprises. The law requires the *Enti di Gestione,* the IRI and the ENI, to place 40 percent of their total investments for all purposes and not less than 60 percent of their investment in new enterprises in the south. This criterion of 40 percent was subsequently used in other sectors, for instance, in the plan for the railroads, which provides that 40 percent of the governmental expenditures for the modernization of the railroads be placed in the south, and in the plan for the development of agriculture, which, again, stipulates that 40 percent of the investments must be in the south.

Apart from the activities described above, the Cassa per il Mezzogiorno is also charged with execution of the special provisions for the city of Naples, which were established by Law No. 297 of April 9, 1953; the provisions for Calabria, established by Law No. 1777 of November 26, 1955 (which provides 204 billion lire ($330 million) for measures to be applied in the 12-year period 1955–67 for the protection of watersheds, rivers, and water sources in the mountains, the stabilization of mountain slopes, land improvement in mountains and valleys, and the protection of houses endangered by floods and landslides); and the provisions for those areas affected by the redevelopment plan for Sardinia.

Coordination of General and Special Policies

At the time of the creation of the Cassa per il Mezzogiorno, a sharp critic warned that "the other branches of the administration will show an attitude of competition and self-defense with respect to the Cassa." [27] This is what actually did happen, underground, of course, but nonetheless obvious; and this has often isolated the Cassa, depriving it of the necessary conceptual and practical integration with national economic policy. This means that very often the Cassa, instead of being a part of a total scheme of development, has been only one among many distinct policymaking organs.

---

[27] Giorgio Ceriani Sebregondi, "La Cassa per il Mezzogiorno," *Cronache Sociali,* 1950, p. 61.

Experience under these conditions demonstrates clearly that "coordination" between the actions of the Cassa and those of the ministries, even with the mediation of the ministerial committee, has been only partially achieved. This failure has not been for lack of determination on the part of those ministers who have served as president of the committee. But the provisions of the law establishing the Cassa are weak, in that the committee is composed of ministers who are individually and personally responsible to Parliament for the conduct of their respective ministries. They cannot therefore, be subjected to a majority decision reached within the committee of ministers. Only the personal consent of the minister concerned can make such a decision operative, and there is no formal way to assure his consent.

Second, the president of the committee does not have extensive powers, aside from those concerning the formulation of the general plan and the appropriations for the annual programs of the Cassa. All the executive powers rest with the administrative council of the Cassa. Consequently, it is much easier to force the Cassa to adjust its policies to those of the ministries than to attain coordination or compromise on the part of the ministries.

Third, the execution of the projects planned often depends on the cooperation in various ways of the local administrations (of communes and provinces). This constitutes another obstacle to integrated planning, since policies of local administrations are subject to political pressures.

Finally, there are many technical administrative problems which constitute further difficulties in the way of coordination of the programs executed by the ministries and by the Cassa per il Mezzogiorno. The first report to Parliament, presented by the president of the ministerial committee for the Mezzogiorno in 1960, pointed out that the programs of the different ministries were not established by uniform methods or at the same time. Rather, each ministry has its own form of planning, and the timing of the development of the programs, whether by legislation or in practice, differs greatly and often depends on procedures in which outside organizations also participate. Moreover, many current measures of the Government are based on particular laws which will be valid for several years and which frequently require action by local public and private entities. It is not easy to harmonize these programs among themselves and with those of the Cassa, which also follow a long-term plan from the technoprocedural point of view. The report states that, for these reasons, the ministerial committee must recognize the need to harmonize the course and, as much as possible, the procedure of the executive planning of the ministries and the Cassa.

This still does not exhaust the preliminary problems, as coordination involves a fundamental political aspect. Obviously, the coordination of the programs has to take place in the final phases of planning, before their definite approval by the ministries, but after they have been established in a rather precise form. However, each program is not simply a list of works to be executed. It expresses a particular policy to aims to achieve definite objectives. The ministerial committee for the Mezzogiorno, therefore, must establish the bases of the programs by means of a prior coordination of *policies*. This clearly makes solutions most difficult, because it throws into the debate the political and institutional prerogatives of the individual ministries.

Nevertheless, in the meeting of July 30, 1959, 9 years after establishment of the Cassa per il Mezzogiorno, the ministerial committee, recognizing that no coordination of programs was possible unless there was some general agreement with respect to ordinary expenditures in the south, "ordered the President to call the committee into session, during the phase of preliminary financial appropriations, in order to analyze, together, the basic criteria for public investment expenditures in the different sectors." According to the report, the truly central problem of coordination was forced upon the committee: The specification and harmonization of the sectoral policies in view of the requirements of the south. Though this decision was taken in 1959, its application was not felt until subsequent years. It is perhaps for this reason that the criterion of *aggiuntiva*—"in addition"—which the policies of the Cassa per il Mezzogiorno are to express, is not always respected. Thus it is said that the ordinary policies; i.e., those of the ministries which depend on state budgets, should maintain a "normal rhythm," which preserves the existing relationship between the populations of the south and of the Centro-Nord. The debates on this subject have been rather heated in recent years, because statistics, in particular those of the annual report in Parliament, have shown that ministerial investments in the south have tended to decrease rather than increase or remain unchanged relative to what they had been before the establishment of the Cassa. These statistical data have been much contested, but here we simply refer to the text of the last report on coordination activity.[28]

For the sake of interpretation, we must emphasize that the figures below show not only the expenditures actually made during the period examined, but also the authorizations to expend the indicated funds in the future. However, the structure of the local administrations in the Mezzogiorno, which very often implement the projects or participate in their financing, is so backward that they frequently do not succeed in realizing the investments that would have been possible; while in the Centro-Nord, on the other hand, the local communities have greater financial means available to participate in the expenditures and have better administrative techniques with which to realize the investments within shorter time periods. Thus the figures given below overstate by unknown amounts the data for the Mezzogiorno.

The report on coordination activity for the past 12 years states that the ordinary administrative investment expenditures of the state in the Mezzogiorno—i.e., those of the Ministries of Labor and Social Welfare, of Public Works, of Transport, and of Agriculture and Forestry—amount to 2,786.9 billion lire ($4.5 billion), or 39.8 percent of the national total. Of these investments 61.1 percent were made by the Ministry of Public Works, 17.1 percent by the Ministry of Labor and Social Welfare, 11.7 percent by the Ministry of Transport, and 10.1 percent by the Ministry of Agriculture and Forestry. A more detailed analysis of these data can be found in table III.

The report also showed data, based on the figures of the Central Statistical Institute, on the public works *actually affected* by the ordinary administration of the state, by the Cassa per il Mezzogiorno, by the INA–CASA, by the UNRRA–CASAS,[29] by the local communities, and by other institutions under public administration (INAM, INAIL, INPS, ENPAS).[30] To

[28] Comitato dei Ministri per il Mezzogiorno, *Relazione sull'Attività di Coordinamento,* vol. II: *Intervento Pubblico nel Mezzogiorno e Bilancio Economico per il 1962,* pp. 5 ff.

[29] These are the institutes for the construction of housing for workers. The second was established with the assistance of the U.S. Marshall plan.

[30] These are the very important national social security institutions which administer many hundred billions of lire.

TABLE III.—*Changes in Ordinary Government Expenditures and Authorizations*

	Mezzogiorno			Centro-Nord			Italy		
	Millions of lire	Index, annual average 1950–55=100	Percent	Millions of lire	Index, annual average 1950–55=100	Percent	Millions of lire	Index, annual average 1950–55=100	Percent
MINISTRY OF LABOR AND SOCIAL SECURITY [a]									
1950–55	180, 863	100. 0	40. 6	264, 117	100. 0	59. 4	444, 980	100. 0	100. 0
1956–60	216, 917	119. 9	37. 2	366, 131	138. 6	62. 8	583, 048	131. 0	100. 0
1960–61	45, 547	125. 9	48. 7	47, 926	90. 7	51. 3	93, 473	105. 0	100. 0
1961–62	32, 020	88. 5	54. 6	26, 618	50. 4	35. 4	58, 638	65. 9	100. 0
Total	475, 347	....	40. 3	704, 792	....	59. 7	1, 180, 139	....	100. 0
MINISTRY OF PUBLIC WORKS [b]									
1950–55	585, 768	100. 0	43. 6	756, 757	100. 0	56. 4	1, 342, 525	100. 0	100. 0
1956–60	815, 616	139. 2	41. 2	1, 166, 198	154. 1	58. 8	1, 981, 814	147. 6	100. 0
1960–61	166, 413	142. 0	36. 4	290, 234	191. 8	63. 6	456, 647	170. 1	100. 0
1961–62	134, 618	114. 9	44. 6	167, 065	110. 4	55. 4	301, 683	112. 4	100. 0
Total	1, 702, 415	....	41. 6	2, 380, 254	....	58. 4	4, 082, 669	....	100. 0

MINISTRY OF TRANSPORT									
1950–55	99, 242	100. 0	29. 1	241, 769	100. 0	70. 9	341, 011	100. 0	100. 0
1956–60	164, 110	165. 4	25. 5	479, 161	198. 1	74. 5	643, 271	188. 6	100. 0
1960–61	24, 477	123. 3	24. 2	76, 864	159. 0	75. 8	101, 341	148. 6	100. 0
1961–62	38, 656	194. 8	32. 0	81, 963	169. 5	68. 0	120, 619	176. 9	100. 0
Total	326, 485	...	27. 1	879, 757	...	72. 9	1, 206, 242	...	100. 0
MINISTRY OF AGRICULTURE AND FORESTRY									
1950–55	81, 385	100. 0	48. 0	88, 042	100. 0	52. 0	169, 427	100. 0	100. 0
1956–60	164, 806	202. 5	57. 0	124, 443	141. 3	43. 0	289, 249	170. 7	100. 0
1960–61	17, 693	108. 7	53. 4	15, 415	87. 5	46. 6	33, 108	97. 7	100. 0
1961–62	18, 720	115. 0	42. 4	25, 431	144. 4	57. 6	44, 151	130. 3	100. 0
Total	282, 604	...	52. 7	253, 331	...	47. 3	535, 935	...	100. 0
TOTAL									
1950–55	947, 258	100. 0	41. 2	1, 350, 685	100. 0	58. 8	2, 297, 943	100. 0	100. 0
1956–60	1, 361, 449	143. 7	39. 0	2, 135, 933	158. 1	61. 0	3, 497, 382	152. 2	100. 0
1960–61	254, 130	134. 1	37. 1	430, 439	159. 3	62. 9	684, 569	149. 0	100. 0
1961–62	224, 514	118. 2	42. 7	301, 077	111. 5	57. 3	525, 091	114. 3	100. 0
Total	2, 786, 851	...	39. 8	4, 218, 134	...	60. 2	7, 004, 985	...	100. 0
Billion dollars	4. 5	...	...	6. 8	...	...	11. 3	...	...

[a] Including management of INA–CASA. [b] Including investments in ANAS.

Source: The Report on Activity of the Ministerial Committee for the Mezzogiorno, 1962, vol. II, p. 6.

lessen the effect of certain abnormalities in one of the years of the series, it was desirable to use as a base of reference, not 1951, but rather the annual average of the first 5 years of the 1950's. The public measures in the Mezzogiorno in terms of the public works *carried out* show an increase of 35.9 percent in 1962 over the annual average for the period 1951–55; the increase has been 100.5 percent in the Centro-Nord, and 68.3 percent for Italy as a whole. (See table IV.) The report continues:

In practice, it appears to be necessary to examine once more what has already been stressed in the preceding report, namely, that in the Mezzogiorno the public works carried through show a smaller increase than those in the Centro-Nord. This means that the programs of the Cassa as a whole have not been "aggiuntiva," as the law prescribes.

* * * The deficiencies of local administrations appear to be the major reason for the differences between the financial statements and the investments actually carried out. These deficiencies consist in the failure to make full use of legislative appropriations for the Mezzogiorno. Furthermore, the difficulties of actually incurring the expenditures over a long term arising from administrative regulations must be kept in mind. * * *

In particular categories of public works, such as road construction, water systems, and public buildings, the expenditures for the Mezzogiorno, though they increased slightly from 1961 to 1962, have never again reached the relative levels of the first years of the decade of the fifties. On the other hand, expenditures for maritime works, housing, hygiene, sanitation, and miscellaneous purposes have increased more rapidly, and, for housing, exceed those of 1951.

The only sectoral expenditures that have continued to increase as a proportion of the national total and that have been over 60 percent of the total in every year of the twelve-year period under consideration are those for land reclamation. In 1962 these expenditures in the Mezzogiorno constituted 76.8 percent of the national total. The reason for this is, obviously, the particular attention the Cassa has devoted to this sector.

An examination of the expenditures for public works apart from those of the Cassa shows that the relative decrease of public expenditures is even more pronounced if no account is taken of extraordinary policies. For example, compared with the period 1951–55, ordinary public expenditures in the Mezzogiorno were up by 24 percent in 1962, constituting 31.6 percent of the national total, while the corresponding percentages for the Centro-Nord are 100.7 percent and 78.4 percent respectively.

Coordination remains one of the most delicate problems of development policy in the Mezzogiorno although industrialization policy has mitigated it somewhat. It is partly for this reason that, within the general debate developing in Italy over suitable measures to plan the entire national economic policy, the role of the Cassa per il Mezzogiorno is much discussed. It is thought that its institutional role should remain as it is, but that it should be subject to the direction, not of the ministerial committee, but of a new institution chosen to direct the whole of the planning process. If such an institution should have real power to coordinate the entire national economic policy, it would make much easier the integration of the special policies of the Cassa with the ordinary programs of the ministries. This view was expressed by Minister Pastore, then president of the ministerial committee for the Mezzogiorno, in an article attributed to him in a journal of which he is editor.[31] He seems to hold that the ministerial committee for the Mezzogiorno should be abolished, while the Cassa per il Mezzogiorno should be maintained as a necessary institution, probably with enlarged responsibilities including those for the depressed communities of the Centro-Nord.

---

[31] *Il Nuovo Osservatore,* October 1962, p. 558.

TABLE IV.—*Public Works Carried Out* [a]

Years	Mezzogiorno			Centro-Nord			Italia		
	Millions of lire	Index, annual average 1951–55=100	Percent	Millions of lire	Index, annual average 1951–55=100	Percent	Millions of lire	Index, annual average 1951–55=100	Percent
INCLUDING THE "CASSA"									
1951–55	1, 029, 809	100. 0	49. 8	1, 038, 803	100. 0	50. 2	2, 068, 612	100. 0	100. 0
1956–60	1, 263, 328	122. 7	40. 9	1, 828, 588	176. 0	59. 1	3, 091, 916	149. 5	100. 0
1961	308, 748	149. 9	38. 6	491, 374	236. 5	61. 4	800, 122	193. 4	100. 0
1962 [b]	279, 824	135. 9	40. 2	416, 622	200. 5	59. 8	696, 446	168. 3	100. 0
Total	2, 881, 709	...	43. 3	3, 775, 387	...	56. 7	6, 657, 096	...	100. 0
Billion dollars	4. 7	...	...	6. 1	...	...	10. 7	...	...

See footnotes at end of table.

TABLE IV.—*Public Works Carried Out* [a]—Continued

Years	Mezzogiorno			Centro-Nord			Italia		
	Millions of lire	Index, annual average 1951–55—100	Percent	Millions of lire	Index, annual average 1951–55—100	Percent	Millions of lire	Index, annual average 1955–51—100	Percent
EXCLUDING THE "CASSA"									
1951–55	759, 071	100. 0	42. 8	1, 015, 333	100. 0	57. 2	1, 774, 404	100. 0	100. 0
1956–60	924, 387	121. 8	34. 0	1, 795, 424	176. 8	66. 0	2, 719, 811	153. 3	100. 0
1961	208, 562	137. 4	30. 2	482, 693	237. 7	69. 8	691, 255	194. 8	100. 0
1962 [b]	188, 273	124. 0	31. 6	407, 507	200. 7	68. 4	595, 780	167. 9	100. 0
Total	2, 080, 293	....	36. 0	3, 700, 957	....	64. 0	5, 781, 250	....	100. 0
Billion dollars	3. 4	....	....	6. 0	....	....	9. 3	....	....

[a] The data refer to public works involving new construction, reconstruction, improvements, structures, and extraordinary maintenance. The amounts are those for the ministries, the INA–CASA and UNRRA–CASAS, local agencies, and other agencies of public law (INAIL, INAM, INPS, ENPAS).

[b] Provisional data.

Source: ISTAT.

Special Policies of the Cassa per il Mezzogiorno

In the preceding sections some of the institutional characteristics and the kinds and extent of the policies of the Cassa per il Mezzogiorno have been outlined. Before analyzing the special types of assistance, certain economic factors and political choices on which the activity of the Cassa is based should be noted, including the fact that the very concept of special consideration of the problems of the south is under question. As Pietro Campilli, who under the direction of De Gasperi, then president of the council, gave life to the Cassa per il Mezzogiorno, has said:

> The successes of the policy for the south, and the benefits they have brought to the whole country because of economic interdependencies and interrelations between the various economic sectors, have helped to clarify what the problem of the Mezzogiorno really represents in the middle of the twentieth century: namely, a development problem of the Italian economy and society.[32]

At the time of its initiation, the special policy for the south was directed mainly toward the establishment of the basic infrastructure, the minimum of *social fixed capital* necessary for further development, and toward the strengthening of southern agriculture, which was still considered to be among the best productive possibilities of the Mezzogiorno. It is true that some supported an immediate industrialization policy. Even today it is still difficult to say whether it was a good choice to concentrate the programs of the Cassa in the "first cycle," i.e., the first 7 years, on the infrastructure and on agriculture, or whether an immediate concentration on industrialization would have had more favorable effects. Many critics of the choice at that time believe that industrial development in the Mezzogiorno during the past few years is evidence that time has been wasted. However, present developments are largely the fruit of the so-called Italian economic miracle of the northern regions. And, notwithstanding the exceptional efforts made to build up social fixed capital, even now industrial entrepreneurs who locate in the south encounter difficulties in transportation, the availability of industrial water supplies, electrical energy, etc.[33]

The Cassa has carried out a series of operations of land reclamation and improvement in southern agriculture. It has developed, and continues to develop, water systems for the communities of the Mezzogiorno. These were very urgent because, at the time the Cassa was established, the proportion of communities which had insufficient water supplies, or none at all, was very great. The water problem has always characterized and emotionally symbolized the life of the Mezzogiorno. At the same time, the Cassa undertook a large-scale program of improvement of roads not normally the responsibility of central government, by the development of interregional roads and the construction of new roads, whether interregional or connecting state roads, and by a dense net of land reclamation roads. After these beginning efforts to "restructure the economic environment and increase the potential of the agricultural sector," the Cassa was given increasing responsibilities. It undertook activities in the fields of public education, vocational instruction, and social assistance, and encouraged private initiative in the industrial, handicraft, hotel, fishing, and agricultural sectors.

---

[32] Pietro Campilli, *Cassa per il Mezzogiorno, 12 Anni—1950–62,* Editori La Terza, vol. 1, par. III.

[33] Comitato dei Ministri per il Mezzogiorno, *Relazione al Parlamento,* Rome, 1960, p. 5.

In sum, the new cycle of activities of the Cassa was now started: The period of actual industrialization began. One should note, however, that even in the first period the Cassa could give incentives to industrial enterprises. But those given were not very important and were not parts of a single plan; thus, they did not yet constitute a policy.

At the beginning of the second cycle, the problem appeared to take the following form: Success in improving agricultural productivity accentuated the release of agricultural labor, but without immediate effects on investment in other sectors. Even as to agriculture, obsolete marketing systems created bottlenecks.

Public expenditures on the infrastructure reduced some but not all of the disadvantages to industrial investment in the south. While they provide the necessary public facilities, they do not create such external economies as proximity of complementary industries, availability of specialized and skilled labor, and well-developed markets.

Thus, public works expenditures do not set off a self-propelling development, nor do they solve the overall problem of unemployment aggravated by the release of agricultural labor. Indeed, they may contribute to the rising cost of living through the increased expenditures of high-wage workers on public projects, without an increase in the output of consumer goods. Hence other employees may suffer declining real wages.[34]

For these reasons, it was decided not to concentrate wholly on "preindustrialization," waiting for the market to respond with a "natural" process of industrialization, and Law No. 634 of July 29, 1957, formally established the Cassa's active industrialization policy.

In this new phase the tasks of the Cassa were extended, while the efforts to improve the infrastructure and the potential of the agricultural sector continued. The programs of the Cassa in the latter areas have been determined by a long-term plan that has not been altered by the new provisions, except in the sense that the new objectives of industrialization have been added. These were to be implemented to a large extent by enlarging the scope of the credits the Cassa could extend for industrial developments; now it was also permitted to give nonrepayable grants in aid. Most important, however, was the fact that now all the policy measures were to be decided upon within the framework of an integrated politico-economic plan, implemented by means of the so-called poles of industrial development (*poli di sviluppo industriale*), to be discussed below.

The activities of the industrial enterprises in which the Government participates have contributed greatly to the industrialization policy. Article 2 of Law No. 634 orders the Minister for Governmental Participation to present each year the investment programs of the institutions and enterprises under his authority to the Ministerial Committee for the Mezzogiorno. The law states that these programs must provide for a regional distribution of the investments so as to achieve a progressively better economic balance between the several regions.

The law provides, as has been noted, that of the investments of the abovementioned institutions and enterprises in *new* industrial plants, no less than 60 percent should be made in the territory of the Cassa per il Mezzogiorno, and that investments in the Mezzogiorno of the *Enti di Gestione,* for whatever purpose, must constitute no less than 40 percent of the total invest-

[34] *Ibid.,* pp. 5–6.

ments in Italy and must be distributed in all the regions of the Mezzogiorno.

The Cassa per il Mezzogiorno operates in three ways: It either directly administers its projects, or it puts local governmental agencies in charge of their execution, or it encourages private initiative by means of a whole series of measures which will be examined in the following section. The relations with local institutions in the second method of operation have given rise to the greatest difficulties, mainly of a procedural nature. The Cassa was established so as to be free from the old controls of the Italian public administration, but when it put local agencies in charge of its public works, it found itself, once again, subject to all the regulations and controls it was to avoid. This situation, together with the low technical efficiency of the research and forecasting facilities of the local institutions, has led the Cassa to emphasize direct administration of the projects through its own technical staff. This staff has reached a high level of efficiency, and has made a whole series of analyses, forecasts, and regional plans of great importance.

In the beginning, the activities of the Cassa were slowed down because of a limited knowledge of the geological structure of the areas and a lack of sufficiently detailed, up-to-date maps. The Cassa has spent much time and energy on the solution of these problems. Conditions in the Mezzogiorno were indeed depressed, even from the point of view of the necessary knowledge of the area.

Thus, the special policies of the Cassa faced many fundamental and complex problems. There was the difficulty due to the economic environment, the difficulty of finding fast and efficient executive instruments, the difficulty of getting up-to-date scientific data on the geological structure of the areas, and, finally, the difficulty of inserting the new instrument of the Cassa per il Mezzogiorno into the context of Italian legal and political institutions.[35] The problems seem to point to the need for even greater autonomy for the Cassa.

Means of Implementation of the Development Policy

AGRICULTURAL POLICIES

The description of the agricultural policies of the Cassa must be preceded by two premises: The first is an economic one and concerns the agricultural situation of the regions analyzed; the second is a legal one and concerns the land reclamation legislation on which the Cassa had to base its actions.

The agriculture of the south can be divided into three distinct areas which are characterized by great differences. There are, first of all, the mountain and hill areas where extensive grain culture and pasture predominate.[36]

---

[35] See Pescatore, *L'Intervento Straordinario,* op. cit., pp. 87–88.

[36] According to Rossi Doria, in the article cited above in the journal *Nord e Sud,* "these areas include over 70 percent of the region and approximately 60 percent of the agricultural families (at least until very recently), while they contribute barely 40 percent to the total agricultural revenue. Thus, family incomes in these areas are lower than average and more uncertain * * *.

In these areas, a revolution is taking place, manifested by the permanent or temporary migration to the north or to foreign countries, a migration which differs greatly in its extent from area to area, even between neighboring regions."

Then there are the coastal plains, whose farms are usually of small or medium size, and which, until very recently, suffered from malaria. These were the depopulated areas with little or no production. Due to the irrigation measures initiated by the Cassa, these areas are about to become modern agricultural centers of relatively high productivity able to reach international competitive levels.[37]

Third, there are the areas which, for many decades or even centuries, have constituted the wealth of the intensive agriculture of the Mezzogiorno, with mixed or specialized production.[38]

Obviously, the Cassa per il Mezzogiorno should apply different measures in these diverse areas. However, it had to act within an already established juridical framework, namely, that of the *bonifica.*

The present concept of land improvement, or *bonifica,* is the result of a long evolution. The policy of the *opere di bonifica* was initially intended to be only a partial measure for the improvement of rivers, the draining of swamps, and the consolidation of the hilly areas. It assumed, therefore, mainly a sanitation function in the swamp and malaria regions. The original concept of *bonifica idraulica* (draining of the swamps) goes back to the Roman *bonifica* of the Fucino, but over time the concept has been enlarged to encompass all the public works necessary for agriculture, including improvement of the soil and resettlement. The state provides the public works, with some supplementary private contributions; the private landholders make soil improvements with government support, and, finally, the resettlements are carried through by the private landholders, but with public support in the form of interest payments on the loans contracted by the former. This measure is accompanied by some exemptions of a fiscal nature.

---

[37] According to Rossi Doria, these plain areas (of which there are about 10) are about to become the new invigorating centers of southern agriculture, due to irrigation. He confirms that, "if the policy of 1950 and the Cassa per il Mezzogiorno had had no other merits, they would still have the one of having started the construction of the reservoirs for hydroelectricity and for irrigation, and the installations for the irrigation of 700,000 hectares (or 1,750,000 acres) in the coastal plains. * * * It is different with the internal regions where, since the extinction of malaria, a relation between population and resources has been created which allows an increase of the agricultural as well as the nonagricultural population. Even before irrigation these plains became populated, the landed property was divided, the land values rose, new types of cultivation were started, and here and there nonagricultural activities began and new industrial plants were established."

[38] Rossi Doria states further that, "the old riches of the Mezzogiorno—which have continuously grown in the past and the present century—were replaced by the intensive cultures and the tree cultures which (wherever they are on the peninsula and on the islands) are of particular significance. They are particularly large in the Campagna Felice and its surroundings, in Puglia, with its wine and olive cultures, in the coastal zones of Abruzzi, Calabria, and Sicily, and here and there in Sardinia and elsewhere. Today, while they cover barely one-fifth of the territory, they produce more than one-half of the agricultural revenue and employ more than one-third of the agricultural population of the Mezzogiorno apart from the fact that four-fifths of the urban population lives in these areas, which have nevertheless a mixed urban-rural character (with all the consequences implied thereby). * * *

"As the modest semi-rural economy of the country becomes more and more industrialized the productive and social organization shows more clearly the signs of the weaknesses of these areas: Old-fashioned and irrational agricultural enterprises, productive structures that are only to a very small degree oriented toward the existing markets, etc."

The concept of the *bonifica* has been enlarged also in the sense that it has become a point of reference for the collaboration between the state and private entrepreneurs; it finds its institutional expression in the *consortium,* composed of private entrepreneurs interested in a specific *bonifica* program and certain public organizations. The *consortiums* are of a public character and have public functions with consequent implications on the legal and administrative levels. A special law of 1933 provides that for each land reclamation zone a general plan of *bonifica* is to be established, containing the principal projects and the basic directives for the agricultural structure of the area. The landholders whose lands are included must carry out the works for the particular benefit of their lands with grants given by the Government, in conformance with the directives of the plan and under the terms determined by the Ministry of Agriculture and Forestry.

However, in the south there have been great difficulties in implementation, for predominantly psychological reasons. Though the system has worked well in the central regions and particularly in the north, the necessary collaboration between the state and private individuals has not been achieved in the Mezzogiorno, partly because of poverty, partly because the local population is unprepared. Moreover, the existence of primitive agricultural areas, of large land concentrations, and of investment deficiencies has brought about, since the Second World War, great social tensions and the political determination to do away with landed estates. This has been accomplished with land reform legislation by which the huge properties were broken up and assigned to small farmers. At the same time, reform institutions (*Enti di Riforma*) have been created which find the new proprietors, transfer the lands, assist agricultural activities through land improvement, and aid in resettlement of the landholdings and improvement of the type of products cultivated.

The law requires the Cassa per il Mezzogiorno to give the funds to carry out the land reform in its areas. Cassa funds for these purposes amounted to 280 billion lire ($450 million) for the decade 1950–60. The Cassa has furnished the funds directly to the reform institutions, which have used them in ways appropriate to their institutional objectives.

A short outline of the agricultural reform actions can be found in tables V and VI. With the exception of the 280 billion lire which the Cassa was required to put at the disposition of the reform institutions, the agricultural development measures of the Cassa have been based on a 12-year plan (1950–62), which, however, was not approved until 1955. Earlier, many public works had been carried through, but without regard for any criterion of organic development. These haphazard measures, though costly, were justified by the very depressed economy and by the psychological condition of the local population, who, with the establishment of the Cassa, again had reason to hope.

The choices made in the general plan of action determined the following order of priorities:

First: Irrigation, if it creates immediate increases in income and productivity.

Second: Completion of land improvement projects (*bonifica*) already begun, in order to save and make productive the capital already invested.

Third: Improvement of mountain forest watersheds which directly affect the condition of land improvement zones chosen for Cassa action.

The 15-year plan (1950–65) has extended the activity of the Cassa per il Mezzogiorno so as to encompass 72.8 percent of the entire land area of the Mezzogiorno.

The zones which the Cassa was to assist were divided into three categories. The first included the "zones of evolution," in which prior public land improvement projects were far enough along to require simply completion and improvement of existing structures and the development of agriculture by irrigation.

TABLE V.—*Land Reform: Area Expropriated and Assigned up to End of 1959*

	North	South (excluding Sicily)	Sicily	Italy
Area expropriated [1] (1,000 hectares)	227.9	419.0	115.1	762.0
Area allotted (1,000 hectares)	202.9	337.6	76.1	616.6
Number of units allotted (1,000)	25.3	66.5	17.5	109.3
Farms (1,000)	13.7	32.1	....	[2] 45.8
"Quotas" (1,000)	11.6	34.4	....	[2] 46.0
Average size of farms (hectares)	11.8	8.2	[3] 4.4	[2] 9.3
Average size of "quotas" (hectares)	3.5	2.1		[2] 2.4

[1] Includes "tied areas," which under certain conditions may ultimately be retained in part by the original landholder, totaling 48,000 hectares for the whole of Italy; and includes 89,000 hectares acquired by the Reform Institution from sources (including ordinary purchases) other than expropriation.

[2] Excluding Sicily.

[3] In Sicily the Reform Institution makes no distinction between "farms" and "quotas."

Source: Vera Lutz, *Italy: A Study in Economic Development*, Oxford University Press, 1962, p. 184.

The second category included the "zones of transformation," in which a coordinated program of both public works and creation of the necessary agricultural structure was required.

The third category was composed of "zones of primary penetration," in which the land-improvement projects were limited to certain public works and improvement in the control of watersheds, that is, programs that would improve the general environment and facilitate subsequent private initiative.

According to the first report to Parliament by the ministerial committee for the Mezzogiorno, the criterion of organic development required that the following types of agricultural programs be undertaken:

(*a*) Measures to achieve good water control. Specifically, this means measures for improvement of high watersheds and water sources for forestry and agriculture, especially those necessary for valley water systems and reservoirs in the course of construction. Included also are programs of dam construction for the coordination of irrigation and production of electrical energy through more rational use of the existing water supply and the harmonization of the function of the reservoirs with irrigation. Also included is coordination of river drainage, sewage, and irrigation systems.

(*b*) Measures to provide the zones with components of the infrastructure to assure agricultural development, such as roads, service centers, electricity, and windbreaks, coordinating these with other public administrative measures in the area.

(*c*) The adjustment of the rules of land improvement legislation, as they concern private resettlement projects, to local difficulties and to the quantities of investments to be carried out.

(*d*) The selection and financing of all undertakings, individual or cooperative, aimed at setting up establishments for the processing or preservation of agricultural products, and the equipment for protecting their commercial value.[39]

The importance attributed to agriculture within the general plan of the Cassa is shown by the amount of funds provided for these purposes. They were, in total, $1.9 billion, or more than 55 percent of the total appropriations.

THE RESULTS OF AGRICULTURAL POLICIES

As indicated above, in the first phase of the 15-year plan for agriculture, the Cassa had to give priority to basic public works, which would make it possible to utilize natural resources economically. For this reason, by June 30, 1962, the date of the last report on the activity of the Cassa, road, civic building, and rural electrification projects had already expended 95.5 percent of the funds appropriated for such works for the entire 15-year period.

As time passed, however, the Cassa has increasingly stressed such measures as irrigation and others which directly increase agricultural production. The quality of the investments is increasingly emphasized. Because many of the basic investments for infrastructure have been carried out, further developments of greater extent have become possible. By June 30, 1962, total funds appropriated for land improvement and control and improve-

TABLE VI.—*Expenditure on Improvements Carried Out by Reform Institutions up to End of 1959* [1]

[Billions of lire]

	North	South	Italy
Farmhouses	42.9	76.5	119.4
Land improvement [2]	12.8	57.0	69.8
Live and other stock	8.7	16.3	25.0
Machinery and implements	11.8	21.1	32.9
Other [3]	14.7	42.8	57.5
Total	90.9	213.7	304.6
Total in millions of dollars	147	345	452

[1] The figures include work in progress but not yet completed.

[2] Includes preparation of ground, planting of trees, irrigation works.

[3] Includes roads to, on, and between farms; water mains and electric cables; schools, churches, and other public buildings; processing plants; technical assistance; training courses, etc.

Source: Vera Lutz, *Italy: A Study in Economic Development*, Oxford University Press, 1962, p. 187.

[39] Paolo Vicinelli, "La strumentazione operativa," in *Cassa per il Mezzogiorno, 12 Anni—1950–62* vol. II, L'attività di bonifica, p. 12.

ment of mountain areas amounted to about $1 billion, and contracts for works carried out in the 12-year period amounted to $0.9 billion. These two figures compare with total appropriations as of that date of $1.2 billion, distributed as follows:

	Percent
Improvement and control of mountain areas and afforestation	23. 9
Water supplies	14. 3
Irrigation	36. 5
Roads and other public works and civic buildings	16. 8
Rural electrification	6. 9
Research, analyses, and advance money for planning	1. 6

The basic data for civil projects completed are given in the last report on coordination activities presented to Parliament by the ministerial committee for the Mezzogiorno:

> At the end of the twelve-year period, the irrigated area amounts to over 210,000 hectares. This is the result of 995 kilometers of major and connective canals and of 5,422 kilometers of secondary canals.
>
> The *bonifica* roads being continued and those ready for use amount to 4,716 km of new roads and 1,690 km of improved roads. *Bonifica* roads are all the country roads directly connected with the plan for resettlement and for the *bonifica*. Thus, these are not important intercommunal, provincial, or regional roads. The activity of the Cassa has been of particular significance in the field of rural electrification. * * * In total, the electrification to date amounts to 125,000 kw, and services a population of over 700,000.
>
> With respect to improvements of the soil and the water systems in the mountain areas, the following data may be cited:
>
> —There are about 442,000 hectares freed from the danger of floods.
>
> —There are about 275,000 hectares of drained swamps.
>
> —There has been afforestation of about 102,000 hectares, to which must be added another 17,000 hectares of redevelopment of neglected forests.[40]

As to the direct land resettlement programs carried out by private entrepreneurs, but with large contributions from the Cassa per il Mezzogiorno, the total funds appropriated by June 30, 1962, amounted to a little over $700 million. But works actually approved amounted to about $400 million, with a Cassa contribution of about $175 million.

Table VII gives a summary in physical quantities of the principal works carried out, as of June 30, 1962.

But what has been the situation of southern agriculture compared to the general agricultural development? Between 1951 and 1959, the physical volume of agricultural production of southern Italy and the islands increased at a rate slightly lower than that of the Centro-Nord of Italy. The percentage increases, according to Barbero,[41] were 2.5 percent in the Mezzogiorno and 3.1 percent in the Centro-Nord. Consequently, the contribution of the southern regions to the volume (but not the value) of the national agricultural production has slightly decreased, from 34 percent in 1951 to 32.7 percent in 1959. In value terms, the Mezzogiorno would appear somewhat better. Nevertheless, it must be concluded that the agricultural development of the south has remained below that of the Centro-Nord.

---

[40] *Ibid.*, pp. 36 ff.

[41] Giuseppe Barbero, "L'evoluzione dell'agricoltura meridionale nel decennio 1950–60," in *Cassa per il Mezzogiorno, 12 Anni*—1950/62, vol. II, part I, pp. 6 ff.

TABLE VII.—*Cassa per il Mezzogiorno: Physical Quantities of Principal Works Approved and Accepted to June 30, 1962*

	Unit of measure	Quantity	
		Approved	Accepted
Rural structures: [1]			
Habitations	Number	134, 175	85, 776
Rooms	....do	373, 497	240, 312
Stables and animal enclosures, fixed and movable	Head	568, 177	364, 545
Sheepfolds	....do	574, 852	332, 515
Manure storage	Square meters	2, 462, 306	1, 411, 640
Silos and haylofts	Cubic meters	4, 785, 454	3, 025, 162
Other agricultural equipment:			
Warehouses	....do	1, 695, 580	1, 026, 334
Workshops and places of shipment.	Square meters	686, 996	421, 011
Installations for the processing and conservation of agricultural products: [1]			
Cheese dairies	Number	123	69
Daily capacity	Quintal of milk	15, 316	5, 149
Oil mills	Number	452	323
Daily capacity	Quintal of olives	76, 248	54, 882
Wine installations	Number	618	416
Storage capacity	Hectoliters of wine.	2, 817, 466	1, 726, 175
Warehouses for the processing of products.	Number	71	43
Capacity	Square meters	50, 108	25, 099
Fruit and vegetable centers	Number	16	3
Capacity for processing and storage.	Quintal	317, 811	33, 900
Rural roads	Kilometers	7, 113	3, 330
Rural aqueducts and Water supply:			
Aqueducts	Meters	1, 611, 124	1, 075, 291
Wells and cisterns	Number	54, 038	32, 921
Rural powerlines	Kilometers	2, 980	1, 350
Resettlement projects:			
Improvement of arable land	Hectares	261, 358	142, 339
Tree plantings	....do	73, 575	30, 626
Irrigation with underground water.	....do	142, 585	89, 926
Irrigation with running water	....do	82, 070	42, 937
Irrigation from lakes	....do	16, 425	10, 468
Pasture improvement	....do	34, 004	17, 924
Acquisition of breeding stock	Head	13, 629	1, 363
Grain storage (capacity)	Quintal	2, 347, 800	2, 195, 500

[1] Improvements or new construction. Source: Cassa per il Mezzogiorno.

Must it therefore be said that agricultural development policy in the Mezzogiorno has failed? In answering this question, the following two observations must be made:

(1) To reach the objective of a rate of agricultural development of the south nearly equal to that of the Centro-Nord constitutes an extremely positive result, in view of their different starting positions. Moreover, in the period since the war, the agriculture of the north has been able to utilize the contributions of technical progress and mechanization of agriculture, the more advanced productive processes which are particularly suitable for the lands of the north.

(2) The investments made in southern agriculture are definitely long-term investments. It is probable that greater results will be obtained in the years to come. Programs capable of major contributions, such as irrigation, notwithstanding the large investments made, have only become effective very recently, and in many cases they have not yet had any impact at all.

The Cassa per il Mezzogiorno has certainly galvanized a world which had been stagnant for centuries, both on the economic and on the socio-cultural levels. But the basic problem remains that the Mezzogiorno has little more than 2 million hectares, or less than one-fifth of the area of the region, which can be developed along the lines chosen.[42] The remaining four-fifths of the land of the Mezzogiorno has been thrown into a crisis by economic developments: A crisis due partly to the migration of the rural population, and partly to the fact that profound changes in the existing situation are necessary to develop the productive potential of these areas. And these changes require people able to carry them out! Yet in these areas of the greatest poverty and misery in the country, it is difficult to find such people.

Aqueducts and sewer systems

Apart from the problem of water for irrigation, drinking water has been the major problem of the south. The picture of the *Mezzogiorno assetato* (the thirsty south) is found again and again in the literature; it is a good reflection of the conditions in which the southern population lives.

In the field of aqueducts the Cassa has had great success, mainly because it could establish large reservoirs with great dikes and canals for distribution. Such projects had been impossible under the previous legislation, which had limited aqueduct projects to only one or a few communities and to a capacity based only on existing needs, without taking the future into account. As a matter of policy, the Cassa attempts to build the necessary aqueducts and sewer systems in all the populated areas of the south, to meet the demand of the next 50 years. Article 5 of Law No. 646, which initiated this legislation, stated that the Cassa was to take over the total construction of the major works necessary for the aqueducts, including the reservoirs but excluding the distribution systems. This policy was subsequently changed and integrated by Law No. 634 of July 27, 1957. Article 6 of this law states that for local communities with a population of less than 10,000 inhabitants, the Cassa can take over the construction and completion of the internal distribution systems from the aqueducts, as well as the necessary installations and the sewer systems, in cases where the

[42] Manlio Rossi Doria, *10 Anni di Politica Agraria nel Mezzegiorno,* Edizioni La Terza, Bari, 1958, p. XX.

communities are unable to get the necessary loans, in part or in their entirety. In addition, it was provided that, for the communities with a population of over 10,000 and up to 75,000, the Cassa could take over the costs, normally the responsibility of the communities, of the primary water and sewer systems.

The Cassa's sphere of authority with respect to water distribution was again increased by Law No. 1462 of September 20, 1962. Article 17 provides that the Cassa per il Mezzogiorno can take over, at full cost, the construction and improvement of the internal distribution systems from the aqueducts and of the sewer systems and plants, and also the improvement of already existing systems if they are connected with those constructed or improved by the Cassa itself. In greatly depressed areas, the Cassa can also provide the internal distribution systems of aqueducts, plants, and sewer systems not connected with those constructed or improved by the Cassa. In sum, the Cassa eventually had to assume the entire responsibility in this sector.

The 15-year plan of the ministerial committee for the Mezzogiorno provides about $500 million for water and sewer systems. The work of the Cassa in these sectors, however, has had some difficulties. The 10-year plan, which provided for the construction of 52 aqueduct complexes, proved to be inadequate from its inception. It became clear that it was necessary to construct external pipelines to the towns and to build up water and sewer systems within them. Furthermore, the growth in number of the communities required an extension of the installations to unforeseen population centers.

By June 30, 1962, expenditures for the works undertaken in these areas, including the aqueducts for tourist centers, amounted to about $350 million. The conduits constructed had reached 8,297 km., and the number of reservoirs 1,554, with a total capacity of about 1,109,000 cubic meters. The regional distribution of these totals can be seen in table VIII. By June 30, 1962, the number of communities with adequate services had been increased to 1,491, and the population served to 5.8 million.

Road and communication systems

At the time of the establishment of the Cassa, southern Italy was extremely poor in communications. The average density of all the state, provincial, and community roads of Italy in 1950 was 0.562 km. per sq. km.; in the Mezzogiorno it was 0.354 km. per sq. km.; in Sardinia 0.199; and in the north 0.827. There was not only a great deficiency of roads, but many were in rather poor condition. With respect to the ordinary roads, which are of prime importance for the industrial development of the Mezzogiorno, the original law gave the Cassa full or partial responsibility for the cost of improving the existing roads, though such projects were not provided for in the contributions planned by the state. In addition, the Cassa could take over the full cost of the construction of new roads, for which there had been no provision at all. To satisfy the "hunger for roads" of the Mezzogiorno, the increase in the appropriations for this sector in the subsequent integrated laws was significant.

The Cassa undertook the improvement of 15,500 km. of provincial roads, which already constituted a rather organic system in themselves and which offered the greatest promise of economical utilization, and the construction of 3,500 km. of new roads, apart from 500 km. of interregional roads leading to the autostrade and 7,000 km. of *bonifica* roads (which we charged to the agri-

TABLE VIII.—*Dams, Conduits, and Reservoirs Constructed to June 30, 1962*

Regions	Dams		Kilometers of conduits	Reservoirs	
	Number	Liters per second		Number	Square meters
Toscana	65	83. 2	52. 3	21	4, 700
Lazio	36	796. 3	1, 066. 9	187	65, 310
Abruzzi	46	2, 890. 2	877. 0	240	79, 095
Molise	51	433. 0	908. 9	178	111, 325
Campania	145	7, 059. 7	2, 162. 8	441	434, 004
Puglia	46	1, 438. 5	320. 7	25	72, 036
Basilicata	26	280. 0	321. 1	17	13, 300
Calabria	253	1, 922. 9	1, 121. 4	207	127, 931
Sicilia	116	2, 374. 1	733. 1	110	91, 661
Sardegna	59	196. 1	733. 2	128	108, 564
Total	843	17, 474. 0	8, 297. 4	1, 554	1, 107, 926

Source: Reports of the Ministerial Committee for the Mezzogiorno.

cultural program). By June 30, 1962, the finished achievements were 14,715 km. of improved provincial roads and over 2,000 km. of other roads; 2,461 km. of new construction of ordinary roads, as well as 6,000 km. of *bonifica* roads. This was truly remarkable progress, particularly considering the geological problems in the Mezzogiorno.[43]

In addition, $60 million have been appropriated for "tourist" roads. By June 30, 1962, about $40 million had been spent or obligated for the construction of 483 km. of new roads and the improvement of another 550 km.

To these investments one must add those for the autostrade, which had undergone a remarkable development in a few years, but which had been concentrated predominantly in the north. In 1961, a new "plan for the construction of new roads and autostrade" was passed which took much better account of the requirements of the south. This plan provides for the construction of toll autostrade of about 3,200 km. and other autostrade of about 1,900 km. (including that between Salerno and Reggio Calabria). The state also contributes to the costs, by means of certain tax exemptions, of the road construction contractors who operate the toll roads. These autostrade *"in concessione"* will become the property of the state after 30 years.

The plan for the autostrade provides for the completion of the so-called *autostrada del sole* which links Milan, Bologna, Florence, and Rome to Naples, Salerno, and Reggio Calabria. In addition, an autostrada along the Adriatic coast will connect Bologna with Pescara, Foggia, and Bari, with extensions by high-speed roads to Brindisi and Lecce. Finally, another autostrada across the Apennines will connect Naples and Bari. In Sicily, two connected autostrade will be built between Messina and Catania, and Catania and Palermo.

In the communication sector, the programs implemented by the Cassa for

[43] Pescatore, *L'Intervento Straordinario* op. cit, p. 147.

the modernization and improvement of certain major southern railroads are of great importance, in particular the double-tracking of the Battipaglia-Reggio Calabria railroad, the electrification of the Bari-Foggia-Pescara railroad, and the modernization of the Taranto-Metaponto-Reggio Calabria railroad. For these projects, which are nearly completed, and for the ferryboat connections with Sicily and Sardinia, about $140 million have been appropriated.

Miscellaneous activities

The policies of the Cassa in making financial contributions for the construction of schools and of kindergartens through the system of the *cantieri di lavoro,* which employs the seasonal unemployed, must be mentioned in particular. These policies, which in the beginning applied only to communities of less than 5,000 inhabitants, have been extended by the 1959 law to all communities of less than 10,000 inhabitants.

The activities of the Cassa extend also into the sectors of handicrafts, fishing, and tourism. By the end of 1960, the Cassa had provided $6.7 million for handicraft enterprises, and nearly $10 million for the development of fishing; in addition, it had provided for works in the tourist sector in the amount of about $60 million. In this sector, the policy of the Cassa has gradually developed. While it began only in areas that promised rapid success, it now plans programs for tourist zones which require large-scale investment and coordination of public and private activities.

THE INDUSTRIALIZATION POLICY

The solution of the problem of the south would constitute a great stimulus to the general development of the country. However, the problem of the south can be solved only by means of industrialization. By now it has been recognized that the lack of entrepreneurial talents lies at the root of the problem, as in many areas the general and particular preconditions do exist for many different industrial activities. In the Mezzogiorno, according to Francesco Curato, the principal objectives to be pursued are as follows:

"(1) Improvement of the natural resources which are still inadequately and irrationally exploited. More precisely:

"(*a*) Agrarian improvements, above all in the coastal plains which are now free from malaria, through land improvement and resettlement, so that these plains may become new centers of intensive cultivation;

"(*b*) improvement of the water system, with the fourfold objective of improving waterways, hydroelectric utilization, the drinking water system, and irrigation;

"(*c*) improved exploitation of mineral resources, which is still only in its beginning phase.

"(2) Integration of the economic potentialities created by the introduction of a sufficient number of new industries, taking account of the productive conditions of the nation as a whole and of the sectors more directly connected with the products produced and consumed in our regions.

"(3) Improvement of tourist facilities, because tourism, if it increases sufficiently, may constitute a factor of great importance within the economic and social framework of the Mezzogiorno.

"(4) Finally, improvement of services in order to make life more civilized for the indigenous population, to improve the means of production, and to facilitate trade so as to achieve a better adjustment of our economy to the economic structure of Europe and of the world." [44]

Friedrich Voechting holds that, in this still largely precapitalistic world, it is of fundamental importance to "create a class of entrepreneurs capable of taking their place in the world economy":

> A large number of the young men and women of the South, who hold themselves intellectually capable of higher tasks, believe that they can find appropriate fields of activity only in the North of Italy. This stream of migrants, which, with little exaggeration, could be called the "intellectual hemorrhage of the South," is being offset in small part by an opposite stream from the North to the South. The latter migrants (who are fewer in number than the former) succeed in establishing themselves rapidly in the Southern centers and in making their weight felt as the elite they are. As this exchange of intellectuals between the North and the South is so unbalanced, people in Southern Italy, though they know the real material and social advantages that can be reaped from this exchange, often have an inferiority complex. At any rate, because of this thinning out of the intellectual groups, it is difficult to perceive from which social stratum a true class of leaders could emerge. This reciprocal migratory movement is directly connected with another important phenomenon: the insufficient technical education of the Southern middle class and the direct aversion—at least until a very short time ago—of this class to a career in the techno-productive sector, an aversion which is both cause and effect of the scarcity of technical institutes and professional schools in these areas.
>
> The factor just mentioned, i.e., the lack of men with the spirit of entrepreneurs, capable of courageous initiative in the business world, often constitutes the greatest negative element in the play of forces causing industrialization; it is, indeed, a much more serious obstacle to the economic development of the Mezzogiorno than the insufficient supply of capital or the deficiency of the credit institutions distributing this insufficient supply.[45]

In the period immediately after the war, the "spontaneous" development of the Italian economy which took place mainly in the industrialized areas of the Centro-Nord, themselves comparable in industrial development to the other countries of Western Europe, could either seek new commercial outlets in foreign countries or rely on the expansion of the internal market. A large obstacle to the latter alternative, however, was the low per capita income of the Mezzogiorno (in 1950 it was still only 42.8 percent of that in the Centro-Nord).

Given the general principles of Western economic policy and the progressive restoration of open markets and free trade, it is obvious why the industrial reconstruction of the period 1945–50 concentrated on the kinds of activities, the conditions of production, and the locations which could best sustain international competition. Though the direction of the Italian economic expansion toward exports rather than toward the domestic market may have retarded the structural transformation of the southern economy, it nevertheless helped to consolidate the general economic development. In the decade 1951–61 Italy, precisely because it already had a developed industrial apparatus, could begin an autonomous process of developing the south and finance it almost completely from internal sources.

At first it was believed that once a small initial stimulus had called forth certain economic forces, the growth process, thus started, would continue autonomously thereafter. But later another view became predominant; namely, that certain natural trends and forces, if left free to unfold, could

[44] Francesco Curato, "I lineamenti e realizzazioni del piano di sviluppo economico," *Centro Studi della Cassa per il Mezzogiorno,* Quaderno 22, pp. 24 ff.

[45] Friedrich Voechting, "Considerazioni sull'industrializzazione del Mezzogiorno—il problema degli imprenditori,' *Moneta e Credito,* Banco Nazionale del Lavoro, June 1958, p. 198.

aggravate the dualism and the divergencies to the disadvantage of the south. Both views had to be considered in order to reach the goal of the economic development of the Mezzogiorno. Whereas, before the war the problem of the Mezzogiorno was held to be limited to the southern region only, now it was thought that the economic growth of the south had to be promoted and realized in the interest of the north as well as the south (i.e., in the interest of a balanced economy), utilizing common national resources to which the entire country, but above all—and in their own interest—the more advanced regions have made and make contributions.

Nonintervention would undoubtedly have led to unfavorable effects on the growth possibilities of northern industry, which would have found itself operating sooner or later in a much smaller market than the geographic area and the population of the country could provide. Moreover, it was clear that the north would soon have to face the liberalization of trade in Europe. Within this framework, and in view of generally rising living standards, the enlargement of the internal market was necessary for the well-being of the entire country. The north was not deprived in order to give to the south, but something was added to the economic capacity of both.

These principles, though they have been stated and accepted slowly and hesitantly, underlie the industrial development policy for the south. The different stages of this development policy, particularly the stress on industrialization, have been characterized by ever more efficient instruments, increasingly coordinated. The legislators in 1950 based their policy on the idea that the depressed state of the south was predominantly a depressed state of agriculture and that the deficiency of the infrastructure rendered an immediate process of industrialization impossible. It was hoped that, through the measures taken to improve agriculture and the infrastructure, it would be possible to eliminate or at least reduce the disadvantages private entrepreneurs encountered in the construction and operation of industrial establishments located in the south. The results were to come from:

"(*a*) the multiplier effect of the 'adjunctive' public expenditures.

"(*b*) the 'external economies' from which industry would benefit when operating in a more accessible and practical economic environment due to the increase in the public services and their greater efficiency." [46]

But in the course of these activities and especially in view of the necessity to absorb the permanently unemployed and the large number of underemployed, criticism of these policies became louder. The sectoral approach proved to be totally inadequate. The global (regional) approach came to be accepted as the only method that would lead to a real solution.

While it is true that investments in agriculture can increase total output, their effects will be felt much more slowly than the effects of investments in the industrial sector. And in order to obtain a high rate of increase of agricultural production, the structure of agrictulture must be rationalized. This involves the freeing of a large proportion of agrictultural labor. Thus, other sectors must be able immediately to absorb these agricultural workers, if the rate of unemployment is not to be greatly increased.

Moreover, parallel to the increase in agrictultural production, measures must be taken in the marketing sector. Because of its high costs, the system of distribution not only contributes greatly to the problem of underemploy-

---

[46] Giuseppe di Nardi, "Provvedimenti per il Mezzogiorno," *Economia e Storia,* No. 3, 1960, p. 494.

ment, but is also one of the causes of the distortion of production in Italy and an obstacle to agricultural development.

Measures improving the infrastructure have long-run productive effects and increase employment and consumption, but they do not guarantee that the development and a permanently higher level of consumption can be maintained. And they do not alone provide those "external economies" which the enterprise derives from the vicinity of other complementary industries, from the availability of specialized and skilled labor, and from established marketing facilities. Because of this lack of incentive, too few new enterprises were started in the south. Moreover, the low rate of saving consequent on low incomes made local capital scarce in the south. These are some of the major reasons which led to a widening of the horizons of the development policy for the Mezzogiorno and of the Cassa.

The new orientation, first expressed in a law of July 1952, caused an evolutionary process in the Cassa: its activities were extended for 2 years and its funds were increased by 280 million lire. In addition, it was authorized to make loans predominantly for the financing of industrial activities. The latter was a real innovation, as it allowed the Cassa to enter the sector of industrial financing with powers of direction and control. Its functions were twofold:

(1) Foreign funds destined for the financing of industrialization were handled by the Cassa.

(2) The Cassa was asked to help in the establishment of the institutes for medium-term credits for the Mezzogiorno (ISVEIMER, IRFIS, CIS), and to participate both in the making of the grants and in the administration of these institutes through its representatives on the administrative councils and board of directors.

Industrialization, however, was still regarded as the fruit of predominantly private initiative linked to the improvement of the agricultural structure. The Government strengthened the policy of direct encouragement to private entrepreneurs by two major measures. On the one hand, it granted exemptions or reductions in direct taxes and in every way tried to reduce the burden of certain cost factors, and on the other hand, it established the means through which particular small- and medium-size enterprises could obtain capital at low rates of interest.

It was thought that these measures would enable the entrepreneur establishing himself in the south to overcome the initial disadvantages and to meet the costs of doing business in the south above those for comparable enterprises in the north. However, even with these new incentives, the percentage and absolute increase in employment was still too small; they alone apparently could not bring forth the volume of investments capable of starting a self-propelling development process.

Therefore, new principles were worked out and enacted in Law No. 634 of 1957. With this measure, industrialization became the focus of public policy for the Mezzogiorno. Actually, internal political events (the elections and the subsequent prolonged struggles before the establishment of a relatively stable government) prevented immediate action by the administrators responsible for the southern policy. For these reasons regulations to implement the law did not appear until the end of 1958, and it did not really become operative until 1959.[47]

[47] The law charged the Ministerial Committee for the Mezzogiorno with the responsibility of setting up the directives or rules of application of the new policy. Regarding matters of industrialization, the law did not become operative automatically.

The policy based principally on credit for the financing of industry was slowly abandoned and replaced by financial development aids in the form of grants which differed by territory and by sector. In addition, the new policy included the formation of poles of development (*poli di sviluppo*) in order thereby to create areas of industrial growth.

To this end, and in order to reinforce the effects of the incentives given to private enterprises, the agencies of state participation (*aziende a partecipazione statale*) were ordered to make large industrial investments in the Mezzogiorno. As stated above, the law provides that 60 percent of the investments in new industrial plants and 40 percent of total investments under the authority of the Ministry of State Holdings must be carried out in the Mezzogiorno. In practice, these figures have been interpreted elastically, because the state holdings, which include many service industries, such as telephone, radio, and television, must necessarily service the entire national territory and make investments in the entire nation, whether for modernization or in new establishments, in accordance with the requirements of economic change. Thus, only the regulation that 40 percent of the total investments have to be made in the south is operative in practice.

Much attention has been given to the location of new investments, in order to follow consistently the concept of the poles of development. The large investments in steel in the province of Taranto, together with the petrochemical investments in Ferrandina in Basilicata (now Lucania) and the mechanical investments in Bari, have created a real pole of development in Puglia. Similarly, the petrochemical plants constructed by ENI in Gela (in connection with the discovery of oil in this area) have made possible the industrial triangle of southwest Sicily. In addition, the investments of many State holdings in the area of Naples have strengthened the growth of the pole of development which, based on Naples, extends from Caserta to Salerno. Other investments have been made in response to particular regional requirements, such as the machinery establishment at Reggio Calabria, the first industrial establishment of any size in this province.

Meanwhile, the extremely favorable general state of business and the appearance of certain bottlenecks in the labor market of the north increasingly confronted northern entrepreneurs with a choice between further investments in the north at increasing costs for some factors of production, or investments in the south under more favorable conditions of availability and cost of labor. Thus, stimulated by the investments of state holdings, by the progressive effects of the entire complex of direct and indirect incentives, and by the cumulative industrial development of some areas, industrial investments in the south have increased at a remarkable rate in recent years. In short, many and complex factors, partly spontaneous and partly brought about by the direct and indirect public policy measures, have altered the locational advantages for new industrial establishments. The new enterprises in the south have taken certain traditional products like grain or olives and rather than producing or processing for local markets only, have created larger industrial apparatuses serving the entire national demand as well as the export market.

The results of all these events can be seen in table IX. The table shows that the average annual rate of increase of industrial investments (at constant prices) between 1951 and 1957 was about 5.9 percent for the country as a whole, while in the Mezzogiorno it was 9.6 percent and in the Centro-Nord a little above 5.2 percent. For the period 1957–62, while the average annual rate of increase for the country as a whole rose to 9.2 percent, in the Centro-

TABLE IX.—*Gross Investments in 1954 Prices, by Sector*

	Investments (billions of Lire)				Annual rate of increase (percent)		
	1951	1957	1959	1962	1951–57	1957–62	1959–62
Agriculture:							
Mezzogiorno....	89. 1	162. 0	182. 3	228. 2	10. 48	7. 09	7. 77
Centro-Nord....	187. 9	211. 0	232. 7	278. 8	1. 95	5. 73	6. 21
Italy.........	277. 0	373. 0	415. 0	507. 0	5. 08	6. 33	6. 90
Industry:							
Mezzogiorno....	91. 8	159. 0	181. 1	368. 0	9. 59	18. 27	26. 66
Centro-Nord....	609. 2	828. 0	831. 9	1, 163. 0	5. 25	7. 03	11. 82
Italy.........	701. 0	987. 0	1, 013. 0	1, 531. 0	5. 87	9. 18	14. 76
Other:							
Mezzogiorno....	219. 2	451. 6	471. 3	701. 6	12. 80	9. 21	14. 18
Centro-Nord....	692. 8	1, 384. 4	1, 668. 7	2, 315. 4	12. 23	10. 83	11. 54
Italy.........	912. 0	1, 836. 0	2, 140. 0	3, 017. 0	12. 37	10. 44	12. 13
Total:							
Mezzogiorno....	400. 1	772. 6	834. 7	1, 297. 8	11. 59	10. 93	15. 85
Centro-Nord....	1, 489. 9	2, 423. 4	2, 733. 3	3, 757. 2	8. 45	9. 17	11. 19
Italy.........	1, 890. 0	3, 196. 0	3, 568. 0	5, 055. 0	9. 15	9. 60	12. 31

Source: ISTAT.

Nord it amounted to 7 percent, and in the south over 18 percent. In absolute amounts, between 1951 and 1962 industrial investments quadrupled in the south while they about doubled in the Centro-Nord.

This difference in the increase of investments is significant, and its effects show up in the differences in the per-capita income of the Centro-Nord and the south. However, it must be stressed that the goal of the industrialization policy for the Mezzogiorno cannot be simply the diminution of differences in regional income or in the per-capita income of the Centro-Nord and the south; this is only one longrun goal. In the short run, the aim is directly to affect the economic structure in order to create an autonomous development mechanism. And one cannot tell merely from an increase in per-capita income whether the dynamic factors causing it will sustain the structural transformation of the economic system, or whether they only reflect temporary chance elements.

In a comparison of the per-capita income of the south and the Centro-Nord of Italy, many of these chance elements are involved. Agricultural income constitutes a much greater proportion of total income in the Mezzogiorno than in the north. Furthermore, because northern agriculture is more modern, its income is less affected by seasonal disturbances, to which southern agriculture is most sensitive. Therefore, a favorable agricultural year can sharply increase the per-capita income of the south, while an unfavorable year can reduce it considerably. In short, per-capita income statistics are a valid basis only for the comparison of reasonably similar economies in reasonably similar environments, and the Mezzogiorno and the north of Italy are not comparable in this respect.

At any rate, the average annual rate of increase of gross national product at constant prices has been lower in the Mezzogiorno than in the Centro-Nord during the entire decade. For the period 1951–57, the average annual increase for the entire nation was 5.24 percent, while it was 5.52 percent in the Centro-Nord and 4.26 percent in the Mezzogiorno. In the subsequent period, 1957–62, the gross national product increased on the average by 6.68 percent for Italy as a whole, by 7.34 percent in the Centro-Nord, and by 5.07 percent in the Mezzogiorno.

However, if the industrial development policy is analyzed in the light of changes in regional income, account must be taken of the fact that the major part of the planned industrial investments has just been completed or is still in progress. In short, the trend of an increasing divergence between the north and the south has been stopped but the actual divergence has not yet been reduced.

Therefore, the development policy for the Mezzogiorno must again be thought over and stated anew, partly because the huge industrial investments (for instance, those for the steel center in Taranto which amount to about $500 million) that have been carried out to date cannot be easily repeated. Thus, it will be difficult to attain the same volume of industrial investments in future years. Perhaps for this reason, Pastore, the President of the ministerial committee for the Mezzogiorno, noted in his report on the "activities of coordination" for 1962 that:

> It is necessary to re-examine the different forms of incentives applied on the national and on the local level, with the goal of establishing on the national level a unitary system of positive and negative incentives which can be easily handled and periodically revised in view of the actual course of the industrial investments carried out.
>
> In particular, continuation of the special credit and tax measures in the Northern regions seems to be incompatible with this goal. For, on the one hand, they destroy the positive effect of the measures favoring the South, and, on the other hand, they stimulate further migrations of the population from the South to the North.
>
> Regarding the central regions, one should take account of the existence of certain depressed zones, with imbalance between the demand and supply of labor, and should consider what type of stimulating actions could be taken.
>
> In addition, the possibility of introducing special kinds of disincentives in order to prevent further concentrations in the already congested zones must be considered.
>
> Because of the rate of industrial development necessary in the Mezzogiorno, the policy of concentrating investments in the areas and nuclei of industrial development must be continued.
>
> The present industrial concentrations alone do not seem to be capable, within a relatively short time, of counterbalancing the forces attracting men and capital to the industrialized regions.
>
> In this context, therefore, it is necessary progressively to reduce the stimuli given to certain areas in the Mezzogiorno where industrial growth has already become self-sustaining, and to increase them in areas and nuclei which have thus far been insufficiently touched by the development process, and in which the existence of an infrastructure already provided by public measures, favorable location with respect to marketing outlets, and above all the availability of labor constitute a good basis for the establishment of an industrial center.
>
> The absolute necessity to stimulate the greatest possible expansion of the small and medium-size enterprises requires particular credit, financing, and fiscal incentives,

related to rural industrial standards and ways of thinking, in the form of participation in risk-capital and, above all, in the form of greater technical and commercial assistance which should go as far as to include the training of technical cadres. In fact, the techno-economic assistance must be directly linked to the financial aids these enterprises receive.

More organic and efficient incentives to private entrepreneurs must be accompanied by direct intervention on the part of the State, be it through the state holdings, or through the financial development institutions, in order to assure the attainment of the planned amounts and types of investment.

Given the undesirability of further industrial concentrations in the Centro-Nord, new industrial undertakings of the state holdings must not be permitted outside the Mezzogiorno. For the next fifteen years it seems absolutely necessary to assure that a greater proportion of the new investments of the state holdings than the 60% now required will be carried out in the South. Within the framework of the policy of the Plan and of the respective institutions, it will be necessary to assure the cooperation of the Ministerial Committee for the Mezzogiorno and of the Ministry for State Holdings in order to determine the increase in the proportion of the state holdings' investments that is to go to the Mezzogiorno within the next fifteen years.

The tasks of the state holdings in the South require not only capital but also entrepreneurial capacities. And the difficulties of acquiring such capacities are the greater, the more the objective of the state holdings becomes the establishment of medium-size manufacturing enterprises.

The policy measures of the companies at the head of the *Enti di Gestione* must be integrated with those of the financial development institutions. Those companies which possess adequate entrepreneurial as well as financial capacities must create new enterprises related to the existing technical and financial capacities of private entrepreneurs, and encourage the latter to participate more and more in these activities. The Cassa has already had one experience in this respect with the INSUD, and the regional financial institutions can utilize this model and coordinate their policy programs among themselves.

These companies must be endowed with the necessary financial means from the very start, in view of the important role they have to play in the next five years. They should develop particular policy measures favoring the rise of small enterprises directly connected to the large industrial complexes which are about to be established in the Mezzogiorno, through minority participation and adequate technical assistance. In this manner they could play a decisive part in the modernization of the structure of the already existing handicraft and other small enterprises, and promote a reasonable amount of transfer of entrepreneurial talents from the North to the South.[48]

In short, this is a more deliberate development policy with more direct Government intervention. As was to be expected, it has aroused further controversy. It is obvious that the development so conceived will involve internal migrations, the elimination of inefficient enterprises, modification of the social structure, and probably also socioeconomic problems in each area. The development policy must take account of these facts and provide for the necessary adjustments.

Now that the priority of industrialization has been established, although the measures for agriculture and for the infrastructure continue to be important quantitatively, three fundamental directives have been formulated:

(1) *The location of industry.* In view of the industrialization processes already started in the Mezzogiorno, poles of development should be created by the consortiums which guide the "industrial development areas" and the "nuclei of industrialization." The industrial development areas are administered by these consortiums composed of local administrative bodies and private business interests. They are to set up the development plan for the area; this is an urban plan which also presupposes an economic program, if

---

[48] Comitato dei Ministri per il Mezzogiorno, *Relazione sull'Attività di Coordinamento,* Rome, 1963, vol. I, pp. 22 ff.

only in broad outline. Through their promotional activities they must attempt to strengthen the first beginnings of industrial development.

(2) *Direct investments.* The state holdings must make their investments in areas which have the preconditions for industrialization. It is evident that their investments must always be in accordance with economic logic, that is, their locational distribution must not be subject to demagogy and provincialism. The policy of the state holdings must conform to criteria which have been well stated by the president of the IRI (the IRI, which administers the state holdings, constitutes the fourth largest industrial group in Europe):

> The feeling of global responsibility of the public authority has found its most mature expression in the creation of the "industrial development areas." We completely agree with those who feel that this policy ends the old controversy regarding the extent of public intervention in regional development. In opposition to those who want the State to take over all industrial enterprises, this policy emphasizes the need to concentrate on well-delimited individual areas in which there are real investment opportunities. On the other hand to the proponents of local autonomy, the policy of the industrial development areas answers clearly that the State cannot and should not intervene everywhere, but that it must promote a geographic mobility within particular regions, which, along with and complementary to occupational mobility, constitutes the determinant element in the development of the entire socio-economic environment, because of structural changes whose revolutionary character requires the modification of many hard-to-change situations.[49]

(3) *Diffusion of industrial enterprises.* It is the goal of this policy that all the southern regions participate more and more actively in the process of industrialization. Therefore, aside from the policy of industrial development areas, incentives are offered to small- and medium-sized enterprises throughout the south, so that the development areas do not run the risk of becoming islands of well-being. Hence, nuclei of industrialization, which receive much more limited assistance than the areas of industrial development, have been established. In order to facilitate the spreading of small- and medium-size private enterprises, the Institute of Development Aid for the Mezzogiorno (*Istituto per l'Assistenza allo Sviluppo del Mezzogiorno*) has been created with the help of the Cassa per il Mezzogiorno and of the special credit institutes. This institute extends the necessary technical assistance to these small entrepreneurs. Along the same lines, action has been taken regarding the vocational training of labor and of the intermediate and higher level technical cadres.

These new legislative directives and this economic policy were designed to create an elastic system in which the initiatives, the burdens, and the risks of industrialization are shared by many different institutions and people who may act independently or in cooperation with each other: Private entrepreneurs, public enterprises, the state holdings, the economic administrative bodies of the state, the consortiums for the industrial development areas and for the nuclei of industrialization, the special industrial credit institutes, all the national banks extending medium-term credits, and, last

[49] Giuseppe Petrilli, "La funzione pilotato della grande azienda nelle politica di sviluppo," *Realtà del Mezzogiorno,* February 1962, pp. 143–144.

but not least, the Cassa per il Mezzogiorno, with its technical or financial assistance to the enterprises and consortiums. The aim was to avoid even the possibility of economic rigidities which could have come about through the concentration of industrialization in a region by the state alone. This could have caused not only economic but also political problems.

The industrialization measures may be classified as follows:

(1) Tax exemptions or reductions.

(2) Medium-term credits on favorable terms, or ownership participation.

(3) Grants for the establishment of new industrial plants or for the expansion of existing enterprises.

(4) Creation of areas and nuclei of industrial development together with the establishment of specific infrastructural services required by the respective area and the construction of industrial buildings to be sold or rented to new entrepreneurs.

(5) Miscellaneous special incentives (such as preferential railroad tariffs, etc.)

Incentives for the construction, conversion, or expansion of industrial establishments

(1) Fiscal incentives

As we have seen, one objective of the industrial development policy in the south is to encourage and maintain private initiative through measures attempting to assure industrial investments in the south a return equal to what they would have earned if they had been located in the industrially more advanced regions. Thus, a large bundle of incentives and cost reductions is necessary, covering the major costs and risks of such establishments, in order to eliminate, at least partly, the disadvantages encountered in constructing and operating plants in the southern regions.

The fiscal incentives are certainly most welcome to the entrepreneurs, not only because of the economic advantage they represent, but also for a psychological reason. The Italian fiscal system is rather backward, and tax evasions are widespread. Since tax evasion always constitutes a risk and requires multiple and difficult accounting procedures, the exemption from the income tax (*Ricchezza Mobile,* or R.M.) is doubly advantageous inasmuch as it allows enterprises to do proper accounting for an entire decade.

An enterprise that intends to set up a new industrial plant in the southern regions, or to expand, modernize, activate, reactivate, transform, reconstruct, or transfer an industrial establishment that already exists, can obtain the following tax exemptions:

Exemption from customs duties (Law No. 634, art. 29): Exemption from the payment of duties on construction materials and equipment for the installation of new plants, or for the expansion, modernization, activation, reactivation, transformation, or reconstruction of industrial establishments.

Exemption from the R.M. (Law No. 634, art. 29): Exemption from the payment of the tax on net income, which applies also in the Centro-Nord, is granted directly in the south for an amount not exceeding 50 percent of the net income declared, if it is reinvested in industrial enterprises, on the condition that the total investment is at least twice the amount of net income thus exempted from the R.M. tax. In addition, the Minister of Finance grants, for a period of 10 years, exemption from the R.M. payment on business income produced in any new or converted establishment in the Mezzogiorno.

Reduction of the General Turnover Tax (IGE): A reduction of 50 percent of the IGE for the materials or equipment required for the above-mentioned purposes, even if they are purchased within Italy, provided they are for fixed investments.

Reduction of the fixed registration and mortgage tax which has to be paid for some transactions—such as the acquisition of real estate and other property, incorporations, grants, etc.—which constitute necessary formalities in many industrial activities.

Exemption from the industrial tax imposed by the communities: The administrations of the communities, which examine the requests for new industrial establishments case-by-case, can grant partial or total exemption of the community tax on industry, including the consumption tax.

The tax on electrical energy can be reduced by 50 percent for the energy used by the respective enterprises.

Giarda has conducted empirical investigations on the effects of the fiscal incentives on regional economic development. Through an interview study he attempted to learn from the experiences of the entrepreneurs concerned to what degree the fiscal incentives have influenced the choice of industrial locations, and to determine the effect of the rate of taxation on the level of development of an area, and thus to establish the relationship existing between regional economic development and the fiscal burden on the regional level. He attempted also to measure the effective burden of local and Government taxes on the costs of the enterprises in various localities. On the basis of his analysis he concluded:

> Differences in taxes can imply important variations in total costs and particularly in profits. On the one hand, the entrepreneurs interviewed attributed to the fiscal element a certain degree of importance in their choice of location; on the other hand, it cannot be demonstrated that high tax burdens have discouraged regional economic development, as the latter was actually greater where the tax burden was higher.[50]

Regarding the efficiency of fiscal incentives, Di Nardi distinguishes between "tax exemptions or reductions" which are made only once—at the time of the purchase of machinery, for instance—and "tax exemptions on business profits." [51] While the former are rather efficient incentives, the latter, though constituting a strong element of attraction for the enterprises situated in special areas, become effective only if there are taxable profits; nevertheless, they seem to encourage the creation of new activities in particular critical zones without great prospect of profits.

(2) Credit incentives

In general, credit facilities are a rather efficient stimulant for the creation of new activities, if they are accompanied by a considerable reduction in the interest rate (relative to the current market rate), and if they are combined with the granting of guarantees for loads by the state or other public authorities and an adequately structured banking system. The existence of financial corporations which in some cases may participate in the capital stock of the enterprise can further increase the efficiency of these measures.

The credit measures adopted in the special legislation for the Mezzogiorno in order to speed up the process of industrialization by assisting the

---

[50] Pietro Giarda, "Incentivi fiscali e sviluppo economico regionale: I risultati di recenti indagini empiriche," *Rivista Internazionale di Scienze Sociali,* May–June 1963, fsc. III, p. 237.

[51] Di Nardi, *Vie e Mezzi della Riconversione Industriale,* Luxemburg, 1961, p. 50.

entrepreneur to obtain capital may be classified as medium-term credits and operating credits.

(*a*) *Medium-term credits for enterprises.* Law No. 634 of July 1957 (integrated and modified by Law No. 555 of July 18, 1959) consolidated and amplified the task of the banking system in aiding industrial development in the South. The medium-term credit institutions specially created for the Mezzogiorno (ISVEIMER, IRFIS, CIS) and all the other medium-term credit institutions operating in the other regions of Italy (IMI, EFI, *Medio Banca, Centro Banca, Banca Nazionale del Lavoro*) were authorized to operate in the South through facilities offered by the Cassa per il Mezzogiorno.

An industrial enterprise that wanted to establish a new industrial plant in the southern area, or to expand or convert an already existing establishment, could obtain medium-term loans from these institutions on the conditions determined by the Interministerial Committee for Savings and Credit. These conditions have been changed several times since 1957, with the intention of further facilitating requests for loans. Today the conditions are the following:

(1) A medium-sized enterprise is defined as one in which the maximum amount of capital invested in each individual productive unit (establishment) is 6 billion lire (about $10 million). There is no limit on the number of employees.

(2) These enterprises are eligible for loans at a special rate of interest of 4 percent for the entire amount of the credit extended.

(3) Enterprises larger than medium-size—i.e., enterprises with investments exceeding 6 billion—may get loans at a rate of interest of 5 percent for the entire amount of the credit, but within the limits of a total appropriation which does not allow for much financing under this condition.

On the basis of Law No. 649 of July 25, 1961, which modified and integrated Law No. 623 (July 30, 1959), the interest rate for medium-sized businesses was lowered to 3 percent for all requests for loans presented before June 30, 1963. This latest interest concession was made by the Ministry of Industry; at the same time, a concession was granted to medium-sized and small businesses of the Centro-Nord which lowered their interest rate from 7–8 to 5 percent. There is a high probability that these concessions will be further prolonged.

Still on the basis of these last two laws; i.e., No. 623 and No. 649, the industrial credit institutes can grant loans in the south up to 70 percent of the actual costs of the initial financing, including expenditures for primary materials and the finished products necessary to the production cycle.

Lending institutions, of course, have established their own criteria. For example, the principal criteria of one special medium-term banking instituton, ISVEIMER, may be classified as follows:

Functional criteria: Preference is given to new establishments relative to the expansion of already existing establishments.

Locational criteria: Through the spreading of industrial enterprises, industrial unity is to be supported.

Sectoral criteria: Preference is given to industries producing capital goods, and secondly to industries transforming agricultural products.

Business criteria: Preference is given to medium-sized enterprises with investments in fixed capital up to the amount of 150 million (about $240,000) and with the number of employees not exceeding 500.

Employment criteria: Preference is given to those enterprises which, within the limits of their economic possibilities, offer the greatest amount of employment.

(*b*) *Operating credits.* The Departments of Industrial Credit of the Bank of Naples and the Bank of Sicily, as well as the CIS, can extend credit for operating costs during the production cycle. These credits must be for at least 1 year and for less than 5 years.[52] Operating credits can be obtained also by the large- and medium-sized enterprises that already have obtained loans for the establishment of new or the enlargement of existing plants. The departments reserve at least 25 percent of the total funds at their disposition for such loans; 50 percent of this reserve is earmarked for operating credits to the businesses financed by ISVEIMER and IRFIS. The rate of interest is 5.5 percent.[53]

(3) Grants

Law No. 634 attacked the difficult problem confronting many small and medium-sized enterprises which could not begin production because of their lack of circulating capital. Often income expectations were most uncertain. Since the banking system could not extend short-term credit without security, it was impossible to solve the problem by bank loans. As it was absolutely necessary to provide these enterprises with a minimum of operating capital at the beginning of their operations, Article 18 of Law No. 634 authorized the Cassa to extend grants "for the establishment of small- and medium-sized enterprises in communities with a population of less than 75,000 inhabitants in which there are not enough industrial activities."

As it was difficult to draw a precise line between "establishment" and "expansion" of small- and medium-sized enterprises, Law No. 555 of July. 18, 1959, permits grants also for the expansion of existing enterprises. In addition, this law extends the maximum population of the communities in which these industrial plants must be located in order to receive assistance to 200,000 inhabitants. Finally, businesses located in communities in areas and nuclei of industrial development may receive grants even if these communities have a population greater than 200,000.

Article 18 states that the "determination of the location and the characteristics of the small- and medium-sized industries which may benefit from these grants, as well as the amounts of the latter, have been established by the ministerial committee for the Mezzogiorno on the basis of a proposal by the Cassa and after having heard the opinion of the Minister for Industry and Commerce." Article 19 specifies that "the amount of the grant is determined by the importance of the industrial establishment and the employment possibilities it will create, as well as the contribution the new plant will make to the economy of the industrially underdeveloped areas."

According to the resolution adopted by the ministerial committee for the Mezzogiorno on the application of article 18, "small and medium-sized enterprises" must be interpreted to mean bona fide industrial establishments which manufacture one or more products from primary or secondary materials, and which involve capital investments not exceeding 6 billion lire (about $10 million).

On the basis of articles 18, 19, and 20 of Law No. 634 and of articles 10 and 13 of Law No. 1462 of September 29, 1962, the grants for industrial enterprises may be extended for the following expenditures:

[52] Art. 4 of Law No. 135 of Apr. 16, 1954.
[53] Art. 25 of Law No. 634 of July 29, 1957.

—for fixed plant (machinery and buildings).

—for building improvement (links to aqueducts, sewers, etc.); electric conduits, oil and gas pipes; road and railroad connections; various social services, and activities.

Fixed Plant

Regarding the expenditures for fixed plant (machinery and buildings) the maximum percentage has been specified by the law:

—10 percent for machinery and buildings produced in the Centro-Nord of Italy.

—20 percent for machinery and buildings produced in southern Italy.

—in each case, foreign machinery is excluded from the grant, as the exemption from customs duties applies here.

Building Improvement

The proportion of the expenditures for "building improvement" that can be covered by a grant is determined on the basis of the average of the number of points assigned to the three following factors:

—the industrial sector and the size of the enterprise.

—per capita investment.

—location.

Factor No. 1 (industrial sector and size of the enterprise). A certain number of points is assigned to the enterprise requesting the grant according to its industrial sector. Priority (i.e., the largest number of points) is given, for example, to the machinery industry, and the smallest number of points is attributed to sectors which are already overabundant in the south, as for instance, *some* sectors of the food industry. A similar criterion is applied regarding the size of the establishment, with priority going to the larger enterprises and less weight to the smaller ones.

Factor No. 2 (per capita investment). The amount of investment per employee; i.e., the relation between the investment expenditures which may result from a grant and the number of new stable "workyears" (a workyear corresponds to 300 annual workdays), constitutes the basis of the calculation of the second factor. A point system proportional to the fixed per capita investment is applied.

Factor No. 3 (location). The location in the industrial development areas is the criterion for the assignment of points in this regard; there are more points for the provinces with less industrial concentration or with a lower ratio of industrial employees to the total inhabitants of the area.

(4) Miscellaneous incentives

The laws providing for the fiscal incentives, particularly Legislative Decree No. 1598 of December 15, 1947, and Law No. 634 of July 29, 1957, have also established a system of miscellaneous incentives.

Reduction of Railroad Tariffs

Differential tariffs for transport and services can encourage the establishment of particular industries in certain localities. The state railroad (according to article 7 of Law No. 1598) grants a reduction in railroad rates and maritime freight rates for the slow transport of industrial material (up to 50 percent) and of semifinished and finished products (up to 20 percent).

Real Estate and Buildings for Industrial Use

The administrations of the communities are authorized (article 33 of Law No. 634) to give away real estate and buildings for industrial undertakings; they may give them away or lease them for a long or short period on easy terms of payment.

Orders and Works of the Government

The central and regional administrations of the state (article 29 of Law No. 634) have to set aside, simultaneously, one-fifth of all the orders and public works carried out under each of their budgeted programs, for competitive bids by enterprises operating in the south only.

Real Property Condemnation

The works necessary for the implementation of the incentive measures for industry are declared to be public utilities, and as such they can take advantage of the law of condemnation with respect to the real estate involved. (Article 4 of Law No. 1598; article 1 of Law No. 1472 of Dec. 29, 1958.) Because these works are designated as urgent and cannot be postponed, the real estate and buildings may be taken over immediately.

The industrial development areas and the nuclei of industrialization.

The most unusual and most important aspect of the industrialization policy for the Mezzogiorno is certainly the effort to establish the new industrial enterprises in the more favorable locations, so that the areas of concentration of these enterprises become real "poles of economic development." This policy goes hand in hand with the effort to bring some new industrial enterprises also to the less favored regions which are less ready for rapid development.

In other words, the industrialization policy follows two seemingly contradictory directives: It is based partly on a concept of *locational diffusion,* with the purpose of spreading out the small- and medium-sized industrial enterprises among the communities; and it is based partly on the concept of *regional concentration,* with the aim of creating a few large "areas of development." Nevertheless, the two concepts can be integrated, with the result that the economic operators have the greatest possible choice of locations, and that no part of the south is excluded from the industrial development. But it is also true that the basic orientation of the politicians interested in and responsible for the problems of the Mezzogiorno is toward "regional concentration."

In the south of Italy, there are already some concentrations of industrial activities, which by now have a limited but effective potential for autonomous development, though still within the framework of the development aids, without which their rate of growth would certainly slow down, if not stagnate. These areas are the following:

(1) The region around Rome which falls within the sphere of authority of the Cassa per il Mezzogiorno. It constitutes a triangle with its vertices at Rome, Latina (with its province), and Frosinone (with its industrial enterprises along the *autostrada del sole;* i.e., the branch from Rome to Naples).

(2) The provinces of Caserta, Naples, and Salerno with a multitude of large- and medium-sized steel, machinery, chemical, and other plants.

(3) The territory of Puglia between Taranto (where a huge steel complex is rising), Ferrandino (which has two companies exploiting local deposits of natural gas), Brindisi (with a large petrochemical plant), and Bari (where important metal-mechanical complexes are rising).

(4) The territory of southeast Sicily; i.e., the coastal area from Catania to Siracusa.

There are other concentrations of minor importance, though they seem durable. Those indicated above are the only ones whose economic conditions are such as to be described legitimately as "poles of development."

The areas and the nuclei of industrialization are much more numerous. Some overlap with the above areas; others are outside these poles and constitute at best a hope.

(1) The industrial development areas

There are a number of communities with the requisite conditions, where new industrial enterprises are concentrated in one or more zones endowed with all the necessary infrastructure. The infrastructure may be *particular* to the zone, or *general;* i.e., extending over a large area and used by all the enterprises in the region.

For the creation of these areas and for the administration of the "infrastructurally endowed zones," special consortiums have been set up by the local administrative agencies (communities, provinces, chambers of commerce, etc.), in which private interests, too, may participate on condition that they represent special "associations," which are usually economic development associations for the respective zone.

The institutional function of the "consortiums for the industrial development areas" is (according to article 21 of Law No. 634) to develop and administer the infrastructural projects within the area, such as roads and railroads, water systems, gas and electricity works for industrial or private use, and sewers. The consortiums may, in addition, arrange for the condemnation of real estate and buildings not only for infrastructural purposes but also for resale to new industrial establishments. Finally, and this factor is important because of the responsibility for initiating activities it places in their hands, they may "carry out any other activity deemed useful for the development of the area."

The Cassa per il Mezzogiorno assists the consortiums with various kinds of grants and loans, such as:

(1) Grants up to a maximum of 85 percent of the expenditure for infrastructural projects.
(2) Grants up to a maximum of 50 percent of the expenditures for the construction of industrial establishments in rural areas.
(3) Grants up to a maximum of 40 percent of the expenditures for the building of dams for industrial use.
(4) Reimbursement of the expenditures incurred in the establishment of the regulatory program for the area.
(5) Contributions, to an extent not yet fixed, to the building of houses for workers in the industries of the areas and nuclei of industrialization.

Apart from the grants, the Cassa may also finance the construction and improvements of harbors and airports which are held to be a necessary part of the infrastructure of the areas and nuclei, and it may, in lieu of the consortiums, take the necessary measures for the condemnation of land destined for industrial establishments.

Through coordination and approval, by the interested governmental bodies, of the regulatory plans which are conditions for the making of loans and grants, an integrated approach to industrial location is provided for. However, despite the large expenditures by the Cassa, the consortiums for the areas and nuclei of industrialization are greatly hampered by the inability or unwillingness of local agencies to make their contribution to the financing of infrastructural projects. Thus far local financing has been minimal.[54]

To be recognized as such, an industrial development area and its consortium must meet the requirements which the ministerial committee, in a circular letter of July 30, 1959, has formulated as follows:

Preliminary requirements: The existence of a minimum of private investment plans ready to be implemented (the workers to be employed in the already existing or definitely planned installations must constitute at least 5 percent of the total of industrial employees as counted in the census of 1951).

Minimum requirements:

(*a*) Number of communities: The communities adjacent to the central community must be part of the consortium.

(*b*) Population: The population of the areas surrounding the central community must be at least 100,000; the total area must have at least 200,000 inhabitants; the central community must have a population amounting to at least one-third of that of the entire area.

(*c*) Nature of the territory: Areas that include plains predominantly are preferred.

(*d*) Safety of the territory.

(*e*) Susceptibility of the area to structural economic changes.

(*f*) Existence of the basic infrastructure, at least in the central community (i.e., means of communication in the form of roads, railroads, and maritime transportation).

(*g*) Nonexistence of particular factors suggesting that the area not be industrialized (areas with panoramic view, archeological zones, etc.).

Secondary requirements:

(*a*) Existence of sufficient supplies of energy and water.

(*b*) Existence of a minimum of industrialization, at least in the central community.

(*c*) Complementarity between the economy of the central community and the economies of the other communities within the area.

(*d*) Existence of other indispensable factors for development, such as the right attitudes regarding industrialization and potential natural resources.

Subordinate requirements: There must be indications of the existence of the following phenomena:

(*a*) Unemployment and underemployment.

(*b*) Industrial employees.

(*c*) Historical development of industrial activities.

(*d*) Educational facilities.

(*e*) Banking facilities.

(*f*) Marketing facilities.

(*g*) Roads.

(*h*) Urban services, telephones, and postal service.

(*i*) Railroad and maritime transportation as well as railroad stations and harbors.

[54] Manna Domenico, "Aspetti territoriali della localizzazione industriale," *Svimez-Formez,* 1963, p. 27.

(*j*) Other kinds of transportation.
(*k*) Electricity distribution systems.
(*l*) Aqueducts and sewers.

The making of the regulatory plan for the industrial development areas is very important, as the regulatory plans are not limited to indication of the zones for industrial establishments and directives for the infrastructural projects, but are derived from appropriate hypotheses about the economic and social development of the respective area. Thus, they are a first step toward the establishment of a regional economic development plan. For this reason, Pastore, president of the ministerial committee for the Mezzogiorno, declared in his latest report to Parliament:

> The regulatory plans of the areas and nuclei must definitely be operative in nature and must attempt the rational utilization of the resources in the area, based on the objectives and provisions of an economic development founded on industrialization. The lack of a national program today can, in some cases, prevent the establishment of the appropriate objectives at the local level, which makes the coordination of the development plans of each area at the regional and interregional level rather difficult. Nevertheless, this fact cannot hold up the passing from the preliminary and planning stages to the operating phase. One should therefore move gradually, while studying progressively the adjustments that have to be made in view of the general hypotheses and objectives.
>
> Hence, it will be necessary to assure (through particular encouragement and assistance) that by 1964 all the consortiums have worked out their basic regulatory plan. It will then be possible to know all the different plans for the entire Mezzogiorno and to coordinate them on the regional level. One can then set up a policy program for the entire South, not as the sum of the different local regulatory plans, but as a synthesis of the various requirements. One must move in two directions: on the one hand, from lower to higher levels of organization thereby progressively achieving a better and better synthesis of the various local needs at the regional level; on the other hand, from the higher to the lower levels of organization when defining the general objectives of local development. Given the provisions of the national development plan and of the regulatory plans, the necessary combinations and integrations can be attained.[55]

(2) The nuclei of industrialization

Though in many parts of the south the preconditions for the establishment of a development area do not exist, certain small industrial concentrations can be found which show pronounced tendencies toward further industrialization. In other words, one can speak of two different kinds of industrial concentrations:

> The "large one," created by many and important industrial enterprises which established themselves in several industrial nuclei within a development area and required large territory and much labor; and the "small one," created through the agglomeration of a limited number of industrial enterprises (small and medium-sized) which used limited markets, local primary materials, and certain natural and infrastructural characteristics which were lacking in the neighboring areas. With the establishment of these nuclei of industrialization, it is intended to further the process of small concentrations. The existence of the necessary infrastructure and the advantages of the greater stability of the area reduce the collective and individual costs of establishment by a large amount and encourage entrepreneurs to locate their enterprises in these zones, while leaving them their free choice of location.[56]

Though originally two different organizations were created for two qualitatively different phenomena, with the progressive increase in the number of recognized areas and nuclei the importance of the qualitative distinction decreased, and it became increasingly apparent that the two were the same

---

[55] Comitato dei Ministri per il Mezzogiorno, *Relazione sull'Attività di Coordinamento,* Rome, 1963, vol. I, p. 25.

[56] Comitato dei Ministri per il Mezzogiorno, Requisiti minimi per la istituzione dei nuclei di industrializzazione," Circolare No. 5621, June 8, 1960.

phenomenon with quantitatively different dimensions. Originally, the areas were to favor the concentration of industrial enterprises of great complexity producing capital goods or products of the large export industries, the demand for which came from outside the southern market. On the other hand, the nuclei were to assist the development of smaller activities of a local nature, more directly connected with the existing economic structure of the respective zones, and intended to create greater balance between the various productive sectors. However, when confronted with requests for the creation of an area for which the minimum prerequisites were lacking, the authorities decided not to reject them completely, but rather to create nuclei which were to be areas of smaller dimension.

The provisions of article 21 of Law No. 634, of article 8 of Law No. 555, and of Law No. 1462 of 1962, apply to the nuclei of industrialization. The ministerial committee has established minimum conditions and requirements for the recognition of an industrial nucleus: In these localities, there must be a clear tendency toward industrial concentration; there must be industrial establishments to which new activities can be easily added; and there must be definite investment plans for new enterprises in the area. In addition, the community and the other interested groups must make every effort to provide the infrastructure necessary for the nucleus. Once a nucleus of industrialization has been planned and recognized as such by the ministerial committee, the promoting groups form a consortium, following the same procedures as those for the consortiums of the areas.

The areas and the nuclei which have already been recognized as having the minimum prerequisites are, by territorial regions, as follows:

Marche:
- Nucleus of Ascoli Piceno

Lazio:
- Area of Roma-Latina
- Nucleus of Frosinone

Abruzzi:
- Area of the Valle del Pescara
- Nucleus of Avezzano
- Nucleus of Vasto
- Nucleus of Teramo

Campania:
- Area of Salerno
- Area of Naples
- Area of Caserta
- Nucleus of Avellino

Calabria:
- Nucleus of the Piana di Sibari
- Nucleus of the Golfo di Policastro
- Nucleus of Crotone
- Nucleus of S. Eufemia Lamezia
- Nucleus of Reggio Calabria

Sicily:
- Area of Catania
- Area of Siracusa
- Area of Palermo
- Nucleus of Messina
- Nucleus of Gela
- Nucleus of Trapani
- Nucleus of Ragusa
- Nucleus of Caltagirone

Puglia:
- Area of Bari
- Area of Taranto
- Area of Brindisi
- Nucleus of Foggia

Basilicata:
- Nucleus of Potenza
- Nucleus of Ferrandina

Sardinia:
- Area of Cagliari
- Nucleus of Sassari
- Nucleus of Tortoli-Arbatax
- Nucleus of Sulcis Iglesiente
- Nucleus of Oristano

As can be seen in table X, the areas and the nuclei together encompass 23.6 percent of the area of the Mezzogiorno and 47.1 percent of its population. They include 62.2 percent of its industrial labor force, 56.2 percent of those working in its commerce sector, and 66.3 percent of those working in other nonagricultural sectors. In 1961 these areas obtained 76.3 percent of the loans of the medium-term credit institutes in the south. These figures all confirm the concentration of industrial establishments in the chosen regions, and a greater concentration in the industrial development areas.

The industrial investments of the state holdings

In an earlier section general reference has been made to the role the state holdings play in the development of the Mezzogiorno. The ownership of these enterprises was transferred to the state during the Great Depression after 1932. At that time, the most important Italian banks were in trouble because the major part of their investments consisted of shares in mechanical and metallurgical enterprises which were on the verge of bankruptcy. In order to save these banks and the enterprises, the state took over the banks and therewith the shares in the enterprises.

Once the enterprises had been made financially sound again, the shares remained with the state and were regrouped in the Institute for Industrial Reconstruction (*Istituto per la Ricostruzione Industriale,* the IRI), which became an instrument of the industrial development policy of the country. To the IRI was added, later on, the *Ente Nazionale Idrocarburi* (ENI), which administers the enterprises operating in the sector of natural gas, petroleum, and their derivatory products. In addition, there are certain enterprises with mixed participation (especially the mechanical enterprises in Breda) and some services administered by other small *Enti di Gestione.*

Altogether, these mixed enterprises invested about $75 million in the Mezzogiorno in 1957; $110 million in 1958; $120 million in 1959; $170 million in 1960; $240 million in 1961; and $400 million in 1962. For the 4-year period 1963–66 further investments in the amount of approximately $1.5 billion are scheduled. (For details see table XI.) To the last figure must be added the investments to be made by the IRI for the autostrade and those of the ENEL (*Ente Nazionale Elettricità*), which was established only recently, after the nationalization of the electrical industry. These amounts are not known at present.

The investments planned for 1963–66 constitute 44 percent of total national investments, so it can be presumed that during the period Law No. 634 applies (1951–65) the minimum requirement of 40 percent of the investments of the state holdings to be made in the south will be reached or surpassed.

As an aid in interpreting these data, it should be noted that in 1957 the investments of the state holdings made up 26 percent of all industrial investments; 74 percent were wholly private investments. In 1961 the share in total investments of the public enterprises had risen to 41 percent.

RESULTS OF THE INDUSTRIALIZATION POLICY—CRITICAL EVALUATION OF THE METHODS USED

At the present stage of development, it is difficult to evaluate the results attained with the industrialization policies for the southern regions. In two different studies, three authors [57] have attempted to evaluate the economic

[57] G. Ackley and L. Dini, "Agevolazioni fiscali e creditizie per lo sviluppo industriale nell'Italia meridionale," *Moneta e Credito,* No. 49, March 1960, pp. 25–51; G. Coppola d' Anna, "Incentivi per lo sviluppo industriale del Mezzogiorno," *Moneta e Credito,* No. 52, December 1960, pp. 552–575.

TABLE X.—*The Areas and Nuclei of Industrialization*

	Area		Population, 1961 census		Population per square kilometer	Number, 1961 (thousands)			Total loans to industry Dec. 31, 1961 [1]			
	Total (thousand square kilometers)	Percent	Total (thousands)	Percent		Industrial establishments	Commercial establishments	Others, excluding agriculture	Number	Percent	Total amount (millions of lire)	Percent
Areas	1, 243. 2	9. 7	6, 363. 1	32. 9	512	411. 1	261. 3	168. 0	2, 573	48. 4	270. 0	56. 7
Nuclei	1, 786. 5	13. 9	2, 752. 0	14. 2	154	143. 0	99. 5	57. 3	672	12. 6	94. 1	19. 7
Total	3, 029. 7	23. 6	9, 115. 1	47. 1	301	554. 1	360. 8	225. 3	3, 245	61. 0	364. 1	76. 4
Rest of Mezzogiorno	9, 823. 2	76. 4	10, 214. 2	52. 9	104	337. 2	281. 7	114. 4	2, 073	39. 0	113. 1	23. 6
Total Mezzogiorno [2]	12, 852. 9	100. 0	19, 329. 3	100. 0	150	891. 3	642. 5	339. 7	5, 318	100. 0	477. 2	100. 0

[1] Made at reduced rates of interest by ISVEIMER, IRFIS, CIS, and the industrial credit departments of the Banco di Napoli and the Banco di Sicilia.

[2] Only the provinces are included.

significance of the locational incentives. They arrive at basically analogous conclusions:

The most important hypotheses are that these measures leave the proportion of the financing of the (reduced) costs of the establishment of new industrial plants unchanged and that the annual amortization rates are constant. After having noted that the exemption from the *Ricchezza Mobile* (R.M.), inasmuch as it is a proportional profit tax, favors the enterprises which need incentives less, the authors calculate the minimum cost for an industrial establishment in the south under the assumptions (*a*) that construction costs without assistance are the same in the north and in the south (rate assistance equalizes the major burden of transport for the south), and (*b*) that the composition of the investments is the same in the north and in the south. They found costs to be less in the south by an amount varying from 3 percent (if the enterprises obtained only an exemption of registration expenses and a reduction of the general turnover tax) to 29.1 percent or 26.8 percent (depending on whether it used Italian or imported machinery) when all the exemptions and reductions applied. These are the major net savings (the *Richezza Mobile* exemption is included here) for the enterprise due to the various development aids. The conclusions are the following: (1) The saving of operating costs is much less than that of construction costs. (2) Due to the tax exemptions, the increase in profits is the greater, the higher these profits would be without development assistance. (3) As these development aids directly reduce capital costs, the increase in profits is the larger, the greater the capital intensity of the investment.

The policies that are expected to be most effective have been in force only a short time. The consortiums for the industrial development areas and the nuclei of industrialization have been functioning for only a short period, yet they already are confronted with financial difficulties, despite the increase in contributions by the Cassa per il Mezzogiorno recently provided for in Law No. 1462.

Though the credit facilities have been working for many years, there are still complaints that they are subject to too rigid banking criteria. Because of this, the ministerial committee for the Mezzogiorno is making every effort to enlarge the possibilities of assistance from financial corporations which combine credit facilities with participation in share capital and with technical assistance for small and medium-sized enterprises. The *Istituto per l'Assistenza allo Sviluppo del Mezzogiorno* (the Institute of Development Assistance for the Mezzogiorno, the IASM) has been established for this purpose. It acts as an information center for both Italian and foreign enterpreneurs and performs many other functions of industrial counseling, without charge. The IASM has had considerable obstacles and problems to face in its operation, to some extent because the requests received have proved to be much greater and more complex than had been expected in the beginning.

For evaluation of the past achievements of the industrialization policy, the available statistics are somewhat ambiguous. If one looks, for instance, at the data on gross investments (see table IX), the general impression is certainly rather favorable, especially in view of the fact that the rate of increase of investments in the south has been much higher than that in the Centro-Nord. The different starting points of the two regions, however, so

TABLE XI.—*Investments in the Mezzogiorno of Enterprises with State Participation, 1957–62, and Planned, 1963–66* [1]

[Billions of lire]

Industry	Year							Percentage composition						
	1957	1958	1959	1960	1961	1962	1963–66	1957	1958	1959	1960	1961	1962	1963–66
Steel, metallurgy and related	9.6	10.9	10.1	13.1	18.0	28.8	429.4	20.9	16.0	13.3	12.3	12.2	12.0	46.2
Cement	0.5	1.5	0.4	0.8	0.3	1.2	14.7	1.1	2.2	0.5	0.7	0.2	0.5	1.6
Machinery	2.1	0.6	1.6	3.3	9.9	17.3	74.4	4.6	0.9	2.1	3.1	6.7	7.2	8.0
Shipyards		1.7	2.2	6.8	1.4	3.0	5.0		2.5	2.9	6.4	0.9	1.3	0.5
Hydrocarbons	13.8	13.5	16.2	26.5	24.8	43.4	119.9	30.1	19.9	21.3	24.8	16.8	18.1	12.9
Petrochemical	......	......	......	4.1	8.3	42.0	76.5	......	......	......	3.8	5.6	17.5	8.2
Electrical and nuclear energy	17.5	25.5	25.9	32.0	60.4	76.4	......	38.1	37.6	34.1	29.9	40.8	31.8	......
Telephone	1.1	11.3	16.2	18.8	22.5	22.0	122.0	2.4	16.6	21.4	17.6	15.2	9.2	13.1
Heating	......	......	......	......	0.6	1.0	3.6	......	......	......	......	0.4	0.4	4.8
Various	1.3	2.9	3.3	1.5	1.8	4.8	84.1	2.8	4.3	4.4	1.4	1.2	2.0	9.1
Total	45.9	67.9	75.9	106.9	148.0	239.9	929.6	100.0	100.0	100.0	100.0	100.0	100.0	100.0
Total in millions of dollars	75	110	120	170	240	400	1,500	......	......	......	......	......	......	......
Steel, metal, and related	......	......	......	......	......	......	......							
Hydrocarbons	......	......	......	......	......	......	......							
Petrochemicals	......	......	......	......	......	......	......	91.5	90.1	90.1	88.4	90.6	88.6	80.4
Electrical and nuclear energy	......	......	......	......	......	......	......							
Telephone	......	......	......	......	......	......	......							

[1] Including the additional plan of the IRI, but excluding the electricity and highway programs.

Source: Ministry of State Holdings.

much higher in the Centro-Nord than in the south, considerably diminish the importance of this fact.

On the other hand, the rate of increase in net industrial production in the Centro-Nord was higher than that of the south. On a basis of 100 for the year 1951, the index of industrial production has risen to 241 in the south and to 255 in the Centro-Nord. But, as has been noted, the more important investments in the south have not yet been made or have been made only recently, and so their effects, which ought to be rather considerable, have not yet been felt.

The greatest stimuli to industrialization have come in the most recent years, some as recently as 1962. A few examples will suffice to confirm this statement, beginning with the statistics of the grants extended by the Cassa per il Mezzogiorno. These funds were made available almost immediately after the enterprises started. In the fiscal year 1961–62 (July 1 to June 30):

> 1,165 applications for grants were received, or 29% of the total number of applications received from the beginning until June 30, 1962. At this time, the total number of applications since the initiation of the policy was 4,004. As for their regional distribution, the greatest number of applications came from Puglia (25%), Campania (23%), and Abruzzi e Molise (14%). On the other hand, classified according to the amount of the grants involved, Campania holds first place with 27%, followed by Puglia with 17% and Lazio with 17%.
>
> Regarding the sectoral distribution of the number of applications, the (agricultural) food industry comes first with 52%, followed by the construction materials industry with 15%, the mechanical industry with 7%, and the wood industry with 6%.
>
> With respect to the amount of the investments, the (agricultural) food industry again occupies first place (30%), followed by the mechanical industry (16%), the construction materials industry (16%), and the chemical industry (9%).
>
> Of the 4,004 enterprises which applied for grants, 2,308 (58%), with a total investment of 302 billion lire (85%), had applied for loans which were granted in the amount of 210 billion lire.
>
> The remaining 1,696 applications (42%), with a total investment of 53 billion lire (15%), were for plants of relatively minor importance, mainly for the processing of agricultural products, with an average investment of about 31 million lire.
>
> In the financial year 1961–62, there has been an increase of 30% over the preceding year in the investigations, considerations, and approvals of grants, while, due to a shortening of the administrative processes, the number of grants actually paid out has doubled.
>
> Thus, the grants appropriated by the Ministerial Committee for the Mezzogiorno have increased from 962 to 1,902, and from 7.9 billion to 17.2 billion lire, of which 8.3 billion lire have been spent already.[58]

This shows that the rate of applications for new industrial enterprises or for the modernization of existing ones has been increasing. A further and better proof of the proposition can be found in the amount of loans granted by the medium-term credit institutions.

> In 1962 the Institutes authorized to extend industrial loans on special conditions with the assistance of the Cassa per il Mezzogiorno * * * granted credits in the amount of 481.3 billion lire, which presumably contributed to investments of another 900 billion lire.
>
> The special Institutes (ISVEIMER, IRFIS, CIS) granted loans in the amount of 215.8 billion lire, which constitutes 44.8% of the total investments for which these applications were made.
>
> There has also been a remarkable increase in the amount of industrial loans granted by the *Istituti Speciali Meridionali* and by the National Institutes. Thus, it may be said that, after an initial period of uncertainty, since 1961 the industrialization of the Mezzogiorno has finally reached an adequate rate of development.

---

[58] Comitato dei Ministri per il Mezzogiorno, *Relazione sull'Attività di Coordinamento,* vol. II, pp. 57 ff.

From July, 1957, to June 30, 1962, the total loans approved by the Cassa in accordance with Article 24 of Law No. 634 of July 29, 1957, amounted to 215.6 billion lire. Of these, 156.1 billion were given through the special Institutes and 59.5 billion through the national Institutes.[59]

The difference between the last figure (the amount approved by the Cassa) and the figures cited before shows that there has been an increase in the length of time required for the administrative processing of loans. It is especially interesting to note that the expenditures of ISVEIMER [60] increased rapidly in the 4-year period 1959–62:

1959—21.3 billion lire ($34 million).
1960—44.9 billion lire ($72 million).
1961—91.8 billion lire ($150 million).
1962—130.0 billion lire ($210 million).

In 1962, these expenditures were distributed as follows:

32.2% for industrial enterprises producing capital goods.
38.2% for industrial enterprises producing intermediate products.
29.6% for industrial enterprises producing consumption goods.

The industrial development of Sicily came to a kind of standstill in 1962, mainly because of the delicate political situation of the island. This is shown by the annual expenditures of the IRFIS:

1959—2.0 billion lire ($3.2 million).
1960—24.4 billion lire ($40 million).
1961—30.4 billion lire ($48 million).
1962—25.9 billion lire ($42 million).

In contrast, a remarkable expansion has taken place in Sardinia, probably partly as a result of the *Piano di Rinascita* (Plan for Restoration) for the island, which was approved a short time ago. The expenditures of the CIS were as follows:

1959—2.9 billion lire ($4.8 million).
1960—5.5 billion lire ($8.8 million).
1961—26.0 billion lire ($42 million).
1962—59.9 billion lire ($97 million).

Finally, the other medium-term credit institutes which operate within the entire nation, and which have been able to participate in the financing of industrial enterprises in the Mezzogiorno only since 1960, granted loans as shown on following page.

From the following table the conclusion may be drawn that first in 1961, and then again in 1962, the rate of industrial development in the Mezzogiorno made a significant jump forward. In 1963 there has been some slowing down of business activities in general, partly due to disturbing political events; however, the investments that have already been started should weaken the effects of the "slowing down" on the Mezzogiorno.

Within the last fifteen years, the increase of industrial employment in the Mezzogiorno has been rather modest, only 200,000, which is equivalent to an annual rate of increase of 2.7%. The rate of increase of gross investments for the same period

[59] *Ibid.*, pp. 62 ff.

[60] One should recall that the ISVEIMER operates only in the continental Mezzogiorno, the IRFIS only in Sicily, and the CIS in Sardinia.

	1960–62		1962	
	Billion lire	Million dollars	Billion lire	Million dollars
Banco di Sicilia (department of industrial credits)	38. 3	62	9. 7	16
Banco di Napoli (department of industrial credits)	60. 9	98	5. 2	8
Banco Nazionale del Lavoro (department of industrial credits)	34. 9	56	10. 4	16
Medio Credito del Lazio (only for the provinces of Lazio which lie within the zone of the Cassa)	4. 9	8	4. 9	8
Efibanca	28. 3	46	9. 1	15
Centrobanca	. 4	0. 7	. 2	0. 3
Mediobanca	31. 9	51	1. 4	2
Istituto Mobiliare Italiana (IMI)	520. 9	840	224. 5	360

has been 18% per annum. The high rate of increase is due to the weight of the investments in the highly capital-intensive sectors (steel, electricity, and petrochemistry) within total industrial investments. Incidentally, the number of new jobs is actually higher than the above figure indicates, due to the increase in full-time jobs, as the processes of transformation and modernization within the pre-existing industrial structure have brought about changes in the jobs of some industrial activities, in particular, in the small local establishments with less than six employees.

Within the next five years about the same increase in the rate of investment must be maintained. However, in order adequately to absorb the labor force, more weight must be given to investments in sectors and for the sizes of plants that have a lower capital-labor ratio. This must be done for the additional reason that the investments for the large plants in the basic sectors of steel and petrochemistry will progressively be reduced.

The increase in total gross industrial output should be at an annual rate of about 12%, which is considerably greater than the 8.9% for the last five-year period.

In order to attain these objectives, an organic industrial policy is needed which can command and use certain basic instruments, i.e., instruments of incentives and disincentives, including control of the financial market, government participation in and financing of development, and the establishment of the infrastructure in the areas of industrialization.[61]

In concluding, it must be said that the instruments of the industrialization policy are operative and tested. They amount to enough quantitatively; perhaps it will be necessary to improve them qualitatively. Above all, their administration must proceed more rapidly or, better, less bureaucratically (the "technical" time it takes for the granting of a loan at favorable terms often amounts to 12 months, which is too much). It is further necessary to reduce the formalities involved in the establishment of a new enterprise, which often discourage entrepreneurs from the Centro-Nord or from foreign countries.

Finally, it is necessary to study carefully the methods that should be applied in order to utilize the instruments efficiently within the policy of planning which is likely to be introduced in the near future. If this policy of economic

[61] Comitato dei Ministri per il Mezzogiorno, *Relazione sull'Attività di Coordinamento,* vol. I, pp. 21–22.

programing is initiated, it should function parallel to the extension of the activities of the Cassa per il Mezzogiorno (which, as has been stated above, is scheduled to be terminated in 1965). This will be a good chance to proceed as the Cassa has done: analyze first, and then implement.

PROVISIONS FOR IMPROVEMENT OF THE HUMAN FACTOR

Before analyzing the policies for the "human factor," it seems appropriate to describe the present relationship between the schools and the economic community. In Italy there is a chasm between the world of education and the world which must use the products of the schools, a kind of incapability of having a dialogue, which prevents one party from knowing what the schools offer and the other from knowing what the world of labor needs.

The complex structure of the labor force demonstrates the great divergence between the actual needs and the kinds and levels of education existing in Italy. For instance, Italian skilled workers (4 million workers of a total labor force of 20 million) are predominantly people who have been educated only in elementary schools, where they learned to read and write, and to a very small extent in the vocational institutes (which have been in existence for only a short time). Thus, it is clear that these workers have been trained more in the factory than by the schools.

Since the establishment of the Cassa, it has been evident that the development of the Mezzogiorno could not be attained without a series of measures concerning the human factor. Without them the rate of economic development would be slowed down by the fact that the southern population would be largely unable to participate in the development policy.

As the law establishing the Cassa did not contain any provisions regarding vocational training and educational institutions, it was provided by the authority of the ministerial committee that the interest earnings of the Cassa on the deposits of the funds at its disposition might be used for these purposes. In April 1954, for the first time, the Cassa took action concerning agricultural training concurrent with other measures then directed predominantly toward agriculture. The first legislation regarding vocational training of handicraft workers in the south was contained in Law No. 634 of July 29, 1957, which was modified by Law No. 555 of July 18, 1959. Under these laws, the Cassa could finance programs and institutes for the training of technicians and skilled workers, specifically designed to meet the particular needs of the developing regions. In addition, the Cassa could give assistance to existing institutions that provided vocational training for these needs.

In order to increase the facilities, the legislators by Provision No. 1349 of December 28, 1957, authorized the Ministry of Finance to set apart (on the basis of the U.S. loan of agricultural surpluses) about $14 million for a fund for the improvement of vocational education in the Mezzogiorno. This provision was made part of Law No. 622 of July 24, 1959, when another $8 million was appropriated for this purpose. And in line with this policy, the Minister for Public Education became a permanent member of the ministerial committee for the Mezzogiorno, according to Law No. 1492 of September 29, 1962.

Within the framework of these laws, the Cassa has financed the construction of elementary schools and of state agricultural training institutes, and to aid the industrialization process, it has established a program of assistance to the education and vocational training of skilled craftmen. Apart from the industrial and handicraft training institutes, assistance has been given to the vocational institutions that offer beginning courses to young people who wish to enter skilled occupations within industry. The Cassa may also help to improve the facilities of the private centers of education which offer introductory courses in the trades.

For the young men and women who wish to qualify for higher positions in southern industry, *Centri Interaziendali,* or centers for vocational training in industry, have been established. The specific function of these centers is to teach the particular work processes of the industrial enterprises to be established in the south. With this end in view, the *Centri Interaziendali* were organized cooperatively by private business enterprises and the schools.

The Cassa also has greatly stimulated professional instruction at the medium and higher levels. Along these lines, the Cassa established the *Centro Residenziale di Formazione e Studi* (the Residential Training and Study Center) at Naples. In view of the need to encourage and maintain managerial and technical talents for industry, this center attempts to aid in the creation of a leading industrial class.

However, it became clear that efforts to upgrade the labor force, and to augment the managerial force, would provide only a partial solution to the problem presented by the low level of sociocultural habits and attitudes of the population of the Italian south. Therefore, an experimental program has been established in an attempt to correct the social and educational deficiencies.

Youth social centers have been founded where exhibitions, debates, information, consultation, travels, and other club activities are organized. Residential centers for the training of prospective teachers for adult education have also been established. In addition, the program provides for educational measures concerning health and hygiene, necessary for those communities in which the people are reluctant to abandon traditional habits. Finally, measures have been taken to improve the administrative apparatus of the numerous public assistance agencies, particularly by means of studies and consultation. Funds in the amount of about $78 million have been expended altogether for these measures. (For details see table XII.)

Recently, the Cassa per il Mezzogiorno considered the problem of migration and established a center of introduction for immigrants at Torino, which is to assist in the vocational education of people from the south who have chosen Torino as their new residence. The Cassa also created a center of assistance to immigrants at Torino, which provides many different types of aid, including the reception of the immigrants at the railroad station, the housing of single youngsters and men, the procuring of work through cooperation with local industry, and family assistance, from which 15,000 families have benefited.

The Ministry of Labor, for its part, has contacted the ministerial committee for the Mezzogiorno regarding the establishment of "Information Centers for Migratory Labor" in places from which there are a large number of emigrants. These centers should function both to control the local labor market and to direct the workers to the appropriate zones and sectors, in order to prevent—as much as possible—indiscriminate migratory movements by uninformed workers.

In particular, the information centers must cooperate with the labor exchanges at the destinations of the migrants, since the latter know about the job openings, the wages and conditions offered, the availability of housing, boarding facilities, etc. The integration and improvement of public policy

TABLE XII.—*Distribution of Funds for Training and Social Programs*

[Millions of lire]

	Post-1959 funds	Law No. 1349,[1] Dec. 28, 1957	Law No. 634, July 29, 1957	Law No. 622, July 24, 1959	Law No. 1177, Nov. 26, 1955	Total
Prevocational instruction	....	....	....	....	1, 200	1, 200
Programs of instruction and vocational preparation:						
Vocational Institute for Agriculture	3, 071	4, 000	....	2, 000	1, 350	[2] 10, 421
Vocational Institutes for Industry and Commerce	1, 520	4, 000	....	1, 650	2, 350	[2] 9, 520
Training centers in the sectors:						
Of public works and services	....	....	1, 000	....	1, 500	2, 500
Of industry and artisan trades	....	....	1, 950	1, 000	500	3, 450
Of agriculture	....	....	500	100	500	1, 100
Interindustrial centers (*Centri Interaziendali*)	....	....	7, 000	....	700	7, 700
Maritime schools and training centers	....	....	....	....	400	400
Preparatory activities for emigrants	....	....	....	....	1, 500	1, 500
Training activities:						
Of intermediate and supervisory personnel	....	....	3, 000	....	300	3, 300
Of teaching personnel for vocational institutes	200	500	....	....	....	[2] 700
Of instructional personnel for training centers	....	....	500	250	....	750
Technical, social and upgrading programs:						
Programs of social education	....	....	2, 000	....	1, 200	3, 200
Assistance to agricultural sector	....	....	1, 000	....	1, 800	2, 800
Studies in the sectors	....	....	50	....	....	50
Total	4, 791	8, 500	17, 000	5, 000	13, 300	48, 591
Total in millions of dollars	8	14	27	8	21	78

[1] Loan of U.S. "agricultural surplus."

[2] In the appropriations for the *Istituti Professionali Agrari e Industriali* under Law No. 1177 are included 30 and 80 millions for the preparation of teachers. This 110 million should be added to the total of 700 million appropriations for these purposes.

measures for the establishment of equilibrium in the labor market and for the orderly movement of labor, and the assistance provided therefor, will certainly be fundamental problems for the next legislature.

Special Legislation for the Naples Area and for Sicily and Sardinia

Another series of legislative measures has been provided for the areas within the realm of authority of the Cassa per il Mezzogiorno. All these special provisions are of an "adjunctive" nature, so far as the intervention of the Cassa is concerned.

THE SPECIAL LAW FOR CALABRIA

The particular hydrogeological problems of Calabria, which suffered from devastating rainstorms in 1935, 1951, and 1953, led to the special law for this area. Law No. 1177 of November 26, 1955, authorizes the administration to carry out an organic 12-year plan (from July 1, 1955, to June 30, 1967), of special projects for the improvement of watersheds and afforestation, control of rivers and mountain water sources, stabilization of the slopes and land improvement in mountains and valleys, as well as relocation of the population. One of the most striking characteristics of the law is that it considers the entire region of Calabria subject to land improvement, that is, there is to be an integrated land program for the areas lying below an altitude of 300 meters and a special improvement program for the mountain areas above this altitude.

The Cassa per il Mezzogiorno is charged with implementation of the law, through a basic regulatory plan for all projects, subject to the approval of the ministerial committee for the Mezzogiorno. During the development of the plan and its application, the law has been interpreted broadly enough to include measures for real economic development.

The law provided 204 billion lire (about $320 million); however, the program for the distribution of the funds actually appropriates 209.8 billion lire, as it includes also the interest earned on the deposits of the funds. The distribution of the funds is as follows:

	Billion lire
Research and studies	3, 200
Technical assistance and vocational education	1, 600
Instruction and vocational training	12, 600
Soil conservation:	
In the mountains	68, 000
Improvement of the waterways in the valleys	18, 400
Increasing salability of agricultural products	25, 800
Improvement of the remaining infrastructure:	
Roads	15, 600
Civic works	3, 600
Consolidation and relocation of the communities	20, 500
Subsidies for private soil improvements	40, 500

To date 117 billion lire have actually been spent on these works. Recently another 50 billion were appropriated which have not yet been allocated.

THE AREA UNDER SPECIAL STATUTE: SICILY

The broad legislative powers given to the area of Sicily by article 4 of the regional statute, with particular reference to agriculture, industry, and tourism, have been exercised in a series of policy measures designed to improve the socioeconomic conditions of the region.

Among the major provisions is the establishment of the Financial Corporation for Industrial Investments in Sicily (*Società Finanziaria di Investimenti Industriali in Sicilia*), or the SOFIS. The SOFIS can participate—usually up to 25 percent of the capital—and give other financial assistance to corporations planning the establishment, expansion, or modernization of industrial plants in Sicily; the exploitation of mineral deposits, oil, and natural gas, as well as the processing of their derivatory products; the construction and administration of dockyards in the harbors of Sicily; and the establishment of chemical plants which use melted and mineral sulfur, as well as sulfur products from the Sicilian mines, and of enterprises utilizing the sulfur.

In addition, other fiscal and financial incentives to industrialization have been provided in various regional laws. The IRFIS, which, with the assistance of the Cassa per il Mezzogiorno, grants loans at reduced interest rates, has also engaged in activities in aid of the Sicilian regions.

With regional Law No. 51 of 1957, a revolving fund was established apart from IRFIS, earmarked for loans for the exploitation of primary materials and the production of finished products that are necessary to their particular cycle of operations and nature of production.

Other measures of considerable importance are those for the establishment of industrial zones in Sicily. For each zone, a plan is to be made for the improvement of roads, hygiene, electricity, railroads, and the general services that are required for the completion of the infrastructure of the zone. Thus, these measures anticipate the areas and nuclei of industrialization.

THE AREA UNDER SPECIAL STATUTE: SARDINIA

The various measures for the social and economic development of Sardinia must be given particular attention. Many ordinary and special, State and regional measures have been instituted for the Sardinian area under special statute (which was established with Law No. 3 of February 26, 1948). To these must be added the special provisions of the "Plan for the Restoration of Sardinia," which was established by Law No. 588 of June 11, 1962.

Article 1 of Law 588 states that, in order to assist in the economic and social restoration of Sardinia, the ministerial committee for the Mezzogiorno, in cooperation with the autonomous region of Sardinia, is to draw up an organic special plan to be in addition to the measures already provided by the State. In order to achieve the results desired under the plan, the regional territory was divided into "homogeneous zones," homogeneous with respect to the predominant economic structure, the possibilities of development, and social conditions. In each zone a "committee for the zone" was established. Thus, a constructive type of cooperation has been created between the local development efforts, as expressed in these committees, and the regional administrative body. The committees analyze the particular situation of the zones, tell the regional planning agencies about their particular requirements, and subsequently carry out the several measures of the plan. The final goal is to attain specific improvements of the economic and social structure of the homogeneous zones, the largest possible amount of stable employment, and more rapid increases in income more equally distributed.

The measures provided by the Plan for the Restoration of Sardinia—measures which are over and above those of the ordinary administration and of the Cassa per il Mezzogiorno—concern the basic infrastructure, vocational training, the system of education, housing rehabilitation, and the three basic economic sectors. Regarding the infrastructure, particular efforts are to be made to improve the transport and communication system. These improvements will end the isolation of certain small local economies, and will attempt, above all, to prevent any interruptions in the transportation of products in and out of the harbors.

Under the provisions of the plan, the region of Sardinia can contribute to the financing of the infrastructural projects in the industrial development areas and the nuclei of industrialization, which already obtain grants up to 85 percent of their expenditures from the Cassa per il Mezzogiorno. Similarly, the sectoral policies permit incentives and assistance greater than those in the rest of the Mezzogiorno. Industrial enterprises can obtain grants up to 40 percent of their investment expenditures, compared to only 25 percent in the other areas within the sphere of authority of the Cassa.

In order adequately to coordinate the multitude of general and special measures, the ministries and the Cassa communicate to the ministerial committee and to the autonomous region of Sardinia the directives worked out to implement the policies and the projects to be carried out in the respective sectors within the region. In view of the relations between the state and the region, it has been ruled that each decision of the ministerial committee for the Mezzogiorno is to be adopted only with the consent of the autonomous region of Sardinia. For this purpose, the president of the regional commission attends the meetings of the ministerial committee.

PROVISIONS FOR THE CITY OF NAPLES

Law No. 297 of April 9, 1953, which is also of an "adjunctive" nature, provides for the planning of development activities for the city and the Province of Naples. These activities involve the reconstruction of facilities destroyed or damaged in the war, and the construction of modern houses for the families now living in miserable conditions in buildings which are to be cleared for the reconstruction of the harbor and market sections of the city. Two billion lire ($3.2 million) have been appropriated for the construction of buildings for the university, and 3 billion ($4.8 million) for the improvement of railroad installations and services.

These works are being carried out according to programs of the provincial administration and of the city of Naples, to which the Cassa per il Mezzogiorno has given its consent and which have been approved by the Ministry of Public Works. However, in practice the annual programs of special projects for Naples are subject to the approval of the ministerial committee for the Mezzogiorno.

Evaluation of the Programs of the Cassa and Future Prospects

The special policies for the Mezzogiorno have reached a turning point of great importance, coinciding with the aproaching expiration in 1965 of the law governing the operation of the Cassa per il Mezzogiorno. Decisions must be taken as quickly as possible in order to prevent an interruption of activities which must be continuous. Moreover, there is always the danger that the economic policy of future governments—which are above all interested in existing institutions, partly because of their political power—may be changed in favor of the northern economy.

At this point in the economic development of Italy and of the southern regions, there can be no doubt that it is necessary to continue and improve on the activities that have been carried on for 13 years. Today, as in 1950, the standards of living and the development potential of the regional economies in the Centro-Nord and in the south differ greatly. Although both qualitative and quantitative changes have occurred, and the trend of an ever increasing divergence has been stopped, real self-sustaining development in the Mezzogiorno is only just beginning. But its preconditions have been established, so that its realization within a short time can be predicted; perhaps the next 5 years will be decisive in this respect.

Therefore, the special policies must be continued; but, for the same reason, they cannot continue with the present methods. They must be adjusted to the new conditions which they themselves have helped to bring about, and to the evolution of the institutional framework within which economic policy is made. It is of the greatest importance, however, that the special policies maintain their organic unity and do not again become isolated measures, like those before 1950, which cannot really change the cultural, social, and economic conditions of the south.

The general principles Pastore stated in 1963 before Parliament in his report on the activities of coordination [62] constitute a first step in the critical revision of the concepts on which the special policy and the activities of the Cassa per il Mezzogiorno are based. Pastore has even indicated (as a first approximation) the finanical requirements of a program for the 5-year period 1964–68 which ought to be borne by the state and administered by the Cassa. These requirements amount to 1,400 billion lire ($2.3 billion), or 280 billion ($450 million) annually, on the average, which constitutes a rate of investment the Cassa has reached and surpassed only in the last 2 fiscal years.[63] The total amount would be distributed among the three basic sectors in the following way:

Industrial activities—510 billion lire ($840 million).
Agricultural activities—490 billion lire ($800 million).
Infrastructure—400 billion lire ($660 million).

On first glance, the expenditures planned for industrialization appear to be considerably increased; however, one must take account of the fact that part of these expenditures will be for the special type of infrastructure necessary for industrial development. Indeed, $240 million are for the infrastructure of the areas and the nuclei, $50 million for workers' housing, and $8 million—which is very little indeed—for the industries in rural areas. The remainder will be divided among grants, credit incentives, and participation in share capital.[64] These estimates are based on realistic analyses

[62] *Ibid.*, vol. I.

[63] See table XIII, which reproduces an estimate (made by the Cassa) of the investments carried out in each of the first 12 fiscal years of the Cassa, subdivided by economic sectors.

[64] Specifically, there are 140 billion lire for grants for the next 5 years, 170 billion for loans, and the remainder for participation in share capital on the part of the existing state holdings. The funds destined for agriculture are distributed as follows: 320 billion for irrigation, 70 billion for afforestation and the improvement of the mountain areas, 25 billion for the establishments attempting to use and commercialize agricultural products, and 75 billion for rural electrification. Finally, it is interesting to note that the program for the infrastructure provides for measures concerning tourism with funds in the amount of about 100 billion lire.

TABLE XIII.—*Investments Made by the Cassa per il Mezzogiorno in Each of the First Twelve Years*

(Billions of lire)

Sectors of intervention	Investments in fiscal year									
	1950–51	1951–52	1952–53	1953–54	1954–55	1955–56	1956–57	1957–58	1958–59	1959–60
For infrastructure:										
1. Land improvements and mountain control	2.3	15.8	39.7	47.2	39.6	33.8	33.4	36.6	40.0	36.9
2. Ordinary roads	.1	14.9	24.3	20.6	12.2	7.7	7.1	4.8	9.8	11.4
3. Aqueducts and sewers	.8	3.2	9.1	13.9	13.9	13.3	14.6	15.1	21.5	18.6
4. Touristic projects	....	.5	1.7	2.2	2.5	2.6	3.5	2.4	1.2	2.3
5. Railroads and bridges	....	....	....	2.6	11.9	14.9	12.2	2.6	15.5	12.3
Total (1–5)	3.2	34.4	74.8	86.5	80.1	72.3	70.8	61.5	88.0	81.5
6. Land reform	.7	6.5	19.3	38.7	60.8	47.0	33.9	20.0	26.8	14.0
Total (1–6)	3.9	40.9	94.1	125.2	140.9	119.3	104.7	81.5	114.8	95.5
For incentives to private enterprise:										
7. Agricultural improvement	.1	9.4	18.4	20.3	24.6	32.6	30.6	38.3	43.6	47.5
8. Industrial enterprise:										
(a) Through funds of Cassa and others	....	....	4.4	11.6	15.1	44.0	36.6	25.7	52.0	67.2
(b) Through capital and interest grants	....	....	....	....	....	....	....	....	.6	12.4
9. Grants for fishing and artisan trades	....	....	....	....	....	....	....	....	.9	6.7
Total (7–9)	.1	9.4	22.8	31.9	39.7	76.6	67.2	64.0	97.1	133.8

For other activities:										
10. Provisions for the city and province of Naples	....	....	....	....	1.1	1.3	1.1	6.9	4.6	5.2
11. Schools, vocational instruction, and grants to social institutions	....	....	....	....	....	.2	.8	2.1	4.9	5.2
Total (10–11)	....	....	....	....	1.1	1.5	1.9	9.0	9.5	10.4
General total	4.0	50.3	116.9	157.1	181.7	197.4	173.8	154.5	221.4	239.7

Sectors of intervention	Investments in fiscal year			Invest-ments chaged to the Cassa	Investments on authority of others			Disburse-ments made	Ratio of invest-ments to disburse-ments
	1960–61	1961–62	Total		Financed by others	Financed by Cassa	Total		
For infrastructure:									
1. Land improvements and mountain control	53.6	56.9	435.8	414.5	9.9	11.4	21.3	426.3	1.02
2. Ordinary roads	13.6	16.2	142.7	142.7	....	....	....	132.8	1.07
3. Aqueducts and sewers	21.1	30.5	175.6	165.0	8.8	1.8	10.6	168.1	1.04
4. Touristic projects	5.2	4.3	28.4	28.4	....	....	....	28.8	.99
5. Railroads and bridges	9.6	12.7	94.3	90.7	3.6	....	3.6	81.5	1.16
Total (1–5)	103.1	120.6	876.8	841.3	22.3	13.2	35.5	837.5	1.05
6. Land reform	....	....	267.7	267.7	....	....	....	278.9	.96
Total (1–6)	103.1	120.6	1,144.5	1,109.0	22.3	13.2	35.5	1,116.4	1.03

TABLE XIII.—*Investments Made by the Cassa per ill Mezzogiorno in Each of the First Twelve Years*—Continued

Sectors of intervention	Investments in fiscal year			Investments charged to the Cassa	Investments on authority of others			Disbursements made	Ratio of investments to disbursements
	1960–61	1961–62	Total		Financed by others	Financed by Cassa	Total		
For incentives to private enterprise:									
7. Agricultural improvement	49. 1	47. 7	362. 2	156. 8	185. 7	19. 7	205. 4	135. 5	2. 67
8. Industrial enterprise:									
(a) Through funds of Cassa and others	99. 4	144. 2	500. 2	....	320. 4	179. 8	500. 2	192. 8	2. 59
(b) Through capital and interest grants	20. 8	32. 3	66. 1	10. 1	56. 0	....	56. 0	9. 8	6. 74
9. Grants for fishing and artisan trades	10. 5	16. 7	34. 8	11. 4	23. 4	....	23. 4	11. 6	3. 00
Total (7–9)	179. 8	240. 9	963. 3	178. 3	585. 5	199. 5	785. 0	349. 7	2. 75
For other activities:									
10. Provisions for the city and province of Naples	2. 1	6. 6	28. 9	....	17. 3	11. 6	28. 9	27. 8	1. 04
11. Schools, vocational instruction, and grants to social institutions	7. 3	11. 4	31. 9	17. 8	13. 1	1. 0	14. 1	17. 6	1. 81
Total (10–11)	9. 4	18. 0	60. 8	17. 8	30. 4	12. 6	43. 0	45. 4	1. 34
General total	292. 3	379. 5	2, 168. 6	1, 305. 1	638. 2	225. 3	863. 5	1, 511. 5	1. 43

by the technical staff of the Cassa.[65] And, though they would represent substantial additional burdens, they merely propose to extend existing institutional devices for implementation. It may be that the time has come for real critical review of the bases of policy.

In the first place, a selection must be made of the "economic zones," whether predominantly agricultural or industrial, on which the Cassa per il Mezzogiorno will concentrate in the future. Up to now, the special policy has affected practically the entire territory. This constitutes a dispersion of energies which possibly might better have been concentrated on specific areas. This is not to say that there were no efforts to differentiate the activities geographically. The establishment of the industrial development areas demonstrates this, even if the kind of measures applied within these areas do not differ much from those applied outside the areas and the nuclei (for the purpose of industrialization).

With respect to agriculture, the report states that new problems are arising for the agricultural policy, which so far has been devoted predominantly to the establishment of the infrastructure for modern, commercial agricultural enterprises in the south. With this policy phase almost entirely completed, the structural problems which the enterprises have to face when attempting to fully utilize the public services created and to achieve a satisfactory level of profits become particularly obvious.

The economic development of the country and the emigration from the southern regions now allow much more freedom in an attack on these problems. There is need for land reform, for more modern contractual relations, for an improvement of the marketing facilities, and for rather large financial and productive capacities on the part of the farmers.[66]

Basically, the agricultural measures of the Cassa must be rethought not only in view of the territorial characteristics of the Mezzogiorno, but mainly in view of the general crisis of the entire agricultural sector. One can say that Italy does not yet have a real agricultural policy; the Green Plan represents only a timid and incomplete beginning of a solution to the problems.

The Cassa per il Mezzogiorno alone cannot make an agricultural policy, even though it has laid solid bases for an understanding of the difficulties involved and for measures to overcome them. The Cassa cannot become a instrument of this policy unless and until the establishment of "Development Agencies" [67] alters the institutional framework for agriculture. In the meantime, the irrigation operations already started must be completed more rapidly. To do this, the Cassa must modify its rules for the implementation of the programs carried out by private entrepreneurs. The latter seem to be very reluctant to take advantage of the public services which would enable them to make substantial changes in the economic organization of their enterprises.

The fact remains that the Cassa has done exceptional work for southern agriculture, the results of which are already evident and will be much more

---

[65] Comitato dei Ministri per il Mezzogiorno, *Relazione sull'Attività di Coordinamento,* vol. I, p. 44, notes.

[66] *Ibid.,* p. 27.

[67] The assignment of new agricultural development activities to the agencies that have administered the land reform and given technical assistance to the new small farmers has been studied for a long time. In the event of this alteration of the activities of the reform agencies, new agencies with regional or interregional authority would be created in those zones in which no reform agencies exist at present, in order to establish a new agricultural policy on the basis of the so-called "agencies for agricultural development."

so within a few years. The future of these policies, as well as of those in the other sectors, depends on the evolution of the institutional framework and of the legislation that will replace the present laws as they become more and more outdated.

The measures concerning the infrastructure are also a great achievement of the Cassa, considering the enormous needs in the Mezzogiorno at the beginning of the 1950's. The construction of water systems is particularly important. These efforts *must* be continued in order to complete the projects already started, to organize the administration and maintenance of existing water systems, and to establish new ones for the new demands created by industrial development. Scarcity of industrial water is a major bottleneck in some areas, while in others industrial uses may make economical provision of water for general purposes.[68]

Thus, we have arrived at the area with the most hopeful prospects—industrial development. The policy of industrialization for the Mezzogiorno started very late, but once started, it had a dynamic impetus, elastic instruments, and an organic coherence which can be found in few other sectors of Italian political life. This is partly because these measures are better understood than are other aspects of development policies.

The areas and nuclei of industrialization not only represent a more up-to-date location policy than that of the past, but they also constitute a solution, which can no longer be delayed, to the problems of urban congestion and the related cultural problems. For this reason, criticism concerning the "excessive" number of areas and nuclei does not appear to be well founded. On the other hand, it is true that appointments to the administrative bodies of many consortiums still have not been made, due partly to a scarcity of funds. Thus, in these areas or nuclei it is impossible to implement the measures provided for by the regulatory plans.

The 5-year plan of the Pastore report requests funds specifically for the infrastructure of the areas and nuclei. However, there are other substantial expenditures which contribute to the general infrastructure. Therefore, it has been proposed to coordinate existing and future plans at the regional level.[69] Along these lines, an even greater problem arises, namely, that of cooperation between the Cassa per il Mezzogiorno and the regional institutions. However, this problem goes beyond our present investigation.

The policy of assistance to industry should now be applied to the entire nation, avoiding deterrents as much as possible, but differentiating in a more refined way the different kinds of incentives and the various degrees of assistance under each policy. The present system is not satisfactory; the grants, for instance, are differentiated on the basis of a certain weighting of various factors,[70] but the applicants learn about this only after the decision is made, even though the information is available to them. Under the future plan, the incentives should be classified in a series of groups, and the cities, regions, or zones that fall into each of these groups should be listed, so that a potential applicant may know what to expect. However, it must be possible easily to alter the classification of the cities, regions, and zones, in order to be able to adjust to changing situations.

The structure of the Cassa per il Mezzogiorno must be reconsidered. The idea of changing the Cassa to a "fund for the development of depressed

---

[68] Comitato dei Ministri per il Mezzogiorno, *Relazione sull'Attività di Coordinamento,* vol. I, pp. 39–40.

[69] *Ibid.*, pp. 151–155.

[70] *Ibid.*, pp. 143–145.

areas" seems sensible. The Cassa, by now, has a degree of experience and competence which cannot easily be reproduced in our intellectual and managerial labor market, which is becoming increasingly tighter. And since the need still exists for some such agency, changes, beyond the scope of this study, in certain of the statutory and administrative provisions and procedures might serve to preserve these in the service of the country and put them to more efficient use.

The Policy of Regional Development in the Centro-Nord

General Economic Policies with Regional Effects

As stated before, there are numerous legislative measures which, though differing considerably in form, have one thing in common, namely, that they are all designed to contribute to the elimination of the serious agricultural problems in Italy and of the widespread underemployment in the agricultural sector.

While these measures will be treated as general policies, given the particular geographic and economic structure of the country, they do have well-defined regional effects.

Before these provisions are analyzed, it should be recalled that, excepting the plains of the Po and a few other areas, the whole of Italian agriculture suffers from most severe problems. Though they are, perhaps, caused primarily by orographic factors, they have been complicated by demographic pressures, the worsening of the ratio between the prices of agricultural and industrial products, the outmoded systems of production and distribution, the inadequacy of certain institutions regulating contractual relations within agriculture, and, finally, the considerable rigidity of the agricultural institutional structure.

The significance of these problems is indicated by the difference in agricultural efficiency between Italy and the other countries of the EEC. The efficiency coefficients in the six EEC countries in 1958 were, at least as a rough approximation,[71] as follows:

	Coefficient for agriculture	Coefficient for industry
Germany	1.0	0.98
Belgium-Luxembourg	2.5	1.19
France	1.3	1.07
Italy	.6	.88
Netherlands	2.7	1.08

[71] A. Fantoli, "Sulla soglia del EEC," *Nord e Sud,* No. 56.

While in the industrial sector the divergency between Italy and the other countries is not very great and is being progressively reduced, in the agricultural sector the disparity is impressive. It is easy to understand the implications of these differences on the social as well as the economic level. The main efforts in this area on the part of the democratic governments have consisted in compensating for the sectoral imbalances, attacking as best they could the major causes of such disequilibria.

THE LAW FOR THE MOUNTAIN AREAS

The legislation for the mountain areas is of particular significance because a large part of the Italian territory consists of mountains and hills. As the inhabitants of the mountains cannot earn an adequate living in these areas, there is much emigration toward the plains below, creating great problems there of reception and absorption. The problem is the more acute because the remarkable physical fitness of the inhabitants of the mountains is not accompanied by adequate vocational training. It was therefore decided to start a policy for the mountains which might solve these problems in the mountains themselves, so that normal emigration might take place at a rate that would allow the emigrants to be absorbed gradually in the plains.

The text of Law No. 991 of July 25, 1952, does not have the exclusive character of other laws, but supplements other provisions directly or indirectly concerning the mountain areas. It is linked to the law on afforestation, to the one concerning the Cassa per il Mezzogiorno, and to those regarding the depressed areas, though only to the extent, of course, to which the provisions of these laws are applicable to the areas designated in article 1 of Law No. 991. These areas include territories at least 80 percent of which lie higher than 600 meters above sea level, as well as the territories with a difference of at least 600 meters between the lowest and the highest point, and in which the average income per hectare (which includes both the income from farming and that from part-time jobs) does not exceed a specified maximum.

Loans in the amount of 1 billion lire (about $1.6 million) were provided for the improvement of the mountain areas in the fiscal year 1952–53, and in the amount of 2 billion for each successive fiscal year. These loans are for farmers (direct cultivators), for small- and medium-sized proprietors, for small- and medium-sized breeders of cattle, and for individual artisans or artisan associations, operating in the mountain areas. The loans must be used for the expansion and development of agricultural and forest enterprises, for manufacturing enterprises using primary materials in the mountain areas, for the improvement of hygiene, and for private housing, apart from hotels, to develop tourism. These loans may cover 80 percent of the technically admissible expenditures; they have to be repaid within 30 years.

The contributions for soil improvement operations which had been provided for by the general land improvement law of 1933 and Law No. 165 of April 23, 1949, have been raised for the mountain areas to 50 percent of the covered expenditures, and the admissible expenditures include those for mountain railways, for dams, and for nurseries and seed selection centers, with particular preference given to feed crops. The contribution was raised to 60 percent for fertilizer and irrigation establishments; and to 75 percent for the cultivation of new forests, for afforestation of woods that had deteriorated, and for afforestation which is to serve as protection for the area or buildings, as well as for the protection of hygienic conditions.

Exemptions are provided from the property tax, from the tax on agricultural income, and from the payment of the uniform agricultural contributions in areas at an altitude of 700 meters and above.

In addition, for such mountain areas, under special conditions, consortiums may be established to administer the land improvement projects in the areas.

For each system of mountain improvements a general improvement plan is established which contains the major projects under the authority of the state and the soil improvement schemes, with particular emphasis on the operations of soil consolidation and the improvements in the water system which are necessary for the resettlement projects in the zone. The approval of the general plan by the Ministry of Agriculture and Forestry, apart from determining which operations and activities are public works under the authority of the state, makes the execution of the projects provided by the plan obligatory for the private entrepreneurs.

THE GREEN PLAN

The most important policy for the agricultural sector is no doubt the "Green Plan" (Law No. 454 of June 2, 1961).

The evermore accelerated development of industry and of the services, the integration of the Italian economy—including its agriculture—into a wider market, the migration of the population from the country to the industrial centers, all these factors, while accentuating the crises within the world of agriculture, also constitute dynamic elements which allow, for the first time in Italian history, positive intervention in agriculture without having to face the dramatic obstacles of overpopulation, underemployment, and unemployment, as in the past. Because Italian agriculture is about to move from a static and closed world, in which only policies capable of attacking particular and most urgent problems were undertaken, or could be undertaken, into a dynamic European economy, it now seems necessary to attack the problem globally on the basis of a broad organic plan.

The Green Plan is the result of a new kind of evaluation of the agricultural sector, which is not limited to the economic parameters of agricultural activities, but which takes account of the sociological aspects of the rural world. This involves the problem of bringing the agricultural population into the social market, in order to draw it out of its traditional isolation and to vitalize it through greater cooperation and greater integration with other social and economic sectors.

Other significant aspects of the Green Plan are the amount of the funds appropriated (550 billion lire, or about $900 million, over a period of 5 years) and the greater authority of the Ministry of Agriculture and other public agencies over the cultivation, conservation, processing, and sale of agricultural products.

For the realization of the production and market objectives of the plan, it is provided that the Ministry of Agriculture and Forestry, with an annual expenditure of about $5 million for the 5-year period 1960–65, shall conduct systematic and continuous market analyses, in order to follow market developments and to provide the agricultural entrepreneurs with adequate information on the situation with respect to both internal consumption and international markets (art. 5).

Special emphasis is put on the organization and improvement of the market. Funds in the amount of about $57 million, over and above administrative expenses, have been appropriated for the period of the plan for credits

761-932 O—65——20

for the agricultural agencies and associations, and—and this is more of an innovation—for the construction, by the Ministry of Agriculture and Forestry, of establishments of national interest for the cultivation, harvesting, conservation, processing, and sale of agricultural products, as well as for expenditures incurred in organizing the markets, and for assistance to and coordination of the activities of the agricultural agencies and associations.

The plan has renewed and modified incentives involving national and certain local taxes, grants, and loans. These may be applied for purposes which include the development and consolidation of small farm property.

With respect to the problem of agricultural imbalances, the variations in the interest rate on loans for operations concerning soil improvement are also of significance. Article 9 establishes a rate of interest of 3 percent for southern Italy, the islands, Venezia Giulia, Maremma Toscana, and Lazio, while it is 4 percent for the remaining territories. For operations involving working farmers, small proprietors, and long-term lessors, the interest rate is reduced to 2.5 percent. It is also 2.5 percent for enterprises in the mountain areas.

About $72 million have been authorized for infrastructure projects and the improvement of agricultural productivity in the areas under the authority of the land reform agencies.

The innovations introduced on the institutional level are also of considerable importance.

The law provides (by decree of the Government) for acceleration of the organization of consortiums for land improvement and for more rapid execution of land improvement programs. Even more interesting is the provision concerning the land reform agencies. These are to intervene (under the supervision and control of the Ministry of Agriculture and Forestry) in "particularly depressed" agricultural zones (even outside the land reform areas) in which there are no consortiums for the improvement of the mountain areas, or in which, to date, the actions of the consortiums have been limited to the implementation of public works or have been inadequate in view of the economic-social objectives. Thus, the transformation of the land reform agencies into development agencies appears to be the real intention of the legislators.

Article 3 provides that the Ministry of Agriculture and Forestry, after having heard the opinion of the superior council for agriculture and the interministerial committee for reconstruction, *and after having consulted with the agricultural labor unions and the agricultural employers' associations,* is to decide, in accordance with the objectives of the 5-year plan, on the basic directives for the application of the incentives and assistance. These general directives are intended to clarify the policies of the Government and the activities of the agricultural operators.

Paragraphs 2 and 3 of article 3 of the law are most interesting in their effects on programing. These paragraphs provide that the basic criteria may be reexamined annually, on the basis of the report which the Ministry of Agriculture must present to Parliament each year and which concerns the particular economic-social requirements that have become apparent during the year. The Ministry of Agriculture is given the power to issue, each year, additional directives in order to implement, in an organic and coordinated manner, the policies of the administration, with due regard to regional conditions.

These directives have been published in the ministerial decree of November 28, 1961, and, upon advice from the regional committees, the national territory was divided into 86 homogeneous agricultural areas. In the first year, the directives have specifically stressed the improvement of enterprises and the relations between enterprises, improvement of the mountain areas, and improvements in the following fields: Breeding, mechanization, coordination between the measures of the consortiums and those of the marketing organizations, irrigation, and the diffusion and consolidation of farm properties.

The Regional Policy in the Centro-Nord

ECONOMIC POLICIES FOR THE DEPRESSED ZONES IN THE CENTRO-NORD

Within the fundamental regional dualism of the socioeconomic structure of Italy, there are great internal differences. In large zones of the Centro-Nord situations of underdevelopment exist, which, since the end of the war, have become increasingly disturbing.[72]

This is a phenomenon which has different characteristics in the north than in the south; in the former, there are not the same deep-seated historical, physical, economico-social, and geographic causes that led to the so-called "southern problem." Nevertheless, depressed areas in the Centro-Nord are becoming more apparent and ever more serious, despite the fact that these areas have a well-developed infrastructural inheritance and a relatively large amount of fixed social capital.

Especially in central Italy, there are many areas with a flourishing agriculture, with ample infrastructures and services, and situated near modern towns or villages, whose economic and social life nevertheless has increasingly deteriorated. Among the principal causes of this phenomenon is the increasing divergence between agricultural and nonagricultural productivity, together with the simultaneous divergence in the rate of growth of the consumption of primary products and that of industrial products and services. Other causes include the fact that the formerly most profitable locations of industry are being affected by economic change and that the economy is being transformed into a more open and competitive exchange economy.

The depression of certain zones in the Centro-Nord led the Italian Parliament to realize (whether for reasons of social justice or because of the need for harmonious development of the entire economy) that special policies were necessary in order to stop the decline of these areas, to reestablish the relationship between their resources and population, and to provide for the establishment of essential local services. This policy provides for the setting aside of funds within the state budget specifically for these areas, in order to carry out additional public works for the improvement of water supplies and forests, land improvement and irrigation, land reform, local and community roads, rural aqueducts and electrification, urban water systems, and other basic services.

The immediate objective of the policy, which was formulated in Law No. 647 of August 10, 1950, was the improvement of the infrastructure. Its final goal is to raise the infrastructure of the poor regions to a level comparable to that of the country as a whole, and at the same time to create the necessary preconditions for the development of productive activities.

[72] See La Malfa, "Nota," *Mondo Economico,* No. 22, June 2, 1962.

Law No. 647 provides for a fund of about $320 million for a period of 10 years.. A subsequent provision (Law No. 543 of July 15, 1954) increased the period to 12 years and the fund to about $400 million.

It must be stressed that this supplementary policy was not thought to require the establishment of a special administrative body, as in the south. The planning of the annual programs of public works and their implementation was to be done partly by the Ministry of Agriculture and Forestry. A "ministerial committee for the depressed areas of the Centro-Nord" was to approve the programs and determine the depressed areas in which the public works were to be carried out.

In the first years of the operation of the law, however, its limited, fragmentary character and its exclusive concern with the infrastructure came to light. Thus, a subsequent law (Law No. 635 of July 29, 1957), which increased the period of operation to 15 years and the funds to about $660 million,[73] provides also, in article 8, for the exemption, for a period of 10 years, from all direct taxes on the income produced by new handicraft enterprises and small businesses[74] which are established in the mountain communities with less than 20,000 inhabitants and in the areas recognized as "depressed" by a formal decision of the ministerial committee for the depressed areas of the Centro-Nord. In the mountain communities, the exemption applies also to the newly established hotels and to the enterprises building ski lifts, chair lifts, etc.

In accordance with this law, by April 30, 1963, the ministerial committee had classified 2,090 communities in the Centro-Nord as "depressed." As for the mountain communities with less than 20,000 inhabitants, an investigation conducted at the end of 1961 showed that by that time, 2,900 communities, 4,000 industrial enterprises with 36,000 employees, and 39,000 handicraft establishments with 66,000 employes had benefited from article 8 of Law No. 635. The recognition of a large number of "depressed" communities in the Centro-Nord, and the imminent exhaustion (in 1965) of the funds destined for infrastructural works, make clear the necessity of a reexamination (in broader terms) of the entire problem of public policy for the depressed areas of the Centro-Nord.

THE INDUSTRIAL ZONES OF THE CENTRO-NORD

Even before the enactment of Law 634, which established the development areas in the south, certain agencies had been put in charge of improvements in the "industrial zones." But these older policies were developed *ad hoc* to deal with particular local situations.

The objectives of the designation of "industrial zones" are:

(1) To promote industrial development in particular localities by means of incentive policies.

(2) To integrate this industrial development with the regulatory plan for the community and with the provisions for specific public works and services.

The policy for the industrial zones has not been incorporated in general regional or national development schemes. The zones have been instituted

[73] Subsequently Law No. 622, July 24, 1959, increased the appropriation to 426 billion. Other legislation in the sequence of development includes: Law No. 841, Oct. 21, 1950; Law No. 949, July 25, 1952; Law No. 10, July 25, 1952; Law No. 677, July 2, 1960; Law No. 526, June 13, 1961.

[74] Except in the mountain communities, where the maximum is 500 employees, small industry is defined as that normally employing not more than 100.

primarily on the basis of the general criterion of the greatest possible industrial equilibrium within the country. Specifically, the areas that are to become industrial zones must be of the following kind:

(1) Areas with an ample supply of trained labor and insufficient industry.
(2) Areas with declining industries.
(3) Areas whose integration with the national community is of particular urgency.

The "industrial zones" are not established on the basis of an organic law, but case by case, by special legal acts which vary greatly in nature. The industrial zones established on the basis of parliamentary legislation prior to 1948 include: Venezia-Marghera, Naples, Messina, Rome, Trieste, Livorno, Pola, Bolzano, Ferrara, Massa, and Verona. Industrial zones established on the basis of the provisions of local agencies (provinces or communities) are: Ancona (1950), Modena (1953), Vicenza (1954), Cremona (1955), and Padova (1956).

The act establishing the industrial zone usually provides for special facilities to induce enterprises to locate in the zone. These facilities may include the following:

(1) Sale of real estate at reduced prices.
(2) Tax exemption or reduction with respect to the profit tax (*Ricchezza Mobile*), the property tax and surtax on buildings and real estate, the tax on profits due to the war, the consumption tax, the tax on the use of construction materials and on energy consumption, the general tax on the installation of machinery and on construction material, the registration, stamp, and mortgage tax, and the tax on property transfer.
(3) Exemption from customs duties on machinery and construction materials and the application of a system of custom-free storage.
(4) Special financing conditions (only for the zone of Trieste).
(5) Reduction of freight rates on the state railroads.
(6) Reduction of water and energy rates.
(7) Grants for links to water and energy systems, the consumption of water and energy, the purchase of real estate, the installation of electricity, etc., in the buildings, the purchase of machinery, and the establishment of industrial social work projects.
(8) Preferences in the distribution of primary material, of energy sources, of railroad materials, and for dock operations.
(9) Priorities with respect to government orders.

All these incentive measures are not enacted in all the zones. The period for which these measures apply usually varies between 5 and 10 years.

Various agencies administer these "industrial zones," depending on the law or decree establishing the zone. In particular, the following may be distinguished:

(1) Zones administered by the administration of the community (examples are Bolzano and Ferrara).
(2) Zones administered by the consortiums of the local public organizations (provinces, communities, chambers of commerce, industrial associations at the provincial level, etc.); the Ministry of Industry supervises the consortiums and approves their budgets.
(3) Zones administered by specific autonomous public bodies (e.g., Trieste).

(4) Zones administered by agreements between the administration and private or semipublic corporations (e.g., Marghera or Livorno).

Within the framework of the general objectives listed above, the consortiums and the other administrative agencies of the industrial zones provide for the following:

(1) Coordination of the public works and public services, which, however, are almost always undertaken by other local bodies.
(2) Acquisition and administration of real estate for entrepreneurs (but advance industrial buildings are not provided).
(3) Administration of the public services of the communities (in some cases, the administration of the harbors is also included).

The most important relations of the consortium for an industrial zone are those with the authorities of the community. The regulatory plan for the zone (which does not require particular legislative or administrative rules of approval) must be incorporated in the regulatory plan of the community; in addition, the community is in charge of the establishment of the basic infrastructure.

Almost all the consortiums must refer legal or administrative disputes to the Ministry of Industry. The relations between the consortiums and the industrial and agricultural chambers of commerce, the regional "productivity committees," the industrial associations, and most recently the large state holdings are also very close.

The sources of the funds for the industrial zones are the following:

(1) State contributions: In some cases the special laws creating the zones have established loans on favorable terms or lump-sum grants; sometimes the state has assumed the responsibility for certain general public works.
(2) Contributions by the local bodies represented.
(3) Obligatory contributions by the enterprises.

The type of policies applied and their results differ greatly from one zone to the next, so that it is very difficult to evaluate them. Moreover, from a technical point of view the concept of the "areas" in the south has rendered the experiences of the old "industrial zones" obsolete.

Results and Critical Evaluation of the Policies in the Centro-Nord

As noted at the beginning of this section, the goal of the legislative measures in the Centro-Nord is above all to remedy the major socioeconomic imbalances by means of methods which are becoming increasingly organic and systematic. As the preconditions for the promotion of regional development policies did not exist in the period immediately after the war, sectoral measures had to be taken in order to eliminate the major causes of the disequilibrium, which threatened to grow at an ever increasing rate.

From this point of view, and apart from general comparisons with the policies for the Mezzogiorno, it may be said that these measures have had a positive effect in all those cases where there were favorable dynamic elements contributing to their success. Among these elements, the progressive increase in industrial employment, in some regions in particular, has been of the greatest importance in alleviating the pressures of underemployment and unemployment in agriculture. Thus, for example, the policies established by the law on the depressed areas of the Centro-Nord have been more effective in the regions at the periphery of the "industrial triangle" than in those in the mountains of central Italy.

A similar statement can be made regarding the law for the mountain areas; however, it is too early to make any judgments on the effects of the Green Plan. But the organic nature of this plan should be emphasized. It supersedes the restricted and sectoral policies of the past and considers the problem from a regional point of view.

Finally, it must be noted that these policies, with the exception of the Green Plan, have been established in and express a socioeconomic context, in which the labor supply was the dominant factor. With the changing situation in the labor market, it seems clear that these policies must be revised in order to put more emphasis on the productivity objective and to prevent certain undesirable phenomena which could result from excessive industrial concentration. Thus, the provisions for the depressed zones of the Centro-Nord could also be used for industrial decentralization, while those for the mountain areas could stress the policies concerning the consolidation of the soil, the provision of water, and productivity increases. In this way the final objectives of these special policies would become even more evident. These objectives are not only the equilibration of the structures and the productive units of the regional economies, but also the promotion of harmonious economic and social development of the nation as a whole.

Appendix I

Summary of Major Legislation (1947–61)

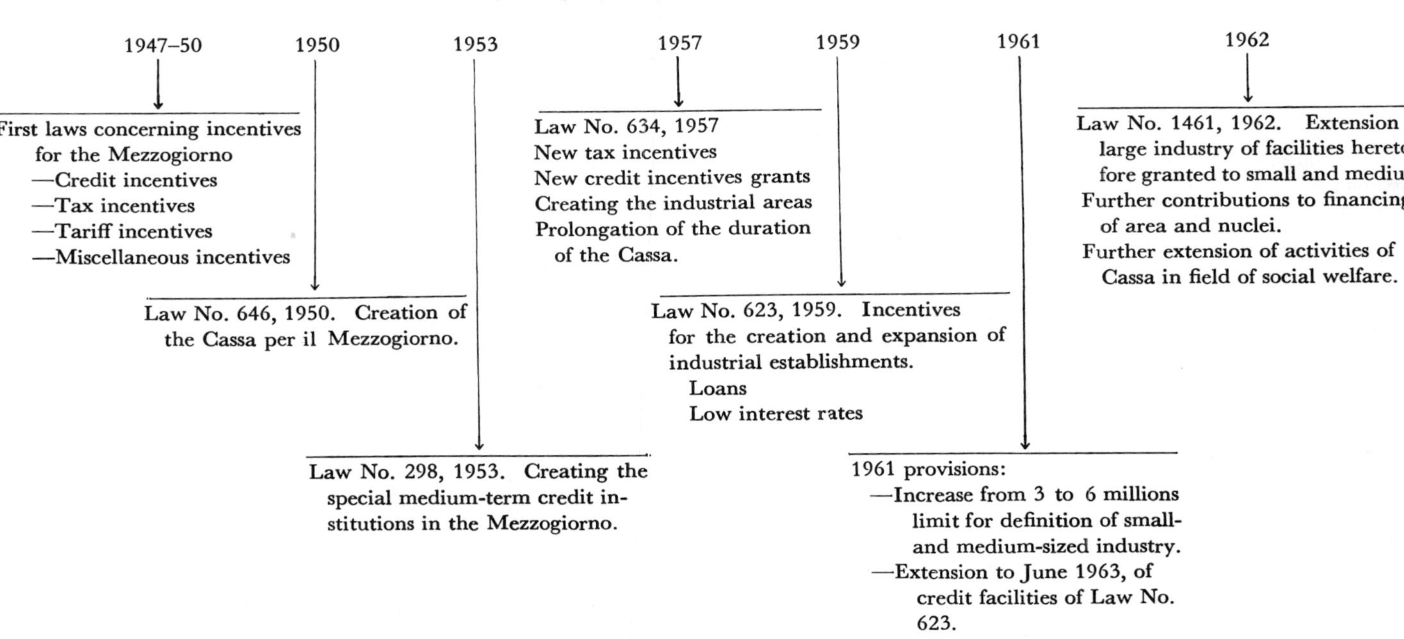

1947–50
1950
1953
1957
1959
1961
1962
First laws concerning incentives for the Mezzogiorno
—Credit incentives
—Tax incentives
—Tariff incentives
—Miscellaneous incentives
Law No. 646, 1950. Creation of the Cassa per il Mezzogiorno.
Law No. 298, 1953. Creating the special medium-term credit institutions in the Mezzogiorno.
Law No. 634, 1957
New tax incentives
New credit incentives grants
Creating the industrial areas
Prolongation of the duration of the Cassa.
Law No. 623, 1959. Incentives for the creation and expansion of industrial establishments.
Loans
Low interest rates
1961 provisions:
—Increase from 3 to 6 millions limit for definition of small- and medium-sized industry.
—Extension to June 1963, of credit facilities of Law No. 623.
Law No. 1461, 1962. Extension to large industry of facilities heretofore granted to small and medium.
Further contributions to financing of area and nuclei.
Further extension of activities of Cassa in field of social welfare.

Appendix II

Summary of Incentives for Industrialization

Incentives for industrialization	Industry in general	Large industry	Small and medium industry	Artisan trades
Financial aid:				
Subsidies and grants	Only in Sicily and Sardinia	...	...	In the whole Mezzogiorno, 30 percent of the cost of building improvement and equipment for conversion of business.
	In Sardinia, grants up to ⅔ either for cost of installation of industry, or for studies and research.	...	Grants up to 20 percent of cost of installation and expansion of industry in communes of up to 200,000 inhabitants.	In Sardinia, grants in accordance with laws of 1950 and 1952.
	In Sicily, grants of 50 percent for construction for social purposes; 40 percent for study and research.	...	Grants up to 20 percent of cost of machinery made in the south and to 10 percent for machinery made in other regions.	In Sicily, 50 percent of cost of installation or modernization of business.
Loans	See appendix III.			
Guarantees	In Sardinia, the regional administration guarantees 75 percent of a loan for industrial installation. In Sicily, the regional administration guarantees 30 percent of loans for purchase of stocks of raw materials, etc.	...	60 percent of the losses sustained by the industrial departments of the southern banks and the CIS are charged to the state.	

Participation		In the Mezzogiorno in general by ISAP; in Sardinia, by FINSARDA; in Sicily, by SOFIS.	
Tax exemptions:			
Exemption from central and communal taxes.		(a) 10-year exemption from profits tax (RM); (b) exemption from RM for earnings reinvested; (c) exemption and reduction of registration and mortgage fees; (d) exemption from various taxes on financing transactions; (e) 10-year exemption from commune taxes.	
Exemption from customs duties.		Exemption from payment of duty on imported machinery and construction material for new or converted industry.	
Reduction of turnover tax		50-percent reduction of turnover tax for machinery and materials for new or converted industries.	
Reduction of tax on electricity consumption.		Reduction of 50 percent of tax on electrical energy for industrial use.	
Miscellaneous benefits:			
Railway rate reduction		50-percent reduction of transportation rates for materials necessary for new or converted industry.	
Declaration of public interest.		Declaration of public interest so as to permit immediate occupation of necessary lands and buildings.	
Cession of land for buildings and for industrial areas and zones.		Various provisions relating to land acquisition by central government, and by consortiums for areas and nuclei. Special provisions in Sicily and Sardinia.	
"Reservation of the fifth" of government procurement.		The central government is to reserve one-fifth of its procurement for southern business.	
Stockholders		In Sicily and Sardinia, bearer shares may be issued for new industrial companies.	
Electricity connections		The Sicilian Electricity Agency provides free connection for establishments in industrial zones.	

Appendix III

Summary of Credit Incentives

	Use of credit	Financing institution	Rate of interest	Amount of financing	Duration of loan	Security
Large industrial enterprises.	New installations	Under consideration at time of preparation				
	Expansions	BIRS and BEI through the Cassa, either directly or by way of ISVEIMER, IRFIS, and CIS.	From 5 percent to 6.3 percent.	Up to 50–60 percent of the total cost of the installation.	Based on the technical amortization of the installation.	
Small and medium-sized industries.	New installations	All institutions authorized to grant medium-term credit.	3 percent up to 1½ million; 4 percent above.	70 percent of the cost, including in the 30 percent the cost of acquiring initial stocks.	15 years	Prior lien on installation and real and personal security.
	Expansions	Industrial credit departments of southern banks.	3 percent up to 1½ million; 4 percent above.	Maximum of 50 million.	15 years	Prior lien on installation and real and personal security.
	Acquisition of machinery.	ISVEIMER and CIS.	5.5 percent (+0.1 percent fee).	75 percent to a maximum of 15 million.	5 years	Prior lien on machinery financed.
		IRFIS	4 percent			
	Purchase of stocks of raw materials and semifinished goods.	IRFIS and CIS	4 percent	100 percent of a maximum of 50 million.	From 1 to 5 years.	Prior lien on inventory purchased.
		Industrial credit departments of southern banks.	5.5 percent (+0.1 percent fee).			

Small and medium-sized commercial establishments.	Acquisition or conversion of equipment.	All institutions authorized to grant medium-term credit.	3 percent—to June 30, 1963.	Up to 70 percent to a maximum of 50 million.	10 years, including "preamortization."	Prior lien on equipment.
Exporters of fruit and vegetable products.	Installation and improvement of equipment.	All institutions authorized to grant medium-term credit.	5.5 percent, reducible by 3 percent by grant from Minister of Foreign Commerce.	Up to 100 million; may be increased to 200 million for certain legal forms of enterprises.	15 years, of which 2 are "preamortization."	Real or personal.

Appendix IV

Income produced by the private and public sectors in the provinces and regions of Italy, total and per capita, 1960

(Thousands of lire)

Provinces and regions	Agriculture and forestry 1	Fishing 2	Construction 3	Industry, commerce, credit, insurance, and transport 4	Professions, industrial, domestic services and other 5	Total income of the private sector 6(1+2+3+4+5)
Alessandria	38, 819, 200	...	6, 482, 900	99, 004, 100	5, 875, 500	150, 181, 700
Asti	23, 206, 500	...	1, 802, 300	34, 218, 000	1, 974, 600	61, 201, 400
Cuneo	56, 862, 000	...	5, 971, 800	88, 510, 600	5, 971, 800	157, 316, 200
Novara	23, 996, 300	...	6, 698, 100	139, 609, 400	8, 500, 200	178, 804, 000
Torino	47, 142, 000	...	49, 738, 100	771, 045, 600	35, 566, 200	903, 491, 900
Vercelli	32, 865, 700	...	6, 375, 300	131, 853, 300	5, 875, 500	176, 969, 800
PIEMONTE	222, 891, 700	...	77, 068, 500	1, 264, 241, 000	63, 763, 800	1, 627, 965, 000
VALLE D'AOSTA	5, 103, 000	...	1, 264, 300	36, 955, 500	1, 276, 200	44, 599, 000
Bergamo	24, 543, 000	...	6, 994, 000	180, 671, 000	9, 824, 700	222, 032, 700
Brescia	50, 422, 500	...	10, 491, 000	172, 915, 000	11, 269, 400	245, 097, 900
Como	14, 033, 200	...	8, 823, 200	191, 164, 600	8, 524, 300	222, 545, 300
Cremona	37, 725, 800	...	5, 137, 900	60, 679, 900	5, 080, 900	108, 624, 500
Mantova	52, 002, 000	...	6, 321, 500	60, 679, 900	5, 369, 800	124, 373, 200
Milano	50, 908, 500	...	90, 195, 700	1, 673, 488, 300	84, 183, 700	1, 898, 776, 200
Pavia	48, 235, 500	...	6, 482, 900	119, 078, 700	6, 549, 800	180, 346, 900
Sondrio	9, 173, 300	...	1, 345, 000	33, 305, 500	1, 637, 400	45, 461, 200
Varese	8, 626, 500	...	10, 033, 700	219, 451, 400	7, 392, 600	245, 504, 200

LOMBARDIA	295, 670, 300	....	145, 824, 900	2, 711, 434, 300	139, 832, 600	3, 292, 762, 100
Bolzano	28, 021, 900	....	6, 049, 200	69, 399, 000	5, 200, 800	108, 670, 900
Trento	23, 009, 800	....	4, 913, 200	67, 646, 500	4, 462, 100	100, 031, 600
TRENTINO-ALTO ADIGE	51, 031, 700	....	10, 962, 400	137, 045, 500	9, 662, 900	208, 702, 500
Belluno	13, 099, 700	....	1, 846, 000	34, 699, 500	2, 511, 800	52, 157, 000
Padova	41, 349, 300	....	9, 684, 400	115, 665, 000	10, 933, 500	177, 632, 200
Rovigo	26, 996, 700	196, 800	2, 612, 800	34, 699, 500	2, 777, 700	67, 283, 500
Treviso	35, 653, 800	....	4, 714, 400	86, 573, 500	6, 796, 500	133, 738, 200
Venezia	33, 489, 500	2, 311, 200	8, 946, 000	193, 476, 000	10, 372, 000	248, 594, 700
Verona	65, 953, 900	....	8, 548, 400	111, 108, 500	8, 658, 200	194, 269, 000
Vicenza	34, 286, 900	....	6, 248, 000	111, 809, 500	7, 269, 300	159, 613, 700
VENETO	250, 829, 800	2, 508, 000	42, 600, 000	688, 031, 500	49, 319, 000	1, 033, 288, 300
Gorizia	3, 645, 100	350, 400	2, 641, 200	28, 390, 500	1, 713, 900	36, 741, 100
Trieste	1, 025, 200	393, 600	10, 053, 600	93, 934, 000	7, 151, 100	112, 557, 500
Udine	36, 906, 800	127, 200	7, 611, 200	105, 150, 000	8, 835, 400	158, 630, 600
FRIULI-VENEZIA GIULIA	41, 577, 100	871, 200	20, 306, 000	227, 474, 500	17, 700, 400	307, 929, 200
Genova	17, 799, 800	1, 052, 900	30, 692, 900	393, 735, 100	24, 657, 900	467, 938, 600
Imperia	43, 679, 200	188, 400	3, 577, 700	36, 955, 500	3, 925, 000	88, 325, 800
La Spezia	6, 439, 500	622, 800	5, 433, 800	41, 974, 000	3, 058, 200	57, 528, 300
Savona	15, 916, 500	535, 900	5, 137, 900	77, 104, 600	4, 286, 300	102, 981, 200
LIGURIA	83, 835, 000	2, 400, 000	44, 842, 300	549, 769, 200	35, 927, 400	716, 773, 900

Appendix IV—Continued

Income produced by the private and public sectors in the provinces and regions of Italy, total and per capita, 1960—Continued

(Thousands of lire)

Provinces and regions	Agriculture and forestry	Fishing	Construction	Industry, commerce, credit, insurance, and transport	Professions, industrial, domestic services and other	Total income of the private sector
	1	2	3	4	5	6(1+2+3+4+5)
Bologna	55, 815, 900	....	15, 563, 200	205, 042, 500	17, 493, 600	293, 915, 200
Ferrara	59, 461, 000	627, 600	4, 544, 000	90, 078, 500	4, 698, 500	159, 409, 600
Forlì	32, 464, 400	717, 600	5, 964, 000	74, 306, 000	5, 821, 300	119, 273, 300
Modena	46, 589, 200	....	7, 014, 800	93, 233, 000	6, 707, 900	153, 544, 900
Parma	42, 716, 200	....	6, 901, 200	74, 306, 000	5, 614, 500	129, 537, 900
Piacenza	35, 084, 300	....	3, 266, 000	55, 379, 000	3, 752, 900	97, 482, 200
Ravenna	33, 717, 400	182, 400	3, 606, 800	84, 470, 500	3, 930, 100	125, 907, 200
Reggio Emilia	35, 312, 100	....	4, 714, 400	65, 894, 000	4, 284, 700	110, 205, 200
EMILIA-ROMAGNA	341, 160, 500	1, 527, 600	51, 574, 400	742, 709, 500	52, 303, 500	1, 189, 275, 500
Arezzo	18, 567, 300	....	2, 612, 800	35, 751, 000	3, 516, 400	60, 447, 500
Firenze	30, 641, 700	....	24, 424, 000	261, 473, 000	22, 133, 000	338, 671, 700
Grosseto	19, 364, 700	619, 200	2, 698, 000	30, 844, 000	2, 009, 400	55, 535, 300
Livorno	8, 657, 200	1, 387, 200	5, 367, 600	84, 470, 500	4, 846, 200	104, 728, 700
Lucca	12, 871, 800	487, 200	6, 588, 800	59, 234, 500	5, 348, 500	84, 530, 800
Massa Carrara	6, 492, 900	9, 600	2, 044, 800	38, 555, 000	1, 950, 300	49, 052, 600
Pisa	23, 351, 600	4, 800	5, 112, 000	62, 038, 500	5, 023, 500	95, 530, 400
Pistoia	9, 910, 200	....	3, 266, 000	38, 555, 000	2, 541, 300	54, 272, 500
Siena	21, 756, 800	....	4, 118, 000	41, 359, 000	3, 900, 600	71, 134, 400
TOSCANA	151, 614, 200	2, 508, 000	56, 232, 000	652, 280, 500	51, 269, 200	913, 903, 900

Perugia	35, 084, 300	....	4, 402, 000	56, 430, 500	6, 796, 500	102, 713, 300
Terni	10, 707, 500	....	2, 044, 800	42, 410, 500	2, 364, 000	57, 526, 800
UMBRIA	45, 791, 800	....	6, 446, 800	98, 841, 000	9, 160, 500	160, 240, 100
Ancona	23, 579, 400	547, 200	4, 657, 600	55, 379, 000	5, 880, 500	90, 043, 700
Ascoli Piceno	24, 035, 000	1, 185, 600	2, 499, 200	28, 390, 500	3, 930, 100	60, 040, 400
Macerata	27, 224, 500	250, 800	2, 783, 200	26, 287, 500	3, 457, 300	60, 003, 300
Pesaro Urbino	19, 934, 200	706, 800	2, 754, 800	29, 091, 500	3, 043, 700	55, 531, 000
MARCHE	94, 773, 100	2, 690, 400	12, 694, 800	139, 148, 500	16, 311, 600	265, 618, 400
Frosinone	25, 401, 900	....	1, 874, 400	31, 895, 500	2, 925, 500	62, 097, 300
Latina	24, 832, 400	835, 200	1, 732, 400	28, 040, 000	2, 068, 500	57, 508, 500
Rieti	16, 972, 600	....	994, 000	12, 267, 500	1, 063, 800	31, 297, 900
Roma	61, 283, 600	1, 059, 600	76, 481, 200	722, 731, 000	81, 026, 100	942, 581, 500
Viterbo	33, 831, 300	....	2, 101, 600	24, 535, 000	2, 689, 000	63, 156, 900
LAZIO	162, 321, 800	1, 894, 800	83, 183, 600	819, 469, 000	89, 772, 900	1, 156, 642, 100
Campobasso	28, 994, 400	172, 900	2, 447, 700	18, 905, 800	1, 842, 600	52, 363, 400
Chieti	21, 193, 300	150, 500	3, 062, 700	30, 625, 100	2, 514, 500	57, 546, 100
L'Aquila	22, 883, 500	....	3, 038, 100	26, 976, 600	2, 371, 900	55, 270, 100
Pescara	12, 807, 000	253, 400	2, 078, 700	31, 620, 200	2, 738, 400	49, 497, 700
Teramo	17, 617, 700	398, 000	1, 931, 100	19, 900, 800	1, 913, 800	41, 761, 400
ABRUZZI E MOLISE	103, 495, 900	974, 800	12, 558, 300	128, 028, 500	11, 381, 200	256, 438, 700

Appendix IV—Continued

Income produced by the private and public sectors in the provinces and regions of Italy, total and per capita, 1960—Continued

Provinces and regions	Agriculture and forestry	Fishing	Construction	Industry, commerce credit, insurance, and transport	Professions, industrial, domestic services and other	Total income of the private sector
	1	2	3	4	5	6(1+2+3+4+5)
Avellino	27, 369, 200	....	2, 177, 100	23, 549, 300	2, 636, 600	55, 732, 200
Benevento	22, 363, 400	....	1, 426, 800	16, 362, 900	1, 669, 500	41, 822, 600
Caserta	41, 021, 300	23, 100	4, 231, 200	36, 484, 800	3, 685, 200	85, 455, 600
Napoli	50, 447, 800	914, 800	47, 711, 700	379, 441, 900	33, 085, 000	511, 601, 200
Salerno	58, 509, 000	611, 100	6, 076, 200	81, 151, 000	6, 810, 400	153, 157, 700
CAMPANIA	199, 710, 700	1, 549, 000	61, 623, 000	536, 989, 900	47, 886, 700	847, 759, 300
Bari	69, 950, 800	1, 454, 700	16, 113, 000	130, 350, 200	11, 931, 000	229, 799, 700
Brindisi	32, 114, 900	313, 500	3, 653, 100	23, 549, 300	2, 382, 100	62, 012, 900
Foggia	41, 541, 400	535, 200	5, 485, 800	45, 882, 400	4, 234, 900	97, 679, 700
Lecce	46, 027, 100	363, 700	4, 477, 200	38, 696, 000	4, 967, 800	94, 531, 800
Taranto	26, 784, 100	621, 000	5, 276, 700	36, 484, 800	3, 634, 300	72, 800, 900
PUGLIA	216, 418, 300	3, 288, 100	35, 005, 800	274, 962, 700	27, 150, 100	556, 825, 000
Matera	15, 082, 300	....	1, 365, 300	12, 935, 500	1, 170, 700	30, 553, 800
Potenza	20, 608, 200	1, 300	2, 115, 600	21, 117, 000	2, 707, 900	46, 550, 000
BASILICATA	35, 690, 500	1, 300	3, 480, 900	34, 052, 500	3, 878, 600	77, 103, 800

Catanzaro	36, 275, 600	277, 200	4, 649, 400	51, 742, 100	3, 909, 100	96, 853, 400
Cosenza	30, 359, 700	180, 900	2, 767, 500	38, 696, 000	4, 122, 900	76, 127, 000
Reggio Calabria	28, 149, 300	328, 700	2, 915, 100	41, 128, 300	3, 471, 400	75, 992, 800
CALABRIA	94, 784, 600	786, 800	10, 332, 000	131, 566, 400	11, 503, 400	248, 973, 200
Agrigento	26, 359, 700	1, 298, 500	4, 624, 000	24, 204, 700	2, 917, 100	59, 404, 000
Caltanissetta	13, 565, 200	35, 700	3, 872, 000	16, 881, 800	1, 635, 300	35, 990, 000
Catania	29, 504, 300	267, 400	13, 424, 000	87, 427, 600	9, 661, 900	140, 285, 200
Enna	16, 247, 400	....	2, 520, 000	9, 447, 100	1, 293, 800	29, 508, 300
Messina	23, 800, 800	350, 000	10, 040, 000	55, 788, 200	5, 924, 100	95, 903, 100
Palermo	33, 635, 500	748, 300	15, 136, 000	124, 265, 700	12, 734, 700	186, 520, 200
Ragusa	22, 043, 400	49, 700	2, 552, 000	23, 086, 700	1, 976, 700	49, 708, 500
Siracusa	31, 878, 200	641, 200	5, 072, 000	49, 415, 600	2, 761, 400	89, 768, 400
Trapani	22, 043, 500	2, 179, 800	5, 216, 000	31, 639, 400	3, 264, 600	64, 343, 300
SICILIA	219, 078, 000	5, 570, 600	62, 456, 000	422, 156, 800	42, 169, 600	751, 431, 000
Cagliari	41, 127, 200	803, 600	9, 952, 000	89, 440, 000	10, 967, 700	152, 290, 500
Nuoro	21, 735, 200	63, 700	1, 992, 000	15, 819, 700	2, 180, 400	41, 791, 000
Sassari	26, 359, 600	562, 100	5, 600, 000	31, 583, 500	4, 582, 300	68, 687, 500
SARDEGNA	89, 222, 000	1, 429, 400	17, 544, 000	136, 843, 200	17, 730, 400	262, 769, 000
ITALY	2, 705, 000, 000	28, 000, 000	756, 000, 000	9, 732, 000, 000	698, 000, 000	13, 919, 000, 000
NORTHERN ITALY	1, 292, 099, 100	7, 306, 800	394, 442, 800	6, 357, 661, 000	369, 785, 800	8, 421, 295, 500
CENTRAL ITALY	454, 500, 900	7, 093, 200	158, 557, 200	1, 709, 739, 000	166, 514, 200	2, 496, 404, 500
SOUTHERN ITALY	650, 100, 000	6, 600, 000	123, 000, 000	1, 105, 600, 000	101, 800, 000	1, 987, 100, 000
ISLANDS	308, 300, 000	7, 000, 000	80, 000, 000	559, 000, 000	59, 900, 000	1, 014, 200, 000
NORD-CENTRO	1, 746, 600, 000	14, 400, 000	553, 000, 000	8, 067, 400, 000	536, 300, 000	10, 917, 700, 000
SOUTH-ISLANDS	958, 400, 000	13, 600, 000	203, 000, 000	1, 664, 600, 000	161, 700, 000	3, 001, 300, 000

Provinces and regions	Duplication and error	Total income of the private sector	Public sector	Total income, private and public	Net income per capita (lire)	Index per capita (Italy=100)
	7	8 (6—7)	9	10 (8+9)	11	12
Alessandria	−10, 892, 600	139, 289, 100	17, 927, 500	157, 216, 600	330, 634	112. 1
Asti	−4, 456, 100	56, 745, 300	6, 124, 600	62, 869, 900	293, 510	99. 5
Cuneo	−11, 429, 000	145, 887, 200	14, 196, 000	160, 083, 200	297, 442	100. 8
Novara	−12, 996, 900	165, 807, 100	11, 965, 100	177, 772, 200	394, 962	133. 9
Torino	−65, 603, 400	837, 888, 500	59, 461, 000	897, 349, 500	512, 566	173. 8
Vercelli	−12, 831, 900	164, 137, 900	9, 126, 000	173, 263, 900	439, 310	148. 9
PIEMONTE	−118, 209, 900	1, 509, 755, 100	118, 800, 200	1, 628, 555, 300	425, 978	144. 4
VALLE D'AOSTA	−3, 218, 300	41, 380, 700	2, 798, 600	44, 179, 300	446, 707	151. 4
Bergamo	−16, 132, 700	205, 900, 000	12, 817, 000	218, 717, 000	295, 643	100. 2
Brescia	−17, 783, 100	227, 314, 800	17, 075, 800	244, 390, 600	278, 064	94. 3
Como	−16, 173, 900	206, 371, 400	12, 898, 100	219, 269, 500	359, 164	121. 8
Cremona	−7, 880, 700	100, 743, 800	9, 896, 600	110, 640, 400	310, 526	105. 3
Mantova	−9, 035, 900	115, 337, 300	9, 856, 100	125, 193, 400	321, 421	109. 0
Milano	−137, 890, 900	1, 760, 885, 300	98, 155, 200	1, 859, 040, 500	603, 728	205. 3
Pavia	−13, 079, 400	167, 267, 500	14, 561, 000	181, 828, 500	354, 165	120. 1
Sondrio	−3, 300, 800	42, 160, 400	5, 962, 300	48, 122, 700	300, 017	101. 7
Varese	−17, 824, 300	227, 679, 900	10, 464, 500	238, 144, 400	423, 443	143. 5
LOMBARDIA	−239, 101, 700	3, 053, 660, 400	191, 686, 600	3, 245, 347, 000	445, 771	151. 1
Bolzano	−8, 164, 000	100, 506, 900	17, 719, 200	118, 226, 100	319, 185	108. 2
Trento	−7, 496, 700	92, 534, 900	14, 894, 400	107, 429, 300	262, 985	89. 2
TRENTINO-ALTO ADIGE	−15, 660, 700	193, 041, 800	32, 613, 600	225, 655, 400	289, 710	98. 2

Belluno	—3, 925, 000	48, 232, 000	6, 163, 200	54, 395, 200	228, 551	77. 5
Padova	—13, 305, 800	164, 326, 400	21, 571, 200	185, 897, 600	267, 671	90. 7
Rovigo	—5, 063, 200	62, 220, 300	7, 618, 400	69, 838, 700	239, 256	81. 1
Treviso	—10, 008, 800	123, 729, 400	14, 723, 200	138, 452, 600	228, 772	77. 6
Venezia	—18, 643, 700	229, 951, 000	33, 726, 400	263, 667, 400	358, 989	121. 7
Verona	—14, 561, 800	179, 707, 200	26, 536, 000	206, 243, 200	311, 875	105. 7
Vicenza	—11, 971, 200	147, 642, 500	14, 808, 800	162, 451, 300	265, 660	90. 1
VENETO	—77, 479, 500	955, 808, 800	125, 147, 200	1, 080, 956, 000	281, 726	95. 5
Gorizia	—2, 747, 500	33, 993, 600	8, 217, 600	42, 211, 200	308, 561	104. 6
Trieste	—8, 438, 800	104, 118, 700	31, 672, 000	135, 790, 700	454, 910	154. 2
Udine	—11, 892, 700	146, 737, 900	30, 987, 200	177, 725, 100	231, 112	78. 3
FRIULI-VENEZIA GIULIA	—23, 079, 000	284, 850, 200	70, 876, 800	355, 727, 000	295, 381	100. 1
Genova	—33, 998, 200	433, 940, 400	54, 066, 500	488, 006, 900	484, 230	164. 2
Imperia	—6, 436, 600	81, 889, 200	6, 530, 200	88, 419, 400	454, 598	154. 1
La Spezia	—4, 167, 300	53, 361, 000	22, 064, 600	75, 425, 600	318, 386	107. 9
Savona	—7, 468, 000	95, 513, 200	9, 653, 300	105, 166, 500	408, 890	138. 6
LIGURIA	—52, 070, 100	664, 703, 800	92, 314, 600	757, 018, 400	446, 250	151. 3
Bologna	—22, 019, 300	271, 895, 900	45, 282, 400	317, 178, 300	383, 807	130. 1
Ferrara	—11, 932, 000	147, 477, 600	11, 470, 400	158, 948, 000	391, 980	132. 9
Forlì	—8, 949, 000	110, 324, 300	14, 980, 000	125, 304, 300	246, 177	83. 5
Modena	—11, 500, 200	142, 044, 700	14, 808, 800	156, 853, 500	309, 376	104. 9
Parma	—9, 694, 800	119, 843, 100	12, 497, 600	132, 340, 700	340, 821	115. 4
Piacenza	—7, 300, 500	90, 181, 700	11, 812, 800	101, 944, 500	349, 416	118. 5
Ravenna	—9, 459, 200	116, 448, 000	9, 416, 000	125, 864, 000	388, 709	131. 8
Reggio Emilia	—8, 281, 800	101, 923, 400	9, 501, 600	111, 425, 000	293, 610	99. 5
EMILIA-ROMAGNA	—89, 136, 800	1, 100, 138, 700	129, 769, 600	1, 229, 908, 300	338, 687	114. 8

Provinces and regions	Duplication and error	Total income of the private sector	Public sector	Total income, private and public	Net income per capita (lire)	Index per capita (Italy=100)
	7	8 (6−7)	9	10 (8+9)	11	12
Arezzo	−4, 553, 000	55, 894, 500	8, 816, 800	64, 711, 300	209, 286	70. 9
Firenze	−25, 394, 700	313, 277, 000	48, 021, 600	361, 298, 600	362, 458	122. 9
Grosseto	−4, 160, 500	51, 374, 800	8, 046, 400	59, 421, 200	270, 835	91. 8
Livorno	−7, 850, 000	96, 878, 700	14, 124, 000	111, 002, 700	363, 467	123. 2
Lucca	−6, 319, 300	78, 211, 500	10, 186, 400	88, 397, 900	246, 302	83. 5
Massa Carrara	−3, 689, 500	45, 363, 100	5, 820, 800	51, 183, 900	254, 141	86. 2
Pisa	−7, 143, 500	88, 386, 900	14, 723, 200	103, 110, 100	286, 020	97. 0
Pistoia	−4, 082, 000	50, 190, 500	6, 420, 000	56, 610, 500	249, 276	84. 5
Siena	−5, 338, 000	65, 769, 400	9, 929, 600	75, 726, 000	278, 917	94. 6
TOSCANA	−68, 530, 500	845, 373, 400	126, 088, 800	971, 462, 200	298, 893	101. 3
Perugia	−7, 693, 000	95, 020, 300	17, 548, 000	112, 568, 300	198, 849	67. 4
Terni	−4, 317, 500	53, 209, 300	8, 902, 400	62, 111, 700	279, 405	94. 7
UMBRIA	−12, 010, 500	148, 229, 600	26, 450, 400	174, 680, 000	221, 563	75. 1
Ancona	−6, 751, 000	83, 292, 700	20, 116, 000	103, 408, 700	256, 026	86. 8
Ascoli Piceno	−4, 513, 800	55, 526, 600	8, 731, 200	64, 257, 800	193, 606	65. 6
Macerata	−4, 474, 500	55, 528, 800	7, 960, 800	63, 489, 600	218, 930	74. 2
Pesaro Urbino	−4, 160, 500	51, 370, 500	9, 501, 600	60, 872, 100	189, 810	64. 3
MARCHE	−19, 899, 800	245, 718, 600	46, 309, 600	292, 028, 200	216, 879	73. 5

Frosinone	−4, 631, 500	57, 465, 800	10, 700, 000	68, 165, 800	154, 152	52. 3
Latina	−4, 317, 500	53, 191, 000	10, 528, 800	63, 719, 800	203, 123	68. 9
Rieti	−2, 355, 000	28, 942, 900	5, 906, 400	34, 849, 300	214, 986	72. 9
Roma	−70, 650, 000	871, 931, 500	263, 305, 600	1, 135, 237, 100	426, 028	144. 4
Viterbo	−4, 749, 200	58, 407, 700	8, 303, 200	66, 710, 900	254, 428	86. 3
LAZIO	−86, 703, 200	1, 069, 938, 900	298, 744, 000	1, 368, 682, 900	355, 974	120. 7
Compobasso	−3, 603, 600	48, 759, 800	9, 080, 600	57, 840, 400	155, 694	52. 8
Chieti	−3, 958, 500	53, 587, 600	9, 434, 400	63, 002, 000	165, 717	56. 2
L'Aquila	−3, 794, 700	51, 475, 400	11, 871, 600	63, 347, 000	190, 804	64. 7
Pescara	−3, 398, 800	46, 098, 900	8, 491, 000	54, 589, 900	225, 020	76. 3
Teramo	−2, 866, 500	38, 894, 900	6, 761, 300	45, 656, 200	176, 143	59. 7
ABRUZZI E MOLISE	−17, 622, 100	238, 816, 600	45, 638, 900	284, 455, 500	179, 399	60. 8
Avellino	−3, 822, 000	51, 910, 200	10, 770, 900	62, 681, 100	132, 771	45. 0
Benevento	−2, 866, 500	38, 956, 100	8, 019, 300	46, 975, 400	149, 413	50. 7
Caserta	−5, 869, 500	79, 576, 100	16, 667, 400	96, 243, 500	150, 828	51. 1
Napoli	−35, 148, 800	476, 452, 400	110, 461, 100	586, 913, 500	246, 965	83. 7
Salerno	−10, 524, 100	142, 633, 600	22, 839, 100	165, 472, 700	183, 797	62. 3
CAMPANIA	−58, 230, 900	789, 528, 400	168, 757, 800	958, 286, 200	203, 830	69. 1
Bari	−15, 779, 400	214, 020, 300	39, 349, 300	253, 369, 600	202, 323	68. 6
Brindisi	−4, 258, 800	57, 754, 100	8, 844, 800	66, 598, 900	195, 937	66. 4
Foggia	−6, 715, 800	90, 963, 900	18, 279, 200	109, 243, 100	162, 685	55. 2
Lecce	−6, 497, 400	88, 034, 400	14, 269, 500	102, 303, 900	153, 218	51. 9
Taranto	−4, 995, 900	67, 805, 000	28, 067, 300	95, 872, 300	208, 554	70. 7
PUGLIA	−38, 247, 300	518, 577, 700	108, 810, 100	627, 387, 800	185, 010	62. 7

Provinces and regions	Duplication and error 7	Total income of the private sector 8 (6−7)	Public sector 9	Total income, private and public 10 (8+9)	Net income per capita (lire) 11	Index per capita (Italy=100) 12
Matera	−2, 102, 100	28, 451, 700	4, 953, 100	33, 404, 800	168, 117	57. 0
Potenza	−3, 194, 100	43, 355, 900	10, 024, 000	53, 379, 900	118, 939	40. 3
BASILICATA	−5, 296, 200	71, 807, 600	14, 977, 100	86, 784, 700	134, 030	45. 4
Cantanzaro	−6, 647, 600	90, 205, 800	16, 510, 200	106, 716, 000	144, 386	48. 9
Cosenza	−5, 227, 900	70, 899, 100	18, 515, 000	89, 414, 100	129, 174	43. 8
Reggio Calabria	−5, 228, 000	70, 764, 800	19, 890, 900	90, 655, 700	149, 203	50. 6
CALABRIA	−17, 103, 500	231, 869, 700	54, 916, 100	286, 785, 800	140, 657	47. 7
Agrigento	−5, 414, 700	53, 989, 300	12, 559, 900	66, 549, 200	139, 956	47. 4
Caltanissetta	−3, 280, 200	32, 709, 800	8, 670, 300	41, 380, 100	137, 384	46. 6
Catania	−12, 778, 900	127, 506, 300	28, 596, 700	156, 103, 000	178, 363	60. 4
Enna	−2, 688, 800	26, 819, 500	5, 671, 500	32, 491, 000	139, 207	47. 2
Messina	−8, 741, 000	87, 162, 100	29, 509, 300	116, 671, 400	172, 132	58. 4
Palermo	−16, 992, 400	169, 527, 800	50, 565, 700	220, 093, 500	199, 668	67. 7
Ragusa	−4, 527, 600	45, 180, 900	7, 431, 700	52, 612, 600	214, 921	72. 9
Siracusa	−8, 177, 400	81, 591, 000	11, 017, 100	92, 608, 100	268, 041	90. 9
Trapani	−5, 858, 200	58, 485, 100	12, 060, 200	70, 545, 300	168, 366	57. 1
SICILIA	−68, 459, 200	682, 971, 800	166, 082, 400	849, 054, 200	181, 628	61. 6

Cagliari	−13, 878, 500	138, 412, 000	28, 727, 000	167, 139, 000	225, 042	76. 3
Nuoro	−3, 806, 800	37, 984, 200	8, 018, 400	46, 002, 600	163, 885	55. 6
Sassari	−6, 255, 500	62, 432, 000	14, 472, 200	76, 904, 200	204, 044	69. 2
SARDEGNA	−23, 940, 800	238, 828, 200	51, 217, 600	290, 045, 800	207, 131	70. 2
ITALY	−1, 034, 000, 000	12, 885, 000, 000	1, 872, 000, 000	14, 757, 000, 000	295, 024	100. 0
NORTHERN ITALY	−617, 956, 000	7, 803, 339, 500	764, 007, 200	8, 567, 346, 700	383, 323	129. 9
CENTRAL ITALY	−187, 144, 000	2, 309, 260, 500	497, 592, 800	2, 806, 853, 300	304, 101	103. 1
SOUTHERN ITALY	−136, 500, 000	1, 850, 600, 000	393, 100, 000	2, 243, 700, 000	181, 463	61. 5
ISLANDS	−92, 400, 000	921, 800, 000	217, 300, 000	1, 139, 100, 000	187, 506	63. 6
NORD-CENTRO	−805, 100, 000	10, 112, 600, 000	1, 261, 600, 000	11, 374, 200, 000	360, 169	122. 1
SOUTH-ISLANDS	−228, 900, 000	2, 772, 400, 000	610, 400, 000	3, 382, 800, 000	183, 454	62. 2

Source: Banca Nazionale del Lavoro, *Moneta e Credito*, No. 59, September 1962, pp. 414–419.

Part 6

Regional Policy in Great Britain

Alan J. Odber*

*In this report I have criticized the words and actions of various members of civil service departments, including in some cases those of personal friends of mine. I am aware that statements made by civil servants before estimates committees reflect departmental views. I am equally aware that civil servants are not able to defend their policies in print, so that academics have an unfair advantage. I hope, however, that if I have been guilty of misinterpreting statements and actions, I shall be told so. My studies of regional policy have already benefited greatly from discussions with policymakers and I hope that this educational process will continue.

Contents

The Development of Policy

Introduction

Regional policy in Great Britain has a history dating back to the 1930's, and over the whole period, under various statutes operated by different governments, it has been an employment policy. The aim has been to reduce unemployment in places where it is markedly higher than the national average, and to reduce it mainly by guiding new industry to those places, so as to diversify their industrial structures. We shall see that, while the details of policy have varied, the main purpose has always been the direct reduction of unemployment. Regional policymakers have, therefore, been applying social or welfare criteria rather than economic ones, and have not, until recently, been greatly concerned with the link between regional employment policy, regional income policy, and national economic growth. This will become clear as the development of policy is outlined. It seems fair to add, however, that ideas are now changing and that over the last 12 months or so evidence has been accumulating that the Government is beginning to think in less rigid terms about regional problems.

In the Benelux study, Professor Klaassen outlined various frictions which prevent market forces from eliminating regional differences in employment and incomes. In Britain these frictions have been much the same as in Holland, but the emphasis may be a little different. To make this point clear a certain amount of straightforward description is necessary.

In Britain unemployment is much lower today than in the 1920's and 1930's, but there are still marked differences in unemployment rates as between different regions of the country, and the areas of higher than average unemployment are much the same as in the interwar years (see app. I for local unemployment rates in various years). These regions are Scotland, Wales, the northern region of England (Cumberland, Westmoreland, Northumberland, and Durham), and certain parts of Lancashire, Cheshire, Cornwall, and Devon (see map 1 at end of text).

For the most part, these are among the regions in which industrialization first occurred in Britain (see map 2 for main industrial areas). In Durham and Northumberland, as in the middle industrial belt of Scotland, local prosperity in the 19th century was built on coal, iron and steel, marine and other heavy engineering, and shipbuilding. In south Wales, there was little shipbuilding, but proportionally greater dependence on coal and iron and steel production. The northwest of England also built up coal and shipbuilding, but its main 19th-century industry was cotton. Finally, it should be added that the less industrialized parts of Wales and, even more, Scotland were and are heavily dependent on agriculture. This is a familiar picture of specialization in a country and of narrower specialization by region, common to most industrialized countries, which pays great dividends during the growth period of the industries.

However, since the 1920's, the textile, coal, marine engineering, shipbuilding, and agricultural industries have all suffered from a persistent, though interrupted, decline in their demand for labor. The situation was made worse by the world depression from 1929. A more fundamental problem, from a long-term viewpoint, was and is that the new industries arising at that time were largely market-oriented consumer durable industries. The wealthiest markets of Britain are in the Midlands and the south, so these new ventures were naturally drawn there. As was pointed out more than 20 years ago by Prof. J. H. Jones, it was not that industries in London and the Home Counties were growing at a faster rate than similar industries in other parts of Britain, but that the London area was "composed almost entirely of expanding industries (and largely of those industries that were growing more rapidly than population in the country as a whole)." [1]

A considerable wage diferential, with markedly lower rates in the areas of industrial decline, would have been necessary to attract the newer industries voluntarily to those areas, even if we were to assume that businessmen were completely logical in their choice of location. This differential did not emerge. The familiar point can be made that wages were inelastic in a downward direction. Heavy unemployment did not bring sufficient reductions in wage rates in the north to attract the businessman. The pattern of expansion thus continued to be largely in the south of England and the Midlands.

Since the second world war, despite lower unemployment rates all round, the uneven pattern of growth has continued and market forces have failed to close the gap. The fact that most of the newer growth industries had established themselves in the more prosperous regions during the interwar years has meant that there has been a marked tendency for growth to continue to be greater there, in absolute terms, since the war. This tendency might have been overcome to some extent if the wage-cost differential had swung markedly in favor of the regions of higher unemployment. Once again, this did not happen. The problem this time, however, has not been the inelasticity of wages in a downward direction, for all wages have been rising in Britain almost continuously since the war. In such circumstances, one might have expected that they would rise much more rapidly in areas of low unemployment than in areas of high. Some widening of the regional earnings differential did occur, but not as much as might have been expected and certainly not sufficient to cause a large voluntary flow of industry northward. The reasons for this will be explored later.

It is arguable, of course, that even if wages were equal in all regions, at least one might expect the unemployed to migrate. In Britain there has been some interregional movement of labor since the war,[2] but not enough to even out unemployment. One reason for this has been that, on the whole, the areas of higher unemployment have had higher than average birth rates for decades. The actual migration from the less fortunate regions has offset only part of the natural increase in population there. A factor hampering migration has been a general shortage of houses to rent, especially in the prosperous areas,[3] coupled with the system whereby local authority houses

---

[1] J. H. Jones, "A Memorandum on the Location of Industry," app. II of the *Report of the Royal Commission on the Distribution of the Industrial Population,* 1940. It is not suggested that this phenomenon arose solely because of the existence of higher incomes in the south. An excellent analysis of how the Scottish industrial economy came to lag behind that of southern England is given in Scottish Council, *Enquiry into the Scottish Economy,* 1961, pp. 30–34.

[2] See, for example, J. Sykes, "Employment and Unemployment in Regions," *Scottish Journal of Political Economy,* November 1959, tables X, XI, XIV, XV; and L. C. Hunter "Employment and Unemployment in Great Britain," *The Manchester School,* January 1963, table IV. See also app. IV, below.

[3] An acute housing shortage in an area where unemployment is high can, of course, help to cause out-migration. For comment on this in relation to parts of Scotland, see Scottish Council (Development and Industry), *Enquiry into the Scottish Economy,* 1961, pp. 110, 130, 132–133 (referred to below as *Toothill Report*).

are heavily subsidized, but would-be occupiers often require long local residence qualifications before becoming eligible for one. An unemployed or low-wage worker may stay put in a subsidized house in one place rather than seek a job elsewhere, because he knows he will be most unlikely to be given a subsidized house in his new location for many years.

The above is a brief and very general survey of the situation, made up of a series of generalizations.[4] Exceptions can be found to many of them, but it is true in essence that the market mechanism has not functioned so as to equalize employment rates between regions of Great Britain, either in the years of heavy unemployment between the wars or in the happier years since. Thus, despite high average rates of employment since the second war, there have continued to be considerable disparities in unemployment rates in Great Britain (see app. I). The Government has, therefore, intervened where the market has failed.

Policy in Practice—the Interwar Years

It is worth while tracing the development of Government policy in relation to the problem of regional unemployment. The early official efforts in Britain were aimed at accelerating the movement of labor from north to south. The start was in 1928 with an industrial transference scheme. The original emphasis was on the transfer of unemployed miners to jobs in the more prosperous regions. Soon, however, the scheme was widened, and men from other industries were being paid small grants to enable them to migrate south and east.

This system was augmented by the establishment of training centers, mainly to retrain workers in new trades, but partly to refurbish the skills of the unemployed. These centers were linked with the transference system, and over the years 1935–38 about one-fifth of the transferees came from them.[5]

Both schemes were operated by the Ministry of Labour and, within their modest limits, they had some success. As Dennison pointed out: "Between 1929 and 1938 the training centers had trained over 70,000 men, of whom about 63,000 are known to have found employment; the 'great majority' were under 35 years old." [6] Moreover, in the same years, more than 20,000 workers were transferred under the Ministry of Labour scheme, and very many were transferred directly to a job. About a quarter of these, however, returned to the depressed areas.

The schemes had other drawbacks apart from the high return rate. In the first place, the older people left behind in the areas of high unemployment saw the prospects of local social and economic revival diminished by the outflow of large numbers of younger and more flexible workers. Second, the schemes worked least effectively in the worst years of the depression, partly because there were fewer jobs available in the south and partly because of a fall off in the quality of the unemployed workers offering themselves for transfer, after the first few years. This fall in quality was emphasized by a decline in the proportion of transferees who retained their new jobs. Third, the achievements of the schemes were small in rela-

---

[4] Certain points will be amplified later.
[5] See S. R. Dennison, *Location of Industry and the Depressed Areas*, 1939, p. 177.
[6] *Ibid.*

tion to the problem of unemployment. Broadly, the two schemes served to spread unemployment more evenly over the country rather than to reduce total unemployment. This last point is obviously linked with the fact that training and transferences were carried out without any attempt being made to raise the aggregate demand for labor. The transferees were going to places where unemployment was substantial by postwar standards, and they were quite likely to slow down the rate at which local labor could be reabsorbed.

This may all now be ancient history, but it still has its relevance for today. Because the training and transference schemes were given tasks which, unaided, they could not carry out, the impression has been indelibly stamped on many people's minds that any geographical transfer of labor is "a bad thing" and that training schemes are a waste of time. For some years, certain academics have argued that economic conditions after the second war are far different from those of the 1920's and 1930's and that a transference scheme could have a part to play again.[7] Yet it still remains true that it would be most difficult for a government to introduce a large-scale transference scheme today. Moreover, there is even resistance to official retraining schemes. Some trade unions look at them with great suspicion. Their attitude was referred to as recently as April 8, 1963, in the budget debate in the House of Commons. A retraining scheme, small by prewar standards, still operates in Britain, and it was announced in the budget statement that the scheme was to be increased. In the debate that followed, one Scottish Member of Parliament, while making it clear that he was not against training centers, stressed that the trade unions were chary of them because of what had happened in the 1930's. He added:

> We have been through all this before. It is more than 30 years since I retrained at a Ministry of Labour training center. At that time, more than half of the insured workers in Lanarkshire were on the dole. There was no shortage of tutors in all the skills, because so many were unemployed. We were learning one another's skills, but there were no jobs for us after we had been retrained. If the Government just go on increasing the number of training centers in areas where there is large-scale unemployment, they will find, as we found, that the new skills in which the workers are retrained are skills already surplus in those areas, that they have unemployed skilled men going into the training centers to teach other unemployed skilled men a new skill.[8]

The speaker went on to reveal that his fear was also that workers after retraining in Scotland would promptly head south.

Granted that, in some cases, this is happening, it is still significant that a Member of Parliament should draw a close parallel between 1962, when unemployment in Lanarkshire was between 6 and 7 percent, and the early 1930's, when the rate was some seven times as great. This is just one example of the staunch resistance to labor migration maintained over the last 30 years, a resistance which is an important reason why the Government abandoned the fostering of migration as a policy in the late 1930's and has concentrated on a "work to the workers" policy ever since.

This policy, of trying to create additional jobs in areas where unemployment is high, began in a small way in the 1930's. The Special Areas Act of 1934 designated four regions of Great Britain, where unemployment was particularly high, as special areas.[9] A commissioner was appointed for

[7] A recent commentator is K. J. Hancock, "The Reduction of Unemployment, 1920–29," *Economic History Review,* December 1962, esp. pp. 338–339, 341.

[8] Thomas Fraser, M.P. for Hamilton, Lanarkshire, *Weekly Hansard,* Apr. 8, 1963, vol. 675, cc. 937–938.

[9] The areas were in North East England, South Wales, West Cumberland, and Central Scotland.

761-932 O—65——22

the English and Welsh areas and one for the Scottish, with the duties of facilitating the economic revival of the areas. They had powers to improve the infrastructure of the regions and to acquire land for industrial development, but could offer no financial incentives to attract industry. Thus almost nothing was achieved, for the economic situation in the depressed areas was hardly attractive to private capital.

Then came two important changes of principle. The first came in 1936, when the Conservative Government, having examined the existing privately developed estates, decided to establish non-profit-making industrial estate companies, one in each special area, with powers to acquire sites and develop them as industrial estates. It was a new departure for a British Government to finance agents so that the latter could buy land, build groups of factories, provide them with sewerage, roads, rail sidings, gas, electricity, water, heating, etc., and to let out those factories to private businessmen.

The second important change came under the Special Areas (Amendment) Act of 1937. This authorized the Treasury to make loans to industrial firms coming into the special areas and granted the commissioners for the special areas powers to pay for a limited period all or part of the rents, rates, and income tax of firms establishing themselves in the areas. This was a breakthrough; for the first time taxpayers' money was to be used in an effort to steer industry to places which were not the first choice of the industrialist.

Despite the new thinking, the results were small. By 1937 Britain had a comprehensive regional employment policy, for the training and transference schemes were still in operation, as well as the new efforts to steer industry to high unemployment areas. This "micro" employment policy, however, was not supported by a "macro" employment policy of reflation in the economy as a whole. Unemployment was falling, generally, in the upswing of the trade cycle from 1932 to 1937, but there was a deterioration from 1937–38, and over the whole period labor remained in surplus supply in almost all of Britain.[10]

There were some shortages of particular skills in the prosperous south and east, but not sufficient to cause businessmen to consider seriously the idea of transferring to, or opening a branch in, the special areas. In all, by May 1939, only some 8,500 workers were employed in 239 factories on industrial estates and sites in the British special areas, and it is significant that many of these were established by refugees from Europe who had no factory in the south of England and whose bargaining power against the authorities was weak.

The outbreak of the second world war supplied the boost to aggregate demand for which the special areas had been waiting. Full employment came to all regions; in the special areas it came largely in the form of an expansion in the basic manufacturing industries whose sag had caused most of the troubles in the interwar years. There was also some expansion in the newer industries and considerable building of Royal Ordnance factories, most of which were to be converted for peacetime use after the war.

---

[10] For data relating to England and Wales, see G. M. Beck, *A Survey of British Employment and Unemployment, 1927–45* (Oxford University Institute of Statistics), esp. table 19, which gives annual unemployment rates by counties.

Distribution of Industry Policy—the Immediate Postwar Years[11]

In the years immediately before and during the war, considerable rethinking occurred about national and regional economic problems. In 1937 the Government appointed the Royal Commission on the Distribution of the Industrial Population (or Barlow Commission as it is more familiarly called). The terms of reference given were: "To inquire into the causes which have influenced the present geographical distribution of the industrial population of Great Britain and the probable direction of any change in that distribution in the future; to consider what social, economic, or strategical disadvantages arise from the concentration of industries or of the industrial population in large towns or in particular areas of the country; and to report what remedial measures if any should be taken in the national interest."

Thus, for the first and, up to now, only time in Britain an official body was implicitly asked to look at the related problems of urban congestion, on the one hand, and regional stagnation, on the other, and to look not only at the existing situation but at the probable trends. Unfortunately, the terms of reference were not wide enough. The commissioners rightly took them to mean that they were not to concern themselves primarily with the problems of the areas of higher unemployment.[12] Their examination of the special areas was therefore brief and limited in scope, and the chance was missed to examine the whole problem of regional unemployment, urban concentration, and economic growth.

Even on the more limited problem of urban concentration, the commissioners were not asked to write a comprehensive and balanced assessment weighing the advantages against the disadvantages, but were merely to look at the disadvantages thereof. Thus another opportunity was missed, that of examining the question whether there were optimum size ranges of particular types of towns from the economic, social, or general point of view.[13]

Despite the limitations imposed by their terms of reference, the commissioners felt able to claim "that the disadvantages in many, if not in most of the great industrial concentrations, do constitute serious handicaps and even in some respects dangers to the nation's life and development, and we are of the opinion that definite action should be taken by the Government toward remedying them."[14]

The commissioners were not in agreement as to the nature of this definite action. The majority report recommended the establishment of a National industrial board with power to refuse consent to the setting up of additional industrial undertakings in London and the home counties.[15] Three of the commissioners who signed the majority report added a note of reservation to

[11] The early parts of this section are based on E. Allen, A. J. Odber, and P, J. Bowden, *Development Area Policy in the North East of England,* chap. 2. That report, published privately by the North East Industrial Development Association in 1957, is now out of print.

[12] *Report, op. cit.,* p 153.

[13] References to the problem do occur in the report, especially in ch. XIII, but there is no systematic analysis.

[14] *Report,* p. 195.

[15] *Ibid.,* pp. 204–206.

the effect that the creation of "more favorable conditions of life and work in other parts of the country" would weaken the inducement to seek work in the London area.[16]

Three other commissioners did not sign the majority report, but presented a brief minority one.[17] The main theme of the minority report was that a new ministry was needed to achieve "a continuous review and a general control over the ever changing industrial and social environment." To insure this, the three Royal commissioners recommended that the power of the commissioners for the special areas should be transferred to the proposed new ministry and that various functions should pass from other ministries of state. The new ministry would thereby be permitted to build industrial estates and factories and to control the building of houses and main roads in relation to them. The ministry was to be supported by a research committee, a permanent body to advise on the development of a systematized national plan for the distribution of industry and to maintain a continuous study of the changes taking place in British industry.

On the basis of this plan, the country was to be divided into three types of areas: First, "free zones" where industry was to be free to develop subject only to local planning requirements; second, areas in which the new minister would control all factory building mainly to prevent scattered developments; and third, areas in which further factory development would be prevented, except for special cases which passed a series of stringent tests. It was proposed to control not merely the establishment of new firms, but also extensions, transfers, and the taking over and conversion of existing premises. To aid the ministry, a board was proposed for each region of Great Britain, such boards to be an integral part of the new ministry and to act as regional agents "for purposes of industrial location and other matters."

It is possible now to say that the three out-of-step commissioners had oversimplified views on the problems of creating a national industrial plan and of redistributing industry. Moreover, they made no reference to the part that local self-help and publicity can play in solving regional problems, no reference to the question of labor retraining, and no reference to the part played by commercial development rather than factories in creating congestion in London. These, however, are criticisms from 25 years on. The fact remains that they grasped the need for research, for a continuing study of emerging problems, and for control to be in the hands of one ministry. Only recently has such research begun.[18]

The Government did not accept either the majority or the minority report. Instead it created a Ministry of Town and Country Planning, with responsibility for physical planning and house building, particularly the building of new towns and the clearing of slums. In 1945 the major responsibility for distribution of industry policy was handed over to the Board of Trade. A third department, the Ministry of Labour, was left with the reduced responsibilities for retraining labor, while all road planning has been left to the Ministry of Transport.

---

[16] *Ibid.*, pp. 208–217. Note of reservation by Prof. J. H. Jones, Mr. G. W. Thomson, and Sir W. E. Whyte.

[17] *Ibid.*, pp. 218–232, by Prof. P. Abercrombie, Mr. H. H. Elvin, and Mrs. H. Hitchens.

[18] Mainly by the National Economic Development Office, from 1962, and in the Ministries responsible for preparing reports on particular parts of Britain.

The wartime Government, did, however, make one vital adjustment in its thinking. It accepted the Keynesian view that the basic cause of unemployment between the wars was a deficiency in aggregate demand, and it added to this the recognition that the solution of the problem of unemployment would involve both a general employment policy for the country as a whole and a more detailed attack on regional unemployment. This rethinking was made public in the famous White Paper on Employment Policy, 1944. The authors of the White Paper saw local unemployment as being more a result of the cyclical instability of certain localized industries than of their secular decline. Thus the solutions proposed were to strengthen the basic industries in the development areas (as the special areas were renamed in the White Paper), to diversify the industrial structure of these areas by bringing new industry to them, and to remove obstacles to the geographical and industrial mobility of labor.

Armed with the report of the Barlow commission and the Employment White Paper, the Government presented the Distribution of Industry Bill to Parliament. This was duly enacted in 1945. The prewar Special Areas Acts were repealed, but four development areas were scheduled with very similar boundaries to the old special areas.[19] These could not be descheduled without the permission of Parliament. The main responsibility for distribution of industry policy, that is, for diversifying the industrial structure of the development areas, was given to the Board of Trade. To this end the board was authorized to buy land in the areas, to render that land suitable for industrial purposes, and to build factories on it. With Treasury consent, the board was able to make loans to the industrial estate companies, of which there was one in each area, to enable them to provide industrial premises for firms coming to or expanding in the areas. The board, again with Treasury approval, could make grants to local authorities toward the cost of clearing derelict land. Any Minister of the Crown responsible for particular basic services could, with Treasury consent, give financial assistance toward improving those services in the development areas. Finally, the Treasury could make annual grants or loans to firms in or moving to the areas, where the firms seemed to have good prospects of success but no access to other capital on reasonable terms. A Development Areas Treasury Advisory Committee was set up to guide the Treasury in this matter.

All this could be said to be a response to the appeal of the three Barlow commissioners who signed the majority report but asked in a note of reservation that more favorable conditions of life and work should be created outside the London area. It clearly did nothing, however, to meet the wishes of the minority of the commissioners who recommended that powers be centralized under one Ministry.

The 1945 act by itself actually enabled a narrower range of financial inducement than had the special areas acts to be offered to businessmen to locate factories in the development areas. There were no longer any *general* rent, rates, and income tax rebates. The only real financial incentives were the prospect of a loan or grant from the Treasury and the offer of an industrial estate factory at a subsidized rent. Loans and grants were rare; the main official attraction to the development areas in the years immediately after the war was the estate factory. The amount of the subsidy offered varied with the remoteness of the location, but only in extreme cases did

[19] The main difference was that the new areas included towns such as Newcastle, Darlington, and Glasgow which had been omitted from the special areas.

it reach as much as two-thirds of the cover-cost rent. Of more fundamental importance to the businessman moving to a strange area was the actual factory, sometimes built in advance of demand, with all basic services provided.

This, then, was the main blandishment to industry. There were, however, certain negative controls which could be used to help push industry out of the areas of high employment. The most important of these in 1945 was the building license system. This was operated by the Ministry of Works and had been designed as a wartime rationing system for building materials. Anyone wishing to use such materials had to obtain a building license. The postwar Labour Government, however, used the system to curb industrial building in the south and Midlands, in the hope that this would force a greater rate of industrial building in areas of higher unemployment.

The whole system of building licenses was abolished in 1954, but they were, in theory, no longer needed as regulators of industrial location. For, under the 1947 Town and Country Planning Act, industrialists were required to obtain from the Board of Trade an Industrial Development Certificate (IDC) before building any new factory or extension over 5,000 square feet. This system still operates in Britain; the IDC is a document which states that the proposed development "can be carried out consistently with the proper distribution of industry." A copy of each certificate issued goes to the relevant local planning authority from which the industrialist must obtain planning approval before building on a particular site. No planning approval is possible for any industrial development over 5,000 square feet, unless an IDC is issued. No IDC's are required for commercial buildings or warehouses,[20] although local planning permission is required.

In addition to this push and pull of Government policy, there were other influences on the relocation of industrial enterprises in the years immediately after the war. Industry in general was in a particularly persuadable condition. Industrial building had been strictly controlled in wartime. Many firms were in old-fashioned and unsuitable premises; others, particularly in London, had suffered bomb damage and wanted to restart or expand production. Above all, business confidence was high; the rush to meet the pent-up demand for civilian goods was on. The main impediments were shortages of factory space, raw materials, and labor.

As far as factory space was concerned, not only was a program of advance factory building launched in the development areas, but of more immediate importance was the fact that there were 13 million square feet of adaptable munition factory space left empty in the areas. These were offered for immediate occupation to firms which had been refused permission to expand or start production in more prosperous regions, especially in the south and Midlands.

The shortages and controls of raw materials enabled the Government to favor firms in, or transferring to, the development areas. Finally, labor was less scarce in the development areas than elsewhere. In brief, a combination of circumstances, some of them temporary, made the development areas seem particularly attractive to industrialists in other parts of the country. In the years 1945–47 the areas, with about one-sixth of Britain's manufacturing employees, obtained about one-half of Britain's new industrial development. It is true that some of these factories were built in advance of demand, but little difficulty was met in finding occupiers.

[20] Except where an existing commercial building is to be converted for use as a factory.

All in all, the situation in those early years after the Second World War seemed almost designed to create the false impression that it was not very difficult to steer industry into regions where unemployment was relatively high, and to suggest that the Government had at last found the right combination of national and regional unemployment policies. More than this, the impression seems to have been created that the momentum of development in the outer regions of Britain would now be taken over by private enterprise so that Government spending could be allowed to taper off. Thus the underlying problem seems to have been both underestimated and partially misunderstood. The policymakers should have recognized that their job was not a once-and-for-all task of reducing regional unemployment, but much more to modernize the industrial structure of certain parts of Britain, and that this would be a long, slow process involving a steady use of powers under the Distribution of Industry Act.

Thus, the active implementation of regional policy was brief. When Britain hit a serious balance of payments crisis, coupled with a materials shortage, in 1947, there clearly had to be sacrifices. Development area policy was one of the first victims. It was unavoidable that the national industrial building program would have to be cut, and insofar as the development areas had been getting the lion's share of such building, it was understandable that they should suffer most. In point of fact the areas suffered a much greater percentage cut in industrial building than did the rest of Britain; the building of advance factories was stopped altogether (for 12 years), and there was a reduction in the pressure on businessmen to build their new factories in the areas.

Free Wheeling

When the crisis was over and the Government allowed the industrial building program to expand, the immediate effect was mainly outside the development areas. The amount of capital spent by the Board of Trade in providing factories to rent in the development areas fell from £23,500,000 in the financial years 1947–49 to £11,500,000 in the financial years 1949–51. Total industrial building in the areas also fell sharply, and their share of the nation's new factory space approved declined from one-half to less than one-fifth. The change of Government from Labour to Conservative saw a further easing of development area policy. Building licenses were abolished, and businessmen found that it was much easier to obtain IDCs in the big urban areas of the southeast and Midlands, so that less and less pressure was put on them to build new factories in the development areas. Thus the inflow of new firms to the areas was greatly reduced. Indeed, it is broadly true that from 1951 to 1958 development area policy was in abeyance. Further details are in appendix II. The justification, from the Government's point of view, was that unemployment in the areas was declining toward the national average over these years as a result of the expansion of the basic industries of the areas, coupled with the growth of many of the firms which had arrived between 1946 and 1949. For example, if we compare 1956 and 1951, we find that in both years average unemployment in Great Britain was 1.2 percent, but that over the 5 years it fell from 2.2 percent to 1.6 percent in the northern region (which was largely made up of the North East development area and the West Cumberland development area) and from 2.7 percent to 2.0 percent in Wales (which included the South Wales development area). It is true that in Scotland unemployment remained at about double the national average, but this, it was argued, was a special case, partly because of the distance from the market in southern England.

Then came a slow rise in unemployment in various places; most of these were inside the development areas but a few were not. There were a number of causes. It could be that the impulse given by the flow of new firms to the development areas in 1946–49 was weakening as they reached the end of their initial growth phases. More important, however, was the fact that almost continuous inflation from the end of the war to 1957 had helped to slow down the long-term decline in employment in certain industries, particularly coal and shipbuilding. Contractions in demand since 1957 have forced these industries to make substantial reductions in the size of their labor forces.

By February 1958 unemployment in Scotland and Wales had reached 3.6 percent and 3.8 percent, respectively, compared with a national average of 1.9 percent. Development area policy was hastily brought out and dusted, and a new act—the Distribution of Industry (Industrial Finance) Act—was passed in 1958. This was in addition to the acts of 1945 and 1950 and created a clumsy system. To the old development areas were added other smaller "development places" to which industry was to be attracted by a somewhat different set of financial inducements.

Regional Policy from 1960

The authorities were not happy about the complexities created by adding new legislation to old. Therefore, in 1960 the Distribution of Industry Acts of 1945, 1950, and 1958 were completely repealed and replaced by the Local Employment Act. This act empowers the Board of Trade to list as development districts any "localities in which in the opinion of the board a high rate of unemployment exists or is expected and is likely to persist."[21] The list is not statutory; the Board of Trade is free to add places to and remove them from the list and no automatic criteria for inclusion are laid down in the act. See map 3 for the location of development districts in the spring of 1963.

The powers given to the Board of Trade to attract industry to development districts are nearly all similar to those in the 1945 act. They include the power to build factories, on or off industrial estates, for lease at a subsidized rent or for sale on deferred terms; the power to make grants or loans to firms which require finance to buy plant or equipment or working capital; the power to clear derelict sites; and the power to make grants to improve basic services. A number of limitations in the old acts have been removed. For example, the power of making loans and grants to businessmen has been transferred from the Treasury to the Board of Trade. The board still has to obtain Treasury approval for its broad financial activities, and it has to consult a Board of Trade Advisory Committee (BOTAC) before making loans or grants. It is clearly better, however, that one department should be responsible for the provision of trading estate factories and of loans to businessmen. Moreover, the loans and grants can now be sought by any type of undertaking in a development district, whether it be a manufacturing firm, shop, commercial house, or hotel.[22] The 1945

[21] *The Local Employment Act, 1960, and Industrial Location,* Note by the Board of Trade, April 1960, p. 1.

[22] This extension was first introduced in the 1958 act.

act limited the offer of grants and loans to manufacturing firms only. Finally, a person seeking a loan need now show only that his undertaking has good prospects of success. Previously, he also had to show that he had no access to alternative sources of capital on reasonable terms. That made the sieve of rather a fine mesh!

In addition to these modifications to the old system, the 1960 act added a new concession. The Board of Trade was empowered to offer a building grant to businessmen building their own factories in development districts. Very often, the cost of building such a factory is greater than its market value when built. The act gave the Board of Trade, after consulting BOTAC, the power to pay the firm 85 percent of the difference between the estimated cost of a new building and its estimated market value.

These are the actual powers at the time of writing, mid-1963. Certain modifications were announced in the budget debate in April 1963, and most of these were presented in the Local Employment bill, 1963. However, it seems clearest to examine the existing powers, their strengths and weaknesses, before considering the possibilities of the proposed new legislation.

It is evident that the present powers are very wide. This will become even more obvious if the system is examined. For the moment, it is convenient to take the method of selection of development districts for granted and to start by assuming an established pattern of such districts. We will consider the selection techniques later.

Industrial Development Certificates

So far, the initiative has come from the industrialist. The Board of Trade does not seek out firms and ask them to develop in particular parts of the country. A firm wishing to build a factory over 5,000 square feet applies for an industrial development certificate to the relevant regional controller of the Board of Trade. If the firm wants to build a development district, the IDC will be granted automatically.[23] If it wishes to build in the prosperous south or Midlands, it will be refused unless there are pressing reasons why the project cannot be anywhere else. Anywhere south and east of Stoke-on-Trent is regarded as a congested area where IDCs are refused unless the firm wants a small extension which is an integral part of an existing works, or unless the firm is in a service industry such as a laundry or a local newspaper. A senior Board of Trade official therefore has to ask himself: "Must this development take place here (e.g., in Coventry) or is it capable in my opinion of being carried out reasonably successfully in a development district? * * *. Even if it can only be done in Coventry that does not mean that we shall approve it if the congestion is so bad that to allow the firm to expand will make life even more intolerable for its neighbors." [24] For factories up to 50,000 square feet the regional controller may refuse or grant a license, but he must inform board headquarters of the application, and they may step in to coordinate it with other plans. Larger applications are automatically referred to headquarters for decision.[25]

Once a firm has secured a development certificate in a development district, the next step is to apply for official aid if the firm feels so inclined.

---

[23] *Seventh Report from the Estimates Committee,* session 1962–63, Administration of the Local Employment Act, 1960, minutes of evidence, question 183. (This committee will be referred to below as E.C.)

[24] E.C., Q. 358; see also Qs. 346, 354.

[25] E.C., Q. 345.

It has a choice of seeking a Government factory or of building for itself and applying for a building grant. In either case, it may also seek a loan and/or a (general) grant. The Board of Trade will discuss all these possibilities with the firm and endeavor to ensure that the firm, however small, understands the whole system. The board must also pay regard to the relationship between the expenditure to which it may be committing itself and the employment likely to be provided by the firm.

The Industrial Estates Management Corporations—Factories to Rent

If the firm plumps for a factory on an industrial estate or site, it is referred to the relevant Industrial Estates Management Corporation.[26] These bodies act rather like responder beacons. They are not expected to advertise their presence or guide firms to them; they come alive to a potential customer only when signaled to do so by the Board of Trade. Prior to the 1960 act, the predecessors of the corporation were able to go out and look for possible tenants.[27] Now they have to wait. Once the Board of Trade informs them that a firm is interested, the corporation officials then meet representatives of the firm. Often a firm, having been refused an IDC elsewhere, has no great desire to come to a development district and may believe that there will be serious disadvantages in doing so. The Management Corporation, with long years of local knowledge behind it, tries to clear up these difficulties, perhaps taking the firm's representatives to other firms on the local estates to show that it is possible "to train former coal miners to deal with electrical machinery," [28] or to discuss how the established factory has learned to maintain efficient contact with its head office in the south.

If the firm decides to settle on an estate, it then has to negotiate with the Management Corp. for a factory. The corporation draws up a sketch plan, with estimate of cost, of a building to meet the firm's requirements. These have to go to the Board of Trade headquarters for approval or rejection. The decision will depend in part on the regional office's view as to whether the employment provided will be appropriate to the needs of the district.[29] In the early days after the second war, there were many fine theories about appropriate employment and the diversification of industry. Theories, however, have had to give way to the hard fact that relatively few firms are prepared to move to, or open branches in, the higher unemployment areas. Gradually a much more realistic approach has been developed. It would now be thought inappropriate to guide a new cotton mill to an area where the cotton trade is declining or to guide a female-employing firm to one where many men, but few women, were available for employment. Other than that, any viable firm seems to be regarded as appropriate.[30]

---

[26] There are three such corporations, for England, for Scotland, and for Wales respectively. The decision not to have a single corporation for Great Britain was apparently taken for political reasons. Even Britain has a mild form of States-rights disease. See E.C. Qs. 701–702, 825.

[27] E.C., Qs. 381–384.

[28] E.C., Q. 384.

[29] E.C., p. 8, par. 28.

[30] E.C., p. 3, par. 9, qq. 47, 145–151, 711, 868–870, 872, 893. But see below, pp. 90–91.

When the Board of Trade has decided that the firm may have an estate factory, the district valuer [31] steps in and negotiates the rent of the proposed new factory with its intending tenant. The valuer's calculations are based on "current market value" which, in development districts, is always below a cover-cost rent.[32] Today, a cover-cost rent would be somewhere around six shillings per square foot, apart from any costs arising from hauling materials to a remote district or building on unstable land. The lowest rent mentioned to the Estimates Committee of the House of Commons for a factory to be built in 1962 was two shillings and fourpence per square foot in parts of Scotland.[33] In some of the more industrialized development districts, rents much nearer to cover-cost are achieved.

In some cases a firm may want a specialized or a very large factory from a Management Corp. The corporation will then build it, but the firm has to buy the factory on amortization terms over 15–20 years.

The actual building of the factory for rent or purchase on amortization is carried out by the Management Corporation. In some cases, a site has to be found (though often a factory is built on an estate already owned by the Board of Trade). Negotiations may have to take place with local landowners, road authorities, and the local planning authority (county or county borough), tenders have to be arranged, water, gas, and electricity supplies laid on, and so on. As one Board of Trade official pointed out, "There is a great deal that is not covered by the bit of paper which they get from the Board of Trade." [34] This is clearly a great load taken off the backs of a firm's board of directors, who may be grappling with problems of recruitment and labor training, buying or transferring machinery, etc.

Even when a firm is settled on an estate, the Management Corporation does not become a faceless landlord. It may be asked by a tenant to suggest names of local suppliers of components or materials or to help the firm contact a "group" with which it can come to an arrangement for finance, or the corporation may even be asked to say if it feels that the firm would be wise to build an extension. The corporations know that this is not within the Local Employment Act, "but it is an essential part of the job." [35]

If the firm does decide to seek an extension, the whole system is repeated from the application for an IDC to the building of the factory by the Management Corporation.

Building Grants

The days are past when firms would not contemplate an estate factory for fear that others would think that such a move was a sign of financial weakness. Even so, numbers of firms that establish themselves in development districts prefer to build for themselves. Moreover, existing nonestate firms in a district may wish to build an extension.[36] If they do, they can

---

[31] The organization and functions of the Valuation Office, Inland Revenue, are briefly described on p. 216 of the estimates committee report.

[32] E.C., p. 15, par. 14.

[33] E.C., p. 143, allowing for Qs. 786–787.

[34] E.C., Q. 443.

[35] E.C., Qs. 714–715.

[36] Occasionally a firm in its own factory rents an estate factory nearby, because of the convenience of so doing. In either case, this is a growth of existing capacity in a development district, which is just as valuable as the arrival of a new firm.

apply for a building grant. This is a new facility under the 1960 act, designed to give a firm roughly the capitalized value of the rent subsidy which would be enjoyed by a firm on an estate in the same district. Here again, the Estates Management Corporations are willing to "give expert advice about the sort of building which can be built," even though the corporation has no formal role to play in this case.[37]

Before offering a building grant, the Board of Trade must seek the advice of the independent Board of Trade Advisory Committee [38] on the viability of the firm requesting the grant. It can formally ignore the advice of BOTAC,[39] but has to obtain the permission of the Treasury before paying out a building grant in excess of £50,000 (about $140,000). So far the Treasury has never refused although "there have been difficulties." [40]

Loans and Grants

In addition to seeking an estate factory or a building grant, a firm may ask for a general grant and/or loan from the Board of Trade. In this case, BOTAC again is required to advise the board, but this time it is advising not only on the viability of the firm, but also on the terms and conditions of the loan or grant. Moreover, the Board of Trade regards itself as having no power to vary a BOTAC recommendation. It may only accept or reject it, and in practice always accepts it.[41] Thus it behooves the members of BOTAC to take their advisory role seriously, and this they certainly do. A firm seeking financial help is brought into direct contact with BOTAC, whose secretary visits the regions where the main development districts are, in order to explain to firms how requests for loans and grants should be presented. This is partly to help any small firm whose owner is not accustomed to filling in the type of form required [42] and partly to try to save time by ensuring that applicants have worked out a fairly clear project before applying for financial aid.[43]

Having received a formal application for a grant or loan, BOTAC promptly refers the matter to the Board of Trade, which must certify that the project will provide employment suitable to the needs of the development district and that the amount of assistance requested is reasonable in relation to the expected additional employment.[44] The great majority of applications are so certified.[45] The firm then receives a longer form to fill in.[46] BOTAC's next move is to send an accountant and a technical officer round to the firm. They may spend 2 or 3 months finding out "if the firm deserves what it is asking for." [47]

At the end of about 3 months, BOTAC members end up with a file on the applicant which contains an accountant's report on the firm's fi-

---

[37] E.C., Q. 384.

[38] There are six members of this committee; the chairman is a chartered accountant, four are industrialists, and one was formerly general secretary of a trade union. See E.C., Q. 1092.

[39] But never has done. See E.C., Qs. 1188–1189.

[40] E.C. Qs. 528–529, 655–656.

[41] E.C., Qs. 1086–1088, 1189.

[42] E.C., Q. 920.

[43] E.C., Q. 2029.

[44] E.C., p. 5, par. 19.

[45] E.C., Q. 466.

[46] E.C., Q. 465.

[47] E.C., p. 6, par. 19, Qs. 467, 475.

nancial past, present, and prospective future; a technical report on equipment, layout, methods, requirements, and the quality of management; references from bankers and possibly customers and suppliers;[48] and the views of relevant government departments about availability of labor and raw materials and the present and prospective national production capacity of the particular industry.[49] Finally, in some cases, independent and informal inquiries are made about the market prospects of the applicant's product.[50]

If the advisory committee feels that the quality of management is suspect, the case is rejected once and for all. There is no appeal, except back to BOTAC.[51] Sometimes, if a management seems inexperienced, financial aid is recommended only on condition that a financial adviser be appointed by BOTAC, or even, very occasionally, a director.[52] Another condition sometimes laid down is that a limitation be put on directors' remuneration.[53] An application may be rejected but the applicant asked to redraft it and scale it down.[54] Very occasionally, the committee recommends that a firm increase the amount it is applying for, because it has failed to take account of the total costs of the planned expansion.[55]

Once aid has been recommended by BOTAC, offered by the Board of Trade, and accepted by the applicant, BOTAC's official interest in the case lapses. In practice, the committee takes a continuing interest in the fortunes of the firms.[56] The Board of Trade sends an accountant around to each firm, usually every 6 months, to talk things over and collect trading figures, and if his report causes the board any anxiety, it will informally discuss the matter with BOTAC. A committee member remarked that a lot of small firms would not have survived without the help of the Board of Trade's accountants and technical officers.[57] A board official appeared to think the same about BOTAC.[58]

A member of BOTAC told the estimates committee that the question of a grant was always looked at much more carefully than that of a loan.[59] It is now necessary to look at these two items separately.

A cash grant may be sought by firms "incurring unusual initial expenses arising from the choice of a development district for the location of their project." Grants are therefore not normally made to firms already in a district and expanding there.[60] The philosophy behind such grants is that firms should be compensated for any unusual costs of moving to or opening a branch in a development district. However, they do not receive the difference in cost between expanding at their existing site in say, Peterborough, and building in Greenock. They are compensated "for the extra costs incurred by going to a development district over what would have

---

[48] The committee may not ask for references in some of the biggest cases. See E.C., Q. 1093.
[49] E.C., pp. 180–181: Memorandum submitted by BOTAC.
[50] E.C., Q. 1101.
[51] E.C., Qs. 482–484.
[52] E.C., Qs. 493, 1153–1156.
[53] E.C., Q. 492.
[54] E.C., Qs. 482, 1205.
[55] E.C., Qs. 1135–1142.
[56] E.C., Q. 1203.
[57] E.C., Qs. 1161–1164.
[58] E.C., Q. 1166.
[59] E.C., Q. 1147.
[60] E.C., p. 11, par. 44.

been incurred by any other move."[61] If this were interpreted precisely, it would lead to no grants being paid, for it would always be possible to find some place outside the development districts where the costs of transfer would be just as great. Thus the Board of Trade Advisory Committee has no precise guide here, but only a very broad hint that it is not expected to be at all generous in recommending grants. Nor has it been. Firms' claims for grants have been scaled down by over two-thirds, and in a little under 3 years, only £5.2 million (about $14.6 million) has been paid out in grants, apparently to between 40 and 50 firms.[62]

These payments may be a general contribution toward exceptional costs or for particular items. They may cover special costs of site clearance, labor training, and removal of plant or machinery, or they may meet a problem of indivisibilities, where a firm has excess capacity in its factory outside the development district, but sacrifices its chance to use that capacity by opening a branch in such a district.[63]

As has been said, BOTAC is responsible for recommending the terms and amount of loans as well as of grants. Assuming that a loan is to be recommended, the first point to decide is the rate of interest. The Board of Trade has instructed BOTAC to "recommend a rate of interest which shall not be higher than the rate currently charged by a commercial lender to a first-class commercial borrower for a well-secured loan."[64]

This is a policy with one open end, which has made it possible, but not obligatory, to follow changes of bank rate. Opinions appear to differ as to whether bank rate has been followed. A Board of Trade official said that the Advisory Committee does not follow bank rate, because it is lending for eight to ten years, and bank rate is a short-term rate.[65] A Treasury official thought that while BOTAC rates did not move precisely with bank rate, either in time or degree, they did move broadly with bank rate. "This has been reflecting the general view or doctrine that what BOTAC should do is to charge a commercial rate."[66] The members of BOTAC who faced the Estimates Committee were a little evasive about the matter. They gave the impression of wanting to keep their recommended rates down a little when bank rate rose, but of being acutely conscious that if they stepped outside "pretty narrow limits"[67] they would be overruled by the Treasury.[68] This point was confirmed by a Treasury official.[69]

What seems to have happened in practice is that when bank rate was "low," i.e., 4½ percent, BOTAC's rate was the traditional commercial banker's rate of 1 percent over bank rate, i.e., 5½ percent.[70] When bank

---

[61] The Local Employment Act, 1960, does not lay down explicit conditions for the making of grants, so this vague criterion must have come from the Treasury or Board of Trade. It is not contained in the "Directions" given by the Board of Trade to BOTAC in April 1960. See E.C., p. 183.

[62] E.C., Q. 390; and p. 164, table IV; p. 181, par. 12.

[63] E.C., p. 11, par. 44, Qs. 388–393, 634–639; pp. 116–117; pp. 181–182, par. 12–13, Qs. 1123, 1147–1152.

[64] E.C., p. 183, par. 2.

[65] E.C., Q. 310.

[66] E.C., Q. 1500. Thus the Treasury mind translates a requirement to charge no more than a commercial rate into a doctrine of charging no less than a commercial rate also!

[67] E.C., Q. 1178.

[68] E.C., Q. 1184. The whole discussion occurs in Qs. 1174–1184.

[69] E.C., Qs. 1500–1511.

[70] E.C., Q. 616, on July 4, 1962.

rate was high, i.e., 7 percent, BOTAC recommended loans at 6½ percent.[71]

This hardly seems a very flexible policy. However, it should be stressed that these are standard rates. There is more flexibility as between applicants. In the first place, certain firms may be charged one-half of 1 percent below the going standard rate.[72] Then, there can be a waiver of interest for an initial period, in which the borrowing firm is not in production. The period of waiver is usually for 1 year, exceptionally for 2, and rather more than half the borrowers have gained this concession, which, on average, would reduce the effective rate of interest by almost 1 percent.[73] The start of the period in which the loan has to be repaid may also be varied. Repayment usually starts 3 to 5 years from the date of the loan.[74] The length of the period in which repayment has to be made may also vary,[75] and occasionally firms are allowed to postpone repayment for a little.[76] Again, the proportion of loan to the firm's permanent capital in the project is not rigid. This is not, however, designed to help the little man. A new firm would have to put up equity capital equal to at least a quarter, and often a half, of the total capital required, while for an established firm BOTAC might recommend a loan to cover the whole cost of the expansion.[77] Finally, there is the question of security. Some security is asked for in 90 percent of the cases, but often it will be a second security after a bank has protected its overdraft.[78] So it would seem that BOTAC, on this item, is not overcautious.

Even so, in the light of BOTAC's whole approach, it is not surprising to learn that second loans to safeguard initial ones are rare and that losses have been light also.[79]

This completes the detailed description of the structure by which the 1960 Local Employment Act is operated. Actual spending, under the act and under previous legislation, is outlined in appendix II(i). The next step is to analyze current policy.

An Assessment of Current Policy

Background

THE RULES OF THE GAME

It is logical to start the analysis by making clear the implicit rules of the game. It has so far been accepted, in Britain, that it is not possible to order workers to move from one part of the country to another, except in time of

[71] E.C., Qs. 490, 616.
[72] E.C., Qs. 616, 1489.
[73] E.C., Qs. 36–40, 616, 618–620.
[74] E.C., Q. 36.
[75] E.C., Q. 306.
[76] E.C., Qs. 306–307.
[77] E.C., p. 181, par. 9, Q. 1115.
[78] E.C., Qs. 172, 491.
[79] E.C., Q. 602. This question refers to losses under the DATAC system, 1945–60. The system was the same, the members were the same, but the committee was answerable to the Treasury, not the Board of Trade.

war. This also appears to mean that a British Government will not order a firm to move to, or locate a branch in, an area of high unemployment. This is partly because it is accepted that the transfer of industry is the transfer of labor, for when a firm moves, managers, foremen, and "key workers" have to go with it, or seek other employment. This rule does not prevent the Government from pressing firms to open branches in areas of high unemployment or from refusing them permission to build a factory where unemployment is low. Such negative controls are "fair," positive direction is not! Moreover, the rule of "no direction of labor" does not apply to the Civil Service. Each individual Ministry is free to transfer numbers of its employees hundreds of miles, and even to relocate a whole department, without being regarded as having broken the rules of the game. Of course, transferred employees are free to resign.[80]

BASIC REQUIREMENTS OF REGIONAL POLICY

So much for the rules. The first step toward achieving a coherent policy within them is to recognize that a balanced approach is needed between a general policy of maintaining a high level of aggregate demand in the country as a whole and a series of regional policies aimed at reducing unemployment in places where it is high. The second step is to find out what the bases of a coherent regional policy are. This implies research, both within each region of higher than average unemployment and, to a lesser extent, in the rest of Britain also.

On the first point, while there is no proof that one can alter the industrial structure of whole regions by combining a comprehensive general employment policy with a local employment policy, there seems to be a strong suggestion that to use either of these alone will not get us very far. In times of national full employment, without an active local employment policy, firms tend to build additional factories in the regions where the new industries are already growing. In times of an active regional policy but less than full employment nationally, firms are growing less rapidly, anyway, and are reluctant to go anywhere strange to them.

All this is obvious enough. What may be more surprising is that, judged by these criteria and despite appearances to the contrary, Britain has not applied a comprehensive policy of industrial relocation except in 1945–48 and 1960.

Looking back, it seems that the prewar years lacked any general Keynesian reflationary policy; the years 1946–48 saw fairly comprehensive national and regional employment policies and, for a brief period in which the situation was favorable, a considerable amount of relocation of industry was achieved; the years 1949–58 were ones of an active general employment policy, but with regional employment policy largely in abeyance (see app. II). From 1958 to 1963 there has been a return to a more active regional policy, i.e., IDCs used to discourage industrial growth in the Midlands and the south, plus government loans, grants, and factory building in areas of higher unemployment. However, this has not been backed by a general high-employment policy except in 1960. Thus, a number of firms which were refused permission to expand on their sites in the Midlands or the south have in turn refused to build an offshoot in an area of high unemployment, and have done one of four things: Not expanded at all,

[80] And the Civil Service unions are free to refuse to cooperate with the policy.

packed men and machines more tightly into existing premises, taken over an existing vacant factory, or developed works in Europe.[81]

THE TENETS OF POLICY

This failure to pursue a continuous firm policy stems from a variety of causes and has a number of symptoms. One central cause is the view widely held in official circles that the main case for eliminating pockets of unemployment is a social one, and that the Board of Trade's distribution of industry, or local employment, activities are a social policy with little economic content. Thus, in May 1962, a Board of Trade official told a subcommittee of the Estimates Committee that in operating local employment policy the Board of Trade did not consider the national economy generally. The board was concerned with the individual firm, and if it received advice from BOTAC that a firm would be viable in Durham or Fife, the board did not consider whether the national economy would be better served by the firm's being placed in the south of England.[82]

Another Board of Trade official told the Select Committee that "in one sense one could say that it [expenditure on local employment policy] is all of a social service nature." [83] The Deputy Chief Valuer for England and Wales made a similar point.[84]

To point this out is not to criticize the officials, for they are carrying out the wishes of Parliament, as enshrined in current legislation. It is, however, most unfortunate that this great emphasis should have been laid on social considerations. This attitude, combined with a marked reluctance to intervene effectively in the decisionmaking processes of private businessmen, has had effects both on the degree of continuity of policy and on the day-to-day execution of policy.

Regional Policy and National Economic Policy

Given the official approach, the lack of continuity is easily understood. Governments, of any color, are prepared to carry out welfare schemes unless they clash with stern economic reality. When they do, the economic forces usually win. The first time this happened with the distribution of industry policy was in 1947, when as stated above, Government spending in the development areas was cut sharply, when Britain faced a crisis in her external balances.

This was by no means the only time that regional policy has been caught in a credit squeeze. The chairman of the Industrial Estates Management Corporation for England told the Estimates Committee that, on various occasions, when the corporation sought money from the Government to build new factories and extensions on the estates, it was informed that:

> Because of a certain credit policy or some other economic or political doctrine at the time we cannot expect to get approval for that kind of scheme. One can cite many, many examples since the beginning of the industrial estates. This is not just something which has happened under the Local Employment Act. This

[81] For an example of this last reaction, see *The Economist,* July 22, 1961, p. 372.
[82] E.C., Q. 264.
[83] E.C., Q. 1323.
[84] E.C., Q. 1366.

761-932 O—65——23

has happened at many times in the post-war period and all that we are saying really about the stop-go system is that as far as possible there should be as little of it as need be because interruptions in the normality of industrial development and management of that sort are bad, both in the short and the long run, for Britain as a whole. It may be necessary; I am not saying that it is not but certainly it is bad. During the period 1956–58 in the northeast there was de-scheduling of the development area administratively and we know that during that particular time the effect was to hold up schemes for extensions to factories for a matter of two or three years. The year 1958 saw the end of the stop period and we got the "go" that we were very anxious to have but then it took us another year or two to build and equip these factories before the benefits came and by that time we were probably in another "stop" year. *Continuity is vital.*[85]

This comment was echoed by a number of witnesses before the committee. A Board of Trade witness mentioned difficulties in getting Treasury approval for extensions to estate factories in 1958–59, and commented that things became much easier in the credit expansion of 1959–60.[86] The idea that the authorities must continue to tackle the problem of local unemployment "just as vigorously, if not more vigorously, in times of industrial expansion than in times when unemployment figures are high" has gained some ground in recent years in Great Britain. The words quoted are from a speech by the then parliamentary secretary to the Board of Trade in May 1959.[87] One feels, however, that the Treasury still has to be converted. Certainly, there was no attempt to exempt the development districts from the credit squeeze of 1961. Moreover, one has the impression that some Treasury officials still cling to the view that regional problems can be solved fairly quickly or at least that they must bow to national economic needs. The senior Treasury witness before the Estimates Committee, 1962–63, rejected the idea that it was possible to look at regions in terms of 10-year periods, for "the situation does change so much." He told the committee, in March 1963, that a year previously he had believed that expenditure under the 1960 act might soon disappear or at least decline. The sharp rise in unemployment in the less fortunate regions in 1962 caused him to think that the prospects for a decline in expenditure were less rosy in March 1963 than they had been in March 1962.[88] Even so, one is left with the clear impression that this official saw no real need for any great continuity of regional policy. His main interest seems to have been in the immediate national economic situation, of which local unemployment was not a part. As an instance of this, one may refer to his assertion that the rate of interest charged by BOTAC to firms which were expanding in development districts should be a commercial rate related, to some extent, to bank rate. He rejected completely the idea that in a credit squeeze interest rates should be kept down in development districts, so as to maintain the level of investment there. He thought that other inducements should be used for that purpose, but did not specify them. Finally, he implied that if BOTAC were so misguided as to keep down its lending rate in development districts when bank rate rose, it would soon receive a directive to raise rates.[89]

---

[85] E.C., Q. 677 (author's italics).
[86] E.C., Qs. 774–778.
[87] *Weekly Hansard,* May 14, 1959, vol. 457, c. 1463.
[88] E.C., Qs. 1536–1537.
[89] E.C., Qs. 1500–1511.

Such inflexible thinking shows a clear failure to understand the need for continuity in regional policy, and to grasp that there are sound economic reasons for a vigorous regional policy in Britain. The case for continuity rests on the simple fact that it takes many, many years to alter the economic structure of a region.

The case for economic vigor is, first, that it is wasteful to permit resources to be idle,[90] a point that needs little amplification, except in one respect. When general unemployment is low, the existence of excess labor in some regions implies that there are unnecessary labor scarcities in others. Such shortages have occurred from time to time in the south and Midlands. As an example, in September 1957, the unemployment rate over the whole of southeast England was 0.8 percent and there were nearly twice as many unfilled vacancies in industry as there were unemployed workers. Such a situation can directly hamper economic growth. It can, of course, be argued that scarcities of labor stimulate investment in laborsaving equipment. This may be desirable when all labor is short, but when unemployment is uneven between regions, a firm in the London area might invest in laborsaving equipment that would be uneconomic if the firm were in an area of higher unemployment, or if the unemployed workers could be encouraged to move south.[91] Since the war, therefore, there may well have been unnecessary investment in laborsaving equipment, a misallocation of scarce resources which, if put to better use, might have made a greater contribution to growth.

Second, uneven unemployment can adversely affect economic growth through its effect on the frequency and sharpness of reversals of economic policy. In recent years, in Britain, attempts to stimulate economic growth by fiscal and monetary measures, where they have succeeded, appear to have led fairly quickly to inflationary increases in wages and prices, which in turn have been followed by balance of payment difficulties. Before long, therefore, the Government has had to reverse its policy. Its actions have called a temporary halt to economic growth and caused unemployment to rise, thereby once more bringing a fairly rapid reversal of official policy.

It seems that these reversals of policy have been made more abrupt and more frequent because the results have been unequal as between different regions of the economy, partly because the regions with higher unemployment rates have also a higher than average dependence on capital goods industries. One may consider first a period of economic expansion, April to October 1959, a time when the Government was stimulating the economy and when unemployment was falling. Table 1 compares the main regions of lower and higher unemployment in this period.

It should be stressed that this and the subsequent table cannot be taken completely at face value, for various random factors can hide the underlying influences. Even so, it appears that within 6 months of the expansion getting properly underway, unemployment in London, the Midlands, and North Midlands was falling about as rapidly as in the less fortunate regions, despite the fact that the initial level in the south was much lower. Thus, by October, unemployment in the south and the Midlands had fallen almost

---

[90] The best recent comment on this appears in National Economic Development Council, *Conditions Favourable to Faster Growth*, pp. 14–19.

[91] Either of these adjustments would involve some retraining of adult workers, of course.

to 1 percent and vacancies exceeded unemployment, while in the northern region, Wales, and Scotland unemployment was between 3 and 4 percent and was still far in excess of notified vacancies.

TABLE 1.—*Changes in Rates of Unemployment and in Vacancies, April to October 1959*

[Percent]

Region	Unemployment, April 1959	Unemployment, October 1959	Change	Average change, April 1951–October 1960 [1]	Vacancies as percent of unemployment	
					April	October 1959
London and South East	1. 4	1. 1	−0. 3	0	72. 5	119. 2
Midlands	1. 9	1. 1	−. 8	−0. 1	53. 5	118. 2
North Midlands	1. 8	1. 2	−. 6	−. 2	56. 6	100. 3
Northern	3. 5	3. 1	−. 4	−. 3	17. 8	20. 2
Scotland	4. 7	4. 0	−. 7	−. 4	10. 4	12. 2
Wales	4. 4	3. 4	−1. 0	−. 3	17. 8	26. 1
Great Britain	2. 4	1. 9	−. 5	−. 2	37. 3	58. 8

[1] This column is put in to permit some judgment on seasonal influences to be made. It is not a "seasonal adjustment factor" for it covers only 10 years and there was a tendency over these years for squeezes to occur in the autumn and relaxations in the spring.

This type of uneven reaction has a particular significance in relation to the balance of the economy as a whole. A rapid fall in unemployment toward 1 percent and a rise in notified vacancies in important manufacturing regions are signs of labor scarcities. These scarcities cause wage costs to rise. There is wage-push inflation, for shop-floor negotiators are able to achieve sizable concessions fairly easily, over and above the nationally negotiated wage rates. There is even an element of wage-pull inflation, for employers offer slacker piece rates when labor is scarce, not so much to attract labor from the emptying labor market, but to protect themselves from the firm down the road. The increase in wages, without comparable increase in output, is clearly inflationary in the high employment areas, but it spreads to other regions, partly as a direct result of the rise in retail prices, but more because union officials in other regions notice when regional earnings differentials get out of line. Regional communications between shop stewards have improved since the war, partly as a result of the greatly increased number of branch factories established in the development areas. It may well be that workers and their stewards in a factory in an area where unemployment stands at, say, 4 percent would find it difficult to win higher local wage rates "out of the blue," but they have a stronger argument when they know that men in factories elsewhere in the same firm or industry are pulling ahead of them. Moreover, even managements can find it difficult to refuse higher rates in such circumstances; indeed, certain multiplant firms have a policy of paying similar wages in different regions.[92] Thus, the increases in wages spread out in ripples and result in greater spending, forcing an early reversal of credit policy at a time when there is still surplus labor available in particular regions.

The next task is to consider a period of credit squeeze, the period after September 1957, when bank rate was raised to 7 percent, reductions were ordered on bank advances, the Capital Issues Committee was told to be tough, and limits were announced on Government expenditure. Table 2 shows regional rates of unemployment before the squeeze began, and 6 months later.

TABLE 2.—*Changes in Rates of Unemployment and of Vacancies, September 1957 to March 1958*

[Percent]

Regions	Unemployment, September 1957	Unemployment, March 1958	Change	Average change, September–March, 1951–1960	Vacancies as percent of unemployment	
					September 1957	March 1958
London and South East	0. 8	1. 3	+0. 5	+0. 3	184. 5	78. 3
Midlands	1. 0	1. 4	+. 4	+. 1	108. 1	75. 7
North Midlands	. 8	1. 5	+. 7	+. 2	198. 8	79. 2
Northern	1. 4	2. 2	+. 8	+. 5	67. 8	37. 8
Scotland	2. 3	3. 6	+1. 3	+. 6	32. 7	17. 3
Wales	2. 3	3. 7	+1. 4	+. 5	43. 6	20. 3
Great Britain	1. 2	2. 0	+. 8	+. 3	106. 1	50. 1

These figures again are capable of more than one interpretation, but they show that, in absolute terms, unemployment rose more in those regions where it was high to begin with than in the regions where labor was scarce. In the latter regions there was a somewhat greater effect on "notified vacancies," which fell by 25 percent, on average, over the 6 months, compared with a fall of 20 percent, on average, in Scotland, Wales, and the northern region. These three regions however, had proportionally far fewer vacancies to start with, and it seems clear that the general effect of the squeeze was undesirable. It must have created a dilemma for the British Government.

To have continued the squeeze until all inflationary tendencies had been removed in the south and Midlands would have brought enormous political opposition, especially in those areas in the north and west where unemployment was already reaching 6, 8, or 10 percent by March 1958.[93] Moreover, it would have brought even higher unemployment of men and machines largely in regions which were not contributing directly to inflation. In any

[92] An outstanding example is the decision of Fords to pay Dagenham rates in their new plant near Liverpool.

[93] This claim is strongly supported by the reaction, including the by-election results, which followed when the more recent squeeze of 1961 got out of hand and became the recession of 1962.

event, the authorities plumped for a quick reversal of policy. In terms of the problem of inflation, it is significant to note that the first cut in bank rate was in March 1958, when unemployment in London, the Midlands, and North Midlands was still as low as 1.3 to 1.5 percent, and notified vacancies were still between three-quarters and four-fifths of unemployment.

Although there is no case for dogmatic assertion on this complicated matter, there is some evidence that the presence of regional disparities in unemployment has caused the Government to reverse its policies more quickly than would otherwise be economically desirable. It appears that pressure of inflation in the south and Midlands brings an early reversal of expansion and that rising unemployment in Wales and the north brings an equally speedy reversal of the squeeze. This is important in that frequent and abrupt changes of policy inhibit growth and make continuing changes of policy unavoidable.

If this argument has any merit, it implies that there are sound economic reasons why official policy in regions with higher than average unemployment should be pressed on, regardless of the general state of the economy. Indeed, it is probably desirable to operate certain parts of regional policy directly out of phase with general policy, for it seems that, over the years, changes in government credit policy have had their main effects in the regions where those effects were not required. To particularize, it would be desirable to take steps to maintain expansion in areas of high unemployment during a credit squeeze, and to maintain something of a squeeze in the areas of lowest unemployment even during a period of general expansion. However, the scope for such out-of-phase activities would be strictly limited in Britain. It would be possible, in a squeeze, to exempt certain regions from cuts in public investment and to lower official lending rates there; but it would not be possible to have regional purchase-tax or hire-purchase differentials in Britain, for they would be much too easy to evade. Discrimination would be possible, however, between industries. If the Government had more detailed and up-to-date statistics of the main shortages and surpluses of materials, labor skills, and other factors, by industry, it could temper a general change in policy by an opposite adjustment in purchase-tax and hire-purchase regulations in those industrial sectors which were out of step, i.e., which still had sizable unemployed resources in a boom or were acutely short of capacity in a recession. By concentrating squeezes and expansions on the sectors where they were most necessary, greater results would be obtained from smaller efforts, the economy as a whole would benefit, and so would the regions of higher unemployment.

The Execution of Policy

So much for continuity. We turn now to the actual execution of policy. This also has been dominated by the belief that the whole aim of policy should be a social one, the immediate relief of unemployment by guiding industry as near as possible to the pockets of unemployment regardless of whether such pockets are in places suitable for industrial expansion or not. Broadly speaking, the main higher unemployment regions of Britain are areas in which there are certain larger towns surrounded by rather more "rural areas." In the northeast of England, South Wales, and Scotland, these rural areas contain small villages based on a declining coal trade (and in South Wales a collapsed hand sheet and tin plate industry). As far as the northeast and South Wales are concerned, the main towns are not great conurbations like Birmingham and there has been no strong case for discouraging industrial growth there on the grounds that they are far beyond their optimum economic size. What has happened, however, is that because towns like Middlesbrough or Darlington are good industrial centers, unemployment there fell to a low level in the early days after the second war. Thus the Board of Trade ceased to induce further industrial growth in such places. As time passed, attention was more and more concentrated on trying to lure businessmen to the economically less attractive parts of the development areas, because basic policy continued to be to try to bring work to the doorsteps of the unemployed.

In 1946, for example, a labor president of the Board of Trade apologized in the House of Commons because mining subsidence in the valleys of South Wales, plus the shape of those valleys, made it impossible to put a firm down in each little area where there was unemployment.[94] This theme was echoed by a conservative parliamentary secretary to the Board of Trade, in 1954, when he told the House that "if there is a limited amount of industry on the move, it is rather natural to try to send it to those parts of the development areas where existing unemployment is the most serious."[95] This view ignores the possibility that one reason why there was a limited amount of industry on the move was that prospective movers were at that time being discouraged from taking the plunge, because they were being shown the industrially least attractive parts of the development areas. This dogma, that industry should go to the exact spots where the unemployed were, even if these places were broken-down pit villages off the beaten track, was also accepted by certain civil servants responsible for executing policy. In 1955, the then northern regional controller of the Board of Trade assured a select committee that "the last thing" the Board of Trade would wish to do would be to encourage firms to go to such places as Tees-side "because there is no unemployment there."[96] This was despite the fact that Tees-side—the Middlesbrough area—was only 25 to 30 miles from the declining coal field of West Durham and was an industrial growing point.

This perverse philosophy was continued under the 1958 and 1960 acts. The now-repealed 1945 legislation had scheduled relatively large regions for economic face-lifts. Even if the authorities wanted to guide industry mainly to particular parts of the development areas, industrialists could seek the benefits of distribution of industry legislation in or near any of the main towns.[97] Both the 1958 and the 1960 acts reduced their ability to do so. Under the 1958 act, the Board of Trade was able to name "development places," as they were unofficially called, in which loans and grants could be made to firms located there or settling there. The basis on which

[94] *Official Report,* Oct. 28, 1946, vol. 428, c. 302.

[95] *Official Report,* July 6, 1954, vol. 529, cc. 1943–44.

[96] *Second Report from the Select Committee on Estimates,* 1955–56, p. 94, Q. 606. Available statistics, such as they are, bear out the controller's claim. It would appear that in 1956 only 3 percent of the 180,000 male workers on Tees-side and the surrounding districts were working in factories on the industrial estates or factories steered to Tees-side under the distribution of industry policy. See House & Fullerton, *Tees-side at Mid-Century,* pp. 424–5.

[97] Except in the northeast of England in 1956–58, where distribution of industry policy was in cold storage.

such places were chosen was usually that they had suffered 4 percent unemployment over 12 months. On April 10, 1959, the Minister of State, Board of Trade, informed the House of Commons that the areas selected contained 15 percent of the insured population and that this was about the limit to which the board should go if it were "to help the worst places." [98] This resulted in a scattering of small areas being listed, most of which were not attractive as industrial centers. At the same time, industrial towns near to areas with 4 percent unemployment were not listed, unless they were "lucky" enough to be enjoying 4 percent also.[99]

The 1960 Local Employment Act, as its name implies, followed the same dogma. In many ways, including the ability to put areas on and off the list, the type of establishment which could be aided, and the range of assistance which could be offered, the new act was more flexible than its predecessors. However, the only criterion on which the board can list an area as a development district is that of unemployment, actual or expected. Very soon after the act was passed, the board went on record as saying that "one of the main principles for deciding whether an area suffers from high unemployment has been that (during the previous year) the average number of wholly unemployed represented about 4½ percent of insured employees." This was roughly double the national average. The use of annual averages was to discount purely temporary and seasonal changes in unemployment. In recognition of the need for flexibility, account "has been taken on the one hand of unfavorable developments to be expected from definite decisions to reduce employment in certain places (for example factory and colliery closures) and on the other of the volume of additional employment likely to be provided by new projects *known* to be going ahead in some places." [1]

So much for flexibility. Only precise changes known to be about to occur were to be taken into consideration. In other words, policy in areas of higher unemployment is still a narrowly defined, geographically narrowly based, short-run affair which lacks any attempt to look beyond the immediate problems of small localities to the longer-run, more fundamental problems of the industrial structure, and possible future trends of regions.[2]

This failure to look ahead seems even more startling when one compares the way the Board of Trade decides on whether to list a place as a development district and the way BOTAC assesses the case for giving a firm some financial help in a development district. Logically, there are two complementary exercises to be carried out with the same care. In fact, one is a rule-of-thumb technique, the other a research project. We have already seen how BOTAC obtains a wide range of detailed reports about a supplicant for aid, and will even seek information about the prospects of his product and his industry.

---

[98] *Weekly Hansard,* Apr. 10, 1959, vol. 453, c. 612.

[99] For a more detailed account of the 1958 Distribution of Industry (Industrial Finance) Act, see A. J. Odber, "Local Unemployment and the 1958 Act," *Scottish Journal of Political Economy,* 1959.

[1] "Statistics of Local Unemployment: Principal Towns and Development Districts," *Ministry of Labour Gazette,* April 1960, p. 134 (author's italics).

[2] The latest defenses of the principle of concentrating aid in areas of highest unemployment occur in the Board of Trade's annual *Report on Local Employment,* August 1962, and in E.C., e.g., p. 29, Qs. 55–58.

It would be idle to pretend that it is possible to outline one ideal regional economic policy in all its perfection. All one can do is to start by admitting that there is a continuum of possible policies and to narrow down the alternatives with reference both to the aims of policy and to the realities of political life in Britain. Finally, one arrives at a suggested policy which appears to make sense to the writer.

The first point that emerges from the preceding paragraphs is that regional policy in Britain should have a social content, but its primary aim should not be merely the reduction of unemployment, but the raising of incomes by facilitating more rapid economic growth in the country as a whole. It is fair to say, however, that an effective regional policy which does have economic growth as its main aim will operate partly by seeking to reduce local unemployment.

THE NEED FOR RESEARCH

The second point is that, to the extent that regional policy should concern itself with unemployment, it should concentrate mainly on the problem of chronic unemployment, and underemployment, actual or prospective. Only where a region has a pattern of industry which is very highly sensitive to official credit squeezes should attention be paid to the question of whether it is possible to guide in cyclically more stable industries. Thus the starting point should be an officially sponsored examination of the basic industrial structure of the regions; the aim of the survey would be to try to assess the regional prospects of each main industry, declining, stable, and expanding alike, the prospects, that is, in terms of future employment and output. This would have to be related to a regional population analysis, dealing not merely with age structure, but with activity rates and migration rates. These combined would give a very broad picture of the relationship between the expected demand and the expected supply of labor. A more detailed analysis would be obtained by examining the actual labor skills required and available.

Obviously, all this would involve a considerable exercise in the collection of data, to permit the buildup in each region, and each industry therein, of indices of employment and of output, of details of the labor content of each industry, etc. Finally, an assessment of the infrastructure of the region would be needed.

A thorough analysis of this nature would, among other things, reveal where, if anywhere, were the growth points of a region of higher unemployment, the points where the expanding industries were economically viable. It would also reveal some of the factors hampering the growth of these industries.[3] However, it would not reveal everything in a changing world. There would be need for smaller, continuing assessments of new or enhanced problems arising both from external causes and from the application of regional policy itself.

It has sometimes been argued in Britain that such an approach is purely academic, that the need is for action, not research. This is a dangerous

[3] One has to stress "some of the factors," for other factors may exist only in the minds of businessmen in more prosperous regions.

thesis, if the action turns out to be misguided. In any case, there is no reason why action and analysis should not coexist.[4]

THE NEED FOR ACTION

We now turn to this question of action. To a small extent it could be "indirect" in the sense that it may be possible to stimulate incomes and employment in region A by, say, Government contracts[5] given to firms in region B which have a high labor-intensive input from firms in region A. There seem to be two sorts of limitations to any large-scale use of this technique. The first is the statistical problem of achieving reliable inter-regional input-output data. The second is that even if these were available, the technique could not be extended to a broader policy of direct financial help to firms. It would be very interesting to stand on the sidelines and watch a British president of the Board of Trade try to persuade Scottish M.P.'s that financial help should be given to certain firms in prosperous areas because this would indirectly help Scotland's unemployed.

The remaining methods of tackling the problem of regional unemployment are the orthodox ones of guiding industry to the workers and encouraging workers to migrate to industry. A sensible policymaker would recognize that there is no reason why these should not be operated simultaneously, with the emphasis rather more on the migration of capital into certain regions of higher unemployment and on the migration of labor out of other regions. In Britain, it seems broadly true that in older industrial areas such as South Wales and the northeast of England the emphasis should mainly be on attracting capital into selected parts of the regions, while in the more sparsely populated regions like mid-Wales and the Highlands of Scotland the chief emphasis would probably have to be on the out-migration of labor plus the offer of loans and grants to help local people employ more workers. This is mainly social policy and expensive, but there are hardly any other alternatives, for "it is very, very difficult to persuade an industry from the Midlands to set up north of Inverness."[6] Fortunately, the total numbers unemployed in such areas are relatively small. The variety of problems suggests that a fairly wide and flexible range of techniques should be available to Government departments which are concerned with ironing out irregularities in unemployment between regions.

Our main concern, however, is with the older industrial areas: The central area of Scotland, Merseside, the northeast of England, and South Wales. These are all areas in which employment is growing less rapidly than in Britain as a whole, and in which there is an overdependence on declining industries as well as varying degrees of shortage of industries that are expanding in employment terms (see app. III).

The first step would be to look at each of these regions, as regions, and not as a series of disconnected pockets of unemployment. The sort of survey

---

[4] Regional surveys were carried out in the 1930's, but no further official work was

[5] See A. T. Peacock and D. G. M. Dosser, "Regional Input-Output Analysis and Government Spending," *Scottish Journal of Political Economy*, November 1959. As the title suggests, Peacock and Dosser limit their analysis to the effects of Government contracts.

done until 1962–63, when surveys of Scotland, the northeast, and southeast of England were made. These have not yet been published.

[6] Controller for Scotland, of the Board of Trade, E.C., Q. 979.

outlined above would almost certainly reveal that, in each region, there are growth industries that are progressing far better in certain locations than in others. Two independent, though not exhaustive, surveys of the northeast of England support the claim that there are definite growth points, or rather lines of growth, in that part of Britain, broadly from Newcastle upon Tyne to Darlington and from Darlington to Middlesbrough.[7] There is evidence that this is also true in other regions of higher unemployment.[8] To concentrate industrial expansion in a few selected areas would be a complete reversal of present policy, but it would have a number of obvious advantages. If good industrial sites were carefully selected, so that expansion were possible without creating new congested conurbations, then the difficulties of operating local employment policy would be reduced and various economies would be achieved, as compared with the present system of encouraging industry in a large number of areas. We will examine first certain difficulties that face those who are responsible for policy, and then go on to consider the economic aspects of the problem.

The Listing and Delisting of Development Districts

The present technique of selecting development districts is to list any local employment exchange area or group of areas as a "district" when the rate of unemployment there is or is likely to become 4.5 percent, and then to delist the district as soon as there appear to be sufficient extra jobs in prospect to bring the unemployment rate down to a reasonable level, provided there is no *immediate* reason to expect it to rise again.[9] This is intended to permit government help to be concentrated on the worst hit areas, in unemployment terms. However, even within the context of the present emphasis on social policy, this approach has its drawbacks. When a firm asks the Board of Trade for financial assistance to move into or expand in a development district, the board always wants to know how many additional jobs will be created as a result of the expansion. Partly this is to meet the requirements of the Local Employment Act of 1960 that the board must pay regard to the cost of official assistance per job created. Partly, however, the information is to help the board keep a check on prospective inroads into unemployment in the development district. Each of these exercises in arithmetic can be tricky, but we are concerned here solely with the question of delisting. Apart from the desire to concentrate assistance, the board's officials are very keen not to oversell an area, that is, they wish to avoid at all costs guiding more firms into a place than can reasonably find labor there. Officials of the board and the chairman of the Industrial Estates Corporation for Wales stressed to the Estimates Committee that it would be ludicrous to offer taxpayers' money to finance the move of several firms into an area and then see those firms fighting each other for the same labor.[10] This is, perhaps, a sound point in theory, but it is exceedingly

---

[7] One survey was the combined effort of several Government departments. It was not published, but was referred to before the recent Estimates Committee. See E.C., Q. 707. The other work was E. Allen, A. J. Odber, P. J. Bowden, *Development Area Policy in the North East of England*, 1957, pp. 65–75, 90–91.

[8] See, for example, E.C., Q. 847, and the report of the Committee on Local Development in Scotland, usually known as the *Cairncross Report*.

[9] E.C., Q. 587.

[10] E.C., Qs. 682–684, 838.

difficult in practice to judge the correct time at which to delist a development district. On a number of occasions, the Board of Trade has been too optimistic about its delisting.[11] It is easy enough, on paper, to calculate that the estimated increase in employment predicted by a firm or number of firms will be enough to justify delisting, but in practice several things can go wrong.

In the first place, the assisted firm's estimate may be wrong. Second, the growth of employment in the assisted firm may be much slower than expected. Third, even if employment growth is as planned, the effect on local unemployment may be less than expected, for any of several reasons. Finally, all may go well in the assisted firm, but something else may go wrong locally. This is quite an impressive list of possibilities, each one of which has actually occurred in one or other of the development districts during the first 2 years of the operation of the 1960 act.

Let us consider the first point, overoptimistic forecasting of labor demand. Though Board of Trade officials check these estimates carefully, in the light of their considerable knowledge of the labor requirements of similar types of firm, they may find it difficult to assess the estimates.[12] While firms may be tempted to exaggerate the extra amount of labor they will employ in a development district, this was not the main cause of error.[13] Calculations had been upset for a wide variety of reasons, including the advent of technical changes after the planning of a new factory, which had reduced the labor to capital ratio. In other instances, there had been changes in the economy after a factory had begun building, changes which had reduced actual sales in relation to expected sales. In some cases, there had been genuine overoptimism in the board room.[14]

A slower-than-planned rate of growth of employment in an assisted firm might arise from any of the above reasons, or from other factors such as bad weather delaying factory building. Again, some businessmen have found the training of labor to take longer than expected. In some cases the pickup of manpower is far slower than planned, and yet there are good reasons to expect that some day the estimated target will be reached. This sort of situation clearly sets a problem, if the estimated increase in employment is likely eventually to mop up most of the local unemployed. The key word is "eventually," for if the area is a fairly remote one to which firms will not go without a Government subsidy, then to delist the area, on the grounds that a firm is growing there and will some day mop up unemployment, is in effect, to earmark the unemployed for that firm and to insure that its labor market is protected. The firm can then man up in a leisurely way. A little more competition for labor might speed things up.

The third point is that even if employment grows as planned the reduction of local unemployment may be less than expected. This can be for one or more of several reasons. New developments may attract migrants back to the region of their birth. Firms may decide to bring in more workers

---

[11] There is a halfway house toward delisting, called stoplisting, but as the chairman of the English Estates pointed out, there is, in effect, very little difference between stoplisting and delisting. For our present purposes they are synonymous. See E.C., Q. 686.

[12] E.C., Qs. 1244, 1306.

[13] E.C., Qs. 265–266, 1306.

[14] E.C., Qs. 670–676, 683, 832–834, 1306–1307.

than originally planned from their factories in other parts of Britain, or they may find surprising numbers of people who are not on the unemployed register at all. Three Board of Trade officials told the Estimates Committee, at different times, that the effect on the local unemployment register of an increase of, say, 1,000 jobs in the locality can vary considerably.[15] The average *local* decrease in unemployment would be less than half the increase in employment, but the precise picture is different from area to area. It would depend first on how many self-employed people, with low income perhaps from farming, might be tempted into factory work for the first time. It would also depend on the activity rates in the local area. Finally, a firm might attract labor from an unexpectedly large area, thus having less effect on local unemployment. This has occurred with the British Motor Corp. factory at Bathgate in Scotland.[16]

The fourth point is that other things are seldom equal. The minutes of evidence taken before the Estimates Committee are full of examples of the unexpected, that is, of a local problem having been "solved" by the advent of a new firm, only to be reopened by the closure of local pits, or shale workings, or steelworks, etc.[17]

One result of these complexities is that several parts of Britain have been listed as development districts, removed from the list (or stop-listed), and put on the list again, all within the space of 2 to 2½ years.[18] It is not surprising that Mr. Sadler Forster, chairman of the English Industrial Estates, should remark, "From the beginning one has felt that the Government were in a hurry to deschedule. There may be good reasons * * * but those of us who are in the firing line think that it is a mistake." [19]

This mistake is no trivial matter of just having to reverse a decision. This "stop and start" policy can deter firms from establishing factories in the development districts. When the Local Employment Act of 1960 replaced the old distribution of industry legislation, certain industrial estates found themselves to be outside the development districts. Firms on these "outside" estates at first had difficulty in obtaining extensions to their factories. When, eventually, the Board of Trade agreed to build extensions, these were at full cover-cost rentals of 10 percent per annum.[20] Discussing this problem with a number of firms, the present writer found a strong feeling among some businessmen that they had been misled. They felt that they had been guided to the estate with Government aid and had thus helped to lower unemployment in the surrounding area to the point where that area was taken off the list. Some of these firms claimed that positive obstacles to expansion had been put in their way, and that expansion was almost as difficult as in the English Midlands. It is hard to assess the sometimes conflicting claims of indignant businessmen, but it is quite clear that the Board of Trade keeps new capital expenditure to a minimum on descheduled

---

[15] E.C., Qs. 175, 338, 835.

[16] E.C., Q. 957.

[17] E.C. Qs. 685, 834, 954–956. These give one example each from England, Scotland, and Wales.

[18] E.C., Report, p. vii.

[19] E.C., Q. 689.

[20] There is no guarantee even of this. It is still possible for extensions to be refused.

estates. Although 40 percent of all estate factories were outside the development districts, during the first 2 years under the 1960 act the board sanctioned the spending of only £0.8 million ($2.25 million) on extensions to these factories, compared with £25 million ($70 million) on factories and extensions on estates inside the development districts.[21] This tough policy had the backing of the Treasury, which has the power, and sometimes uses it, to refuse permission for extensions of approximately 15,000 square feet or over to be built for rent on an estate outside a development district.[22]

All this, and especially the abrupt termination of all prospects of additional subsidies, may seem fair enough to those who think only in rigid terms of a policy of mopping up puddles of unemployment, but it does not seem fair to a firm which has allowed the authorities to persuade it, "with promises of gold," to occupy a factory in a place which was not of the firm's choosing. There may be any number of teething problems in an area which in the long run will turn out to be perfectly suitable for the firm. The mere fact that unemployment around the firm falls to less than 3 or 4 percent does not remove these temporary high costs overnight. Indeed, a fall in unemployment may add to the individual firm's problems.

These events were taken as a lesson by certain firms outside the regions of higher unemployment. The resistance of these firms to moving to a development district was heightened by the fear that the district might soon come off the list, and they would then find themselves stuck in a high-cost location, with no chance of financial help for future expansion from the Government.[23]

Sometimes, in a development district, the board encourages a firm to put in a project in two phases. The firm will then receive financial help for phase two even if the area is taken off the list before phase one is completed. This is a useful technique, but is not enough. Perhaps it should be made explicit that when a district is delisted, there can be no *new* building grants, ordinary grants, loans, or subsidized rents. Firms in their own factories are affected just as are firms on the estates. The former, however, have no spokesmen, so their feelings are rarely revealed. The firms on the estates have their management corporation to express their views to.

The chairman of the Industrial Estates Management Corporation for Scotland was particularly critical of this "stop and start" policy. He pointed out that his estate company was interested in the expanding firms which would want extensions, and might wish more certainty about future subsidized rents. He was quite sure that the uncertainty about delisting was one of the reasons why "quite a number of desirable firms" had not settled in Scotland, and he mentioned certain American firms which had put great emphasis on the need to be clear about the prospective costs of expansion.[24] A witness from the Welsh Estates commented that listing, delisting, and listing again created "uneasiness more than anything else" in the minds of businessmen.[25]

---

[21] E.C., p. 16; p. 19, tables I and II.

[22] E.C., Qs. 584–586.

[23] E.C., Q. 666.

[24] E.C., Qs. 950–953.

[25] E.C., Q. 828.

Although another member of the Welsh Estates Corporation felt that changes in policy did not have very harmful effects,[26] a broad pattern emerges. The three management corporations for England, Scotland, and Wales attack the whole policy of quick delisting because of its deterrent effect on potential clients for their estates, while the three relevant regional controllers of the Board of Trade defend the policy on the grounds that one must not have subsidized firms competing for labor[27] and that the economically more attractive areas must be delisted as quickly as possible so as to concentrate aid in the less attractive ones.[28]

There is a genuine dilemma here, but on balance it seems that policy has been overhasty. One point that has to be faced is that some businessmen in the south and Midlands have a lurking conscience about their failure to do anything to help reduce unemployment in the north. At the same time they know that to open a factory there would be a troublesome business in the initial stages. When cajoled by the Board of Trade to do so, they are glad of excuses for staying put, for packing the machines in the workshop a bit more closely, and adding to the inflationary situation in the Midlands. Thus, they seize on the vagaries of policy as an excuse to sit tight.

Concentration of Development

The obvious way to tackle this whole problem is to concentrate development in the main lines of growth in each region of higher unemployment.[29] If one takes an oversimplified situation, one can visualize an imaginary region made up of 24 "districts." This region is dependent largely on a number of different declining industries. Under present policy one might find that for a year or two areas 5, 6, 9, are scheduled, and are then replaced by areas 8, 12, 20, and then by 17, 18, 22, and so on. The main industrial belt of the region, however, is made up of 7, 11, 15, 19, districts which have better chances of attracting new industry (because this is the area of main roads and large industrial towns), but no chance of being listed, because unemployment in these parts never rises above 4.5 percent. It would be far better to list these areas as development

1	2	3	4
5	6	7	8
9	10	11	12
13	14	15	16
17	18	19	20
21	22	23	24

[26] E.C., Qs. 836–840.

[27] E.C., Qs. 682, 684–685.

[28] E.C., Qs. 831, 838, 954–959.

[29] Except where the sheer size and congestion of the central area makes this impossible. Glasgow is the obvious example. Here the solution must be to build up existing smaller towns which are good industrial locations and, if necessary, build new ones. See *Toothill Report,* especially chap. 18. If new towns must be built, it would seem better to launch one or two big ones than a dozen small.

districts and concentrate the main effort to build up employment in them. As they are central to the various areas which may have "patches" of trouble at various dates, the central area could be guaranteed a 10-year period of development district status. This would be economical in overheads and would help the towns to grow nearer to their optimum economic size. Above all, however, it would, at one stroke, break through the dilemma of not overselling a region while at the same time guaranteeing continuing help to firms which deserve it. For clearly, as there is a 10-year guarantee, there would have to be no hurried rethinking if a firm failed to expand as it had expected, or if it drew its labor from further afield, or if it brought in an unexpected batch of workers from the Midlands, or if a firm elsewhere in the region unexpectedly closed. To build up growth lines would be to give British regional policy something it has lacked for over a decade, a basis of solidarity.

It is important to add that this change of policy would also be desirable on economic grounds. The costs of the operation would be reduced for a number of reasons. First, if we think of the matter from the viewpoint of an Industrial Estates Corporation running a series of estates and sites, it is clear that big estates are cheaper to administer than little ones.[30] This, however, is a small matter compared with the second point which concerns capital costs. Almost any industrial expansion may come up against barriers in the form of capital deficiencies. Whatever these may be, whether shortages of social capital in the form of schools or roads, or more direct capital in the form of gas, water, or electricity, it is cheaper to supply them in a few large places than in a large number of small ones. For example, the recent Estimates Committee was told of a small factory in a fairly remote area of West Durham for which a special electricity cable, 6 miles in length, had to be laid at a cost of £20,000.[31] In Wales, the committee heard of firms at Treforest, the largest industrial estate in the principality, obtaining water and electricity without having to pay a capital contribution and thus finding it cheaper to subsidize the fares of employees who came from a distance rather than to locate the factory near to the source of labor.[32] In addition to these savings in terms of services, firms in or near important industrial towns may have the advantage of proximity to some customers or suppliers, to repair facilities, and to research know-how. Discussions with firms on Tees-side suggest that external economies of scale are very real forces and are wider than is sometimes thought. For example, firms new to the region can pick up advice about apprentice training or about local transport facilities from adjacent firms in completely different industries. On the other hand, new arrivals that are branches of powerful firms established in other regions can bring invigorating ideas to an area and cause existing firms to rethink their attitudes to such things as recruitment and training. In brief, the successful buildup of industry in a few carefully selected centers in a region can have a cumulative effect. Moreover, it will attract workers from the surrounding areas and will increase the population of those centers more nearly to their various optimum population sizes.[33]

---

[30] E.C., Q. 842.
[31] E.C., Qs. 707–708.
[32] E.C., Q. 847.
[33] As defined by Professor Klaassen in part II of this study on the Benelux countries.

There are other advantages of concentration, especially in coal mining districts—and many of Britain's problem areas are in or near mining areas. If the coal has yet to be extracted, then each scattered factory means that a core of coal has to be "sterilized" and compensation paid to the coal board. Grouped factories need in aggregate a smaller area of sterilization. Better still is to locate the factories just off the coalfield.[34] The perils of erecting an isolated factory above worked coal seams were vividly outlined to the committee by the deputy-chief valuer for England and Wales. By the time piling has been carried out and a lot of reinforced concrete has been put in, one ends up with a factory that has cost farm more than its value in the market.[35]

It is clear that, in many cases, the total costs of operating a factory on an isolated site will be higher than in an industrial town in the same region. The solution cannot be to charge all extra costs, where identifiable, to the Treasury. Apart from the accounting problems involved, this would still leave the firm mallocated and would involve extra taxation which again might help to damp down economic growth. Moreover, although there is no fixed limit to the amount of financial help the Board of Trade may offer annually under the Local Employment Act, there must be broad financial limits for any policy of this sort. Thus if the assistance were concentrated in selected towns rather than scattered around the industrial regions of the north of England, Scotland, and Wales, more help could be given in real terms and more employment and growth generated.[36]

ADVANCE FACTORIES

Once this point is firmly taken, other elements in the problem begin to come into line. One of them is the tricky subject of advance factories. These played a part in the first postwar burst of distribution of industry policy in 1945–47, when 55 were built in northeast England alone. Then the policy of building factories in advance of specific demand was abandoned until 1959, when a small start was made with three little units, each of 25,000–30,000 square feet and each in a different rather remote part of Britain. The following year a further three were begun and in mid-1962 it was announced that 10 more would be built. These were again small, 20,000 square feet on the average, and again were away from the main towns of the regions. Then in November 1962 a change of policy occurred. It was announced that nine rather bigger factories, of about 60,000 square feet on the average, would be built "in places which are regarded as being potentially attractive to industry, though at present suffering from unemployment, such as Sunderland and Dumbarton." [37] This appears to be a half-step

---

[34] E.C., Q. 707.

[35] E.C., Q. 1365. In one extreme case, an isolated factory in Wales which cost £780,000 to build, in stages, between 1948 and 1955 was sold to its tenant in 1959 for £400,000, after a careful valuation. Another smaller factory was sold after 7 years at a cost of 40 percent of the initial cost (E.C., p. 46 and Qs. 242–244).

[36] It may be necessary to recall that the present discussion concerns industrial areas, in which the words "remote" and "isolated" refer to places from 10 to 30 miles from an industrial town. It has already been conceded that a genuine social policy may be necessary for genuinely remote areas such as the Scottish Islands. It is fair to say that a small fraction of the increase in national income gained from a more coherent regional policy in the industrial areas would be sufficient to offer considerable subsidies in the truly remote ones.

[37] E.C., Memorandum from Board of Trade, p. 161.

761-932 O—65——24

toward a growth point policy but it is probably only a tiny move forward, because there are still many official doubts about the wisdom of advance factories. It has been argued that it is difficult to tell when a tenant will want a factory, that tenants want much more specialized factories than they did 5 or 10 years ago,[38] that to suit particular tenants may involve the Board of Trade in expensive conversion programs, and that such factories are really needed only "when trade is good." [39]

The Treasury controls the advance factory program,[40] and it is no use telling its officials that the objections are exaggerated. They know that recently built factories and recently vacated ones have been let with surprising ease,[41] they know that expensive modifications to advance factories to meet a tenant's requirements have been very rare.[42] They presumably know that the Estates Management Corporations have considerable experience in knowing what not to put in a factory until a tenant has been acquired. They should know that it is highly desirable that trade be good as often and for as long periods as possible in areas where unemployment is high, for, as argued above, there is no point in applying disinflationary policies to regions which are not suffering from inflation. No matter, for, as one Treasury offical remarked, the risks of building advance factories are such that "the Treasury has kept a pretty firm grip on the program." [43] Certainly, the decision to build 19 new advance factories was clearly not good news to him, for he told the committee that "the program is being stepped up very fast in different business conditions and I would not be too confident about what will happen." [44]

This is a fair example of the timid approach which has hampered regional policy for the last 10 years. If the authorities would take the full stride toward a growth point policy, they might then see that the advance factory program fits squarely at the growth points. Under such a policy, it would be safe to build advance factories wherever they were needed in the growth lines, because these would be the places shown first to visiting businessmen who were contemplating building factories in the region. The effect of concentration of effort would be to reduce risk, for it would greatly increase the number of possible tenants who would look with interest at any one standard advance factory.

The existence of an empty factory, almost ready for occupation, can be an important factor in attracting new industry to a region. This was certainly the situation in the northeast of England in 1945–47, and it could be so again. It is sometimes said that times are different from those early postwar days, for a stock of estate factories has been built up.[45] In actual fact, even in the recession period of mid-1962, only 12 out of over 1,000

[38] E.C., Qs. 937–939.
[39] E.C., Q. 930.
[40] E.C., Q. 1466.
[41] E.C., Q. 1476 (letting of advance factories), Qs. 9–16, 768–776 (letting of vacated factories).
[42] E.C., Q. 1477.
[43] E.C., Q. 1466.
[44] E.C., Q. 1476.
[45] E.C., Q. 567.

estate factories were empty, including at least two tiny ones,[46] so the stock is small. Moreover, one important point which has not been emphasized is that despite the heavy decline in the textile industry in East Lancashire and in Yorkshire, there has been less unemployment resulting there than in Scotland and northeast England from the decline in coal and shipbuilding. This was true between the wars and is true now. There are various reasons for this, one being that a declining textile industry releases married women who are not eligible for unemployment pay and therefore do not register as unemployed. Another reason, however, is that a declining textile industry releases factories suitable for other industries; abandoned mines and shipyards do not, except on a tiny scale. Even in the 1930's some 200 redundant Lancashire cotton mills were occupied by new industries, others followed during the war, and of the 550 cotton mills closed between 1951 and 1960, 400 have been reoccupied by a range of firms estimated to employ 120,000 people,[47] which is more than half of the numbers employed in all the government-owned industrial estates and sites in England, Scotland, and Wales combined.[48]

It is fair to add that the price per square foot of a cotton mill is lower than that of a new factory,[49] but so is the degree of fitness-for-purpose of most mills, in terms of location, age, and general layout. The running costs in terms of maintenance, heating, and lack of compactness are often high.

TRAVEL TO WORK

The acceptance of a growth-line policy implies the acceptance of more travel to work and more transfer of workers from outlying locations in a region. These are the snags which have helped prevent the policy being developed. There would have to be a change of attitude on the part of the local authorities outside the growth lines.[50]

Present policy does recognize that some travel to work is necessary, but only on a limited scale. A firm located or locating in a place near to a development district can obtain aid from the Board of Trade, if it meets other criteria, and if it can show that its plans will provide substantial employment for people living in a development district. The board usually judges the validity of a firm's claim by considering how many of the firm's existing employees live in the development district. Apart from the dubious nature of this assumption that the marginal will be closely related to the average, the whole exercise seems another example, like the 4.5 percent-rule, of the sacrifice of the rational for the administratively convenient. There are all sorts of objections to this approach. The first is that "travel to work distance" interpreted in this way turns out to mean the distance which people in a particular area are accustomed to traveling.[51] It should mean

[46] E.C., Qs. 770–772, 784.
[47] E. G. W. Allen, "Industry in the North West," *Financial Times*, Dec. 4, 1961.
[48] There were approximately 215,000 people employed in Board of Trade owned factories on Feb. 28, 1962. A number of factories, formerly owned by the Board, had been sold to their tenants and the employment therein is not included in this total.
[49] In some cases, mills have changed hands at 5 shillings per square foot compared with a building cost of £3 for a new building.
[50] E.C., Q. 707.
[51] E.C., Q. 136.

the distance which they could reasonable be encouraged and expected to travel. At present, the system strengthens the hand of those people who argue that a factory should be guided to each little pocket of unemployment, regardless of the effects on industrial costs and on the capacity of industry to grow.[52] Second, this approach ignores the "indirect" effects on unemployment in outlying districts. Most simply, a new factory at a growth point will help the surrounding villages if it offers employment to people who are living beside the factory gates but who previously traveled daily to work in one or other of the villages.[53] There are, of course, far more complex ways in which prosperity in one place can spill over into others, as Professor Peacock and Mr. Dosser have indicated.[54]

HOUSING

If growth lines require that more workers be encouraged to move into the more industrialized parts of a region, then they mean more housing. The Toothill report remarks that, according to a Ministry of Labour review commissioned by the Scottish Council, the biggest barrier to the geographical movement of labor is a shortage of housing.[55] This was confirmed by the National Economic Development Council (NEDC) in discussions with industries which had sought to persuade workers to move to jobs in other areas.[56] The need, say these two reports, is to insure that more private and local authority houses are built for workers moving into growing areas. This is a difficult problem; local authorities often have long waiting lists of their own residents for houses. The NEDC report suggests that local authorities should receive a special housing subsidy to build houses for transferred workers and that the existing system of granting certificates of housing need to "key workers" should be extended "to cover suitable unemployed workers willing to transfer to growth areas in the less prosperous regions and other less congested areas subject to the approval of the Ministry of Labour."

The report goes on to advocate bigger transfer grants to the workers themselves. This point will be taken up in the next section. Here two comments need to be made about the NEDC housing suggestion. The first is that in Britain most public authority housebuilding is in the hands of the local authorities: County boroughs, urban districts, and rural districts, some very big, some very small. The Government retains a general control of public authority housebuilding by regulating the supply and price of credit for the purpose, but, within the framework, each local authority is free to build as it decides, and the willingness and ability to build vary very widely.[57]

---

[52] E.C., Q. 844. Two witnesses from the Welsh Estates answered this question on the merits of having more travel to work. The first thought that if travel of half an hour each way were encouraged, a more centralized factory-building policy would ensue. The second witness reflected the more old-fashioned point of view that factories must be near the home.

[53] This was pointed out by a Member of Parliament before the present legislation was enacted. See *Weekly Hansard,* July 2, 1959, vol. 462, cc. 685–686.

[54] A. T. Peacock and D. G. M. Dosser, "Regional Input-Output Analysis," *Scottish Journal of Political Economy,* 1959. See also their article on "The New Attack on Localized Unemployment," *Lloyds Bank Review,* January 1960.

[55] Pp. 110, 188.

[56] NEDC, *Conditions Favourable to Faster Growth,* 1963, pp. 10–11.

[57] This point will be taken up later in conjunction with local authorities' willingness and ability to build roads.

This creates a difficulty for a growth-line policy. It sometimes seems as if certain local authorities in the outlying parts of the regions of higher unemployment have pursued an almost desperate housing "fling" in order to be able to point to their "social capital" as justifying new industry to replace their moribund pits or other declining trades. In a country where the building and contracting industry may turn out to be a bottleneck hampering the efforts to achieve the NEDC's 4 percent-growth target, it may not be possible to continue the complete decentralization of public authority housebuilding decisions. It may be necessary for the Government to take over the decisionmaking, saying where public authority housing shall be built, or at least to create some form of regional authorities to decide for it. This is one aspect of the general point that regional planning needs regional authorities.

The second comment refers to privately owned houses. A worker in a declining area who owns his own house may or may not be willing to move to a growth area; but even if a house is available there, he will be deterred from moving by the knowledge that he will have great difficulty in selling his present home. Indeed, experience indicates that he will inevitably take a loss on the transfer.[58] The answer may be a Government scheme to buy up such houses at some notional regional valuation, for the scheme can hardly be left to local authorities who would be understandably reluctant to operate it.

TRANSFER GRANTS

Many people are strongly opposed to transfer grants, believing that work should always be brought to the workers. As this is not always possible, the compromise in effect at present is to have a tiny resettlement transfer scheme, operated by the Ministry of Labour, in which recipients are given "no more than a contribution to the minimum necessary expenses of removal." [59] If the main emphasis were put on short-distance transfers to growth areas in the same region, public opposition to an enlargement of the scheme might be reduced. In any case, much bigger transfer and resettlement payments are necessary.

TRANSPORT AND COMMUNICATIONS

It is obvious that a growth point policy would mean changes in transport and communication. Bus services would have to become geared to increased commuting to and from the growth points by workers from outlying districts. There is no need to develop these matters in general here, particularly as they have been examined in considerable detail in the Toothill report.[60]

Training

With or without a growth policy, it is clear that a considerable amount of labor retraining will be needed to make workers from declining industries suitable for expanding ones. Since the war, there has been an almost con-

[58] See "Housing and Mobility," *Financial Times,* Apr. 25, 1963.

[59] *Conditions Favourable to Faster Growth,* p. 11. There is, in addition, a National Coal Board scheme for financing the movement of workers from high-cost to low-cost pits.

[60] Ch. 7, "Personal Communication," and ch. 8, "Transport of Goods," together with app. 5–7.

tinuous shortage of skilled labor in this country. The prosperous regions have felt this most acutely, but there are problems in the less prosperous areas too. The Estimates Committee was told by a senior Board of Trade official that "skilled labor is becoming increasingly the main factor preventing a larger dispersal of industry." [61] He later referred again to this problem in relation to Scotland.[62] Over the last few years, if official statistics of unemployment and of vacancies are any guide, Scotland has had an excess of unemployed over vacancies in most skilled trades, and a greater excess than in either Wales or the northern region. However, there is always the question of the "quality" of the unemployed. Skills rust and rapidly get out of date. Moreover, even a recently unemployed electrician from the mines may need retraining before being fitted for a light electrical firm. And, in two important trades, precision fitters and turners, there has been a considerable shortage in Scotland for some years in that the numbers unemployed fall short of the vacancies. In Wales and northern England, these trades are less scarce, but there has been a greater shortage of electrical fitters, sheet metal workers, toolmakers, press toolmakers, and machine tool setters than in Scotland.[63] Many of these trades are "key" trades in the sense that a shortage of such people prevents the employment of a greater number of other skilled and semiskilled men and discourages firms from establishing factories in a region.

As for the supply of labor in the regions of unemployment, since these are areas in which the industrial structure is out of date, there will continue to be a flow of adult labor requiring training in the newer trades. In addition, there is a need for enlarged and improved apprentice training in these regions, for they almost all have had higher-than-average birth rates since before the war.

The point is often made that it is not the Government's job to train workers. If this merely means that "the best place to learn is on the job," it is axiomatic, but it is still an oversimplification. It ignores the fact that industry has for many years failed to train enough skilled men for particular trades. To some extent, this is bound up with Britain's archaic apprenticeship system.[64] In addition, however, there appears to be insufficient retraining in industry.

Recently, the British Government seems to have accepted that training is its business. In a White Paper, reference is made to the continuing shortages of skilled labor, and to the fact that the rise in numbers of apprentices recruited since 1961, though welcome, will still not meet future needs. The report goes on: "A serious weakness in our present arrangements is that the amount and quality of industrial training are left to the uncoordinated decisions of a large number of individual firms. These may lack the necessary economic incentive to invest in training people who, once trained, may leave them for other jobs. While the benefits of training are shared by all, the cost is borne only by those firms which decide to undertake training themselves." [65] Thus one aim of the Government is to break down

[61] E.C., Q. 346.

[62] E.C., Q. 369.

[63] All this ignores the artificial rise in unemployment and fall in recorded vacancies brought about by the abnormally bad winter of 1962–63.

[64] See Lady Gertrude Williams, *Training for Skilled Trades,* 1957, and *Toothill Report,* pp. 114–116, 121–122.

[65] H.M.S.O., *Industrial Training: Government Proposals,* Cmnd. 1892, December 1962, pp. 1–2.

this system whereby firms which do not train batten on those which do.

The Government therefore proposes an improved partnership between itself, industry, and the education authorities so that, first, the scale and range of needs will be better understood; second, the quality of training will be raised; and third, the costs will be more evenly spread. To achieve this, the intention is to enact legislation empowering the Ministry of Labour to set up boards to be responsible for all aspects of training in individual industries. Such boards might establish a general training policy in the industry on such matters as standards for admission; length and standards of training; syllabuses; test for trainees and instructors. In addition, advice and assistance could be available to individual firms, and courses might be established in Government training centers.

On the financial side, the Boards would receive loans or grants from the Ministry of Labour, but the aim is that most of the cost should come from industry by means of a levy on individual firms. On the other hand, firms providing approved training would receive from the board "all or part of the costs incurred" and could earn a rebate from the levy.

In trying to assess the usefulness of these proposals, it is necessary to remember that there are really two problems here. The first is the need to meet immediate labor shortages; the second is to try to plan for the 1980's. Neither of these related tasks is simple; it is difficult to predict even the short-run expansion of demand for certain familiar skills and the contraction in demand for others. However, these difficulties are small compared with trying to judge what the industrial scene will be like in 20 or 30 years' time. Yet it is essential that some attempt be made. Young people starting apprenticeships in the next few years will still be under 40 in 1985, and will then still have over 20 years' working life ahead of them, but the pace of technical change suggests that in many industries today's training will be irrelevant to them.

It is essential, therefore, that we develop a new approach to training. As we cannot hope to know precisely what skills will be needed in the future, we must develop a two-pronged attack. The first aim is to improve the quality of current basic training so as to produce people who are highly skilled and yet still adaptable. The second is to start creating a climate of opinion in which it becomes accepted that it is normal for many people to retrain once or more in their working life.

It is not clear whether the white paper on industrial training is aimed mainly at the short- or the long-run problems. References do occur to the existence of technological progress and to the need for greater adaptability. From the long-term point of view, it is encouraging that the tenor of the white paper suggests that for a start the main emphasis will be on apprentice training and on improving the quality of first year training in particular. The point is made that "if young people on leaving school are given a systematic course of training in the basic skills of their trade, their progress thereafter to full skill will be more rapid and their adaptability within their trade much greater than if they started out on a narrow range of production work." [66]

On the other hand, the white paper says nothing constructive about retraining. Moreover, while it would be overoptimistic to expect any reference to the actual content of courses, it is hardly reassuring to learn

[66] White Paper, p. 5.

that "the major part of the representation [of the boards] would have to be provided by employers and trade unions."[67] These are the very people who have not provided a lead so far. Some representation will come from Government departments and from education. It is to be hoped that persons will be found with experience of training difficulties in countries which have advanced further than Britain in the field of automation. It is often said that we lost our industrial lead because other countries took short cuts by learning from our mistakes. However oversimplified this may be, we now have the chance in the sphere of labor training to learn from theirs. Finally, the Ministry of Labour has a research unit which investigates forward movements in labor demand and supply. This, presumably, will have links with boards and will be given a chance to help modernize British training.

As for the problem of creating a climate of opinion in which it is regarded as normal for people to retrain, we must start from the fact that the present climate is variable to poor. Indeed, the systematic retraining of adults is not nearly so common as it should be. In the northeast of England, the minority of firms which really try to establish a retraining program find that they seem to be training for the whole region, as one industrialist expressed it, and keeping only a small proportion of their output of trained men. This has an inhibiting effect, especially as a 6-month training course may cost about £500 ($1,400) per man.[68] It may be argued that grants can be paid under the Local Employment Act to meet retraining costs. It should be remembered, however, that such grants are only in or near the development districts and are intended to cover only extra costs as compared with the position outside the development districts. Moreover, they are only for specific projects of expansion either by established firms or by newcomers to a development district. What is wanted is that a much greater proportion of the cost of retraining should be taken off the shoulders of individual employers, and that firms should be eligible to claim this reimbursement whether they are undergoing a considerable expansion program involving the building of a factory or extension, or are merely improving the numbers and quality of a particular craft skill. In aggregate, the small contribution of 50 firms to labor retraining is more important than the large contribution of 1. It thus seems highly desirable that the idea of collecting levies from all establishments in an industry and reimbursing those which train should be extended to approved retraining schemes in all areas of Britain regardless of the level of unemployment.[69]

This is one way of helping to break the vicious circle. Another is to establish more Government retraining centers. A few training centers are

---

[67] *Ibid.*, p. 6.

[68] NEDC, *Conditions Favourable to Faster Growth*, p. 25.

[69] Long before the white paper was published, the *Toothill report*, pp. 113, 116, argued for training grants, but only for firms new to a region where unemployment is relatively high. This seems to be an unnecessary limitation, for two reasons. The first is that established firms in areas of high unemployment are entitled to existing grants (except building grants) under the Local Employment Act, and they are logically just as entitled to special training grants as are new arrivals. Of course, it could be that as all but one of the Toothill committee members were businessmen with factories in Scotland, they were reluctant to plead for subsidies for themselves. The second point is that it is just as important that people become used to the idea of retraining in the Midlands as in Scotland. It may be that there is less immediate need for retraining in the Midlands now, but the industrial pattern of this prosperous region suggests that in the fairly near future there will be considerable difficulties arising from technological change. Thus a nationwide scheme is needed.

already operated by the Ministry of Labour. In some, a small number of boys are taking a first-year apprenticeship course before going into the engineering industry for the remaining 4 years of their apprenticeship. Most of these boys are sponsored by engineering employers, so they are really taking part in a demonstration course. Only one center has boys, 24 in all, who are technically unemployed; other centers are for retraining of adults. The Ministry of Labour integrates these courses with Board of Trade policy, for most training is in areas of higher unemployment. Two types of courses are operated. Conversion courses are for people, for example, from the shipyards, who are already skilled, but who need training to work to finer limits. These are short courses. Others, of 6-months' duration, are for people hoping to come into a skilled trade for the first time. Courses vary between centers according to the needs of the region. The 13 centers combined had only 3,000 trainees in them in April 1963, and most of these were disabled or ex-service. Over the whole of Britain only 800 able-bodied unemployed were training in Government centers.

However, in April the Minister of Labour announced in the House of Commons an expansion of facilities in Government training centers.[70] There were to be 18 new centers, two-thirds of them in the less prosperous areas, mainly Scotland and the northeast of England. These 18 new centers will train about 5,000 men a year, mainly in engineering and building crafts. Thus they will not make any great impact on the problem of modifying the climate of opinion, and they do not seem likely to have any great effect on unemployment. As has been said, one difficulty is that there is considerable trade-union opposition to such training schemes, usually at the local level. Opposition takes various forms and is sometimes contradictory. One is told in areas of high unemployment that training encourages migration; that 6 months is not enough to learn a trade, so that employers will not take the men;[71] and that these "dilutees" cause unemployment among skilled craftsmen. Obviously, we are now back to the point that regional growth policy operates best when a national full employment policy is in operation.

It may well be that it is only possible to proceed with caution in building up Government training facilities while both sides of industry become more accustomed to this innovation from the early 1930's. This idea of buildup may not be in the Government's mind, however. The amount of retraining has been small since the second war, but some centers were actually closed in the credit squeeze of 1961—another piece of shortsightedness. The new scheme, 18 centers for 5,000 men, is obviously a policy of a large number of little centers. It is to be hoped that this, instead of the more economical choice of fewer big centers, is not so as to make closure of centers possible in the next credit squeeze. It is also to be hoped that an effort will be made to attract attention to these training centers. The closure of centers in the past on the ground that there was no local demand for their facilities may have been due in part to insufficient local advertising of them. There are signs of a change. The Ministry already operates a scheme with the cooperation of employers under which redundant workers are registered

---

[70] *Weekly Hansard,* Apr. 8, 1963, vol. 675, cc. 930–932.

[71] In point of fact, the trainees are not regarded as fully trained when they leave the center. Even so, it is fair to say that some employers are suspicious of men from the centers. In one firm, management solemnly assured us that they would not take such men because the workers and their stewards would not stand for it. Shop stewards equally solemnly claimed that they were prepared to see a few recruits from the centers, but the managers would not look at them.

at the works before being discharged so as to speed up reemployment. It is now proposed that such workers be told of the existence of retraining centers at the same time. Of equal importance is the question of pay during retraining. The rates have recently been raised. A single man will receive £7 10s. per week and a married man with two or more dependents £9 10s. These figures are still well below the average industrial wage. The principle of maintenance of income during training should be accepted. This could be regarded as part of the price of making retraining acceptable.

The next point to consider is the location of the centers. As far as can be judged from the places named, the 11 centers in the areas of high unemployment reflect a careful balance between "training to the workers" and "training at growth points." While it may be that not all centers should be at growth points, the main emphasis should be there. The aim should be an integrated one of putting the main accessories of growth at the growth points.

The Question of Coordination

It has been argued that to develop growth lines would be a desirable way of tackling regional unemployment. It would facilitate continuity of policy, it would help industrialists to achieve external economies of scale, and it would save in outlay on social capital such as roads and schools. However, it would involve a considerable degree of coordination between Government departments. It is true that the department charged with the main responsibility for raising local employment rates is the Board of Trade. However, we have seen that a more effective approach would involve: a change in housing policy, the responsibility of the Ministry of Housing and Local Government; changes in the resettlement transfer scheme and in training, the responsibility of the Ministry of Labour; a rethinking of our transport and communication policy, the responsibility of the Ministry of Transport. Nor are these all. Other Ministries, from Education to War, could play a part in a coordinated policy of breaking the various bottlenecks which hold back the rate of regional growth. To say this is not to argue that all administrative decisions should bow before the need to develop certain regions of Britain, but merely that there should be sufficient collaboration between departments and awareness of each other's aims to ensure that their actions are consistent with each other.

This is platitudinous enough, except that coordination has not always been achieved in the past. One curious example of this arises in the famous Beeching report on the railways.[72] Though this is not the work of a Ministry, it was called for by the Ministry of Transport in 1961, over a year after the Local Employment Act had been placed on the statute book. It is clear, however, that Dr. Beeching was not asked to worry about that. He says:

> The point has been made in the previous section that there is no proposal to weaken the main line network within the country, so that there will be no inhibition of a general relocation of industry and population as a result of the proposals put forward. It can be argued, however, that relocation on a smaller scale may be affected by closure of lightly used branches and extensions of the main route.
>
> This may conceivably be true, but it must be recognized that most of the lines to be closed have already been in existence for some fifty to a hundred years and their existence has not induced development so far. Indeed, in most cases the trend has been in the opposite direction. Therefore, in formulating proposals for line closure,

---

[72] British Railways Board, *The Reshaping of British Railways,* part I, Report H.M.S.O., April 1963.

all the Railway Regions have taken account of any developments which are sufficiently specific to be probable, but have not been influenced by quite unsupported suggestions that something might happen some day.[73]

This may be a case of "doing good by stealth," for it is clear that by proposing the keeping open of the main lines and the closing of a large number of branch lines, Dr. Beeching is advocating a policy that would make the buildup of scattered development districts more difficult and would increase the need for a growth point approach. Even so, these are proposals that go directly against the policy to which the Board of Trade was committed during the whole time the Beeching report was being prepared.[74] However, there is little here which would clash with the development of growth lines, except for the possibility that the closure of certain railway branches might reduce the ability of workers to commute from the outlying parts of the region. This would probably mean more buses and more houses at the growth points.

While on the problem of communication, it is worth examining the findings of the Select Committee on Estimates, Trunk Roads, in 1959.[75] These suggest a disturbing lack of coordination even in the road program itself. In its report the committee comments:

The concept of a "national route system for through traffic" which the Trunk Roads Act (1946) and Special Roads Act (1949) have sought to create implies a centralized direction and the assessment of priorities amongst competing regional claims which should result in a balanced and fair allocation of the resources available throughout the country. No special organization exists to administer this program direct and the Ministry have avowedly taken advantage of the pre-existing local authority system. * * * Your Committee have considered whether this system is adequate to meet the nation's needs.[76]

The result of their considerations reveals the weakness of using local authorities, large, medium, and small, as agents of the Ministry.[77] In the first place, small authorities may lose their place in the queue because of a shortage of first-rate staff. Second, wealthy authorities may seek to jump the queue of road plans by preparing schemes in advance of the Minister's request.[78] Third, the committee commented that while many county boroughs are only too anxious to carry out works, they had discovered "one case of a major trunk road scheme being endangered by the reluctance of an Authority to continue the development satisfactorily within their boundary." [79] The committee was therefore understandably "concerned at a situation where certain local bodies are in a position to frustrate the full implementation of a national plan at points, generally speaking, where improvements are most urgently needed."

This uneven attitude of local authorities to road-building is very similar to their approach to house-building. Writing in the same year as the Trunk

---

[73] *Ibid.*, p. 57.

[74] It is amusing that this direct clash with Board of Trade policy should arise from an approach so similar to that taken by the Board of Trade in selecting development districts—in both cases, only specific future developments are allowed to influence policy proposals.

[75] *First Report from the Select Committee on Estimates,* Session 1958–59, Trunk Roads.

[76] *Committee on Trunk Roads report,* p. IX, par. 21.

[77] *Ibid.*, pars. 22–26.

[78] For a successful example of this, see p. VII, par. 12 and Qs. 237–259.

[79] See also *ibid.*, Qs. 787–788.

Roads report, but without having seen it, the present writer criticized the Minister of Housing for failing to ensure that most house-building in the less fortunate regions was in the expanding areas thereof. To quote, "it is not enough for the Minister of Housing to say that he has 'told nearly every local authority in England and Wales that it can have the full program [of house building] it was asked for.' He unwittingly condemns his own policy by adding in the next sentence, 'If more houses are needed, the initiative lies with the local authorities to ask for them.' *This ignores the fact that not all local authorities are farsighted, not all are willing or able to build sufficient houses for future local needs and some are far too willing.* Moreover, showing the green light to all now may mean that their plans will be mutually incompatible again by 1960. There is thus a case for more central control of publicly-owned house building to determine the locations, even if the actual building and letting is left largely in local hands."[80]

These experiences suggest the need in Britain for regional governments. *The Economist* recently pointed out that the British people think of their town and then of the Nation; between the two there is nothing except county boundaries which lack any logic.[81] The article goes on to advocate regional bodies with power to pick their growth points for the future. One would add that they would also need power to insure that houses are built at those growth points and roads built to them.

This would still fail unless government departments are mindful of the needs of growth points in the less fortunate regions. Regional governments, however eager, cannot insure that trunk roads are built or improved unless the relevant Ministry decides to sanction the road. On this point, the "Memorandum on behalf of the Ministry of Transport and Civil Aviation" submitted to the Committee on Trunk Roads is disturbing.[82] It states that the major constructional program has concentrated on the needs of heavy industrial traffic. This is based on the latest information about traffic trends, in turn partly based on inadequate research on urban traffic flows.[83] The memorandum makes no reference to future possible industrial developments or to Board of Trade policy, though the resurrection of distribution of industry policy had been heralded a few months previously by the enactment of the Distribution of Industry Act, 1958.

The weakness of the Ministry of Transport's technique of predicting the future from the past is enhanced by the fact that the whole road-building program in Britain is in arrears in relation to needs. Thus the main pressure on traffic flows is in the congested south. Therefore, this method of approach puts the emphasis on building in the south, too. The first motorway of any length built in Britain was that from Birmingham to London, and it retained its lonely eminence 3 years later, thus helping to perpetuate the pattern of southern prosperity and northern recession.

The sharp rise in unemployment in the northeast in 1962 brought the decision to build the Durham motorway earlier than had previously been planned. However, this decision does not seem to be the beginning of a

---

[80] A. J. Odber, "Local Unemployment and the 1958 Act," *Scottish Journal of Political Economy,* 1959, p. 227. The quotations within the quotation are from *Official Report,* June 30, 1959, vol. 462, c. 225.

[81] "Working up Britain," *The Economist,* May 11, 1963, p. 520.

[82] *Committee on Trunk Roads, Report,* pp. 1–8.

[83] *Ibid.,* p. VI, par. 8. It should be noted that more research has gone on since.

new phase of coordination between departments. It is, instead, a piecemeal public works approach, mainly designed to mop up local unemployment.

In addition to their role in developing the infrastructure, government departments are able to influence the level of employment in less fortunate regions directly. The Ministry of Aviation, the Admiralty, and the War Department are all able to do this by their placing of munitions contracts. On the whole, however, these Service departments have stuck to the economic doctrine of buying in the cheapest market.

An example of this is a reply of the Civil Lord of the Admiralty to a question in the House of Commons. When asked would he offer a disproportionately heavy share of the naval shipbuilding program to Scotland, he said he would bear in mind Scotland's position, but that the allocation of orders depended primarily on the prices quoted in reply to tenders.[84]

On the same day, the Secretary of State for War had refused to enable Scottish firms to manufacture, under license, the new Belgian machinegun. This gun was to be made at the Royal Ordnance factory in Enfield near London.[85] This was a small order, but it is fair to say that the decision is typical of the War Ministry, which seems to adhere strictly to commercial principles.

A slightly more flexible attitude is sometimes shown by the Ministry of Aviation. Two days after the replies from the two other Service Ministries, the Minister of Aviation told a questioner that the V.C. 10 contract for the R.A.F. had been divided between a firm in Belfast and one in Weybridge. The division would involve duplication of tools and would add about 9 percent to the cost of the program. The Government had authorized this additional expenditure in order to help provide employment in northern Ireland (where unemployment is well above the national average).[86]

There is a clear need to be careful about this. There are limits to any policy of not giving production contracts to the lowest bidder. The Toothill report, while advocating that specifications should be drawn up in such a way as to enable firms not previously in the field to tender, advocates that there should be no change in the present rules.[87] At the same time, it advocates that more Government research establishments should be located in the problem regions and that more of the funds expended on research carried out for the Government in private industry should be in such areas.[88]

This division between production contracts and research contracts is an artificial one. Many production contracts enable a firm to achieve a knowledge without which a research contract cannot be efficiently executed, and vice versa. The present system of awarding production contracts to the lowest bidder is based on too short-run a point of view. On the whole, it is easier for firms near to the Ministries and Research Departments to win contracts. This is not necessarily to argue the importance of lobbying, but rather the advantages of close liaison once contracts are awarded. Given that, the firms winning contracts acquire "know-how" which is useful

---

[84] *Weekly Hansard,* Apr. 3, 1963, vol. 675, cc. 438–439, corrected by Apr. 5, 1963, c. 779.

[85] *Weekly Hansard,* Apr. 3, 1963, vol. 675, oral answers, c. 441.

[86] *Weekly Hansard,* Apr. 5, 1963, vol. 675, written answers, c. 84.

[87] *Toothill Report,* p. 165.

[88] *Ibid.,* pp. 166–9.

to further contracts. The result is that a closed circuit is set up, or rather a happy ingroup and a not so happy outgroup. This is important not merely for war work, as many electronic contracts facilitate processes and products which are of great value to civilian production. Thus, the ingroup has a considerable advantage. A coordinated regional policy would require Service Ministries to take a long-term view and to offer both research and production contracts to firms at or near growth points, and in the case of production contracts, to offer them at tender prices slightly above the minimum. No enormous change of principle would be involved, for already, where it is thought advisable to increase the production capacity of an industry, firms may be encouraged to become more solidly based in that industry by the granting of contracts on a negotiated basis for a while.

Firms given a contract at a slightly lenient price would have to show promise of becoming competitive in a number of years. It would probably be necessary to burden BOTAC with the duty of assessing this. It might even be necessary to overcome the inhibitions of the Service departments by empowering the Board of Trade to meet the extra cost of such contracts out of its expenditure under the Local Employment Act.

These comments in no way invalidate the argument in the Toothill report that more Government research establishments should be located in the regions of higher unemployment to help boost the growth of new technologies there. Indeed, the policy could go further than that. There is a strong case for transferring more Government departments or sections of departments from London to the less fortunate provinces of Britain. This point, however, can be left until we come to consider the whole problem of controlling commercial developments.

One obvious danger, if much of the effort to stimulate economic growth in problem regions is initiated by Government departments, is that local initiative may be reduced. Already in certain areas of high unemployment there is far too great a tendency for people to say that "they" should do something. It is vital to insure that local morale does not falter. Thus, encouragement and finance should be given for local self-help in making an area more attractive to industry.

For example, the Board of Trade has power under the Local Employment Act to acquire and improve derelict land. These powers are hardly ever used,[89] for the responsibility rests mainly on local authorities, which receive only 50 percent of the cost from the National Exchequer. Local authorities in declining areas cannot generate sufficient income for such purposes. The Toothill committee, in criticizing the 50 percent rule, advocated that the central grant should be raised to 80 or 90 percent.[90] The Government accepted this in the budget of 1963. The actual grant will be 85 percent in development districts. There seems to be no good reason why the grant should not be 100 percent of the reasonable cost of approved improvement schemes. Finally, while priority should be given to removing industrial scars in or near growth points, there is no reason why the 100 percent grant should be limited to such locations or even to regions of higher than average unemployment.

---

[89] About £5,000 was spent in 1961–62, and the estimate for expenditure in 1962–63 was £500. See E.C., Qs. 945–946.

[90] *Toothill Report,* pp. 147–148.

Having considered the creation of growth points, it is logical now to take up the matter of how to get firms to go there. This problem will be tackled in two sections. The first will consider the question of financial inducements; the second, that of the active approach to businessmen.

The first point, of course, is that the amount of subsidization and of loans should be known precisely and quickly to the firms seeking them. There have been many complaints of delays and uncertainties in the past. However, these seem to have been caused partly by certain firms coming forward with vague schemes; partly by shortages of land; partly by the official channels, including BOTAC, being flooded by a sudden surge of demand for finance after the resuscitation of policy after 1958; and partly, particularly for building grants, by the clumsy nature of the concession. There is every reason to assume that each of these causes of delay has been reduced recently. Certainly the responsible authorities seem to be aware of the problems and to be tackling them constructively.[91] Further improvements could be made. For example, the system under which Estates Management Corporations draw up plans for prospective tenants while District Valuers negotiate rents seems to be unnecessarily cumbersome.[92]

A second improvement would arise if more authority were delegated from the Treasury. For example, any industrial estate factory or extension costing over £150,000 ($420,000) has to have individual Treasury approval. Although the majority of factories are below this size, the majority of estate employment is in factories above it. Moreover, as costs rise, smaller and smaller factories will need individual approval, and as techniques change, a given factory size means fewer and fewer workers.[93] At present, on the Scottish estates this rule means that on average a factory for more than about 200 workers has to be approved by the Treasury.[94] The figure of £150,000 should be doubled or trebled. Equally, in view of the Treasury's timid approach to advance factory building, there seems good reason for delegating authority to the Board of Trade for the erection of advance factories up to, say, 75,000 feet at growth points. Indeed, the whole range of policy should be reviewed to see how much loosening up is possible for the financial chains which bind the Board of Trade and the Estates Management Corporations. This would not lead to extravagance or even to increased errors in advance estimating of expenditure. The senior Treasury witness told the Estimates Committee: "Sometimes we cut down too much. In 1961–62 the Board [of Trade] had to come for a supplementary as a result of our reducing the estimate." [95]

Perhaps the best solution to the problem would be radically to modify the whole system under which finance is made available to the Board of Trade. Finance for all expenditures under the Local Employment Act comes from above the line in the annual budget. This means that it is all

[91] E.C., Qs. 854–862, 876–877, 927–936, 940–944, 1209–1212. See also the section on Recent Changes" below, where the replacement of building grants by a simpler system is discussed. This impending change was announced in the April budget.

[92] See E.C., Q. 904.

[93] E.C., Q. 891.

[94] E.C., Qs. 584, 972.

[95] E.C., Q. 1524.

regarded as current expenditure, despite the fact that probably the bulk of it goes into the highly tangible form of factory buildings. If expenditure were transferred to below the line, so that the Board of Trade, in its execution of local employment policy, were put on the same more flexible basis as the Post Office and nationalized industries, two advantages would follow. The first is that the board would be able to concentrate a little more on a long-term policy and a little less on getting annual estimates right and on trying to convince the Estimates Committee that it is not possible to show how many jobs have been created today by money spent yesterday. The second point is that the change would make possible a more sensible approach to the question of cost per job.

On the first point, one can hardly blame an Estimates Committee for worrying about estimates, but the Board of Trade demonstrated that there are many reasons why it is never possible to predict the level of spending over 12 months. One official pointed out that it may take several years to plan and build a factory and to get the final bill in. Thus, while it was possible to predict the total cost, it was not possible to tell how much expenditure would come into a particular year. "The difficulty arises owing to the constitutional requirements of estimating for Parliamentary purposes on an annual basis when the practical planning has to be done over a period of perhaps 4 to 5 years.[96] Again, as the estimates are in water-tight compartments, they may be thrown out by the decision of a big firm to ask for an estate factory on an amortization basis instead of a building grant.[97] As a result, the Board of Trade has to lend 100 percent of the cost of the factory, instead of making a gift of 10 percent. There are many other ways in which estimates may go astray; the only thing they seem to have in common is that they show the futility of the system of annual estimating, for the errors are certainly in no way fundamental to policy.[98]

The other way in which a transfer to below the line accounting would help is that it might encourage the creation of a more sensible method of calculating "cost per job." The Board of Trade is required by the Local Employment Act to have regard "to the relationship between the expenditure involved and the employment likely to be provided." As we have seen, each firm applying for help has to estimate the number of jobs likely to result from the project. The Board of Trade assesses the amount of Government expenditure involved. Neither of these two concepts of "employment" or "cost" is at all clear, and when they are brought together a most confused and confusing picture emerges. Here, although they are the two sides of the same equation, they will be treated separately, taking the problem of measuring cost first, and assuming for the moment that the word "job" is meaningful. To quote from the report of the Estimates Committee:

> In general they [the Board of Trade] regard as reasonable any develoment on which the total gross expenditure of public money does not exceed £1,500 [$4,200] for each job estimated to be provided. Only in very exceptional circumstances is expenditure above £2,500 [$7,000] per job considered as reasonable.

---

[96] E.C., Q. 538.

[97] E.C. Q. 558.

[98] E.C., p. XIV; pp. 6–7, pars. 23–27; pp. 8–9, pars. 31–32; p. 10, par. 39; p. 11, pars. 45–46; p. 12, par. 52; Qs. 82–88, 533–538, 553–560, 604–611, 642–648, 1055–1074, 1521–1524, 1531–1535.

The Treasury are also concerned with the question of cost per job. All projects estimated to cost more than £1,000 [$1,400] per job—the Treasury regard this as a more normal cost than the figure of £1,500 chosen by the Board of Trade—have to be submitted to them for approval.[99]

We are not concerned here with the usual Treasury supercaution, but with the whole fantastic way of calculating cost per job. For this disagreement between the Treasury and the Board of Trade as to whether £1,500 or £1,000 per job is reasonable is almost meaningless. This is the *gross* cost, the aggregate of factory building costs or building grant, plus loans plus grants. Thus, it is a horrible jumble of unaggregatable figures.[1] If a firm which ran its accounts in this way applied for a loan BOTAC would almost certainly have no hesitation in refusing it.

The Board of Trade, of course, is aware that the real cost per job to the taxpayer depends on how the aid is offered,[2] that is, that grants are very different from loans, and that the relevance of the cost per job depends on the degree of capital-intensity in the firms applying for financial aid.[3] At the same time, in operating the assessment of cost per job, the Board of Trade approach seems to be somewhat mechanical. One official told the select committee that "the practice is to allow £1,500 fairly much on the nod and to look more closely between £1,500 and £2,500 at which point we say it is too expensive." [4] Moreover, the board does not attempt to cost out the net charge to the taxpayer of total grant plus building grant (or capitalized value of subsidy on estate factory rent) plus capitalized value of loan interest rate subsidy. These, together with a risk element, are the true long-run costs to the taxpayer. The Board of Trade argued that such calculations cannot be made.[5] Agreed they are difficult, and would involve a little guesswork about future bad debt, but it is surely better to work out a range of meaningful figures than to operate on a precise, but meaningless, calculation.

This is not a quibble; the present system could lead to unjustified refusals of aid. That it apparently has not done so yet may have arisen from the fact that the Board of Trade Ministers gave instructions that for certain motorcar firms their officials were not to consider "the reasonableness of the cost per job." [6] The officials themselves apparently accepted that their own criterion, of over £2,500 per job being too expensive, was unreasonable for such firms,[7] but they still had to have a ministerial rule. All in all, the gross cost per job system is misleading and should be scrapped, and one

---

[99] E.C., *Report,* p. VIII.

[1] It would seem, for example, that a firm asking for an estate factory might come out with "too high" a cost per job ratio, while if, for the same project, it planned to build its own factory and wanted a building grant, the calculation would come out on the right side. This is because the whole cost of an estate factory is put into the cost-per-job equation, while for the private factory only the building grant, i.e., 15 to 20 percent of factory cost, is so included. This may bias firms into choosing to build for themselves, when it would be more sensible for them to rent an estate factory.

[2] E.g., E.C., Qs. 278–279.

[3] E.C., Qs. 162, 166, 173, 257–260.

[4] E.C., Q. 1309. See also Q. 162.

[5] E.C., Qs. 1049–1053.

[6] E.C., Q. 317.

[7] E.C., Q. 318.

761-932 O—65——25

feels that if board officials were not subjected to the pressures of annual estimating, they would have found a better guide for themselves.[8]

So much for the cost side of the equation. Now we can consider the job side. The point that it is exceedingly difficult to predict how many jobs will be created by a given amount of capital expenditure has been examined in the section on the listing and delisting of development districts in this chapter. There is no need to add to the arguments, except to say that they were concerned solely with the creation of employment in the firm spending the money. Just as meaningful is the local multiplier effect. Occasionally this can be more important than the direct effect. One such instance is a proposed new paper mill at Fort William in Scotland. As the president of the Board of Trade said, "the mill itself would not provide sufficient employment to qualify for facilities under the Local Employment Act to se the project through. On the other hand, if we get the project going it will provide a great deal of employment in the forests and ancillary transport industries * * * . If we could have done this under the Local Employment Act, we would have done so." [9] To achieve this "invigorating and permanent effect on the economy of the Highlands," [10] therefore, needed special legislation to itself.

So we now have instances, in the motor industry, where the "cost" limitations of the equation, imposed by the Treasury, had to be overriden by a Minister of the Crown, and one instance where the "job" side of the equation, imposed by the act itself, had to be overridden by a special act of Parliament. The concept of "cost per job" is well-nigh meaningless. The best solution would probably be to repeal this hampering section of the legislation.

Finally, in this whole question of the operation of financial inducements, we come to the question of discrimination between applicants. The official line is that there can be no discrimination, in similar locations, between applicants. Of course, each firm must pass the test of creditworthiness and, within the limits discussed above, attention is paid to the question of capital intensity. Beyond this, the official policy is not to give special concessions to small firms, or to firms in particular industries.[11] In fact, this principle seems to be strictly adhered to for estate factory rents, but not for loans. The curious situation arises that a small firm which borrows money may be allowed a little "tempering of the wind," [12] while a small firm in an estate factory pays the same rent per square foot as a large one.[13] This is on the ground that if one firm is offered a concession, all must be. Otherwise there is discontent among tenants.[14]

Either rents and interest rates should be equally flexible or equally rigid. On the whole, it seems best to aim for a little flexibility. Provided that estate rents, in general, reflect current market value, there is no reason why small firms in nursery factories (or nest factories as they are called in Scot-

---

[8] The author of sec. C of NEDC, *Conditions Favourable to Faster Growth,* seemed to find no great difficulty in describing the problems of subsidies to firms in terms of net cost.

[9] *Weekly Hansard,* Apr. 4, 1963, vol. 675, cc. 665–666.

[10] *Ibid.*

[11] E.C., Qs. 33–36, 60–62, 257, 571–572, 582–583.

[12] E.C., Qs. 616, 1499.

[13] E.C., Q. 62.

[14] E.C., Qs. 571–572, 578–583.

land) of 1,200 to 5,000 square feet should not receive a rent concession. This would hardly cause the big motorcar firms to gnash their teeth in envious rage. Moreover, although in the past there have been a number of failures of small estate tenants, there have also been firms, on a number of estates in England, Scotland, and Wales, which have started in a small way and come to have 500, 700, or 900 employees. It needs only a minority of small firms to do this for the whole exercise in flexibility to be worth while.[15]

Discrimination could have a second and more important aspect, that of choosing between industries to be encouraged at the growth points. At present, with the emphasis on the social policy of steering industry to the place where unemployment is highest, little or no attention is given to the question of selection.[16] However, it is now timely to recall that regional policy should have more than one objective, that the aim should be partly to remove unemployment as a social evil and partly to facilitate national economic growth. Thus, it is important to take up a point made by Peacock and Dosser when critically examining present policy in Britain. They argue that an expansion of employment and incomes in a region, as a result of Government policy, will generate a demand for consumer goods, but the benefit to the region of this multiplier effect will depend on the patterns of consumption and production. Thus, if incomes and employment rise in parts of Scotland, much of the extra income may be spent on goods made in England. Indeed, as the production of consumer durables is largely concentrated in the areas of lowest unemployment in England, any *general* attempt to cure northern unemployment will lead to increased inflation in Birmingham and London.[17] In brief, in so far as one important reason for reducing the irregularities of income between regions is to facilitate economic expansion without inflation, this form of cure is worse than the disease. The answer, say Peacock and Dosser, is to try to guide to the areas of higher unemployment industries that make products for which there is a high income elasticity of demand in the country as a whole.

Given the apparent political difficulties of discrimination, the most that could be expected would be some form of loose, informal quota system, designed to insure that a larger proportion of the expansion at growth points was in industries with a high income elasticity of demand. This would be much easier, of course, if rather more firms were interested in locating factories in the less fortunate regions.[18] On this, four comments can be made. The first is that continuing high employment and activity in the country as a whole makes firms more aware of the bottlenecks in the more prosperous regions. Second, a policy of building up growth points, and of eliminating bottlenecks there, would make more firms aware of the advantages of locating at them. Third, this problem posed by Peacock and Dosser may strengthen the case for the Service Ministers having a slightly lenient approach to tenders for production contracts put in by firms located in areas of higher unemployment. Many of the skills acquired by electronics firms through such contracts are of great value in the production of modern

---

[15] E.C., Qs. 904–912.
[16] E.C., Qs. 33, 47, 65–67, 145–151, 872.
[17] See A. T. Peacock and D. G. M. Dosser, "The New Attack on Localised Unemployment," *Lloyds Bank Review,* January 1960, p. 24.
[18] See E.C., Qs. 47, 145–151, 868–872.

electronic equipment for which the income elasticity of demand is high. Fourth, if there is to be any policy of selection of firms to be guided to growth points, the Board of Trade will have to play a more active part in finding new customers than it does at present.

The Guidance of Industry to Growth Points

Before considering the need for a more active role by the Board of Trade, one or two more general points need discussing. The resistances to moving on the part of businessmen are an amalgam of prejudice, inertia, and economic and social considerations. Here again, research can help by trying to find out why firms which have contemplated opening a factory in an area of high unemployment have decided not to do so. There is also the question of why so many firms in congested areas have apparently never contemplated moving. Such research might give the authorities some idea as to priorities among the various ways in which both the regional infrastructures and liaison between Government departments could be improved.

Beyond this, a knowledge of how businessmen view the matter might give the Board of Trade a more positive approach to local unemployment problems. At present, its main weapon against industry is the industrial development certificate.[19] It is generally accepted, in Britain, that there is a good case for this power to prevent firms establishing new factories or extensions in the more congested parts of Britain, and over the last few years it has been applied fairly stringently. It is curious, however, that the policy is limited to a control over building factories.[20] There is no reason why there should not be a control over the taking over of empty factories, and a control over the building of offices. Consideration of the latter will be deferred to the next section.

The control over the purchase of existing factories might not be easy to operate. It would involve the development of a system under which the Board of Trade could buy up premises which are being vacated. The main snag is that this would bring the District Valuer into the picture in order to calculate "current market value." One feels that in congested London, where prices are rising steadily, the valuer's assessment of "current market value" would always lag behind actual value in the market. This would act as a deterrent to any firm which wanted to transfer out of London to a growth point in the regions of high unemployment. It would seem, therefore, that for such a firm a special bonus would have to be awarded, as a reward for good conduct, over and above "current market value."

We can now turn to the question of initiative, in relation to the transfer of firms to development districts. It seems that regional controllers of the Board of Trade sometimes remind firms in the Midlands which show "signs that they are thinking about expanding" that their chances of being allowed an IDC in that region are poor, and that there are such places as development districts.[21] There does not, however, appear to be any concerted plan about this. The normal procedure is to sit back and wait for firms to apply for an IDC and then to refuse it, or at least to write indicating

---

[19] See pp. 15–16 and p. 53, above.

[20] And the conversion of storage space to factory premises.

[21] E.C., Qs. 342–343.

that a refusal will be highly likely.[22] This was true even of the motor vehicle firms, the guidance of whose expansion plans to the development districts has been the biggest action under the 1960 act.[23] Moreover, the Board of Trade does not regard as part of its duties the actual encouragement of suppliers and customers to locate factories in development districts near to where key firms are building. They did not, for example, go out after the subcontractors of the motor car industry. Chasing them is regarded as the duty of the car firms themselves and of the regional development councils.[24] These councils include the Scottish Council (development and industry), the Lancashire and Merseyside Industrial Development Association, the North East Development Council, etc. These are voluntary bodies, backed with finance from local authorities, industry, and trade unions in their region, which carry out research,[25] try to keep government departments on their toes, and seek out firms in the prosperous areas which they think can be encouraged to open a factory in the region for which the particular council is acting. They do valuable work and are encouraged (but not financially) by the Ministries. The Government line seems to be that the development councils should find the new firms for their region, the Board of Trade should supply the subsidies, and the Industrial Estates Management Corporation should look after the new tenants, if they opt for estate factories.

The big weakness of this system is that it hands over the initiative for finding newcomers to the development districts to bodies which have not had years of experience in administering to estate tenants, as have the management corporations, and which have no access to Government funds and so cannot talk authoritatively about the subsidies available to firms moving to the districts.

The Estimates Committee, 1962–63, recommended that more use should be made of the experience of the Management Corporations and that these bodies "should be given a positive part to play in the task of encouraging industry to settle in development districts." [26] It is clear that this would be welcomed by the corporations themselves,[27] and it would seem to be a useful move. There remains the question of the Board of Trade. The committee did not make any suggestions as to changes in its role, beyond recommending an even tighter use of IDCs. The committee commented that "the use of industrial development certificates is clearly the cheapest way of achieving the objects of the act." [28] This may not be true. If the use of IDCs leads to a firm expanding nowhere, the results may be cheap for the Government accounts and expensive for the nation. Thus, IDCs ought to be used as part of a coordinated process. The present technique of waiting for firms to apply for IDCs in the low unemployment areas, of refusing a certificate, and of advising firms to go to a development district is much too piecemeal. The result of this system is that numbers of firms make a grand tour of the development districts with no intention of settling

---

[22] E.C., Qs. 518–522, 1108.
[23] E.C., Q. 325.
[24] E.C., Qs. 924–925.
[25] Outstandingly, the *Toothill report* of the Scottish Council.
[26] E.C., *Report*, p. X.
[27] E.C., Qs. 694–700 (English Corporation), 849–853 (Welsh Corporation).
[28] E.C., *Report*, p. XV.

there, but solely to be able to strengthen their claim for an IDC on their existing site in the south. Such firms occupy the valuable time of development councils and of Board of Trade staffs in the north—time which could have been better devoted to the serious seekers after sites in the less fortunate regions.

More coherence would emerge if the Board of Trade went out to sell the growth points to the right sort of industry. It should seek access to the investment plans of all major firms in the relevant trades, in each region. After all, if it knows the plans of all the electrical goods firms in one prosperous area, it may know that collectively these firms would run into an acute shortage of labor. By calling a conference, the board could exhort the firms, collectively, to direct at least some of their expansion to other places. There is more hope of cooperation from businessmen who are shown, together, that their schemes are incompatible than from men who are individually refused permission to execute their seemingly achievable plans.[29]

Commercial Employment and the Congested South

The point was made earlier that there was a good case for transferring certain government departments, or parts thereof, from London to the regions where unemployment is relatively high. In certain of these areas there is a shortage of office jobs.[30] There is some evidence that the present Government is coming round to this view. Already, it has started to transfer the Post Office Savings Certificate Division to Durham City, and in April it was announced that Sir Gilbert Flemming, a former civil servant, was reviewing all the headquarters work of government departments located in London, and would advise the Government on what work could be moved elsewhere. The aim was "to obviate the great overcrowding of office space in London" and to give employment outside.[31] There is some scope for Sir Gilbert, for only 25,000 of some 125,000 headquarters staff in the civil service work outside London.

This, however, is only part of the problem of employment in congested London. The main problem is the growth of employment in offices. A recent white paper makes the point that since the mid-fifties, nearly 40,000 new jobs a year have been created in the London conurbation, of which only 20 percent were in manufacturing industry. The big increase has been in service employment, particularly office employment, and at least 15,000 new office jobs are being created annually in central London alone.[32]

---

[29] The policy of waiting for firms to apply for an IDC was modified for the first time in April 1963, when the president of the Board of Trade announced that he and his colleagues would meet the chairmen of 100 major companies with growth prospects in order to tell them about the development districts. *Weekly Hansard*, Apr. 4, 1963, vol. 675, c. 664. This is a useful first step, but it ignores the need to build up a high local income multiplier in regions with idle resources. It also ignores the fact that such individual meetings will not be as effective as a number of local conferences. There will still be no point at which it becomes obvious to the chairmen that the total local planned expansion is impossible, no point at which to seize the initiative and propel some of these plans into areas of higher unemployment.

[30] For a period prior to the recession of 1958, the unemployment rate among white-collar workers in the Newcastle area was greater than among manual workers.

[31] *Weekly Hansard*, Apr. 2, 1963, vol. 675, c. 247.

[32] *London, Employment: Housing: Land*, Cmnd. 1952, February 1963, pp. 3–4.

It is worth making the point that not only are there far more offices than factories in central London, but that, area for area, an office block creates far more employment, and thus congestion, than does a factory. It seems that over the years 1946–58 each thousand square feet of factory space in Metropolitan London was for 1.3 workers, while each thousand square feet of office space in the central area was intended for 8 workers. Moreover, offices are usually multistory, while factories usually have only one or two floors. It is clear, therefore, that if IDC's are a necessary weapon in Britain, commercial development certificates are even more essential barriers to urban congestion. Yet the authorities have consistently refused to implement a system of CDC's. Indeed, until 1963, it can be said that the control of commercial building has been a problem which the Central Government in Britain has always ducked. When challenged, Board of Trade officials either take shelter behind the local employment act, by pointing out that it limited the IDC to factories, or they say that commercial development certificates are impracticable.[33] This claim is based on the argument that IDC's are awarded or withheld on the test of what is to be made in the proposed factory. Unfortunately, most offices are built by speculators and "one has very little information about what particular company will operate in that office." The only sensible reply to that comment is "so what?" One has very much information about what particular consequences have arisen from the spate of office buildings in London. The fact that most offices in London are built to let is no real problem. The solution is to put the onus on the would-be developer to show that his proposed office block is indispensable enough to merit a commercial development certificate.

The authorities will not recognize this.[34] Despite the admission that the main growth of employment in London is in offices, and that this "is bringing formidable transport, housing and financial problems in its wake",[35] which affect the lives of every Londoner, the white paper proposes only relatively slight alternations in the present system of trying to regulate commercial development. Indeed, one commentator thinks that "the new policy amounts to little more than exhortation to move to the suburbs or beyond." [36] And it is true that of the four proposals made, two of them reflect the continuing faith in exhortation, for the Government proposes, first, "to encourage provision of more office centers" outside London, and, second, "to make a major effort to dissuade employers" from coming to or extending their offices in London, as well as trying to get existing offices out of London.[37] This is harking back to 1934 when powers were given to the commissioners for the special areas to exhort industrialists to locate factories there, and with singularly small results.

The third proposal is to increase the powers of local authorities to refuse planning permission for the redevelopment of a site on which an office building has stood or for the building of extensions to existing offices. If

---

[33] Or they advance both these arguments; see E.C., Qs. 181–182.

[34] White paper, pp. 4–5.

[35] *Ibid.*, p. 4.

[36] Patrick Coldstream, "The Scope Left for Offices Now," *Financial Times*, Feb. 27, 1963.

[37] White paper, p. 5.

this Government proposal becomes law, then for redevelopment schemes a local planning authority will be able to "refuse to allow an increase in floor-space of more than 10 percent of the amount devoted to a particular use in the building being replaced," [38] without becoming liable for heavy compensation to the person seeking planning permission. Similarly, for existing buildings, planning authorities will be able to refuse any extensions, without compensation, for buildings erected since 1948, and to refuse enlargements of over 10 percent without compensation, for older buildings.

The fourth proposal is that a location of offices bureau be set up by the Ministry of Housing to inform management about rents and the availability of suitable employees, etc., in the proposed new office centers outside London, and to make sure that firms understand what effects their own and other expansion proposals in London are likely to have on congestion, costs, and staff difficulties and therefore on their own working efficiency.

Thus the curious situation is that, for offices, the Government is taking this step, which they have not taken for factories, while refusing to use development certificates, which have applied to factories for nearly 20 years. Once more, then, an unbalanced policy is being developed. There should be power to refuse, in suitable cases, any new office building, and this power should be in the hands of the same department, the Board of Trade, which is responsible for offering subsidies and loans to firms building offices in development districts. To give partial powers of control to local authorities, as is proposed, is to run a grave risk of failing to achieve a coherent policy.

Recent Changes

Since the writing of this report was started, a number of changes in policy have been announced. There have been hints of changes in attitude to the whole problem of the outer regions. Before attempting a summary of the new proposals, it is necessary to consider certain background happenings. The crucial point is that the 1960 Local Employment Act was not followed by any improvement in the regional employment situation. Indeed, the situation deteriorated as a result of a number of linked events. In the first place, the credit squeeze initiated in July 1961 was, as usual, unselective, so it created unemployment where it was already highest.

The squeeze helped to bring about a general fall-off in investment in Britain and thus to slow down the rate at which workers released from the declining industries could be absorbed by the expanding ones. The squeeze thus served to highlight certain structural changes which had been taking place in recent years in some of Britain's older industries. First, there was the steady decline in employment in the older parts of the Scottish and Durham coalfields, a decline brought about by the closures of pits which were economically worked out and the drastic mechanization of other old mines. Second, there was a fall in employment in shipbuilding, as order books dwindled as a result of a slower rate of expansion of world trade at a time of an acute surplus in world shipbuilding capacity. The decline in shipbuilding naturally affected adversely the marine engineers and the steel-

---

[38] *Ibid.*, p. 15. In the past, the rule has been that firms could be prevented from increasing the cubic capacity by more than 10 percent. This allowed increases of up to 40 percent in lettable floor space.

plate rollers. Meanwhile, the cut in capital investment, inspired by the credit squeeze, was hitting the constructional steelrollers.

It soon became clear that this was 1929 *in miniature,* and that here there was an unpleasant mixture of the cycle and the trend, with certain more modern overtones, such as the effects of increased automation in certain parts of the chemical and steel industries. It would be possible to argue at length whether the main cause of unemployment in Great Britain today is cyclical or secular. The present writer believes that, as often, the two are linked. For example, it seems that the long years of inflation from the end of the war to 1958 deferred part of the long-term decline of coal and shipbuilding. Pits that were long past the end of their economic life were kept on, churning out coal at a loss of £3 ($8.40) per ton. Shipyards long past any hope of modernization were given a breathing space by the temporary inflation of demand. With the cyclical recession, these industries accelerated their secular decline.

It soon became clear that the industrial pattern of parts of Britain was not sufficiently altered, as compared with the 1930's. In the northern region in 1961, for example, 15.8 percent of the total working population were still employed in coal, shipbuilding, and marine engineering, compared with a national average of 4.4 percent. Percentage unemployment in the northern region rose as follows:

	1961			1962				1963		
	Apr.	July	Oct.	Jan.	Apr.	July	Oct.	Jan.	Apr.	July
Northern region......	2. 4	1. 9	2. 5	3. 5	3. 4	3. 2	4. 3	6. 5	5. 1	4. 0
Great Britain.........	1. 5	1. 2	1. 6	2. 0	2. 0	1. 8	2. 2	3. 6	2. 7	2. 0

Other areas also suffered, but not so sharply, because none was so heavily dependent on the basic declining industries.

As a result of the sharp climb in unemployment, nationally and regionally, a certain amount of Government rethinking has occurred. The first important event was the appointment of a Cabinet Minister, Lord Hailsham, as "Minister for the North East," with the task of preparing a plan for the region. This is the first time that any part of England has had a Minister to itself and the first time that a plan has been prepared for any of the less prosperous regions of Great Britain. There have been the privately sponsored *Toothill Report on the Scottish Economy,* 1961, and the official *Report of the Joint Working Party on the Economy of Northern Ireland,* 1962,[39] but the latter is outside our present geographical limits.

So far, the most important result of the Hailsham appointment has been that it has caused senior officials of various government departments to travel round together looking at the same problems. This has helped to create a greater awareness of the need for coordinated policies. Events will show how deeply this awareness has gone.

There are other hints that the Government is thinking in terms of a more constructive approach, combined with signs that the battle for such an ap-

[39] Cmnd. 1835.

proach is not yet completely won. These are particularly striking in the speeches made by various Government spokesmen during the budget statement and the subsequent debate thereon in the House of Commons in April 1963.

In his budget speech, the Chancellor of the Exchequer announced improved capital allowances on taxation. The combined effect is to give businessmen an investment allowance of 30 percent on plant and 15 percent on buildings. This is for firms everywhere in Britain. In addition, firms in development districts will receive certain special concessions. The first is to be called "free depreciation." The idea is that "the businessman making an investment in these qualifying areas can write off for tax purposes the expenditure he incurs after today on new plant and machinery at any rate he chooses. He need not, therefore, pay a penny piece of taxation until he has written off his entire investment in new plant and machinery plus the 30 percent investment allowance." [40]

In addition, the old method of calculating a building grant, introduced in the 1960 act, is to be abolished and will be replaced by a fixed grant in development districts of 25 percent of the cost of a new building or extension or of adapting an existing building, excluding expenditure which is judged by the Board of Trade to be unreasonable for the purposes for which the building is needed. In addition, industrial undertakings in a development district will receive a fixed 10 percent grant toward the cost of acquiring and installing machinery. The cost per job rule will still apply, and BOTAC will still have to satisfy itself in the case of building grants and large machinery grants that the firm is credit-worthy. The other forms of loan and (general) grant, discussed on page 343 above, will still apply, but BOTAC will be asked to take account of the new fixed-rate grants when recommending a general loan and/or grant to a firm.[41]

In addition, a program of 11 new advance factories was announced to follow the program announced in November 1962, and legislation on the problem of redundancy was promised in the autumn. Finally, increased grants were promised to local authorities to help the clearance of derelict land.

These are important changes. The most significant is the new "free depreciation" allowance. This is in no sense a cash grant to firms; it is equivalent to an interest-free loan by the Government, for it simply means that firms in development districts are able to deduct the cost of investment from taxable profits more quickly than previously. The important points are two. First, it is not linked with any measurement of cost per job. It is for all investment in fixed plant and machinery for replacement and modernization regardless of whether it creates employment.[42] This is a move away from the self-imposed restrictions which have hampered policy. Second, it is a change of principle. As a Conservative back-bencher said, "it introduces for the first time in this country the acceptance of the prin-

---

[40] Chancellor of the Exchequer, *Weekly Hansard,* Apr. 3, 1963, vol. 675, c. 482; also Economic Secretary to the Treasury, *Weekly Hansard,* Apr. 8, 1963, vol. 675, c. 1047.

[41] Local Employment bill, April 1963; also *Weekly Hansard,* Apr. 3, 1963, vol. 675, cc. 481, 659–662, and Apr. 8, 1963, vol. 675, c. 993.

[42] *Weekly Hansard,* Apr. 4, 1963, vol. 675, c. 662.

ciple that differential taxation on a geographical basis is possible."[43] Moreover, it does so despite the fact that Treasury officials have consistently argued that there were great problems and administrative difficulties in giving special tax incentives to areas of high unemployment.[44] Thus, here we appear to have a victory for the Chancellor of the Exchequer over the "dead hand" of his own Treasury, a victory which opens up the possibility of a more coherent policy in Britain of squeezing only the sectors of the economy where there is inflation and expanding mainly the sectors where there is slack. This will be a long road, but the first step has been taken.

Turning to the new fixed rate building grant, this is an improvement on the old 85 percent of the difference between "x," the cost of building, and "y," the market value when built. The new rule is still imprecise in that the businessman merely knows that he will get 25 percent of "x," the reasonable building cost, but this is an improvement psychologically, for most people will feel more certain with one unknown, which is in a form familiar to him, than with two, one of which is in the lap of the gods of the inland revenue. Moreover, the new grants will be bigger than the old, which on average have been 14 percent of cost in England, 17 percent in Wales, and 19 percent in Scotland.[45]

There are more important considerations than the mere simplification of the system and the fact that the degree of subsidization has been increased. The first is that if the above figures are in any way representative of the long-term situation, the new system will be more of a boost for development districts in England than for those in Wales and, especially, Scotland. The second point is not so obvious, and may have escaped the notice of the Government and its advisers. This is that, compared with the old system of building grants, the fixed-rate 25 percent rule will enhance the attractiveness to businessmen of a central, economically more suitable development district vis-a-vis that of a more remote one in the same region. This is made clearer by considering the old system, under which a firm received 85 percent of the difference between the estimated cost of a suitable building and the estimated market value. If one thinks of two development districts in the same region, one, say, 25 miles from any important industrial town and one right in or close to the town, the certainty is that market value will be lower in the "remote" location and there is a very strong probability that building costs will be higher because of the greater haulage of raw materials and the greater likelihood of having to build on unstable land. Thus, the former type of grant was likely to be proportionately greater for locations in remote places.

There are signs, throughout the budget debate, of rethinking of regional policy in Government circles. The Chancellor of the Exchequer said at the end of the section of his speech on development districts: "I have been dealing with the human element in a growth program."[46] The next day he was echoed by the president of the Board of Trade in the words: "One of the most important things to do is to get a more even spread of economic growth throughout the various regions of the country. In this way we shall

[43] *Weekly Hansard*, Apr. 8, 1963, vol. 675, c. 989.

[44] *Weekly Hansard*, Apr. 3, 1963, vol. 675, c. 551.

[45] E.C., p. 164, table III; of course, this covers a fairly short period, Apr. 1, 1960–Jan. 31, 1963.

[46] *Weekly Hansard*, Apr. 3, 1963, vol. 675, c. 484.

grow faster and more surely."[47] The economic secretary to the Treasury put it as follows: "The economy as a whole cannot realize its full potential expansion until regional disparities are reduced. The advantage Parliament is giving, if it so decides, to these areas must not be dissipated by extending their definition more unjustifiably."[48]

Thus, on the one hand, we have the beginning of a recognition of the link between regional employment and national growth, for which thanks is due to the officers of the National Economic Development Council. On the other hand, we have this same old harping on the "unjustifiable" extension of the boundaries of the development areas. If by this, as seems apparent, the Ministers mean sticking to the least attractive places, and if they want a more even spread of growth throughout each nook and cranny of each region, we are left with the old mixture in a new pudding basin.

At the same time, the Minister of Labour, who is not *responsible* for local employment policy, did say that "the growth point concept has its attractions."[49] Moreover, the Newcastle area, which did not quite have 4.5 percent unemployment over 12 months, has been added to the list of development districts since the budget, and rumor has it that other growth points in the northeast are soon to be added, though they are below the magic 4.5 percent also.[50] So the lines of policy seem to be becoming crossed.

Another related point is that the change of policy announced in the budget cries out for longer-period listing of development districts. The bigger the subsidy, the bigger the let down when a firm finds it is no longer eligible for help. Yet the president of the Board of Trade still believes in the quick delisting technique. He said, "We shall deschedule (delist) in the future just as we have in the past. On descheduling, the standard of benefits and other benefits under the 1960 act will no longer be available. Perhaps even more important, free depreciation will no longer be available either for expenditure undertaken thereafter. Prudent industrialists, I suggest, will have this in mind when making their plans."[51] To add to the confusion in the minds of industrialists, the new bigger building grant is for development districts, excluding those which are stoplisted,[52] while the new system of free depreciation is for development districts, including those which are stoplisted.[53]

Finally, there are hints of a lingering hope that the attack on regional economic problems need be only a brief one, that the main difficulty is that there is a recession at the moment and what the less favorably placed regions need is a shot in the arm. This is shown by the decision of the Government to increase the rate of help given to local authorities in development districts toward the cost of clearing derelict land. This now goes up from 50 to 85 percent, but only for all tenders approved in the 9 months

---

[47] *Weekly Hansard,* Apr. 4, 1963, vol. 675, c. 655.

[48] *Weekly Hansard,* Apr. 8, 1963, vol. 675, c. 1048.

[49] *Weekly Hansard,* Apr. 8, 1963, vol. 675, c. 934.

[50] Since this was written, other parts of the main industrial belt of the northeast of England, with unemployment rates below 4.5 percent have been listed. See app. V.

[51] This example of trying to treat businessmen in the way stores treat the housewife in bargain fortnight is in *Weekly Hansard,* Apr. 4, 1963, vol. 675, c. 664. It brought protests from both sides of the House. See *Weekly Hansard,* Apr. 8, 1963, vol. 675, cc. 935–936, 964, 988, 1036.

[52] Stoplisting is a halfway stage between being an actual development district and being taken off the list altogether.

[53] *Weekly Hansard,* Apr. 8, 1963, vol. 675, cc. 935, 1024.

after the date of the announcement. One wonders what the point of this is. Policy has dictated that many development districts are small, relatively impoverished places, some of them short of the technical staff capable of making such plans quickly.[54] To them, this must be a tantalizing offer with no substance to it. To repeat, the answer should be a 100 percent grant with no time limit, as in 1945–50. The importance of clearing derelict land is twofold. This first point is that dereliction is repellent to resident and visitor alike, including the visiting industrialist looking for a factory site. The second is that in some of the older parts of Britain much of the land available for new industry is covered by the wreckage of old industry. So there is a vicious circle of no space for new industry without expensive clearances and insufficient funds for clearance without new industry.

Summary and Conclusions

We have seen that regional policy has had a long history in Britain and that so far it has not been entirely successful even in achieving its limited aim of reducing unemployment in the outer regions of Britain. The significance of the resurgence of higher unemployment in particular regions after regional policy had been rested for some years is that the market cannot be expected to solve this sort of problem. There are too many frictions preventing the price mechanism from operating. Moreover, it would seem that the solution cannot be in terms of the Government overcoming initial inertia and then expecting private enterprise unaided to take over. Private enterprise has a large part to play in solving the difficulties, but it must be backed up by a continuing and coherent policy.

First of all, there must be coordination betwen a general full employment policy and a regional renovation policy. This involves a large number of related actions. There is the need to ensure that credit expansions do not quickly lead to inflation in the areas of high employment. Equally, squeezes must not hit the areas where employment is low. This is particularly important in view of the long timelag which usually occurs between a businessman's decision to build a factory and the actual creation of employment and income by that factory.

Further, there is need for research to ascertain the best ways of helping particular regions by identifying the bottlenecks that are hampering economic expansion and by trying to assess the longer-term prospects of the regions. Such research should be backed by a broad policy which links subsidies for firms moving into or expanding in areas that are temporarily high cost to them, training grants, transfer grants, house building, road improvements, etc. All this would involve coordination among government departments on a level not so far achieved. It may also imply the creation of regional governments, although that is a point about which one may be permitted to have reservations. Regional governments are not bound to act in the national interest.

Above all, the need of the country in this matter is for less emphasis on a social policy of work to the workers wherever they may be and more emphasis on a growth point policy combined with a willingness to take a few risks. This would mean concentrating attention first and mainly on particular parts of regions; attention, that is, on encouraging industry to

---

[54] *Weekly Hansard,* Apr. 8, 1963, vol. 675, c. 945.

move and expand there, providing training facilities, and building up social capital.

As far as the guidance of industry is concerned, a broader and more active policy is needed. One Government department should be responsible for the control of all industrial expansion in the congested areas, whether manufacturing or service in old buildings or new. Furthermore, that department should be prepared to call regional conferences for selected industries to demonstrate the bottlenecks that face them in the Midlands or the south and to explain the inducements available in the north. As far as the inducements are concerned, abolition of the cost per job rule would help. "Free depreciation" is a step in the right direction here, but the whole policy should be one of seeking to modernize the industrial structure of particular regions, not merely of creating employment. Underlying this, there is a need to escape from the overcautious attitude of the last 30 years. The Treasury and, to a less extent BOTAC are reluctant to take risks. A growth point policy would make more risks justifiable, for there need be less fears about building too many advance factories if these are needed in the more attractive parts of the regions, less fears about buying land near to estates, and less fears about marginal firms in a good industrial location than in a remote area. Beyond this, however, the authorities should steel themselves to face a few losses. The bankruptcies of 10 small assisted firms would be well balanced by one new Lord Nuffield. Even so, bankruptcies would be less if the present, admirable technical and advisory services operated by the Board of Trade were widened to cover small firms which were not paying back loans in development districts.

The next point is that the actual subsidies should be looked at again and widened a little. For example, the new building and machinery grants are available to new and old firms alike in development districts. The older form of general grant, however, is still limited to covering part of the extra cost of moving to a development district. There is no reason why, first, these grants should not be interpreted a little more generously and, second, why firms expanding in a development district should not be entitled to seek a general grant, particularly when a firm in an older industry is seeking to diversify its output into expanding lines of production.

Beyond this suggestion of wider use of existing grants lies the question of whether other types of subsidy should be used. At present, most subsidies seem to be offsets to high fixed costs: Building and machinery grants, rent subsidies, loans at slightly favorable rates of interest are the order of the day. The NEDC report [55] mentions the idea of wage rate subsidies to firms, rejects them if applied to all labor in firms in development districts, but leaves open the question of whether they should be paid for increases in employment. We must do the same. There is an obvious logic in having subsidies which vary directly with variable costs where such costs are high for an initial period, and a strong case for yet more research on the question of what are the most effective and economical forms of subsidy. It is doubtful whether they have yet been found.

However subsidies are paid, there does not seem to be a particular need for special subsidies for growth points. A given level of subsidy is more attractive in a lower-cost part of a region than in a higher-cost one. Moreover, it has already been argued that most new social capital should be at or

---

[55] *Conditions Favourable to Faster Growth,* p. 24.

for the growth points. However, there does seem to be a need for to strike a balance between the help offered to firms on their own sites and that offered to estate firms. The present Government seems to prefer that firms should build their own factories and qualify for a building grant rather than move into an estate factory at a subsidized rent. This is said to be largely because a policy of offering building grants can be switched off quickly while rent subsidies cannot, because leases run for 21 years. It has been argued above that much damage has been done by the quick delisting of development districts. Growth points guaranteed for 10 years would involve the acceptance that no form of subsidy could be switched off suddenly. At the same time, if sensible points were chosen, the rent subsidies paid would be smaller than in remote areas and need keep no civil servant awake at night. Having said this, however, it should be pointed out that the new 25-percent building grant is a far better bargain in a prospective growth point than in a remote location. Clearly, growth points under the present rules would mean that building grants would be more attractive than estate factories from a purely financial viewpoint. This does not mean that artificially high subsidies should be offered on estate factory rents at growth points. It does mean, however, that management corporations should be allowed to go out and look for tenants for factories on central sites and to explain the real advantage of life on such estates. This would go a long way toward redressing the balance which has been upset by the new 25-percent building grant.

This report is clearly a serial story which necessarily must end before the final installment. Moreover, it ends at a particularly exciting point. The question has still not been answered as to whether the British Government will take a step roughly equivalent to the breakthrough of 1934–36 when industrial estates and official subsidies were launched. The new breakthrough would be the reversal of policy advocated above—the adoption of a long-term coherent policy of concentrating development in the economically most suitable parts of the problem regions and of thinking more in terms of economic growth than unemployment. If the policy makers are brave enough to do this, they may find that if they look after the growth some of the employment will look after itself.

Introduction to Appendices

The following appendices offer a certain amount of statistical data on the regions of Britain. Not a vast amount of information can be offered. Research workers frequently complain of the shortage of regional statistics. Peacock and Dosser remarked on the "almost complete lack" of regional economic statistics on which to base the application of the policy changes they had proposed.[56] The position has improved a little since 1960, for example, some information about regional incomes is now available. Even so, it is still reasonable to complain of "a paucity of systematic regional statistics" and to stress the need for improvements in their supply.[57]

If regional statistics are inadequate, those for parts of regions are almost nonexistent, even for important localities like Merseyside. Thus one is often forced either to use data for much wider areas than is desirable or to neglect certain subregions altogether.

---

[56] "The New Attack on Localised Unemployment," *Lloyds Bank Review,* January 1960, pp. 27–28.

[57] NEDC, *Conditions Favourable to Faster Growth,* pp. 14–15.

The Standard Regions of England and Wales as Delimited in 1946

Reproduced from C.B. Fawcett, *Provinces of England*, P. 39

Main Industrial Areas

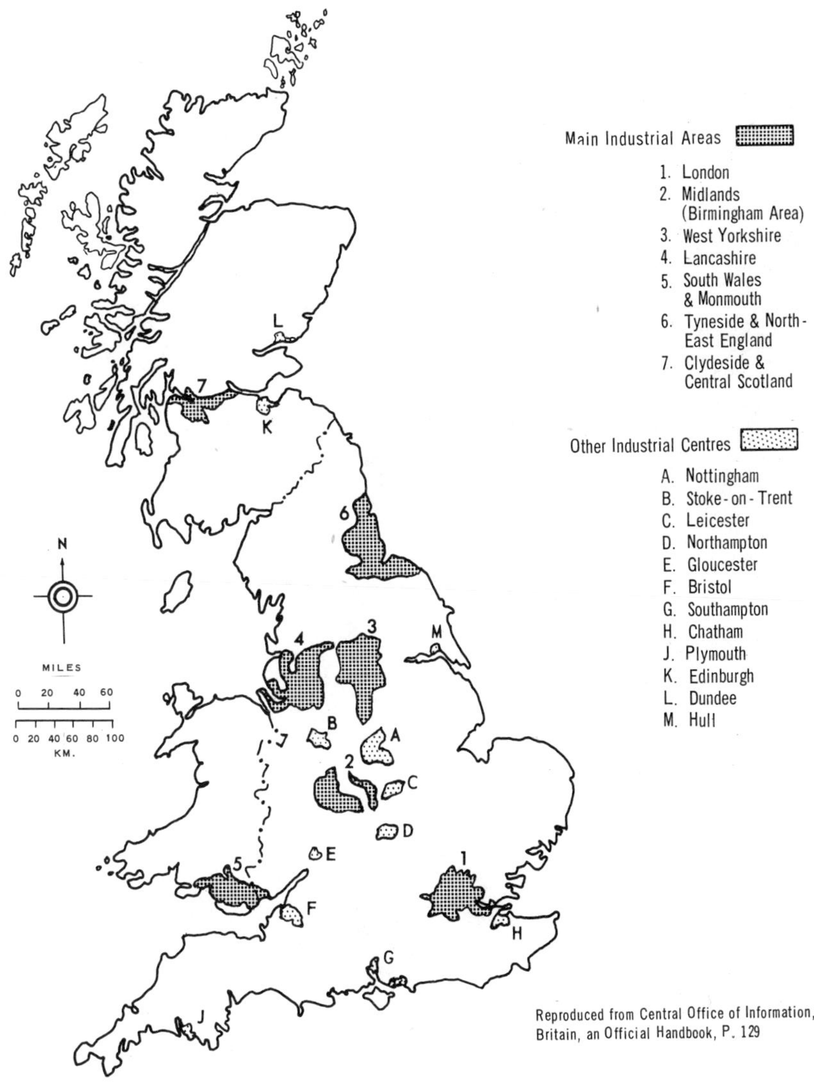

Reproduced from Central Office of Information, Britain, an Official Handbook, P. 129

The Development Districts in Great Britain—Spring 1963

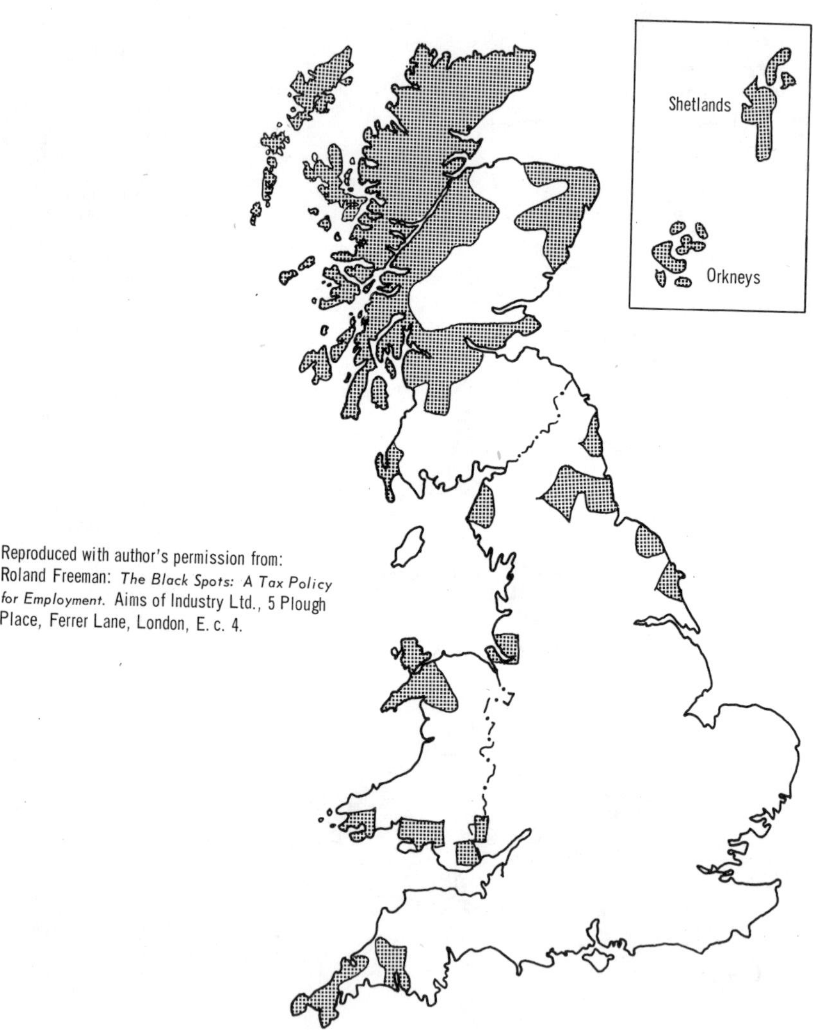

Reproduced with author's permission from:
Roland Freeman: *The Black Spots: A Tax Policy for Employment.* Aims of Industry Ltd., 5 Plough Place, Ferrer Lane, London, E. c. 4.

Appendix I

Regional Unemployment Rates, Personal Incomes and Activity Rates

Unemployment Rates

Tables 3 and 4 show, respectively, unemployment rates in selected interwar years, in the then divisions of Great Britain; and unemployment rates in a run of postwar years in the regions of the country. It is not easy to compare the interwar and the postwar periods. For one thing, nearly all the present regions have different boundaries from the old divisions. For another, rates of unemployment in Britain are calculated by dividing the number of persons registered as unemployed (times 100) by the total number insured by the state against unemployment. Nowadays, all wage and salary earners are covered by the national insurance scheme. In the interwar years shown in table 3, most nonmanual workers and various others in occupations thought to be relatively immune from unemployment were outside the then unemployment insurance scheme. In all, less than two-thirds of all employees were covered.

Even so, while this means that precision is impossible, the tables show that broadly the same parts of Britain have suffered from higher than average unemployment under the various economic conditions of the last 30 years.

June 1929 was a prosperous month by interwar standards; June 1932 was the worst June for unemployment on record; June 1936 was in a period in which unemployment was rising again. Under all these varying conditions, unemployment in the London and South East, South Western and Midlands divisions was below the national average. In the other divisions, it was above average.

Table 3.—*Unemployment Rates, by Division, Selected Interwar Years* [1]

Division	June 1929	June 1932	June 1936
London and South Eastern	4. 5	13. 0	6. 2
South Western	6. 8	15. 8	7. 7
Midlands	9. 1	21. 5	9. 0
North Eastern	12. 6	29. 8	18. 1
North Western	12. 6	25. 9	16. 6
Scotland	11. 0	26. 8	17. 1
Wales	18. 2	37. 4	30. 4
Great Britain	9. 6	22. 4	12. 8

[1] From G. M. Beck, *A Survey of British Employment and Unemployment, 1927–45*, table 18, p. 36a (from unpublished Ministry of Labour data).

Table 4 shows that the regions with low unemployment since the war have been London and South Eastern; Eastern and Southern; Midlands; North Midlands; East and West Ridings of Yorkshire. In each of the last

14 years, the average annual unemployment rate [58] in each of these regions separately has been below the national average, and has been on average, noticably below it, as the final two columns of table 4 show.

The South Western region, despite the fact that it is hardly a microcosm of Great Britain, has reflected the national average unemployment rate with great regularity. In 9 out of 14 years, the average in this region has been within ±0.1 percent of the national average.[59]

The North Western region has had an average rate in excess of the national in 12 of the last 14 years, and has never succeeded in getting below the average. Even so, only in 5 years has average unemployment exceeded the national average by more than 0.3 percent. The pattern in the region, over time, has been of unemployment running a little above national average with an occasional kick up to 0.5 percent or 0.6 percent above it, as textiles, electronics, and/or shipbuilding suffer a recession. Within the region, however, there are important areas of higher unemployment, in particular, Merseyside. It has already been pointed out above, that few useful statistics exist for subregions and one must follow the National Economic Development Council's lead [60] and treat the North West as being not one of the high unemployment regions of Britain, despite the fact that Merseyside is an example of one of the trickiest problems of regional policy—a larger conurbation with relatively high unemployment rates.

This leaves the Northern region, Scotland, and Wales, regions in which unemployment has never been down to the national average. The Scottish position can be summed up as one of consistency. Unemployment, almost every year, comes out at between 1¾ and 2¼ times the national average. In Wales, after a period in 1949–51, in which unemployment was running at a higher rate than in Scotland, the situation improved relatively and over the last 10 years, unemployment has stayed at between about 1.6 to 1.9 times the national average.

In the Northern region, the situation has been a little more complex. For the most part, the unemployment rate has been a little less than in Wales, at about 1.5 to 1.8 times national average, except for the years from 1956–58, when unemployment threatened to get down to the national average, thus causing the Government to completely abandon what little was left of development area policy in the region.[61]

Regional Incomes

Little information is available about regional income patterns. What there is has emerged almost entirely in 1962–63, and is for relatively recent years only.[62] The most detailed information is in the latest annual report

---

[58] Calculated as the average of the 12 separate monthly returns published in the *Ministry of Labour Gazette*.

[59] There are a number of small areas of relatively high unemployment in the region, and it also suffers from seasonal unemployment as a result of its importance as a tourist center.

[60] *Conditions Favourable to Faster Growth*, pp. 14–15.

[61] See above, pp. 36–37.

[62] See *Ministry of Labour Gazette*, March 1963, and Ministry of Labour, *Statistics on Incomes, Prices, Employment and Production* (first published 1962), for details of regional earnings of manual workers. For information about taxable incomes, by regions, the only information is in the *105th Report of the Commissioners of Internal Revenue*, January 1963. This gives regional breakdowns of personal income before tax for 1959–60. No comparable data exist for earlier years.

TABLE 4.—*Unemployment Rates, by Region 1949–62 Monthly Averages* [1]

Regions [2]	1949	1950	1951	1952	1953	1954	1955	1956	1957	1958	1959	1960	1961	1962	Average 1949–62	Average ranking
London and South Eastern	1.1	1.1	0.9	1.3	1.2	1.0	0.7	0.8	1.0	1.3	1.3	0.9	1.0	1.3	1.1	3
Eastern [3]	1.1	1.2	.9	1.3	1.3	1.2	.9	1.0	(1.3)							
Southern [3]	1.4	1.4	1.1	1.4	1.4	1.1	.9	1.0	(1.3)	1.6	1.5	1.2	1.1	1.4	1.2	4
South Western	1.4	1.4	1.2	1.5	1.6	1.5	1.2	1.2	1.8	2.2	2.2	1.7	1.4	1.8	1.6	6
Midland	.6	.5	.4	.9	1.1	.6	.5	1.1	1.3	1.6	1.5	1.0	1.4	1.8	1.0	2
North Midland	.6	.6	.5	1.0	.7	.6	.5	.6	1.0	1.5	1.5	1.1	1.0	1.4	.9	1
East and West Ridings of Yorkshire	.9	.9	.9	1.9	1.2	.9	.7	.8	.9	1.9	1.9	1.2	1.0	1.6	1.2	4
North Western	1.7	1.6	1.2	3.6	2.1	1.5	1.4	1.3	1.6	2.7	2.8	1.9	1.6	2.6	2.0	7
Northern	2.6	2.8	2.2	2.6	2.4	2.2	1.8	1.6	1.7	2.4	3.3	2.8	2.5	3.8	2.5	8
Scotland	3.0	3.0	2.5	3.3	3.1	2.8	2.4	2.4	2.6	3.7	4.4	3.6	3.1	3.8	3.1	10
Wales	4.0	3.7	2.7	2.9	3.0	2.5	1.8	2.0	2.6	3.8	3.8	2.7	2.6	3.8	3.0	9
Great Britain	1.5	1.5	1.2	2.0	1.6	1.3	1.1	1.2	1.4	2.1	2.2	1.6	1.6	2.1	1.6	6

[1] Monthly figures appear in Ministry of Labour Gazette.

[2] These regions are made up of the following counties. London and South Eastern: London (administrative county), Middlesex, Kent, Surrey, Sussex, and parts of Essex and Hertfordshire. Eastern: Rest of Essex and Hertfordshire, Bedfordshire, Cambridgeshire, Huntingdon, Norfolk, and Suffolk. Southern: Berkshire, Buckinghamshire, Dorset, Hampshire (including the Isle of Wight), and Oxfordshire. South Western: Cornwall, Devonshire, Gloucestershire, Somerset, and Wiltshire. Midland: Herefordshire, Shropshire, Staffordshire, Warwickshire, and Worcestershire. North Midland: Derbyshire (except High Peak District), Leicestershire, Lincolnshire, Northamptonshire, Nottinghamshire, and Rutland. East and West Ridings: East and West Ridings of Yorkshire and the City of York. North Western: Cheshire, Lancashire, and High Peak District of Derbyshire. Northern: Cumberland, Durham, Northumberland, Westmorland, and the North Riding of Yorkshire. Wales: Wales and Monmouthshire. Scotland.

[3] Amalgamated in 1958, for Ministry of Labour purposes.

of the Commissioners of Inland Revenue, which gives details of net taxable personal incomes by county. This covers incomes over £180 a year, only and treats married couples as one "person." A systematic sampling technique was used.

Table 5 has been calculated from table 135 of the commissioners' report. These figures are only rough indicators of the spread of incomes between regions. They tell us nothing about the inequalities of incomes within regions. Moreover, they are influenced by differences in activity rates, and in the age structure of the tax-paying population in different parts of the country. Nevertheless, whether we take employment incomes or total net incomes, it appears that the five regions with highest average taxable personal incomes are also the five regions which have had lower than national average unemployment rates over the last 14 years. The three regions with markedly higher than average unemployment (Northern, Scotland, Wales) also have lower than average incomes in 1959–60. There is nothing remarkable about this. Indeed, the only two points which deserve mention are first, that while unemployment in the South West of England is consistently close to the national average, incomes seem to be well below it, and secondly that employment income in the North West of England is lower than in the Northern Region or Wales.

Incomes in the South West region are pulled down partly by the fact that its relatively mild climate attracts large numbers of retired people. Pensions and retirement pay are included in table 5 under "employment income" because they are taxed under schedule E. In addition, however, this is probably a low earnings region, because of the importance of farming and of seasonal trades.

The relatively low employment income in the North West reflects, in part, the fact that there are problem areas in this region. There is also the fact that the ratio of employed females to total employed population is higher in this region than in any other, and that of the 1,100,000 females employed in the region, in 1959, approximately 130,000 were in the relatively low-wage cotton spinning, doubling, and weaving trades.

Activity Rates

This comment on female employment in the North West is a reminder that activity rates vary between regions. The figures in table 6 are taken from the second NEDC report,[63] with the exception of the Great Britain totals.

Activity rates, like personal income before tax, need some interpretation. In the first place, an activity rate of 77.5 percent for males in Great Britain does not mean that 22.5 percent of British males over the age of 15 are available for employment. Some of them will be over the age of retirement, and some will be self-employed, as doctors, architects, farmers, and chimney-sweeps. Moreover, the percentage of retired people and self-employed, especially farmers, will vary from region to region. Another factor which influences the activity rate of females is that in some parts of Britain there is a stronger belief than in others that the woman's place is in the home. This attitude is strong in Wales.

It is not possible to allow for these influences, and thereby to reach an assessment of the numbers available for employment in each region, or more precisely to assess the aggregate supply curves for labor in each region.

[63] *Conditions Favourable to Faster Growth*, p. 16, table 1.

TABLE 5.—*Survey of Personal Incomes (before Tax) 1959–60*

[Income totals by region [1]]

	Schedule E—employment income			Total net income including employment			
	Number of cases (1,000)	Amount (£M)	Average income per case (£)	Number of cases (1,000)	Total amount (£M)	Average income per case (£)	Ranking
London and South Eastern	3, 908. 6	2, 756. 8	705	4, 475. 3	3, 643. 9	814	1
Eastern and Southern	2, 212. 3	1, 417. 4	641	2, 560. 6	1, 869. 5	730	3
South Western	881. 2	520. 0	590	1, 079. 0	745. 0	690	7
Midland	1, 697. 6	1, 139. 3	671	1, 865. 2	1, 402. 0	752	2
North Midland	1, 217. 0	773. 3	635	1, 371. 0	984. 1	718	4
East and West Riding	1, 435. 5	898. 4	626	1, 598. 1	1, 137. 3	712	5
North Western	2, 187. 5	1, 352. 3	618	2, 472. 3	1, 752. 0	709	6
Northern	1, 013. 6	630. 7	622	1, 131. 1	776. 2	686	8
Scotland	1, 636. 5	957. 4	585	1, 864. 6	1, 257. 7	675	10
Wales	766. 3	478. 4	624	897. 4	608. 5	678	9
Great Britain [2]	16, 956. 1	10, 924. 0	644	19, 314. 6	14, 176. 2	[3] 734	....

[1] The figures contained in this table are aggregated from county data in the commissioners' report. This means that the small part of Derbyshire which is actually in the North West region appears in this table under North Midland, and that the parts of Essex and Hertfordshire which lie in the South Eastern region have had to be included in the Eastern region.

[2] Excluding incomes of civil servants, the armed forces and merchant navy; these are not allocated to regions in the official tables in Cmnd. 1906.

[3] Average income outside London and the South East was £710.

TABLE 6.—*Percentage Activity Rates by Regions mid-1961* [1] *(see following page)*

	Males	Females
London and South Eastern / Eastern and Southern	79. 3	40. 8
South Western	66. 6	30. 9
Midland	81. 6	42. 0
North Midland	76. 0	36. 8
East and West Riding	80. 2	39. 3
North Western	79. 7	42. 0
Northern	75. 0	32. 4
Scotland	76. 6	37. 6
Wales	69. 6	27. 5
Great Britain	77. 5	38. 5

[1] "Estimated number of employees (employed plus unemployed) as a percentage of the total population over the age of 15." Part of footnote to original text.

However, it is interesting to note that in the combined London and South Eastern and Eastern and Southern regions, as well as in the Midlands and the East and West Ridings, all regions of low unemployment and high taxable incomes, the activity rates are higher than in the country as a whole. In the three low-income, high-unemployment regions of Northern England, Scotland, and Wales, activity rates are consistently below the national average.

Low activity rates in the South Western region are probably brought about by the same causes as low incomes. Lower than average activity rates in the North Midlands, despite the lowest average unemployment rates in Britain over the last 14 years, are less easy to explain, but one would first want statistics of self-employed persons in the region, before making any comment.

Granted first, that statistics of unemployment, incomes, and activity rates all have their imperfections and secondly that two or three regions do not fit neatly into the categories of "more prosperous" and "less prosperous", it still remains true that for most of the regions of Britain, the statistics briefly examined in this appendix seem to be consistent with each other. It would seem, that by nominating areas for assistance by reference to unemployment figures, the authorities have not missed many areas of low income, etc., for the development districts are in the Northern, Welsh, Scottish, South Western, and North Western regions. As has been said, however, the use of the unemployment criterion has led to other inadequacies of policy. One of these will be looked at in appendix II.

Appendix II(i)

Official Expenditure on Distribution of Industry Policy and Local Employment Policy

There is some tendency for people to assume that there has been a steady pursuance of development area policy since the end of the second war. In particular, the stimulating arguments of A. T. Peacock and D. G. M. Dosser for a new look at policy were unfortunately weakened by their claim that "Unemployment in the Development Areas has been consistently above the national average, *although efforts were concentrated entirely on them up till 1958.*" [64]

Efforts in this sense can mean the use of Industrial Development Certificates and/or the expenditure of official subsidies. IDC's will be looked indirectly at in Appendix II(ii). The present task is to show that as far as official spending is concerned, distribution of industry policy was well-nigh suspended for 10 years.

Government expenditure on helping to create employment in development areas or, since 1961, development districts, is shown in table 7. Board of Trade expenditure from 1946 to 1960 was under the Distribution of Industry Acts 1945 and 1950 and was almost entirely devoted to the provision of factory buildings on the industrial estates. Treasury expenditure from 1946–60 was under the Distribution of Industry Acts of 1945 and 1958, and consisted largely of grants and loans to firms. Since 1960, all expenditure has been by the Board of Trade under the Local Employment Act, 1960, but the table maintains the separation between "factory buildings" and "grants and loans":

This table shows the fall in spending which occurred during the 10 years 1949–59. However, it does not reveal the extent of the decline in real terms, because of course, building costs were rising during the period under review. As a rough guide, one may deflate the Board of Trade's expenditure on factory buildings by an "Index of New Non-House Building Costs" [65] and thus obtain an index of official expenditure on factory buildings at constant costs. A similar exercise for Treasury spending permits the construction of an index of total expenditure on factories, grants and loans at constant costs, as in table 8.

This table shows that distribution of industry policy was in abeyance for about 9 or 10 years. Moreover, the table does not reflect the full story. Over the period, there has been a steady rise in the capital-to-labor ratio, including a rise in the average square footage of factory space required per worker. Thus, there has been a steady rise in the official spending and lending required, in real terms, to generate one unit of employment.[66] Perhaps the clearest illustration of the hibernation of distribution of industry policy in the 1950's comes from the following calculations. Board of Trade

---

[64] "The New Attack on Localized Unemployment," *Lloyds Bank Review,* 1960, p. 18 (author's italics).

[65] This appears as a graph in *The Builder,* Aug. 31, 1962, p. 427. The graph was based on actual instances of building costs. Some doubts on its accuracy as a general guide to changes in building costs in the last few years were expressed by C. F. Carter, *The Builder,* Oct. 19, 1962, p. 773. However, it does give an indication of broad changes over the postwar years.

[66] See E.C., Q. 891.

TABLE 7.—*Official Expenditure on Distribution of Industry and Local Employment Policy, 1946–62* [1]

[In £M]

	1946–47	1947–48	1948–49	1949–50	1950–51	1951–52	1952–53	1953–54
Board of Trade	5.7	12.5	11.0	6.5	5.0	5.0	3.7	3.1
Treasury	.2	.3	.5	.6	.8	.8	.3	1.1
Total	5.9	12.8	11.5	7.1	5.8	5.8	4.0	4.2
	1954–55	1955–56	1956–57	1957–58	1958–59	1959–60	1960–61	1961–62
Board of Trade	4.5	5.9	4.9	2.7	1.5	5.6	7.0	11.0
Treasury	1.7	.4	.3	.1	2.1	3.0	4.8	21.8
Total	6.2	6.3	5.2	2.8	3.6	8.6	11.8	32.8

[1] This table is compiled from official report, Apr. 24, 1958; vol. 586, c. 1139, and from E.C., p. 166. The figures cover financial years, April–March.

TABLE 8.—*Constant Cost Indexes of Official Expenditure on Distribution of Industry and Local Employment Policy*

[1947–48=100]

Financial year	1946–47	1947–48	1948–49	1949–50	1950–51	1951–52	1952–53	1953–54
Expenditure on estate factories	48	100	82	47	35	30	20	17
Total expenditure including factories loans and grants	48	100	84	50	40	34	21	22
Financial year	**1954–55**	**1955–56**	**1956–57**	**1957–58**	**1958–59**	**1959–60**	**1960–61**	**1961–62**
Expenditure on estate factories	24	30	24	13	17	27	33	49
Total expenditure including factories loans and grants	32	32	24	13	17	40	54	142

officials told the Estimates Committee, 1962–63, in a written memorandum [67] that, on average, between April 1960 and April 1962, some £970 of official expenditure of all types was required "per job," i.e., for every additional worker *expected* to be hired by the firm receiving the assistance. Deflating for rising costs and rising capital intensity, a figure of £600–700 per estimated job would seem in the right range for 1952–59. Thus, it would seem that the official expenditure of £32.3M in that period would lead to expectations of some 45,000–55,000 additional jobs, or sòme 6,000–8,000 per annum over all the development areas of Great Britain, with their 4 million insured workers. Moreover, these figures are expectations of employment. We have already seen that expectations are almost always sharply disappointing and, further, that actual increases of employment reduce unemployment by a further fraction again.

In brief, one can say that the achievements in the development areas during the 1950's were trifling, and that an important reason for this was that efforts were far from being concentrated there.

Appendix II (ii)

Industrial Building by Region

Another test of the extent to which development area and local employment policies have been effective is to consider the distribution of industrial building by region. This is attempted in table 9. Column 1 of this table shows the distribution of building, in terms of square footage, from January 1, 1945, to September 30, 1962, the latest date for which figures are available. Columns 2, 3, 4, break this down for various periods. The division between columns 2 and 3, at June 30, 1954, is not ideal, but it is unavoidable, because at that date, the Board of Trade altered its method of analysis from a value basis to a square-footage basis and thus it is not possible in the time available to break the series at any point earlier than mid-1954.[68] This is unfortunate, a break somewhere between 1950 and 1951 would bring out the change in policy after the early postwar years more sharply than is possible in table 9. The division between columns 3 and 4 marks the start of local employment policy. Moreover, it is a good point at which to break, as it is 2 years—a typical factory gestation period—after the revival of development area policy under the 1958 act.

Columns 6 and 7 show the distribution of the insured population in 1952 and 1962. The former is a convenient date for comparison with columns 2 and 3. The latter gives the latest available in information.

A comparison between columns 1 and 7 appears to show that in the more prosperous regions factory building has been restricted since the war. The London and South Eastern, Eastern, Southern and South Western Regions, combined, which have a greater weighting of growth industries than in the country as a whole, have secured some 31.4 percent of postwar industrial building, whereas they have some 35.8 percent of employees in manufacturing industry.[69] Similarly, the Midland, North Midland and East and West

[67] E.C., p. 56.

[68] See *Board of Trade Journal,* Oct. 2, 1954, and *Monthly Digest of Statistics,* September 1954, p. 71.

[69] Even here, it should be noted that part of the effect of the sharp control of factory building in the London and South East Region has been that there has been considerable building in the eastern and southern regions, much of it "in the vicinity of the London conurbation." M. Chisholm, *Location of Industry,* planning vol. XXVIII, No. 466, P.E.P., p. 343.

TABLE 9.—*New Building for Manufacturing Industry—Percentage Distribution of Total Floor Area, by Region*

Region	(1)	(2)	(3)	(4)	(5)	(6)	(7)
	New building completed				Under construction at Sept. 30, 1962	Distribution of Insured Employees in Manufacturing Industry	
	Jan. 1, 1945 to Sept. 30, 1962	Jan. 1, 1945 to June 30, 1954	July 1, 1954 to Mar. 31, 1960	Apr. 1, 1960 to Sept. 30, 1962		May 1952	May 1962
	Percent	*Percent*	*Percent*	*Percent*	*Percent*	*Percent*	*Percent*
London and South East	13.3	8.7	16.5	13.5	14.9	22.1	21.2
Eastern	8.4	6.1	10.0	8.5	15.2	4.5	10.1 (Eastern and Southern combined)
Southern	5.1	4.7	5.0	6.0	6.1	3.6	
South Western	4.6	3.5	4.6	6.5	4.5	4.2	4.5
Midland	13.1	11.5	14.6	12.4	9.7	12.8	[1] 31.3 (Midland, North Midland and East and West Riding combined)
North Midland	7.4	7.3	7.4	7.8	6.1	7.2	
East and West Riding	7.9	8.3	7.7	7.9	9.5	10.2	
North Western	14.3	14.4	13.8	15.3	17.1	17.4	15.8
Northern	8.4	11.9	6.5	7.4	2.9	5.1	5.1
Scotland	9.6	11.7	8.8	8.2	7.0	9.5	8.5
Wales	7.7	11.9	5.3	6.4	6.9	3.4	3.4
Great Britain	100.0	100.0	100.0	100.0	100.0	100.0	100.0
Total floor area, Great Britain, thousand square feet	579,411	188,092	269,544	121,775	81,071	...	...

[1] It is necessary to amalgamate these regions' figures for 1962, because the Ministry of Labour has closed its North Midland regional office and has allocated part of the region to the Midlands and part to the East and West Ridings, which it now misleadingly calls Yorkshire and Lincolnshire.

NOTE.—Some columns do not total precisely 100.0 because of rounding off errors.

Riding of Yorkshire divisions, with 31.3 percent of manufacturing industry's employees in 1962 secured 28.4 percent of industrial building. In contrast, the Northern Region, Scotland and Wales, with only 17.0 percent of manufacturing employees in 1962 achieved 25.7 percent of industrial building space between 1945 and 1962. This appears to be regional policy in action.

However, when one examines columns 2, 3, 4 of table 9, it becomes obvious that this apparent achievement of regional policy arose very largely in the years immediately after the second war. Table 10 below is a summary of table 9 and brings out the pattern of events more clearly.

This table really speaks for itself. Column 2 shows the curb on industrial building in the south of England in the years immediately after the war and the factory building boom in the areas of higher unemployment. It also shows that the three Midland regions did not suffer from the same degree of regulation as did the south. Column 3 shows the main period of relaxation, with the south now getting its "share" and the higher unemployment areas getting very little more than theirs.[70] Columns 4, and more especially 5, show that the genuine efforts to steer industry, under the Local Employment Act of 1960, have had no great success. Indeed, column 5 suggests that progress has been in a reverse direction. It should be remembered that Britain has been passing through a recession since 1961, although it is fair to add that the volume of industrial building under construction at September 1962 was little below the average of recent years.

All in all, columns 4 and 5, of tables 9 and 10, go a long way toward explaining the sharp change in regional policy in 1963, including the bigger building grants, the discovery that it is administratively possible to discriminate fiscally between regions and the murmurs of an impending growth point policy for the north east.

Appendix III

The Growth in Numbers Employed by Region

Having sighed long enough in appendix II over opportunities missed, it seems reasonable to examine what has happened in recent years to the pattern of employment in the three problem regions of Scotland, Wales, and the Northern region of England, as compared with the Midland region and Great Britain as a whole.

For many years, Scotland, Wales, and the Northern region of England have had slower rates of increase in numbers employed than has Britain as a whole. See table 11. It was thought worthwhile to try to assess whether these lags arose mainly from the regions' having unfortunate industrial structures or from a failure of the growth industries to grow proportionally as rapidly in the regions named as in the country as a whole.[71]

---

[70] In one sense, this statement is unfair. The main growth industries are in the south. A complete lack of regulation, by IDC's, would have led to the south of England obtaining a greater proportion of total new factory building than its percentage of total industrial population would appear to "warrant." Even so, policy was supposed to be trying to redress the uneven regional balance of growth industries. It has clearly not been having much effect since the early 1950's.

[71] Here, as in the whole of this section, the concepts of growth and growth industries refer solely to increases in numbers employed, between particular dates. Though this is only one measure of growth, it is the most suitable one for the present purposes. It is realized that, for example, some of the industries deemed below to be declining have in recent years been growth industries in terms of their volumes of output.

TABLE 10.—*New Building for Manufacturing Industry—Distribution by Grouped Regions*

[In percent]

Region	(1)	(2)	(3)	(4)	(5)	(6)	(7)
	New building completed				Under construction at Sept. 30, 1962	Distribution of Insured Employees in Manufacturing Industry	
	Jan. 1, 1945 to Sept. 30, 1962	Jan. 1, 1945 to June 30, 1954	July 1, 1954 to Mar. 31, 1960	April 1, 1960 to Sept. 30, 1962		May 1952	May 1962
London and South East, East, South, and South West	31. 4	23. 0	36. 1	34. 5	40. 7	34. 4	35. 8
Midland, North Midland, East and West Riding	28. 4	27. 1	29. 7	28. 1	25. 3	30. 2	31. 3
North Western	14. 3	14. 4	13. 8	15. 3	17. 1	17. 4	15. 8
Northern, Scotland, and Wales	25. 7	35. 5	20. 6	22. 0	16. 8	18. 0	17. 0
Great Britain	100. 0	100. 0	100. 0	100. 0	100. 0	100. 0	100. 0

It was decided to take, as base year, 1952 and to try to measure, by industry, the change in numbers employed between then and 1961, first in Great Britain and then in each of the three regions named, plus the Midland region where employment had been high throughout the period and the growth in numbers employed had exceeded the national average.

TABLE 11.—*Percentage Increase in Numbers Employed 1952–61*
[End of May]

Great Britain	Scotland	Wales	Northern Region	Midland Region
8. 6	2. 1	4. 6	5. 6	10. 8

1952 was taken as base year because it was thought to be the first year in which the teething troubles, in the collecting of regional employment data, inevitably associated with the changes brought by the National Insurance Act of 1948, had been eliminated. It is also statistically less prone to short-term influences than the years immediately after the Second World War or during the Korean War. At the same time, there was a slight depression, mainly in textiles, in 1952 while the first half of 1961 was fairly buoyant, so the 2 years were not at the same point of the trade cycle. However, the differences between the 2 years in the percentages of wholly unemployed workers were slight:

TABLE 12.—*Unemployment Rates mid-June*

	Great Britain	Scotland	Wales	Northern Region	Midland Region
1952........	2. 1 (1. 4)	3. 2 (2. 6)	2. 6 (2. 4)	2. 3 (2. 1)	1. 0 (0. 8)
1961........	1. 2 (1. 1)	2. 8 (2. 6)	2. 1 (1. 9)	2. 0 (1. 9)	. 8 (.7)

NOTE.—The figures in parentheses are for the wholly unemployed, i.e., they exclude the temporarily stopped.

Regional figures of "number of employees" by industry are calculated by the Ministry of Labour annually for end of May. We are grateful to the Ministry for making these available to us. These figures are for employed plus unemployed. We have subtracted from each figure the number of unemployed for the nearest available date, mid-June, to give an approximate figure for number employed.

The Ministry compiles their employee figures from the number of national insurance cards exchanged at their local offices in each region. In some cases, cards may be exchanged in a region different from that in which a worker is employed. Since 1955, the Ministry have adjusted their figures as far as possible to correct for this. They have also compiled tables of adjustments by industry and by region at May 1955, to permit broad corrections to be made to regional figures prior to 1955. We have used these 1955 figures to adjust the 1952 totals.

One major difficulty in trying to measure regional employment changes by industry between 1952 and 1961 is that the British Standard Industrial Classification was modified in 1958.[72] This classification was first compiled in 1948; it then contained over 160 minimum list headings or "industries" grouped into 24 industrial orders. The revised 1958 classification still has 24 orders, but the number of headings has been reduced to 152. Moreover, while there were some straight forward transfers of headings from one order to another, plus certain separations and amalgamations of headings, there were also transfers of parts of headings to other headings and similar complicated reorderings. Finally, although the figures for Great Britain, 1959, by orders, were calculated and published on both the 1948 and 1958 classifications so as to create a "bridge", this double exercise was not carried out for the regional figures. Thus it is not possible to use this "bridge" for the present purposes.

It was decided that, in the circumstances, the 1952 figures, by regional and minimum list headings, should be re-sorted as far as possible to fit the 1958 SIC. This is clearly an imperfect method. The errors have been reduced by aggregating certain minimum list headings so that these are 133 industries, instead of 152, but some errors still remain, particularly amongst industries in which our figures show a very large increase or decrease in numbers employed over the 9 years. However, it was judged better to make a tentative effort than none at all. An attempt will be made later to compare the results with other calculations.

First, however, we have the 133 industry analysis. We decided to adopt the same method as in appendix 2 of the *Report on the Scottish Economy*. That is to say, we calculated, for each of the 133 industries, the apparent percentage change in numbers employed in Great Britain, between the relevant years. We then ranked these industries from those with the greatest apparent percentage increase to those with the greatest apparent percentage decline, grouping them into eight categories. Each category consists of those industries in which, between May 1952 and May 1961, the numbers employed in Great Britain had changed between certain limits. The limits are shown on page 414.

We thus have five groups, or categories, of industries in which numbers employed in Great Britain apparently increased between 1952 and 1961 and three groups of industries in which employment apparently fell. These will be referred to as the five growth categories and the three decline ones.

In each category, the totals of numbers employed in each industry in 1952 were aggregated, then the aggregate for 1961 was calculated, and finally, for each category the average percentage change in employment over the 9 years, in Great Britain, was calculated.

The whole of the above exercise was then repeated for Scotland, Wales, and the Northern region, as well as for the Midland region. The 133 industries were, in each region, ranked in the same order as the Great Britain figures, that is by national rates of change of employment 1952–61. Here again, the figures within each category were aggregated for 1952 and 1961,

---

[72] The classification is based on industries and the unit is the establishment. Each establishment is allocated to the heading appropriate to its major activity, unless it has separate departments for which separate records are kept. For further details see Central Statistical Office, *Standard Industrial Classification,* HMSO, August 1958.

Category [1]	I	II	III	IV	V	VI	VII	VIII
Change in numbers employed, 1952–61, Great Britain.	Increase of over 50 percent.	Increase of over 30 to 50 percent.	Increase of over 20 to 30 percent.	Increase of over 10 to 20 percent.	Increase of 10 per cent or less.	Decrease of less than 10 percent.	Decrease of 10 percent and less than 20 percent.	Decrease of 20 percent or more.

[1] The industries in each category are listed at the end of this appendix.

and for each category, the average percentage change in employment was calculated, and the results compared with the national rate of change.

Finally, the whole process was repeated nationally and regionally for the 98 primary and manufacturing industries combined. The results are shown in tables 13 and 14 below.

Leaving aside the Midlands, for a time, we will concentrate on Scotland, Wales, and the Northern region. The tables suggest that these three regions have had rather different patterns of change from each other. If we take the "All Industries" table first, the least complicated picture appears to be that of the Northern region. The percentage rate of increase in employment seems to have exceeded the national rate in all the growth categories except the first. The average growth of employment in the five groups combined appears to have been much the same as in Britain as a whole. As the declining industries seem to have shrunk at a slightly slower pace than in Britain, we apparently cannot blame divergencies between regional and national rates of change for the fact that total employment in the Northern region rose by only 5.6 percent compared with a national average of 8.6 percent. The main cause of the slow growth of employment appears to be the unfortunate industrial structure of the region, which would seem to have had only 52.4 percent of its workers in growth industries in 1952, compared with a national average of 62.5 percent.

The Welsh situation seems similar. In each of the five growth categories, the percentage increase in numbers employed in Wales is very close to the national average. The failure of the Welsh economy to achieve more than a 4.6 percent increase in employment in 9 years appears to arise, to a small extent from the fact that the declining industries have shrunk at a rather faster rate than in Britain as a whole, but much more, again, from an unfavorable industrial structure. The pattern in 1952 was not as adverse as in the Northern region, but the Principality has 43.7 percent of employment in decline industries compared with a national average of 37.5 percent.

The picture in Scotland seems more complex. Total employment growth over the 9 years was only 2.1 percent, only one quarter of the national average. When one examines the individual categories, it would seem that in each of the five growth ones, the Scottish achievement was poorer than that of either Wales or Great Britain, and in four out of five poorer than in the Northern region. Moreover, although the Scottish distribution of employment between categories was not as favorable as the total British one, in 1952, it was better than the Welsh one and markedly better than in the Northern region.

If for Scotland, Wales, and the Northern region, the percentage change of employment in each of the eight categories between 1952 and 1961 is reweighted by the percentage distribution of employment by category in Great Britain in 1952, the results come out in table 15.

In presenting this table, it is not intended to imply that such achievements would have been possible. In the Northern region, for example, it is highly probable that if the industrial pattern had been nearer to that of the country as a whole, certain bottlenecks in labor skills and availability of factory sites would have emerged. Moreover, some of the growth achieved was in small firms building up from scratch. On the other hand, some industries in the region might have grown more rapidly if they had been more strongly represented and had thus secured more external economics of scale. A number of electrical and electronic goods manufacturers in the area firmly believe that they would gain from having more firms of a similar

TABLE 13.—*Changes in Numbers Employed, 1952–61, by Minimum List and Grouped Minimum List Headings*

[All industries]

Categories	Index of numbers employed, 1961 (1952=100)					Numbers employed 1952 (thousands)					Percentage distribution of employment 1952				
	Great Britain	Scotland	Wales	Northern region	Midlands	Great Britain	Scotland	Wales	Northern region	Midlands	Great Britain	Scotland	Wales	Northern region	Midlands
I	171. 3	155. 0	170. 8	152. 4	180. 1	1, 182	102	41	54	83	5. 8	5. 0	4. 5	4. 4	4. 1
II	137. 1	128. 5	136. 8	143. 2	141. 6	2, 283	256	81	131	210	11. 1	12. 4	8. 9	10. 9	10. 4
III	125. 8	121. 2	125. 8	131. 1	124. 8	2, 542	217	95	104	370	12. 4	10. 5	10. 4	8. 6	18. 4
IV	114. 8	109. 6	116. 2	116. 2	113. 7	4, 476	414	207	238	536	21. 8	20. 1	22. 7	19. 7	26. 7
V	104. 4	101. 3	104. 9	109. 4	110. 7	2, 338	218	90	107	153	11. 4	10. 6	9. 8	8. 8	7. 6
VI	94. 0	80. 8	85. 2	86. 1	87. 0	1, 248	124	59	69	159	6. 1	6. 0	6. 5	5. 7	7. 9
VII	84. 7	85. 2	83. 1	86. 2	82. 0	4, 204	466	263	403	354	20. 5	22. 6	28. 8	33. 3	17. 6
VIII	71. 6	69. 0	66. 6	71. 5	76. 5	2, 236	264	77	104	145	10. 9	12. 8	8. 4	8. 6	7. 2
Total	108. 6	102. 1	104. 6	105. 6	110. 8	20, 510	2, 061	912	1, 211	2, 008	100. 0	100. 0	100. 0	100. 0	100. 0
I+II+III	139. 0	130. 5	138. 4	139. 2	137. 1	6, 007	576	216	290	662	29. 3	27. 9	23. 8	23. 9	32. 9
I to V	124. 2	118. 0	123. 6	124. 9	124. 8	12, 821	1, 207	513	634	1, 350	62. 5	58. 6	56. 3	52. 4	67. 2
VI to VIII	82. 4	79. 6	80. 2	84. 4	82. 0	7, 688	854	399	577	657	37. 5	41. 4	43. 7	47. 6	32. 7

NOTE.—Certain columns in tables 13 and 14 differ slightly from their totals because of rounding off errors.

TABLE 14.—*Changes in Numbers Employed, 1952–61, by Minimum List and Grouped Minimum List Headings*

[Primary and manufacturing industries]

Categories	Index of numbers employed, 1961 (1952=100)					Numbers employed 1952 (thousands)					Percentage distribution of employment 1952				
	Great Britain	Scotland	Wales	Northern region	Midlands	Great Britain	Scotland	Wales	Northern region	Midlands	Great Britain	Scotland	Wales	Northern region	Midlands
I	168.1	205.4	194.1	160.9	163.8	350	16	6	10	22	3.6	1.7	1.3	1.6	1.8
II	143.0	146.7	135.9	168.5	140.1	451	51	10	23	73	4.6	5.2	2.2	3.6	5.9
III	124.7	114.1	120.9	126.2	124.4	1,305	100	51	53	286	13.3	10.3	11.4	8.3	23.0
IV	114.7	108.5	111.7	114.8	109.4	2,354	180	113	132	382	24.0	18.6	25.2	20.7	30.7
V	103.6	100.8	101.2	113.0	111.0	944	83	21	35	44	9.6	8.6	4.8	5.5	3.5
VI	94.3	82.1	92.5	88.5	87.6	784	79	35	38	148	8.0	8.2	7.8	5.9	11.9
VII	85.2	85.9	80.5	86.0	81.8	1,752	230	149	263	168	17.9	23.7	33.2	41.2	13.5
VIII	72.7	70.5	68.6	72.1	79.1	1,854	229	64	84	122	18.9	23.6	14.1	13.2	9.8
Total	103.3	95.6	95.9	98.7	106.4	9,792	970	450	637	1,245	100.0	100.0	100.0	100.0	100.0
I+II+III	135.8	133.0	129.6	141.1	129.7	2,105	167	67	86	381	21.5	17.2	14.9	13.5	30.7
I to V	121.0	116.6	116.5	122.8	119.1	5,402	431	202	252	807	55.2	44.4	44.9	39.7	64.9
VI to VIII	81.6	78.8	79.1	83.0	83.0	4,390	538	248	385	438	44.8	55.5	55.1	60.3	35.2

TABLE 15.—*Regional Employment May 1961 All Industries*

[May 1952=100]

	Scotland	Wales	Northern region	Great Britain
Actual employment	102. 1	104. 6	105. 6	108. 6
Notional employment, reweighting by distribution of employment in Great Britain by category	103. 6	107. 6	109. 5	

nature near to them. In brief, table 15 is far from being meaningless, but it is nothing more than the very broadest indication of the extent to which adverse industrial structures have held back the growth of employment. Perhaps the most interesting point is the degree of difference between the notional calculations for Scotland and the Northern region. It would certainly seem that, for Scotland, the presence of an unbalanced industrial structure is only part of the story.

Finally, a brief reference to the Midlands of England is worthwhile. This is the most prosperous manufacturing region of Britain, regarded as the success story of the Islands, with an increase of employment of 10.8 percent in 9 years. Before taking this point any further, it is necessary to stress that the region has suffered from chronic shortages of various types of skilled labor over the period under review and that this fact has encouraged capital intensive investment projects. Moreover, in manufacturing industry, official attempts have been made, from time to time since the war, to damp down industrial expansion by the refusal of IDC's.

We have already seen that these attempts have just about succeeded in keeping the Midland region's share of factory building since the war in step with its share of manufacturing employment (app. II, table 9). Similarly, the rate of growth of growth industries has been much the same as in Britain as a whole. The higher rate of total employment growth seems to have arisen from the fact that the industrial structure, with 67.2 percent of employment in 1952 in industries which expanded in the next nine years, was even more favorable than in Britain as a whole.

As a brief check on the above, it is worth making a comparison with an earlier exercise of the same type. Prof. J. Sykes[73] compares growth of insured employees by region between 1949 and 1957. For each region, he compares the actual increase in employment against what the increase would have been if each industry group had expanded or contracted at national rates.

It is possible to carry out a similar exercise for the 1952–61 figures, using the eight "categories" as weights. The results are in table 16.

The drawbacks of the Sykes method were that he was using employees (employed and unemployed) as a basis, was operating with the 24 industry groups, not minimum list headings and was basing his calculations on 1949, a year relatively near to the end of the war and very near to the introduction

[73] J. Sykes, "Employment and Unemployment in Regions," *Scottish Journal of Political Economy,* 1959, esp. p. 195, table IV.

TABLE 16.—*Percentage Increase in Insured Numbers by Region*

	Scotland	Wales	Northern region	Midlands
Sykes: 1949–57:				
Actual percentage increase in employees	3. 7	4. 9	5. 5	9. 7
Increase if each industry group had expanded or contracted at national rates	6. 7	6. 8	5. 2	9. 2
Present paper: 1952–61:				
Actual percentage increase in employment	2. 1	4. 6	5. 6	10. 8
Increase if employment in each category had expanded or contracted at national rates	6. 8	5. 8	4. 8	10. 5

of the national insurance scheme. The main drawbacks of the method used in the present paper are that it cuts across the 1958 SIC change and it uses categories of grouped minimum list headings. Despite the different sources of error, the picture from both sets of calculations seems much the same, except that the Scottish picture seems less unfavorable and the Welsh one a little more unfavorable in Professor Sykes's table.

It is sometimes argued that tertiary industries are broadly dependent for their growth on the success of local primary and manufacturing ones, so that the true employment history of a region or country emerges best from an examination of primary and manufacturing industries only. This argument is overstated. The most that can be said is that probably a greater proportion of tertiary industry in a region, than of primary and secondary, is mainly dependent for its growth on the growth of total income in the region. However, it remains true that much of the present report has been concerned with primary and manufacturing industry. Therefore it is worth comparing the regional and national structures and employment changes in primary and secondary industries only. This is done in table 14 above. This table shows an apparent national increase in employment of 3.3 percent in primary and manufacturing industries over the years 1952–61. This is an understatement because in the 1958 SIC change, certain subgroups within minimum list headings were transferred from manufacturing to tertiary industries. It is possible to adjust for these changes in Great Britain, but not in the regions.

We are concerned, however, mainly with regional comparisons. Once again, as in table 13, the Northern region appears to come out quite well. The average employment growth of growth industries is again at about national average, and it would seem that the poor showing in terms of aggregate employment change arises from a particularly adverse pattern of industry, only 40 percent of primary and manufacturing employment in 1952 appears to have been in industries in which employment was to increase in the country as a whole over the next 9 years, compared with a national average of 55 percent.

On the other hand, Scotland's showing seems rather better for primary and secondary industries, than for all industries, while Wales' seems rather worse. This is brought out by calculating the national percentage change in employment in each region for primary and manufacturing industries, in the same way as was done for all industries in table 15. The result is:

TABLE 17.—*Regional Employment, May 1961, Primary and Manufacturing Industries*

[May 1952=100]

	Scotland	Wales	Northern region	Great Britain
Apparent employment	95. 6	95. 9	98. 7	103. 3
Notional employment	100. 3	100. 6	104. 8	

It must be emphasized that this table pushes the statistics rather far. Certainly one would be much happier if regional bridges were prepared for 1958. Even so, if the same reweighting exercise is performed on the Scottish figures for 1950–58, given in appendix II of the Toothill report, a very similar picture to that in table 17 emerges, with the Toothill figures slightly less unfavorable to Scotland.

All in all, if the figures in this appendix are even approximate guides to what is going on in the outer regions of the British economy, it would seem that the pattern of progress has been quite different between them. It would seem that, in the Northern region, the main problem is the industrial structure. Growth industries are not as well represented as in Britain as a whole, but they appear to be growing at the national rate, whether we take all industries or primary and manufacturing. In Wales, also, it would seem that the main problem is the industrial structure but that the growth of primary and manufacturing industry is also lagging slightly behind that of Britain as a whole. In Scotland, again, the chief problem is a structural one, but there is a tendency for the growth rate of primary and manufacturing and of tertiary industry to lag behind. A considerable research program would be needed to check these very tentative claims and, if they were verified, to assess the causes. For a start, one would very much like to know what percentage of growth industry has been located in remote areas as opposed to industrial ones in Scotland, Wales ,and the Northern region of England respectively.

Finally, a few comments can be made about the progress of firms on industrial estates in the Northern region. The figures in the last column of table 18 were prepared for us by members of the English Industrial Estates Corporation, to whom we are very grateful. Without their cooperation, the exercise would have been impossible, for they are unable to divulge information about individual firms. However, it can be said that the total employment in the estate firms referred to in table 18 was 40,500 in 1952 (out of a total of 637,000 workers in primary and manufacturing industries in the Northern region) and 66,000 in 1961 (out of a total of 630,000). Thus, over these years, of the total increase in employment of 68,000 in the region (including tertiary industry) the primary and manufacturing firms in the estates have contributed over 25,000.

The column headed "Industrial Estates in Northern region" is not strictly comparable with the other two columns, although it is as near as is possible. The main snag is that it was not possible to obtain all the SIC numbers of estate firms in 1952. Therefore, the 1961 SIC numbers have been used. In other words, it has been assumed that firms did not change their pattern of production sufficiently to change their SIC number between these years. This is not, in fact, true; some firms which we have visited have made considerable changes. Most adjustments will have been into growth trades, however, from declining or more slowly growing ones. Thus we have almost certainly understated the rate of growth of employment in categories I–III and also understated the decline of employment in categories VI–VIII.

TABLE 18.—*Changes in Numbers Employed 1952–61, by Minimum List and Grouped Minimum List Headings*

[Primary and manufacturing industries]

Categories [1]	Great Britain [2]	Northern region [2]	Industrial	Estates in Northern region
I	168	161		214
II	143	169		177
III	125	126		197
IV	115	115		209
V	104	113		187
VI	94	88		96
VII	85	86		105
VIII	73	72		82
Total	103	99		163

[1] As in tables 13 and 14.

[2] As in table 14.

In calculating the last column in table 18, the figures for 1952 include employment in all estate firms which ceased to operate in the region between then and 1961. The figures for 1961 include the firms which began production in the region between 1952 and 1961. The only nontertiary estate firms which have been excluded from the calculations are the four which were on an estate in 1952 but moved to nonestate premises in the Northern region before 1961. These had to be disregarded because the estates corporation had no record of their 1961 employment figures. In addition, all tertiary firms on estates were ignored. Approximately 360 firms were involved in the calculations, of which about 50 closed down, or transferred outside the region, between the relevant dates. Most of these were small. About 90 of the 360 firms settled on the estates between 1952 and 1961. The remaining 220 were there over the whole period.

All in all, it would seem that there is something in the claim made by the chairman of the estates that the industrial estates are the growth points of the Northern region.[74]

Minimum List Headings and Grouped Headings, 1958 SIC

[Ranked according to apparent growth in numbers employed, 1952–61, Great Britain]

Category I

SIC No.	*Industry*
899	Other services.
214	Bacon curing, meat and fish products.
889	Hairdressing and Manicure.
474	Shop and office fitting.
364	Radio and other electronic apparatus.
351	Scientific, surgical and photographic instruments, etc.
334	Industrial engines.
706	Air transport.
709	Miscellaneous transport services and storage.
872	Educational services.
272	Pharmaceutical and toilet preparations.

Category II

482	Cardboard boxes, cartons and fibre-board packing cases.
332 }	{ Metal working machine tools.
333 }	{ Engineers' small tools and gauges.
341	Industrial plant and steelwork.
483	Manufacturers of paper and board not elsewhere specified.
887	Motor repairers, distributors, garages and filling stations.
239	Other drink industries.
820	Retail distribution.
496	Plastic moulding and fabricating.
499	Miscellaneous manufacturing industries.
419	Carpets.
832	Dealing in other industrial materials and machinery.

Category III

494	Toys, games and sports equipment.
486	Printing, publishing of newspapers and periodicals.
874	Medical and dental services.
217	Cocoa, chocolate and sugar confectionery.
871	Accountancy services.
361	Electrical machinery.
860	Insurance, banking and finance.
274	Paint and printing ink.
365 }	{ Domestic electric appliances.
369 }	{ Other electrical goods.
395 }	{ Cans and metal boxes.
399 }	{ Metal industries not elsewhere specified.

[74] Made in a paper read at Newcastle at a meeting called in April 1963 by the Town and County Planning Association.

411 Production of man-made fibres.
422 Made-up textiles.
492 Linoleum, leather cloth, etc.
481 Paper and board.
363 Telegraph and telephone apparatus.
312 Steel tubes.
879 Other professional and scientific services.
469 Abrasives and building materials, etc., not elsewhere specified.
213 Biscuits.

Category IV

491 Rubber.
275 } Vegetable and animal oils, fats, soap and detergents.
277 } Polishes, gelatine, adhesives, etc.
218 Fruit and vegetable products.
103 Chalk, clay, sand and gravel extraction.
381 Motor vehicle manufacturing.
382 Motorcycle, three-wheel vehicle and pedal cycle manufacturing.
383 Aircraft manufacturing and repairing.
464 Cement.
873 Legal services.
810 Wholesale distribution.
271 } Chemicals and dyes.
276 } Synthetic resins and plastics materials.
394 Wire and wire manufactures.
396 Jewelry, plate and refining of precious metals.
602 Electricity.
500 Construction.
603 Water.
417 Hosiery and other knitted goods.
393 Bolts, nuts, screws, rivets, etc.
336 } Contractors' plant and quarrying machinery.
337 } Mechanical handling equipment.
338 } Office machinery.
339 } Other machinery.
349 } Other mechanical engineering not elsewhere specified.
449 Dress industries not elsewhere specified.
882 } Sport and other recreations.
883 } Betting.
311 Iron and steel (general).
463 Glass.
262 Mineral oil refining.

Category V

231 Brewing and malting.
831 Dealing in coal, builders' materials, grain and agricultural supplies (wholesale or retail).
703 Road haulage contracting.
707 Postal services and telecommunications.
414 Woolen and worsted.
261 Coke ovens and manufactured fuel.

450 Footwear.
886 Drycleaning, job dyeing, carpet beating, etc.
906 Local government service.
211 Grain milling.
489 Other printing, publishing, bookbinding, engraving, etc.
415 Jute.
444 } Overalls and men's shirts, underwear, etc.
445 } Dresses, lingerie, infants' wear, etc.
352 Watches and clocks.
362 Insulated wires and cables.

Category VI

479 Miscellaneous wood and cork manufactures.
421 Narrow fabrics.
471 Timber.
002 Forestry.
493 Brushes and brooms.
313 Iron castings, etc.
704 Sea transport.
472 } Furniture and upholstery.
473 } Bedding, etc.
433 Fur
881 Cinemas, theatres, radio, etc.
429 Other textile industries.
321 } Light metals
322 } Copper, brass and other base metals.
705 Port and inland water transport.
432 Leather goods.
240 Tobacco.
461 Bricks, fireclay and refractory goods.

Category VII

370.2 Marine engineering.
495 Miscellaneous stationers' goods.
431 Leather (tanning and dressing) and fellmongery.
475 Wooden containers and baskets.
216 Sugar.
885 Laundries.
441 } Weather-proof outerwear.
442 } Men's and boys' tailored outerwear.
443 } Women's and girls' tailored outerwear.
385 Railway carriages and wagons and trams.
875 Religious organizations.
702 Road passenger transport.
423 Textile finishing.
370.1 Shipbuilding and ship repairing.
389 Perambulators, hand-trucks, etc.
884 Catering, hotels, etc.
101 Coal mining.
901 National government service.
701 Railways.

462	Pottery.
331	Agricultural machinery (except tractors).
601	Gas.
416	Rope, twine and net.
888	Repair of boots and shoes.

CATEGORY VIII

384	Locomotives and railway track equipment.
412	Spinning and doubling of cotton, flax and man-made fibres.
219 }	{ Animal and poultry foods.
229 }	{ Food industries not elsewhere specified.
418	Lace.
003	Fishing.
001	Agriculture and horticulture.
102	Stone and slate quarrying and mining.
335	Textile machinery and accessories.
212	Bread and flour confectionery.
391 }	{ Tools and implements.
392 }	{ Cutlery.
109	Other mining and quarrying.
446	Hats, caps and millinery.
215	Milk products.
891	Private Domestic service.
273	Explosives and fireworks.
413	Weaving of cotton, linen and man-made fibres.
342	Ordnance and small arms.
263	Lubricating oils and greases.

Appendix IV

MIGRATION

Over the last decade, the net flow of workers between regions has been mainly to the London and South East, Eastern Southern and South Western regions, combined. There has also been a very small net movement into the Midlands and North Midlands. The main outflow has been from the Northern region, Scotland, Wales, and the East and West Ridings. Thus broadly, the movement has been from areas of higher unemployment to areas of lower. See table 19.

It is generally accepted that the problem of migration from regions of higher unemployment is not just the actual number of workers who are lost to the area, but that there is a tendency for the younger, more skilled people to go. There are no statistics of the skills of migrants, but it is clear that when particular localities suffer from high unemployment, some firms in areas where labor is scarce send personnel officers to recruit skilled men. As far as ages are concerned, "an analysis by age of the net outflow from Scotland of insured employees to other regions over 6 years showed that 88.4 percent were in the age-group 20–44; 10.8 percent were aged 15–19; 0.8 percent were aged 45 or over." [75] As for graduates, it seems that between

[75] *Toothill Report,* p. 108.

TABLE 19.—*Net Movement of Employees Between Regions* [1]

Region	Net gain (+) or loss (−) of employees by migration 1951–61	Net gain (+) or loss (−) as percent of 1950 employee population	Average unemployment rate 1951–61
London and South East; East, South and South West [2]	+279,000	+3.4	1.1
Midlands	+1,000	+.1	1.0
N. Midlands	+2,000	+.1	.9
East & West Ridings	−42,000	−2.3	1.2
North Western	−42,000	−1.4	2.0
Northern	−59,000	−4.8	2.3
Scotland	−98,000	−4.6	3.1
Wales	−41,000	−4.4	2.8
Great Britain	...	...	1.6

[1] This table, except for the "average unemployment rate" column is taken straight from L. C. Hunter, "Employment and Unemployment in Great Britain," *Manchester School*, January 1963, p. 33 table IV.

[2] "It is not possible to separate out movement between London and South East, East, and Southern and South Western regions." (Footnote to original table).

1954 and 1959, two-thirds of the Arts graduates and three-quarters of the Science ones who went direct from Glasgow University into industry, found their first employment outside Scotland.[76]

This presents an alarming picture of regions unable to expand because of a shortage of ability. Certainly, the big weakness of the argument that migration presents a solution to a region's problems is that if the loss of younger skilled people goes beyond a certain point, the effect of migration may be more and more migration. At the same time, it would be utterly wrong to consider the possibility of discouraging individuals from moving. There is all the difference in the world between "forced" migration arising from the lack of job opportunities in a region and voluntary migration in search of a change in climate, or in job. It is possible to visualize considerable cross-movements of workers, seeking their individual ideas of a better location and job.

On this, one point must be made. The net outflow of workers from any part of Britain is already the result of much larger movements of labor inwards and outwards. For example, in Scotland, between 1951 and 1960, the net loss of 87,000 workers to other parts of Britain was the result of 297,000 going out and 210,000 coming into the country. Similarly, in the same years, 298,000 insured employees left and 253,000 entered the Northern region. Moreover, as far as Scotland, at least, is concerned, the quality of migrants in was thought to be as high as that of migrants out, in terms of skills, managerial grades, etc.[77] Thus, the outer regions of Britain are

[76] *Ibid.*, pp. 108–109.
[77] *Ibid.*, p. 109.

not faced with the problem of creating an in-migration of skills but of bringing about an increase of an existing flow.

Clearly, however, raising the rate of migration into a region is a part of a bigger problem. The authors of the Toothill report argued that the main thing is to seek a general improvement in the regional economy. One important point should be added, however. The effort to raise the migration rate of skilled workers into the outer areas of Britain would probably be more effective if the general improvements were first concentrated at particular points. There is evidence in the North East of England that the recruitment of technicians and other key workers, and their retention by the firm which brings or appoints them, is much less expensive and more successful if the firm is in one of the industrial towns of the region rather than on a rural site.[78] Thus, we are back to the argument for growth points and for the need for capital spending there on amenities as well as on services of more direct use to industry. Furthermore, such growth points might help to reduce out-migration.

Appendix V

These six maps show, first, the employment exchange areas of the North East of England, excluding a few rural areas, secondly, the slow buildup of development districts as the employment situation deteriorated from 1961 to early 1963, and thirdly, the decision to list the whole of Tyneside (in May 1963) and Birtley, Washington, and Durham (in May 1963), at a time when unemployment in the region was falling. It is not yet clear whether this was merely a rounding off, or the first step toward a new policy of listing industrial areas near to areas with high unemployment.

The maps also show the listing, stoplisting, and relisting of a small number of areas. The most curious incident was the listing of Haswell in October 1960, when unemployment rose there followed by the stoplisting of the adjacent area of Houghton-le-Spring in the following year.

---

[78] E. Allen, A. J. Odber, P. J. Bowden, *Development Area Policy in the North East of England,* pp. 46, 67–68.

North East of England

By Employment Exchange Areas

LEGEND

1. Hexham
2. Morpeth
3. Bedlington
4. Blyth
5. Seaton DeLaval
6. Newcastle
7. West Moor
8. Whitley Bay
9. Prudhoe
10. Newburn
11. Elswick
12. Walker
13. Wallsend
14. North Shields
15. Sarrow
16. South Shields
17. Blaydon
18. Cateshead
19. Felling
20. East Bolden
21. Consett
22. Stanley
23. Birtley
24. Washington
25. Sunderland
26. Chester – le – Street
27. Houghton – le – Spring
28. Seaham
29. Crook
30. Durham
31. Haswell
32. Horden
33. Bishop Auckland
34. Spennymoor
35. Wingate
36. Hartlepools
37. Shildon
38. Darlington
39. Stockton & Thornaby
40. Stokesley
41. Middlesbrough
42. South Bank
43. Redcar
44. Guisborough
45. Saltburn
46. Loftus
47. Whitby
48. Scarborough

SCALE

0 5 10 Miles

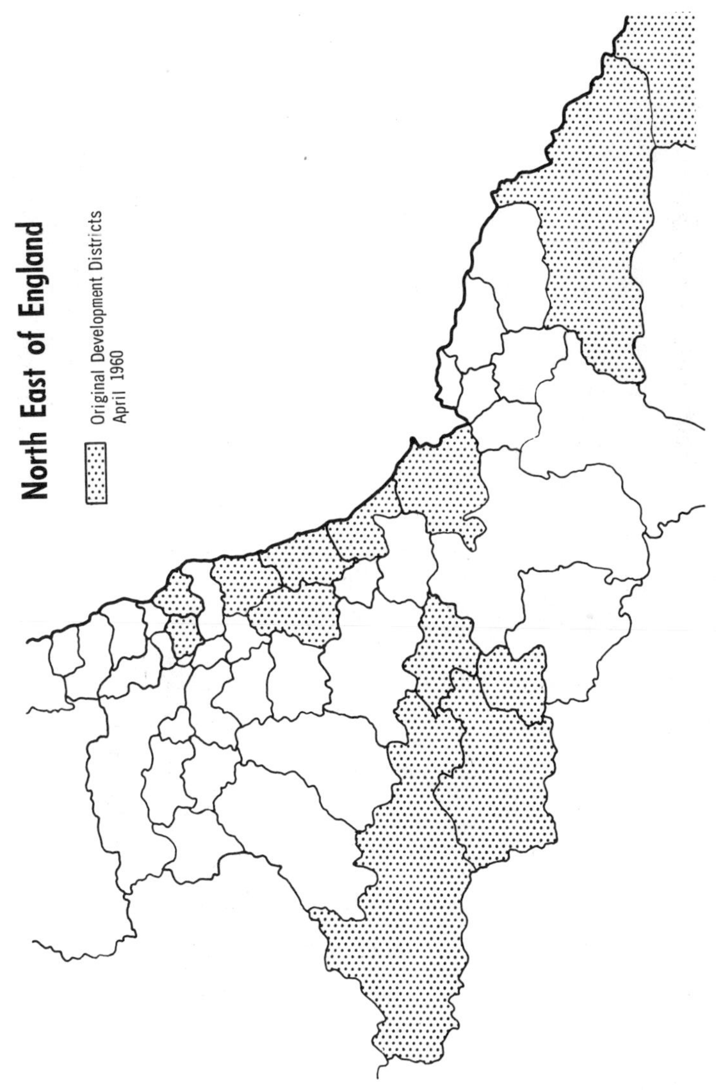
North East of England
Original Development Districts
April 1960

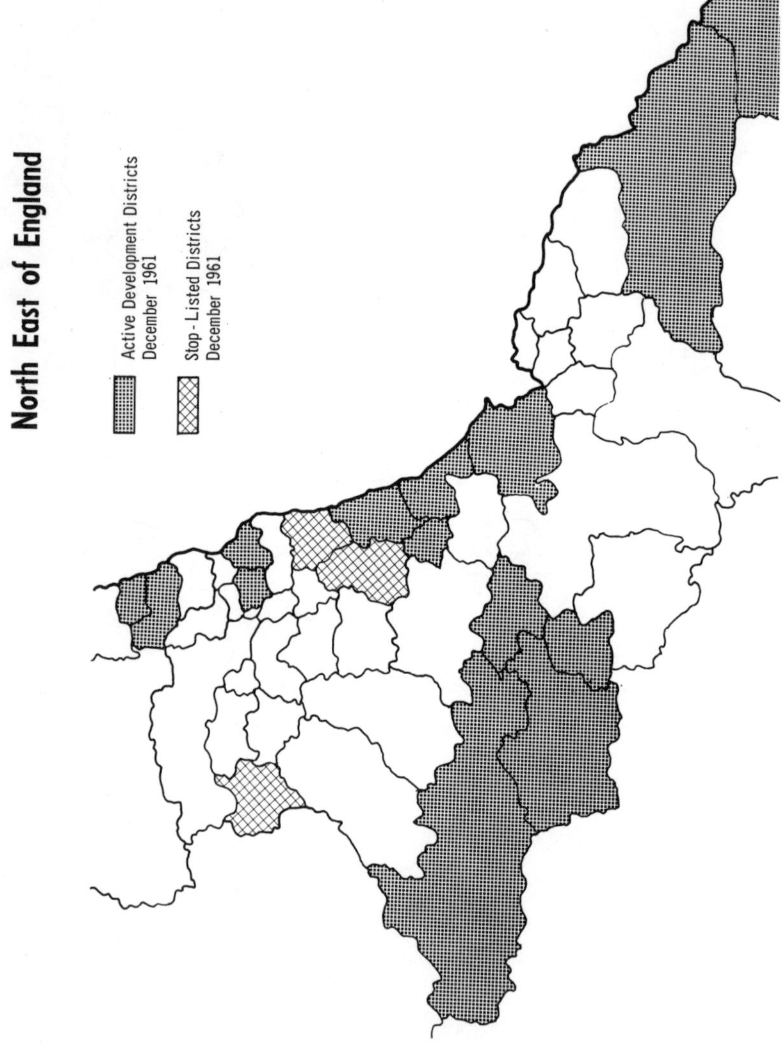
North East of England
Active Development Districts
December 1961
Stop-Listed Districts
December 1961

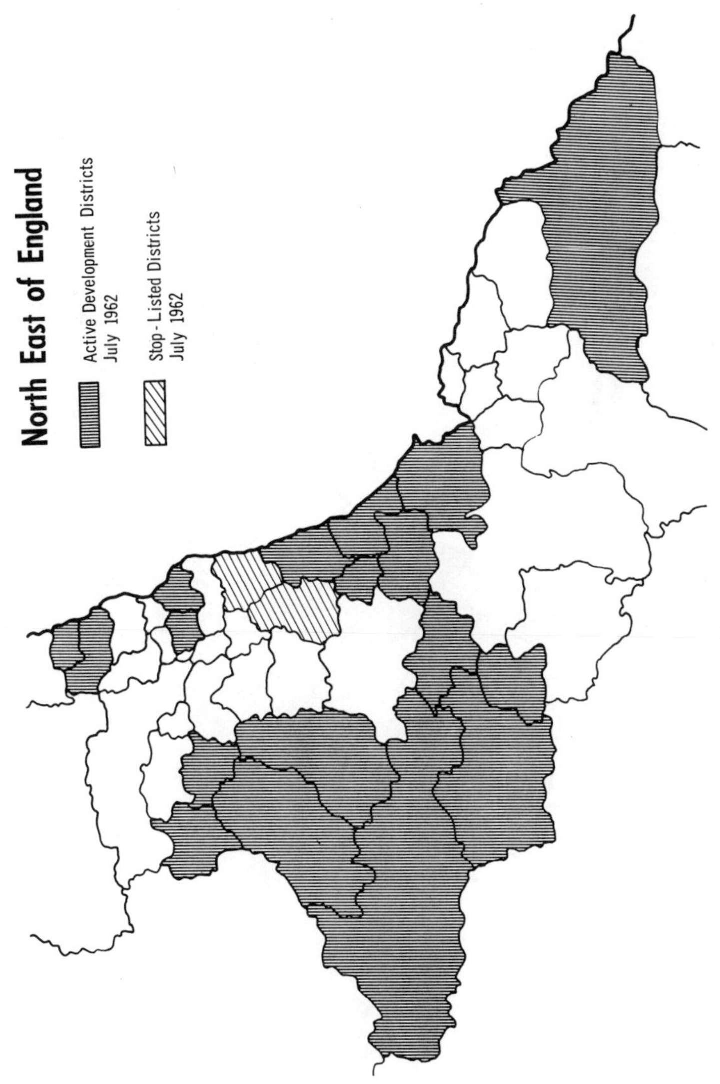
North East of England
Active Development Districts
July 1962
Stop-Listed Districts
July 1962

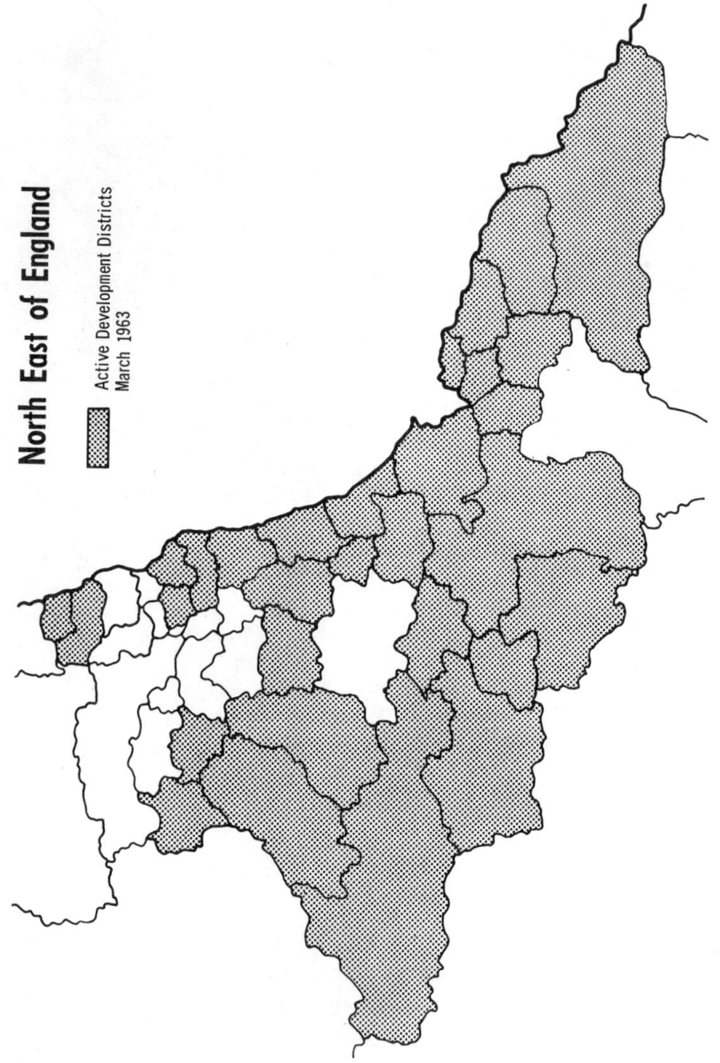
North East of England
Active Development Districts
March 1963

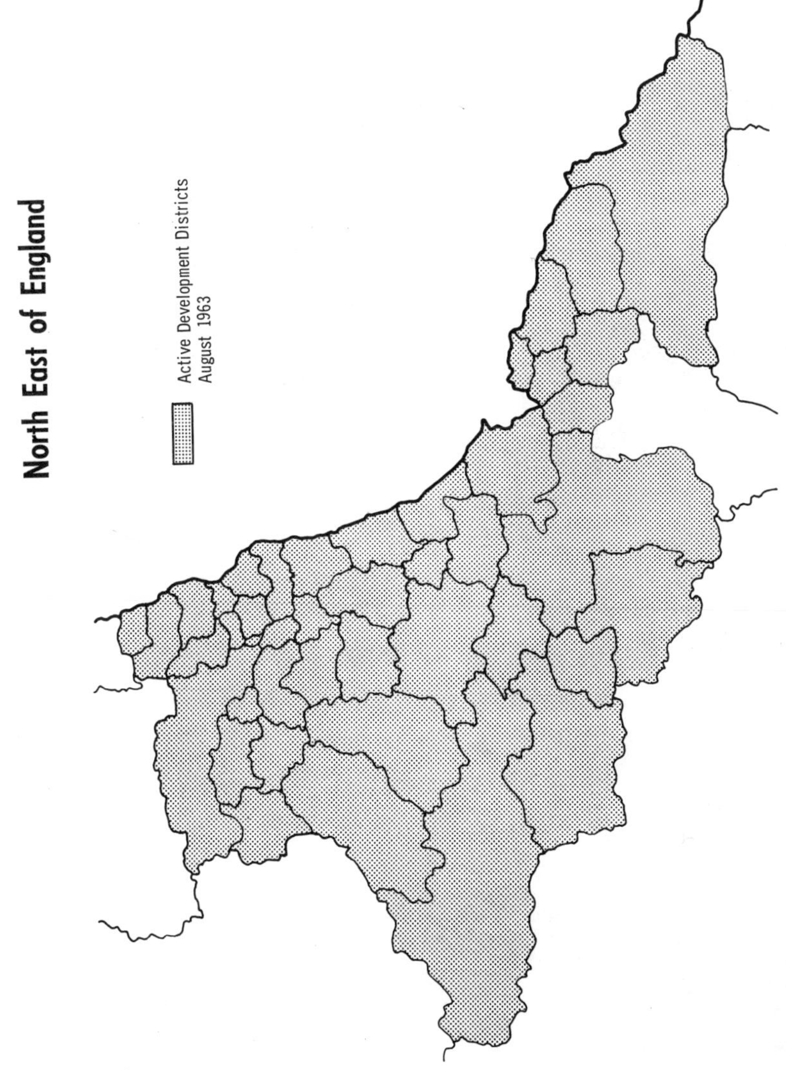
North East of England
Active Development Districts
August 1963

Part 7

The Role of the European Coal and Steel Community and the Common Market in Regional Policy

Yves Delamotte and Erika Georges

Contents

Section A

Section B

Section A

The European Coal and Steel Community

Introduction

National area redevelopment policy, as any policy, must be analyzed in view of (1) its objectives, and (2) the instruments used to attain these objectives. Today, the experts on area redevelopment policies agree to a great extent on the kind of instruments that may profitably be used. However, no such agreement exists regarding the objectives, and, consequently, regarding the criteria according to which the areas to be redeveloped and the instruments to be applied in each are to be selected. In the literature on national area redevelopment policy, the objectives are assumed—explicitly or implicitly—to be either of a predominantly social nature (i.e., regional income redistribution), or of a predominantly economic nature (e.g., maximum possible growth of *per capita* income), or a combination of both. As the last comes closest to the national policymakers' intentions, it appears to be the better criterion for an analysis of the instruments of national area redevelopment policy.[1] However, for an analysis of supranational regional policy measures, and in particular for the analysis of the policy of the European Coal and Steel Community (ECSC), this criterion is not necessarily the only appropriate one.

While all institutions are continuously changing, this holds to a much greater degree for supranational institutions which have been established for only a short time or are still in the process of being established; and the policy goals of supranational executive bodies change together with the institutions.

The reasons for such changes are the following: In the first place, while the policy of supranational executives must be based on their respective treaty which purports to demarcate the realms of national and supranational authority, particular provisions of the treaty may be interpreted in various ways, and they are interpreted at different points in time, i.e., whenever the question of their application arises. Because of these interpretations, policy, goals, and instruments may be changed. Secondly, as a result of developments beyond the control of the supranational authority, new problems may arise which had not or could not be anticipated at the time the treaty was

---

[1] The authors recognize, of course, that, at the present time it is practically impossible to conduct this type of analysis in a strictly scientific manner because of both the lack of knowledge on the marginal rates of substitution between social and economic goals on the part of the policy makers, and the lack of data on the reaction coefficients to changes in economic and social data on the part of the various economic and social operators. While extensive research in all disciplines of the social sciences is required to furnish some of these data, at the present time some explicit assumptions on these reaction coefficients and rates of substitution ought to be made in the analysis of national regional policy. In the analysis of supranational regional policy, however, this does not seem to be appropriate (for reasons given in the introduction of this paper).

drafted. Thus, policy goals and instruments may be altered again. Thirdly, in any practical economic integration scheme, like the ECSC, there are strong forces making for further integration. As certain treaty provisions cannot be implemented because the policy instruments of the supranational executive prove to be insufficient, new instruments may be given to the supranational authority which can again affect and alter other policy goals and means. Finally—and this applies particularly to the area redevelopment policy of the ECSC—while practical experiences of policymakers and administrators and the theoretical concepts regarding a particular policy always mutually influence each other, this occurs in an especially high degree when this policy is first attempted. In continental Europe, national area redevelopment has become a matter of policy only very recently; it was born practically at the same time as the idea of the ECSC, i.e., in the late 1940's and early 1950's. It is therefore not surprising that the policy of the High Authority of the ECSC was influenced by and did influence national area redevelopment policies, and that both national and supranational experiences had effects on and were affected by simultaneous developments in the theory of regional policy—which again led to changes of regional policy objectives and instruments.

The area redevelopment policy of the ECSC can therefore be analyzed in view of (1) the application of the provisions of the treaty of the ECSC under changing exogenous conditions, (2) the limitations of partial integration, (3) the mutual influences of national and supranational policies, (4) the effects of ECSC policies on those of other supranational institutions, e.g., of the European Economic Community (EEC), and (5) the development of regional thinking of theorists, policymakers, and administrators.

In the following, we shall concentrate on an analysis of the High Authority's regional policy mainly in view of aspects (1) and (5), while assuming that the High Authority has been pursuing both social and economic objectives.[2] Occasional references to aspects (2), (3), and (4) will be appropriate. Yet it appears that changes in market conditions and techniques of production in the coal and steel industries, as well as the gradual development of a more regionally-oriented concept of area redevelopment policy, have been the most important determinants of the evolution of the High Authority's area redevelopment policy.

The Legal Framework of the ECSC and Regional Policies

Social Policy Provisions and the Objectives of the ECSC

Article 2 of the ECSC treaty states that the objectives of the creation of the common market for coal and steel are "* * * to contribute to the expansion of the economy, *the development of employment and the improvement of the standard of living* in the participating countries * * *," by assuring "* * * the most rational distribution of production at the highest

[2] With the rates of substitution between social and economic objectives, and between different economic as well as between different social objectives, changing over time.

possible level of productivity, while safeguarding *the continuity of employment* and avoiding the creation of fundamental and persistent disturbances in the economies of the member states."[3] These objectives were to be realized by means of eliminating, for the products included in the Common Market, all discriminatory duties, quantitative restrictions, taxes, and other restrictive practices, including subsidies or special charges of the member states.[4]

Thus, apart from the full employment provision and certain other exceptions, the ECSC treaty was made on the basis of predominantly liberal economic concepts.

In addition, at the time the treaty was drafted, it was generally held—by the majority of labor as well as industry representatives—that not too many social policy powers should be concentrated in the new supranational agency. On the one hand, there was, at the time, a great lack of information regarding the comparative social situations within the member countries. Thus the High Authority would not have had an adequate basis for its actions. On the other hand, the national social groups and governments did not want to be restricted in their own freedom of action. And, because of the partial nature of integration, a community-wide common social policy for the employees of the coal and steel industries alone would have had disturbing effects within the national economies.[5]

Thus, apart from repeated general statements to the effect that the ECSC was to contribute to the continuity of employment and the improvement of working conditions and the standard of living, not many specific social policy instruments can be found in the treaty. The only significant social provision was contained in article 56 which, for the first time in the history of the western industrialized nations, established policy instruments regarding the compensation of workers who had become unemployed as a result of *technological* change.[6] Yet article 56 could be applied only if a number of rather strict conditions were found to hold simultaneously in a particular area.[7]

However, added to the treaty was the *Convention Containing the Transitional Provisions* which set forth the measures necessary for the creation of the common market during a 5-year period of transition. According to these transitional provisions, complete trade liberalization was to be established only gradually for certain products and member countries under the treaty in order to avoid great disturbances in some national markets. Along the same lines of thought, section 23 of this convention contained provisions

---

[3] *Treaty establishing the European Coal and Steel Community,* subsequently cited as *ECSC Treaty,* art. 2 [authors' italics]. The treaty was signed in April 1951 and went into force in January 1952. The institutions of the ECSC include the High Authority, the executive of the Community and the administrator of the provisions of the treaty, the Council of Ministers, a court, and the European Parliament. The Consultative Committee, which the High Authority is to consult on various problems, in particular those of a social nature, is composed of an equal number of producers, workers, and consumers and dealers of the ECSC industries.

[4] *Ibid.*, art. 4.

[5] ECSC, High Authority, *Die EGKS 1952–62, Die ersten 10 Jahre einer Teilintegration,* Vorlaeufige Ausgabe, Luxembourg, 1963, subsequently cited as *Die EGKS 1952–1962,* pp. PSoc. 1/1–1/2.

[6] *Ibid.*, p. PSoc. 1/2.

[7] *ECSC Treaty,* art. 56. *Cf.*, pp. 8–9 of this report.

for workers who had become unemployed due to the introduction of the ECSC. These provisions played an important part in the development of the regional policy of the ECSC.

Section 23 of the Convention [8]

It has been said that the readaptation provisions of section 23 of the convention constitute one of the most significant innovations of the treaty in view of their influence on subsequent national and international policies concerning structural unemployment.[9]

When the treaty was being worked out—after consultations with representatives of labor and industry—readaptation policy was considered the necessary "social counterpart" [10] of the economic measures creating the common market. For, as the ECSC was to increase productivity in the coal and steel industries through the elimination of customs barriers leading to increased competition, the weakest enterprises were expected to be unable to continue their operations or to be able to do so only after substantial reorganization or modernization. In either case, workers would become unemployed. The report of the French delegation on the treaty well reflects the ideas which led to section 23 of the convention. "It cannot be considered desirable to maintain in each particular industry or even in each particular enterprise a given volume of employment. This would lead * * * to stagnation * * *. Full employment * * * is compatible with economic progress only if it is combined with the necessary relocation of workers * * * from declining to expanding industries, and from industries with higher increases in productivity than in output, where, consequently, the demand for labor decreases, to industries with higher increases in output than in productivity, where the demand for labor increases. However, the burden this essential determinant of economic progress * * * implies for labor, cannot be ignored, and every possible effort must be made to protect the latter from this burden." [11]

Section 23 of the convention provides that if, during the transition period, certain enterprises or parts of enterprises had to cease or change their activities *as a consequence of the introduction of the common market,* "* * * the High Authority, at the request of the governments concerned * * * must help to protect the workers from the burden of readaptation and assure them productive employment, and may grant nonrepayable assistance to certain enterprises * * *. [It] shall participate in a study of the possibilities of reemploying the unemployed workers either in existing enterprises or by creating new activities. * * * [It] shall assist the financing of approved programs submitted by the governments concerned for the readaptation of enterprises or for the creation, either in the industries subject to its jurisdiction or * * * in any other industry, of new, economically sound activi-

---

[8] *Convention Containing the Transitional Provisions,* subsequently cited as *Convention,* sec. 23.

[9] "Structural unemployment," in this report, is defined to mean long-term unemployment caused by either technological change or shifts in demand.

[10] *Die EGKS 1952–62, op. cit.* p. PSoc. 3/1.

[11] *Rapport de la Délégation française sur le Traité instituant la Communauté Européenne du Charbon et de l'Acier,* Paris, October 1951, p. 124 (authors' translation from *Die EGKS 1952–62,* p. PSoc. 3/1).

ties capable of assuring productive employment to the workers thus discharged.* * *"[12]

Furthermore, section 23 authorizes the High Authority to grant nonrepayable assistance to contribute (1) to the payment of compensation to tide unemployed workers over until they obtain new employment, (2) to the payment of resettlement allowances to the workers, (3) to the financing of technical retraining, and (4) to enterprises to assure the payment of their personnel in the case of temporary layoffs due to reconversion. These grants are subject to a contribution by the respective state of at least an equal amount, unless an exception to this provision is authorized by a two-thirds majority of the Council of Ministers of the ECSC.[13]

Thus section 23 of the convention provides the High Authority with the two basic instruments of area redevelopment policy: (1) Bringing labor to industry, or the "readaptation policy," and (2) bringing industry to labor, or the "reconversion policy." And it authorizes the High Authority to participate in studies on the possibilities of reemploying the unemployed.

Of course, these provisions were intended to relate only to situations arising in particular enterprises due to the establishment of the ECSC, regardless of their location. Consequently, section 23 of the convention can hardly be said to entitle the High Authority to any real area redevelopment policy. Nevertheless, it so happened that many of the enterprises and of the unemployed benefiting from section 23, in particular the collieries and the mineworkers, were located in single-industry areas or in other regions suffering from structural unemployment. Thus the general measures of section 23 tended to become regional ones in practice. Moreover, experience in the application of section 23 led the staff of the High Authority more and more to view the problem of structural unemployment as a regional problem.

Readaptation Provisions of the Treaty

STUDIES

The treaty authorizes the High Authority to undertake various kinds of studies concerning readaptation and reconversion possibilities. Although these provisions do not directly refer to area studies, they can and have been interpreted in this sense.

Under article 46.4 it is only at the request of the governments that the High Authority may "* * * participate in the study of the possibilities of reemploying, either in existing industries or through the creation of new activities, workers unemployed by reasons of the development of the market or technical change." However, under article 46.5 the High Authority, on its own initiative, can "* * * gather any information required to assess the possibilities of improving the living and working conditions of the labour force in the industries under its jurisdiction, and the *risks* menacing their living conditions. * * * [It] may publish the studies and information. * * *[14]

FINANCIAL ASSISTANCE

Article 56 of the treaty contains the provisions for financial readaptation assistance of the High Authority. According to the original text of this

[12] *Convention*, sec. 23, pars. 1–3.
[13] *Ibid.*, pars. 4 and 6.
[14] *ECSC Treaty*, art. 46.5 [authors' italics].

article, the High Authority could grant such assistance only if all of the following three conditions were present: (1) The unemployment had to be caused by the introduction of technical processes or new equipment "within the framework of the general objectives laid down by the High Authority"; (2) the unemployment had to be exceptionally large; and (3) reemployment of the discharged workers had to be especially difficult. The grants, which were again subject to an equal contribution by the respective state, could be made for the payment of unemployment compensation, of resettlement allowances, and for vocational retraining.

From 1952 to 1959, the readaptation provision of article 56 was never used because of the restrictive nature of its conditions. The few applications for assistance received under article 56 had to be rejected by the High Authority, as all three of the conditions were never fulfilled simultaneously.[15] Thus, before 1960, all readaptation assistance was granted under section 23 of the convention. Section 23, however, was to expire on February 9, 1960,[16] while structural changes in the coal and steel industries in the late 1950's—in particular the competition of other fuels and the cheapening of iron ore from third countries—made the continuation of readaptation measures rather desirable. Members of the Consultative Committee—particularly representatives of labor—and of the European Parliament, as well as experts on the staff of the High Authority felt that article 56 was totally inadequate and that readaptation and reconversion measures had to be taken also in cases of structural unemployment that had been caused by shifts in demand and that did not necessarily constitute "an exceptionally large reduction in labour requirements."[17] In 1957, upon request of the European Parliament and of various professional groups, the High Authority began to study the possibilities of a revision of article 56. After a first amendment to article 56 (which was limited to the coal industry and to a period of 3 years) had been rejected by the court of the ECSC, the amendment in its present form was finally adopted as section 2 of article 56 on January 26, 1960. It provides for the same kind of readaptation assistance as section 23 of the convention, for the entire period of the treaty,[18] if an enterprise has to cease, reduce, or change its activities due to great changes in the market conditions of the coal and steel industries (which are not directly connected with the establishment of the common market).[19]

This amendment, which was called the "Little Revision" of the treaty (it is the only revision to date), was a large step forward in the develop-

---

[15] F. Finck, "L'action de la Haute Autorité pour le réemploi des travailleurs," in ECSC, *Collection d'Economie et Politique Regionale, I, La Conversion Industrielle en Europe,* vol. III (Les Financements des Investissements et les Aspects Sociaux de la Réconversion), subsequently cited as *La Conversion Industrielle en Europe,* vol. III, p. 160.

[16] As provided for in par. 8 of sec. 23 of the *Convention,* sec. 23 had been extended for 2 years after the official termination of the transition period in February 1958. *Cf.*, ECSC, High Authority, *Sixth General Report,* 190. Hereafter, all the General Reports of the High Authority will be cited as "ECSC, (*First*) *General Report.*"

[17] Cf., e.g., ECSC, *Réadaptation et Réemploi de la Main-d'Oeuvre,* Rapport de la Mission aux Etats-Unis des Syndicalistes de la Communauté, Luxembourg, 1956, pp. 110–111.

[18] I.e., for a period of 50 years.

[19] ECSC, *Eighth General Report,* 144–148.

ment of the area redevelopment policy of the High Authority, as it incorporated effective readaptation and reconversion provisions into the treaty.[20]

Reconversion Provisions of the Treaty

STUDIES

Article 46 authorizes the High Authority to conduct reconversion as well as readaptation studies. Paragraph 5 of article 46 has been particularly important with respect to area studies, as it allows the High Authority, on its own initiative, to gather information on the *risks* menacing the living and working conditions of labor in the coal and steel industries; i.e., it enables the High Authority to accumulate, for any area where such risks are in the offing, the basic economic and social data required for any reconversion and redevelopment project.

In addition, article 55 of the treaty states that the High Authority must encourage technical and economic research concerning "* * * the production and the development of consumption of coal and steel, as well as workers' safety in these industries." [21] While this article does not authorize reconversion studies, it may indirectly facilitate reconversion. On the one hand, the High Authority must place the results of its economic research on the production and the development of consumption of coal and steel products at the disposal of all the interested parties in the Community. On the other hand, the High Authority may conduct primary technical research which results in a new type of utilization of coal and steel products.

FINANCIAL ASSISTANCE

The history of the treaty provision for financial reconversion assistance from 1952 to February 1960 has, of course, been the same as that for readaptation assistance. However, while readaptation assistance had been extended under section 23 of the convention before the "Little Revision," reconversion assistance did not begin until about 1960.

Article 56, in its original form, provided that the High Authority could facilitate "* * * the financing of such programmes as it may approve for the creation, either in the industries subject to its jurisdiction or, with the agreement of the council, in any other industry, of new and economically sound activities capable of assuring productive employment to the workers * * * discharged; * * *" Again, however, such assistance could be extended only if the three conditions mentioned above were present simultaneously. Under the revision of article 56, the same kind of assistance may now be granted also to relieve structural unemployment that has been caused by shifts in demand, and that is not "exceptionally large" and "especially difficult" to eliminate.

It is only because of this reconversion provision in the "Little Revision" that one can actually speak of an "area redevelopment policy" of the High Authority. For only when the High Authority was authorized to grant

[20] Due to the partial nature of integration of the ECSC, it is, of course, never quite correct to speak of an "area redevelopment policy" of the High Authority, as regional policy should be an integral part of overall economic policies, and the High Authority has such policy powers only to a limited extent for the coal and steel industries. *Cf.*, the conclusion of this report.

[21] *ECSC Treaty,* Art. 55, Section 1.

financial assistance to reconversion and redevelopment schemes in the coal and steel industries or any *other* industry, was it able to participate in constructive regional redevelopment programs.

Other Treaty Provisions

Certain other policies of the High Authority have direct regional implications, e.g., those concerning investments and transportation. However, the treaty certainly did not intend these policies to be used in favor of regional development. While there is growing concern for regional problems among the staff of the High Authority, and while regional considerations sometimes have played a part in the policies of the High Authority, e.g., with respect to granting loans and giving opinions, it is not very likely that these policies will take account of regional considerations to a much greater extent in the future.[22]

The provisions for free mobility of labor in the coal and steel industries of the ECSC, however, could have been an important instrument facilitating readaptation. In order to eliminate the obstacles to such mobility, article 69 of the treaty prohibits any discrimination in payment and working conditions as between national and foreign workers.[23] However, this provision applies only to skilled labor of the coal and steel industries, and changes in the immigration regulations regarding unskilled workers are to be made only "* * * where an expansion of production in the coal and steel industries might be hampered by a shortage of suitable labor. * * *"[24] Thus, the mobility provision of the treaty, all by itself, does not constitute much aid to readaptation.

However, article 69 provided also that the member states were to work out among themselves the arrangements necessary to prevent the differing social security measures of the member countries from being an obstacle to the free movement of labor.[25] With the cooperation of the International Labour Office, a group of experts began to work out these arrangements in July 1954. While they were originally intended to apply only to skilled workers of the coal and steel industries within the ECSC, once the Treaty of Rome was signed establishing the EEC and providing for the free mobility of all workers within the EEC,[26] the social security arrangements were extended to become the *European Convention on Social Security for Migrant Workers.*[27] This is one example of the preparatory work of the

---

[22] E.g., art. 70.4 of the *Treaty* provides that the High Authority may give its consent to temporary special domestic tariffs in the interest of one or several coal or steel producing enterprises. The High Authority has applied this article to facilitate adaptation of the collieries in the Centre-Midi of France. However, this kind of measure is generally considered inappropriate and will not commonly be applied. *Cf.*, ECSC, *Moyens d'intervention des pouvoirs publics pour faciliter la réconversion industrielle.* Travaux preparatoires à la Conférence intergouvernementale sur la réconversion industrielle, Luxembourg, September 1960, p. 121.

[23] *ECSC Treaty,* art. 69, par. 4.

[24] *Ibid.,* par. 3.

[25] *Ibid.,* par. 4.

[26] *Cf., Treaty establishing the EEC,* subsequently cited as *EEC Treaty,* arts. 48–51.

[27] *Cf.*, EEC, Commission, *First General Report on the Activities of the Community,* p. 88. For further details on the European Convention *cf.*, sec. B of this report, pp. 59–60.

partial integration scheme of the ECSC being taken over and expanded by the larger common market of the EEC. In this sense, inasmuch as a general increase in the mobility of labor facilities adaptation and reconversion, one can say that article 69 indirectly assists area redevelopment within the European Communities.

Most of the social activities of the High Authority indirectly facilitate readaptation and reconversion. This is particularly true of its measures regarding vocational training, workers' housing, industrial health and safety, and the data collections and studies in these areas.

Activities of the High Authority Concerning Area Redevelopment

Readaptation Assistance

TYPES OF ASSISTANCE

The High Authority classifies its policy instruments for readaptation into "active" and "passive" measures. Active readaptation measures are those which assist the unemployed to obtain a new job without great loss of income. F. Vinck lists the following active readaptation measures to which the High Authority has contributed under section 23 of the convention as well as under article 56.2(b):

(1) reemployment allowance: Workers accepting a new job at a salary below their former pay may receive, for a period of 12 months, the difference between their new and a specified percentage of their former salary;
(2) resettlement allowance: Workers accepting a new job in a different region are reimbursed for the transportation and moving expenses incurred for themselves and their families;
(3) supplementary transportation subsidy: Workers accepting a new job at a greater distance from their place of residence may, in certain cases, be reimbursed for their additional transportation costs;
(4) separation allowance: Workers accepting a new job in a different location who must be temporarily separated from their families may be reimbursed for the additional expenses they thereby incur;
(5) retraining assistance: Workers taking occupational retraining courses obtain a specified percentage of their former salary; the institutions or enterprises providing these courses are reimbursed for the costs of administering these courses.

"Passive" readaptation measures consist predominantly of the High Authority's supplementary contribution to unemployment insurance in the amount of a certain percentage of the former salary for the period of at least 1 year. Vinck points out that passive readaptation assistance, apart from protecting the standard of living of the unemployed, helps to maintain purchasing power within the respective area.[28] Thus, this measure also

[28] *La Conversion Industrielle en Europe*, *op. cit.*, vol. III, pp. 161–162.

facilitates area redevelopment in the narrow sense, if accompanied by reconversion activities.

Active and passive readaptation assistance of the High Authority is not the same for all workers within the ECSC. The High Authority has been well aware that this would be neither possible nor desirable in view of the present state of integration of the economic and social policies of the member countries. In the first place, one-half of the expenditures for readaptation assistance must be borne by the goverments applying for such assistance, and thus the High Authority cannot dictate to the governments the kind of assistance it prefers. For each application, the form and extent of the readaptation assistance is arrived at by special agreement between the High Authority and the respective government. Secondly, equal assistance for all workers in a particular occupation would not constitute equality, inasmuch as the social legislations of the member countries differ (e.g., regarding amount and duration of unemployment insurance which is supplemented by the High Authority). Thirdly, the general economic situation of the respective country, in particular the conditions in the national labor markets, must be taken into consideration (e.g., in a country in a state of recession or where there is a relatively large amount of structural unemployment, unemployed workers will, on the average, need more time to find a new job, and thus readaptation assistance should be given for a longer period). For these reasons, the High Authority itself desired a plurality of readaptation measures.[29]

FINANCIAL ASSISTANCE

As stated above, until February 9, 1960, the High Authority granted readaptation assistance only under section 23 of the convention. While during the first years of the ECSC there were only a few applications for readaptation assistance, the number increased rapidly in the late 1950's. Over the entire 4-year period 1953–57, only 19 applications from member governments were received, 16 of which were accepted by the High Authority. By contrast, in 1958 alone, the High Authority received 16 applications, and in the first 9 months of 1959, 35. The slow start had been due partly to the boom conditions prevailing in the ECSC countries and their coal and steel industries, partly to the new administrative and budgetary formalities the national administrations had to comply with, and partly to enterprises and labor unions being insufficiently informed.[30]

The total amount made available under section 23 of the convention came to 42,518,000 units of account,[31] benefiting 115,085 ECSC workers. Ninety-five thousand two hundred and eighty-five Community coal miners received the major share of these grants, or 31,536,000 units of account; 19,300 steelworkers about one-third as much, or 10,876,000 units of account; and 500 iron-ore miners a total of 106,000 units of account. The unit of account is

---

[29] *Die EGKS 1952–62, op. cit.,* p. PSoc. 3/5.

[30] ECSC, *Sixth General Report,* 191–192; *Seventh General Report,* 182; *Eighth General Report,* 141. The unusually large number of applications in 1959 was of course partly due to the fact that section 23 was to expire in February 1960, and, until January 1960, art. 56.2 had not yet been adopted.

[31] A unit of account corresponds to the value of 1 American dollar, or 0.88867088 grams of fine gold.

the equivalent of 1 U.S. dollar. The distribution by countries was as follows: The Federal Republic of Germany received the greatest amount of financial assistance for a total of 55,100 workers, mostly coal miners; Italy and Belgium came next with respect to total grants received, although more Belgian than Italian workers benefited from the assistance. The grants to Belgium were for coal miners only, those to Italy and France for both coal miners and steelworkers. Iron-ore miners received adaptation assistance in Germany and France.[32]

In several instances, the Council of Ministers has exempted the respective government from its contribution,[33] in particular Italy and Belgium. The major areas in which workers received readaptation assistance under section 23 were the Borinage in Belgium; the Ruhr and Saar, Lower Saxony, and Aachen in Germany; Lorraine, Auvergne, and the Centre Midi in France, as well as the Atelier et Forge de la Loire and some iron mines in Western France and the Pyrenees; the Sulcis mines in Sardinia and steelworks in northern Italy.[34]

Under article 56.2(b), the total readaptation assistance made available by the High Authority from February 1960 to January 1963, amounts to 11,170,000 units of account, benefiting 42,156 ECSC workers. Again, the major proportion went to German coal miners; French and Belgian coal miners were next in line, while the relative amounts going to steel workers were less than they had been under section 23, and the proportion received by iron-ore miners had considerably increased. These changes are due to the recent developments in the world market of iron-ore.[35] Compared to the assistance extended under section 23, and taking account of the respective periods (71 and 24 months), the number of workers receiving assistance has increased under article 56.2(b).[36]

---

[32] For further details regarding the distribution of the High Authority's readaptation assistance under sec. 23, *cf.*, table I, p. 18 of this report. According to the *Ninth General Report* of the High Authority (432), the figures in table I include four different categories of workers: (1) Workers whose assistance had already been terminated in 1960; (2) workers who were still receiving assistance; (3) workers who were to receive assistance in the near future, because they would definitely be laid off; and (4) workers who were to receive assistance in 1960, but who did not actually receive it as they were not discharged. The amounts made available by the High Authority, as shown in table I, do not correspond to the actual amounts disbursed. For instance, by Sept. 30, 1960, actual expenditures for readaptation on the part of the High Authority amounted to only 15,760,000 units of account, while the amounts made available by February 1960 are 42,518,000. The rather large difference between these figures is due to the following reasons: (1) Certain readaptation programs extend over several years and had not yet been terminated in 1960; (2) the governments of the member states first extend the total amount of assistance to their workers and ask for reimbursement from the High Authority only after the national expenditures have actually been made; (3) workers originally expected to become unemployed have found new jobs on their own either in the same or in other areas. *Cf. La Conversion Industrielle en Europe, op. cit.*, vol. III, p. 162.

[33] This is possible according to par. 6 of sec. 23 of the *Convention*. *Cf.* also, ECSC, *Sixth General Report,* 191.

[34] ECSC, *Fifth General Report,* 238–241; *Seventh General Report,* 183–185; *Eighth General Report,* 142.

[35] For further details see table II, p. 18.

[36] *Die EGKS 1952–62, op. cit.*, p. PSoc. 3/4.

Reconversion Assistance

As previously noted, it was only in the last years of the 1950's that the High Authority began serious efforts in the field of reconversion. The experience with readaptation assistance under section 23 of the convention, particularly the realization that for economic and social reasons it was neither easy nor always desirable to encourage unemployed workers in depressed areas to move to industries in other locations, caused members of the European Parliament, of the Consultative Committee, of the national governments, and of the High Authority to concentrate more and more on the possibilities of industrial reconversion. The "Little Revision" was both a result and further encouragement of this tendency, as was the Intergovernmental Redevelopment Conference which was organized by the High Authority in the fall of 1961.

THE INTERGOVERNMENTAL REDEVELOPMENT CONFERENCE

The High Authority decided to hold an intergovernmental redevelopment conference because (1) the problem of the collieries was recognized as a structural problem, (2) divergent national policies in this area are inappropriate within the ECSC, and (3) while the High Authority could assist reconversion measures for the reemployment of workers of the coal and steel industries on the basis of article 56.2(a), it had to obtain the consent of the Council of Ministers if the reconversion programs included industries not under the authority of the ECSC, and it had no means to do anything about the indirect depressing effects of the pit closures (i.e., effects other than the unemployment of miners) on entire regions.[37]

Among the 160 participants in the Conference were experts and administrators of regional policies, representatives of industry and labor organizations, and members of the commission of the EEC, the European Investment Bank, the Council of Ministers, and the High Authority. The Conference was to study the problems of the areas affected by pit closures, the appropriate reconversion measures for their redevelopment, the different kinds of assistance that could be extended by the national governments and the European institutions, and the forms of cooperation necessary between the governments and the European institutions.

The major conclusions of the Conference, which determined to a considerable extent the subsequent reconversion activities of the High Authority and other European institutions, were the following:

1. Reconversion projects should preferably be carried out during boom periods. In general, reconversion is much easier if started before decline has actually begun; thus reconversion projects may be long-run or short-run.
2. Reconversion policies must be adjusted to the socio-economic characteristics of the respective areas. It is absolutely necessary that a whole series of measures be concentrated in time and space in order to provoke the required "shock."
3. Infrastructural improvements, prefabricated industrial buildings, and industrial parks are important reconversion techniques.
4. Tax measures seem to be less effective than the extension of credits and of investment grants.

---

[37] ECSC, *Ninth General Report,* 444.

TABLE I.—*Readaptation Assistance of the High Authority Under Sec. 23 of the Convention* [1]

[Mar. 18, 1954–Feb. 9, 1960]

Country	Coal mining industry		Iron ore industry		Steel industry		Total	
	Number of workers assisted	Amount (1,000 units of account)	Number of workers assisted	Amount (1,000 units of account)	Number of workers assisted	Amount (1,000 units of account)	Number of workers assisted	Amount (1,000 units of account)
Belgium	28, 900	10, 560	....	....	....	....	28, 900	10, 560
Germany	54, 200	17, 061	250	59	650	226	55, 100	17, 346
France	6, 655	1, 551	250	47	5, 000	914	11, 905	2, 512
Italy	5, 530	2, 364	....	....	13, 650	9, 736	19, 180	12, 100
ECSC	95, 285	31, 536	500	106	19, 300	10, 876	115, 085	42, 518
Total number of workers in the ECSC in 1955	902, 000	....	33, 600	....	427, 000	....	1, 362, 000	....

[1] Source: ECSC, High Authority, *Ninth General Report*, 433.

TABLE II.—*Readaptation Assistance of the High Authority Under Art. 56, Par. 2* [1]

[Feb. 9, 1960–Jan. 31, 1963]

Country	Coal mining industry		Iron ore industry		Steel industry		Total	
	Number of workers assisted	Amount (1,000 units of account)	Number of workers assisted	Amount (1,000 units of account)	Number of workers assisted	Amount (1,000 units of account)	Number of workers assisted	Amount (1,000 units of account)
Belgium	12, 010	2, 363	....	....	135	85	12, 145	2, 448
Germany	17, 324	4, 105	3, 687	666	2, 056	259	23, 067	5, 030
France	4, 455	2, 845	847	362	1, 642	485	6, 944	3, 692
ECSC	33, 789	9, 313	4, 534	1, 028	3, 833	829	42, 156	11, 170
Total number of workers in the ECSC in 1961	676, 000	....	43, 000	....	483, 000	....	1, 202, 000	....

[1] Source: ESCS, High Authority, *Eleventh General Report*, 487.

5. Financial assistance should generally be extended only in the form of a once-and-for-all incentive to investments in order to avoid market distortions.
6. Decentralization of credit institutions should be promoted in order to avoid red tape and to comply better with regional needs. The establishment of special semi-public credit institutions for industrial redevelopment loans might be advantageous in certain cases.
7. Information on the various types of subsidies available ought to be centralized, so that entrepreneurs do not have to address many different institutions in order to obtain this information.
8. Various kinds of readaptation assistance must be provided for the miners, and should be available at the time the redevelopment program is started.
9. The progressive integration of the six member countries requires Communitywide actions. There should be more intergovernmental exchange of information on the national programs, and national policies ought to be coordinated, especially those for depressed areas alongside common national frontiers within the ECSC (e.g., those for the reconversion of the Département du Nord in France and the Borinage in Belgium).
10. The European institutions, while recognizing that the initiatives and the major responsibility for redevelopment programs lie with the member governments, must assist in the planning and financing of redevelopment programs and attempt to harmonize the various national policies.
11. The High Authority is to keep in mind that coordination of reconversion policies of the Community level is the necessary counterpart of a coordinated energy policy.[38]

The Conference was considered a great success because of the quality of the reports presented, the atmosphere of cooperation created, and the personal contacts it made possible.[39] One of the practical results was the establishment of a Joint Working Party on Coalfield Redevelopment of the High Authority, the EEC Commission, and the European Investment Bank, which is to coordinate the activities of the European institutions regarding coalfield redevelopment schemes and which examines the redevelopment programs for which governments are seeking financial aid.[40]

STUDIES, INFORMATION, AND COORDINATION

Since the beginning of its reconversion activities, the High Authority has held that reconversion schemes should be based on long-run redevelopment plans and be started long before layoffs and shutdowns occur. For it is much easier to counteract the gradual decline of an area than to try to revive it when it is already depressed, economically and psychologically. Thus, in examining applications for reconversion assistance, the authority has considered not only the actual but also the potential future unemployment, as well as the problem of coordinating in time the closure of enterprises and the start of new operations.[41]

---

[38] *Ibid.*, 447.
[39] *Ibid.*, 446.
[40] ECSC, *Tenth General Report*, 528.
[41] *Die EGKS 1952–62, op. cit.*, p. PSoc. 3/8.

From this view derives the High Authority's emphasis on regional studies, such as those on the *Bassins du Centre-Charleroi et du Borinage,* on *Brescia-Udine,* on *Auvergne-Aquitaine,* etc. Fifteen area studies had been completed by June 25, 1963 (most of them published in 1962 and 1963) under article 46.4 and 5. Four studies were then in preparation, and another four under consideration.[42]

In addition, there have been studies on the production of "new products" in the redevelopment areas. The *Tenth General Report* states that, in order to stimulate new departures in industry in the redevelopment areas, "research should be undertaken with a view to encouraging the more extensive use of treaty products, by facilitating the selection and development of new production lines," [43] and the *Eleventh General Report* describes a study of new products with good prospects for success in certain redevelopment areas for small or medium-sized enterprises. In this study, "new products" are taken to mean (1) products that have not been produced before in the particular area, (2) products that are being produced already (e.g., in the U.S.A.) but not yet within the ECSC, and (3) products that can be produced with new techniques. After a group of experts has chosen a dozen such products, market studies will be made for each one. Following the final selection of the new products, prospective investors will be provided with complete information on each. By means of this study, the High Authority also hopes to establish a practical method for periodically receiving information on new products.

Apart from the area studies, the High Authority, in 1962, established a committee of six experts—one from each member country—on industrial reconversion under article 46 of the treaty, in order to be able to consult the experts on current problems. In addition, the committee is to (1) continue the study of particular redevelopment problems, e.g., regarding zonings or prefabricated industrial buildings, (2) make studies on the coal and steel areas that are depressed or about to become depressed, (3) inform the High Authority on the reconversion activities carried through by the member countries, and (4) act as an information exchange center between the High Authority, the study groups, and the experts of the six member states.[44]

FINANCIAL RECONVERSION ASSISTANCE

By January 31, 1963, the High Authority had participated in eight reconversion schemes, four of which were in Belgium (Liège and Borinage), three in France (Champagnac, Béthune, and Saint-Eloy-les-Mines in the Puy-de-Dôme), and one in Italy (Genoa). It has guaranteed the loans of two enterprises in the amount of 1.04 million units of account, one being for the transfer of an enterprise to Béthune, France, the other for a steelworks in the region of Genoa. Credits were extended in the other six cases in the amount of 9.3 million units of account. The rate of interest on the loans never exceeds 5 percent; the term of the loans is usually between 15 and 20 years.

According to a rough estimate which does not take into account the multiplier effect of the investments, about 6,500 new jobs have been created by

[42] For a complete list of the area studies of the High Authority, see app. I.
[43] ECSC, *Tenth General Report,* 536.
[44] ECSC, *Eleventh General Report,* 490.

these measures, predominantly for unemployed mineworkers. The investor obtaining a loan or a guarantee must agree to employ a certain number of unemployed workers from the coal and steel industries, the number to equal a specified percentage of his total employment.

The programs assisted by the High Authority made use of various reconversion instruments, such as the creation of new and the expansion of existing enterprises, the construction of industrial buildings, the restoration of deserted mining areas, etc.[45]

The following two examples of reconversion programs assisted by the High Authority illustrate the great variety of redevelopment possibilities to which the High Authority may contribute.

One of the earliest reconversion applications concerned the intended closure of a small mine at Champagnac in central France. The situation in this area was specifically examined in the study on Auvergne and Aquitaine in the series of regional employment studies. In July 1959, the High Authority agreed to readaptation arrangements under section 23 of the convention on behalf of 220 workers who had lost their jobs due to the closure of the mine. With the consent of the council, the High Authority decided in February 1960 to grant a loan for the installation of a new enterprise (under section 23.3) in the amount of 365,000 NF at 3¾ percent interest, repayable in 21 equal annual installments. The loan is secured by collateral pledged to the High Authority and the Charbonnages de France, which participated in the scheme with a loan of 740,000 NF "As the object of the operation is to provide alternative employment for former mineworkers who have not yet succeeded in finding any for themselves, the enterprise in question has undertaken to sign on by December 31, 1962, not less than 80 such men, and to retain them for at least 2 years, except in the event of serious misconduct."[46]

While the Champagnac scheme is interesting for reasons of timing and the sequence of study, readaptation, and reconversion assistance, the program of the Société Provinciale d'Industrialisation for the Liège area is probably the most impressive one assisted by the High Authority in view of its scale and the wide range of redevelopment techniques to be tried out. The Société was established in February 1961 as a joint public/private corporation, under the Belgian Act of July 18, 1959, concerning economic expansion and regional development. Its first projects are to result in the creation of approximately 4,000 new jobs. The program includes the building of factory premises, the establishment of industrial belts, and the utilization of disused colliery sites. The High Authority, after consent of the council, granted a loan of BF 115 million at 4⅞ percent interest for a term of 20 years, with an initial redemption-free period of 4 years. The loan is guaranteed by the Belgian Government. The latter also provided for interest reductions which, in some cases, bring the rate down to as low as 1 percent. "The Société Provinciale is to submit to the High Authority all applications by enterprises wishing to set up on sites prepared with ECSC participation. Enterprises receiving assistance from the Société

---

[45] *Die EGKS 1952–62, op. cit.,* p. PSoc 3/10.

[46] ECSC, *Tenth General Report,* 534.

must recruit some of their personnel from among discharged mine-workers." [47]

In addition to assisting particular reconversion projects, the High Authority instituted compensation and subsidy schemes for the reorganization and modernization of Belgian and Italian collieries. The convention had provided that the Belgian and Italian coal industries were to be integrated into the Common Market only gradually, in order to allow their high-cost collieries sufficient time for modernization.[48] Thus, a compensation scheme was established which was financed by means of a special levy on the coal production of member countries whose average production costs were below the weighted average for the Community. "Up to April 30, 1957, this levy was payable on the production of the German and Netherlands collieries; from May 1 to December 10, 1957, it was collected only from Germany * * *, and the system was ultimately discontinued altogether from this last date. * * *" [49] The yield of the levy from March 1953 to November 1957 amounted to 56.6 million units of account, 52.09 million having been collected from German and 4.48 million from Dutch collieries.[50]

For 2 years, the Italian collieries at Sulcis received compensation assistance in the amount of 13 million units of account, one-half of which was furnished by the Community and one-half by the Italian Government. "After paying over a number of advances * * *, the High Authority made the final settlement of the compensation conditional upon the acceptance by the Italian Government and the Carbosarda Co. (which runs the Sulcis mines) of a reconstruction programme which it had approved." [51] Between 1952 and 1957, underground output per man/shift in the Sulcis mines rose from 618 to 959 kg., and underground and surface output per man/shift together from 450 to 784 kg.[52]

To facilitate the integration of Belgian coal into the Common Market, section 26 of the convention provided for compensation payments to the Belgian coal industry. The latter were to make it possible to reduce the prices of Belgian coal to the price level prevailing in the Common Market generally, and to offset to some extent losses incurred in the sale of Belgian coal in the Community. In 1954, the High Authority established a joint commission of experts from the High Authority and the Belgian Government, which was to analyze the situation in the Belgian coal market. On the basis of its findings, the compensation scheme was altered several times in an attempt to distribute the funds more rationally.[53] Furthermore, the High Authority requested the Belgian Government to introduce a number of reorganization measures aimed particularly at "* * * securing the financing of reequipment programs, supervising their implementation, encouraging a more rational layout of the workings, and valorizing production." * * * [54] These measures were partly financed with credits granted

[47] *Ibid.*, 532.

[48] Special precautionary measures were also provided for the French coal industry, but they never had to be introduced. *Cf.*, ECSC, *Sixth General Report*, vol. II, 14.

[49] *Loc. cit.*

[50] *Loc. cit.*

[51] *Ibid.*, 38.

[52] *Ibid.*, 39.

[53] *Ibid.*, 17.

[54] ECSC, *Fifth General Report*, 180.

by the High Authority out of the funds it had raised in the international capital market. In addition, the High Authority authorized and contributed to subsidies by the Belgian Government to the especially high-cost Borinage Collieries in southern Belgium. Based on the joint commission's reports, the High Authority, in 1956, laid down a definite reorganization program for those collieries which provided for the overhaul of pits whose operating results could be improved, and for the gradual closing-down of those which could never be operated at a profit. The subsidies were designed to facilitate the reorganization program. The High Authority was of the opinion "* * * that the closures imposed under the reorganization scheme must be effected at a rate carefully calculated not to involve undue economic and social hardship, and that subsidization is the means of enabling pits scheduled for closure to carry on until their time came. Furthermore, it was felt that some Belgian collieries should ultimately be able thanks to subsidies to qualify for full integration into the Common Market." [55] Total compensations and subsidies paid to the Belgian coal industry under section 26 of the convention amounted to 117 million units of account, 48.8 million of which had been contributed by the ECSC and 68.2 million by the Belgian Government.[56] Between 1952 and 1957, 23 pits were closed and output per man/shift increased, from 1,051 to 1,150 kg. for Belgium as a whole, from 1,300 to 1,450 kg. in the Campine, yet only from 965 to 1,032 kg. in southern Belgium. [57] Thus, although the High Authority had contributed both directly (by granting loans for modernization projects) and indirectly (by operating the compensation scheme) to the reorganization of the Belgian coal mining industry, the latter was still in difficulties at the end of the transition period. However, thanks to the payment of compensation, "* * * it was possible to prevent widespread unemployment in the Belgian collieries during the minor recession of 1953–54." [58]

The compensation payments under section 26 of the convention ended with the transition period, and Government subsidies were to be scaled down and ultimately abolished. However, just at that time, the coal crisis began to develop, and the High Authority applied article 37 of the treaty in favor of Belgium,[59] granted a special ECSC allowance to Belgian miners placed on short time, and authorized the Belgian Government to continue its subsidization of part of the industry's production.[60] The measures taken under article 37 provided "* * * that the reorganization of the coal mining industry should be continued by the closure of pits which had no prospect of ever qualifying for integration into the Common Market; in return, it afforded protection to the Belgian coal market by placing restrictions on trade in Community coal, on imports of coal from third countries, and on

---

[55] ECSC, *Tenth General Report,* 212.
[56] ECSC, *Sixth General Report,* vol. II, 23.
[57] *Ibid.,* 25, 28.
[58] *Ibid.,* 34.
[59] Art. 37 of the *ECSC Treaty* states that if a member state "* * * considers that in a given case an action of the High Authority, or a failure to act, is of such a nature as to provoke fundamental and persistent disturbances in the economy of the said State, it may bring the matter to the attention of the High Authority. The High Authority, after consulting the Council, shall if it is appropriate recognize the existence of such a situation, and decided on the measures to be taken * * * to correct such a situation. * * *"
[60] ECSC, *Ninth General Report,* 182.

the selling-off of stocks." [61] As a result of the new reorganization program, 57 additional pits of the southern coalfields had been closed by December 1961. And while the problem of the coal crisis has by no means been solved, underground output "* * * increased substantially in the south, the overall underground average exclusive of managerial and supervisory personnel rising from 1,125 kg. in 1957 to * * * 1,635 kg. in November 1961." [62]

Other Activities of the High Authority

Other activities of the High Authority have probably indirectly facilitated readaptation and reconversion, in particular those concerning the free movement of labor, vocational training, workers' housing programs, and industrial health and safety measures.

Article 69, which provides for the free movement of skilled labor within the coal and steel industries, became effective in September 1957, after the convention on social security had finally been worked out.[63] At that time, only 56 selected skilled jobs could receive labor cards enabling the workers to take up employment offers in other Community countries. However, in May 1961, a second schedule of 118 additional occupations was incorporated in the decision of the Council of Ministers concerning the implementation of article 69.[64] By September 30, 1962, 1,695 labor cards had been issued, and 423 of these cardholders had obtained employment in othe ECSC countries.[65] These figures certainly look disappointing and do not constitute much direct assistance to readaptation. In view of the limitation of article 69 to skilled workers within the ECSC industries, they should not represent a great surprise. As mentioned above, article 69 is of greater significance for the European Convention on Social Security for Migrant Workers and its application within the mobility provision of the EEC.[66]

The High Authority has been rather active in the field of studies and the exchange of information on vocational training. For instance, regarding the training of supervisory personnel, the High Authority, together with the member governments, encouraged cooperation between educational institutions and the ECSC industries and the elimination of customs and administrative impediments to the exchange of teaching aids within the Community. Two studies were made to serve as background information for discussion by the High Authority and the Government experts on the harmonization of vocational training.[67] More recently, new studies were started with the objective "* * * to support the measures now being taken in the different member countries to adapt the training of miners and steelworkers to the requirements of technical and social progress and provide systematic advanced training for technical sales and administrative executives." [68]

[61] ECSC, *Tenth General Report,* 201.
[62] *Ibid.,* 195.
[63] ECSC, *Sixth General Report,* 187–189.
[64] ECSC, *Tenth General Report,* 514–516.
[65] ECSC, *Eleventh General Report,* 456.
[66] *Cf.,* footnote 27 above.
[67] ECSC, *Tenth General Report,* 502.
[68] *Ibid.,* 510.

No positive statement can be made on the extent to which the activities of the High Authority in the fields of vocational training, as well as workers' housing and industrial health and safety, have facilitated readaptation.[69] The dissemination of information and the results of the studies conducted, as well as the exchange of ideas between member governments and the High Authority and among experts at the various conferences organized by the High Authority, certainly has stimulated the activities of the member governments in these areas and contributed to some extent to their harmonization. However, whether—and, if so, to what extent—the small degree of harmonization achieved to date in these areas has facilitated readaptation and reconversion, is impossible to say.

Conclusions

The area redevelopment policy of the High Authority of the ECSC has undergone a rather fascinating evolution in view of the application, interpretation, and amendment of the provisions of the ECSC treaty and the gradually growing tendency to regard area redevelopent as a regional problem.

In the development of its area redevelopment policies, the High Authority—partly on its own initiative and partly at the request of interested groups of the consultative committee and the European Parliament—has made the most of the provisions of a treaty whose major intent was to increase competition and productivity within the coal and steel industries rather than to take into account regional social and economic considerations. The studies made, assisted, or encouraged by the High Authority, the promotion of the gathering and exchange of information and ideas, and the actual assistance given to readaptation and reconversion programs—measures which were started primarily to further European intergration by creating a "European spirit" among the citizens of the member states—have been more and more a direct response to the requirements of changing economic and social conditions within the ECSC. So was the development of the High Authority's regional thinking, which, in turn, stimulated the development of member governments' regional concepts and policies.

Regarding the criteria used in the choice of the areas to be assisted and in the selection of the instruments to be used in each, the powers of the High Authority are rather limited due to the partial nature of the economic integration of the ECSC and due to particular treaty provisions. In the partial integration scheme of the ECSC, the High Authority does not have the power of overall economic policy, it cannot, therefore, make its regional policy a rationally integrated part of overall policy. In addition, the initiative for readaptation and reconversion programs lies with the member governments. Furthermore, as area redevelopment policy is still only in its beginning stages, one may suspect that, particularly with respect to the choice of the areas to be assisted and to the total amounts of assistance provided within the budget of the High Authority, few, if any, explicit economic-social criteria were applied. On the other hand, with respect to the choice of redevelopment techniques for a given area, the emphasis of the High Authority on long-term programs, on the study of the development possibili-

[69] For an account of the High Authority's activities concerning workers' housing, *cf.*, ECSC, *Eleventh General Report,* 550; regarding its contributions to industrial health and safety provisions, *cf.*, *ibid.*, 551–587, and earlier general report.

ties of a given area, and on the careful planning of redevelopment schemes has certainly increased efficiency in the use of the subsidies given to particular areas.

The reader may have been surprised by the authors' stress on the High Authority's studies, conferences, and collection and exchange of information and ideas. While the effects of these activities cannot be measured, the authors believe that it is in this area that the High Authority has made its major contribution to the development of concepts and instruments of regional policy—and of *European* regional policy—on the part of experts and policy makers of the member states and of other supranational institutions, in particular the EEC. While, originally, there existed only a treaty and the determination of the High Authority to contribute to the creation of European unity, activities of the High Authority as a study, information and communication center and social and economic changes (brought to the attention of the High Authority by political operators from the member countries), led to the development of regional policies and regional policy concepts on the one hand, and to the recognition of the need for cooperation, coordination, and integration on the other.

Appendix

Studies and Reports on Industrial Reconversion Financed Wholly or Partly by the High Authority

Studies and Reports Completed

1. *Auvergne-Aquitaine* (*cf.*, doc. no. 7057/62), July 1957, series "Etudes et Documents," collection "Etudes régionales d'emploi"; author: M. Gravier.
2. *Liguria* (*cf.*, doc. no. 7057/62), November 1957—idem; author: M. Parenti.
3. *Limbourg néerlandais* (*cf.*, doc. no. 7057/62), December 1957—idem; author: M. Winsemius.
4. *Bassins sud-belges* (*cf.*, doc. no. 7057/62), November 1957; preliminary edition: doc. no. 8695/58; author: M. Gottschalk.
5. *Possibilités de réemploi et création d'activités nouvelles au Borinage* (*cf.*, doc. no. 7171/62), 1958, series "Etudes d'Économie Régionale" of the Université Libre de Bruxelles, Institut de Sociologie; author: Solvay.
6. *Salzgitter* (*cf.*, doc. no. 7057/62), August 1960; preliminary edition doc. no. 7062/60; author: M. Bauer.
7. *Repertoire sur les Dispositions pour faciliter la création d'activités nouvelles dans les Etats membres et le Royaume-Uni* (*cf.*, doc. no. 7438/62), 1960, 1962; author: several experts.
8. *Brescia-Udine* (*cf.*, doc. no. 7172/62), July 1960; preliminary edition, doc. no. 7246/60; author: Prof. Vito.
9. *Bassins du Centre-Charleroi et du Borinage* (*cf.*, doc. no. 7434/62), 1963; author: Socorec.
10. *Acier inoxydable-ALUMSTAL* (*cf.*, doc. no. 7437/62), 1962; author: Sema.
11. *Sites Charbonnieres désaffectées* (*cf.*, doc. no. 7688/62), 1962; author: Socorec.
12. *PIOMBINO* (*cf.*, doc. no. 7435/62), 1962.
13. *Montesau-les-Mines* (*cf.*, doc. no. 7436/62), 1963; author: Battelle Memorial Institute.

14. *Umbria* (*cf.*, doc. no. 7351/62), 1963; author: Centro regionale per il piano di sviluppo economico dell'Umbria.
15. *Sud-Luxembourg belge et Nord de la Lorraine* (*cf.*, doc. no. 3837/62), 1963; author: M. Gendarme et Socorec.

Studies and Reports in Preparation

1. *Fabrications Nouvelles* (*cf.*, doc. no. 7572/62 and 4203/63); author: Directeur de Recherche M. Savary; Institutes: Sobemap, Civi, Sodic, GFK.
2. *Logements ouvriers* (*cf.*, doc. no. 3851/62); author: Socorec.
3. *Tarento* (*cf.*, doc. no. 962/63)—participation of the High Authority in the study of the EEC.
4. *L'Usine de Boucau* (doc. no. 852/63 and 3841/63).

Studies and Reports Under Consideration

Studies of the Expert Committee on Industrial Reconversion (doc. no. 3842/63).

1. *Le bâtiment industriel dans la politique de développement régional.* M. Parodi.
2. *Analyse de la structure socio-économique des régions minières et siderurgiques.* M. Van Os.
3. *Zones industrielles.* M. Massacesi.
4. *Les organismes d'action régionale.* M. Detroz.

Section B

The European Economic Community

Introduction

In analyzing the regional policy of the European Economic Community (EEC), or the "European Common Market," [70] one must take account of the fact that the EEC differs from the European Coal and Steel Community (ECSC) with respect to form and degree of integration as well as the political setting within which regional policy is made.

In the first place, the EEC aims not at partial, but at complete economic integration, while future social and political integration of the member countries is hoped for. Economic integration is to be accomplished, during a transitional period of 12 to 15 years, through (1) the elimination of all obstacles to the free movement of goods, services, capital, and persons; (2) the inauguration of a common agricultural and transport policy; (3) the coordination of other economic policies of the member states, e.g., monetary policies, etc.; (4) the approximation of their respective municipal law to the extent necessary for the functioning of the Common Market; (5) the

[70] The members of the EEC are the same countries as the member countries of the ECSC.

creation of a European Social Fund for improving the possibilities of employment for workers and raising their standards of living; and (6) the establishment of a European Investment Bank to facilitate the economic growth of the Community through the creation of new resources.[71]

Secondly, the EEC has a much shorter history than the ECSC. The EEC went into effect in January 1958, so that, today, it is still in its period of transition. Thus, the elimination of all the obstacles to the free movement of goods, services, capital, and persons has not yet been completed, and many of the common policies, particularly in the field of agriculture and transport, are still in the process of being formulated.

Thirdly, at the time the EEC treaty was drafted, the idea that policies aiming at economic integration and rationalization of production had to be accompanied by corresponding social policies as their necessary counterpart was much more generally accepted than at the inception of the ECSC. Indeed, when the signatory governments submitted the EEC treaty to the Parliaments of the six member states, "* * * their purpose was not to attain merely economic objectives which at a later date would have the effect of improving the living conditions of the populations; the governments allotted the Community its own role in social affairs. The first phrases of the preamble to the treaty make it clear that the aim is to assure both economic and *social* progress and that the essential purpose is that of *constantly improving the living and working conditions of their peoples.* * * * From this it is clear that the objectives of a social character are placed on the same footing as those of economic character * * *" [72]

Fourthly, by 1958, the problem of depressed areas and the necessity for regional policies had been recognized by all the governments of the member states. While regional policy has not yet become an integrated part of the entire set of national policies—which is the necessary premise for a rational regional economic and social policy of a nation—there is a growing tendency for the states to make policy along these lines. At the same time, there is growing understanding that within the EEC, too, regional considerations ought to be a part of general policies.

Therefore, at present, regional policies of the EEC are best analyzed in view of (1) the applications of the treaty provisions concerning regional policy, (2) the progressive coordination and harmonization of national regional policies, and (3) the incorporation of regional policy considerations in the Community policies and the ultimate objective that regional policy should become a truly integrated part of the common policies of the EEC.

Regional Policy Coordination and Controls

Article 2 of the treaty of the EEC states that it is the aim of the Community, "* * * by establishing a Common Market and progressively approximating the economic policies of the Member States, to promote

---

[71] *Treaty establishing the European Economic Community,* subsequently cited as *EEC Treaty,* art. 3.

[72] EEC, Commission, *First General Report,* 102. Subsequently, all general reports of the Commission will be cited as "EEC, (*First*) *General Report.*"

761-932 O—65——30

throughout the Community a harmonious development of economic activities, a continuous and balanced expansion, an increased stability, an accelerated raising of the standard of living, and closer relations between its Member States." And the preamble of the treaty sets forth that the "harmonious development of economic activities" and the "balanced expansion" shall be achieved by "* * * reducing the differences existing between the various regions and by mitigating the backwardness of the less favoured. * * *"

Thus, the treaty specifically makes regional policy a part of the tasks of the Commission of the EEC,[73] and article 2 lists the two major policy instruments for the *direct* assistance of the EEC to readaptation and reconversion programs of the member states, i.e., the European Social Fund and the European Investment Bank.[74] In addition, the Commission has also been given powers of coordination and control regarding regional policy within the EEC.

On the one hand, certain regional policies of the member countries may be directly incompatible with the Treaty. The Commission is to point out these incompatibilities to the governments and have the respective national policy abolished. These controlling powers of the Commission have been called its "competences négatives." On the other hand, the treaty provides the Commission also with "competences positives": [75] In the first place, as any general national policy measure has regional implications, so do the common Community policies of the Commission concerning agriculture, transport, energy, etc., which are in the process of being worked out. These regional implications must be investigated by the Commission and called to the attention of the member governments. When framing the common EEC policies, the Commission is to give due consideration to their regional effects, while "* * * care must be taken that these common policies foster more rapid development of the less favoured regions." [76] In addition, while it is recognized that the authority for regional policies lies

[73] The Commission of the EEC is the administrative counterpart of the High Authority of the ECSC. However, its policy powers are more limited than those of the High Authority of the ECSC relative to the sphere of authority of their respective Council of Ministers. In the ECSC, the High Authority must assure the achievement of the purposes of the treaty, and the council is to harmonize the actions of the High Authority and those of the member governments. In the EEC, on the other hand, it is the council who must decide on many of the regulations implementing the treaty provisions and ensure the coordination of the general economic policies of the member states, while the Commission has a power of decision only in certain areas specified by the treaty, may formulate recommendations or opinions, assure the application of the treaty provisions and of the regulations enacted by the Community institutions, and "* * * exercise the competence conferred on it by the council for the implementation of the rules laid down by the latter." *EEC Treaty,* arts. 145 and 155. Also, *cf., ECSC Treaty,* arts. 8 and 26. Since the establishment of the EEC and Euratom in January 1958, these two institutions and the ECSC have assembly and court in common. The counterpart of the Consultative Committee of the High Authority is the Economic and Social Committee of the EEC.

[74] The direct regional policy measures of the EEC will be analyzed in part III of sec. B of this report.

[75] This classification of the Commission's policy powers of coordination and control has been suggested to the authors by an expert on regional policy of the staff of the Commission.

[76] EEC, *Fifth General Report,* 101. Also, *cf.,* EEC, *Third General Report,* 221–222.

at present essentially with the national governments,[77] their individual regional policies may conflict with each other. As the economic policies of the member states must be approximated to promote a harmonious economic development, the Commission ultimately will have to attempt to coordinate the regional policies of the member countries and point out any incompatibilities between them. In view of this end, the Commission endeavors to make the member governments and their regional experts aware that the dimensions of the problem are changing, i.e., that at the end of the transitional period, it will no longer be appropriate to view regional difficulties within the national framework, but that they must be viewed within the framework of the Community.[78]

In the following, we shall consider the "competences négatives" and the "competences positives" in turn.

Competences Negatives

Article 92 of the EEC treaty states that, in general, any subsidy of a member government which distorts or threatens to distort competition to the extent that it adversely affects trade between the member countries is incompatible with the Common Market. However, the following categories of aids are deemed to be compatible with the Common Market:

> "(*a*) aids of a social character granted to individual consumers, provided that such aids are granted without any discrimination based on the origin of the products concerned;
>
> "(*b*) aids intended to remedy damage caused by natural calamities or or other extraordinary events;
>
> "(*c*) aids granted to the economy of certain regions of the Federal Republic of Germany affected by the division of Germany, to the extent that such aids are necessary in order to compensate for the economic disadvantages caused by such division." [79]

In addition to these types of special subsidies, which may have strong regional implications, the following kinds of direct regional assistance are also deemed to be compatible with the Common Market:

> "(*a*) aids intended to promote the economic development of regions where the standard of living is abnormally low or where there exists serious underemployment;
>
> "(*b*) aids intended to facilitate the development of certain activities or of certain economic regions, provided that such aids do not change trading conditions to such a degree as would be contrary to the common interest * * *
>
> "(*c*) such other categories of aids as may be specified by decision of the Council. * * * [80]

---

[77] Robert Marjolin, "Rapport introductif," *Documents de la Conférence sur les économies régionales,* published by the Commission of the EEC, Brussels, 1961, vol. I. p. 29. Marjolin continues as follows: "Our ambition in this regard is to keep ourselves sufficiently informed in order to be able to accomplish the tasks given to us by the Treaty of Rome. But it is also our ambition to assist the national governments as much as possible and to create all the contacts between them which are necessary for the realization of the Common Market." [Authors' translation.]

[78] Statement of a staff member of the Commission.

[79] *EEC Treaty,* art. 92.2.

[80] *Ibid.,* art. 92.3.

According to article 93, it is the task of the Commission to constantly examine all systems of aids existing in the member states. If it finds that any of these aids is not compatible with the Common Market, in view of article 92, it shall order the state concerned to abolish or alter it. In addition, the Commission must be informed by the member governments of any plans to modify such aids or to establish new ones, so that it can submit its comments before their implementation.

To date, mainly the last-mentioned provision of article 93 has been applied. Whenever a member county passed new regional policy legislation, the Commission was informed of the kind of subsidies involved and examined them in view of (*a*) their compatibility with the functioning of competion within the Common Market, and (*b*) their economic and social "justifiability." Up to now, none of the newly instituted regional laws or regulations of the member countries has been rejected by the Commission on either ground. This is not too surprising in view of the short period evolved since the inception of the Common Market and the political problems connected with such an action by the Commission.[81] In the future, however, it is likely that the "competences négatives," if based on a medium or long-term policy program [82] and on a more detailed specification of the categories of aids falling under articles 92 and 93, might considerably increase the efficacy of regional policies within the EEC.

Competences Positives

REGIONAL ASPECTS OF COMMON EEC POLICIES

The most important Community policies that must be examined by the Commission with respect to their regional implications are the common agricultural, transport, energy, and social policies of the EEC.

The common agricultural policy can contribute to the development of areas suffering from low agricultural productivity through (1) the planned structural improvements of agriculture with financial assistance from the European Agricultural Guidance and Guarantee Fund established by the Commission for the purpose,[83] and (2) the creation of employment for the agricultural labor set free through the structural agricultural improvements in industries established in the same or other regions.[84]

The common transport policy is based on Community-wide projections of future demands and supplies of transportation services. It constitutes an attempt to unify the road, rail, and inland waterway communication facilities, e.g., by gathering and disseminating information on the various national projects and coordinating their termination dates, or by financial assistance from the European Investment Bank to such coordination projects. EEC policies in this area can further the development of underdeveloped regions at the peripheries of the Community" * * * chiefly by influencing the choice of the main arteries of communication. The develop-

---

[81] Statement of a staff member of the Commission.

[82] In August 1963, the Commission handed a document to the member governments asking for the establishment of a medium-term policy program for the EEC as a whole. *Cf., Die Zeit,* No. 32 (Aug. 9, 1963), p. 17.

[83] EEC, *Fifth General Report,* 112.

[84] *Documents de la Conférence sur les économies régionales, op. cit.,* vol. I, p. 30. Also *cf.,* EEC, *Fifth General Report,* 112.

ment and modernization of the networks serving outlying areas can help to secure a more balanced distribution of economic activity throughout the Community."[85]

The common energy policy will have two regional aspects: On the one hand, underdeveloped areas situated far from the coalfields, which formerly have been at a disadvantage with respect to cheap energy supplies, may profit from the lower cost of energy due to the growing use of petroleum products in Europe and the establishment of new energy-producing centers. On the other hand, in areas affected by the closure of coal mines, rationalization and conversion measures can be assisted by the European institutions.[86]

To the extent that regional problems are due to an imbalance on the regional labor market, the common social policy can facilitate their solution through the improvement of labor mobility and of training and retraining facilities. The common policy of occupational training, provided for by article 128 of the treaty, is of particular significance in this regard.[87]

It appears that regional considerations have actually played a part in the framing of these Community policies.[88] However, to the exent that the latter have not yet been agreed upon, future developments in the establishment of these and other common policies must be awaited.

COORDINATION OF NATIONAL REGIONAL POLICIES

To date, there has not been much, if any, actual coordination of the regional policies of the member countries. The Commission has made no statements regarding any incompatibilities between their respective regional measures. At this time, the experts of the Commission are only in the study phase of this problem.[89]

To coordinate existing policies within the EEC is already very difficult. In this rather new field of policy, which is just becoming recognized as an integrated part of the entire set of national policies, coordination is even more difficult, especially if attempted by means of direct changes of national policies. Thus, the work of the Commission in collecting and disseminating information on member countries' regional policies and experiences and in encouraging studies, conferences, and the exchange of ideas is particularly emphasized at present. For the Commission hopes that through the establishment of closer relations between the national regional experts and policy makers, the kind of "atmosphere" can be created which is the necessary precondition for the development of regional thinking from a Community point of view.[90]

An important factor contributing to the "creation of atmosphere" was the Conference on Regional Economies organized by the Commission in Brussels in December 1961, which was attended by approximately 300 participants: Politicians, administrators, representatives of labor and industry groups, of regional development organizations, of the Community

[85] EEC, *Fifth General Report,* 101.
[86] *Documents de la Conférence sur les économies régionales, op. cit.,* vol. I, p. 30.
[87] *Ibid.,* pp. 30–31.
[88] Statement of a staff member of the Commission.
[89] Statement of a staff member of the Commission.
[90] Statement of a staff member of the Commission.

institutions, and of various international institutions. The objectives of the Conference were (1) to establish close relations between the national regional policy experts, (2) to point out the lessons learned from individual member country's experiences with regional policies, (3) to set forth the regional problems of common interest to the member states, including the effect of the Common Market on the regions of the Community, and (4) to establish principles on the basis of which the Commission is to assist the redevelopment efforts of the member states.[91]

As a framework for the analysis of regional problems, the member states' regional policies, and their coordination at the Community level, the staff of the Commission, assisted by experts from the member countries, produced a paper on *The Regions within The EEC* for the Conference, which constitutes an attempt to define "regions" within the Community. The Treaty of Rome had used this term in various ways. In the preamble, the term seems to denote an area of a certain unity due to its "natural conditions" and the complementarity of its economic activities. Other parts of the treaty, such as the protocol on Italy, speak of the regions as delimited by legislative decisions or administrative regulations of the member governments. And in articles 92 and 226 of the treaty, the term seems to refer to areas suffering from declining industries or the elimination of tariff protection. This confusion "* * * demonstrates the difficulty of placing the various regional policies carried out within the Community within a homogeneous regional framework. * * * Therefore, a definite division of the EEC territory into regions according to inflexible criteria would certainly create more problems than advantages. * * * However, a territorial framework is absolutely required for the understanding of regional problems, the influence of geographical conditions, the measuring of the relative extent of these problems, and the attempts to solve them. * * *"[92] Accordingly, 31 "large socio-economic regions" were defined within the Community on the basis of certain not very precise economic and social criteria. The concept that economic activities give rise to certain polarizations in space due to their geographic, economic, and social interdependency and complementarity was one of these criteria. In addition, "* * * the notion of a region seems to have also a social meaning to the extent that the human milieu of a region has certain characteristics of its own in comparison with other regions. * * * Thus, one can maintain that one of the criteria for the delimitation of the socio-economic regions is the fact that it is possible for a worker to move from one location to another without losing his 'home' or his roots. * * *"[93] The large socio-economic regions, however, are subdivided into the so-called "basic regions," which are nothing more than the regions used by the member countries in applying their regional policies. Thus, the national regional frameworks of the "régions de programme" of France, the "regioni" of Italy, the "Laender" of Germany, etc. have been basically retained, as "* * * suited both to the coordination of these (regional) policies and to the appraisal of the various stages reached in regional development,"[94] while the delimitation of the large socio-economic

---

[91] *Documents de la Conférence sur les économies régionales, op. cit.*, vol. I, p. 9.
[92] *Ibid.*, vol. II, p. 67. [Authors' translation.]
[93] *Ibid.*, vol. II, p. 68. [Authors' translation.]
[94] EEC, *Fourth General Report*, 100.

regions was intended for structural analyses on a Community scale and as "* * * the setting for a regional policy in the EEC." [95] In addition, because of the diversity of the economic activities within the areas thus defined, the mining, farming, textile, tourist, and other "problem areas" were singled out as "specific zones." The classification of the latter is to be revised periodically in view of the dynamic nature of their particular problems.[96]

This delimitation of the regions within the EEC is certainly far from any theoretical ideal. It is a preliminary compromise solution which combines the existing national administratively defined regions with certain vague economic and social criteria. The experts of the Commission are well aware of this and *The Regions within The EEC* has been called a pure experiment.[97] Nevertheless, this paper presents a great deal of information on the nature of smaller areas within the Community; and the fact that it was written called the attention of the national experts to the importance of and the difficulties involved in the establishment of homogeneous definitions of regions within the Community.

Apart from an analysis of the probable effects of the Common Market on particular regions within the EEC, the majority of the 20 reports of the Conference were presented and discussed in two Commissions. One of them examined specifically the problems of certain agricultural areas, regions at the periphery of the Community, and regions alongside common frontiers within the Community. The other analyzed the instruments of regional development, in particular certain industrialization techniques such as the creation of "poles of development" and industrial reconversion.[98]

The major conclusions of the Conference, as stated by Robert Marjolin, vice president of the Commission, were the following:

(1) The objective of establishing closer relations between the various national experts and administrators concerned with regional development was attained. Particularly, it was realized that, whatever ideology predominated in any member country, the regional policy techniques applied were very similar, and so was the mixture of free competition and government intervention. "There is not much difference between the convinced 'dirigiste' who agrees to the necessity of competition on the enterprise level * * * and the convinced liberal who admits the necessity of the principal government interventions for economic development." [99]

(2) Among the lessons learned from each other's experiences with regional development policies, three stand out in particular:

(*a*) There is growing interest in regional problems and there is a growing tendency for regional policy to become an integrated part of national economic policies, while, before, it had been only a sort of corrective measure for the centralizing effects of general economic policies.

---

[95] *Loc. cit.*
[96] *Documents de la Conférence sur les économies régionales, op. cit.*, vol. II, p. 69.
[97] Statement of a staff member of the Commission.
[98] *Documents de la Conférence sur les économies régionales, op. cit.*, vol. I, pp. 25–28.
[99] *Ibid.*, vol. II, p. 59.

(*b*) There are great differences between the various depressed areas, so that generalizations should be made only on the basis of the most careful analysis. In particular, it has become clear that the question whether to concentrate investments in a few poles of development or to disperse them among a greater number of areas must be answered differently in the north and the east of Europe, on the one hand, and in the south and the west, on the other. In the former areas, which are already industrialized, one has a real choice between the two methods. In the large underdeveloped areas of the south and the west, however, only the concentration of investments and the creation of poles of development seem to lead to an effective solution.

(*c*) The development of the social and cultural infrastructure has not been emphasized enough in most development projects.

(*d*) With respect to regional problems of common interest, it was pointed out that there are great divergencies between the full-employment areas of the great "central block" within the Community—which extends from the Netherlands to northern Italy—and the regions at the periphery of the Community. Thus, more incentives should be provided to attract entrepreneurs to the peripheral areas, and the channels of information on these incentive measures should be improved. In addition, while mobility of labor within the same region is important, migrations from region to region or from country to country, though sometimes still necessary, * * * are accompanied by unfavorable sociological, political, and human phenomena. Therefore, my colleagues and I believe that whenever it is possible to move industry to labor, this ought to be done. Industry should move to labor, and labor should move to industry only under exceptional conditions." [1]

(*e*) The Conference did not attain its fourth objective, i.e., to establish the principles on the basis of which the Commission is to assist the member States' redevelopment policies. Marjolin states only that the necessity for increased cooperation between the Commission and the member Governments was recognized; that smaller groups of experts should now attack particular problems, such as the redevelopment of common frontier areas, the question of dispersion versus concentration of new investments, and the development of social and cultural infrastructures; and that the Commission should continue and intensify its analyses of particular areas, concentrating especially on studies leading to the creation of industrial poles of development.[2]

Thus, while the Conference did create some of the "atmosphere" required for future actual coordination of national regional policies, it has not succeeded in arriving at *the* necessary condition for such coordination, i.e., the establishment of rational Community-wide socio-economic criteria for the selection of the areas to be developed and the investment priorities within

[1] *Ibid.*, vol. II, p. 61.
[2] *Ibid.*, vol. II, pp. 62–63.

each area thus selected. To date, no progress seems to have been made in this regard.[3]

On the other hand, partly as a consequence of the Conference, and partly in response to demands of the European Parliament for the development of common regional policy concepts and the establishment of a consultative committee on regional policy, the Commission appointed three expert groups to study (1) development techniques for the peripheral areas of the Community, (2) the problems of the areas with declining industries, and (3) the efficacy of the various development techniques. Once these experts have arrived at some results, common meetings of the three groups and other regional experts are to be held, which could be the beginning of the consultative committee on regional policy the European Parliament desires.[4]

Direct Regional Assistance of the EEC

Readaptation Assistance

The Commission of the EEC can assist national readaptation measures directly through the European Social Fund and indirectly through the implementation of the treaty provisions on vocational training, labor mobility, and other social policies.

THE EUROPEAN SOCIAL FUND

The European Social Fund was established in order to contribute to the raising of living standards by promoting employment facilities and the georaphical and occupational mobility of workers within the Community.[5] According to article 125 of the EEC treaty, the fund is to attain these ends by covering 50 percent of the expenses incurred by a member state or by a body under public law for (1) occupational retraining of unemployed workers, (2) resettlement, and (3) the maintenance of the wage level of workers who are temporarily or permanently laid off due to the conversion of their enterprise to other production.[6] Occupational retraining assistance by the fund is conditional upon "* * * the impossibility of employing the unemployed workers otherwise than in a new occupation and upon their having been in productive employment for a period of at least 6 months in the occupation for which they have been retrained."[7] Resettlement assistance may be granted if the unemployed had to change their residence within the Community and after they have been employed for a period of at least 6 months at their new place of residence. The maintenance of the wage level of workers affected by reconversion of their enterprise is subject to the conditions:

"(*a*) that the workers concerned have again been fully employed in that enterprise for a period of at least six months;

"(*b*) that the Government concerned has previously submitted a plan, drawn up by such enterprise, for its conversion and for the financing thereof; and

[3] Statement of a staff member of the Commission.
[4] EEC, *Sixth General Report,* 107.
[5] *EEC Treaty,* art. 123.
[6] *Ibid.,* art. 125.1.
[7] *Ibid.,* art. 125.2.

"(*c*) that the Commission has given its prior approval to such conversion plan." [8]

The fund is made up of contributions by the member states. In view of the differing employment situations in the member countries, these financial contributions are fixed in proportions different from those of other contributions to the budget of the Community; i.e., the respective payments of the member countries are as follows: [9]

	Contributions to the budget of the social fund	Contributions to the remainder of the EEC budget
	Percent	*Percent*
Belgium	8. 8	7. 9
Germany	32. 0	28. 0
France	32. 0	28. 0
Italy	20. 0	28. 0
Luxembourg	. 2	. 2
Netherlands	7. 0	7. 9

For the adoption of the section of the annual EEC budget relating to the social fund, the votes of the members of the council are weighted in accordance with the respective financial contributions to the fund, and a majority of at least 67 votes is required for the adoption of any conclusions.[10] The annual budget of the social fund is proposed by the Commission on the basis of the member states' applications for reimbursements received or estimated. While the European Parliament may propose amendments to the draft budget, the final approval lies with the council.[11] The fund is administered by the Commission with the assistance of the committee of the social fund; the latter is a tripartite consultative committee of representatives of the member governments, trade unions, and employers' associaions, which must approve all the applications for readaptation assistance.[12]

After the legal, administrative, and financial status of the European Social Fund had been decided upon in regulation No. 9 of the council, which became effective on September 20, 1960, the fund began its operations. As of December 31, 1962, readaptation reimbursements granted amounted to 12,291,798 units of account for the retraining and resettlement of approximately 183,000 EEC workers (in 1959, the total labor force of the EEC—employed and unemployed—was 74,038,000.)[13] The distribution of these funds by country and type of assistance is shown in table I. While France

[8] *Loc. cit.*

[9] *Ibid.,* 200. 1, 2.

[10] *Ibid.,* 203.5.

[11] *Ibid.,* 203.2–4.

[12] EEC, *Fifth General Report,* 143.

[13] Statistical Office of the European Communities, *Basic Statistics for Fifteen European Countries,* Luxembourg-Brussels, 1961, p. 20.

received the largest total amount of readaptation assistance, the number of Italian workers benefiting from the fund was greater than the number of French workers. This divergence is due to the fact that in the individual member countries different amounts are expended per worker resettled or retrained.[14] Of the Italian workers resettled, 48,000 obtained new employment in France, 27,000 in Germany, and 4,000 in Benelux (predominantly in Luxembourg).[15]

By December 31, 1962, the activities of the fund involved a transfer of revenues from Germany, Belgium, and Luxembourg to Italy, France, and the Netherlands, in the amount of 2,578,305 units of account.[16]

As of the same date, applications for readaptation assistance received and not yet decided upon amounted to approximately 20 million units of account, 16.2 million being for retraining, and 3.4 million for resettlement assistance. Of the 17.8 million of expenditures planned for the financial year 1963, 11.6 million are for retraining, 5.9 million for resettlement, and 228,000 units of account for assistance to workers affected by reconversion of their enterprises.[17]

TABLE I.—*Readaptation Assistance by the European Social Fund as of Dec. 31, 1962*

Countries	Reimbursements (in units of account)	Number of workers retrained—resettled (in 1958 and 1959)	
Belgium	461, 421	1, 400	....
Germany	1, 999, 912	19, 700	....
France	4, 624, 641	9, 700	....
Italy	3, 733, 198	69, 000	79, 200
Luxembourg	....	....	....
Netherlands	1, 472, 626	3, 500	....

Source: EEC, Commission, Sixth General Report, p. 207.

Apart from the screening of readaptation applications, the committee of the social fund adopted a list of the "recognized bodies under public law"[18] whose readaptation expenditures may be reimbursed by the fund, and it established a definition of "underemployment" on the basis of which the fund can also be used to assist the underemployed (e.g., in agriculture).[19] The fund also participated in a vocational training program which was started as a cooperative scheme by Italy, Germany, and the Netherlands: the training of approximately 10,000 Italian workers was to begin in southern Italy and to be completed in Germany and the Netherlands. However, the

[14] *Cf.*, EEC, Commission, *Tableau des Frais Moyens Remboursables par Ouvrant-droit.* Document de la Direction du Fonds Social et de la Formation Professionnelle, CFS/S4/62, Doc. No. 6–F, Brussels, November 1962, p. 5.

[15] EEC, *Sixth General Report,* 187.

[16] *Loc. cit.*

[17] *Loc. cit.*

[18] *Tableau des Frais Moyens Remboursables par Ouvrant-droit, op. cit.*, p. 5.

[19] EEC, *Sixth General Report,* 187.

scheme was not fully carried out, as most of the Italian workers were able to obtain reemployment in Italy.[20]

While the Commission is of the opinion that experience to date with the European Social Fund is too limited to warrant a basic revision of regulation No. 9, the European Parliament favors a considerable expansion of the operations of the fund in the field of retraining, particularly for underemployed persons desiring to remain in an independent occupation and for workers whose jobs are about to disappear. The Commission itself, holds that the fund should be more than an automatic reimbursement mechanism for the vocational retraining schemes of the member states and should initiate programs of its own. A proposal to this effect will be submitted to the Council of Ministers in the near future.[21]

In addition, article 126 of the EEC treaty provides that, at the end of the transitional period, the council, on the basis of a proposal of the Commission and after consultation with the Economic and Social Committee and the European Parliament, may

> "(*a*) acting by means of a qualified majority vote, rule that all or part of the assistance referred to in Article 125 shall no longer be granted; or
>
> "(*b*) acting by means of a unanimous vote, determine the new tasks which may be entrusted to the Fund within the framework of the mandate as defined in Article 123."

It seems, however, that, to date, the staff of the Commission has not given much thought to this possibility of extending the operations of the European Social Fund.[22]

VOCATIONAL TRAINING

Article 128 of the EEC treaty provides that

> The Council shall, on a proposal of the Commission and after the Economic and Social Committee has been consulted, establish general principles for the implementation of a common policy of occupational training capable of contributing to the harmonious development both of national economies and of the Common Market.

These general principles were established by the decision of the council of April 2, 1963. The double objective of the common policy on vocational training is (1) to realize everybody's right to adequate vocational training, and (2) to provide the various economic sectors with the labor supplies required. The Commission, assisted by a tripartite consultative committee, may propose to the council and the member states policy measures furthering these objectives, particularly regarding the gathering and dissemination of information on employment opportunities and training facilities within the Community and the establishment of appropriate training programs in individual member countries and on the Community level. Progressive harmonization of the training facilities and levels will be sought.

This decision of the council authorizes the Commission also to propose additional retraining measures: "Everyone must have the opportunities for appropriate training and retraining, if necessary, during all phases of his

---

[20] *Documents de la Conférence sur les Économies Régionales, op. cit.*, vol. I, p. 31, and statement of a staff member of the Commission.
[21] EEC, *Sixth General Report,* 187.
[22] Statement of a staff member of the Commission.

professional life." [23] Thus, the future implementation of this policy could considerably facilitate readaptation within the Community.

FREE MOBILITY OF LABOR AND OTHER TREATY PROVISIONS FACILITATING READAPTATION

Other provisions of the treaty indirectly facilitating readaptation are those concerning the free movement of workers within the Community,[24] the social security regulations necessary to effect free labor mobility,[25] and collaboration between the member states in the fields of employment, labor legislation, working conditions, protection against occupational accidents and diseases, industrial hygiene, and the laws on trade unions and collective bargaining.[26]

As the free movement of labor is to be ensured by the end of the transitional period and as the European Social Security Convention had already been signed by the member governments on December 7, 1957 (due to the preliminary work of the High Authority of the ECSC and the International Labour Office), the implementation of the mobility and social security provisions progressed relatively fast. Under the terms of the ECSC treaty, the European Social Security Convention could come into force only after ratification by the Parliaments of the member states. However, as article 51 of the EEC treaty provides for measures similar to those established by the convention but is part of a treaty already ratified by the six Parliaments, it was possible "* * * for these measures to be adopted by a Community procedure, which is more rapid than the process of ratifying the Convention. * * * The European Commission * * * proposed to the Council in April 1958 that the Convention should be turned into a regulation, a possibility that had in fact been provided for in a Protocol annexed to the Treaty." [27] The council accepted the Commission's proposal and the convention became Council Regulation No. 3, which, together with regulation No. 4—which specifies methods and procedures for the implementation of regulation No. 3—became effective on January 1, 1959.[28] The application of these two regulations "* * * will put an end to one of the handicaps facing workers in situations outside their home country. In effect, equality of rights between natives and foreigners is made general, insurance periods are added together, and in certain cases benefits are paid out in another member state. Consequently, frontiers no longer prevent wage-earners from benefiting from the rights acquired in the field of social security." [29] Regulation No. 3 covers all branches of social security (including sickness and disability benefits, old-age pensions, payments to dependents, insurance against industrial accidents and occupational diseases, family allowances, and unemployment insurance), and migrant workers are assured that for the calculation of each of these benefits all the periods for which the recipient

---

[23] Décision du Conseil du 2 avril, 1963. Published in the Journal Officiel des Communautés européennes, Apr. 20, 1963, No. 63 [Authors' translation].

[24] *EEC Treaty,* arts. 43–49.

[25] *Ibid.,* art. 51.

[26] *Ibid.,* art. 118.

[27] EEC, *First General Report,* 117, 118.

[28] EEC, *Second General Report,* 164, 165.

[29] *Ibid.,* 164.

has been insured in one or more Community countries are taken into consideration.[30] The regulations are implemented by the EEC Administrative Committee for the Social Security of Migrant Workers, which attempts to settle the various problems arising in the application of the regulations and to simplify the administrative relations between the social security organizations in the six countries. In addition, the committee has published an initial series of guides for migrant workers informing them of their rights and the formalities necessary to obtain them. At present, 1,500,000 insured persons and beneficiaries are covered by regulations Nos. 3 and 4, involving annual payments in the amount of 40 million units of account.[31]

Regarding the implementation of articles 48 and 49 concerning the free mobility of workers, regulation No. 15 of the council, which became effective on September 1, 1961, "* * * defines the right of workers from a Community country when they enter, reside in, or are employed in another member country, sets up clearing machinery for employment offers and applications, gives priority to the Community labour market, ensures the necessary cooperation of the National administrations with each other and with the Commission and, finally, takes a first step towards the elimination of the administrative procedures and practices which hinder the free movement of manpower." [32] In addition to the European Coordination Office which acts as a Community clearing house for vacancies and applications for employment, advisory and technical committees were set up which are working on certain practical studies, including "* * * the technical examination of the comparative glossary of the trades in which migration is most frequent. This glossary * * * will make clearing operations between national labour exchanges considerably easier." [33] Several other provisions for the mobility of particular categories of workers have been and are being worked out.[34]

It is, of course, impossible to measure the quantitative impact on readaptation of these and other social policies of the Commission. However, there can be no doubt that they do indirectly facilitate readaptation.

Regional Development Assistance

When the EEC treaty was being framed, it was expected that, in the process of integration, difficulties would arise due to inadequate communication facilities, the lack of electrical power, and the existence of underdeveloped areas and industrial and agricultural sectors suffering from low productivity. "To overcome these obstacles, as well as to give birth to the new activities and installations necessary on the scale of the Community, big investments have to be made. * * * Actually, these countries together form one of the regions of the world where the rate of investment, expressed in relation to gross national product, is very high and where banking machinery is the most developed. But if care were not taken * * * the favourable factors might not in themselves be sufficient to enable the recessed sectors to be financed at the desired rhythm. * * * The six member

[30] For further details on specific benefits *cf.*, ECSC, *Sixth General Report,* 187.
[31] EEC, *Fifth General Report,* 32–34.
[32] EEC, *Fourth General Report,* 59.
[33] EEC, *Fifth General Report,* 28.
[34] *Cf., Ibid.,* 28–31, and EEC, *Sixth General Report,* 27–28.

countries, therefore, decided to found a bank between themselves. At Community level, and along the line of action of the Community, this bank would be able to examine these new problems of financing in common and help to solve them."[35]

THE EUROPEAN INVESTMENT BANK

Purpose and principles governing the policy of the Bank

The purpose of the European Investment Bank (EIB) as set forth in article 130 of the EEC treaty is

> * * * to contribute, by calling on the capital markets and its own resources, to the balanced and smooth development of the Common Market in the interest of the Community. For this purpose, the Bank shall by granting loans and guarantees on a non-profit-making basis facilitate the financing of the following projects in all sectors of the economy:
>
> (*a*) projects for developing less developed regions,
>
> (*b*) projects for modernizing or converting enterprises or for creating new activities which are called for by the progressive establishment of the Common Market where such projects by their size or nature cannot be entirely financed by the various means available in each of the Member States; and
>
> (*c*) projects of common interest to several Member States which by their size or nature cannot be entirely financed by the various means available in each of the Member States.

The EIB must work in close cooperation with the Commission of the EEC. The Bank is administered and managed by a board of governors, a board of directors, and a management committee. Its capital stock in the amount of one thousand million units of account is subscribed to by the member states[36] and paid up to 25 percent, each payment being one-quarter in gold or a freely convertible currency and three-quarters in national currency. Apart from obtaining loans from the capital markets of the member countries, the board of governors may, by a qualified majority vote[37] on a proposal of the board of directors, decide to borrow from the member states if the Bank needs such loans for the financing of specific projects and is unable to obtain them in the capital markets on suitable conditions.[38]

While all applications for loans and guarantees must be screened by the management committee of the EIB, applications made through the intermediary of the Commission must be submitted for an opinion to the member state in whose territory the project is to be carried out, and are to be rejected if opposed by this state. Applications made through a member government must be examined by the Commission. If the Commission or the management committee of the EIB give an unfavorable opinion on a project, the board of directors may grant a loan or guarantee only by means of a unanimous vote. If both the management committee and the Commission view the financing of a project unfavorably, the board of directors may not grant such a loan or guarantee.[39]

---

[35] EIB, *Annual Report 1958,* pp. 15–16.

[36] Germany and France: 300 million units of account each; Italy: 240 million; Belgium: 86.5 million; Netherlands: 71.5 million; Luxembourg: 2 million. *Cf., Protocol on The Statute of The European Investment Bank,* subsequently cited as *EIB Protocol,* art. 4.

[37] I.e., a majority of at least eight votes of the 12 governors. Cf., *EIB Protocol,* art. 12.

[38] *Ibid.,* art. 6.

[39] *Ibid.,* art. 21.2, 5, 6, 7.

The basic principle the Bank is to observe in its financing operations for the three categories of projects specified in article 130 is "* * * to ensure that its funds are employed in the most rational manner in the interest of the Community"; [40] i.e., the selection of projects is to be based on their economic profitability. The Bank may participate in the financing of projects only if funds from other sources are also used, and

(*a*) where the the service of interest and amortisation is guaranteed, in the case of projects carried out by enterprises in the sector of production by earnings, or in the case of other projects by an obligation of the State in which the project is carried out or by any other means; and

(*b*) where the execution of the project contributes to the increase of economic productivity in general and promotes the development of the Common Market." [41]

The total of outstanding loans and guarantees granted by the Bank is not to exceed 250 percent of the subscribed capital. The rates of interest on the loans extended by the Bank and the guarantee commissions must be adapted to the conditions prevailing in the capital market and calculated so that the receipts resulting therefrom enable the Bank to meet its obligations, cover its expenses, and build up a reserve fund of 10 percent of the subscribed capital. The EIB is not to grant any reduction in interest rates. Where such a reduction appears desirable, the respective member State or a third party may grant a rebate on the interest, if this is compatible with article 92 of the treaty.[42]

Apart from these directives and the resolution to concentrate on large projects and on loans rather than guarantees in the initial phase of its operations,[43] no specific criteria for investment priorities have been established by the EIB. The regional policy orientation of the Commission determines in a general way to what sectors and projects the Bank ought to devote its principal attention[44]—in addition to the Commission's examination of each particular project. However, if basic criteria for the EIB's own investment decisions exist, they have certainly not been publicized. In the Conference on the Regional Economies in December 1961, the president of the EIB stated only that the directors and administrators of the Bank are well aware of the importance of area studies (the only basis on which rational investment decisions can be made), of infrastructural investments, and of the necessity of concentrating investments to the extent required for a self-sustaining development process. Furthermore, the Bank realizes that any criteria for policies in depressed areas must be continuously revised and that, within the Community, the regions of the future will lie across national frontiers, thus posing new problems which must be analyzed as early as possible.[45]

Credit operations and other EIB activities concerning regional development

The EIB reports that, in the beginning of its operations, many of the applications for loans did not comply with the conditions governing the

---

[40] *Ibid.*, art. 20.

[41] *Loc. cit.*

[42] *Ibid.*, arts. 18, 19, 24.

[43] *European Investment Bank*, Brussels, May 1962, p. 7, *Cf.*, also EEC, *Second General Report*, 75.

[44] *Documents de la Conférence sur les Économies Régionales, op. cit.*, vol. I, p. 44.

[45] *Ibid.*, pp. 40–44.

Bank's activities, i.e., to be situated in underdeveloped areas, to promote the development of the Common Market, or to be of interest to several member countries. Other applications were deferred as they concerned economic sectors on which the studies of the Commission had not yet been completed.[46]

The majority of the loans the Bank did grant were for projects in the underdeveloped areas in the Community, particularly in southern Italy. While the earliest loans were predominantly for projects in the fields of basic industries and energy production, later on the Bank also contributed to the financing of investments in processing industries, in agriculture, and in transportation—once the Commission had established certain priorities in the last field.[47] And while the Bank held in the beginning that "* * * the initiative of creating new industries can, in practice, come only from fairly large concerns or groups of concerns * * *,"[48] its annual report for the year 1962 shows that an important fraction of the total loans in this year concerned medium-sized projects.

The number and amounts of the credits extended have increased over the years, as can be seen in table II. In total, 37 loans have been granted, amounting to 254.3 million units of account and contributing to total investments of 1,250 million units of account. Only one of the 37 loans was for a reconversion project, the other 36 being for the financing of new investments. With respect to distribution by country, Italian enterprises received the greatest share of the loans: 164.1 million units of account, or 64 percent of the total; France and Germany followed with 21 percent and 11 percent, respectively. For details, see table III. As to distribution by economic sectors, 53 percent of the total, or 135 million units of account, were for the industrial sector, with the chemical industry receiving almost one-half of this amount (71.9 million for nine individual projects). Credits for investments in the transport and power sector were next in line, amounting to 66.2 and 42.6 million units of account, or 26 percent and 17 percent, respectively. Agricultural investments were assisted with only 10.5 million units of account, or 4 percent of total loans. For further details, see table IV.

TABLE II.—*Historical Distribution of Loans*

Year	Number	Amount (in million units of account)
1959	7	52. 1
1960	5	41. 3
1961	10	66. 2
1962	15	94. 1

Source: European Investment Bank, annual reports (1958–62).

[46] EIB, *Annual Report 1959*, p. 14.
[47] *Documents de la Conférence sur les Économies Régionales, op. cit.*, vol. I, p. 44.
[48] EIB, *Annual Report 1959*, p. 15.

761–932 O—65——31

TABLE III.—*Distribution of Loans by Country, as of Dec. 31, 1962*

Countries	Number of projects	EIB loans (million units of account)	Share of total
			Percent
Belgium	1	4.8	2
Germany	2	27.4	11
France	8	54.0	21
Italy	25	164.1	64
Luxembourg	1	4.0	2
Total	37	254.3	100

Source: European Investment Bank, annual report 1962, p. 30.

TABLE IV.—*Distribution of Loans by Sector, as of Dec. 31, 1962*

Sector	Number of projects	EIB loans (million units of account)	Share of total
			Percent
Agriculture	2	10.5	4
Transport	4	66.2	26
Power	6	42.6	17
Industry	25	135.0	53
Iron and steel	1	24.0	....
Building material	3	9.1	....
Paper	2	12.8	....
Mechanical industry	3	11.2	....
Chemical industry	9	71.9	....
Food stuffs	4	4.8	....
Other industries	3	1.2	....
Total	37	254.3	100

Source: European Investment Bank, annual report 1962, p. 31.

The repayment period of the Bank's loans is determined according to the nature of the project and the normal period of depreciation in each individual case. For the loans granted thus far, this period varied from 7 to 20 years, including an interval between the date of disbursement and the commencement of the repayment, which usually corresponded to the period required for the construction and establishment of the project.[49]

Apart from its lending activities, the EIB has participated in the two conferences organized by the EEC and the ECSC and in various regional

[49] *European Investment Bank, op. cit.*, p. 15.

studies of the Commission. In connection with the latter, the Bank examined the conditions under which it might assist projects for the improvement of the infrastructure of transport. In addition, the Bank has undertaken a number of studies of its own, which mainly concerned its financing of medium-sized firms and the social and economic problems raised by the development of agricultural regions.[50]

Furthermore, due to the fact that the capital of the Bank is paid up in several currencies and that the Bank floats loans on various national markets, the EIB, from the beginning, had to deal with monetary problems the solutions of which "* * * may effectively contribute to the liberalisation of capital movements between the six countries. * * *" [51]—thus indirectly facilitating regional development.

REGIONAL STUDIES AND PROJECTS

As the Commission considers regional analyses and the gathering and dissemination of information on regional problems to be of the foremost importance, it has participated in various regional studies and projects. As prevously mentioned, the EEC, the EIB, and the ECSC have set up a Joint Working Party on the Industrial Reconversion of Mining Areas, while the Commission created three study groups on the problems of areas with declining industries and the relative efficacy of different development techniques in general, and for the peripheral areas of the Community in particular. In addition, the Commission initiated a number of Community-wide industry studies, three of which are already completed (i.e., those on the paper, the automobile, and the brewing industry). These industry studies, although mainly intended for use in market forecasts on which Community policies can be based,[52] constitute valuable information for regional development objectives as well.

Furthermore, in accordance with the suggestions of the Regional Development Conference, the Commission has started specific studies on the redevelopment of common frontier areas within the Community and on the creation of industrial poles of development. At present, analyses of the French-Belgian frontier area, which includes Belgian Luxembourg and North Lorraine, are being made with the intent to create a common economic region through the development of existing and potential complementarities of the frontier areas of the two countries (e.g., regarding water supplies, the training of labor, means and ways of communication across the frontier, and the promotion of investments in the less developed zones within this region).[53]

The most important project of the Commission, however, is the creation of an industrial pole of development in the Taranto-Bari area in southern Italy. On the basis of various studies, a group of industries was selected, centering on steel production, with which a self-sustaining development process is to be started. This project of investment concentration constitutes an experiment in the use of an efficient industrialization technique which could be extended to other regions of the Community.[54] In Septem-

---

[50] EIB, *Annual Report 1960,* p. 20.
[51] EIB, *Annual Report 1958,* p. 17.
[52] EEC, *Sixth General Report,* 104.
[53] *Ibid.,* 105.
[54] *Loc. cit.*

ber 1962, another specific regional development project was started with the creation of an Action and Liaison Committee for the sulphur industry in Italy: The committee is to examine the actual and potential employment situation in Sicily and the possibilities of developing the sulphur industry in the most rational way.[55] In addition, studies are being made on the development of the Eifel-Hunsrueck area and other regions in the Community.[56]

Conclusions

An evaluation of the regional policy of the EEC is a rather difficult undertaking in view of the short period since the establishment of the Common Market. Several Treaty provisions concerning readaptation and redevelopment have been implemented; some of the regulations regarding the free mobility of labor and social security have been instituted relatively fast; and regional considerations seem to play a part in the framing of the common Community policies. There are proposals to extend the activities of the social fund with respect to the number of employees benefiting from readaptation assistance as well as with respect to vocational training. And there are plans for the establishment of a consultative committee on regional policy.

On the other hand, in the area of coordination and harmonization of national regional policies, the political situation apparently has not yet allowed much progress. The EEC still seems to be predominantly occupied with attempts to create the necessary "atmosphere." Thus, studies, conferences, and the gathering and dissemination of information on regional problems and policies in the member countries are given priority.

However, even the studies and conferences have not yet led to the establishment of rational Community-wide socio-economic criteria for the selection of the areas to be developed and the investment priorities within each area thus selected—as the paper on *The Regions within The EEC* and the EIB's and the Commission's redevelopment policies show. For instance, the concept that, in general, industry should move to labor wherever possible, must be criticized. In the first place, Marjolin's statement could be interpreted to contradict the spirit of the free mobility provisions of the treaty. More importantly, a decision with respect to who is to move where can be made only on the basis of the above-mentioned criteria and a detailed analysis of the redevelopment areas and their interrelationships with the other regions of the Community.[57]

To date, no progress seems to have been made in this respect.[58] If the Commission and the EIB use any criterion at all, it must be that of regional harmonization. For they have concentrated most of their regional development efforts on the least developed areas within the Community, particularly in southern Italy.[59] Whether this policy of income redistribution can

---

[55] *Ibid.*, 106.

[56] EEC, *Fifth General Report*, 102.

[57] The authors are aware of the conceptual and practical difficulties involved in such analyses and in the development of these criteria. Yet they believe that more appropriate compromise solutions should be attempted than the ones chosen by the Commission.

[58] Statement of a staff member of the Commission.

[59] Statement of a staff member of the Commission, *Cf.*, also the regional distribution of EIB loans as shown in table III of part B of this report.

be considered rational in view of the overall Community policies is impossible to tell. For there does not yet exist a consistent set of Community policies based on Community marginal rates of substitution between economic and social goals, which would indicate the socio-economic criteria necessary for regional development policies.

Regarding the total amount of financial regional development assistance, it must be noted that by choosing for this task, "* * * not a fund which would simply have distributed its allocations, but a bank, which can itself make loans * * * the six member countries set aside more direct financial intervention methods. * * *"[60] However, in view of the 37 loans in the amount of 254.3 million units of account the EIB has granted in its 5-year operating period, the Bank has been criticized for being too conservative. The answer to this charge by the president of the EIB is: (1) That the Bank is to assist not only redevelopment projects, but also projects contributing to the realization of the Common Market and to the economic development of the Community as a whole; (2) that, according to the treaty, the loans of the EIB are to constitute only a fraction of each individual investment project; (3) that, in the beginning, the Bank had concentrated on relatively large projects; (4) that the formalities involved in obtaining a loan from the Bank take time—e.g., the examination of a project by the respective member government, the Commission, and the Management Committee of the Bank; and (5) that the EIB does not object to being called "conservative," as it considers it important to observe customary, sound banking policies.[61] Again, lacking the above-mentioned criteria, it is impossible to judge whether the Bank has indeed been too conservative.

However, as the EEC is still in its period of transition, it is perhaps premature to expect Community policies already to be guided by explicit socioeconomic criteria. Possibly these criteria might be developed when the proposed medium-term policy program for the EEC is being realized. In the meantime, it must be recognized that the Community's readaptation and redevelopment aids as well as its studies, conferences, and the dissemination of information, constitute important assistance and stimulation to the regional policies of the member states.

---

[60] EIB, *Annual Report 1958,* p. 16.

[61] *Documents de la Conférence sur les Économies Régionales, op. cit.,* vol. I, pp. 46–47.

U.S. GOVERNMENT PRINTING OFFICE: 1965 O—761-932